P9-DXE-795

Insiders' Guide®
to Boulder

and Rocky Mountain National Park

SIXTH EDITION

By Roz Brown and Linda Cornett

Guilford, Connecticut
An imprint of The Globe Pequot Press

The prices and rates in this guidebook were confirmed at press time. We recommend, however, that you call establishments before traveling to obtain current information.

Maps by Eric West

ISBN: 0-7627-1058-6

Manufactured in the United States of America
Sixth Edition/First Printing

Contents

Directory of Maps

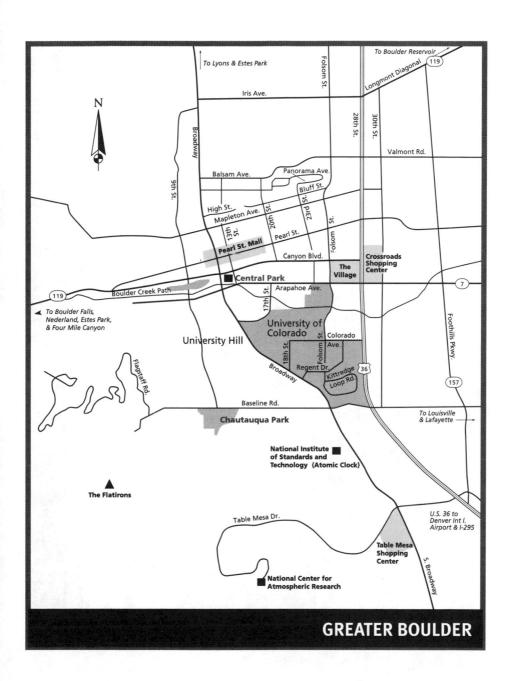

GREATER BOULDER

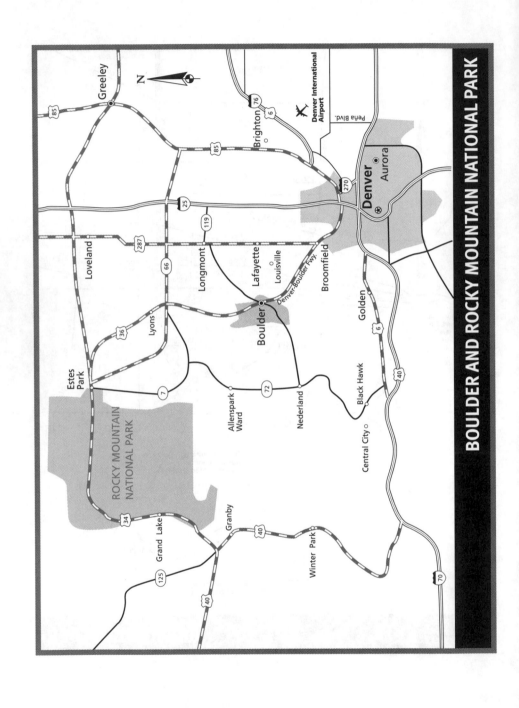

Preface

What you'll notice first about Boulder isn't Boulder itself but the beautiful land that cradles it—the great upthrust slabs of rock that line the city's western border, shoved from the horizontal to almost vertical during a period of geologic violence peaceful now as a picket fence; the gently rolling plains, emerald in spring, dun for most of the year, with a texture that from a distance resembles raw silk; the long, glittering threads of creeks and streams that attract and sustain a remarkable wealth of wildlife.

Boulder is where it is because of the natural bounty, and some of that bounty is preserved because the people of Boulder recognized what could be lost if they were not very careful. What's here is not the grandest, the tallest, the widest, the largest, or the only. It is simply a community, stitched firmly to the land that gave it birth.

Why visit Boulder? It's not exactly a tourist spot, nor a mountain resort—though it's close to many of Colorado's most popular ones. It takes an hour or a little more to drive to Rocky Mountain National Park, the Indian Peaks Wilderness, and many of the ski areas, including Winter Park, Breckenridge, and Keystone. A couple of hours more takes you to Vail, Aspen, and Steamboat Springs. Just up Boulder Canyon, Eldora Mountain Resort, a smaller ski area, is less than an hour away.

Boulder has all the attractions of a big city—art and culture, fine educational institutions, an interesting populace, many excellent restaurants, and points of attraction—but without the hassle of the big city.

But Boulder is also an attraction unto itself. It's a national model for municipally owned open space and controlled growth. It's an inspiration for cities that want to preserve and revitalize their historic hearts, while nurturing commerce, the arts, and entertainment. It's an outdoor recreation mecca for regular folks and professional athletes alike. Anyone who enjoys hiking, backpacking, bicycling, rock climbing, mountaineering, running, and skiing will love Boulder. The annual Bolder Boulder 10-kilometer footrace is one of the nation's largest.

Most visitors to Boulder come to see family and friends—not your typical tourists on a vacation adventure—though adventure possibilities abound in the area. The University of Colorado attracts families for graduation, holidays, and ski vacations, with many of the graduates staying in the area. After its early days as a mining supply town—there was no gold discovered right in Boulder, but nearby in the mountains—Boulder's identity became firmly established as a university town in the late 1800s and continues to be so, with the university comprising about one quarter of the city's population. With its various scientific institutes, including the National Oceanic and Atmospheric Administration, the National Institute of Standards and Technology and the National Center for Atmospheric Research, Boulder attracts an international population of scientists and engineers.

Many of us moved to Boulder because it's such a great place to live. It has Colorado's sunny dry climate, is close to the mountains, and is a manageable size. We enjoy the health-promoting attitude, good schools, recreational opportunities, and wholesome atmosphere for raising families and living the good life. Athletes from all over the world live and train in Boulder for many of the same reasons, plus the high elevation gives them a competitive edge.

Boulder also hosts many annual events and festivals such as the Colorado Dance Festival, Colorado Shakespeare Festival, and Colorado Music Festival, welcoming a whole entourage of performing artists and audiences each summer.

So read on and explore all of Boulder's fine offerings.

Acknowledgments

Original settlers in Boulder were determined to create an "Athens of the West." With such a lofty goal, you can imagine how challenging it is to "keep up" with this ever-changing community at the beginning of the twenty-first century. I have lived in Colorado for 25 years, but updating this *Insiders' Guide* was an educational experience, as the state's Front Range continues on a path of rapid change and growth. Thanks to my co-author, Linda Cornett, for keeping me on deadline, and to previous authors Reed Glenn, Claire Walter, and Shelly D. Schlender for the original text that made my job easier. A special thanks to editor Erika Serviss for her patience.

To the organizations and individuals who offered me assistance or information: the Boulder Chamber of Commerce, *Boulder Magazine, Nexus,* and the *Daily Camera*. To Realtor Irene Shaffer at RE/MAX of Boulder and the many public relations people and communications officers in Boulder. Thanks also to the Boulder Media Women's group for all the "connections" they support. To the late Maria Rogers for instilling an interest in Boulder's history. And to Phyllis Smith for her one-of-a-kind book, *A Look At Boulder: From Settlement to City*. To my friends for their encouragement and my mother, Hope, whose faith in my abilities is essential. And to my daughters, Collier and Grey, who commented only infrequently when trying to locate something on my desk and more regularly encouraged me to "hurry up" so we could find time to take part in Boulder's diverse cultural activities.

—*Roz Brown*

My heartfelt thanks to:

The people who lived here originally and kept the place so beautiful for the rest of us.

The visionaries who recognized that Boulder had become a town well worth planning and shaping and preserving.

The citizens who agreed, and continue to support that effort.

The residents of 1973, who graciously made room for one more.

The visitors who come and appreciate, richen the mix for a while and leave us some of their money.

My dear, old friends, who have shown me so many unsuspected facets of our shared home over the years.

My children and their young friends, who have taught me things I never thought I'd want to know about the younger side of town.

The elders who put in the hard work for decades, defining what a quality community should be, and the younger generation who are taking up the reins. May they be wise and courageous in their turn.

My father, who taught me that there is joy in braving the wilderness and equal joy in returning home safe, who could pinch a penny until it squeaked but could coax a wanton generosity from his garden, who loved an open road and the far side of a hill, but hated it so much when I took that road to the far mountains. I miss you, Daddy.

—*Linda Cornett*

How to Use This Book

Most people, even those who have never been to Colorado, believe they have a pretty clear image of the state. Chances are it involves a skier flying down a mountainside with a fan of lighter-than-air powder rooster-tailing behind.

The fact is there's a whole lot more going on here, geographically, socially, economically, and recreationally. Oh, the skiing is still here, and it's great. But Colorado is also a place of flat-as-a-pancake plains—upthrust tables that bare a geologic history of inundation and drought, rich alluvial plains that nourish fields of potatoes and onions, tomatoes and corn, and orchards heavy with apples and peaches. The Rockies draw a handy north-south line through the state, dividing Colorado into the Eastern Slope and Western Slope. Although the line is blurring somewhat, a shorthand description puts the state's agriculture primarily on the West and its population and growing high-tech industry along the Front Range on the East.

Boulder lies tight against the Front Range at an elevation just over a mile above sea level. It's not a ski town, although skiing is not far away. More than anything, Boulder is characterized by the education, scientific research, and technological innovation that goes on here. It also has a well-deserved reputation for recreation and fitness, with kayaking, running, hiking, bicycling, hang gliding, fishing, in-line skating, and street skiing just the beginning of the list of popular activities. Boulder is considered part of the Denver metro area and is linked to Denver by the increasingly crowded U.S. Highway 36, but Boulder residents have spent upwards of $140 million buying a ring of undeveloped land (a "greenbelt") to ensure that the city maintains a unique identity. And boy, does it. The generally liberal attitudes fostered by the presence of the flagship campus of the University of Colorado have won Boulder the nickname "The People's Republic of Boulder" from others in this politically conservative state.

This book is designed as a guide for visitors or newcomers to the unique, independent enclave that is Boulder. Chapters reflect logical areas of interest, from how to get around the place to where to eat, sleep, shop, listen to music, take a hike, worship, or find a good dentist. There are specialized chapters for children and for the elderly, for house hunters and for sports fans. All the chapters are independent and can be read in any order. They are cross-referenced where appropriate, so if you find only a sentence in one chapter about something that sounds intriguing, it's likely there's an expanded paragraph elsewhere.

Insiders' Tips in each chapter will have you behaving like a native in no time. Close-ups provide a little more information about the places and people that the locals love to talk about. There are also chapters devoted to the glories of Rocky Mountain National Park to the north and the cities of Estes Park and Grand Lake that flank the park.

We update the guide regularly, so let us know what you like and don't like or if we've missed something. Write us at the *Insiders' Guide® to Boulder*, The Globe Pequot Press, P.O. Box 480, Guilford, CT 06437, or visit our website at www.insiders.com.

Overview

Cresting the scenic overlook on U.S. Highway 36 from Denver, first-time visitors gaze down upon Boulder and know they've arrived someplace special. Snuggled serenely against the pine-covered foothills, punctuated dramatically with the red Flatirons, and crowned with the gleaming white halo of the Continental Divide, Boulder looks to some like the Promised Land.

That's how it appeared to early settler Capt. Thomas Aikins, who, in 1858, peered at the Boulder Valley through his field glasses and remarked, "The mountains looked right for gold, and the valleys looked rich for grazing." Aikins and his party did find gold in the hills above Boulder, and many have driven the highway over the hill and found their Shangri-la.

A mere 29 miles from Denver, Boulder is sometimes considered part of the Greater Denver Metropolitan Area for statistical purposes. But Boulder considers itself a world apart—and indeed it is.

This green haven at the foot of the Rocky Mountains is a unique enclave of science, education, research, outdoor enthusiasm, elite athletic training, health food, bicycling, recycling, the arts and New Age culture—a kind of Berkeley of the Rockies, sometimes jokingly dubbed "The People's Republic of Boulder."

Boulder is home to Celestial Seasonings tea company, the Naropa Institute (started by Tibetan Buddhists), the Boulder School of Massage Therapy, the Rolf Institute (international headquarters), Ball Aerospace, the National Center for Atmospheric Research, the National Oceanic and Atmospheric Administration, the National Institute of Standards and Technology (home of the atomic clock, by which all U.S. time is set), and one of the four campuses of the University of Colorado (referred to throughout this book as CU-Boulder). The university's student and staff population of more than 35,000 (28,000 students and 7,000 employees) makes up more than one-third of Boulder's total population of 96,727. The median age in Boulder is 29; Boulder County's median age is 31.6. The *Denver Post* once described Boulder as "The little town nestled between the mountains and reality."

Boulder People: A Confluence of Cultures

Boulder is full of old and new refugees from congested East and West Coast cities and Chicago—many of them professionals—seeking a better life. And they find it here, along with compatible company and culture in what many longtime residents feel is near-utopia: low crime, high mountains, plentiful blue skies and sunshine, glacial-melt drinking water, good schools, a lively arts scene, an enlightened city government, and a wholesome, healthy outlook. In fact, parents often urge their college-age offspring away from Boulder for an eye-opening dip into "the real world." Escapees from the Midwest find

3

Boulder sits in a valley below the Rocky Mountain foothills. PHOTO: DAILY CAMERA/JAY QUADRACCI

the cultural milieu they were missing—and mountains! Boulder natives do exist, but they're rare creatures. (They're usually the ones who don't ski, while almost everyone else in Boulder does.)

Though Boulder has a predominately white, upper-middle-class population, there's a cosmopolitan element provided by the staff and students from foreign countries at the many scientific institutions and the university. Sixty-four percent of Boulder adults attended four years of college; 59 percent have had five or more years of college.

Unfortunately, plentiful well-paying jobs and affordable housing are not among Boulder's amenities. Many local engineers and scientists came to work at IBM or one of the national centers. But most people who live in Boulder have deliberately chosen to do so for the mountains and general ambiance, not necessarily for the job opportunities—and they pay the price in underemployment and a daunting real estate market. Compared to prices in California or Washington, D.C., Boulder's average single-family home price of $335,000 (the overall figure for

the year 2000 from the Boulder County Assessor's Office) might seem affordable. But for those operating within the local economy, surviving in Boulder can be a real challenge. Students vie for all the low-paying jobs and affordable housing, and many CU-Boulder graduates, originally from other states, like it so much that they stay here.

Traditionally, many people, both young and old, have worked for next to nothing just to live in Boulder. But as rents and housing costs continually escalate, it becomes more difficult. Rock-climbing bums, writers, certified massage therapists (there are hundreds), teachers, psychotherapists, and scientists are some of the colorful—often unemployed—clients lingering in local coffeehouses. Some of these same folks may deliver your pizza, drive your cab, or sell you skis at a local mountain sports shop. Boulder unemployment is only 2.7 percent, but *under*employment is much higher.

Boulderites participate in a number of humanitarian and volunteer efforts including local government, environmental activism, and a strong Sister Cities program. Among Boulder's sister cities are Jalapa, Nicaragua; Lhasa, Tibet; Yamagata, Japan; and Dushanbe, Tajikistan. The Sister Cities programs include cultural exchange as well as humanitarian aid shipments; environmental projects; and exchange of students, doctors, and technicians. Boulder families and other organizations host foreign students and sponsor Bosnian refugees. In past years many Vietnamese refugees were also brought to Boulder, and they have since succeeded professionally here. Habitat for Humanity has a local contingent, and there's a controversial local program to help the trade-embargoed, economically stressed Cubans.

Despite the natural beauty outside their back door, Boulderites do love to travel. Go to a remote island in Fiji, and don't be surprised to bump into someone from Boulder.

Boulder Ethnic Demographics

Note: Based on 1994 data, the most recent available.

White	89.7%
Hispanic	4.8%
Asian	3.8%
Black	1.2%
Native American	0.4%
Other	0.1%

Open Space, Limited Growth, and Enlightened Development

Unlike sprawling Greater Denver and other Colorado communities mushrooming to infinity, Boulder is a sort of fixed island surrounded by the protective reefs of open space. In 1967, Boulder became the first city in the United States to tax itself for funds to be used specifically for the acquisition, management, and mainte-nance of open space—and it's an ongoing program. To date more than $40 million has been spent on the acquisition of open space. But even earlier, at the turn of the nineteenth century, Boulder's city government and citizens established a mountain park system by purchasing portions of the city's dramatic mountain backdrop, often called the greenbelt, to protect it from development. (See our History chapter for details.)

Today, Boulder's citizens enjoy more than 30,000 acres of open space in and around the city (another 9,000 acres is slated to be purchased in the next few years), 7,000 acres of adjacent city-owned mountain parks, and about 60,000 acres of county open space, some of which is under agricultural lease and is not open to the public. Residents of Greater Denver and nearby communities frequent Boulder's 78 miles of trail-laced open space, too. The city of Boulder itself encompasses 27.8 square miles.

In 1977 Boulder instituted a limited-growth ordinance called the Danish Plan, the brainchild of then-city councilman (now county commissioner) Paul Danish, restricting new building to 2 percent annual growth. In 1985 it was replaced with another growth moratorium, which is still in effect.

There's no getting around the fact that this makes Boulder a more desirable, yet more expensive, place to live. Because of limited growth, affordable housing is one of the biggest problems in this small city where the student population occupies most of the lower-priced dwellings. Many people find less-expensive housing in the nearby smaller cities of Louisville and Lafayette, currently bursting at the seams with new development. See our Boulder Neighborhoods and Real Estate chapters for more information.

Because so much natural habitat has been preserved, more than 1,200 deer share the environs with residents. Deer grazing in neighborhood yards is a common sight. Though undeniably picturesque, the deer wreak havoc on local gardens. Gardeners have been distressed to find their tomatoes trampled, peas pilfered, and tulips nipped off at the bud. Smart gardeners plant a wildlife garden and build a tall fence around the human garden. Mountain lions and bears occasionally wander into town, too. In one case, a concerned citizen fetched his futon to provide a soft landing pad for a treed bear, tranquilized by wildlife officials. Another young bear led police on a chase right down the Pearl Street pedestrian mall. Skunks, raccoons, and coyotes are regulars in areas near open space. A city-sponsored backyard wildlife program promotes landscaping that will attract and accommodate songbirds, butterflies, and bats.

Outdoor-Sports Capital

Look in any Boulder garage and you're likely to find several bicycles (mountain, touring and racing), several pairs of skis (downhill and cross-country), snowshoes, perhaps a sailboard and/or kayak, crampons (climbing spikes), an ice axe and mountaineering gear, rock-climbing ropes and harnesses, backpacks, in-line skates, a fly-fishing rod, and a plethora of running shoes. It's no coincidence that *Outdoor Explorer* magazine listed Boulder among the 25 "best places to raise an outdoor-loving family" in 2000.

Residents also engage in more traditional pursuits, such as tennis and golf. Boulder's population of couch potatoes is probably one of the nation's smallest. A 1992 survey by the Centers for Disease Control found that Colorado had fewer overweight people per capita and more people who exercise than any other state. In 2000, the International In-line Skating Association named the Boulder Creek Path one of the top 10 places to skate. That same year, *Seventeen* magazine listed Boulder among the country's top 10 places for teens. Dubbed "Winter Wonderland" by the magazine, Boulder was chosen for its unique location between the metropolis of Denver and the spaciousness of the mountains.

Why Boulder? The mountains seem to attract outdoors-oriented people. Perhaps Boulderites felt obliged to lead the way when citizen Frank Shorter became the first American ever to win an Olympic medal in the marathon—gold in 1972 in Munich, silver in 1976 in Montreal. "When Frank won the gold, everybody in America started running," says Neill Woelk, a veteran sports reporter at Boulder's *Daily Camera* newspaper. Shorter, now a Boulder attorney, also sells a line of athletic wear and is a frequent Olympics commentator. Another famous Boulder runner, Arturo Barrios, held the world record for 10 kilometers until 1993.

Boulder is also known nationwide for its huge bicycling population and local celebrities. Boulder cyclist Connie Carpenter won Olympic gold in 1984 for the road race, and her husband, Davis Phinney, was the first American ever to win a Tour de France stage. Alexi Grewal won an Olympic gold medal in 1984 for the road race. With more than 90 miles of bike lanes and off-street bike paths, citizens can cycle almost everywhere, sometimes faster than by car—and without the parking hassle.

Elite athletes from all over the world, including mountaineers Pete Athans and Jon Krakauer, move to Boulder specifically to train in its health-promoting atmosphere and high altitude. Dozens of outdoor recreation publications, including *Rock and Ice, Trail Runner,* and *Ski* magazines, and *Velo News* are based here, as are hundreds of outdoor recreation–oriented businesses.

The University of Colorado's football team, the Golden Buffaloes, was the 1990 co-national champion and is considered one of the nation's most successful programs. The women's basketball team is also tops. CU-Boulder's alpine and Nordic ski teams train at nearby Eldora Mountain Resort, only 21 miles away. The Denver-Boulder Metroplex has been named the No. 1 metropolitan area for sports fans in the nation (ahead of Dallas, Los Angeles, New York, and Chicago).

In fitness-crazed Boulder, biking is a popular mode of transportation. PHOTO: DARCY KIEFEL

For mere mortals there are health clubs galore, the most popular being the great outdoors. Boulder boasts 100 miles of hiking trails in the mountain parks, literally outside our back doors. One of the world's largest 10-kilometer footraces, the annual Bolder Boulder through the city's streets, attracts more than 40,000 runners. The Flatirons, numerous rock formations, and nearby Eldorado Canyon make Boulder a rock-climbing mecca. Read this book's chapter on Boulder Sports for a full description.

Heart and Soul

Boulder's Pearl Street Mall forms the heart and center of the city. Historic buildings, housing shops, galleries, offices, and sidewalk cafes line this photogenic, four-block, open-air walkway—formerly part of Pearl Street. Sadly, since the mall was completed in 1976, constant "upscaling" and rising rents have driven out many of the older businesses, replacing them with a musical-chairs array of new establishments. But Boulder's downtown mall still lures as many locals as visitors, especially on summer evenings when string quartets, bagpipers, Peruvian bands, and all manner of performers stake out spots by storefronts. One musician hauls his piano in on a wheeled platform. Jugglers, fire and sword swallowers, tightrope walkers, and even a Rastafarian contortionist complete the circus-like scene. Lively entertainment, people-watching, and the piney aroma of the summer breeze make mall strolling a warm-weather favorite.

The Boulder Creek Path, two short blocks from the Pearl Street Mall, meanders along Boulder Creek as a peaceful but sometimes perilous thoroughfare for bicyclists, in-line skaters, joggers, and strollers. Seven-and-a-half miles of scenic path follow the creek as it tumbles down from Boulder Canyon and out onto the plains.

Bicycling is so highly regarded in Boulder that sometimes the city plows the snow off the bike path before it plows the streets.

During spring runoff and early summer, kayakers and kids of all ages take tumultuous rides down the creek in boats and innertubes. Also along the path, adjacent to Central Park, the Boulder County Farmers' Market operates on Saturdays and Wednesdays from spring through fall, offering local, organically grown vegetables, fruits, and flowers as well as crafts and baked goods.

No Boulder summer is complete without a concert and meal at Chautauqua. Chautauqua Park, with its 100-year-old dining hall and barn-like concert hall, houses some of the best music and meals anywhere, including the Colorado Music Festival with artists from around the country. Elsewhere in town, summertime offerings include the Colorado Dance Festival, Colorado Shakespeare Festival, Colorado Lyric Opera, Boulder Creek Festival, and less lofty, the Kinetic Sculpture Challenge—a crazy land and water race along and across Boulder Reservoir in wildly imaginative, but not-so-navigable, human-powered conveyances.

Industry and Economics

To dispel any notion of Boulder as a bedroom community to Denver, consider this: 78 percent of Boulder County's population works in the county, 45 percent of the City of Boulder's population works in the city, and 45 percent of the city's workforce commutes in from surrounding communities. Boulder industry focuses on education, scientific research, and technology at such places as the University of Colorado at Boulder, the National Oceanic and Atmospheric Administration, the National Center for Atmospheric Research, and various other government and university scientific institutes.

Celestial Seasonings tea company, the largest U.S. herbal tea manufacturer, makes its home here on Sleepytime Drive. The company revolutionized the tea industry, and founder Mo Siegel literally picked his way to an herbal tea fortune—he started out gathering herbs in Boulder's foothills. He is renowned as the hippie who became a millionaire. A bicycling aficionado, Siegel also brought international bicycle competition to Boulder for more than a decade with the Red Zinger Bicycle Classic race. Started in the mid-1970s, it eventually became the now-extinct Coors Classic.

The University of Colorado, IBM Corp., and Storage Technology Corp. are the top three employers in Boulder County, with more than 38,000 employees. Other top county employers are the Boulder Valley School District (3,176 employees), Ball Aerospace (2,500), and Centrobe

Since 1951, Boulder's City Hall has sat at the busy corner of Broadway and Canyon Boulevard. City offices have spread to two nearby towers, north on Broadway, east into the county, and south into a shopping center, but City Hall is still the heart of it all. PHOTO: LINDA CORNETT

(2,600). Centrobe's employees are distributed among Boulder, Denver, and Colorado Springs; the company is a nationwide subscription and mailing service for magazine publishers. California-based Sun Microsystems is relocating from Silicon Valley to Boulder County and will employ 5,000 people here by the year 2002.

Boulder Notables

The University of Colorado has in the past housed such scholars as Robert Bakker, a world-renowned paleontologist who transformed the study of dinosaurs with his now widely accepted theory that they were warm-blooded and more closely related to birds than reptiles. Movie mogul Steven Spielberg consulted Bakker during the filming of *Jurassic Park*. CU-Boulder is currently home to Patricia Nelson Limerick, renowned teacher and historian of the American West and a leader among the "new Western historians." Limerick's groundbreaking work on the roles played by women, Native Americans, and other ethnic groups in settling

the West won her the 1995 MacArthur Fellowship, a "genius grant" of $275,000 over a five-year period with no strings attached.

Also at CU-Boulder is Nobel laureate Thomas Cech, who received that prize for his work proving that the genetic messenger RNA can also function as an enzyme, leading to the speculation that RNA could have played a key role in the origin of life. Nationally recognized as a leader in the field of educational testing, professor of education Robert Linn received the university's highest honor, a distinguished professorship, in 1996. He is an advisor to key professional and governmental committees as an expert in evaluating test reliability and validity; test comparison, bias, and ethics; and the strength and weakness of the mathematical models that define testing. CU physics professor Carl Wieman was one of two people who created the coldest temperature in 1995. The other scientist was Eric Cornell, a staff physicist with the National Institute of Standards and Technology in Boulder. They led the scientific team that created the long-sought Bose-Einstein condensation—a state that occurs when individual atoms meld into a "superatom" at a few billionths of a degree above absolute zero. Wieman is considered to be one of the premier physicists of his generation and to have achieved some of the most important successes in atomic physics in the past two decades.

CU law professor Charles Wilkinson is a nationally renowned attorney and expert in natural resources management. He has won awards from the National Wildlife Federation and served as special counsel to the Department of the Interior in connection with the recent creation of the Grand Staircase-Escalante National Monument in Utah. The author of many books, he is also an expert in Western land and water issues and Native American law and rights.

CU is fourth among U.S. universities in the number of astronauts it has produced (excluding the military academies), exceeded only by MIT, Purdue, and Stanford.

Atmospheric scientist Walter Orr Roberts, who died in 1990, founded the National Center for Atmospheric Research (NCAR—pronounced "en-car") in Boulder, and his work in solar physics established Boulder as an atmospheric science center, attracting such other scientific facilities as the National Bureau of Standards and Technology (now known as NIST) and Ball Aerospace. He helped found CU-Boulder's Joint Institute for Laboratory Astrophysics and Department of Astrophysical, Planetary and Atmospheric Sciences. Roberts also helped bring Boulder's greatest architectural gem into being: the stunning mesa-top NCAR laboratory, designed by architect I. M. Pei, who also designed the National Gallery in Washington, D.C., and the pyramid-shaped entrance to the Louvre in Paris. NCAR is also known for being the futuristic setting of Woody Allen's 1970s comedy film *Sleeper*.

Climate

It's no wonder that weather and climate are two big topics of study at local scientific institutes: Boulder's climate is marked by unusual extremes. Foot-deep

When the sky meets the mountaintops, the Boulder Valley can look like a pretty ominous place, but old hands know the adage, "Don't like the weather? Wait five minutes." PHOTO: LINDA CORNETT

snow and below-zero temperatures can suddenly transform to breezy 60-degree T-shirt weather by Boulder's capricious Chinook "snow-eater" winds. These warm, dry winds blast down from the eastern slope of the mountains and melt the snow with blinding speed. Boulder's winds have also been known to blow in gusts exceeding 120 miles per hour, removing roofs and toppling telephone poles.

Because of these strong winds, Native Americans chose not to make permanent settlements in the area and mainly visited for summer hunting. The dreaded high winds, Boulder's biggest weather affliction, can come at any time but are the worst in winter and can continue for days. It can be so windy that schools won't let young children leave the building without an adult. Safeway supermarket sometimes posts a note on the door asking that shopping carts be returned to the store so errant, wind-blown carts don't damage cars in the parking lot. The winds can make people irritable, and there are tales of pioneer women wandering off onto the prairie or committing suicide, driven insane by the gales. Similar winds (in Europe called the *foehn* or *mistral*) are common throughout the world near high mountain ranges.

Sometimes it seems like Boulder has only two seasons: summer and winter. The tulips do bloom in spring, and the leaves change in fall for a brief but spectacular show. But these two fickle seasons are often accompanied by a foot of snow, burying the crocuses and lilacs or blackening fall's golden aspen leaves. Halloween is often one of the most miserable nights of the year, with the poor trick-or-treaters braving the freezing rain or snow. Then again, Thanksgiving and Christmas can sometimes have outdoor cafe weather. It rarely rains in Boulder except for summer afternoon thunderstorms and the August monsoon—a week or two of rainy weather.

Boulder's high elevation, 5,430 feet, keeps temperatures cool at night even on the hottest summer days. Mountain breezes and low humidity help, too. Tor-

Insiders' Tip

Boulder's backdrop and trademark, the Flatirons, are Pennsylvanian red sandstone and conglomerate that were deposited as alluvial fans and aprons along the edges of the ancestral Rockies. They were dragged upward at their current angle by the rebirth of the Rockies about 65 million years ago. The Third Flatiron (third from the north) is one of Colorado's and the nation's premier, classic rock climbs. It towers 1,400 feet high, a couple hundred feet higher than the Empire State Building, and has been climbed by people without using their hands, on roller skates, naked, and in 8 minutes (all separate climbers).

nadoes generally stay well to the east, though hailstorms occasionally shred summer flowers and vegetables.

The record low temperature in the Boulder area is –33 degrees (1930) and the record high is 104 degrees (1954). Boulder has an average of 33 days above 90 degrees and 133 days below freezing. January, the coldest month, averages 21 degrees; July, the warmest, averages 88. Average precipitation is 18.24 inches. The most snow in a season was 142.9 inches; the least, 20.8 inches. Though it may snow or blow, low humidity and a higher-than-California average of sunny days make Boulder's climate one of the most pleasant in the nation.

From the foothills, the Boulder Valley stretches to a far horizon on the high plains. PHOTO: LINDA CORNETT

Area Geography

The foothills of the Rocky Mountains divide Boulder County from north to south. Eastern Boulder County lies on the western edge of the Great Plains, with rolling terrain, small ridges, and the Davidson Mesa, which runs northeast from south of Boulder to Louisville. Western Boulder County rises from the foothills to the Continental Divide, to a breathless summit of 14,255 feet atop Longs Peak in Rocky Mountain National Park in the extreme northwestern part of the county.

Boulder Environs

Roughly 20 towns dot the mountains and plains of Boulder County, ranging from rustic, high-country settlements like Eldora and Raymond, with only a handful of year-round residents, to sizable burgs like Longmont, the second-largest city in Boulder County after Boulder. A former sugar beet and canning capital, Longmont—northeast of Boulder—is now home

to Longmont Foods, a turkey-breeding and meat-processing company.

Nothing could be farther from Longmont in both locale and flavor than lofty, funky Ward, former mining boom-and-bust town, now a home for old and young hippies and other escapees from the system. After Longmont, the small plains cities of Broomfield, Lafayette, and Louisville are the most populous.

The small towns of Lyons (north of Boulder) and Eldorado Springs (south of Boulder) lie at the mouths of spectacular canyons. Eldorado Springs is also the site of a state park and mineral springs and is a famous rock-climbing area. Hygiene and Allenspark are unincorporated small settlements of a few hundred residents each. Jamestown was once a mining boom town with a population of 10,000; now it has less than 300 residents. Its picturesque mercantile cafe is a popular bicycling stop.

Spectacularly sited at the top of Boulder Canyon on Barker Reservoir, Nederland is Boulder County's largest mountain town and an odd mix of eccentric mountain folk, young families, old hippies, conservative Republicans, environmental activists, self-sufficient rugged individualists, and a small contingent of out-of-staters who fall in love with it during the summer move in and beat a fast trail out after their first winter.

Of course a lot more can be said about each Boulder County town and its unique character and history. See our chapters on Boulder Real Estate and Neighborhoods and Nearby Communities for more information.

Niwot's Curse?

Though Boulder has been utopia for many residents for many years, the city (like the rest of the planet) is currently experiencing an uncomfortable population expansion. Since the late 1970s, the population has increased by about 45 percent, or 30,000 people. Three million people—75 percent of Colorado's population—live in a 60-mile-wide swath along the Front Range, from Fort Collins to Colorado Springs. By 2020, that number is projected to reach four million. "Too many people and too many cars," is the complaint of residents who remember traffic-free streets and the ability to get anywhere in town in 10 minutes. Gone are those days, and in their place are frustrating waits in traffic jams, rude drivers, a dearth of parking spaces, and long lines at supermarkets, restaurants, and movies.

Unfortunately, Boulder is inheriting some of the problems of a bigger city: increased crime, pollution, traffic, and overpopulation. The current challenge is how to deal with them. Growth-cap initiatives on the ballot and emphasis on bicycling and public transportation versus automobile use continue to be some "driving issues" for the future.

Insiders' Tip

Those who spend any time in Boulder are bound to hear about Niwot's Curse. There are various versions, though no evidence that Chief Niwot (the name means "Left Hand") of the Southern Arapaho tribe ever said any of them—or even proclaimed a "curse"—according to Boulder's Carnegie Library for local history. Nevertheless, the library's official-unofficial version reads: "The Boulder Valley is so beautiful that people seeing it will want to stay and their staying will be the undoing of the beauty." Another less-official but more common version is: "Once you gaze upon the Flatirons, you will never be happy anywhere else."

Boulder residents are determined to ensure that Arapaho Chief Niwot's curse, "that people seeing the beauty of the Boulder Valley will want to stay and their staying will be the undoing of the beauty," will not come true.

Boulder Vital Statistics

Detractors accuse Boulder of obsessively contemplating its own navel, fascinated by all things Boulder to the exclusion of the rest of the world. While that stereotype is much out-dated (if it ever was true), Boulderites do like to know just what their reflection shows. To that end, the community surveys itself regularly and collects and releases statistical infor-mation on an ongoing basis. Among the reflected facts:

Median age: 29 City of Boulder, 31.6 Boulder County

Ethnicity: 92.5 Caucasian City of Boulder, 93.3 Caucasian Boulder County

Average household size: 2.18 City of Boulder, 2.59 United States

Median income (1999): $68,700 City of Boulder, $51,800 Colorado

Average rental cost (excluding utilities): $570 efficiency, $950 two-bedroom apartment City of Boulder

Average cost of new single-family detached home in Boulder (1999): $366,823

Average annual rainfall: 28.49 inches

Average annual snowfall: 158.7 inches

Top 10 employers:
    University of Colorado, 7,500 employees
    IBM, 4,100 employees
    StorageTek, 3,450 employees
    Sun Microsystems, 3,000 employees
    Centrobe, 2,700 employees
    Ball Aerospace, 2,130 employees
    Boulder Community Hospital, 2,040 employees
    Level 3 Communications, 2,000 employees
    Maxtor, 1,500 employees
    NCAR, 1,000 employees

Average annual in-migration to Boulder County:
    37.9% from Colorado
    18.6% from the West
    14.9% from the Midwest
    13.9% from the South
    12.1% from the Northeast
    2.5% from another country

Average annual out-migration from Boulder County:
    53.9% to Colorado
    18.2% to the West
    11.1% to the South
    8.1% to the Midwest
    7.5% to the Northeast
    1.2% to another country

Marriages and divorces (1998): 2,192 marriages, 1,340 divorces

Marital status:
  Married, 49.8% in 1970, 36.3% in 1990
  Single, never married, 41.5% in 1970, 48.9% in 1990
  Divorced, 4.6% in 1970, 9.4% in 1990

Education level of resident adults:
  Didn't finish high school, 5%
  Graduated high school, 11%
  Some college or associate degree, 25%
  Bachelor's degree, 33%
  Graduate or professional degree, 26%

Library circulation (1999): 1.3 million items

University of Colorado enrollment (fall 1999): 26,318 students

Boulder Valley Public Schools enrollment (1999-2000): 13,526 students

Scholastic Aptitude Test (SAT) scores for Boulder Valley students:
  Verbal, 553 in Boulder Valley, 505 nationally
  Mathematics, 569 in Boulder Valley, 511 nationally

American College Test (ACT) scores for Boulder Valley students:
  English, 22.3 in Boulder Valley, 20.5 nationally
  Mathematics, 23.5 in Boulder Valley, 20.7 nationally
  Reading, 23.1 in Boulder Valley, 21.4 nationally
  Science/Reasoning, 22.8 in Boulder Valley, 21 nationally
  Composite, 23.1 in Boulder Valley, 21 nationally

Employment by industry (1999):
  Goods producing, 41,000 employees
  Services, 129,600 employees
  Construction and mining, 8,000 employees
  Manufacturing, 32,900 employees
  Transportation/public utilities, 4,900 employees
  Wholesale, 5,900 employees
  Retail, 29,200 employees
  Finance/insurance/real estate, 6,700 employees
  Other services, 56,300 employees
  Government, 26,500 employees

Unemployment rate (1999): 2.7%

Boulder's deer population (1998-1999): 686 (est)

Mean temperature (1999): 53

Motor vehicle registration (1999): 62,946; 0.66 vehicles per person

Reported crime (1999):
  Aggravated assault, 111
  Arson, 46
  Burglary, 560
  Forcible rape, 39
  Larceny theft, 2,991
  Motor vehicle theft, 186
  Murder, 0
  Robbery, 36

Getting Here, Getting Around

Boulder is about 25 miles northwest of Denver, via Interstate 25 and U.S. 36, better known locally as "The Turnpike" because it was once a toll road. Most visitors arrive here by car or by plane into Denver International Airport, about an hour's drive south and east.

In the city, the car is the favorite mode of transportation, but more than most cities, Boulder offers and encourages use of alternative modes of transportation to the car and has a city agency, the Transportation Planning Group, also known as GO Boulder, to promote, set, and achieve such goals. Pay close attention to alternative modes. In 1992, nearly 26 percent of work-related trips within Boulder were made by bus, bike or on foot. Among 14 comparable cities, Boulder ranks No. 1 in people who walk to work, work at home, and drive with more than one person in the car. It ranks second among those who bike. (The TPG of Boulder says Davis, California, probably ranks first, with Boulder right on its heels.) Alternative modes of transportation can become one of your favorite things about Boulder.

Getting to Boulder

Getting Here By Air

Denver International Airport (DIA)

Opened in 1995, Denver International Airport, 8400 Peña Boulevard (303-342-2200, 800-247-2336), is the biggest in the nation and one of the biggest in the world. Twenty-three carriers service the airport: United Airlines dominates, with some 70 percent of the flights out of DIA, but American, American West, Continental, Delta, Frontier, Northwest, TWA, US Airways, and Vanguard also serve the airport. Others include Air Canada, British Airways, Lufthansa, Mexicana, and Sky West. DIA is posh, with polished granite floors, $7.5 million worth of artwork, and an expansive main lobby roofed with 34 translucent, Teflon-coated fiberglass tent canopies designed to invoke snow-covered peaks and cast light like stylized, billowy clouds. Those canopies were canted in different directions for structural efficiency in the wind and heavy weather. Despite its monumental 5 million-square-foot interior, walks are short. The ticket counters are a short way from passenger drop-offs on both sides of the main terminal. Common carriers (i.e., buses and vans) use a separate level, off-limits to private cars. There are three concourses. You have the option of walking to Concourse A via an air bridge over a taxiway, but a swift subway whisks you to all concourses. Stand near the front windows if you want to see the little propellers along the walls whirl as the train passes.

DIA has excellent shops, including some not usually found in airports: Images of Nature, a national wildlife photographer's store; Benjamin Books, a well-stocked bookstore; and Susan Vale Sweaters, offering handmade sweaters from $200 up. You can also find a travel agency and a massage therapist at DIA. An interfaith airport chapel opened in 1996. Fast food includes McDonald's, TCBY, and specialty pizza, croissant, and espresso shops, all by contract required to sell their goods at prices no more than 10 percent higher than they would sell in a regular mall. Most of these are open daily from 7 A.M. until 10 P.M.

If you need information on Denver International Airport's ground transportation, call (303) 342-4059; for parking information, call (303) 342-7275; for luggage storage and lost and found, call (303) 342-4062.

Driving time between DIA and Boulder takes one hour, minimum, and can take longer if traffic is thick. There is currently no direct or easy route from Boulder to the new airport, so allow plenty of time for getting there (see directions below).

Airport Shuttles

There is currently only one van service that offers scheduled airport shuttle service to and from Boulder. Super Shuttle Boulder (formerly the Airporter; 303-444-0808) picks up at Boulder's major hotels, CU-Boulder, and your own front door. The service departs the Boulder Broker Inn hourly between 4:30 A.M. and 9 P.M. (if you order door-to-door, they'll schedule your pick-up to coincide with a departure from the Broker) and from the airport at 10 minutes past each hour between 8:10 A.M. and 11:10 P.M. Door-to-door service is $22 one-way; hotel service is $18 one-way. It is $10 for each additional person, and those under 12 years of age ride free.

Bus Service

The Regional Transportation District, also known as RTD (303-299-6000), also operates hourly buses between DIA and Boulder. The bus trip takes about 90 minutes, with intermediate stops including the Louisville-Superior and Table Mesa Park-n-Ride lots. The fare is $8 one-way (it's free for CU-Boulder students), and you can grab advance $13 round-trip tickets at King Soopers or Safeway.

RTD also offers a family plan that allows up to three children 15 and younger to ride to or from DIA free with an adult. Children even get a free set of plastic airline-style wings with each ride.

Taxis and Limos

Boulder Yellow Cab (303-442-2277) charges around $50 for an airport trip for one to five people and also picks up in Lafayette and Louisville. If you are feeling flush, you can call an on-demand limo service. Airport Luxury Express (303-938-1234) provides transportation in four-wheel-drive Chevrolet Suburbans, each equipped with cellular phone, television, beverage service, and ski and luggage racks. It operates as an on-demand airport charter, particularly for business travelers and groups. By-the-hour rates are $72 during the day and evening, and $84 between midnight and 5 A.M. for trips between Boulder, Denver, Louisville, or Lafayette and DIA. Prices are higher to Centennial Airport south of Denver and from Eldorado Springs, Gold Hill, Gold Lake, Lake Valley, Longmont, Pine Brook Hills, Walker Ranch, and Ward. Airport Luxury Express also will take you to or pick you up from Colorado Springs, general-aviation airports, and mountain towns. Other limo services include Elegante Limousine (303-443-7723); Foothills Limousine (303-530-0781); and Prestige Transportation Services (303-678-8471 or 800-215-4667).

Car Routes

It's easier to travel to or from the airport with someone else at the wheel, but if you need to drive, here are four options. To choose a route, tune in to KOA radio (850 am), which has the most frequent traffic-condition reports. The distances listed are based on a *Daily Camera* reporter's story when the airport opened in 1995.

We've found Option B to be the fastest from central, north, or south Boulder. Once you're on U.S. 36, you won't encounter a single traffic light, and the high-occupancy-vehicle (HOV) lane from Westminster practically to the I-25 interchange speeds things along even during rush hour. At peak times, you are most likely to encounter congestion on the

I-270 leg, and if KOA tells you that route is jammed, your best alternative is Option A. Of course, reverse these directions to drive from DIA to Boulder. Though driving times vary, allow at least an hour for the trip.

Option A (38.5 miles): Take U.S. Highway 36 to Sheridan Boulevard. Exit at 104th Avenue/Church Ranch Boulevard and follow 104th Avenue east all the way to Tower Road. Until you get well east of I-25, which is still rural, tremendous growth is happening along this route, which has about two dozen traffic lights. At Tower Road, along the airport's western edge, turn right and take it south to Peña Boulevard, turn left and go east into the airport.

Option B (45 miles): Take U.S. Highway 36 to Denver. Go south briefly on I-25, then take I-76 for about a mile to I-270, heading southeast. It merges into I-70 east. Exit at Peña Boulevard and go east into the airport.

Option C (45 miles): This option is best for travel from East Boulder. Take Arapahoe Road (Colo. Highway 7) east to U.S. Highway 85. Take U.S. 85 south to Henderson Road. Go east on Henderson to Tower Road. Take Tower south to Peña Boulevard and go east into the airport.

Option D (42.5 miles): Take U.S. Highway 36 to Broomfield. At Broomfield, take 120th Avenue east to Quebec Street. Jog north on Quebec to Henderson Road. Take Henderson east to Tower Road, turn south to Peña Boulevard and then east on Peña into the airport.

General-Aviation Airports

If you have a private plane, you can fly into one of the region's smaller general-aviation airports. Some also have air taxi services that can fly you quickly to a town not on a regular commercial air route.

Boulder Municipal Airport
3300 Airport Rd., Boulder
(303) 440–7065

Like most airports in Colorado, Boulder's airport is uncontrolled, meaning it has no control tower. Private propeller planes

and a few smaller turbojets land here. There is a comfortable lobby where a selection of videos about flying are for sale. A courtesy car will take you to your Boulder destination. To reach the airport, take Valmont Road east to Airport Road.

Flatirons Aviation (303–440–6522), at the Boulder Municipal Airport, offers flight instruction ranging from recreational to commercial and is a contact for renting hangars or getting airport information. Depending on the aircraft you choose, lessons range from $66 to $100 per hour plus a $33 per hour instructor fee. The tie-down fee is dropped when fuel is purchased. If needed, hanger space is usually available.

Dakota Ridge Aviation (303–444–1017) is another flight school based at the Boulder Municipal Airport. Private, commercial, and instructor lessons are all available and cost $52 per hour to as much $152 per hour, plus the $35-per-hour instructor fee. They don't charge for tie-down if the customer is refueling. Maintenance for all types of planes is ongoing here.

Tri-County Airport/
Crosswind Aviation
395 Airport Dr., Erie
(303) 661–9146

Located in east Boulder County, this airport has a runway big enough for small jets, but most of its air traffic is single-

and twin-engine propeller planes. A full range of flight instruction is available. Experimental and unique home-built airplanes occupy many hangars. And the jet-set—that is, the propeller-set—has settled nearby. More than a dozen houses adjacent to the airport sport private hangars with taxi lanes connecting to the runway.

Vance Brand Municipal Airport
10383 N. 85th St., Longmont
(303) 651–8431

This is an uncontrolled landing field with full services for business and pleasure aircraft. There is a small lobby with snacks available and pilot supplies. They do not have a courtesy car but can arrange for a local rental-car company to transport guests to their destination. To reach Vance Brand, take the Diagonal Highway or U.S. 36 northeast of Boulder to Airport Road and go north 1.5 miles.

Air West Flight Center Inc. (303–776–6266) is a flight school based at Vance Brand Airport. They have nine planes and teach flying lessons ranging from private pilot to instructor. Depending on the plane you choose, lessons start at $50 per hour and go as high as $160 per hour, plus a $32-per-hour instructor fee. Tie-downs are $3 per night or $35 per month.

Another flight school based at Vance Brand Airport is Twin Peaks Aviation (303–776–8467). Lessons start at $65 per hour and go as high as $135 per hour, plus the $30-per-hour instructor fee. They offer scenic rides and rent planes to those who have a license. Tie-down is free with the purchase of fuel, or $35 on a monthly basis.

Jefferson County Airport (Jeffco)
11755 Airport Way, Broomfield
(303) 466–2314

Located just outside Boulder County, this airfield is nonetheless used by many Boulderites. Also known as Jeffco, it's the fourth-largest airport in the Denver area and can handle corporate jets and aircraft up to 70,000 pounds. No scheduled commercial passenger flights leave Jeffco, but it has plenty of general aviation. The tower is staffed by 10 controllers and has the best navigational landing aids near Boulder. There two cafes open to the public.

Getting Here by Car

To drive to Boulder from Denver, take I–25 north to U.S. Highway 36 west, better known as "The Turnpike." The last hill is Davidson Mesa, where you'll get a view of town and find a visitor center kiosk.

If you ask for directions and someone says "Foothills," clarify whether they mean Foothills Highway (U.S. Highway 36), which starts as 28th Street and leads to Estes Park, or Foothills Parkway (Colo. Highway 157), which links U.S. 36 with Colo. Highway 119 and leads to Longmont.

If you are driving to Boulder from the ski areas on I–70, you have two options. The first is to take the Morrison/Golden exit (exit 259) to U.S. Highway 40. Go north toward U.S. Highway 6, turn left on U.S. 6, then head north on Colo. Highway 93 to Boulder. The second, and to us preferable, option is the Central City/Golden exit (exit 244) off of I–70. Follow U.S. 6 east for about 15 miles through beautiful Clear Creek Canyon. At the second traffic light, just on the outskirts of Golden, turn left (north) on Colo. Highway 93, which becomes Broadway in Boulder.

Getting Around Boulder

The No. 1 rule of thumb to help newcomers orient themselves in Boulder is: The mountains are to the west. Most of the north/south streets are numbered, starting with Third Street on the west side of town then going beyond 75th Street as you head east. Broadway is a major north-south thoroughfare on a slight diagonal, and Folsom Street is a significant north-south street from North Boulder to the University of Colorado campus. Other important roads are U.S. 36, which becomes 28th Street through Boulder, and Foothills Parkway, a divided roadway on the eastern edge of town, but with some traffic lights at major intersections, which connects U.S. 36 and the Longmont Diagonal (Colo. Highway 119). It is a way to bypass Boulder, though we wonder why anyone would wish to bypass our wonderful city.

Baseline Road is a significant east-west route, not just to Boulderites, but also to cartographers, for it marks the 40th parallel on maps of the Earth. If you made a beeline down this road, after a few hundred miles you'd hit the boundary between Kansas and Nebraska. The major east-west cross-streets are Table Mesa Road/South Boulder Road and Baseline Road in the southern part of the city; Arapahoe Avenue in central Boulder (and, to an extent, Canyon Boulevard, a short but important major street); and the Alpine Street/Valmont Road routing and Iris Avenue in the northern part of the city.

North Boulder's alphabetical "tree streets"—Alpine, Balsam, Cedar, and so on—are easy to find and remember. Making your way through cul de sac–filled subdivisions, however, requires good directions. Broadway and 28th Street converge in North Boulder, again becoming U.S. 36 toward Lyons.

You'll find basic orientation maps in the front of this book, and more detailed street maps in the front of local phone books. A variety of easier-to-tote maps is available from the city's Transportation Planning Group, GO (303–441–3266), on the second floor of the Park Central Building, 1739 Broadway, including free pocket-size maps for streets and bus and bicycle routes. And remember, it never hurts to ask for directions.

Driving Around Boulder

If you just arrived from a congested metropolitan area on either coast, Boulder might not seem to have much traffic, but if you've been in town a while, you would notice the change over the past few years. More than 200,000 cars flow through the city daily, and people drive a cumulative 2.2 million miles in this little valley every day. That's loads of cars, especially at a higher altitude more prone to air pollution. It's also unsettling to people who don't like the way roads and parking lots eat up land and create canyons clogged with vehicles and the accompanying din and exhaust fumes.

Boulder has given itself a mandate to reduce the car and traffic problem while enhancing its residents' ability to get around. In a classic example of Boulder's foresight and compulsive worrying about quality-of-life issues before they become crises, the city developed its first Transportation Master Plan in 1989, when, believe it or not, the city was still suffering under a regional recession and few people were worrying about too many commuters, too many jobs, or too many homes. The Transportation Planning Group tracks traffic patterns, keeps statistics, creates charts, and most important, tries to use these figures to solve the congestion conundrum. Periodic studies confirm that what most people like about downtown Boulder is its atmosphere and pedestrian orientation, and what most people don't like about Boulder is the parking dilemma. The latest version of the Transportation Master Plan, designed to take Boulder through the year 2020, includes a whopping $1 billion worth of projects (including more than $250 million for improved bus service and $30 million for better bike paths), proving that Boulder takes its traffic and growth issues seriously and is willing to back them up with big bucks.

Individuals do their bit, too. Some people dream about or design supercars,

Insiders' Tip

More than 200,000 cars come and go from Boulder daily.

Electric cars are a common sight in environmentally aware Boulder. PHOTO: ROZ BROWN

which would be quieter and safer than current cars and get more than 150 miles to the gallon. Others want better mass transit, including light rail and improved bus service. A few of them serve on the city's Transportation Advisory Board, which studies the issues in depth and makes informed proposals to the city. Planners strive for small-scale neighborhood centers so people don't have to drive as far to reach necessary services. And many people take public transportation whenever possible or get around town on bicycles or on foot as often as they can. A few even put their commitment into action by living carless.

Plans and dreams aside, the majority of Boulder residents still depend on their cars, even if they secretly wish there were a better way. Don't feel guilty if your car's packed with visiting sightseers or your kids' soccer teammates; you're being a carpool! But if you're all alone, at least try to consolidate your errands so you drive less often.

Boulder has many designated bike lanes, but where there are none, bicyclists may occupy a lane of traffic, just like cars. Pedestrians at crosswalks have the right-of-way, which means you are supposed to stop when you see someone waiting to cross the street.

Except where posted or where there is a red-arrow traffic light, right turns on red are permitted. Wherever the streets are wide enough to make it feasible, which means most arterials, left-turn lanes have been designated. As anyplace else when you're turning left at a green light, pull into the intersection and wait for a gap. Once you are in the intersection, it is still legal to turn on yellow. If you try to zip into an intersection after the light turns red, however, you are asking for a stiff fine, to say nothing of risking an accident.

Car Rentals

The overwhelming majority of fly-in visitors to Boulder rent cars at Denver International Airport or from agencies near the old Stapleton Airport and drive to Boulder, but rental cars are also available in town. Locals whose cars are undergoing major repairs, business travelers in the area for several days but only requiring a car for part of the time, CU-Boulder students (you must be 25 or older to rent), and visiting academicians are among those who might wish to rent a car in Boulder for the short time they really need one.

The Yellow Pages list local and out-of-town agencies under Automobile Renting. Choices include such national firms as Hertz (303-413-8023); Avis (303-499-1136); National (303-442-5110); and Budget (303-341-2277). Smaller regional and local companies abound, too.

Rush Hour

Most cities get only two rush periods. Boulder has three. Morning rush spans 7 to 9 A.M. Also, because many of the new commercial and business parks are lacking in restaurants, workers often drive somewhere for lunch, creating a noon mini-rush that starts around 11 A.M. and lasts until 2 P.M. Traffic really swells between 4 and 7 P.M. A fourth rush sometimes revolves around CU-Boulder home football games, which jam streets around campus. If you hate traffic, make your car trips outside these most popular times or (hint-hint) consider other ways of getting around (see this chapter's subsequent "Alternative Modes of Transportation" section).

Weather Hazards

Boulder's normally benign climate often lulls us into thinking that the driving, like the living, is easy. But meteorological aberrations can be hazardous. Summer hailstorms can pock windshields, impair visibility, and temporarily cause slippery road surfaces. Snowstorms often start with drizzling rain that freezes before the snow falls, and that snow can undergo several days of melt-to-slush, freeze-to-ice cycles before melting and evaporating completely. Hilly streets and intersections are generally sanded rather than treated

If it's too snowy to drive or bike, some Boulder residents take to their skis. PHOTO: DAILY CAMERA

with chemicals. Highways and arterials are plowed, but snow on most residential streets is left to be taken care of by the sun. Several years ago, a child walking to an elementary school was killed by a car that had stopped at a red light but was hit from behind by a driver who skidded on the ice. Good snow tires are a must for Colorado winters.

If you drive a camper or sport utility vehicle or are moving your belongings into town in a rental truck, you'll want to pay attention to high-wind warnings. Colo. Highway 93 between Boulder and Golden is especially vulnerable to wicked crosswinds and is occasionally closed because of them. Mountain driving can be pleasurable or terrifying, depending on the individual driver's skill and confidence. Shifting into a lower gear helps save wear and tear on the engine while ascending and on the brakes while going downhill.

Accidents

As elsewhere, serious accidents demand a 911 call to dispatch emergency police, ambulance, and even fire units. The Boulder Police accident investigation unit deals with non-injury-producing accidents. For information, call the department's general information line, (303) 441-4444. Vehicle insurance is mandatory in the state of Colorado, with current minimum required coverage of $25,000 for bodily injury, $50,000 per accident, and $25,000 property damage. Motorists who leave the scene of an accident without exchanging license, registration, and insurance information may have their driver's licenses suspended. (There are other offenses that can result in loss of license, too, including driving while intoxicated, reckless driving, and possession of certain firearms.)

Emergency Services

You only need to use the American Automobile Association (AAA) emergency road service once to make your membership pay off. AAA Colorado (303-442-0383), provides a variety of services, including changing a flat tire, refueling an empty gas tank, pulling vehicles out of snow drifts or mud, and towing a broken-down vehicle to a repair center. Because of the distances involved, anyone who drives in the mountains is probably wise to sign up for AAA Plus, offering towing services from as far as 250 miles from home. In addition to road services, AAA maintains a walk-in center at 1933 28th Street (upstairs from Blockbuster Video), with a travel agency, traveler's check sales, discount luggage, book sales, and routing assistance. Many of the services are available for nonmembers as well as members. In addition, AAA sells insurance and provides a locator service for good deals on new cars, bail bonds (not than any Insider would ever need one!), and other services.

Parking

If Boulder accommodated every single driver who wanted a quick trip to a perfect parking space, we would need so many roads and parking spaces that little room would remain for buildings, sidewalks, trees, or flowers. On the other hand, for retail businesses and restaurants to remain viable, there must be reasonably convenient customer parking. Periodic studies confirm that what most people like about downtown Boulder is its atmosphere and pedestrian orientation; what most people don't like about Boulder is the parking dilemma. Four downtown blocks of Pearl Street are pedestrian-only, so obviously there's no parking there, and meters limit parking on adjacent commercial streets. A new parking program was initiated in 1997 on adjacent neighborhood streets to discourage daylong parkers. Two- to three-hour nonresident parking is permitted.

Boulder maintains several staffed parking garages and metered surface lots, which are in great demand. If you get a downtown job, you can get on a waiting list for reserved, long-term parking by checking with the city's Parking Services; call (303) 413-7300.

In addition to downtown, another problematic parking area is The Hill, the area around the university. There are metered spaces on retail and commercial streets, but long-term parking is also restricted here. Your best bet is to park in the large CU visitor lot on Euclid, just east of the University Memorial Center (UMC). All other lots on the campus are permit-only parking. CU has its own Parking Services for students, faculty, and staff, call (303) 492-7384.

Alternative Modes of Transportation

For information about alternative modes of transportation, including pedestrian, bicycle, and carpool options, call the

Alternative transportation in Boulder includes just about anything with wheels. PHOTO: DARCY KIEFEL

Transportation Planning Group, a city agency that offers multiple transportation options. It offers easy-to-read maps of bus routes, bike paths, and open-space trails. The pocket-size maps are free, and the larger full-scale ones are a good value at $2. Call the TPG at (303) 441-3266, or stop by its offices on the second floor of the Park Central Building, 1739 Broadway, two blocks south of the Pearl Street Mall.

If you only need a car for an occasional errand or trip to the mountains, call Boulder's Car Share (303-543-1273). Car Share has two cars, titled and licensed, that are shared, free of charge, by local residents.

To encourage bus use, participating businesses and the Downtown Management Commission (303-441-4000), provide ECO-Passes so their employees can ride the bus for free. So far more than 12,000 residents have ECO-Passes. One of the great perks of the program is the guaranteed ride, which uses taxis to take people directly to their door at night. In addition, three Boulder neighborhoods have Neighborhood ECO-Passes, and new neighborhoods join the program yearly.

Boulder's Pathways

Boulder has been ranked among America's most walkable cities by *USA Today*. It's also a wonderful city for runners, bikers, in-line skaters, and wheelchair users. The most pleasing "roads" are the pedestrian and bicycle paths. They follow streams. They go by parks where you can hear birds sing, and they pass pretty homes with kids playing or adults gardening. Many people along the way smile. The major non-motorized-vehicle thoroughfare is the Boulder Creek Path (see the Boulder Attractions and Boulder Parks and Recreation Centers chapters), which is primarily an east-west route.

Walking some of these pathways to your destination often is faster than driving. Try it with a friend. Eat at some lovely spot on the Pearl Street Mall, then plan to meet on the CU-Boulder campus. You start walking while your friend gets the car. As you head up Broadway, look for a

Insiders' Tip

If you are a pedestrian, cyclist, in-line skater, skateboarder, or motorist and have too close a brush with another pedestrian or anyone on wheels who is unmindful of the rules of the road, you can report it to the Close-Call Hotline (303-441-4272). This is a message line, not to be used to report an accident or emergency.

little sidewalk just up the hill from Arapahoe Avenue. You'll probably have time to stop at Andrews Arboretum, an area once occupied by train tracks. You can take this pleasant pathway to the university and enjoy the sights on your stroll. You'll get lung-filling exercise and might even have time to read a chapter in your book before your friend gets the car, drives up to the university, parks, and finally joins you.

The Transportation Planning Group has several programs designed to increase walking by improving pedestrian facilities. Many neighborhood sidewalks are being replaced for safety reasons and intersections have been made more pedestrian-friendly.

Bicycling

Boulder is one of America's best cycling cities. At this writing, the city boasts more than 100 miles of off-street bike paths, bike lanes on city streets, and bike routes. That includes an underpass that allows university students safe biking to outlying dormitories and a climbing lane exclusively for bicyclists on Table Mesa Drive. Savvy locals know that errands-by-bike sometimes go faster than errands-by-car.

The whole idea of the bicycle as transportation is promoted heavily by the TPG, especially during the annual Boulder Walk and BikeWeek in late June.

Boulder Walk and BikeWeek is a major undertaking designed both as an incentive to exercise and a showcase for the benefits of the bicycle as mode of transportation. In 2000, about 25 restaurants and bakeries—mostly in Boulder but also one each in Longmont, Louisville, Lafayette, and Niwot—offered bicycle commuters free continental breakfasts from 6:30 or 7 to 9 A.M. Volunteer mechanics from local bike shops offer $10 tune-ups and bike safety checks. At least one event is held each day, including Walk and Bike to Work Day, Walk and Bike to Ice Cream Day, Walk and Bike to Market Day, Sunrise Breakfast Walk, Walk and Bike to Downtown Day, Intergenerational Walk, and finally, Walk and Bike to Music Day. Clinics cover topics from "Bike Safety for Kids" to "Zen and the Art of Bicycle Maintenance." And of course, there are free gifts and prize drawings to launch the peak summer cycling season. Expect a bigger, better event every year. More than 3,000 residents participate in Walk and BikeWeek.

Spokes for Folks is a program still in transition, but nonetheless a model for city officials from Fort Collins to San Francisco. In 1997, a fleet of more than 150 loaner bikes was launched to provide people with easy pedal power for errands around town. The donated bikes are fixed up by high-school students and painted a rather terrible shade of bright green so they can't possibly be mistaken for anything else. The Spokes for Folks idea is simple: people are supposed to pick up a bike, ride it to their destination, and then leave it for the next person. While 50 percent of the bikes are vandalized in some way, most are fixed and returned to the streets. Spokes for Folks was modeled after a similar program in Portland, Oregon, which because of its size has had less success than Boulder in keeping track of the bikes. Many cities are trying to start their own program based on Boulder's lessons.

Buses, Limos, and Taxis

The Regional Transportation District, also known as RTD, is the greater Denver metropolitan area's public transportation agency. RTD recorded-information lines are (303) 299-6000, (800) 366-RIDE, and (303) 299-6034 (TDD).

RTD buses are promoted as "The Ride." The main bus station in Boulder, currently the hub of RTD's hub-and-spoke system, is at 14th and Walnut Streets. Rides within Boulder cost 75 cents (exact change only), 25 cents for seniors 65 and older (off-peak hours), and 25 cents for disabled individuals with an RTD card; a 10-ride ticket book costs $5.75. Various monthly passes are also available at the bus station and at King Soopers and Safeway grocery markets. Boulder students can buy reduced-rate bus passes, and CU-Boulder students get RTD passes paid for by their student activity fees. Seniors are also eligible for discount passes.

RTD buses on Boulder city routes operate every half-hour. The schedules and prices vary for intercity service to Broomfield, Denver, Golden, Lafayette, Longmont, Louisville, Nederland, and Westminster. RTD also offers rush-hour express buses to the Denver Tech Center, hourly express buses to Denver International Airport, and special buses to the Eldora ski area via Nederland. Buses for Colorado Rockies and Denver Broncos

Insiders' Tip

RTD runs special buses to Rockies and Broncos games and many other big events. For information call (303) 299-6000 or (800) 366-RIDE; (303) 299-6034 (TDD).

games depart from the main Boulder terminal and various Park-n-Ride lots for $4 round-trip.

Many buses are equipped with wheelchair ramps, and many allow some bicycles on board. Call one of the RTD numbers for details on these amenities or for information on how to reach your destination by bus. Tell the RTD operator where you need to be, when, and from where you're starting. Schedules are available on buses and downtown at the main Boulder terminal.

The Hop (303–441–3266) is a fantastic idea for unclogging traffic without greatly inconveniencing people. It uses midsize buses operating frequently instead of infrequent runs by often-empty behemoths. The Hop's circuit has 40 stops, including Crossroads Mall, the University Hill shopping area near CU-Boulder, and the Pearl Street Mall. Buses drive both clockwise and counterclockwise on the circuit. The Hop runs every 10 minutes Monday through Friday, 7 A.M. to 7 P.M., and every 15 minutes Thursday and Friday, 7 to 10 P.M., and Saturday, 9 A.M. to 7 P.M. The University of Colorado Student Union also sponsors Night Hop, which runs a CU–Pearl Street Mall loop Thursday through Saturday from 10:30 P.M. to 2:30 A.M., free to CU students with ID and ECO-pass holders. The fare is 75 cents, 25 cents for seniors during off-peak hours, or free for folks with a CU ID or any RTD pass. Some merchants also give out Hop tokens to their customers, good for a complimentary ride.

The Hop has been so successful, the RTD Board of Directors has introduced smaller, brightly colored buses in other metropolitan areas. A similar service called The Skip debuted in August 1997. The 22-passenger buses operate every 10 minutes (every 6 minutes during the rush hours), running north-south on Broad-

With Boulder's traffic congestion, getting around by bus is a good alternative. PHOTO: DAILY CAMERA

The Skip bus runs every 6 to 10 minutes up and down Broadway. PHOTO: DARCY KIEFEL

way. The Jump shuttle began service in 2000 on Arapahoe Avenue between Boulder and Lafayette. The Leap serves Pearl Street commuters, while The Bound, with its Superman-inspired graphics, travels a route along Boulder's 30th Street.

Other transportation companies go beyond the RTD network. Estes Park Shuttle (970-586-5151) runs year-round shuttle service between any Estes Park location and the Denver International Airport. The ride costs $39 one-way, and $75 round-trip. Call ahead for a schedule and reservations.

The best way to the ski resorts is via SkiXPress, new weekend service to five ski areas within two hours of metro Denver. The service is being underwritten by the Colorado Department of Transportation and the ski areas. This leaves passengers with a tab of just $15 for round-trip transportation from Boulder (or Denver) to Copper Mountain, Loveland, Keystone, Vail, and Winter Park on luxurious buses with reclining seats and restrooms—plus

the opportunity to buy discounted lift tickets on board.

Need a taxi? Boulder Yellow Cab (303-442-2277) can pick up in Lafayette and Louisville as well as Boulder. Drivers charge around $1.60 per mile. Boulder Freedom Cabs (303-292-8900) is a new service competing with Yellow Cab. Rates are $1.60 per mile. There are no taxi stands for either company, so call for service. Town and Country Taxi (303-776-0496) serves Longmont, Niwot, and Lyons. Rates are around $1.50 per mile.

For people with disabilities, life would be all the more challenging without wheelchair-lift-equipped, door-to-door, on-demand transportation service. More than 2,000 people use Boulder's Special Transit (303-447-9696), which offers low-cost rides to people with disabilities. Call well in advance for reservations and prices. The LIFT (303-665-9085) is a Lafayette-based volunteer program for people who have trouble getting around. Call 24 hours ahead.

History

Pre-Human History

On a high, hot and arid Boulder summer day, it may be comforting to remember that a mere 70 million years ago, this was beachfront property. For hundreds of millions of years, inland seas rose and receded in central Colorado, pushed around by the emerging Rocky Mountains. When the mountains became the unquestioned victor, the ocean drained away east and west, leaving the western edge of an endless high prairie pressing against an abrupt wall of mountain where the region's history is written in rock.

For far longer than humans have recorded, plants and animals lived, fed, were fed upon, reproduced, and adapted to the complex ecosystem of the high plains, the mountains, and the wetlands. In the areas where they've been left to it, the cycles continue.

The increasingly frantic scribbling of human settlement on that big canvas may now seem to dominate the landscape, but the mountains and the prairies remember where they came from.

First Humans

The first humans passed through Colorado about 10,000 years ago, on foot and armed with stone-tipped spears. They are believed to have descended from Asians who migrated over the Bering Land Bridge 10,000 years earlier. University of Denver scientists found the first signs of human activity in North America near the New Mexico—Colorado border. The Ice Age Folsom man, named for the nearby New Mexican town, was unearthed in 1924. Such early "Westerners" hunted mastodons, woolly mammoths, and giant sloths.

Colorado's first-known settlements were those of the Anasazi in southwestern Colorado's Four Corners area around A.D. 550. The Anasazi are known for their basketry and distinctive pottery, but most of all for Mesa Verde, the spectacular cliff-side dwellings they built and inhabited around A.D. 1150. It's not known why the Anasazi abandoned their cliff dwellings around 1300 and disappeared, but researchers suspect they over-farmed the thin prairie soil, and a great drought forced the tribe to migrate to literally greener pastures in the Rio Grande Valley to the south. Today's Acoma, Sandia, Taos, Zuni, and other Pueblo peoples are believed to be descendants of the Anasazi.

During the 16th and 17th centuries, Colorado was home to several tribes descended from the Shoshone and Algonquins. The Utes were Shoshonean mountain-dwellers. Plains tribes included the Cheyenne, Comanche, Arapaho, and Kiowa. Other tribes in the area were the Pawnee, Sioux, Navajo, Blackfoot, and Crow.

American Indians throughout the Southwest visited Colorado for such things as clay for their pottery, fossil seashells for their medicine men's magic, and turquoise for adornment. Bands of Cheyenne and Arapaho traveled to the Boulder Valley regularly to collect flint for arrowheads and colorful clays for war paint.

By the mid-19th century, the Comanche and Kiowa had been driven out of the Boulder Valley by the Cheyenne and Arapaho, who came originally from the Minnesota–Great Lakes area, where they, in turn, had been driven west by the Sioux. The Arapaho wintered here because the game was plentiful and the winters mild. They also enjoyed and venerated the warm thermal waters at Eldorado Springs. The

Utes, the oldest continuous residents of Colorado, still lived in the mountains above the Boulder Valley and ranged west to the Salt Lake Basin, lending their name to the state of Utah.

First Europeans and Pioneers

Gold brought the first European explorers to the area. Perhaps the first to venture into Colorado was Francisco Vásquez de Coronado, who arrived in New Mexico in 1541 searching for the mythical Seven Gold Cities of Cibola.

During the 17th and 18th centuries, both the French and Spanish alternately claimed the territory that included all present states on the Mississippi River plus Montana, Wyoming, the Dakotas, and part of Colorado. For a while the territory was called Louisiana after King Louis XIV of France; it became New Spain when the Spanish defeated the French in the French and Indian War in 1762. In 1800 Napoleon gave the Spanish an Italian kingdom for the territory, reclaiming it again for France.

American adventurer James Purcell of Kentucky explored the area in the early 1800s, before it became U.S. territory, and found gold along the Platte River. Then, in 1803, President Thomas Jefferson paid $15 million to France for some 830,000 square miles of the region in the famous Louisiana Purchase, doubling the size of the United States. At the time, Jefferson was maligned for squandering money on questionable, unexplored land.

U.S. Army Lt. Zebulon Pike and Maj. Stephen Long were commissioned to explore the territory, and later, John Fremont came looking for a route across the Rockies. One of Fremont's men, William Gilpin—later to become the first governor of the Colorado Territory—reported that gold could probably be found in the area, stirring some initial interest in what was then considered "the Great American Desert . . . totally unfit for cultivation and, of course, uninhabitable by a people

depending upon agriculture for their subsistence," according to Long.

A wave of loners—fur traders, trappers, and mountain men—followed the explorers, establishing trading posts in the Arkansas and South Platte Valleys, including Bent's Fort, one of the most important trading posts in the West.

Mexico, hoping to win friends and maintain its claims in the territory, ceded land to wealthy settlers in the 1840s but abandoned its claims after the Mexican-American war.

In 1836 Texas, enjoying brief status as an independent republic, also claimed a strip of Colorado extending northward to the 42nd parallel. The federal government bought out the Texas claim in 1850, but Texans have been recapturing the territory ski condo by ski condo ever since.

Colorado's first permanent non-native settlement was established in 1851. Determined farmers began irrigating the arid plains under the increasingly concerned watch of area natives, who realized that the influx of newcomers was not abating.

The Gold Rush

The next gush of settlers came in 1858 after gold was discovered in the sands of the South Platte River near present-day Denver. Prospectors worked their way north, panning Cherry Creek (Denver), Clear Creek (Golden), Boulder Creek, and others. As these lower "placer deposits" of gold were eventually mined out, prospectors and miners followed the creeks up into the mountains, sometimes finding the "mother lode" in such places as Central City and Black Hawk, then even higher to Breckenridge, Gold Hill (above Boulder), Empire, Aspen, Leadville, and Cripple Creek. Along with gold, they would also find silver, iron, tungsten, molybdenum, and on the plains, oil and coal. Among the most notable beneficiaries of the mountains' largesse were the unsinkable Titanic passenger Molly Brown and "Baby Doe" Tabor, who became a wealthy socialite, thanks to her mine above

Leadville. (Unfortunately she later froze to death there penniless and alone.)

The arrival of the miners encouraged a rash of organization in the region. On the present site of Denver, towns named Montana City, St. Charles, Auraria, and Denver City were founded. The first stagecoach carried mail to Cherry Creek settlements in 1859. The region's first newspaper, the *Rocky Mountain News,* published its first edition on April 23, 1859. Bypassing Congressional approval, settlers organized the Jefferson Territory to govern the gold camps.

First Boulder Settlement

In 1858, Capt. Thomas Aikins, a Missouri farmer, led a gold-prospecting group of farmers and merchants to the area. From Fort St. Vrain to the northeast, he peered through his telescope and saw "bands of Indian Ponies and bands of deer and antelope grazing close up to the high foothills; . . . and could see that [it] was the loveliest of all the valleys . . . a landscape exceedingly beautiful, those mountains are so high and steep . . . " (There's some debate about what Aikins actually viewed through his telescope; the Boulder Valley cannot be seen from Fort St. Vrain because of the topography. There's also "first settler" John Rothrock, about whom less is known.)

In October or November, Aikins and party camped near the mouth of Boulder Canyon beneath the jagged vertical red rocks—an area now designated as Settlers Park. According to Aikins, before they had bedded down for the night, Chief Niwot of the Arapaho paid a visit, encouraging the company to move along and commenting prophetically, "Go away; you come to kill our game, to burn our wood, and to destroy our grass." But the miners fed and flattered the tall, handsome Niwot (whose name means Left Hand), and he eventually agreed to coexist in peace.

Boulderites love to tell newcomers the story of another of the chief's comments, which became known as Niwot's Curse.

Popular legend has it that Niwot warned the white settlers that they would never be able to leave the Boulder Valley. The number of students who make their lives in Boulder after graduation, the professionals who return after retirement, and the vacationers who come back year after year seem to prove the legend true. What Niwot actually said, however, was, "Boulder Valley is so beautiful that people will want to stay and their staying will be the undoing of the beauty"—a prediction that Boulder policymakers and citizens have been working hard to disprove.

In January 1859, the Aikins party found gold in a small creek bed between Sunshine and Four Mile canyons. Word got out and within a month there were 2,000 men and 17 women in the Boulder area.

A bust of Chief Niwot, who welcomed the first white settlers in the Boulder Valley with the warning that they would never be able to leave, greets similarly smitten newcomers to the Boulder Courthouse lawn. PHOTO: LINDA CORNETT

Town Development

Winter closed in, making mining difficult and causing many miners to leave. In February, Aikins called a meeting to form a "Town Company." Later that month, A.A. Brookfield became the first president of the Boulder City Town Company, and 56 shareholders divided 1,280 acres along Boulder Creek into 4,044 lots. Each shareholder received 18 lots; a few lots were given for free to those who promised to provide such services as sawmills. The remaining lots were for sale at $1,000 each. Other homesteading lands at the time cost $1.25 an acre, so the Boulder lots weren't hot sellers, and further settlement was quite slow. Other camps and settlements in the area grew much faster.

Boulder, named after the area's plentiful rocks, began as a raw frontier settlement of tents and crude log cabins along the creek. Roofs and doors were made of split pine, and the floors were dirt.

True to its later identity as a seat of education, Boulder built the territory's first schoolhouse in 1860, at the southwest corner of Walnut and 15th Streets. The first Boulder Post Office was established that same year. Originally part of the Nebraska and Kansas territories, Boulder became part of Colorado when Congress established the Colorado Territory in 1861. South of present-day Baseline Road—the 40th parallel—was the Kansas Territory; north was the Nebraska Territory. In

1867, Boulder became the county seat, and the town was incorporated in 1871. Unlike the region's boom-and-bust mining towns, Boulder's economy remained stable because the city functioned mainly as a supply and transportation center for the miners and prospectors—and, later, as a hub for plains farmers. Boulder's population from 1860 to 1870 remained at about 350.

Boulder's first newspaper, the *Boulder Valley News*, began publication in April 1867. Telegraph service was established in 1874. The town's first hospital was built in 1873 and the first bank a year later.

Land Grabs and the Sand Creek Massacre

The technicalities of stealing the land from the Native Americans were set forth in the Pre-emption Law of 1841, which stated that a person had prior right to purchase a piece of land if he occupied it and improved it. The Kansas-Nebraska Act of 1853, which referred to preemption of "the public lands to which the Indian title had been at the time of such settlement extinguished," further assisted settlers in laying claim to the area. In 1866 Congress validated various settlers' claims to these lands.

Land "ownership" and "improvement" were not understood in the American Indian culture as they were by Europeans. If anything, the American Indians believed the land owned them and didn't need any "improving." The result was a classic clash of cultures, East versus West—living in harmony with nature versus controlling it. In the 1850s and 1860s, the clash became more and more violent. Natives attacked caravans of supplies, sending the cost of food soaring. Forts were built around the state to shelter settlers and house troops brought in to fight the Indians.

In the summer of 1864, reports of natives attacking some wagon trains and express wagons led to the creation of the "100 Day Volunteers," a group commis-

Insiders' Tip

Why does Boulder, which is nowhere near the ocean, have a Marine Street? It was named for Marinus Smith, one of Boulder's first citizens and a local farmer.

sioned under Capt. David Nichols, along with other citizens. Friends of Chief Left Hand (Niwot) in Boulder refused to take part in this brigade, which found and attacked peaceful American Indian families camped, in accordance with treaties, at Sand Creek in eastern Colorado. Thinking the attack was a mistake, the besieged Indians raised the American flag, but were ruthlessly massacred nonetheless. Women and children were scalped, and gentle Chief Niwot, who met with the first settlers, was killed.

Bold Miners, Blizzards, Boom, and Bust

The original gold deposit that fueled Boulder's early economy was depleted after about a year. Next, silver from mines in Caribou, west of Boulder and almost twice as high, stimulated Boulder's growth.

Four miles from the Continental Divide at 10,500 feet, life was cold and tough at Caribou, but in the early 1870s the lure of silver had drawn nearly 500 residents, who built houses two stories high so they could find them in the 25-foot-high snow drifts that followed winter storms. The second story also allowed citizens to come and go through their bedroom windows in the deep snow. A rope ran from the mine to the town's center so miners could feel their way home in blizzards. When asked about Caribou's winters, one miner remarked that he did not know how long winter lasted, because he had only been there three years. Perhaps mercifully, Caribou was eventually destroyed by fire, diphtheria, scarlet fever, and the mining bust over the next few decades.

Mines popped up all over the area: Sunshine, Salina, and Magnolia—today the names of a local canyon, town site, and road. Many booming mountain mining towns, such as Ward, soon went bust when the gold ran out. A smelter built at Black Hawk in 1868 renewed interest in deeper mining in the area, because ores containing gold could be processed. A few years later, a gold-silver ore was found at Gold Hill, and

during 1892, the peak year, more than $1 million in gold and silver was produced.

In 1900, ferberite, an ore of tungsten, was identified in Nederland, starting a new rush to the area. (Nederland, meaning "low lands," was named by the Dutchmen who bought the higher Caribou mine.) By 1918, Boulder County had become the main producer of tungsten in the United States, with a total production of 24,000 tons of tungsten trioxide worth $23 million. By 1910, $20 million in silver had come from Caribou, but it finally ran out. "Caribou, like the reindeer it was named after, pawed its food—silver—from beneath the frozen snow. The lifeblood of its silver veins pinched out, and the town stumbled to a stop, and died," wrote historian John Buchanan.

Trains and Transport

Trains were the lifeblood of the mining industry and early settlement of the area. Railroad service connected Boulder with the bigger world in 1873, connecting the town to Denver and Golden and the mining camps to the west. A depot was built near Boulder Creek at 14th and Water Streets (now named Canyon Boulevard). One of the old trains now sits near the site, in Central Park, and the depot has been preserved in a commercial area at 30th and Pearl Streets, although the narrow-gauge tracks are long gone.

By 1883 Union Pacific Railroad had 14 miles of narrow-gauge track to Four Mile, Salina, Wallstreet, Sunset, and later, Ward. By 1904 the line went all the way to Eldora and was known as The Switzerland Trail. It became a popular tourist attraction that provided an additional source of revenue to the railroads. But the route had financial problems by 1909, and then-owners Colorado and Northwestern folded. The line continued to be operated by the reorganized Denver, Boulder and Northwestern Railroad, which spent the next 10 years debating whether to close The Switzerland Trail line. In 1919 a cloudburst washed out

Boulder is home to Colorado's flagship university. PHOTO: DAILY CAMERA/KAREN TOTH

2,500 feet of track, and the line was never rebuilt.

Colorado's First School and the University

Boulder citizens lobbied fiercely to have the city chosen for the territorial (later, state) university. The same Capt. Nichols involved in the Sand Creek Massacre served as a horseback mediator, making an overnight ride from the capital in Denver to secure a pledge of local funds from Boulder businessmen and then back again in time to secure the university for Boulder. (In honor of that ride, a University of Colorado dormitory was named for Nichols. In the 1980s, in recognition of his involvement in the massacre, the dormitory was renamed Cheyenne-Arapaho Hall.)

Boulder's citizens donated 44.9 acres of land and money to match the $15,000 appropriated by the state legislature for construction of the university on a barren, windswept hill south of town.

Construction began in 1876, the same year Colorado became a state. Completed in 1877, Old Main, the university's first building, housed the entire university—a

The Midnight Ride of Capt. David Nichols

A little-known episode in the founding of the University of Colorado became one that sealed Boulder's fate as the chosen site for the state's institution of higher education. In 1874 various cities and communities in Colorado were vying for the university, and the situation developed into a bitter rivalry with political intrigues. But the state Territorial House had not yet even passed an appropriation bill for the university, much less decided where it would be.

An 1872 bill for an act appropriating money for a university in Colorado had been defeated. Mountain mining districts opposed the bill, saying that Colorado had no use for a university. Republican members of the legislature had agreed in caucus to vote against any but the most necessary appropriations.

Capt. David Nichols of Boulder had been elected Speaker of the Territorial House and put a bill for the university before the legislature again. He got the assembly to approve a bill that said the territory would give $15,000 toward a university on the condition that Boulder contribute an equal amount. In those days $15,000 was a lot of money, and the legislature probably thought that Boulder would be hard put to come up with it. If the bill were tabled again, there would be no telling what would happen to the university.

Nichols jumped on his horse at 6 P.M. that rainy, late-January night and rode from Denver to Boulder, arriving around 11 P.M. He banged on the door until he woke Capt. Frank Tyler, a prominent Boulder citizen, who promised Nichols he would personally take responsibility for raising the funds. Nichols then visited other prominent citizens discussing the situation. Nichols stopped only long enough to change horses, then rode the five hours back to Denver. At 10 A.M. the next morning he addressed the legislature and announced that he had visited Boulder and obtained promises for the funds.

Capt. David Nichols secured Boulder as the site for the state university. Also shown is a promissory note from a prominent Boulder citizen, which served as backing for the proposed University of Colorado. PHOTO: L. P. BASS

With a stronger assurance of monetary backing than the other cities, Boulder got the go-ahead for the university with the passage of the new appropriation bill.

few classrooms along with living quarters for the president, and janitor and their families. With much ceremony the university opened its doors in September 1877 to 44 students, a president, and one instructor. The students lived with families in town and hiked daily up the hill to class.

When Mary Rippon of Detroit was invited to be CU's third faculty member, Ann Sewell, wife of first CU president Joseph A. Sewell, predicted that Rippon "would not stay two days in this lonely place." Rippon decided to come West and give it a try after reading about Colorado's wildflowers in the *Atlantic Monthly* and hearing that banker Charles Buckingham had donated $2,000 for a university library. She was a French and German professor for 57 years—the first woman in the United States to teach at a state university. She also helped open Boulder's first public library. CU's lovely outdoor theater, site of the Colorado Shakespeare Festival (see our Festivals and Annual Events chapter), is named for her.

To beautify CU's barren, windswept campus, Ann Sewell ordered 50 wagon loads of soil for landscaping purposes. The dirt promptly blew away with the first high wind, but she ordered another 50 wagon loads, and by 1881 the university had 2 acres of lawn with trees and flowers. The rest of the barren town took heart from Mrs. Sewell's persistance, and soon the grassland was dotted with young trees.

The first private school in Boulder, Mount St. Gertrude Academy, was opened in 1892 west of the university. Nuns and students reported falling asleep in the isolated building to the sound of coyotes howling.

Saloons, Red Lights, Religion, and Law

Meanwhile, Boulder began to take on the features of a permanent settlement. By 1872, various churches had been built: Presbyterian, Baptist, and Methodist-Episcopalian. Some citizens became concerned that the town's young men spent too much time in saloons and opened a reading room, where the men could come and peruse the newspapers while inspecting the genteel young ladies occasionally invited in as an inducement.

By the 1870s, Boulder residents had acquired money and real estate and needed a government and laws to protect their assets. In 1871, Capt. Aikins' son, Lafayette, was appointed town marshal and paid a salary of $72 a year. The only previous law enforcement was the mining district's "club rules," whereby a wrong-

> ### Insiders' Tip
> Boulder's red-light district ran from the present-day municipal building to the library but was wiped out by the 100-year flood.

doer would have the hair shaved off half his face and head (opposite sides) and be expelled from town.

A stately county courthouse was built in 1883 at Pearl Street between 13th and 14th Streets. It burned to the ground in 1932, a fire that also destroyed many county records. The current courthouse was built on the same site in 1934. Liquor licenses costing $100 per saloon were established to raise some revenue for the fledgling town. Loose dogs were a big issue; in 1871 a dog-control program was initiated, along with a formal tree-planting program.

By 1875, local Republican, Democratic, and Prohibition parties had formed. Well-educated and feisty, Boulder's women started lobbying for the right to vote that year. In 1893 Colorado became the second state after Wyoming (then a territory) to grant women voting rights, although the motivation was more a desire to pack the polls over issues of advantage to Colorado than a recognition of women's equality.

Less-liberated women (or, perhaps, more—depending upon one's perspective) occupied a red-light district, which stretched from the north side of Boulder Creek at Canyon Boulevard (formerly Water Street) to the present-day library. Pearl Street, Boulder's original main street for commerce, was reportedly named for a well-respected madam. Prostitution and gambling were declared illegal in 1873, but the law was reversed in 1878. Some houses of "ill repute" closed down temporarily and others not at all, and the so-called "brides of the multitude" continued their business.

The increasing number of buildings and the fear of fire—a great danger with the high winds—finally brought about the construction of a waterworks in 1874 and the first hook-and-ladder company in 1875. Bucket brigades were the first means of firefighting. The first volunteer firemen were the cream of Boulder society and popular at firemen's balls, parades, and fire-fighting tournaments. So important and highly regarded were the firemen, the election of the firemen's officers drew more attention than city elections.

By the late 1870s, increased mining activity was bringing in more crime, and Boulder needed a jail. Prisoners had been kept everywhere from the basement of the fire department to the sheriff's hotel room.

Water also became an issue by the late 1870s, as the population increased and Boulder Creek became polluted with mine tailings. People who didn't have wells had to use the creek water. A reservoir had been built in 1874 at the base of Boulder Canyon, but it too had become increasingly polluted. In 1884 horses were found dead in the creek, and the reservoir was shut down. To avoid the mine-tailing runoff, a new reservoir was built at the mouth of Sunshine Canyon. The Boulder City Improvement Society formed in 1881. By 1882, Boulder's population had reached 3,000.

Coal, Oil, Newspapers, and an International Population

In the late 1860s, there were 77 buildings in town. Local businesses included sawmills, a brickyard, several blacksmiths and general stores, stables and liveries. Downtown Boulder had a wobbly boardwalk that rose and fell to a different height in front of each different shop—ripping ladies' skirts and gouging shoppers with loose nails.

The business of mining was expanding to other minerals. Coal was discovered east of Boulder on David Kerr's farm. Coal prospector Louis Nawatny bought nearby land, registered a town plat in 1878 and named it Louisville after himself. Two years later, 500 people had settled there. In 1887 a coal mine was dug in Lafayette (named for Lafayette Miller), and by 1892 there were five mines and 200 homes. Polish, Italian, Greek, and French immigrants joined the Welsh, Scotch, and English miners who

The art deco–style 1934 Boulder County Courthouse on the Downtown Boulder Mall replaced the original courthouse, which burned to the ground in 1932. PHOTO: ROZ BROWN

had been here since the 1860s. By the 1920s the coal industry would be Boulder County's largest employer, with 1,000 men.

Oil was discovered in 1901 near Boulder, and for a while Boulder had its own oil stock exchange and a specialized newspaper, *Oil News*. Wells sprang up all over east of Boulder, and it was predicted that the oil field would stretch to Wyoming. By March 1902 there were 92 oil companies operating near today's Longmont Diagonal. Natural gas was also discovered along with the oil, but it was considered a nuisance. Ultimately, 183 holes were drilled in Boulder County, but only 81 were functioning. Of these, 76 produced oil; five produced gas.

The weekly *Camera* newspaper, so named because it printed photographs on its front page, became the *Daily Camera* in 1891 and still publishes today (see our Media chapter).

The 100-Year Flood

Just when Boulder was getting its feet on the ground and becoming an established city with various amenities, disaster struck. The winter of 1894 was long, cold, and snowy. The heavy snowpack still plastered the Front Range at the end of May. Easterly winds brought a warm spring rain that lasted for 60 hours and melted the snow too quickly. The creeks began to rise in the early morning hours of May 31, soon unleashing an awesome display of nature's power.

"One seething mass of black water, bowlders [sic] and crushed buildings. Nearly every tree has been torn out by the roots and the road bed is entirely destroyed," read the *Daily Camera*, describing the scene at Left Hand Creek near Glendale.

Boulder was experiencing a 100-year flood—so called because there is only a 1 percent chance of such a devastating disaster occurring in any year.

All the mountain roads, bridges, rooming houses, and even mines broke

apart on Four Mile Creek, Boulder Creek, Jim Creek, Left Hand Creek, and the St. Vrain. Buildings washed away at Sunset, Jamestown, Crisman, and Ballarat. Jamestown's church floated downstream with its bell ringing. The 2-year-old boom town of Copper Rock was washed off the map. The raging waters destroyed the road at Estes Park and a section of Lyons.

The flood roared down Boulder Creek into town, first wiping out the railroad bridge at Fourth Street then the bridges on Sixth, Ninth, 12th, and 17th streets—each piling up on the other in a maelstrom of boulders, buildings, railroad tracks, and trees. Witnesses recalled the terrifying sound of the rock- and wreckage-filled water.

"From the Boulder Hotel to University Hill was one vast lake with here and there a small patch of an island," read the *Camera*. After the waters calmed, one resident caught a 7-inch trout on Water Street (now Canyon Boulevard).

For five days, Boulder was cut off from the outside world, and residents on one side of the creek couldn't get to the other side. CU commencement was postponed, and the first mail arrived after five days with news of flooding all over the Front Range. Afterward, miners were out of work because of flooded mines. Amazingly, no one was killed in the flood, and no crimes were committed except the ransacking of someone's trunk. Boulder cleaned up and rebuilt.

More than a hundred years later, the city has embarked on a campaign to gradually buy buildings in the Boulder Creek floodplain and clear a path for the inevitable next major flood. Pedestrian bridges across the creek are designed to break away and swing to the side so they don't become dams for flood debris. Canyon highways are marked with signs telling motorists to abandon their cars and climb to higher ground in case of flood. In the spring and summer, alarms are tested weekly, reminding residents of the continuing possibility of flood.

Tuberculars, Tourists, and Trolleys

As the 19th century came to an end, Boulder was beginning to draw visitors and newcomers other than miners. From its earliest days, Boulder, like other places in the Southwest, attracted people with tuberculosis who hoped the pure air, dry climate, and vigorous life would restore their health. One such transplant was gunman Doc Holliday, who eventually succumbed to his illness in Glenwood Springs on Colorado's Western Slope. Many eminent CU professors were recovered tuberculars.

In 1895 Seventh-Day Adventists built a sanitarium (later to become Boulder Memorial Hospital and now the Mapleton Rehab and Sports Medicine Center) for tuberculars on Boulder's west side.

Along with the tuberculars came a group of Texas professors in 1897 looking for an airy summer camp and retreat to escape the Texas heat. Boulder, by then accessible to visitors by railroad, was known as a community with a prosperous economy, a comprehensive educational system, and well-maintained residential neighborhoods. The Texans chose Boulder as a site for their proposed Chautauqua; the creation of these family summer camps, which emphasized culture, nature, recreation, and sometimes religion, was part of a respected national movement at the time. They were named after Lake Chautauqua, New York, site of the first such camp. The city bought its first park land and named it Texado Park for the

Texans; it is now called Chautauqua Park. The dining hall and auditorium were completed for the grand opening of Colorado Chautauqua on July 4, 1898, and the first Chautauquans camped in tents, later replaced by cottages. A 1903 brochure described the camp as "not a casino," offering "retirement without loneliness," and "quiet without ennui."

Well-known Boulder photographer Joseph Bevier Sturtevant ("Rocky Mountain Joe")—who produced many memorable photographs of the city's early years—was the official Chautauqua photographer. Chautauqua had a full and varied program, from music and art to political and ethical discussion groups and well-known speakers and performers such as William Jennings Bryan and John Philip Sousa. Operas, magic shows, displays of military tactics, lace-making demonstrations, baby shows, food booths, fish hatchery exhibits, photo contests, children's races, and gypsy camps were but a few of the offerings. Physical health and exercise were emphasized from the start, and the Chautauqua Climbers Club made annual hikes to local landmarks and the higher mountains. Boulder druggist Eben Fine, one of Chautauqua's regular climbers, literally stumbled upon the discovery of Arapaho Glacier in 1900 when he nearly fell into one of its crevasses.

The Switzerland Trail railroad was a popular excursion for Chautauquans, who would ride into the mountains for a picnic and snowball fight. The more adventurous rented handcars and pumped their own way up for a day's outing.

Transportation to and from Chautauqua was difficult, so for the camp's second season in 1899, the city inaugurated its first electric streetcar, which for a nickel "sped" visitors from downtown to the Chautauqua gate at 15 miles per hour. A few years later a line to the sanitarium was put in, and others followed.

The railroad brought more tourists to Eldorado Springs, south of Boulder, where a popular resort developed around the area's thermal springs. It attracted such rich or famous—or soon to be—visitors as young Dwight and Mamie Eisenhower (who honeymooned there), budding musician Glenn Miller (a CU student), actress Mary Pickford and her husband, actor Douglas Fairbanks Sr. (a Jamestown native), writer Damon Runyon, fighter Jack Dempsey, and gossip columnist Walter Winchell. From 1907 to 1948, Ivy Baldwin performed his famous high-wire walk 600 feet across the canyon on a steel cable averaging 582 feet high. He made his last trip at age 82.

More Parks and City Planning

Chautauqua began Boulder's golden age of land and park acquisition. The day after the camp opened, the city bought the eastern slope of Flagstaff Mountain from the U.S. Government. Shortly after, the city purchased another 1,800 acres of Flagstaff Mountain west to Four Mile Creek and from Sunshine Canyon south to South Boulder Creek.

The Boulder Women's Club planted trees in town, and in 1907 a parks board became an official city department. Next, the city slowly acquired the land along Boulder Creek from the Colorado and Southern Railway. At the time, the parks board wanted a park along Boulder Creek stretching from the mouth of Boulder Canyon to the eastern edge of town. Central Park land was acquired in 1906, and steadily the town purchased more lots and parcels from the railroad. Citizens gave gifts of land. Dr. and Mrs. William J. Baird donated 160 acres of their Gregory Canyon holdings in 1911. Hanna Barker and other citizens gave parcels of land. Boulder bought Arapaho Glacier after a battle with U.S. Park Service, which wanted to add it to Rocky Mountain National Park.

A City Vision

In 1908, the Boulder City Improvement Association hired Frederick Law Olmsted, Jr., Harvard-educated in the new field of landscape architecture. Olmsted's father had designed New York City's Central Park. The city asked Olmsted how he thought the city could be improved "to help make it increasingly convenient, agreeable and generally satisfactory as a place in which to live and work?"

Olmsted said Boulder should not arrange itself for the benefit of the tourists, "who hastily pass through…and often conducting themselves so as to interfere seriously with the comfort and welfare…of the permanent residents." Olmsted was suspicious of developers, saying they were usually from out of town. He said that dirty industry only denigrates a community, and to keep it out of Boulder.

On parks, he said, "As with the food we eat and the air we breathe, so the sights habitually before our eyes play an immense part of determining whether we feel cheerful, efficient and fit for life, or the contrary." He was concerned with the "mental and nervous condition of the people." Order was the goal, but "We aim at Order and hope for Beauty," he said.

He envisioned Boulder as a city of homes surrounded by small farms and gardens and advised preserving that feeling of "coziness and quiet attractiveness." He recommended underground wiring and making the Boulder Creek floodplain into a park—"the cheapest way of handling the flood problem." He said the sign of civilized society was the effectiveness of "police" powers to ensure good land use, and he recommended the city manager form of government. Boulderites liked what Olmsted said and, to a large extent, followed his advice.

Slow Growth, Sobering Legislation, War, and Depression

Apparently taking Olmsted's advice to heart, Boulder became notable for its lack of industry except for the necessities: sawmills, lumberyards, blacksmith shops, brickyards, flour mills, a brewing company, and a foundry. Before World War I, Boulder's biggest industry was Western Cutlery and Manufacturing Company. The CU student population had grown to 6,000, and small businesses began opening in the area around the university known as "The Hill."

By 1905 the economy was faltering, and Boulder counted heavily on tourism for city-sustaining income. What was needed, civic leaders decided, was a first-class hotel. Local business owners contributed to a fund to fill that need, and on Dec. 30, 1908, the Hotel Boulderado invited Boulder to its grand opening. The hotel still welcomes a steady stream of visitors to downtown Boulder.

By 1908 Boulder's population was 10,000, including enough teetotalers to outlaw liquor 13 years before national Prohibition. Boulder remained "dry" from 1907 until 1967. During that period "liquor islands," where people could purchase packaged goods, grew up outside the city limits. (Not until 1969 did it become legal to serve liquor in a public establishment; the Catacombs Bar in the Hotel Boulderado was the first to do so.)

After World War I came the Great Depression. During the 1930s the Civilian Conservation Corps built and improved trails, made fire lanes in mountain parks, pulled out diseased trees, and rebuilt Flagstaff Road up Flagstaff Mountain, overlooking Boulder. They built the Sunrise Amphitheater on Flagstaff, a lodge on Green Mountain, and a rock garden at Chautauqua. The Works Progress Administration built the Mary Rippon Outdoor Theater at the university, a golf course at Flatirons Country Club, and other buildings around town.

Small-Town America and the Fabulous '50s

To try to raise Depression-weary spirits, the Boulder Pow Wow was begun on August 1, 1934, to celebrate Colorado's statehood day with a rodeo and various contests, including pie-eating and greased-pole climbing. Ladies had rolling pin and slipper-throwing contests and needle-threading relays. Men tested their strength and skills at hay-pitching, hog-calling, and hard-rock drilling.

In 1937 Boulder High was dedicated, and its "modern" nude sculptures entitled "Strength and Wisdom" caused a brief but heated controversy. The stunted, muscular figures were called everything from "powerful and effective" to "wads of chewing gum," but were finally accepted as harmless and have since been nicknamed Minnie and Jake.

By 1945 Boulder was beginning to wake up after the Depression and war. During World War II, 4,077 Boulderites went to war and 77 were killed. The CU campus became a training center for young officers, and their pre-dawn fitness runs were cheered on by coeds from the dormitory windows.

In 1946, 340 parking meters were installed downtown, and a group of young CU graduates founded Arapahoe Chemicals (bought by Syntex in 1965). Chicago-based *Esquire* magazine moved its subscription operations to Boulder in 1949, the first "Eastern" business to relocate here. In 1950 the National Bureau of Standards (NBS) chose Boulder as its main base after considering 26 cities. Boulder's citizens voted to buy 217 acres of land for the bureau and gave it to the United States. Fifteen years later, NBS was a major employer. Initially at an isolated site south of town, NBS was soon surrounded by small ranch houses in a regular suburbia.

The Boulder-Denver Turnpike (U.S. Highway 36) opened in 1952 and was the first toll road in the nation to pay for itself—13 years ahead of schedule in 1967.

CU's enrollment increased after World War II as returning military personnel took advantage of the GI Bill. In 1947, someone named "Joe" autographed the northernmost Flatiron formation and began a series of Flatiron-painting pranks,

The upthrust slabs of rock reminded early settlers of the clothes irons that weary women heated by the fire. The Flatiron formations reminded enterprising University of Colorado students of a canvas; the letters have since been covered by camouflage paint. PHOTO: LINDA CORNETT

Soon after, Automation Industries moved to town. That same year, Beech Aircraft bought 1,500 acres north of Boulder and started its Aerospace Division there.

The chamber of commerce bought 18 acres east of town for Boulder Industrial Park, and Ball Brothers Research Corp. became the major tenant starting in 1957. The Muncie, Indiana, canning-jar company expanded into aerospace technology in Boulder and designed the Hubble telescope.

With all the new enterprise, Boulder's population shot up in the 1950s, and water became a concern. The population in 1950 was 19,999; by 1960 it was 66,870. In 1959 the Blue Line was established as the first project of the newly formed PLAN-Boulder, an early group of environmentally concerned citizens who wanted to preserve Boulder's unique natural assets. An imaginary boundary line was drawn along the mountain backdrop at an average of 5,750 feet, above which no city water service would be supplied.

usually by university students who painted a giant "C" or "CU" on the First and Third Flatirons. (Look closely at the Third Flatiron and you can still see a faint, slightly orange CU.)

In 1948, an 850-foot ski tow ran up the Chautauqua meadow, but it operated only a few seasons due to poor snow.

Industry continued migrating to the area. The Atomic Energy Commission chose an area south of Boulder to install its secret weapons plant, Rocky Flats, in 1951—despite many misgivings of area residents. In 1955, "Tommy" Thompson of Thompson Engineering Co.—builder of the short-lived Chautauqua ski lift—began building respirators for polio victims.

The Early 1960s

In 1940, a young solar physicist named Walter Orr Roberts began manning the Harvard-run High Altitude Observatory in Climax, Colorado (near Leadville). Twenty years later, Roberts was offered the directorship of a new National Center for Atmospheric Research (NCAR), and he recommended Boulder as the site. The state donated 530 acres of mesa land south of town for the new laboratory, which was designed by noted architect I.M. Pei. Though controversial at the time, an exception was made to the new Blue Line ruling to give NCAR water. NCAR was to become a jewel in Boulder's crown, and a setting for Woody Allen's futuristic comedy, *Sleeper*.

The U.S. Department of Commerce established its Environmental Sciences Service Administration (ESSA) in Boulder in 1966. ESSA became part of the National Oceanic and Atmospheric Administration (NOAA) in 1970.

Shopping centers began springing up around town during this period, and the Crossroads Shopping Center opened in 1963 outside the city limits funded by Texas money.

Boulder's water supplies were increased in 1964, which spurred a controlled-growth plan along several "spokes" radiating outward from the city: one east on Arapahoe, one northeast along the Diagonal Highway, and one south. In 1969, there were controversial referendums concerning fluoridation of water, a bond issue for a new library, and an amendment that would allow the sale of liquor-by-the-drink. All three passed. Though citizens rejected a $500,000 parks bond that same year, two years later they passed a $1 million bond to build the north and south recreation centers.

Historically, both liberals and conservatives have agreed on greenbelt acquisition, supporting the continued purchase of land in the mountains and plains to "belt" the city with undeveloped land. To stop the building of a luxury hotel atop Enchanted Mesa, citizens approved the purchase of 155 acres of that land for $105,000.

In 1967, Boulder citizens made history by becoming the first in the country to vote to tax themselves for open-space purchases. The initial 0.6-cent sales tax has provided for purchases totaling $140 million, and the 30,000 acres of open space have been merged with the 7,000 acres of mountain parks land to provide a true green belt around the city.

The Turbulent Late '60s and Early '70s

The late '60s brought the hippies, the "transient problem," and general turmoil to Boulder. The first gentle flower children camped out in Central Park, which had to be closed because it became a health hazard. Later came the more militant anarchists, whose bombs exploded in the Hall of Justice Building, United Bank, and Flatirons Elementary School. The Board of Education's auditorium was fire-bombed. Fortunately, no one was killed in these incidents. Riots in 1971 on University Hill left stores looted and windows broken. Police tear-gassed the mob and arrested 40 people. In 1972, 3,000 anti-war demonstrators barricaded the Boulder Turnpike at the Baseline interchange to protest President Nixon's blockade of North Vietnam and the mining of Haiphong Harbor. Also during this time, politically active Mexican-Americans were seeking to assert their identity and demand equal treatment, recognition, and respect. In 1974, six activists in the Chicano movement were killed in two separate bomb explosions in cars, one at Chautauqua Park and the other in front of a business on 28th Street. The explosions were believed by police to be accidental and meant for some other target.

More quietly, the first gay human rights ordinance law was passed by City Council in 1973, but when it had its second reading some citizens objected vociferously. Mayor Penfield Tate and Councilman Tim Fuller, the most outspoken supporters, received death threats, and Tate, a dignified heterosexual black man, was dubbed "The African Queen" by detractors. Fuller was recalled from office and Tate barely kept his seat. The ordinance was overturned by voters. (Boulder voters later approved a gay rights ordinance and were overwhelmingly opposed to the state constitutional amendment that would have prevented protection for gays.)

During this period new County Clerk and Recorder Clela Rorex attained notoriety after issuing licenses for several same-sex marriages. To express his opinion, one citizen appeared with his horse, Dolly, saying, "If a boy can marry a boy, and a girl can marry a girl, why can't a lonesome old cowboy get hitched to his favorite saddle mare?" He was refused because the horse was under age. Ultimately, same-sex marriage licenses were declared illegal in 1975 by the state attorney general.

PLAN-Boulder County helped write part of Boulder's first Comprehensive

Plan in 1970. In 1971 a height-limit ordinance was passed so that, in the wave of new construction, residents could keep their mountain views. New buildings could not exceed a height of 55 feet—the height of most mature trees. Voters that year also chose a growth-control study plan to prevent the kind of rapid growth that had occurred in the 1950s.

The "New Wave" Plus Growth and Limitations in the '70s and '80s

The late '70s saw calmer times but also a huge influx of newcomers, particularly from the Northeast, as many young adults tired of life in the drab, polluted, often politically corrupt and overcrowded big cities. Most were well-educated and hopeful of finding jobs in one of Boulder's clean industries. Many had visited the area during vacations and were delighted (or requested) to be transferred here by IBM or Ball Aerospace. Many were single parents starting new lives and seeking gold of another sort: good schools and neighborhoods for their children and a happy life.

By word-of-mouth and the "underground" communications network, Boulder had also become known nationwide to neo-Buddhists, bicyclists, runners, the urban disenchanted, spiritual seekers, health food converts, and just about every New Age religion as a great place to live. And it's no wonder. Boulderite Frank Shorter became the first American ever to win Olympic gold and silver in the marathon (1972 and 1976); Celestial Seasonings founder Mo Siegel began the international Red Zinger Bicycle Classic through Boulder streets and surrounding country roads; Tibetan Buddhist leader Chögyam Trungpa Rinpoche founded the Naropa Institute in 1974; and the Boulder School of Massage Therapy opened its doors in 1976.

Meanwhile, fearful of urban sprawl and uncontrolled shopping center con-

struction, PLAN-Boulder County campaigned in the late '70s for preservation of open space throughout the county. In 1976, almost $2 million was spent to complete Boulder's downtown pedestrian mall on Pearl Street to draw people back into the city's center. In 1977, the Danish Plan—originated by City Councilman Paul Danish—was approved to limit residential growth to 2 percent annually. To discourage the building of a mega-mall in Louisville (which Danish described as an "environmental pig"), City Council approved a controversial expansion of Crossroads Shopping Center (now within the Boulder city limits) in 1979.

When a California-based computer software company, System Development Corporation, announced its plans in 1980 to locate on a plateau at the city's southern entrance, on county land designated as open space by the Boulder Valley Comprehensive Plan, city officials nixed it and ultimately decided to buy the land to put the issue on hold until Boulder residents could vote on it. SDC packed up its plans and left Boulder County.

A furious public art debate broke out in 1983 when a New York sculptor, Andrea Blum, was chosen to design an outdoor sculpture at Ninth Street and Canyon Boulevard. Blum's stark, urban-styled white concrete design reminded many citizens of a subway station or public restroom, and it was ultimately rejected as being inappropriate for Boulder's site.

During the 1980s some of Boulder County's plentiful high-tech industries began to falter. Louisville-based Storage Technology Corporation laid off 1,300 people in October 1984, the largest single-day cutback in county history. By the end of the year it had trimmed another 1,290 employees and filed for reorganization under federal bankruptcy law. The ripple effect was felt throughout the county's economy.

The late 1980s brought changes affecting Boulder's runners and readers. The Boulder Creek Path, which runs from Eben Fine Park at the mouth of Boulder

Canyon east to 55th Street, was completed in 1987 and remains one of the most popular walking, biking, and in-line skating avenues in town. After bitter debate in 1988, Boulder voters approved expansion of Boulder's public library at its current site, a beautiful setting next to Boulder Creek and in the path of a major flood.

An actual natural disaster—the largest fire in the county—burned 2,300 acres and destroyed 44 homes in July 1989 on Sugarloaf Mountain. The fire was believed to have been caused by careless campers, but the cause was never definitely identified.

In 1989, federal agents raided Rocky Flats nuclear weapons plant (8 miles south of Boulder) and brought health and safety questions about the plant to local and national attention, much to the satisfaction of activists who targeted the plant with anti-nuclear demonstrations for many years.

Shutdowns, the 1990s

By 1991, in the warm glow of glasnost and following several massive demonstrations, the beginning of the end had come for Rocky Flats. The U.S. Energy Secretary eliminated 1,000 jobs in non-radioactive work at the plant and revealed plans to move the whole operation to Kansas City. Many of the plant's employees accepted the government's offer to retrain them at local colleges for new careers.

Later, Rocky Flats operators pleaded guilty to 10 environmental crimes after more than two years' investigation by a grand jury, and the nuclear plant's official work was ended in mid-1992. The building and site are still being decontaminated, and officials are still trying to figure out what to do with it all.

Also in 1992, a Colorado Springs–based group, Colorado for Family Values, promoted a constitutional amendment that would prohibit state or local governments from passing laws or policies that would allow a claim of discrimination based on homosexual orientation. The amendment was directed at Boulder, Denver, and Aspen, which all had approved anti-discrimination laws for homosexuals. Colorado voters passed the amendment, which was overwhelmingly defeated in Boulder. Within days of the election, Boulder, Denver, Aspen, the Boulder Valley School District, and individuals including tennis star Martina Navratilova filed a lawsuit challenging the constitutionality of the amendment.

Passage of Amendment 2 initiated a nationwide boycott of Colorado. CU-Boulder football coach Bill McCartney created a statewide furor when, speaking from a University of Colorado podium, he called homosexuality an "abomination of almighty God." McCartney served on the advisory board of Colorado for Family Values and organized the massive Promisekeepers gatherings of Christian men. McCartney was censured by CU-Boulder's president, Judith Albino, for using his position as coach to espouse negative views of homosexuality. McCartney left his coaching position at the end of the 1994 football season.

In mid-December 1993, a Denver district judge ruled the controversial Amendment 2 unconstitutional, and in 1996 the U.S. Supreme Court did the same.

Also around this time, neighbors of the National Institute of Standards and Technology (NIST, formerly the Bureau of Standards) were upset with the government facility's plans to expand on 205 acres they had come to think of as permanent open space. After intensive wrangling, the building was built, but in somewhat modified form to reduce its impact on the view of the mountain backdrop.

In February 1993, the Boulder City Council stunned developers by imposing a building moratorium; the council decided it needed time to develop the Integrated Planning Project to determine "what's best for what's left" of developable land in Boulder. County commissioners also initiated a moratorium on mountain building. In September of that year the City Council put a hold on developing large parcels—

Good Books on Colorado

Geology

Prairie Peak and Plateau by John and Halka Chronic
Roadside Geology of Colorado by Halka Chronic

History and Good Reading

A Colorado History by Carl Ubbelohde, Maxine Benson, and Duane A. Smith
A Lady's Life in the Rocky Mountains by Isabella Bird
A Look at Boulder: From Settlement to City by Phyllis Smith
Stampede to Timberline by Muriel Sibell Wolle (stories and legends of Colorado's gold camps)

Other Reference Works

The Coloradans by Robert Athern
The Colorado Guide by Bruce Caughey and Dean Winstanley
Colorado Handbook by Stephen Metzger
Colorado: Off the Beaten Path by Curtis Casewit
Glory Colorado! by William Davis (University of Colorado history, 1853–1963)
Our Own Generation by Ron James (CU-Boulder history, 1963–1976)

the so-called last 10 percent of developable land—and firmly established a population-growth cap of 2 percent a year by imposing a limit on the number of building permits issued.

In the same spirit, in 1993, Boulder County voters passed a .25 percent sales and use tax to buy open space, which could amount to as much as $90 million in the next 16 years. The county's first purchase with the funds was the 5,000-acre Heil Ranch in the Foothills between Left Hand Canyon and Lyons.

Several corporations moved into town in the 1990s. Schwinn Cycling and Fitness arrived in Boulder hoping "to update its stodgy image with a Boulder address and new attitude," according to the *Daily Camera*. Warren Miller Entertainment, a California ski- and sports-movie maker, also put down roots in Boulder—the company already shoots most of its ski footage in Colorado. Two new subsidiaries of IBM set up shop. Centrobe, formerly Neodata,

the world's largest magazine subscription fulfillment service (located in Boulder since 1963), moved its corporate headquarters from Dallas to Louisville (Boulder County) in 1993.

Stock in Celestial Seasonings, another local company, sold like hotcakes when 2.1 million shares went on the block in July 1994. Local investors complained that large investors snapped up all the shares before locals had a chance.

In 1995, scientists at the University of Colorado and National Institute of Standards and Technology created a form of matter never before seen but predicted by Albert Einstein 70 years ago. Called a superatom, the matter was created by cooling rubidium atoms to within a fraction of a degree above absolute zero, where theoretically all atomic motion ceases. The scientists created the coldest temperature on earth—and possibly the universe—for the experiment. Practical applications are not yet clear.

Later that year, Boulder voters made national headlines and created a local uproar by expanding the city's smoking ordinance to ban smoking in all indoor public places except dwellings, sites of private social functions, and tobacco stores. Some bars and restaurants have built fully enclosed, separately ventilated rooms for smokers. The Boulder Dinner Theatre had to get special dispensation so an actor could light up on stage, as called for in a play.

Bould-ly into the Future

Its destiny dictated by geology—gold, silver, and other minerals—Boulder still attracts contemporary settlers because of its spectacular mountain setting. Though settled by miners, farmers, and fortune seekers, Boulder somehow identified the importance of education, environmental preservation, and quality of life from its earliest days. Holding onto these values, the city has nurtured a major university, internationally known research centers, clean industries, and an interesting assortment of citizens who have come from around the country and the world. Boulder has seen many changes from its rustic and humble beginnings, but then again, the more things change, the more they remain the same.

Boulder leaders today continue to deal with the same issues as the town's founders: dog control, water, the price of land and housing, and what to do with all those newcomers "looking for gold."

Coyotes still howl, soaring raptors still dive onto plump prairie dogs, streams still gush dangerously with spring snow melt and subside to drowsy trickles in the heat of summer through carefully preserved open land. Beneath a growing sea of houses and highways, the prairie still stretches to the horizon and beneath the shush of racing skis, the mountains remember where they came from.

Restaurants

American

Asian

Barbecue

Breakfast and Lunch

Cafes/Coffeehouses

Caribbean

Central and Eastern
   Europe

Continental

Creole

French

Indian

Irish

Italian

Mediterranean/
   African

Mexican

Natural

Pizza

Pubs and Brewpubs

Boulder has earned a nationwide reputation for fine dining. In fact, many of the "best restaurants of Denver" lists include a fair number of Boulder restaurants. Good spots abound in the Pearl Street Mall area, but stupendous possibilities also exist in other shopping areas, the mountains, and plains. This chapter is organized by type of restaurant rather than by geographic region, since they're all within an easy drive of Boulder.

You could enjoy a different Boulder eatery every day and not repeat for weeks. Boulder has a stunning variety, from rollicking party places to quiet and intimate restaurants perfect for conversation or romance. Basic food, served fast, suits some people, especially families. Others prefer meals custom-prepared, and some folks like to linger over a gourmet meal.

In addition to your taste buds, you need to consider your budget. Our price-code key uses dollar signs to give the range for the likely cost of dinner for two, not including cocktails, beer or wine, appetizer, dessert, tax, and tip. Please remember that these symbols provide only a general guide.

Price-Code Key

$	less than $25
$$	$26 to $50
$$$	$51 to $75
$$$$	$75 and more

If you live in Boulder, you've become accustomed to smoke-free dining. If you're new or visiting, Boulder's rigid no-smoking regulations might come as a shock. While all restaurants in the city of Boulder must provide nonsmoking areas, none of them accommodate smokers except in a separate (and separately ventilated) room.

Wheelchair accessibility is common, but it makes sense to call ahead. And if a restaurant sounds elegant, eclectic, or spicy, you can bet your booster chairs that your kids will get a fidget attack unless the place also caters to children—or unless your children are used to finer dining than the usual pizza and burger joints that parents often choose in the name of family dining. Many places have special children's menus and entertainment tricks for the kids, so ask about them.

Unless otherwise noted, these restaurants take Visa and MasterCard. Some also take American Express, Diner's Club, and Discover.

For more on takeout or informal food service, or lively nightspots, check our Shopping and Nightlife chapters. Our Estes Park and Grand Lake chapters include details on dining and might provide you with an excuse to explore those mountain towns.

American

Traditional/Casual

The Boulder Broker Inn
555 30th St., Boulder
(303) 449–1752
$$$

The English atmosphere, with dark wood and stained glass, is a perfect complement to entrees such as filet Wellington, prime rib, or Alaskan king salmon. A complimentary bowl of in-the-shell Gulf shrimp on ice accompanies each meal, as do a choice of soup or salad plus dessert, often a French pastry or other tempting treat (it varies daily). The Broker has consistently been chosen "Best Sunday Brunch in Denver and Boulder" for more than two decades. Reservations are recommended. There is nightly dancing at Bently's. The inn is open for breakfast, lunch, and dinner daily.

Boulder Cork
3295 30th St., Boulder
(303) 443–9505
$$

The Cork is Boulder's oldest steak house, specializing in excellently prepared prime rib and steak since 1969. Southwestern dishes, including chicken enchiladas and fresh stuffed chiles, are complemented by the Southwestern decor. The award-winning wine list has been acknowledged with the Wine Spectator Award. The strong presentation of all the meals makes it as popular for a business lunch as for a special dinner. You also can stop for a sip and a light bite at the bar; choices include angel-hair pasta, fresh steamed artichokes, fresh fish, and salads. The Cork is open for dinner daily and for lunch on weekdays.

Chautauqua Dining Hall
900 Baseline Rd., Boulder
(303) 440–3776
$$

This historic 1898 dining hall has been serving summer visitors for more than 100 years in beautiful Chautauqua Park. Since 1997 the restaurant has featured the Rocky Mountain cooking of acclaimed chef Bradford Heap. The interior dining room was beautifully renovated in 1999. The vistas from the wraparound porch are breathtaking, and the overall experience has earned this gem "Best Outside Dining" awards. Fresh soups, salads made with organic Boulder County greens, lamb, griddle-seared ahi tuna, pan-roasted venison, fresh vegetables from local organic farmers, and dry-aged New York steak are just a few of the offerings. A children's menu and award-winning fresh fruit pies make this a memorable family dining experience. The Dining Hall's days and hours change with the seasons, so call ahead.

ChriSar's Grill & Pasta
543 Terry St., Longmont
(303) 651–2772
$$

ChriSar's is mostly American but with a definite Italian overlay. "Sea of Hearts"—shrimp, scallops, and artichoke hearts tossed with linguine—is just one of the many fine seafood, chicken, and pasta meals made from scratch in this quaint and casual 1910 Victorian house. There are several small dining rooms and a patio full of flowers that is open in summer.

This restaurant is open for breakfast and dinner daily except Monday, for lunch weekdays except Monday, and for champagne brunch Saturday and Sunday.

Corner Bar
2115 13th St., in the Hotel Boulderado, Boulder
(303) 442–4560
$$

This is the ideal location for a quick lunch, a lively happy hour, a late-night meal, or a perfectly poured martini. One block off the Pearl Street Mall, the Corner Bar is less formal than Q's (also in the Hotel Boulderado), but features the same award-winning menu from chef John Platt. Fresh salads, superb sandwiches, house-made pastas, and unique appetiz-

Chautauqua Dining Hall is very popular during summer. PHOTO: DAILY CAMERA

ers are served. Enjoy the intimate Corner Bar atmosphere, or savor the award-winning wine list, exceptional cuisine, and premium cigars under the stars on the heated patio. Open for lunch Monday through Friday, and dinner daily.

Foolish Craig's Cafe
1611 Pearl St., Boulder
(303) 247–9383
$

Just one block east of the Pearl Street Mall, this eatery specializes in crepes and omelets. The "Amazing Homer" is a crepe wrapped around onions, Feta cheese, Greek spices, olives, artichokes, mushrooms, tomatoes, spinach, and sour cream. The caramelized three-onion soup is too good to miss. Everything is homemade, and the menu items are served throughout the day. Open for breakfast, and lunch, and dinner daily.

Gold Hill Inn
Gold Hill
(303) 443–6461
$$$, no credit cards

This family-owned restaurant has served six-course dinners in an old-style log inn since 1962. The menu depends on what

chef Chris Finn deems good and fresh. One June day, the offerings included hot and sour duck soup, a cold banana bisque, a salmon soufflé appetizer, venison with blackberry sauce, and a choice of chocolate torte or apricot-strawberry pie.

The inn opens in May, when the mountain snow flurries abate, and it closes at the end of October, when the snow starts again. During summertime, it's open for dinner all week except Tuesday. Reservations are recommended. It's a 20-minute drive into the mountains from Boulder, straight up Sunshine Canyon, and about an hour from Estes Park.

JW's Steakhouse
2660 Canyon Blvd., Boulder
(303) 440–8877
$$

The restaurant at the Boulder Marriott in central Boulder has made steak the centerpiece of its menu. The roasted prime rib of beef is a 10- or 16-ounce cut and can be served with a Madeira-laced herb butter sauce. Or try the grilled chicken breast with roasted potatoes and papaya relish. An appetizer could be a meal by itself, with escargot, grilled shrimp in garlic butter, and crispy onion straws on the menu.

Dessert can be accompanied by one of several espresso drinks, and a full bar and extensive wine list are available. Breakfast, lunch, and dinner are served daily.

Karen's Country Kitchen
700 Main St., Louisville
(303) 666–8020
$$

A historic building with tin walls, cozy rooms, and decorative gift items sets the tone for Karen's homestyle cooking. Karen's has won too many baking awards to list here, so if you go, try the breads, cakes, cookies, pastries, and rolls, all of which are baked fresh daily on the premises. And don't leave without a slice of pie, voted "Best" by *Daily Camera* readers in 1998. If you're still hungry, breakfast can include thick-sliced bacon, charbroiled local sausage, hash browns, pancakes, and Belgian waffles with fresh fruit. Patrons love the liver and onions so much it has stayed on the menu for 20 years. "Scramlets" are all the ingredients you want folded into eggs. Karen's is open for breakfast, lunch, and dinner weekdays, and breakfast only on Saturday and Sunday.

Karen's in the Country
1900 Plaza Dr., Louisville
(303) 666–8503
$$$

The country is more elegant than the kitchen, for Karen's second restaurant is in a three-story Victorian house. It offers many of the same baked goods as Karen's Country Kitchen but adds more continental inspirations, including pasta and chicken dishes. With a seat on the enclosed deck, you've got a view of the beautifully landscaped yard with a sooth-

ing waterfall and fountain. It's open for breakfast, lunch, and dinner Monday through Saturday, and for brunch on Sunday.

Murphy's Grill
28th St. and Iris Ave.,
Willow Springs Shopping Center, Boulder
(303) 449–4473
$

Even if it's not your neighborhood, this is has been a favorite neighborhood restaurant since 1985. A varied menu offers Mexican dishes, fresh salads, pasta, and burgers; appetizers include nachos and hot chicken wings. The walls are covered with nearly every "Murphy's Law" you've ever heard. Murphy's has a full bar and wine list and is open daily for lunch and dinner.

Mustard's Last Stand
1719 Broadway, Boulder
(303) 444–5841
$, no credit cards

Chicago-style hot dogs, German bratwurst, hamburgers, and thick homestyle fries are served in this Boulder institution, and the place provides a funky view of Broadway. Okay, they've bowed to popular demand and added veggie-dogs and tempeh burgers, but you don't have to eat them if you don't want to. The "best hot dogs" winner in all the local publications, Mustard's is open for lunch and dinner daily. You can also find a second Mustard's in Denver.

Oliver's Restaurant
800 28th St., in the Ramada Inn, Boulder
(303) 443–3322
$

This is a great place to test a wide selection of domestic and imported beers while you chow down on the popular buffalo burger and watch the Broncos. Or try the free appetizers while you play pool during the daily happy hour from 4 to 7 P.M. For breakfast the menu offers blueberry pancakes and a breakfast burrito smothered in green chili. Breakfast, lunch, and dinner are served daily.

Insiders' Tip
If the kids are part of your dinner plans, order take-out food and head to a park.

The Sink has been a college hangout since the 1930s. PHOTO: DAILY CAMERA/NICO TOUTENHOOFD

**Omni Interlocken Resort Meritage
Restaurant and Wine Bar
500 Interlocken Blvd., Broomfield
(303) 464-3330
$$$**

If you seek breathtaking views and have a voracious appetite, you'll find all you're looking for in this comfortable restaurant offering innovative, unpretentious cuisine. There's a first-rate selection of wines to accompany your meal. Begin with an appetizer such as roasted portobello mushrooms, bacon-wrapped prawns, or jumbo lump-crab cakes. Move on to the entree, which could be peppercorn-seared salmon, mint-and-mushroom-crusted rack of lamb, or ruby-red trout. To complete your meal, gaze on the majestic Flatirons and Longs Peak while lingering over a selection from the extensive dessert tray. Breakfast, lunch, and dinner are served daily.

**Pioneer Inn
15 First St., Nederland
(303) 258-7733
$**

Built during Nederland's historical mining days, this landmark offers hearty American fare. Funky and fun, the rustic inn is known for traditional, filling breakfasts, Mexican-accented favorites, great charcoal-grilled burgers, homemade green chili, and varieties of beer.

When you come to the Pioneer, you get to hang out at the big bar with gritty local mountaineers as well as skiers and hikers who stop in to be part of the fun. It's open daily for breakfast, lunch, and dinner. The bar is open until 2 A.M. every night (see our Nightlife chapter for more information).

**Red Robin Spirits Emporium
2580 Arapahoe Ave., Boulder
(303) 442-0320
$**

Enter one of Boulder's major family and teen hangouts. It's a place with high energy, fueled by a variety of burgers, sandwiches, and fries. Features include their trademark "smiling" chicken. There's a bar up front and a video game room off to the side. It's open for lunch and dinner daily.

The Sink
1165 13th St., Boulder
(303) 444–7465
$

This college hangout has been gathering character since the 1930s. But without that college grunge, it just wouldn't be authentic. "Ugly Crust Pizzas" with various toppings; a huge selection of munchies, including nachos and pizza bread sticks; Sink-Burgers; soups and salads fill the menu. There's live music, great beer, happy-hour specials, and an unsurpassed youthful exuberance. After all, many of the patrons have only recently reached legal drinking age. Organized graffiti serves as decor. Robert Redford was the janitor here before he scuttled art at CU-Boulder and went on to make a few major motion pictures. The Sink is open for lunch and dinner daily.

Tom's Tavern
1047 Pearl St., Boulder
(303) 442–3893
$

A perennial "best burger" winner in the *Daily Camera*'s "Best of Boulder" competition, Tom's has a reputation for the juiciest hamburger in town. The friendly neighborhood tavern has been around since 1959; Tom Eldridge, a somewhat eccentric City Council member, says he opened it as a young dreamer of 21 and never got out of it. Tom's is so well-known, some people use it as a landmark when giving directions. In addition to its popular burgers, Tom's dishes up steaks, pork tenderloin, ribs, and chicken. It's open for lunch and dinner daily.

Turley's
2350 Arapahoe Ave., Boulder
(303) 442–2800
$$

This friendly and unpretentious restaurant is the keeper of the flame, preserving a particular kind of Boulder eating place. Paul Turley has operated three restaurants in Boulder, all of which were immediate hits. Entrees here include lots of vegetables, served with a choice of quinoa or brown rice, plus grilled tuna, a chicken and black bean burrito, scrambled tofu, and other Boulderish offerings that eschew red meat or anything resembling gravy. Turley's offers comfort food, too, including chicken pot pie and buffalo meat loaf served with knockout mashed potatoes. All entrees come with a choice of soup or salad and a roll or the muffin of the day. There's a good selection of microbrews and wines as well as full bar service, and the restaurant does fine with smoothies and desserts as well. Turley's is open for breakfast, lunch, and dinner daily.

Contemporary Cuisine

Alice's Restaurant
3371 Gold Lake Rd., Ward
(303) 459–3544
$$$

This is a romantic, honeymoon kind of place about 35 minutes up the mountain and over a country road. The 100-year-old lodge is charming and rustic, yet it is big enough to hold a private party for 350 people for special occasions such as wedding receptions. Generally, it's a more intimate crowd, with about half the people staying at the Gold Lake Mountain Resort and the other half coming up from Boulder.

The cuisine is innovative American with Pacific Rim overtones, such as Thai crab cakes with lemongrass. Fare includes gourmet vegetarian dishes, seafood, wild game, and juicy steaks. The wines are reasonably priced, and the meal is well worth the trip. You can have a cocktail before dinner at Karel's Bar or retire there for an after-dinner drink, but the best treat is to retire to your own quaint cabin for the night instead of driving back to town.

Alice's is open for lunch and dinner daily during summer, with somewhat shortened winter hours. Reservations are highly recommended.

Dandelion
1011 Walnut St., Boulder
(303) 443–6700
$$$

This rather expensive, very stylish restaurant has ratcheted Boulder up another notch on the culinary scale. In a light and airy high-ceilinged room, it draws its stylistic influence from Manhattan's best and most sparkling SoHo restaurants, but it also has a definite Rocky Mountain pedigree. Favorites here include shrimp and blue crab cakes with mango-orange chutney and a spicy mango sauce, sesame-seared tuna with stir-fried cabbages, wasabi, tobiko, and ginger cream, and chipotle-glazed pork chops with roasted-corn mashed potatoes and caramelized apples. Beautiful presentation is a hallmark of this excellent restaurant. The wine list is excellent, and the desserts will make you rethink the concept of "sinful." Reservations are recommended for busy times. Dandelion serves lunch Monday through Friday and dinner daily.

Dolan's Midtown Restaurant
2319 Arapahoe Ave., Boulder
(303) 444–8758
$-$$

Boulder business people voted Dolan's the best lunch restaurant, with the prime rib special featuring mashed potatoes a sure bet for closing the deal. There's a cozy wood-paneled bar, perfect for watching sporting events in the afternoon and yet elegant enough for appetizers or dinner in the evening. There's also a separate dining room. Both the bar and restaurant serve seafood and steaks, soup and salads. The ahi tuna quesadilla with sliced blackened rare tuna, cilantro, Monterey Jack cheese, and pickled ginger is a huge hit. Live Maine lobster is the special every Wednesday and Sunday. Lunch and dinner are served Monday through Friday; dinner only on Saturday and Sunday.

EnVie
1738 Pearl St., Boulder
(303) 417–1240
$$$

If you appreciate a novel, modern, up-to-the-minute restaurant environment, go east from the Pearl Street Mall 3 blocks to discover EnVie. It's the latest entry in the category of places people go to "see and be seen." The menu is billed as New Orleans–style, but beyond gumbo there are contemporary salads, basic breakfast fare, and a full espresso bar. Small tables, jazz or acoustic music almost daily, and a huge selection of wine make EnVie a rich addition to Boulder's downtown scene. Open for breakfast, lunch, and dinner Monday through Friday, and brunch and dinner on the weekend.

14th St. Bar and Grill
1400 Pearl St., Boulder
(303) 444–5854
$$

Another people-watching spot, this bustling, sunny restaurant serves gourmet pizza baked in a wood-burning oven, along with fine salads and rotisserie chicken. Salmon might be accompanied by a cantaloupe salsa during the summer. The turkey sandwich is like a Thanksgiving meal. The vanilla-bean cheesecake is only one example of the knockout desserts. Everything is consistently good, fresh and innovatively prepared. The patio seating lets you be part of the mall scene. It's open for lunch and dinner daily except Sunday, when it's dinner only.

Jax Fish House
928 Pearl St., Boulder
(303) 444–1811
$$

The winner of several awards, Jax is the place people want to be when they're hungry for fresh seafood. Or is it the martinis? Local newspaper readers say Jax makes the best martini in town. Owner/executive chef David Query's restaurant resides on trendy Pearl Street, just west of the Pearl Street Mall. The raw oysters and clams are exceptional. You can doodle on your crisp butcher-paper "tablecloth" while you wait for your spicy gumbo, clam chowder, soft-shelled crab linguine, steamed mussels, and vegetarian specials. Save room for the Key lime pie. Jax is open daily for appetizers and dinner only.

Limbo
2719 Iris Ave., Boulder
(303) 544-1464
$$

This bright and friendly eatery has great appeal to the younger crowd. The menu includes 35 different "little plates"—a concept imported from Europe to allow customers to sample the various dishes, including grilled eggplant, grilled asparagus, and roasted red peppers. Lunch and dinner are served daily.

Q's Restaurant
In the Hotel Boulderado, 2115 13th St., Boulder
(303) 442-4880
$$-$$$

From Fred's to the Fleur de Lis to Winston's, one of the nicest places to dine in downtown Boulder has undergone several diverse changes in the past 20 years. Hotel owner Frank Day ascribes to the belief that a restaurant becomes stale after a few years and has the deep pockets to make dramatic changes that rarely fail to please customers. Q's is regarded as one of Colorado's finest restaurants. Chef John Platt offers changing monthly menus that might include grilled asparagus with arugula, lobster stuffed gold potato, roasted pheasant breast, chile-crusted Colorado trout, or adobe-grilled pork loin with peach salsa, all presented like a 3-D food sculpture. Organically grown green salads accompany all dinners. A fabulous dessert menu and wine list are standard procedure at the hotel. Breakfast, lunch, and dinner are served daily.

Trilogy Wine Bar and Lounge
2017 13th St., Boulder
(303) 473-9463
$$

Why the name Trilogy? This casual restaurant featuring live music and an international wine selection is owned by triplet sisters. Tempura-style coconut shrimp and a variety of bruschetta are perfect appetizers to accompany entrees such as seafood and chicken paella, house-made exotic-mushroom ravioli, seared Colorado lamb chops, and a nut-crusted salmon. Many Trilogy fans stay until 9:30 P.M., when the back room features a blues jam, salsa jam, or Brazilian music Tuesday through Sunday. Trilogy is open for dinner daily.

Trios Grille and Wine Bar
1155 Canyon Blvd., Boulder
(303) 442-8400
$$

This restaurant is oh-so-sleek and its food is oh-so-delicious. Stylish and contemporary, it enchants both in the way it looks and what it serves. Lunch offers a selection of soups such as sweet corn, fresh salads with baby greens, Caesar salad, gourmet pizza, and pasta. Dinner entrees include rack of Colorado lamb, steak frites, Angus porterhouse, pan-seared ahi tuna, and double-thick pork chops. A jazz trio or blues band might perform, and the sommelier certainly will have some excellent selections from the wine bar to offer. The restaurant features an award-winning wine list, with 50 vintages by the glass and more than 400 by the bottle.

Trios has its own private parking lot, a special bonus for a large and lively downtown restaurant. It's open for lunch and dinner Monday through Saturday. Bar hours are later. Trios serves Sunday brunch as well.

The Twisted Vine
1709 Pearl St., Boulder
(303) 442-2542
$$

Bullfrog's has made way for the Twisted Vine at this accessible downtown location. Owned and operated by executive chefs Richard and Salvatore Manzo, both graduates of the Culinary Institute of America, this eatery offers fare with flair. The appetizer menu includes Prince Edward Island mussels in Thai coconut broth, vegetable spring rolls with Asian ponzu, and tea-smoked duck breast over sweet potato-apple puree with black plums and blackberry jus. The entree menu is still more eclectic, with cornmeal-crusted catfish over ancho mashed potatoes with black-bean salsa, and Australian rack of lamb. For dessert, there's chocolate everywhere—chocolate terrine with fresh cream, chocolate with raspberry sauce, chocolate shavings on the coffee. Lunch is served Tuesday through Friday, dinner Tuesday through Saturday, and brunch only is available on Sunday.

Zolo Grill
2525 Arapahoe Ave., Boulder
(303) 449-0444
$

Zolo Grill is regularly named the "Best Southwestern Restaurant" in Boulder, and regulars rave over the duck tacos and chicken enchiladas. Since opening in 1974, Zolo has become known not only for its food but for its decor, which is eclectic electric, from the copper wires crossing the ceiling to the huge abstract murals on the walls, all with a hip Santa Fe underpinning. The food is spicy and visually exciting, with lots of zigzag saucy accents, sort of like Zorro marks . . . or Zolo marks. Start with a Zolorita, the bartender's special margarita, and finish with a dessert from a list that includes incredible grilled banana cream pie. Zolo is open for lunch and dinner Monday through Saturday and for brunch and dinner on Sunday.

Asian

Bangkok Cuisine
2017 13th St., Boulder
(303) 440-4830
$$

This pleasant restaurant off the Pearl Street Mall features fresh food of Thai and Vietnamese origins. Vietnamese spring rolls, vegetarian curries, spicy Dungeness crab, chicken sauteed with lemongrass, and an excellent noodle dish called pad thai are among the best dishes. There's also an interesting Southeast Asian version of stuffed grape leaves. Prices are moderate. There is full bar service, including a new back bar where smoking is permitted—which is newsworthy in Boulder. Bangkok Cuisine is open for lunch Monday, and Wednesday through Friday, and for dinner daily.

Boulder Dushanbe Tea House
1770 13th St., Boulder
(303) 442-4993
$$

If you can take your eyes off the decor you will find a variety of distinctive entrees as well as unique bakery and dessert items here. Mapo tofu (a spicy Chinese dish), eggplant, wild mushroom pasta, Thai curry noodles, salads, and soups are just a few of the menu items. And don't forget the huge varieties of tea.

The Tea House was a gift from Boulder's sister city of Dushanbe in 1986, but money to erect the elaborate structure was not approved until 1997. The Tea House was an instant hit, in part because it's on the Boulder Creek Path, next door to the Museum of Contemporary Art, across from Central Park, and adjacent to the Farmers' Market. Artisans from Tajikistan spent most of 1997 living in Boulder to complete the intricate assembly. The Tea House even won an award from readers of

Boulder's *Daily Camera* in 1998 as "Best Evidence That Boulder is Different." The creekside patio is a great place to people-watch. The Tea House is open daily for breakfast, lunch, and dinner.

Chez Thuy
2655 28th St., Boulder
(303) 442–1700
$$

This pretty restaurant, with deep green, brocade booths and a big, carved dragon-and-peacock motif mural, dishes up elegant Vietnamese food so well it regularly makes one of the "best" lists. Specialties include quail stuffed with seafood served with vegetables and noodles, pork sauteed in a clay hot pot, curried chicken and vegetarian specials, all cooked by owner/chef Thuy Twee. The portions are generous, and you can dine in or take out. It's open daily for lunch and dinner.

Chinese Dumpling House
WaterStreet Center, Canyon Blvd. and
Folsom St., Boulder
(303) 413–1089
$

This whistle-clean establishment has a limited menu and fast service. Order at the counter, and your food will be brought to your table. The family-owned casual eating spot serves just four varieties of steamed Chinese dumplings (beef, pork, chicken, and vegetarian), plus soups, noodles, and salads. There are a few tables inside and a couple more outdoors. Dumpling House is open Monday through Saturday for lunch and dinner.

Golden Lotus
1964 28th St., Boulder
(303) 442–6868
$

A casually elegant restaurant featuring authentic Chinese fare, including Szechwan, Cantonese, and Mandarin dishes, the Golden Lotus uses the freshest ingredients and no MSG. Enjoy the dim sum

daily at lunch and Chinese "small bites" on the weekends. This is a large restaurant with plenty of parking just outside the door. It's open daily for lunch and dinner.

Lee Yuan Chinese Cuisine
4800 Baseline Rd., Boulder
(303) 494–4210
$

Boulder has a tremendous selection of good, small, family-owned restaurants. Lee Yuan is one of them. Two decades ago, this was Lee Yuan Burger Hut, serving both burgers and carry-out Chinese food. Now the restaurant, in the Meadows shopping center, is a morning-glory-decorated, sit-down establishment that is popular for its less-than-$5 lunch specials as well as its dinner selections. It's very friendly to families. Wine and beer are available. It's open for lunch weekdays and for dinner daily.

Orchid Pavilion Chinese Restaurant & Lounge
1050 Walnut St., Boulder
(303) 449–4353
$$

Voted "Best Chinese Restaurant" in the *Daily Camera*'s reader's poll for more than a decade, the Orchid Pavilion is staffed by New York–style Chinatown chefs, who cook sesame chicken in huge chunks, crispy whole fish, champagne beef, and eggplant in garlic sauce. There are also gourmet seafood dishes and Szechwan vegetables. MSG is never used—you don't even need to ask. The soothing, peach-colored interior includes a huge, genuine Chinese silk screen and fine reproductions of Tang Dynasty horses. Children are welcome. The restaurant's early-bird specials take the most popular menu items and add a choice of soups, chicken wings, egg roll, or fried wonton, as well as a choice of steamed or fried rice for one price. Orchid Pavilion is open for lunch and dinner daily.

PanAsia Fusion
1175 Walnut St., Boulder
(303) 447–0101
$

This section of Walnut Street has been transformed in recent years to include a brewery, an upscale pool hall, a Mexican restaurant, and now Asian fare. East meets West at this restaurant featuring Pacific Rim cuisine made with authentic recipes. Favorites include the Korean-style baby back ribs, garlic and soya beef tenderloin, a salad with spicy tempura prawns, and a warm spinach salad with lime vinaigrette and scallion goat cheese. A bonus is the brewed premium loose-leaf tea, served in cast-iron pots. Open for lunch and dinner Monday through Friday and for dinner only on the weekend.

Sawaddee
1630 30th St., Suite B, Boulder
(303) 447–3321
$

Sawaddee was named "Top of the Rockies" in the 1999 *Zagat Survey* and is a regular on the "Best of Boulder" list. Garlic pepper shrimp and Thai iced tea, made with spices and sweetened milk, will tempt you. Lemongrass and curried vegetables add their distinctive flavors to many dishes. The food is mildly spicy, but you can ask for it to be hotter or not spicy at all. The chefs will add more vegetables when requested, which is one reason the spot earns high points from Boulder's many health enthusiasts. Sawaddee is open for dinner daily except Monday and for lunch daily except Sunday and Monday.

Insiders' Tip

Even Boulder's finest restaurants often have room for drop-ins. Call ahead, or if it's a weekday, try your luck and just stop by.

Siamese Plate & Sumida's Sushi Bar
1575 Folsom St., Boulder
(303) 447–9718
$$

Recognized by the Thai government for its delicious Thai cuisine, the Siamese Plate gives diners a choice of Western seating or benches with bright cushions. Try the spicy green curry with vegetables and coconut milk, the green-lipped mussels with spicy garlic sauce, or the exceptional red curry with chicken, and get an appetizer from Sumida's Sushi Bar one level below. Sumida's also offers happy-hour sushi specials and two-for-one sake midday on weekdays, in the early evening, and all evening on Sunday and Monday. If you sit down at Sumida's, you can also order from the Thai menu. Both the Plate and the Sushi Bar are open for lunch Monday through Saturday and for dinner daily.

Silver Palace
3100 Arapahoe Rd., Boulder
(303) 447–3828
$$

The Silver Palace is a fine-dining Chinese restaurant, related to Silver Palaces in, of all places, Vermont and Florida. Boulder's is a lovely and tranquil spot that includes a secluded, romantic patio and service with fine china and silverware on crisp white tablecloths. Signature dishes include Hunan Popcorn, which is very light tempura-style fried calamari with jalapeno peppers and onion; crispy pork with Grand Marnier sauce; and Chicken Gwin Jin, pan-seared with a smoky teriyaki flavor. Silver Palace is open for lunch and dinner daily.

Sushi Tora
2014 10th St., Boulder
(303) 444–2280
$$

This is Boulder's most authentic Japanese sushi restaurant, from the low cloth curtains you walk through to enter during good weather to the excellent raw fish, beautifully presented. This quiet restaurant offers tempura, soups, and appetizers, too. It's open weekdays for lunch and daily for dinner.

Sushi Zanmai
1221 Spruce St., Boulder
(303) 440–0733
$$

There is nothing quiet or low-key about this brassy sushi bar and Japanese restaurant. The sushi is first-rate, the owner, chef Nao-San, is a shameless extrovert, and the restaurant is rarely without a line out the door. This most popular Japanese restaurant was voted by *Daily Camera* readers as the best place for karaoke singing in the metro area. One part of the bustling restaurant features the sushi bar and wood-top tables. At the bar, you can watch the flamboyant Japanese chefs prepare miniature boatloads of artistic sushi. Another part of the restaurant features tatami rooms and grill tables where the chef performs cooking magic.

Sing-along karaoke starting at 10 P.M. on Saturdays make a noisy place noisier—and that much more enjoyable. Lunch and happy-hour specials bring down the cost of good Japanese food and great Japanese-accented fun. This restaurant is open for lunch weekdays and dinner nightly.

Tra-Ling's Oriental Cafe
1305 Broadway, Boulder
(303) 449–0400
$$

Boulder newspaper readers who don't vote for Orchid Pavillion as the area's best Chinese restaurant instead vote for Tra-Ling's. The place is nothing special but the food is. The sweet and sour pork is a favorite, as is the Kung Pao Chicken. The egg rolls are always excellent, and you can never order enough wontons. It's convenient to the Pearl Street Mall, but with free and reliable delivery why not stay home? Tra-Ling's is open daily for lunch and dinner.

Barbecue

Daddy Bruce's Bar-B-Que and Catering
2000 Arapahoe Ave., Boulder
(303) 449–8890
$, no credit cards

This place is usually packed with folks, so it's fun to carry-out after sniffing the maple-stoked stove, where ribs get slathered with sauce that's tangy—not sweet. Not exactly health food, but, oh, what a decadent treat. The beef sandwiches are popular with a side of potato salad. Eat a slab of pork ribs and you'll sweat for two hours . . . with a smile on your face. This place is run by Bruce Randolph Jr., an associate minister of Boulder's Second Baptist Church and son of the late and greatly missed Denver philanthropist "Daddy" Bruce Randolph. Daddy Bruce's is open for lunch every day except Sunday.

Hickory Sticks Smokehouse & Grill
1000 S. Boulder Road, Louisville
(303) 661–9896
$$

Hickory Sticks replaces the Kaddy Shack, a popular barbecue restaurant for 15 years. New owners have wisely kept barbecue on the menu, but have also added steaks and seafood. It's all served in a 100-year-old trio of railroad cars that includes a caboose. It is open for lunch and dinner Monday through Saturday and for dinner only on Sunday.

KT's Barbecue
7464 Arapahoe Rd., Boulder
(303) 786–7608
$

Hickory-smoked barbecue (fat trimmed) gets served with sweet to spicy sauces rated like ski runs—easy way down, more difficult, and double diamond for experts only. KT's is open for lunch and dinner Monday through Saturday.

KT's Barbecue Outback
2675 13th St., Boulder
(303) 442–3717
$

Barbecue comes to North Boulder, specifically to one of the new shops on the "backside" of Community Plaza. KT's serves filling hickory-smoked pork and chicken and all the fixin's. It's open for lunch and dinner daily except Sunday.

Breakfast and Lunch

Annie's Cafe
20 Lakeview Dr., Nederland
(303) 258–3600
$

Perched atop the Nederland Shopping Center, Annie's is a popular local hangout that serves eggs, pancakes, omelets, sandwiches, salads, and homemade soups. It is open for breakfast and lunch daily.

Bart's Restaurant
585 South Boulder Rd., Louisville
(303) 665–2060
$

Sandwiches, steaks, and seafood get served here under pictures of WWII airplanes. This spot is especially appealing to families or to anyone who loves aviation. The restaurant, which is inexpensive to begin with, offers early-bird specials, with hours varying according to the day of the week. Bart's is open for lunch Monday through Saturday and brunch on Sunday.

The Buff
1725 28th St., Boulder
(303) 442–9150
$

It might be the slogan "Eat In the Buff" or the unique breakfast items, but either way *Daily Camera* readers have voted this restaurant the "Best Breakfast in Boulder." Frittatas, panini sandwiches, muffalettas, and breakfast chimichangas are offered along with traditional breakfast items. There's a full espresso bar, or you can sip a mimosa or bloody Mary with a Denver omelet. A children's menu makes this a great weekend stop for families. A pleasant atmosphere and fast service are the norm. The Buff is open for breakfast and lunch daily.

Dot's Diner
2716 N. 28th St., Boulder
(303) 449–1323
1333 Broadway, Boulder
(303) 447–9184
$, no credit cards

Dot's was a fixture at 8th and Pearl for 20 years, but a developer's offer in 1998 was just too good to refuse. The restaurant has moved to north Broadway, with a second location on busy 28th Street. The ambiance doesn't match the old gas station, but the menu is still much the same. It has some of the best buttermilk biscuits in town, along with huevos rancheros, and cinnamon rolls. Dot's is open for breakfast and lunch daily.

Le Français
2570 Baseline Rd., Boulder
(303) 499–7429
$

Real French chefs bake their authentic breads and pastries in stone ovens. The breezy, close-to-CU cafe offers an assortment of croissant sandwiches, French bread, onion soup, spinach salads, and those wonderfully decadent French desserts. The ambiance is cafe-casual (after all, the pastry counter is right there), but the breakfasts and lunches are restaurant-fine. You can order beer or wine. Do you like Grand Marnier cake with butter-cream frosting? How about a thick, rich chocolate mousse shaped like a mouse? This restaurant is open for breakfast and lunch Monday through Sunday.

Lick Skillet Bakery
5340 Arapahoe Ave., Boulder
(303) 449–7775
$

A big old range is center stage at this bakery, where you can eat in or carry out. The fare demonstrates how innovative chefs can elevate basic ingredients. A descendant of a popular spot in Gold Hill that has since closed, this rendition of the Lick Skillet is an informal cafe. The fresh-baked goods, washed down with strong coffee or good tea, are an excellent way to start the day. The muffins and omelets are delicious, as is the chocolate mousse cake—for later, of course. Lick Skillet is open for breakfast and lunch daily.

Marie's Cafe
2660 Broadway, Boulder
(303) 447–0320
$, no credit cards

Marie's is open through lunch (a hearty Middle European one at that), but it is at breakfast that this cafe really shines. Pancakes, eggs, and huge pastries abound. None of the regulars, who include medical professionals from the nearby Boulder Community Hospital and assorted medical groups and support services, seem shy about slathering on the butter or piling on the jam. Maybe they know where to get help if they need it! The atmosphere is luncheonette-basic, with bright lights for perusing the morning paper, and suitably efficient service. Marie's is open daily for breakfast and lunch.

Rocky Mountain Joe's Cafe
1410 Pearl St., Boulder
(303) 442–3969
3980 N. Broadway, Boulder
(303) 444–8510
$

Breakfast, lunch, and Boulder's first espresso bar can be found at the Pearl Street upstairs cafe with high ceilings, exposed brick walls, and if you're at a window table, a bird's-eye view of the Pearl Street Mall. Home fries, breakfast burritos with chorizo, huevos, and a half-dozen salads are on the menu, along with pancakes. Breakfast dishes are available at lunchtime, as are soups, sandwiches, daytime burritos, and salads. There is also a children's menu. The restaurant was named to honor one of Boulder's first photographers, and historic photos line the walls. A second restaurant opened in the North Boulder Village in 1998. Both are open for breakfast and lunch daily.

Cafes/Coffeehouses

Boulder has become a coffee town. Great java is everywhere, and even food and gourmet stores serve eye-opening, high-caffeine espressos right next to the fresh vegetable juices. There's even an espresso bar in the Boulder Public Library. Boulder's coffee craze is most apparent in its abundance of coffeehouses and cafes.

Most of these places sell only coffee. You can get a regular coffee for around a dollar at most of these places, while something like a latte can range from $2.25 to around $3.

The Bookend Cafe
1115 Pearl St., Boulder
(303) 440–6699
$

This hip cafe is connected to the Boulder Bookstore. It's a see-and-be-seen place for the cellular-phone set, especially those who want a little lunch with their coffee. The scones, spelt muffins, and coffeecake start the day off sweetly, and there's a good selection of salads and other light fare for lunch and supper on a daily basis.

The Brewing Market
2525 Arapahoe Ave., Boulder
(303) 444–4858
1918 13th St., Boulder
(303) 443–2098
Crossroads Mall, Boulder
(303) 444–6141
$

This shop has been around for 20 years, but only in recent years has an in-house master roasted the beans. The atmosphere is simple, but it opens daily at 6 A.M., and the crowds line up because they love the coffee and the excellent chai—black tea, sweetened milk, and spices. Don't be mislead by the Arapahoe Avenue address; the Arapahoe Brewing Market is actually a half-block off Arapahoe, next to McGuckin's on the southwest corner facing Folsom.

Buchanan's
1301 Pennsylvania Ave., Boulder
(303) 440–0222
$

On the path between student apartments and CU, this conveniently located shop serves all types of coffee specialties and various pastries from local bakeries. Students in a hurry can even have copies made in Buchanan's copy center downstairs while they wait for the milk to foam. Buchanan's is open daily and stays open late at night; there's outdoor seating, weather permitting.

Espresso Roma
1101 13th St., Boulder
(303) 442–5011
$

This is the Hill's version of Cheers—with caffeine. Students hang here for hours in between classes, savoring the extensive espresso beverage offerings plus bagels, cake, cookies, biscotti, and pastries. Espresso Roma is open daily.

The Foundry
1107 Walnut St., Boulder
(303) 447–1803
$

Known for honey-vanilla latte, poppy-seed cookies, sandwiches, and cakes, this coffeehouse occupies a small space at the front of Boulder's hippest billiards hall. It has limited seating but adequately serves its pool-playing customers, plus the crowd exiting from several new restaurants on Walnut Street.

Javastop
301 Main St., Longmont
(303) 772–1731
$

Longmont's answer to Boulder's burgeoning coffeehouse business, this elegant spot is located in the Old Imperial Hotel. It has a wide assortment of coffees and serves fresh pastries daily. Lunch, including soup, sandwiches and salads, is also served. Javastop closes at 4 P.M. on weekdays, at 2 P.M. Saturdays, and at 1 P.M. Sundays.

Nederland's Acoustic Coffee
95 E. First St., Nederland
(303) 258–3209
$

This quaint coffeehouse is located in a redbrick house with a summer patio and decorated rocking chairs on the porch. Inside are tables printed with chess boards where customers can play, a sitting area with a tattered Victorian couch, and an old wooden ironing board holding the milk and sugar. Used books and new magazines are for sale, and the artwork is both original and daring. In addition to coffee you can buy herb tea, fresh scones, and specials such as mango-apple pie and Italian potato-vegetable soup. Locals come here for poetry readings, too. The cafe is open 7 A.M. to 5 P.M. on Monday,

The Pearl Street Mall offers a variety of eateries, including Panera Bread, a traditional European bakery and cafe. PHOTO: ROZ BROWN

Tuesday, and Thursday; 7 A.M. to 2 P.M. Wednesday and Friday; and 8 A.M. to 5 P.M. on Saturday and Sunday.

Panera Bread
1207 Pearl St., Boulder
(303) 545-2253
$

If you miss the Farmers' Market, the place to buy a reasonably-priced loaf of delicious European-style bread is Panera, formerly Alleycatz or Potter's, depending on how long you've lived here. It offers an assortment of pastries, bagels, and freshly baked bread. In addition to the bakery up front, there's a restaurant in the back with one of the most pleasant dining rooms on the Pearl Street Mall. A variety of salads are made fresh upon order. Hot panini sandwiches are made with focaccia and fresh ingredients and are pressed on a hot grill. Specialty coffees and espressos contribute to the Old World atmosphere. Open daily for breakfast, lunch, and dinner.

Peaberry Coffee, Ltd.
2721 Arapahoe Ave., Boulder
(303) 449-4111
2400 Baseline Rd., Boulder
(303) 499-7337
$

Boulder's three locations are among the metro area's growing number of Peaberry's sites. The owners are from Boulder, but they started their stores in Denver, then expanded to Boulder when it became clear Boulderites love gourmet coffee, too. Especially known for their own coffee concoction, Polar Bears, they serve fresh baked goods, bagels, scones, desserts, and more daily.

Penny Lane
18th and Pearl Sts., Boulder
(303) 443-9516
$

Boulder's historic hippie and teen hangout offers not just coffee and pastries but local music and poetry. Also available are a full juice and smoothie bar, bagels and sandwiches, and both indoor and outdoor seating.

Starbucks
3033 Arapahoe Ave., Boulder
(303) 440–5090
1402 Broadway, Boulder
(303) 442–9199
1427 Pearl St., Boulder
(303) 245–9368
$

The Seattle purveyor that launched the coffee craze has three Boulder locations. They are clean-cut stores, for Boulder that is, and serve a full range of coffees plus pastries and bagels. For the coffee lover in your life, Starbucks is sure to please with great gift items.

Trident Booksellers and Cafe
940 Pearl St., Boulder
(303) 443–3133
$

Regularly voted the best by *Daily Camera* readers, Trident attracts endangered bohemians who love to converse over coffee. It's Boulder's answer to Greenwich Village, or as close as you can get in these parts. A full range of coffees and pastries and lots of interesting conversation at the next table are the draws here. The attached bookstore helps promote the sought-after intellectual feeling.

Vic's
2680 Broadway, Boulder
(303) 440–8209
3305 30th St., Boulder
(303) 440–2918
$

Everybody who's anybody knows Vic doesn't exist. But North Boulder baby boomers who frequent Vic's all know the owner, Mike, and he never forgets a name. Vic's serves coffee and pastries, with Ella Fitzgerald on the CD player. Local artists show their work here, and a Friday open house is common. The new 30th Street store's decor is still more Art Deco/New Age/Retro than the original.

Caribbean

Rhumba
950 Pearl St., Boulder
(303) 442–7771
$$

A taste of the islands comes to Boulder at the Rhumba, a much-praised restaurant serving innovative Caribbean cuisine. Jerk

This Starbucks coffee shop is in a remodeled gas station on University Hill. PHOTO: DAILY CAMERA/DAVID P. GILKEY

chicken with black beans, coconut rice, and grilled pineapple and mango, and garam masala-crusted halibut on yucca whipped potatoes with a candied-ginger beurre blanc are among the menu offerings. Exotic desserts and tropical drinks complete the picture. It's open for lunch and dinner Tuesday through Sunday and closed on Monday.

Central and Eastern European

Andrea's Fine Food and Spirits
216 E. Main St., Lyons
(303) 823–5000
$$

Since 1977, German favorites have been offered by Bavarian native Andrea Liermann, one of the bubbliest, most beloved hostesses in the area. Even if you can't spell them, you know the sauerbraten, spatzle, rouladen, and Matjesfilet are authentic. There are also steaks, seafood, pasta, and vegetarian dishes. Homemade desserts include cinnamon rolls, apple strudel, and walnut torte. On weekends accordion and bell musicians play, and dancers perform the "Lederhosen Slapptanz." Andrea's is open for breakfast, lunch, and dinner daily except Tuesday and Wednesday.

Black Bear Inn
42 E. Main St., Lyons
(303) 823–6812
$$$

Classic European cuisine with a French touch appears on the menu, which changes seasonally. Wiener schnitzel is especially popular. In the wintertime, patrons with a sweet tooth prefer the chocolate taco. In the summer, they go for homemade ice cream. Black Bear is open Wednesday through Sunday for lunch and dinner.

Copperdale Inn
10 miles up Coal Creek Canyon from Colo. Hwy. 93, Boulder
(303) 642–3180
$$$

Sauerbraten, beef stroganoff, wiener schnitzel, and venison medallions are all real central European dishes, prepared by chefs who love Austrian and German cooking. It's a cozy inn, with red booths and fringed lamps, antler motifs, and a family feel. It's open for dinner Wednesday through Saturday, and for lunch and dinner Sunday.

Old Prague Inn
7521 Ute Hwy. (Colo. Hwy. 66), Longmont
(303) 772–6374
$$$

Bohemian plates and hand-stenciled walls give this pre-1900 schoolhouse an elegant, homey ambiance. Entrees include roast duck or pork, Czech-style, served with dumplings and sweet-and-sour cabbage. Reservations are recommended. Old Prague is open for dinner daily except Tuesday.

Continental

Amuse
1430 Pearl St., Boulder
(303) 415–0001
$$$

The Russian Cafe held court at this location for nearly two decades, but the east end of Pearl Street Mall is changing dramatically with the arrival of Borders Books, eclectic boutiques, and high-end housing. The seasonal menu at this new dining spot includes baby arugula and whipped Spanish blue-cheese salad, free-range beef with confit potatoes, and Dover sole with fennel, pearl onions, caperberries, and a Dubonnet reduction. Delicacies on the dessert menu include mascarpone parfait with coffee crème anglaise, and fallen chocolate cake with ice cream and raspberry sauce. Amuse serves lunch and dinner daily except for Sunday.

Emiliana
1739 Pearl St., Boulder
(303) 545–2526
$$$

Those who embrace the "life is short, eat dessert first" approach to life will appreciate Emiliana's. Calling itself a "dessert house and restaurant," Emiliana's features an eclectic continental menu with innovative appetizers and unique entrees. Wild mushrooms and smoked Gouda strudel might begin your meal, followed by walnut-crusted salmon or orange-currant stuffed quail. There's also a full children's menu for ages 11 and under. The specialty, however, is the "Sweet Dreams for Two"—a delectable chocolate platter with a soft, mousse-like cake inside a chocolate tower. The addition of espresso, cappuccino, a specialty coffee, wine, a cocktail, or a microbrew complete a special dining experience. Dinner and dessert are served nightly except Monday.

European Cafe
2460 Arapahoe Ave., Boulder
(303) 938–8250
$$–$$$

Epicures and critics usually call this one of the top four restaurants in town—and the only stratospheric one that's in a strip shopping mall. What it lacks in exterior charm is compensated for inside, where the decor is delightful and the food is outstanding.

What's on the menu depends on what's fresh and in season. Your meal might begin with smoked salmon roll with crab meat and angel-hair pasta, followed by roasted tenderloin with shallots in a sweet soy sauce and a lobster meat garnish, served with a honey-ginger vinaigrette. A popular dessert is the light, cool and refreshing crème brûlée. Beautiful plates and presentation are part of the package; homemade mashed-potato wreaths frame many entrees. The waiters dote on customers. Even if dinner at the European Cafe is beyond the normal budget, you can get a darned good, dinner-caliber lunch here for about $15; try the fish stew. European Cafe is open for lunch and dinner daily.

The Fancy Moose
1345 28th St., in the Millennium Hotel, Boulder
(303) 443–3850
$$$

Enjoy your meal in the elegant dining room decorated in the spirit of a mountain lodge, or dine on the heated outdoor terrace by the waterfall. Rocky Mountain–inspired feasts include Angus beef, cold-water trout, wild game, and freshly harvested vegetables. The Sunday brunch features rotisserie-roasted prime rib, peel-and-eat shrimp, and a lavish display of fresh fruit, vegetables, salads, pastries, and delicious desserts. After dinner, relax by the pines near the open-pit fire and sip a cappuccino with something delightful from the Chocolate Shoppe. Breakfast, lunch, and dinner are served Monday through Saturday; on Sunday, just brunch is served.

Fawn Brook Inn
Colo. Hwy. 7 Bus., Allenspark
(303) 747–2556
$$$$

This tiny mountain hamlet isn't where you'd expect fine continental dining, but it's been served here since 1978 by Chef Hermann Groicher and his wife, Mieke, who hail from Austria and Holland, respectively. Secret ingredients include the crisp mountain air and beautiful flower garden, but even if the surroundings weren't so inviting, the Fawn Brook's exquisite homemade fare, from beef vegetable soup through dessert, would be memorable. All that attention to homey mountain detail just makes it better. Venison served with wild berries and mushrooms, and roast duckling are favorite meals.

Hours vary by the season. During summer, it's open Tuesday through Sunday for dinner. During fall and winter, it's open weekends, depending on the weather. Reservations are recommended. Call ahead for directions. It's about 45 minutes from Boulder and a half-hour from Estes Park.

Flagstaff House
1138 Flagstaff Rd., Boulder
(303) 442–4640
$$$$

When the Emperor and Empress of Japan came to America in 1994, they dined at only one restaurant on their entire national itinerary: Boulder's Flagstaff House. Chef Mark Monette offered their entourage pan-smoked salmon salad with caviar, tossed with local greens in wasabi vinaigrette, along with lobster consommé with spring vegetables and black truffles. Entrees were Boulder trout from the Cline Trout Farm and rack of Colorado lamb with Provencale vegetables, goat cheese, and Japanese eggplant chips. Desserts included Golden Egg Surprise, a cocoa sorbet wrapped with 24-karat gold leaf to make it look like a gold egg.

When legendary French chef Paul Bocuse set up a cooking event with great American chefs from both coasts, he chose the Flagstaff House. Zagat calls it one of Colorado's top 20 restaurants and it makes every "best" list that covers the Rocky Mountain dining scene. You get the idea?

The Flagstaff House, perched high on Flagstaff Mountain, has the most romantic, panoramic view of Boulder around. The Monette family has owned it for nearly 30 years, and chef Mark Monette has trained at the Taillevent in Paris, the Trogois Brothers in Roanne, La Poularde in southern France, and also in Singapore, Tokyo, Thailand, and Hong Kong. His rich blend of culinary knowledge has brought the restaurant increasing fame. More than 40 entrees grace the menu, which changes daily but always includes a commendable selection of meat, seafood, and game. The food is extraordinarily well prepared and artfully presented, and service is excellent, too. The wine list is nationally renowned, and the sommeliers are knowledgeable and helpful. The tasting menu with paired wines is a fine way to tap into the best and freshest ingredients that have inspired the chef's creativity that very evening.

The Flagstaff is by and large an expense-account restaurant, where a full-course dinner for two will easily run into the three figures, but it is definitely worth a once-in-a-blue-moon, all-out grand dinner. Wise locals drive up at sunset or after the lights start twinkling in the valley below and order just appetizers and wine or dessert and wine or coffee—not as grand as a full-course meal but easier on the pocketbook. It's open daily for dinner. Reservations are highly recommended, although drop-ins often can be accommodated.

The Greenbriar Inn
U.S. Hwy. 36, Boulder
(303) 440–7979
$$$

Picture an English earl strolling home with his spaniel to his grand estate, and you're close to the ambiance of this country inn. It has stained glass, dark wood decor, and the vote from one Denver newspaper as the most romantic restaurant in the area. Executive Chef Edwin K. Wiles II presents lordly traditional fare, great for special occasions. Game is well prepared, but rack of lamb is the signature dish. Among the seafood entrees, the shrimp and scallops ambrosia is divine. Follow with white chocolate cheesecake, or make your own combination for a memorable meal.

The Greenbriar is in the country but only 6.5 miles north of Boulder and about 45 minutes from Estes Park. It's open for dinner Tuesday through Saturday and for Sunday brunch. Reservations are recommended.

John's Restaurant
2328 Pearl St., Boulder
(303) 444–5232
$$

If the Flagstaff is No. 1, John's is always No. 2 when Boulder voters choose best restaurant or best place for an extravagant dinner. It doesn't have a comparable view but makes up for it in sophisticated ambiance and charm. Since 1975, chef/owner John Bizzarro has garnered Best Chef awards from *Daily Camera* readers. John's has been featured in novels, and national restaurant critics consistently give it top reviews. The *Daily Camera* calls it "a tranquil eye in the trendy hurricane of food fashions." To quote all the great reviews about John's would fill more than a chapter. John's, in short, is a Boulder institution.

This gem is just a stroll east of the Pearl Street Mall. Set in a small house with herbs and flowers in back and flowers in front, the restaurant is elegant but understated. We have never dined there without being delighted with the service and with each dish.

Classic French, Italian, and Spanish influences are strong, and so is contemporary American influences. Basque-style seafood stew, with perfectly cooked clams, salmon, and shrimp comes in a deliciously sea-flavored broth. If you're feeling more decadent, the creamier and meatier entrees are succulent. The filet mignon is fork-tender and rich, while the wild mushroom ravioli with rosemary porcini is a tender melding of pasta, several species of mushrooms, and sun-dried tomatoes under a sprinkling of fresh parmesan. And from sorbet through cheesecake and the dark chocolate desserts, the final tastes are melt-in-the-mouth good. The wine list is on a par with the cuisine, which is beautifully presented and gracefully served.

There's a magic about John's that can make your spirits glow. Newspaper readers always give John's the award for "Best Restaurant for an Intimate Dinner." Thanks to the attentive staff, engagement rings have even popped up in desserts. But this place can elevate any encounter.

Walk-ins can often be seated promptly. John's is open for dinner daily.

Red Lion Inn
38470 Boulder Canyon Rd., Boulder
(303) 442–9368
$$$

This Old World inn is just 4 miles up Boulder Canyon. The rambling country inn is popular for family gatherings, business dinners, banquets, and weddings. A specialty is wild game, such as venison or pheasant. Much of the menu is devoted to American cuisine, but there are such decidedly Austro-German influences as red cabbage and spaetzle noodles, a good accompaniment with entrees; meals are followed by a tasty dessert tray. The restaurant offers early-bird specials. It's open for dinner daily.

Creole

Lucile's Creole Cafe
2124 14th St., Boulder
(303) 442–4743
$

Sashay up the porch steps of a side-street Victorian house, open the door, and you're in Cajun country. It's just that easy. Faded calico napkins, tables in every nook, and a casual, bustling atmosphere provide a perfect setting in which to enjoy the red beans and grits. Try eggs sardou or a lunch of crawfish etouffé. Rice pudding porridge with currants and raspberry sauce is comfort food, Lucile-style. It's open for breakfast and lunch daily.

Redfish New Orleans Brewhouse
2027 13th St., Boulder
(303) 440–5858
$$

Voted the "Best New Restaurant" by *Daily Camera* readers when it opened in 1997, Redfish features Louisiana Creole–influenced cuisine with a menu that changes frequently. Appetizers include seafood gumbo, crawfish Caesar, fresh oysters on the half shell, spiced shrimp, and oysters Rockefeller. If there's time for dinner, fresh seafood and house-aged steaks head the list. Desserts include "Chocolate Love" and Louisiana bread pudding with bourbon sauce. The brewmaster offers handcrafted beers including Wild Magnolia Pale Ale, Angry Monk Belgian-Style Ale, and Gaston's Swollen Delta Big Easy. Live music Thursday through Saturday is the draw for many. Redfish is open for lunch weekdays and dinner nightly.

French

Bistro 119
**1520 S. Hover Rd., Intersection of Colo. 119
and Hover Rd., Longmont**
(303) 678–0708
$$

Bistro 119 is irresistible for its endless possibilities. Diners can enjoy a smoke-free, casual, candlelit meal in the dining room or on the open-air patio. If you prefer your own patio, Bistro 119 offers specialty items for takeout and several items that can be taken home and prepared for dinner in minutes. Lunch selections include crepes, unique salads, pastas, and seafood. Among the dinner menu choices are Alaskan halibut Wellington, marinated grilled pork loin with caramelized onions, and swordfish with cayenne crawfish cream. A house-prepared white chocolate mousse is just the beginning of the dessert selections. Lunch is served Monday through Saturday, and dinner is served daily.

Indian

Delhi Darbar
826 Pearl St., Boulder
(303) 443–3929
$$

This dimly lit downstairs restaurant, a branch of a popular Denver establishment, serves aromatic and exquisite Indian specialties, including outstanding tandoori offerings from a special clay oven. Chicken, lamb, and vegetarian items grace the huge menu. The inexpensive, all-you-can-eat lunch buffet is a winner with the bottomless-pit crowd. In summer, there are also tables on a pleasant brick patio. Delhi Darbar is open daily for lunch and dinner.

Himalayas Restaurant
2010 14th St., Boulder
(303) 442–3230
$

Authentic Indian, Nepalese, and Tibetan food such as tandoori breads and thali, a vegetarian sampler, are available here. You can order the chicken and lamb curries milder or hotter. There's live Indian music on Sundays. The restaurant is open for lunch and dinner Monday through Saturday; on Sunday, it's dinner only. Reservations are recommended on weekends.

MijBani
2005 18th St., Boulder
(303) 442–7000
$-$$

This small side-street restaurant has a loyal following. The focus here is on meatless meals from southern India, featuring legumes, vegetables, and rice. You won't get regular chicken curry in this interesting eatery, which offers both conventional and futon seating, and live or recorded Indian music that adds to the ambiance.

The menu is divided into themes. You can order from a selection of thali combination plates, entrees that come paired with suitable side dishes. Exotic varieties of ice cream finish the meal in equal style. Beer and wine are served, but many diners opt for the excellent chai tea, just about Boulder's best. In addition to reasonably complete and a la carte dinners, MijBani also sets out an inexpensive all-you-can-eat buffet lunch. MijBani is open for lunch and dinner daily except Monday.

Royal Peacock
5290 Arapahoe Ave., Boulder
(303) 447-1409
$$

Each year, the owners, who are Bombay natives, add yet another peacock decoration to their beautiful restaurant. Hot curried Indian dishes are served, along with vegetarian choices in rich cream sauces, good basmati rice (order lots for anyone who prefers mild food), and yogurt/cucumber salads. The chai (tea with spices and sweetened milk) is delicious. Service is impeccably polite. The staff loves kids, although the leisurely pace here can make the meal a bit long for the youngest tykes. Royal Peacock is open for lunch weekdays and for dinner daily.

The Taj
2360 Baseline Rd., Boulder
(303) 494-5216
$$

The sights, sounds, smells, and tastes of this Indian restaurant are so genuinely Indian that it seems strange to see the Basemar shopping center's acres of asphalt just outside the windows. This large space is divided into a rambling procession of dining areas brought to intimate scale by the personal service and excellent food. Note that we said "personal," not "speedy" or "efficient," for The

Taj is a place for dining and lingering. Everything is custom-prepared at dinner. The opulent, inexpensive lunch buffet provides a sampling if you're in a hurry. There is a full bar. The Taj is open for lunch and dinner.

Irish

Conor O'Neill's
1922 13th St., Boulder
(303) 449-1922
$$

If you're only going to have one Irish restaurant, let it be as close to authentic as possible. This one is, right down to the wood paneling, bar, and antiques all shipped directly from the isle known for its traditional pubs and hearty beer. Speaking of that, you'll find a large selection of draft imported beers and a wide variety of Irish and Scotch whiskeys. Entrees include traditional fish and chips served with coleslaw and malt vinegar, shepherd's pie with lean ground beef, lamb, leeks, carrots, peas, and onions simmered in Bass Ale and topped with roasted garlic mashed potatoes, and steak-and-cheddar boxty. Along with daily beer specials, there is also live music. The restaurant is open daily for lunch and dinner.

Italian

Antica Roma
1308 Pearl St., Boulder
(303) 442-0378
$$

This is one of the Pearl Street Mall's most atmospheric restaurants, a stylish trattoria painted and decorated to look like a piazza in a residential quarter of Rome. There's even a fountain in the middle of the room. With its good food, nice selection of matching wines, and knockout atmosphere, it's no wonder Boulderites have flocked there for years.

The selections are a bit overwhelming, with panzanella, pizza made fresh and

One of the newer additions to Boulder's lively restaurant scene, Bácaro serves traditional and contemporary Italian fare. PHOTO: ROZ BROWN

cooked in a wood-burning oven, and authentic Italian entrees such as saltimbocca ala Romana. The homemade lasagna, ravioli, and tortellini, and the rotolo di pasta have received "Best of Boulder" awards. Antica Roma has even made *Wine Spectator* for its award-winning wine list. If you sit on the patio in summer, you can watch the Pearl Street scene to your heart's desire. It is open for lunch and dinner daily.

Bácaro
921 Pearl St., Boulder
(303) 444-4888
$$$

A fairly recent addition to Boulder's Italian restaurant scene, Bácaro has a simple decor and more complicated Northern Italian cuisine. A house antipasto specialty is carpaccio, thinly sliced raw meat drizzled with olive oil and lemon juice. Fresh homemade pastas include spinach and ricotta cheese ravioli, angel-hair pasta with fresh tomato sauce, and black and white tagliolini with mixed seafood in a lightly spiced tomato sauce. Entree highlights include veal scalloppine topped

with prosciutto and sage, served with creamy baked potatoes. The desserts are as extravagant as the pastas, and the wine list is comprehensive. The service is also excellent. Open daily for lunch and dinner.

Blue Parrot
640 Main St., Louisville
(303) 666-0677
$

Long before "ethnic" food became trendy, this family-run restaurant was providing locals with informal, inexpensive Italian food. The restaurant opened in 1919, when Louisville's coal mines brought many Italian families into the area. For decades, a special evening in Boulder often would end with a trip to the Blue Parrot for a homestyle Italian meal. Today, the noodles are still homemade, including the gnocchi, made with mashed potatoes.

The atmosphere here has stayed unpretentious, so it's a good choice for casual family dining, especially for finicky young eaters who prefer bland to zesty. You can even buy Blue Parrot pasta sauce at grocery stores these days. Blue Parrot is open for breakfast, lunch, and dinner daily.

Café Gondolier
1738 Pearl St., Boulder
(303)443–5015
$

Owned by the same family for more than 40 years, this Boulder restaurant has moved to a new space at 17th and Pearl Streets but still offers fresh, homemade, and affordable Italian cuisine in a casual atmosphere. A variety of Italian breads, soups, and antipasti are served as appetizers. Eggplant parmigiana, lightly breaded and fried eggplant, spaghetti, fettuccine Alfredo, and fettuccine pesto are just a few of the entrees. Desserts include homemade lemon cheesecake and tiramisu. The special on Tuesday and Wednesday is all-you-can-eat spaghetti for $4.99. Open for lunch and dinner Monday through Friday and for dinner only on Saturday and Sunday.

Carelli's of Boulder Ristorante Italiano
645 30th St., Boulder
(303) 938–9300
$$

When this restaurant moved to its new location a few years ago, theatergoers lost a wonderful pre-movie dining spot to south Boulder. But it's worth the drive to sample menu items prepared with the finest imported and domestic ingredients and all-natural chicken and beef. Specialties include pesto di penne, shrimp scampi, chicken picatta, and steak pizziola. Carelli's has a cozy fireplace for winter dining and a garden patio in the summer. The restaurant is open for lunch and dinner weekdays, dinner only on Saturday; it's closed Sunday.

D'Napoli Ristorante
835 Walnut St., Boulder
(303) 444–8434
$–$$

Filling Italian fare, mostly of the traditional Southern Italian variety, is served in this amiable, casual restaurant. Spaghetti, ziti, and fettuccine, the most popular pasta shapes, dominate the menu and are available with an assortment of sauces. Perennial favorites including eggplant parmigiana, lasagna with or without meat, and shrimp fra diavolo. Some seafood, some poultry, and some meat dishes are served, and there's pizza, too. D'Napoli is open for dinner from 4 to 10 P.M. Tuesday through Sunday.

Full Moon Grill
2525 Arapahoe Ave., Boulder
(303) 938–8800
$$–$$$

If it's Italian food you love, you've come to the right town. Full Moon is listed in the *Zagat Survey* of America's top restaurants. Inspired Northern Italian cuisine is prepared by chef Brad Heap, who trained in top French and Italian restaurants and at the Culinary Institute of America before settling into Boulder. His artistry shows. Appetizers include steamed Prince Edward Island mussels and Maine crab cakes. Main courses feature both classic and modern preparations of meat and seafood. Pasta and risotto specials are served and fresh fish is brought in daily for dishes such a pepper-corn-crusted ahi tuna. Great decorative touches such as wooden Balinese pigs serve as visual garnishes to Heap's creations. Full Moon is open for dinner daily and for lunch weekdays.

Laudisio Ristorante Italiano
2785 Iris Ave., Boulder
(303) 442–1300
$$$

Named "Best of Boulder" by two local papers for 10 years straight, Laudisio has also received numerous excellence awards from the *Wine Spectator*. It's one of the most flamboyant dining spots around. And why not? The whole Laudisio family is flamboyant, and their namesake restaurant is a metaphor for their passions. They focus on fresh, local ingredients, exquisitely prepared and generously served. The bustling open kitchen puts forth outstanding food as well as a real sense of family celebration. In addition to the dining rooms, there's a stylish piano lounge. The wine list is extensive, comprehensive, and served with knowledge and grace. There's no grace but a lot of potency to the Italian liqueur called grappa, which seems to come from vials of an ancient laboratory. Yes, the pasta is superb, and so is the risotto, the perfectly cooked seafood, and the chicken. And of course, the desserts—tiramisu, champagne zablagioni, and innovative glacés. Ask for a table on the patio, under the grapevines, or in the quiet dining room with antique Tiffany-style lamps. Laudisio is open for lunch weekdays and for dinner daily.

Millsite Inn
44365 Peak to Peak Hwy., Ward
(303) 459–3308
$

They make the dough for their calzones and pizzas fresh here, with a good sauce and anything in them. There are homemade pies and good desserts as well. Friends give high ratings to the chicken marsala and other full dinners. The food tends toward Italian-American with a few Mexican dishes, and pizza and burgers thrown in. Add to that a comfortably rustic, log-cabin atmosphere. The locals hang out here, meaning residents of the nearby funky town called Ward, along with skiers, and hikers. The guys in the bar have an amiable grubbiness to them and usually pay close attention to the TV broadcasting a game. The Millsite Inn is open for lunch and dinner daily, with the bar open until 2 A.M. when someone's still thirsty.

Neapolitan's
1 W. First St., Nederland
(303) 258–7313
$$

There's a variety of Italian food here just 20 minutes west of Boulder in a cozy family-style restaurant. The stuffed shells are delicious, as are the tasty pastas covered in cream or marinara sauces and combination plates. Homemade garlic rolls are always a nice accompaniment. Neo's serves an outstanding white pizza in addition to the traditional red—both are available with a variety of toppings. Reservations are taken, and carry-out is available. Neapolitan's is open for dinner daily and for lunch and dinner Saturday and Sunday.

Pasta Jay's
1001 Pearl St., Boulder
(303) 444–5800
$$

There was no joy in Boulder when Pour La France Café & Bistro decided the rent at this east Pearl Street location was too high, and Pasta Jay's stepped in to claim the space. But many were just glad it was a popular local eatery and not another chain moving in.

If the atmosphere was perfect for a French restaurant, it suits Italian food just as well. The exposed brick walls, nooks and crannies for dining, the south-facing windows, and the outdoor patio combine to create a pleasant and lively scene. The menu is constructed on a solid foundation of the most popular Italian dishes: manicotti, spaghetti, and various tubular pastas with several flavorful sauces, and pizza, too. Fans love Pasta Jay's mixed salad, drenched in a flavorful dressing, and warm herb and garlic bread. A decent selection of robust domestic and imported wines is available. Pasta Jay's serves lunch and dinner daily.

Salvaggio's Italian Deli
2609 Pearl St., Boulder
(303) 938–1981
$, no credit cards

Looking for the best sandwich in town? Boulder newspaper readers say you'll find it here. Try the hot prime rib or pastrami; both are served on freshly baked rolls. Salvaggio's serves special Italian sausages and Boar's Head–brand meats—among the highest-quality domestic cold cuts you can buy. Prime-rib sandwiches are slow-roasted in the rotisserie oven, and when it comes to popularity, they blow everything else away, hands down. The cajun roast beef and mortadella ham are knockouts. Roasted red bell peppers and fresh mozzarella can be added, too. The sandwich bread is homemade. Order your meal to go, or eat it on the premises. The deli is open for lunch and dinner daily.

Mediterranean/African

Mataam Fez Moroccan Restaurant
2226 Pearl St., Boulder
(303) 440-4167
$$

This richly decorated, exotic restaurant is as much about entertainment as fine dining. While sitting on plump pillows under tented ceilings and listening to Moroccan drums, you will eat with your fingers, but you won't be eating what we think of as finger food.

Dine sumptuously on five-course meals such as couscous with vegetables, lamb with artichokes, and delicious Moroccan tea and pastries. There is a selection of meat and vegetarian dishes.

But best of all, belly dancers entertain Thursday through Sunday. Belly dancing originated to encourage women through childbirth—hence the focus on strong abdominal movements. This is not Las Vegas belly dancing, which is why children are welcome. This restaurant serves dinner daily.

The Mediterranean
1002 Walnut St., Boulder
(303) 444-5335
$-$$

From the bright-red trim to the beautiful iron gate and the avant-garde wood-burning brick oven, this place is stylish and lively. The Mediterranean is another grand restaurant operated by the large Laudisio family. It has been voted "Best Mediterranean Restaurant in the Denver Area" by *Westword* magazine, and "Best Appetizers" by *Daily Camera* readers. It's what you want it to be: a romantic spot, a congenial gathering place with a good bar and summer patio, or a family spot—kids

get kind treatment here.

Spanish tapas, which are small plates of interesting appetizers, include croquetas de gambase y pollo (shrimp and chicken) and lovely mini pizzas. These are served at the bar or at the table. Light dishes include well-prepared calzones and perfectly dressed salads. Spaghettini di Mare is especially popular. The chefs know how to cook chicken and fish without leaving the heat on a moment too long. Spanish friends say the saffron-gold paella is pretty close to authentic. The Mediterranean is open for dinner daily and for lunch Monday through Saturday.

Ras Kassa's Ethiopian Restaurant
2111 30th St., Boulder
(303) 447-2919
$

A Boulder favorite since 1988, Ras Kassa's recently moved into the city from Eldorado Springs. Meat and vegetarian dishes are served with a big slab of injera, a crepe-like Ethiopian sourdough bread, which you use to scoop up the rest of the food. Use the bread like a spoon to capture every drop of the hot, red sauces or the milder ginger and garlic sauces. Entrees include chicken or lamb, sweet potato stew, and butternut squash. You can eat in the Ethiopian-decorated interior, with authentic basket-woven tables, or enjoy the creekside patio. It's open for lunch Monday through Friday and dinner daily.

Shishkabob
Crossroads Mall Food Court, Boulder
(303) 443-8844
$, no credit cards

Enjoy charbroiled kabobs or inexpensive vegetarian dishes such as tofu kabob, spinach delight, and eggplant and mixed vegetables. Basmati rice (always fresh and fragrant), cucumber and yogurt salads, vegetarian spinach casseroles, and lamb dishes are served here, too. Also some of the best lemonade in town, with rose water adding a special bouquet to the sweet tangy drink. Shishkabob is open for lunch and dinner daily.

Triana Tapas Bar and Restaurant
1039 Pearl St., Boulder
(303) 449–1022
$$

Spanish tapas, which are small plates of interesting Mediterranean-style appetizers, rule the menu at Tiana's, formerly the site of Stagehouse Books. Named "Best New Restaurant" by *Westword* magazine in 2001, it offers such tasty treats as baby artichokes baked with cheese, and oysters with roasted chiles. If you prefer a full meal, there's crispy red snapper with baby spinach, and oven-roasted chicken with goat-cheese whipped potatoes, garlic, and shallots. Enjoy your choice of more than 50 Spanish wines while listening to tunes provided by local and international DJs. There is a private dining room available for parties of up to 40 people. Triana's is open for lunch Monday through Friday and for dinner daily.

Mexican

Casa Alvarez
3161 Walnut St., Boulder
(303) 546–0630
$

No sooner did Casa Alvarez open in a corner of the Walnut Garden shopping center than people started raving about its chili—and the honors started pouring in, including winning the Boulder Chile Olé Contest. The red and green chili are each just about the best of their type around, but the restaurant has a way with other Mexican specialties, too. When it's mild out, the patio is a pleasant place to enjoy your meal. Casa Alvarez makes good margaritas and sells them two-for-one during happy hour, from 4 to 6 P.M. every evening. There are also beer and drink specials. Takeout is available, too. They are open for lunch and dinner daily.

Efrain's
101 E. Cleveland St., Lafayette
(303) 666–7544
$$

Efrain's is in an old farmhouse, where the dining area is relaxed and homey. The great tamales, green chiles, and sizzling tostadas make Efrain's one of Boulder County's favorite Mexican restaurants. There are also costillas, which are Mexican ribs in chile verde sauce. Efrain's is open for lunch and dinner daily.

Gustavo's
357 Main St., Longmont
(303) 678–8814
$

Those in the know say that Gustavo Saenz is just a doll, and the fresh-cooked food he serves at his restaurant is a bargain. Gustavo's has homemade guacamole and delicious enchiladas, and you can get a tostada for less than $3. The green chile that smothers burritos and tamales is mild and freshly made. Gustavo's is open for lunch and dinner Tuesday through Saturday.

Juanita's Mexican Food
1043 Pearl St., Boulder
(303) 449–5273
$

Juanita's, one of Boulder's favorite Mexican restaurants, is tucked between Tom's and Stage House Books. This place is noisy and usually packed, so don't expect a quiet, intimate meal. The front half is slightly more formal. The back half is good for families, if you're not too distracted by loud music, pool playing, or a TV screen in every corner; kids love to sit in the back where wooden booths make it easier to color the children's menu. Enjoy the traditional Mexican food, which is always hot; fast service; icy, cold margaritas; and a huge selection of beer. Lunch and dinner are served daily.

Masa Grill Mexican Taqueria
1265 Alpine Ave., Boulder
(303) 440–9511
$

Step up to the counter and order yourself the Burrito Grande, an aptly named, humongous fresh-made burrito in various combinations, which can be tailored to your liking. Tostadas, fajitas, and tacos are also on the menu, and there are daily specials as well. The taqueria's distinctive cilantro rice is an interesting variation on a common theme. There are also decent fresh lime margaritas, served at bargain prices during the daily happy hour, plus good beer and soft drinks. This good-size restaurant is inexpensive and family-friendly, combining the best elements of fast preparation and service with fine, filling food. Olé! It's open for lunch and dinner daily.

Rio Grande Mexican Restaurant
1101 Walnut St., Boulder
(303) 444–3690
$

The old Piccolo's has undergone a huge renovation to become the new Rio Grande, a popular margarita dispensary and Mexican restaurant. Juanita's may win the best Mexican restaurant contest, but the Rio Grande always wins top votes for the best margarita. Colorful Tex-Mex burritos, enchiladas, and fajitas with loads of cheese, black beans, and Spanish rice are featured. The restaurant also offers tortilla chips and pico de gallo, a spicy vegetable relish. The restaurant is open for lunch and dinner daily.

Terrace Maya
4929 N. Broadway, Boulder
(303) 443–9336
$$

You have to travel to the very northern edge of Boulder to find Terrace Maya, but the authentic Mexican fare and festive cantina atmosphere make it worth the trip. Appetizers include chili con queso, bowls of pork or veggie green chili, nachos, jalapeno poppers, and chicken wings. The menu features traditional enchiladas, bean burritos, flautas, fajitas, and chimichangas, too. If you're more adventuresome, try Especial Mexican Barbecue, Mexican rib-eye steak, or house favorites such as Acapulco shrimp or pescado Veracruz. A full bar pours delicious mango margaritas, Mexican cervezas, and microbrews. There's a large outdoor patio with live music every Saturday night. Open daily for lunch and dinner.

Tia Bennie
450 Main St., Lyons
(303) 823–5014
$$

James Arroyo, a Lyons native, named this casual, family restaurant after his Aunt Bennie. It occupies a 125-year-old flagstone, ranch-style building on the west end of Lyons' main thoroughfare. The Cook's Combination—cheese enchilada, chile relleno, beans and rice—and the burritos supreme are especially popular. It's open daily for lunch and dinner in summer (closing at 6 P.M. Sunday) but closed on Sunday during the off-season.

Natural

Rudi's Restaurant
4720 Table Mesa Dr., Boulder
(303) 494-5858
$$

This is a natural-food restaurant that looks and feels like a "normal" place, not like a granola-and-tofu dispensary. It offers fine dining based on a variety of influences from all over the world but with natural and organic ingredients. Samosas, a type of Indian snack food made with mildly spiced vegetables, are a fine starter. Thai vegetable curry and crab-stuffed trout are typical entrees and are served with homemade soup or salad and brown or basmati rice. The tenderloin filet is organically grown. If you come for brunch, try the gingerbread pancakes with whipped cream. Homemade desserts include coffee toffee and Key lime pie. Vegans and people on special diets can get made-to-order food here. Rudi's is open for lunch and dinner daily except Monday and also for weekend brunch.

Souper Salad
2595 Canyon Blvd., Boulder
(303) 447-8272
$

A change of name from the Boulder Salad Company hasn't changed the steady stream of diners who flock to this restaurant for a healthy, diverse, and filling meal. All-you-can-eat salads, soups and pasta, potatoes, baked goods, and fruits are strung along this very popular, very healthful grazing bar. You get in line and choose your items cafeteria-style. It's a super choice for groups who can't agree on what to eat. For all the good eating, you can reward yourself with a big, fresh chocolate-chip cookie. Souper Salad is open for lunch and dinner daily.

Sunflower Natural Fine Dining
1701 Pearl St., Boulder
(303) 440-0220
$$$

Natural food fans can enjoy contemporary fine dining in two spacious dining rooms. The menu features fresh natural ingredients, including organic produce, free-range poultry, fresh seafood, and vegetarian and vegan items. Pesto-stuffed portobello mushrooms and pepper-seared ahi tuna salad can serve as starters. Entrees include sesame-crusted seared Atlantic salmon on Thai rice noodles with miso-sake glaze and ginger broth, and tempeh-mushroom scalloppine with mashed organic Yukon gold potatoes and steamed organic vegetable medley. Seasonal desserts include Key lime cheesecake and tempura bananas. There are fresh salads and sandwiches for lunch, or choose one of several daily specials. Try an organic coffee drink or fresh-squeezed juice. Sidewalk patio dining or delivery service is available. Sunflower is open for lunch Monday through Saturday, dinner nightly, and brunch on Sunday.

Pizza

Abo's
1911 Broadway, Boulder
(303) 443-9113
$

Abo's has been a Boulder institution for more than 20 years. Stop in for a slice or call ahead for a whole pie. Because of its great two-for-one plus free drinks special, this pizzeria has a huge following with the college crowd. Abo's is open daily for lunch and dinner.

Lefty's Pizzeria
641 Main St., Niwot
(303) 666-6200
$, no credit cards

The favorite pizzas at this down-home local pizza parlor are the California veggie (artichokes, broccoli, sun-dried tomatoes, spinach, mozzarella, garlic, and olive oil) and Craig's Cardiac Arrest (pepperoni, ham, sausage, and bacon). But you can also get a pie with pineapple, jalapeños, and/or black olives. Best of all, the pizzeria delivers in Niwot and the surrounding 80 square miles, ranging from Longmont to north Lafayette. A percentage of all proceeds goes to Niwot's youth team sports. This little pizza parlor is open for lunch and dinner daily.

Nick-N-Willy's Take-N-Bake Pizza
801 Pearl St., Boulder
(303) 444–9898
4800 Baseline Rd., Boulder
(303) 499–9898
$

Hands down, *Daily Camera* readers favor Nick-N-Willy's pizza to anything else around. You can buy pizza by the slice and eat it in the store, or call ahead and, 20 minutes later, pick up a whole pizza to take home and bake in your oven. It all started when a friend of Keith McQuillen and Terry Jones opened a great pizza store in California. Keith and Terry found the take-and-bake pizza so delicious, they brought the idea to Boulder. Over the years, different pizzas and toppings have been added, and Nick-N-Willy's has expanded into a dozen different Colorado locations. The Aegean vegetarian pizza is one of the most popular, with olive oil, feta, mozzarella, garlic, spinach, sun-dried tomatoes, and oregano. There's a big cooler with soft drinks and pre-made salads if you need something to complement your pie. Nick-N-Willy's is open daily for lunch and dinner.

Pubs and Brewpubs

The Hungry Toad
2543 Broadway, Boulder
(303) 442–5012
$$

This is Boulder's original English pub. Four English beers are on tap, and eight

Insiders' Tip
Sample local microbrews—on the sites where they are made—at the Walnut and Oasis Breweries.

are available by the bottle. Fish and chips, shepherd's pie, salads, and burgers are popular. The food's not arty, my lad, but it's hearty, and accompanied by comfortable chatter and a pint at your elbow. The pub is open for lunch and dinner daily.

Mountain Sun Pub and Brewery
1535 Pearl St., Boulder
(303) 546–0886
$, no credit cards

This bustling place is Boulder's New Age brewpub, with seven made-on-the-premises fresh brews that burst onto the microbrew scene by winning awards. The food is a winner too. Most of it is vegetarian, including meatless salads, chili, soup, garden burgers, burritos, and pizzas, so you might call it a health-food brewpub. There are shelves of books that patrons can peruse while listening to live folk music on Sunday. Mountain Sun is open for lunch and dinner daily.

Oasis Brewery
1095 Canyon Blvd., Boulder
(303) 449–0363
$$

Award-winning ales are brewed fresh on the premises and served from two full bars. Excellent munchies plus commendable ribs, seafood, and pasta go with the beer. There are popular chef's specials at night, and at lunch the "Brew Plate" should fit the bill. Patio seating, free parking, and a pool parlor upstairs are other pluses. Oasis is open for lunch and dinner through 2 A.M. daily every night except Sunday, when it closes at midnight.

Old Chicago
1102 Pearl St., Boulder
(303) 443–5031
$

It's hard to decide whether to describe this spot on the west end of the Pearl Street Mall as a pub that serves popular Chicago-style pizzas or a pizzeria with a whopping beer selection. More than 110 beers are available from the bar, and the deep-dish pizza is buttery crusted and delicious; whole-wheat crust is also available. The main part of the restaurant truly has a pub feel, while the seating in the back is more spacious. There's also a small patio in the rear. Old Chicago's stout mud pie has layers of coffee and chocolate ice cream, flavored with Australian Sheaf Stout beer. It's open for lunch and dinner through midnight on weekdays and until 1 A.M. on weekends; unlike many brewpubs, the kitchen stays open until Old Chicago closes.

Rockies Brewing Company
2880 Wilderness Pl., Boulder
(303) 444–8448
$

Eight different fresh ales are made on the premises, including the namesake brew, concocted for the Colorado Rockies baseball team. Three are gold-medal winners, pronounced the best beer in the country at the Great American Beer Festival. Sandwiches and salad go with the fresh beer, and if you arrive around 2 P.M., you can tour the establishment, see the whole beer-making process, and sample the current brews. This was formerly the Boulder Brewery, the first microbrewery in the city. Rockies is open for lunch and dinner daily except Sundays.

Walnut Brewery
1123 Walnut St., Boulder
(303) 447–1345
$$

This was Boulder's first true brewpub, and it's still the best. The brewing process is on display here, and you can watch while you drink and dine. The brewmaster concocts six original and seasonal ales, including Buffalo Gold, brewed in small batches to provide a malty, floral happiness . . . we mean, hoppiness. The Walnut Brewery pioneered the practice of donating leftovers from the brewing process to feed happy livestock and to enrich soil in flower beds on the downtown mall. Sometimes, walking the mall is a truly heady experience.

Salads, tenderloin, seafood, pastas, and vegetarian entrees help draw the crowds to this distinctive, tall-ceilinged, lively space. The brewery is open for lunch and dinner daily.

West End Tavern
926 Pearl St., Boulder
(303) 444–3535
$

This is more a bar than a pub, for it is really basic and ungentrified—just the way fans like it. It serves good basic salads, soups, and plenty of burgers, along with 20 different beers and concoctions from the full bar. There's live music or comedy five nights a week—sometimes seven. The rooftop, with the view of the Flatirons, is the most popular summer spot at this friendly neighborhood tavern. Open for lunch and dinner daily, the West End closes at 2 A.M.

Nightlife

Boulder isn't particularly known for its wild nightlife, though there's plenty to do and plenty of places to go after dark. The college crowd has its hangouts, as do the single professionals and families. Most residents and visitors looking for a night out go to a restaurant, concert, or movie—or to one of the many spots listed below.

Because our state is so beautiful and the weather so fine, Boulderites and Coloradans thrive on the out-of-doors. Therefore, many cafes and concert halls are alfresco. On warm evenings from spring through fall, one of the most popular activities, unrivaled in entertainment value (not to mention free), is strolling on the Pearl Street Mall. During summer weekends the pedestrian mall is transformed into a six-ring circus on every block with jugglers, musicians, magicians, bagpipers, and a dreadlocked man in tights who folds himself into an impossibly small box. Though the mall entertainment is free, performers usually have a donation "hat" and appreciate financial support (they have to pay for permits to perform on the mall).

Another uniquely Boulder form of entertainment is *E-Town*, a locally produced weekly public radio show that focuses on the environment and is recorded live with audience participation at the historic Boulder Theater. It's our own homegrown, eco-version of Garrison Keillor's *A Prairie Home Companion*. *E-Town* is aired weekly by National Public Radio on various stations across the country and has featured such celebrities as James Taylor, Dan Fogelberg, Dave Barry, Emmylou Harris, Rickie Lee Jones, and The Persuasions. Tickets are quite inexpensive, and it's fun to play a part in a nationally broadcast radio show. Audience members also get to enjoy the beauty of the restored art deco former movie theater.

Those in search of the really bright lights and big names will usually have to travel to the magnificent Red Rocks amphitheater near Golden, or to Denver's park-like Fiddler's Green amphitheater, its Paramount and Ogden Theatres, or other venues larger than what Boulder has to offer. Some top Denver hot spots regularly frequented by Boulderites are listed among the Boulder nightspots; for a complete Denver listing see the *Insiders' Guide® to Denver*.

Don't forget that the legal drinking age in Colorado is 21, and that drinking and driving don't mix. Don't jeopardize your life—and ours—by getting behind the wheel after you've been drinking. Boulder police have a very low tolerance for alcohol-related offenses. Make sure your group includes a designated driver.

Note that most Boulder bars don't have a cover charge. Those that do usually only charge for admission a couple nights a week, when there's live music or a special event such as dance lessons.

Acoustic Coffee House
95 E. First St., Nederland
(303) 258-3209

Folks drive all the way from Denver up to the mountain town of Nederland—even on weeknights . . . in winter—to enjoy various performers at this pleasantly funky little coffeehouse. Among those who perform here are such nationally known musicians as Chuck Pyle, Tim O'Brien, Peter Rowan, Cheryl Wheeler, and Catie Curtis. Ticket prices for the bigger names range from $5 to $15, but local performers often play for tips. Microbrews and wine are served in the evenings. The Acoustic is open until 10:30 P.M. Friday and Saturday when there is live music. There's a bluegrass jam Sundays at 3 P.M., and other performances generally start around 8. It's also a great stop during the day for fancy coffees, baked goods, and tasty sandwiches; it opens weekdays at 7 A.M. and weekends at 8 A.M. Try a breakfast bagel or one of the delicious scones or brownies. For lunch there are grilled panini sandwiches (focaccia combos grilled in a press). Though the food is a bit Boulder, the atmosphere is definitely Nederland.

Barrel House
2860 Arapahoe Ave., Boulder
(303) 444-9464

Boasting 30 televisions (including 2 HDTVs) with full satellite capabilities, all tuned to one game or another, the Barrel House works hard at proving its claim to be Boulder's best sports bar. There's a rooftop deck for dinner, and 25 microbrewery beers on tap for those who can't tear themselves away from the game. The restaurant also has pool tables outside on the porch to accommodate smokers. A recently completed $200,000 renovation gives the Barrel House the largest number of big-screen TVs in Colorado. Happy hour is from 3 to 6 P.M. daily, with discounts on beer, well drinks, and chicken wings.

Bentley's Nightclub
The Broker Inn, 555 30th St., Boulder
(303) 444-3330

In disco days, Bentley's Nightclub at the Broker (see our Accommodations chapter) vibrated to the dance-dance-dance beat of Donna Summer and the brothers Gibb, an experience complete with lighted dance floor and a DJ with a diamond stud. Today, it remains a favorite spot for less frenetic dancing and meeting interesting people. It attracts an older, more professional baby-boomer crowd (versus college kids). Dancing is popular Wednes-

day through Saturday, with salsa Thursday and swing Saturday. There's a $5 cover on Thursday and Saturday. The bar menu is available every night until 11 P.M. and the bar closes an hour or two later.

Boulder Theater
2032 14th St., Boulder
(303) 443-8696, (303) 786-7030 (Boulder Theater Box Office, noon to 6 P.M. weekdays; noon to 5 P.M. weekends)

An art deco gem (along with the county courthouse across the street, one of only two in Boulder), the former movie theater has evolved into a lively venue for everything from classical performances by the Colorado Music Festival to world music from Kitaro to concerts by former John Coltrane jazz pianist McCoy Tyner. Lately, the theater has returned to its roots with classic and art movies.

The theater is best known, though, as the home of the nationally broadcast radio program *E-Town.* "Live from the historic Boulder Theater in the foothills of the Rocky Mountains, it's *E-Town,*" begins the radio show, which focuses on entertainment and environmental issues—a sometimes difficult twosome. *E-Town* celebrated its 10th year in 2001. The show is taped live to be run by National Public Radio and commercial stations. The audience is part of the show, clapping and cheering on cue, sometimes for several takes. It's interesting to see how a radio show works. The show recognizes individuals from around the country, nominated for their grassroots work for better communities and environment, with the E-chievement Awards.

E-Town records about 35 shows a year. It features musicians, environmentalists, politicians, authors, and others, including Rickie Lee Jones, Taj Mahal, Sweet Honey in the Rock, Paul Winter, Joan Baez, cowboy poet Baxter Black, Earth Day founder Denis Hayes, Bruce Cockburn, Arlo Guthrie, and Leftover Salmon. Run on a shoestring and volunteer efforts, *E-Town* is the brainchild of Boulder husband-and-wife co-producers Nick and Helen Forster. Nick was formerly principal bassist, gui-

The Boulder Theater began life as an art deco movie house. After some uncertainty about its fate, the lovely building is now a popular live performance hall and, in a return to its roots, has begun showing movies again. PHOTO: LINDA CORNETT

tarist, and vocalist for the bluegrass group Hot Rize (which still plays reunion concerts), and Helen, an actress and singer, has provided harmony for performers from Michelle Shocked and John Gorka to Rosanne Cash.

Drinks and snacks are available, so the audience can sip their favorite beverage while they watch the show. Part of the theater has cafe tables and chairs.

Tickets are available at at the Boulder Theater Box Office, at Whole Foods market at 30th and Pearl Streets, or from the theater website at www.bouldertheater.com. See the website at www.etown.org for more information. Come early for dinner on the Downtown Mall and grab a handy parking space before the crowd arrives.

The Catacombs
Hotel Boulderado, 2115 13th St., Boulder
(303) 443–0486

The appropriately named Catacombs was the first bar in Boulder to legally serve liquor in 1969. It has had several incarnations, including one as an inexpensive Italian restaurant and another as an expensive continental restaurant but has now resumed its original identity as an easygoing local bar catering to a mixed-age crowd (average age 35). There's live music Monday, Friday, and Saturday

Insiders' Tip
Some of Boulder's best nightlife is along the Pearl Street Mall on warm evenings from spring through fall. String quartets, bagpipers, magicians, and other street performers keep the crowd entertained for hours. And it's free (donations are suggested for the performers).

nights, with an open blues jam on Monday and a blues bar the rest of the week. Live music continues from 9:30 P.M. to 1:15 A.M. with a $1 cover on weekends. Happy hour is daily from 4:30 to 8 P.M., and snacks and appetizers are served until midnight. Pool tables are scattered through the underground warren of stone-walled rooms. A smoking section is available—a rarity in Boulder, where bars and restaurants may have smoking sections only if they are completely shielded from nonsmoking patrons.

Comedy Works
1226 15th St., Denver
(303) 595–3637

"See tomorrow's stars today" is the slogan of this intimate downtown Denver club where Roseanne Barr got her start. Comedy Works regularly runs headliner shows. Tuesday is improv and new-talent night; Wednesday through Sunday are for established performers. Nonsmoking performances are Wednesday and Friday at 8 P.M. and Saturday at 6:30 P.M. Other Saturday shows are at 8:30 and 10:30 P.M. Reservations are recommended (only ages 21 and older are admitted). Tickets range from $7 to $25 based on who is performing. Cocktails and a limited food menu are available during the show.

Conor O'Neill's Irish Pub and Grill
1422 13th St., Boulder
(303) 449–1922

Since 1978, The James Pub & Grille was the closest thing to a real Irish pub in Boulder—red potatoes were a popular dish, live music filled the bar with the trill of traditional folk tunes. Now the restaurant and bar is a step closer to Tipperary in its new incarnation as Conor O'Neill's Irish Pub and Grill, with an interior created in Ireland and brought to Boulder piece by piece for assembly. The bar has returned to its entertainment roots, too, with live music every night and an open mike on Tuesdays. The pub is open 11 A.M. to 1:30 A.M daily and serves lunch and dinner, including Irish stew and shepherd's pie, teas, and 20-ounce English pints of beer from England and Ireland.

Corner Bar
Hotel Boulderado, 2115 13th St., Boulder
(303) 442-4560

An extensive list of wine by the glass, a variety of martinis, and eight microbrews on tap (five made in Colorado) are available in this historic bar decorated in dark wood. Upstairs from the Catacombs (see previous entry), the Corner Bar has a casually elegant atmosphere. In the summer, the bar spills onto a charming sidewalk cafe along Spruce Street, one block off the Downtown Mall. Food, from macho nachos to elegant rock shrimp and crab cakes, is served until midnight.

Fiddler's Green
6350 Greenwood Plaza Blvd., Englewood
(303) 220-7000 (mid-May through mid-September)

About an hour's drive from Boulder, Fiddler's Green, southeast of Denver, offers summer performances by all types of top nationally known groups, including rock, classical, and oldies (a recent season included James Taylor and the Foo Fighters). Enjoy these outdoor events either from reserved seats or with a picnic on the lawn. The usual types of food and drinks are sold in the amphitheater, but the Green is strict about allowing no outside food or drink—no coolers, picnic baskets, or thermoses. Also outlawed: cameras, tape recorders, lawn chairs, knives, and firearms. You may bring small backpacks and blankets, umbrellas, and binoculars. No exit is allowed once you enter the concert area; if you forget your ID for alcoholic beverages, you can't go out to your car and get it. Concert season is mid-May through mid-September. For tickets call the box office at (303) 770-2222 during the concert season or Ticketmaster at (303) 830-8497.

Flagstaff House
Flagstaff Rd. (west end of Baseline Rd., partway up the mountain), Boulder
(303) 442-4640

Even those who can't afford dinner at the Flagstaff House—one of Boulder's most elegant and expensive restaurants, perched high on Flagstaff Mountain (see our Restaurants chapter)—can still enjoy the great view and wonderful, outdoor terraced bar for the price of a drink. Overhead heating units are installed for comfort on cool evenings. If you're lucky, you might catch a fantastic summer lightning show out on the plains. For a really romantic drink with someone special, choose this beautiful spot. Flagstaff is open Sunday through Friday from 6 to 10 P.M., Saturday from 5 to 10 P.M.

The Foundry
1109 Walnut St., Boulder
(303) 447-1803

A full bar with wine, cognacs, beer, mixed drinks, and cigars, along with 11 full-size Brunswick pool tables make this upscale spot a favorite. It's a great place to meet people and mingle in a comfortable, spacious yet intimate atmosphere. There's free live music Friday and Saturday, with a blues and jazz band starting around 9:30 or 10 P.M. and playing until closing at 2 A.M. Happy hours are 11 A.M. to 7 P.M. daily and drinks are served until 1:30 A.M. Foundry staff get an early start, opening the coffee bar at 7 A.M. An interesting group gathers at the Foundry—people of all types. Free pool is available with lunch daily. Light fare such as nachos, sandwiches, pizza, bagels, and muffins are served.

Fox Theatre and Cafe
1135 13th St., Boulder
(303) 447-0095, (303) 443-3399 (box office)

Nominated for Club of the Year by *Performance Magazine* and several others, the Fox has become one of the top clubs for live music in North America, with acts like Fat Mama, Disco Inferno, Hootie and the Blowfish, and Run-D.M.C. Another converted movie house, this cafe/concert hall on University Hill holds more than 600 people and has three full bars and nightly live music by local, national, and international performers. People of all

Live music can be enjoyed at many Boulder nightclubs, including the Fox Theatre and Cafe.
PHOTO: LINDA CORNETT

ages attend the shows (those over 21 get a bracelet to indicate they can order alcoholic drinks). The lobby sushi bar, Hapa on the Hill Sushi Grill, serves up raw fish and sake from noon 'til the music ends. Call the box office for ticket prices.

The Grizzly Rose Saloon & Dance Emporium
5450 N. Valley Hwy. (I–25), Denver
(303) 295–2353,
(303) 295–1330 (for concert information)

Voted the nation's No. 1 country music dance hall by the Country Music Association, Grizzly Rose has a 5,000-square-foot dance floor and gets such top names as Merle Haggard and Wynonna. There are free introductory dance lessons Wednesdays at 7, with various contests and specials other nights. Call (303) 42–DANCE for contest information. Thursdays are ladies' nights from 8 P.M. to midnight with free wine, well and draft drinks, and no cover charge for women (men pay $5 cover). Concert tickets are available through Ticketmaster (303–830–8497), or at the door; advanced ticketing is necessary for national acts. The Grizzly Rose is open from 11 A.M. (serving lunch) to 1:30 A.M. Monday through Friday, from 5 P.M. until 1:30 A.M. Saturday and Sunday.

Jax Fish House
928 Pearl St., Boulder
(303) 444–1811

Jax is known for its fresh seafood, but savvy Boulderites have latched onto it as a place for a quiet after-dinner drink and plate of raw oysters or shrimp. The full, fishy menu is served in the bar. Jax opens at 4 P.M. daily, closing at 9 P.M. Sunday, 10 P.M. Monday through Thursday, and 11 P.M. Friday and Saturday. Happy hour is from 4 to 6 P.M. daily, with East Coast oysters for 85 cents.

Jose Muldoon's
1600 38th St., Boulder
(303) 449–4543

This popular Mexican restaurant also has a sports bar and claims to serve the "biggest margarita in town" in numerous versions (due, perhaps, to its selection of tequila, Boulder's largest). There's an all-you-can-eat tostada bar in the restaurant during the day, and on Sundays from 10 A.M. to 2 P.M. Jose's serves one of the best brunches in town. The restaurant is open weekends until midnight, and weekdays until 11 (serving meals until 10 P.M.). There's a happy hour from 3 to 7 P.M. weekdays and all day Saturday and Sunday. Fiesta Fridays feature free appetizers from 4 to 7 P.M. The restaurant's patio, billed as the largest in town, is a great place to spend a warm summer evening.

Lazy Dog Bar and Grill
Iris and 29th Sts., Boulder
(303) 440-3355

The old folks who used to come to this edge-of-town location when it was Furr's Cafeteria wouldn't know the place now. The line for fish slabs and fried okra has been replaced with video games, pool tables, and the TVs that mark Lazy Dog as a sports bar. The ribs—a full baby back slab—have been voted the best in Boulder for four years running by the consumers who ought to know. Lazy Dog is open 11 A.M. to midnight every day.

Mercury Cafe
2199 California St., Denver
(303) 294-9281, (303) 294-9258 (dinner reservations/information)

Dinner, dancing, drinks—you name it, the Mercury Cafe has it. The cafe serves an "international, organic, healthy menu for carnivores and vegetarians" 5:30 to 11 P.M. Tuesdays through Sundays. All the soups, breads, and desserts are homemade. The bar is open until 1 A.M. and serves neighborhood microbrews. In a separate concert hall, there's nightly dancing. Tuesday nights bring the Lindy Hop, with $2 classes at 6:15 P.M. Wednesday nights are open stage, with the sign-up beginning about 8:30 P.M. Swing nights are Thursdays and Sundays, with free swing classes at 6 P.M. Thursday and 5 P.M. Sunday. Swing bands start playing about 7:30 P.M. and the cover is $7. Open poetry night is every Friday at 10 P.M.; it's preceded by Argentine tango with a beginners' class at 7 and intermediate class at 8 P.M., each $5. Dances are smoke-free and open to all ages.

Murphy's Bar and Grill
28th St. and the Diagonal Hwy., Willow Springs Shopping Center, Boulder
(303) 449-4473

A casual, not-too-expensive restaurant with burgers, salads, and nachos, and a bar with 36 brands of beer make Murphy's a laid-back destination. Happy hour is 4 to 7 P.M. daily with discounts on well and tap drinks and house wines. Hours are 11 A.M. to 11 P.M. Monday through Thursday, 11 A.M. to midnight Friday, 11 A.M. to 11 P.M. Saturday, and 11 A.M. to 10 P.M. Sunday.

Oasis Brewery
1095 Canyon Blvd., Boulder
(303) 449-0363

Now brewing five of its own beers plus specialties, this large, attractive microbrewery bar and restaurant has Egyptian decor, complete with gently waving papyrus fans over the bar. The Oasis has daily happy hours from 3 to 6 P.M. and 10 P.M. until closing, offering discounted beer, wine, and mixed drinks made from house liquors. Thursday nights the bar serves $1.50 pints and $3.50 Red Bull and vodka. There's free pool during early happy hour every day in the full game room that includes foosball, darts, pool, and video games; on Monday free pool runs from 3 P.M. to 2 A.M. The restaurant serves all types of dishes and has a late-night menu; it opens at 11 A.M. for lunch. The Oasis is open until 2 A.M. Monday through Saturday and until midnight Sunday. Month-to-month specialty beers are served, such as Belgian Strong Ale and Doppelbock.

Ogden Theatre
935 E. Colfax Ave. (nine blocks east of the State Capitol), Denver
(303) 830-2525 (box office and recording of upcoming shows)

Big names and performers appear at the Ogden, among them George Clinton, Los Lobos, Great White, and A Flock of Seagulls. Call for information on tickets and upcoming shows. Most shows at the Ogden are general admission, with no reserved seating necessary, and tickets generally run from $14 to $25. Most shows start at 8 P.M., and the box office opens one hour before shows. Ogden tickets are also available in Boulder at the Albums-on-The-Hill ticket counter at

1128 13th Street (303-443-3399), and by phone from Ticketweb at (800) 965-4827 or (303) 825-4TIX.

Old Chicago
11th and Pearl Sts., Boulder
(303) 443–5031

Known far and wide for its World Beer Tour and Hall of Foam, Old Chicago has more than 110 international and micro-brewery beers, with 24 on tap. It's also known for its deep-dish, Chicago-style pizza, its pleasant patio (ask former *Saturday Night Live* comedian Kevin Nealon, who has been spotted there), and "the big cookie," a delicious, deep-dish, fresh-baked chocolate-chip cookie served hot. Old Chicago opens daily at 11 A.M. and closes at 2 A.M.; last call is 1:15 A.M.

Paramount Theatre
1631 Glenarm Pl., Denver
(303) 534–8336 (tickets/information)

Built in the 1930s by Temple Hoyne Buell, a renowned Colorado architect, this beautiful art deco theater opened as a vaudeville house and was later a movie theater. It still houses one of only two Mighty Wurlitzer organs in the country (the other is in New York's Radio City Music Hall). The theater averages 10 to 12 shows a month, including comedy (Tim Conway and Harvey Korman shared the stage in February 2001), pop music (Kenny Loggins to Alanis Morrissette), children's programming, ballet, noted speakers and rock concerts. During rock concerts the front row of the 2,015 seats is sacrificed to make room for fans who just have to bounce to the beat, dance, mosh, etc. The box office is open 10 A.M. to 9 P.M. the day of events only. Tickets may be purchased through Ticketmaster outlets or charged by phone at (303) 830-8497.

Penny Lane
1795 Pearl St., Boulder
(303) 443–9516

For 20 years, Isidore Million's coffee shop has been a gathering place for Boulder's avant-garde crowd, a warm shelter for kids on the road, a casual venue for local talent, and just a place to get a good cup of coffee and a snack. The daunting hours are 6:15 A.M. to 11 P.M. weekdays and midnight Friday and Saturday. The menu includes juices, ice cream, tea, coffee drinks, bagels and scones, and other goodies—no alcohol. Tuesday and Thursday from 8 to 10:30 P.M. is open mike night for whoever has the chutzpah. Mondays, poets share their latest verses. Other nights of the week, Penny Lane offers an eclectic mix of performers, from jazz to folk to African drumming. When it's warm enough—and even when it isn't—the cafe's outdoor patio offers a view on the passing just-off-the-Mall scene. It's also a good place for a pick-up chess match.

Pioneer Inn
First St., Nederland
(303) 258–7733

For some entertainment with great mountain atmosphere, stop at the rustic "P.I.," where you can dance to live music Friday nights. The Big Tick—bluegrass acoustic music—is scheduled every Wednesday night, and there's an open mike every Thursday night. The Pioneer also serves great burgers and Mexican food and has a pool table, foosball table, and other games. The bar closes at 1:30 A.M. and the kitchen closes at 10 P.M.

The Pub and Cellar
1108 Pearl St., Boulder
(303) 939–9900

This cozy bar offers one of the few smoking areas in the city. The pub opens daily at noon (11 A.M. Saturday and Sunday during football season) and stays open 'til 2 A.M. The Cellar, right on the Downtown Mall next to Old Chicago, is the only place in Boulder where you can get a late-night snack, according to those who have tried elsewhere to no avail. The Cellar really serves food until 1:30 A.M. nightly. On Tuesday all burgers are $3; on Wednesday there's a live soul and country duo; and a variety of live musicians per-

The mountain town of Nederland is the site of some favorite Boulder-area nightspots, including the Pioneer Inn. PHOTO: DAILY CAMERA/VERN WALKER

form on Sunday and Monday. Pool tables, upstairs and down, keep patrons busy. A dart room attracts pick-up games.

Red Rocks Amphitheater
Off I–70 W. (north of Denver), Morrison
(303) 640–7334, (303) 830–8497 (ticket information)

This spectacular natural-rock amphitheater is the venue for many top performers (a recent summer line-up included Dave Matthews, John Mellencamp, and Blues Traveler). Red Rocks information and tickets are available through Ticketmaster (303-830-8497). Or check local newspapers for more concert information.

'Round Midnight
1005 Pearl St., Boulder
(303) 442–2176

This dark, downstairs, nicely urban-feeling nightclub/bar features live music, dancing, pool, and good local performers Thursday, Friday, and Saturday from 5 P.M. to 2 A.M. Cover charges are $2 to $5. Another nice feature is the more than 50 different varieties of single-malt Scotch. Only drinks (no food) are served, and there are happy-hour specials from 5 to 8:30 P.M. daily, with $1.50 well drinks, $1.25 domestic beers, and 50 cents off everything else. It's one of the few remaining places in Boulder where you can go to dance.

Rhumba
950 Pearl St., Boulder
(303) 442–7771

This stylish new hot spot for the youngish crowd opens daily at 4 P.M., with happy hour from 4 to 6 P.M. Lunch is served from 11:30 A.M. to 2:30 P.M. Tuesday through Sunday. The imaginative Caribbean cuisine includes everything from seviche with plantain chips to conch fritters to yam and shiitake bammy cakes at surprisingly affordable prices. Specialty drinks include the yummy Kahana Moru cream soda, a mix of vanilla rum and Sprite that goes down way too smoothly, and the Dark & Stormy that was written up in *Playboy*.

Rio Grande Mexican Restaurant
1101 Walnut St., Boulder
(303) 444–3690

The Rio is a restaurant, no question about that, but mention it to anyone in town

rare venues that offer dance space to younger partiers. House and guest DJs spin the music every night of the week. Soma is open Tuesday, Thursday, Friday, Saturday, and Sunday. It opens at 8 P.M. each night, except Fridays, when doors open at 5 P.M. and free sushi is served until 8 P.M. On Thursdays, there are $2 drinks for adults, and two-for-one draft beers are served Sunday. No cover is charged unless there's a special event.

Sundown Saloon
1136 Pearl St., Boulder
(303) 449–4987

A little off the beaten path in atmosphere but right on the Pearl Street Mall, the Sundown is for those who are sick of the typical Boulder scene. It's a bit more blue collar overall but has an unlikely mix of patrons. College students might find themselves having a beer with a hard-core Harley Davidson biker in black leather or a lawyer in pinstripes. Sundown opens at noon daily and serves snacks until closing at 2 A.M. There are six pool tables and a big-screen TV to pass the time between.

Tom's Tavern
1047 Pearl St., Boulder
(303) 443–3893

Ask longtime Boulderites where to find the best burger, and they'll usually say Tom's. This unpretentious corner tavern has been a favorite spot for more than 30 years. Besides great burgers, there are great beers on tap including Fat Tire, Sam Adams, Sunshine Wheat, and Guinness. A full menu is available daily until about 10:30 P.M. Tom's closes at 11 P.M. on Friday and Saturday, 9 P.M. on Sunday, and 10 P.M. the rest of the week. There's a jukebox back by the kitchen and a television over the bar, but mostly the entertainment is conversation and people-watching.

Trios
1155 Canyon Blvd., Boulder
(303) 442–8400

An elegant, upscale bar, restaurant, and gallery of high-end home furnishings,

and their first reaction will be, "Oh, yeah, margaritas." Double-shot margaritas in birdbath-size glasses have been winning the Rio awards since 1986. The place opens daily at 11 A.M. for lunch and at 5 P.M. for dinner, and it stays open until 10 P.M. Tuesday through Saturday and 9 P.M. Sunday and Monday. The Rio won't sell you more than three margaritas, but if even that number proves overwhelming, the restaurant has a designated-driver program to help you get home safely.

The Sink
1165 13th St., Boulder
(303) 444–7465

For a venerable institution (it opened in 1949), The Sink on University Hill is a funky piece of work, with exposed pipes, concrete floors, walls splashed with bright cartoons referring to Boulder institutions and events, and ceilings and bathroom stalls covered with the graffiti greetings of several generations of CU students. In addition to a traditional hungry-student menu of burgers and pizza, The Sink offers beer and potent mixed drinks (limit two) and historical significance—Robert Redford used to sweep floors there when he was a CU student. Food is served from 11 A.M. until 9:45 P.M. and the bar stays open until 2 A.M. Choose from a selection of 18 beers on tap.

Soma
1915 Broadway, Boulder
(303) 938–8600

With a bar upstairs for the 21-and-over crowd and nonstop dancing for 18-and-olders downstairs, Soma is among the

Trios could be equally at home in Seattle or New York. It attracts an older (than the college kids), more sophisticated professional crowd. There's live jazz from 7 to 11 P.M. Tuesday, Wednesday, and Thursday, and 8 P.M. to midnight Friday and Saturday; no cover charge. Trios also makes good pizza and other light fare for the nightlife patrons. The late-night menu is served from 9:30 P.M. until midnight Sunday through Thursday and 10 P.M. to 2 A.M. Friday and Saturday. The wine bar is open the same hours, with 60 wines by the glass and more than 300 bottles to choose from.

Tulagi
1129 13th St., Boulder
(303) 938-8090, (303) 443-3399 (tickets)

Tulagi is a cozy pool hall with a small stage and dance area that is reviving its 1970s popularity with a seemingly endless stream of local and national performers, including Yo, Flaco!, and Juice; karaoke nights on Tuesdays; and hip-hop on Thursdays. Hours are 4 P.M. to 2 A.M. The cover charge depends on the fame of the performers: some nights are free; when Big Head Todd and the Monsters perform it's $30.

Twisted Vine Grill and Wine Bar
1709 Pearl St., Boulder
(303) 442-2542

Although it's only been open since 2000, Twisted Vine is already making a name for itself as a gathering spot for fans of jazz and good seafood. The eclectic American restaurant offers live music Tuesday through Saturday beginning at 7 P.M. In addition to jazz, the play list includes blues, R & B, and light classic rock; there's no cover. The menu includes fresh seafood, steaks, pasta, and a large selection of appetizers with Italian and Asian influences. Twisted Vine is open 11:30 A.M. to 10:30 P.M. Monday through Thursday, 11:30 A.M. to midnight Friday, and 4 to 11 P.M. Saturday (hours change with the seasons).

The Underground
1360 College, Boulder
(303) 544-1718

Head down the long flight of stairs and into the booming beat and flashing lights to reach the appropriately named Underground, a dance club for people who really, really like to dance. The only after-hours, underage dance club in Boulder, the Underground is open Fridays and Saturdays (and some Sundays) from 10 P.M. to 6 A.M. Because no alcohol is served, the club is open to all ages. The beat is driving, the celebrity DJs relentless, the parties long and loud. The exhausted can take a break in a black-lit room with couches that regulars refer to as "the cud-

On warm evenings from spring through fall, one of the most popular evening activities in Boulder is watching the street performers on the Pearl Street Mall. PHOTO: LINDA CORNETT

dle puddle." Energy-boosting snacks and drinks, including bottled water, are available for sale. Cover varies from $5 to $25, depending on who's playing the music; tickets are available at the door or in advance at The Root of the Hill clothing, jewelry, and pipe store across the hall.

Walnut Brewery
1123 Walnut St., Boulder
(303) 447-1345

This very popular microbrewery is in a tastefully redecorated old warehouse and makes its own six fresh, delicious beers. Order a sampler and try them all. The complete dinner menu is served until 10:30 P.M. every night (see our Restaurants chapter for details). The Walnut Brewery is open until 2 A.M. Thursday through Saturday and until 1 A.M. Sunday through Wednesday. Go early on weekends (before 6 P.M.) if you don't want to wait in a line that often stretches out the door and down the block. The Walnut Brewery also provides beer to go and catering services.

Walrus
11th and Walnut Sts., Boulder
(303) 443-9902

The Walrus has been around for many years, undergoing various changes of personality and clientele from a fancy restaurant to a neighborhood bar. Currently it's a late-night college bar, with pizza, burgers, and appetizers served along with bar drinks and beer. There are six pool tables, air hockey, and foosball for fun. Last call every night is 1:15 A.M., and food is served until 11 P.M. on weekdays and 1 A.M. on weekends.

West End Tavern
926 Pearl St., Boulder
(303) 444-3535

A typical neighborhood tavern and burger restaurant, the cozy West End has a delightful surprise—a rooftop area where diners and drinkers can watch the sun set behind the mountain backdrop or enjoy the coolness of a Colorado summer night under the stars. The menu tends toward burgers and tasty fries. The West End is open daily from 11 A.M. to 2 A.M.

Wit's End Comedy Club
8861 Harlan St., Westminster (halfway between Boulder and Denver)
(303) 430-4242

Stand-up comedy is offered Wednesday through Sunday nights, featuring national performers like Fred Anderson and Greg Phelps from shows like *Leno, Letterman, A&E,* and *Caroline's.* Shows begin at 8 P.M., with additional shows at 10:30 P.M. on Friday and Saturday nights. Ticket prices are $6 on weekdays and $8 on Friday and Saturday.

Accommodations

Bed and Breakfasts
and Country Inns

Hotels and Motels

RV Hookups and
Campgrounds

Meeting Spaces

A Place for Your Pet

Boulder proper offers more than two dozen places to stay, with nearly 2,500 rooms ranging from bargain-rate facilities to luxury hotels and romantic bed-and-breakfast inns. The choices expand when you head for the hills, where country cabins, great adventure ranches, and mountain retreats beckon. Many of the accommodations are popular way stations for travelers planning to continue on to Rocky Mountain National Park and Estes Park (see the chapters on those destinations for more information). In fact, Boulder itself is only 35 miles from Estes Park, which means roughly an hour's drive up, down, and around the mountains. Many country places are even closer, so for these, we've listed the approximate driving time to reach both Boulder and Estes Park.

Towering over the Denver-Boulder turnpike just minutes from the city, the Omni Interlocken Resort is the area's newest luxury hotel, complete with a 27-hole championship golf course. The long-vacant lot at Ninth and Canyon, on the southwestern edge of Boulder's downtown, has sporadically been proposed as a hotel site; however, every development proposal thus far has been defeated, often by requirements that changed mid-scheme. Don't be surprised to ultimately see a hotel in this convenient spot; then again, don't be surprised if you never do.

Get Your Reservation Early

Where Boulder accommodations are concerned, it pays to start working on your reservations early. From May through October, it's wise to reserve a month in advance. Dates that sell out early include CU-Boulder fall football weekends (especially when the Buffaloes play Nebraska), graduation in mid-May, and the Bolder Boulder Memorial Day weekend, all of which pack the town. Since it's not a ski destination, Boulder's slowest season is November through February. Rates are usually lower then, too.

Whether you need a room two years from now or right away, the Boulder Chamber of Commerce (303-442-2911 or 800-444-0447) can send you an updated packet of information about Boulder, plus the latest hotel/motel rate sheet. The Chamber does not operate a central reservations service, but on busy weekends it will assist visitors seeking a place to stay by calling around to see if anyone has canceled, making a room available. If you're desperate, this sometimes can help.

A Word About Smoking

Boulder policy-makers figured out early the harmful consequences of America's legal drug—tobacco—and established many smoke-free zones. In 1995, smoking was banned in all public places. Many accommodations also prohibit or restrict smoking. Most bed-and-breakfast inns, for instance, don't allow any smoking indoors. While most hotels provide some smoking rooms, there are fewer and fewer all the time; so if you want the freedom to smoke, be sure to ask for a smoking room.

Price Information

Prices may vary throughout the year, dropping in late fall and winter. Some places offer rooms at various price levels. Some properties also offer discounted business rates for extended stays or discounts for AAA members, senior citizens, or others. Individual properties can provide more details. Unless indicated otherwise, assume that local lodging places accept cash, traveler's checks, personal and company checks (both in-state and out-of-state), and major credit cards.

Price-Code Key

Our price-code key, shown in dollar signs ($), is based on average daily summer (peak) rates for a standard room for two adults.

$ .... Less than $55
$$ .... $56 to $75
$$$ .... $76 to $100
$$$$ .... $101 to $125
$$$$$ .... $126 and more

Bed and Breakfasts and Country Inns

If you've never stayed at a bed and breakfast or a country inn (though often a distinction is not made between the two, in this area, a country inn is generally bigger), try one in Boulder. Each room is individually decorated with special treasures, antique furnishings, and paintings. Most rooms have private baths, often lavishly appointed. Many are in former mansions or mountain lodges. No, most Boulderites don't live this way, but plenty of us would like to. These homes are so peaceful and romantic, you may wish you could linger for years. Extra details of decor and service can add immeasurably to the richness of your stay. No wonder these are popular for honeymoons and anniversaries. Keep to yourself or relax in the living room and strike up a conversation with the staff and other travelers. Most bed and breakfasts offer what they now tend to call "continental-plus breakfast," with homemade breads or rolls, a choice of beverage, fresh fruit, and perhaps cereal. Some prepare a full breakfast each morning, with a hot entree and cereal available, too.

Bed and breakfasts rarely permit smoking or pets, and most inns don't allow children younger than 12. If you book your family somewhere that does permit children, make sure the kids are well-behaved—and brace them for the absence of standard hotel offerings such as televisions and indoor, heated pools. If you might be arriving during one of Boulder's infrequent hot spells, ask about air conditioning. Some rooms have it, some don't need it, and others do.

Several of Boulder's best bed and breakfasts belong to an association called the Distinctive Inns of Colorado (800–866–0621), which can send you a directory including evocative photographs of many member properties.

City of Boulder

Many Boulder bed and breakfasts are near the center of the city, often in mostly residential areas. In a way, they make you an instant resident, for they give you a lovely, distinctive neighborhood to call your own during your stay. A central location means fun just outside your door. It can also mean traffic and other urban noise. Mention a desire for total quiet to the staff if you want a room where you won't notice traffic at all.

The Boulder Victoria Historic Inn
1305 Pine St., Boulder
(303) 938–1300
$$$$$

The Dwight-Nicholson House, one of Boulder's earliest mansions, was renovated in 1889 and turned into a gorgeous bed-and-breakfast inn more than a century later. Seven distinctive rooms have queen-size brass beds with down comforters, private baths (three with steam showers), and televisions. This wonderful inn is just a block from the Pearl Street Mall. Here you'll find charming Victorian hospitality and plush comfort. The innkeeper serves a complete breakfast

Some Boulder bed-and-breakfast inns have gardens, courtyards, or other spots in which to enjoy a quiet moment outdoors. PHOTO: DAILY CAMERA/VERN WALKER

with homemade fruit breads and muffins, as well as afternoon tea and evening port. In summer, the beautiful front garden is ablaze with flowers.

Briar Rose Bed & Breakfast
2151 Arapahoe Ave., Boulder
(303) 442–3007
$$$$$

This was Boulder's first bed and breakfast, established in 1981, and it remains one of the coziest. This English-style inn has a landscaped courtyard and garden complete with lovely little pond and waterfall. Each of the nine guest rooms has Boulder-made featherbed comforters. Two of the rooms feature wood-burning fireplaces. Tea is served in the afternoon, and a homemade breakfast—delicious baked goods, granola, and fresh fruit—greets the morning. The inn is within walking distance of Crossroads Mall, CU-Boulder and downtown, Naropa University, and the Village Shopping Center.

The Earl House Historic Inn
2429 Broadway, Boulder
(303) 938–1400
$$$$$

The landmark Greene-Earl House is a spectacular 1882 Gothic-style stone mansion. It is also Boulder's newest bed and breakfast, opened in November 1995 with a trellised, wrought-iron fence. Original woodwork and tiles, handpainted by the original owner's wife, make the interior a treasure, too. One room has a double bed, and the rest have queens. All the bathrooms have handpainted tiles and either a steam shower or jetted tub. The parlor and dining room seem a million miles from the bustle of Broadway. Under the same ownership as the Boulder Victoria, the Earl House has adopted the practice of serving continental breakfast, afternoon tea, and evening port. Two carriage houses on the property each have three bedrooms, two bathrooms, a full kitchen living room with TV/VCR and stereo, and a washer/dryer. Each can accommodate up to six people; there is a two-night minimum stay. Carriage house guests are welcome at the main house for afternoon tea, but they're on their own for breakfast and evening port.

The Inn on Mapleton Hill
1001 Spruce St., Boulder
(303) 449–6528, (800) 276–6528
$$$$$

Five rooms with private baths and two rooms sharing a bath make up this 1899 home in the Mapleton Hill historic neighborhood. The inn received the Historic Preservation Award from the Boulder Historical Society in 1992. It's just a minute's walk down tree-lined streets to the Pearl Street Mall, and it has a view of both the Flatirons and the downtown area. Each room has its own romantic decor, with a queen-size bed and fireplace. Basil the hound may greet you as you join other guests in the comfortable back parlor. A generous breakfast is served daily.

Pearl Street Inn
1820 Pearl St., Boulder
(303) 444–5584, (888) 810–1302
$$$$$

Each of the eight Victorian-style rooms here has a wood-burning fireplace. The location is superb, just three blocks east of the Pearl Street Mall, but the inn is tucked behind a high fence and feels private and secluded. There's a lovely garden courtyard for guests to enjoy. Full breakfast, including excellent baked goods and exceptional oatmeal, is served. The innkeeper also puts out afternoon refreshments, which could be hot spiked apple cider, wine and cheese, or tea. The Pearl Street Inn's rates are the same year-round. In-house catering is available for weddings, receptions, business meetings, and retreats for up to 125 people.

The Mountains

The peace and quiet of a mountain lodge can be incredible. Some of these places are just a short drive from Boulder. Others are way, way up where the spring flowers bloom in August. Some locations are even secrets—the owners will give you directions when you inquire. Many are open all year, but check in advance, for some close during winter.

Above Boulder Wildlife Safari Lodge
Sugarloaf Mountain, Boulder
(303) 258-7777
$$$$, no credit cards

Three guest rooms are all you'll find in this very secluded, European-style, big mountain hunting lodge with handmade aspen-log beds, three fireplaces, designer decorations, and 300 full-mounted trophies, including grizzly bears, African lions, and other wildlife. The owner describes himself as a big-game hunter, professional outdoorsman, and environmentalist. Breakfast is continental-plus and often includes wild-game sausage. Children are welcome, and there is a kennel for pets. It's a five-minute drive from Nederland, 25 minutes from Boulder, and 50 minutes from Estes Park.

Allenspark Lodge
184 Main St., Allenspark
(303) 747-2552
$$$

Six rooms with private baths, six rooms with shared baths, and three cabins with private baths and full kitchens make up this authentic 1933 log lodge. Construction is of ponderosa pine on the first two levels inside and out, with knotty pine inside on the top floor. Many of the furnishings are the same vintage as the buildings. There are hot tubs, a gift shop, a wine and beer bar, and a TV in the great room near the flagstone fireplace. Views from this mountain lodge are tremendous, and Wild Basin and its wonderful hiking trails are nearby. Children younger than 14 are welcome in the cabins, and older kids may stay in the lodge, too. It's about a 45-minute drive from Boulder and a 25-minute drive to Estes Park. The lodge includes continental-plus breakfast in its rates.

Alps Boulder Canyon Inn
38619 Boulder Canyon Dr., Boulder
(303) 444-5445, (800) 414-2577
$$$$$

When you look at this beautiful inn today, it's hard to imagine that it was once a run-down old lodge that housed the Fraternal Order of the Moose. You enter via a log cabin that was originally a stagecoach stop and bordello during the late 1870s, wander into the lounge that was the old Moose Lodge bar, then head to your room. The inn's 12 enchanting guest rooms are done up with heirloom furnishings. All the rooms are different, as are their private bathrooms: six with jetted tubs, two with claw-foot tubs, one with a soaking tub for two, and the others with showers. Each room also has a fireplace, and some feature stained-glass doors. Several rooms are honeymoon-perfect, such as "Wallstreet," which includes that vintage-style tub for two. The inn serves a gourmet breakfast, and cheesecake is available in the evening. You can always help yourself to tea and coffee, and hot cider is also available in winter. The TV room has a satellite system and VCR with dozens of videos available, and the lounge features a huge stone fireplace, big card table, and popular games. There are also fireplaces in the breakfast room and the lobby. The large, rustic dining room has a capacity of 100 people and can host weddings, receptions, and meetings. Children older than 12 are welcome. Hiking and biking trails are close by this inn, which is also near Boulder Creek. The inn is just a five-minute drive from Boulder and less than an hour from Estes Park.

Best Western Lodge at Nederland
55 Lakeview Dr., Nederland
(303) 258-9463, (800) 279-9463
$$$

This oversize log lodge, in the heart of Nederland, is a convenient mountain retreat from Boulder. Accommodations include 23 nonsmoking rooms with king-size beds for couples, and rooms with two queen-size beds or a queen and a set of bunk beds for families. All rooms are equipped with hair dryers, coffeemakers, and small refrigerators; suites also have fireplaces. The spacious lobby has a fireplace, and there's an outdoor hot tub on the deck. There is no restaurant, but Nederland's most popular eating places are within a short walk. In winter, the Lodge at Nederland offers reasonably priced ski packages in cooperation with nearby Eldora Mountain Resort. It is also a great jumping-off place for snowshoeing, backcountry skiing, and summer hikes. The activities desk can arrange guided hikes, horseback trail rides, and other diversions.

Insiders' Tip

If you're traveling to Boulder via Denver International Airport, consider Super Shuttle Boulder as an alternative to renting a car. The shuttle transports travelers to nearly all of the city's hotels or motels for $18; it's $22 if you want to be delivered directly to your own front door. (Each additional person headed for the same location pays only $10 and children under 12 ride for free.) The shuttle is easy to locate at the airport, and if you won't be needing a car during your stay, it's a mostly hassle-free and extremely time-saving transportation option.

Boulder Mountain Lodge and Campground
91 Fourmile Canyon Dr., Boulder
(303) 444–0882, (800) 458–0882
$–$$

Twenty-two rooms, many with kitchenettes or full kitchens and all with whirlpool-jetted bathtubs, are available at this rustic motel with homey touches. The campground has 25 first-come, first-served sites with electricity and access to water for RVs (25-foot-maximum) or for tent campers. The lodge is in the mountains, and the office is in an old narrow-gauge train depot. The property features a private fishing pond for kids, a heated outdoor pool (open seasonally), and hot tubs. Smoking is allowed in some rooms, and pets are welcome with a deposit. The lodge is less than 10 minutes from Boulder and about an hour from Estes Park.

Gold Lake Mountain Resort
3371 Gold Lake Rd., Ward
(303) 459–3544, (800) 450–3544
$$$$$

This mountain hideaway can be a wonderful escape for honeymooners (or second honeymooners), or the perfect spot for a pleasant, close-by family retreat. Eighteen charming and distinctive cabins are tucked amid the pine trees. They feature artistically decorated accommodations ranging from single rooms to three-bedroom suites. All guests enjoy a Swiss-style continental breakfast. The resort's spa offers massages and facials, and you can book a spa package. The 35-acre lake is beautiful for catamaran sailing, canoeing, kayaking, and fly fishing in summer. In the winter there's ice skating, cross-county skiing, and snowshoeing; those who prefer the indoors can head for the billiard room. The lakeside hot tubs are a dreamy treat. Summer brings opportunities for horseback riding on mounts you can rent by the hour or day, great mountain biking on challenging trails, volleyball, and hiking. Children are more than welcome. Guests and visitors can dine in the excellent and stylish restaurant, Alice's (see our Restaurants chapter), or enjoy cocktails at Karel's Tavern. Gold Lake Mountain Resort is a 45- to 60-minute drive from either Boulder or Estes Park.

Goldminer Hotel
601 Klondike Ave., Eldora
(303) 258-7770, (800) 422-4629
$$$$

Three rooms with private baths and four with shared baths are in this historic log hotel, which dates from Eldora's mining days. The rooms reflect their original character, with antiques and homemade quilts. There is also one cabin with a kitchenette. This is an away-from-it-all place in a quaint old mining town surrounded by mountains. You can enjoy beautiful views from the hot tub. There is no smoking in the hotel or cabin. Pets are only permitted in the cabin; children are welcome. A full breakfast is part of the deal. It's about 30 minutes from Boulder, about an hour from Estes Park, and a short drive from the Eldora ski area.

Inn at Rock N River Bed and Breakfast & Trout Pond Fishing
16868 N. St. Vrain Dr., northwest of Lyons
(303) 443-4611, (800) 448-4611
$$$$-$$$$$

This delightful riverside complex has seven rooms near the pond, and The Carriage House, which is a two-story cabin accommodating up to four with a large bedroom, a Jacuzzi tub for two, and a fireplace. All units include kitchens. Though it's near busy U.S. Highway 36, the inn is quiet and pretty, with great views of the trout ponds and the St. Vrain River. Full breakfast is included. People stay overnight for the nature and the trout fishing. (You're guaranteed a fish!) Children are welcome. The inn is usually full from May through mid-December, but you can always hope for a cancellation—or come in the off-season. It is three miles northwest of Lyons (take U.S. 36), 25 minutes from either Boulder or Estes Park.

Nederhaus Motel
686 Colo. Hwy. 119 S., Nederland
(303) 444-4705, (800) 422-4629
$$$

The twelve rooms at Nederhaus are all furnished with antiques. This little hotel with a Swiss-looking facade is within an easy walk of downtown Nederland and is also a short drive to hiking spots and Eldora skiing. Smoking is allowed in some rooms. Children and pets are welcome. The property is about 25 minutes from Boulder and about an hour from Estes Park. There is a coffee shop and a pizza parlor.

Peaceful Valley Ranch
475 Peaceful Valley Rd., Lyons
(303) 747-2881, (800) 955-6343
$$$$$

This family-owned, family-run guest ranch, on the site of an old homestead, is a "got everything" facility with 12 cabins, rooms in the main lodge, and various other guest buildings as well as a stable and indoor riding arena and other facilities. This is a classic dude ranch that can house more than 100 people, and conference facilities are available. Staying overnight is dandy, but longer stays are what most seek at Peaceful Valley. Half-week stays are around $800 per person, and full-week packages, including all meals, use of ranch facilities, and all recreational programs begin at $1,650 per person during the summer. During the off-season Peaceful Valley offers a bed and breakfast for $175 a night, or a visit that includes three full meals a day for $225 per night. (The chef makes ranch-style meals such as prime rib and lemon-flavored catfish.)

The children's program is extensive. There's an indoor hot tub, indoor swimming pool, and children's petting farm as well as activities that include horseback riding, jeep tours, and square dancing. The mountainside chapel, with a view of the Indian Peaks behind the altar, is a gorgeous wedding site. In winter, Peaceful Valley offers sleigh rides; stocks cross-country skis, snowshoes, and snowmobiles; and maintains a small track on the property. The trailhead for extensive marked but ungroomed trails around Camp Dick lies just across the highway. This outstanding resort is just a bit less than an hour from Boulder and about 40 minutes south of Estes Park. No smoking or pets are allowed.

The Eastern Plains

These motels, bed and breakfasts, and country inns are open all year and offer good variety and reasonable prices.

Briarwood Inn
1228 N. Main St., Longmont
(303) 776–6622
$$

The 17 rooms in this motel include 10 kitchenettes. The owner calls his the best backyard in town, with a quiet patio area, a fish pond, and a gazebo. Smoking is allowed. Children are welcome. It's a half-hour drive to Boulder and about 45 minutes to Estes Park.

Ellen's Bed & Breakfast in a Victorian House
700 Kimbark St., Longmont
(303) 776–1676
$$$, no credit cards

Two guest rooms, each with a private bath, are in this beautifully shaded, quiet, 1910 Victorian-style house, with eclectic furnishings including several interesting art deco pieces collected by the well-traveled owners. Full breakfast is included; there's a hot tub; smoking is allowed; and children and pets are welcome. It's a half-hour drive from Boulder and 45 minutes to Estes Park.

Sandy Point Inn
6485 Twin Lakes Rd., Gunbarrel/Boulder
(303) 530–2939, (800) 322–2939
$$$

With 33 air-conditioned studio suites, each with a mini-kitchen and cable TV, this is a great place for people relocating or traveling with families. There's one common kitchen with a house-style range, an oven, and utensils for preparing full-scale meals. A membership at Synergy, a full-service sports club, is complimentary for guests. A cold breakfast buffet, served in the common kitchen from 6:30 to 10 A.M. daily and from 8 to 10 A.M. on weekends and holidays, is included in the rate. It's a 10-minute drive to Boulder and about an hour from Estes Park. The inn owners also rent one- and two-bedroom condominiums, normally on a monthly basis.

The Victoria Inn
20400 W. 17th Ave., Longmont
(303) 772–4667
$$$

Each of this inn's 30 executive suites includes a full kitchen, full bath, and sitting room. They are set in three-story, blue Victorian-style buildings with contemporary furnishings. There's a heated outdoor pool. Smoking is allowed. Children are welcome. Cats are considered with a deposit. It's a half-hour from Boulder and 45 minutes to Estes Park.

Hotels and Motels

Boulder hotels and motels all offer non-smoking rooms (ask if you need a smoking room). Most have pools, but if it's cold, check when you call to see whether it's a heated indoor pool. The places we've listed have the usual hotel/motel amenities such as televisions and air-conditioning. Some are simple and sweet, others are lavish. Most don't allow pets. Unless noted, all take major credit cards.

Note that most hotels and motels in Boulder are wheelchair-accessible. Some of the mountain properties may have more difficulty accommodating a wheelchair. Call ahead to be sure.

Best Western Boulder Inn
770 28th St., Boulder
(303) 449–3800, (800) 233–8469
$$$

This motel's 112 rooms are right across the street from the south end of the CU-Boulder campus. Room options include units with two queen-size beds, or just one queen-size bed, or upgraded rooms that have a king-size bed and a wet-bar area. Admission to the nearby health club is included in the rate, as is continental breakfast daily. The motor inn has a hot tub, sauna, and outdoor pool (open seasonally). The Fanatics sports bar is also on site.

Best Western Golden Buff Lodge
1725 28th St., Boulder
(303) 442-7450, (800) 999-BUFF
$$$

This comfortable, well-located business and family motel has 112 guest rooms with king- or queen-size beds; some suites; and conference/banquet space accommodating up to 40 people. On site is The Buff Restaurant, which is open for breakfast and lunch daily. There is a seasonal outdoor pool and an indoor hot tub. The motel is convenient to Crossroads Mall.

The Boulder Broker Inn
555 30th St., Boulder
(303) 444-3330, (800) 338-5407
$$$$$

This ornately decorated contemporary hotel has 116 guest rooms and four suites. Rooms feature brass beds, leather recliners, and cable TV with free HBO and Showtime. Services include valet parking, room service, and bell staffs. The acclaimed Broker Restaurant and Bentley's nightclub are on site. Full breakfast is included in room rates, as are free passes to the nearby 24 Hour Fitness center. There's also a hot tub, and the hotel is equipped with conference rooms. Just south of the campus, The Broker Inn is a short walk or a CU-Boulder shuttle bus (take your pick) away from the university. It is also normally the location where passengers leaving and arriving via the Super Shuttle Boulder transportation service switch from smaller city vans to the larger

vehicles that run hourly between Denver International Airport and Boulder.

Boulder International Youth Hostel
1107 12th St., Boulder
(303) 442-0522
$

Visitors from all over the world have stayed at this hostel, which is a member of the American Association of International Hostels. Accommodations are scattered among several buildings on University Hill. The hostel has separate dormitories for men and women, where beds are only $36 a night, as well as private rooms for couples and families that go for $50 a night for two people. Apartments are available for those wanting longer-term facilities. Each room has a phone, but televisions are located only in common areas. Cable TV hookups are provided, but you must bring your own apparatus. Kitchen and laundry facilities are on site.

Boulder Marriott
2660 Canyon Blvd., Boulder
(303) 440-8877, (800) 228-9290
$$$$$

This business and meeting hotel opened in 1997 with 155 deluxe guest rooms and suites. It is tucked into a shopping center in central Boulder with magnificent views of the Flatirons, especially from the rooftop terrace. Facilities include underground parking, an indoor pool, a whirlpool, a health club and gift shop. JW's Steakhouse and a lounge are inside the hotel, which also houses a jewelry store, an art gallery, and the Essentials Beauty Clinic. The Boulder Marriott is within walking distance of shopping, restaurants, movie theaters, and the CU campus.

Coburn Hotel
2040 16th St., Boulder
(303) 545-5200, (800) 858-5811
$$$$$

There are 12 rooms in this boutique hotel, where wrought iron and leather

Boulder has a wide range of lodging options, including boutique hotels. The 12-room Coburn Hotel offers cozy accommodations in a downtown Boulder neighborhood. PHOTO: ROZ BROWN

furnishings create a turn-of-the-20th-century elegance. Stained-glass windows, old City of Boulder renderings, authentic oil paintings, and Western prints make the interior a visual delight, while the widow's walk on the roof gives you a bird's-eye view of downtown and the Flatirons. Guest rooms offer fireplaces, Jacuzzis, private balconies, televisions, and phones. Continental breakfast is included in all room rates.

Colorado Chautauqua Cabins
Ninth St. and Baseline Rd., Boulder
(303) 442-3282
$

More than two dozen lodge rooms and about 60 cottages are available for rent, with a four-night minimum stay. The one- to three-bedroom cottages offer full kitchens but no telephones, air-conditioning, TVs, or swimming pools. What you get here is a great deal on lodgings, one of the most beautiful locations in town, hiking and superb cultural events right outside your door, and a wonderfully nostalgic step back in time. Bookings start in November for the following summer. All but two of the cabins are summer-only rentals. Ask about

pets. For more information about Chautauqua Park, see our Attractions chapter.

Comfort Inn
1196 Dillon Rd., Louisville
(303) 604-0181, (800) 228-5150 (nationwide reservations)
$$$

The 68-room Comfort Inn is next to the Mann 12-plex movie theater, just off U.S. 36. Rooms have one or two queen-size beds, and there is also one luxury room with Jacuzzi and queen-size bed. Continental breakfast, included in all room rates, is served in the breakfast room. This motor inn also has a meeting room and an exercise facility; for those who want a more comprehensive workout, the Louisville Recreation Center is a short drive away.

Courtyard by Marriott
4710 Pearl E. Circle, Boulder
(303) 440-4700, (800) 321-2211
$$$$

This business hotel has 12 suites and 137 rooms with either a king-size bed or two doubles; there are work desks and coffee-makers in every room and separate seating areas in the suites. The hotel offers conference rooms, the in-house Courtyard Cafe and Lounge, and an indoor pool, whirlpool, and workout room. It's right next to the Boulder Creek Path in a quiet location just east of Foothills Parkway (Colo. Highway 157) on Pearl Street.

Courtyard by Marriott—Louisville
948 W. Dillon Rd., Louisville
(303) 604–0007, (800) 321–2211
$$$$

Just off U.S. 36, this hotel offers 154 guest rooms and suites, a heated indoor pool with a whirlpool, an exercise room, and in-room coffee service. There are also numerous banquet and reception facilities. The affordable restaurant features a full breakfast buffet served daily.

Days Inn
5397 South Boulder Rd., Boulder
(303) 499–4422, (800) 329–7466
$$$

This newly remodeled motel is on a main thoroughfare, just off U.S. 36 and near the Table Mesa Park-n-Ride. It is just about the most convenient lodging to the National Center for Atmospheric Research and the National Bureau of Standards and Technology. Some of its 76 rooms have mountain views. Free local phone calls, TV with HBO, and complimentary continental breakfast are included.

Foot-of-the-Mountain Motel
200 Arapahoe Ave., Boulder
(303) 442–5688
$$

Each of the motel's 18 rooms is in a red-trimmed log cabin, making this place a quaint and rustic charmer. The mountain against whose foot the property nestles is Flagstaff. On a quiet street near the pretty Eben Fine Park and the Boulder Creek Path, it is also just nine blocks west of CU-Boulder and the downtown Pearl Street Mall. All rooms have refrigerators and free HBO. Pets are welcome.

Hampton Inn
912 W. Dillon Rd., Louisville
(303) 666–7700, (800) HAMPTON (nationwide reservations)
$$$$

The Hampton Inn is suited to multi-day business or leisure stays. Each of its 80

One of the rustic cottages at Chautauqua welcomes visitors with potted flowers, wide steps, and the screened-in front porch typical of the summer retreat. PHOTO: LINDA CORNETT

The famous staircase at the Hotel Boulderado is a favorite spot for weddings. In December, a huge Christmas tree soars to the stained-glass dome. PHOTO: DAILY CAMERA/JAY QUADRACCI

spacious, traditionally furnished rooms has a king-size bed or two queens, along with a refrigerator, microwave, coffeemaker, hair dryer, two-line speaker phone, and television with Nintendo. All rooms feature fine designer furniture and working desks for business travelers. In addition, there is one hospitality suite for small meetings, an indoor swimming pool, a hot tub, and an exercise facility. Continental breakfast is included in all rates. It's within walking distance of restaurants, bars, and shopping.

Holiday Inn Express
4777 N. Broadway, Boulder
(303) 442–6600, (800) HOLIDAY
$$$

This North Boulder motor inn has 106 rooms, some with microwaves and refrig-

erators. Extras include a seasonal outdoor pool, an exercise room, a guest laundry, and complimentary continental breakfast. Free local phone calls also are included. The property is a short walk from the intersection of U.S. 36 (28th Street) and Broadway.

Homewood Suites by Hilton
4950 Baseline Rd., Boulder
(303) 499–9922, (800) 225–5466
$$$$$

The 100 apartment-style suites each include a full kitchen and separate living and sleeping areas. Other highlights are an outdoor pool, the fabulous view of the Flatirons, complimentary continental breakfast, and a free social hour, including food and drinks, on Monday through Thursday nights. We know one couple who liked the lifestyle so much they went back home, sold their big house, and moved into a place about the size of a Homewood Suite! Children are welcome, and pets are allowed. The Flatiron Athletic Club is just next door, and Homewood guests pay only $5 per day. The bottom line here is good, basic living for extended-stay guests and business travelers.

Hotel Boulderado
2115 13th St., Boulder
(303) 442-4344, (800) 433-4344
$$$$$

Built in 1909, this is a local landmark as well as the city's finest hotel. It offers old-style grandeur and is famous for the stained-glass canopy in its huge mezzanine. Robert Frost and Louis Armstrong are among its past guests. Its 160 lavishly decorated, Victorian-style rooms are divided between the historic older section of the hotel and the new wing. The VIP suites are the largest and fanciest lodgings. Each has a wrought-iron or four-poster bed, its own stereo, and a separate living room furnished with a Victorian-style desk and sofa. The fanciest, biggest one goes for more than $200 a night, and it's booked almost constantly. The hotel has one of Boulder's best restaurants (see our Restaurants chapter), two bars, a mezzanine entertainment area, lots of conference space, a gift shop, and a sensational location just one block from the Pearl Street Mall.

La Quinta Inn & Suites Louisville/Boulder
902 Dillon Rd., Louisville
(303) 664-0100, (800) NU-ROOMS
$$$$

This hotel has three spacious room choices, with in-room coffeemakers, 25-inch televisions, over-size desks, voice mail, and dataport phones. There are 120 rooms total, some with microwaves and refrigerators. Summer visitors will enjoy the beautifully landscaped courtyard with gazebo, while winter visitors can take advantage of the heated pool and spa.

Omni Interlocken Resort
500 Interlocken Blvd.,
StorageTek/Interlocken Loop, off U.S. Hwy.
36, Broomfield
(303) 438-6600
$$$$$

If it's a view you're after, this new hotel along the Colorado Front Range (opened in 1999) will win you over. The Omni features 390 guest rooms, 13 suites, and a 34,000-square-foot conference center. Guests can dine in comfort at the Meritage restaurant or more informally at the hotel's sports bar; there's also 24-hour in-room dining. Other amenities include a 27-hole championship golf course with clubhouse and pro shop, a health club, and a full-service spa. Running, biking, and hiking trails surround the property, which also features a year-round outdoor swimming pool and whirlpool.

Quality Inn & Suites—Boulder
2020 Arapahoe Ave., Boulder
(303) 449-7550, (800) 228-5151
$$

Forty-six rooms compose this tidy and pleasant family-owned motel (formerly the Econo Lodge). All rooms have king- or queen-size beds and offer cable TV, dataports, coffeemakers, hair dryers, free local calls, and full baths. Just six blocks from downtown's Pearl Street mall and minutes from the university, the property features a 33-foot indoor pool, hot tub, and sauna. A complimentary hot breakfast buffet is served in the lobby each morning. Refrigerators and microwaves are available.

Quality Inn & Suites—Louisville
960 W. Dillon Rd., Louisville
(303) 327-1215, (800) 228-5151
$$-$$$

A stone's throw away from Colorado's newest "shopping experience," this Quality Inn is close to shops, theaters, and restaurants, minutes from downtown Boulder, and less than a half-hour drive from downtown Denver and Coors Field. The spectac-

extended-stay rooms, each with a full kitchen, fireplace, and living room. The hotel also has a 42,000-square-foot conference center, a restaurant, and a heated, outdoor swimming pool. Guests get free breakfast and evening cocktails. The hotel is popular with business travelers, families, and conventions. It's a 15-minute drive to Boulder and an hour to Estes Park.

Ramada Inn—University Area
800 28th St., Boulder
(303) 443-3322, (800) 542-0304
$$$$

By the time you read this entry, this popular and convenient hotel should have finished its transformation from a Holiday Inn to a Ramada Inn. In addition to 165 newly renovated guest rooms, the property features an indoor atrium with a pool, hot tub, sauna, exercise room, and game room. Fortunately for guests, Oliver's casual restaurant and pub is still right next door. Like all hotels along this strip of 28th Street, it's very close to CU-Boulder.

Regal Harvest House
1345 28th St., Boulder
(303) 443-3850, (800) 545-6285
$$$$$

This is Boulder's biggest hotel, with more than 269 high-quality rooms and great business facilities on 16 acres right next to the Boulder Creek Path. It's an easy walk from CU-Boulder and the Pearl Street Mall. It has resort-type recreation facilities, including indoor and outdoor swimming pools, 15 indoor and outdoor tennis courts, mountain bike rentals, and a workout room. The beautifully landscaped inner courtyard is a lively hangout after a Buffs game. Champs lounge and sports bar and The Fancy Moose restaurant are on site.

ular, still-in-progress Flatirons Crossing Mall, featuring Nordstrom and Lord and Taylor, is just a mile away. Not a shopper? Each of the inn's 17 king suites, 39 standard rooms with either one king- or two queen-size beds, and four wheelchair-accessible rooms features a refrigerator, microwave, two-line speaker phone with dataport and voice mail, 25-inch TV, an in-room safe, a coffeemaker, and a hair dryer. When you're not at the fitness center you can enjoy your continental breakfast with your complimentary newspaper or, later in the day, a cocktail next to the outdoor pool and Jacuzzi.

Raintree Plaza Hotel
1900 Ken Pratt Blvd., Longmont
(303) 776-2000, (800) 843-8240
$$$$$

This is Longmont's only full-service hotel. It housed the Emperor of Japan's entourage during the summer of 1994. There are 295 rooms, of which 86 are

Residence Inn by Marriott
3030 Center Green Dr., Boulder
(303) 449-5545, (800) 331-3131
$$$$$

This village-like complex has 128 studio suites, all with full kitchens and fireplaces, designed for extended stays or for families who want a comfortable, relaxing refuge. The Residence Inn provides a complimentary continental breakfast buffet daily and has an outdoor, seasonal pool and whirlpool. It offers easy access to central Boulder, and it's close to many of the high-tech and other companies there.

Super 8 Motel
970 28th St., Boulder
(303) 443-7800, (800) 525-2149
$$

Seventy-one rooms are in this clean, pleasant motel close to CU-Boulder. Some people have stayed as long as three months in the motel's 12 apartment units, at reduced monthly rates. These relocation units have full kitchens and sitting rooms. Children 14 and younger stay free in their parents' room, and pets are welcome in some rooms.

University Inn
1632 Broadway, Boulder
(303) 442-3830, (800) 258-7917
$$$

This neat little inn at the corner of Broadway and Arapahoe Avenue has 39 rooms with refrigerators, cable TV with free HBO, and a guest laundry. It's within easy walking distance of both downtown and the university—and right across the street from Alfalfa's Market (see our Shopping chapter). Although the property is close to a busy intersection, the rooms are fairly quiet if you keep the doors and windows shut. A free continental breakfast is provided.

RV Hookups and Campgrounds

If you're planning to stay in your RV or tent in Boulder, check our Sports chapter (see the "Camping" section under "Participatory Sports").

Boulder Mountain Lodge and Campground
91 Fourmile Canyon Dr., Boulder
(303) 444-0882

This campground has 25 first-come, first-served sites with electricity and access to water for RVs (25-foot-maximum) or tent campers. The fee is $14 a night, with a two-week maximum stay. Shower facilities are available.

The Boulder County Fairgrounds
9595 Nelson Rd., Longmont
(303) 678-1525

The fairground site has 92 campsites and can handle nearly 100 RVs. Costs change minimally from year to year. A site for an RV with no hookups or for one tent costs approximately $10 a night. A site with electricity is $12; one with water and electrical hookups is $13. The maximum stay is two weeks. Showers are available free for registered guests. The dump station fee is $2.

The Denver North Campground
Intersection of I–12 and Colo. Hwy. 7, Broomfield
(303) 452-4120

This campground has space for 104 RVs, with 80 full hookups at $29.50 a night for two people, 24 tent sites at $20.50 a night, a meeting area, and hot showers. Call for reservations.

The Colorado Agency for Campgrounds, Cabins and Lodges
5101 Pennsylvania Ave., Boulder
(303) 499-9343

This statewide directory service offers free information on camp sites, cabins, lodges, bed and breakfasts, and fun things to do.

Meeting Spaces

In addition to the number of hotels, motels, and conference centers that offer space for meetings and other get-togethers, these places offer space for rent in and around town.

The Boulder Broker Inn
555 30th St., Boulder
(303) 444-3330

There are several rooms on the second floor of the hotel with a maximum capacity of 250. There are also three private meeting rooms.

Boulder Chamber of Commerce
2440 Pearl St., Boulder
(303) 442-2911

A huge family reunion, a big convention, or a bonanza of a business meeting should start with a phone call here. Be sure to check on available space as soon as possible. Chamber members have access to meeting space for 50 or more at the Pearl Street location.

CU-Boulder's Glenn Miller Ballroom
CU Campus, Euclid Ave. and Broadway, Boulder
(303) 492-8833

This is a great space for a reunion, reception, or any kind of social gathering, and is therefore usually booked a year in advance. It has room for 1,200 people seated theater-style, 800 seated banquet-style with rectangular tables, or 450 seated at round tables.

Hotel Boulderado
2115 13th St., Boulder
(303) 442-4344

An addition to this historic hotel houses a full-service meeting and conference center. It offers an elegant first-floor space that seats 350 and has a separate street entrance from the hotel.

Omni Interlocken Resort
500 Interlocken Blvd., off U.S. Hwy. 36, Broomfield
(303) 466-9799

The newest conference facility at the Omni Interlocken Resort hotel (between Boulder and Denver, just off U.S. 36) can accommodate 1,100.

Raintree Plaza Hotel and Conference Center
1900 Ken Pratt Blvd., Longmont
(303) 776-2000

Boasting easy access and plentiful parking, the Raintree offers a 42,000-square-foot conference center with seating for 1,100. There are also several smaller meeting rooms.

The Regal Harvest House
1348 28th St., Boulder
(303) 443-3850

Centrally located, the Harvest's Grand Ballroom can seat 650 theater-style, and there are 10 other conference rooms of varying sizes.

A Place for Your Pet

Most of the accommodations we've listed do not allow pets. But never just leave them in your car. Even with the windows left open a bit, Colorado's strong sun can zoom the temperature in the car to a fatal level within minutes. Check the Yellow Pages under "Kennels" for a complete list of accommodations for your traveling animal companion.

Cottonwood Kennels
7275 Valmont Rd., Boulder
(303) 442-2602

Cottonwood calls itself "A Bed & Breakfast for Pets." This is one of the largest kennels in Boulder, boarding both dogs and cats. But it's always a busy place. Generally, if you're traveling during the time when the kids are out of school, call six months in advance for a kennel reservation. During non-holidays in the winter, give two weeks' notice. When Cottonwood fills, they offer other suggestions.

Shopping

Shopping Areas
Specialty Shops

The Boulder shopping scene is going through some changes at this writing. Items that are unusual, eclectic, handmade, imported, upscale, or sporty are available in abundance. If you're in the market for a couch or a housedress, however, the pickings are a bit skimpier. Once the shopping hub for the region, Boulder has been losing ground to neighboring communities and the big-box stores that are springing up in the region. The city's shopping scene took a heavy hit when the 1.5 million-square-foot Flatirons Crossing Mall opened in 2000 just down Highway 36. At the same time, the city's primary shopping center, Crossroads, was struggling to redefine itself and losing scores of businesses. The happy news is that smaller businesses continue to thrive in the community, and many residents are confident the city will emerge with an even richer mix of shopping options.

Shopping Areas

Pearl Street Mall
Pearl Street between 11th and 15th Sts., Downtown Boulder

Boulder's Pearl Street Mall, also known as the Downtown Mall, was the city's original retail area, and is still the heart and soul of the city. This photogenic, four-block, open-air walkway is for pedestrians only—no dogs, no bikes, no skateboards, just leisurely strollers. It is lined with historic buildings that house numerous shops, galleries, microbreweries, offices, and sidewalk cafes, as well as newer buildings of a style and scale that harmonize with the old. During the warm months, street entertainers abound, including a rubber-jointed Rastafarian who obligingly packages himself into a plastic cube several times a day, jugglers, professional musicians, and kids with their first violin trying to pick up a few bucks. A pickup band of drummers gathers periodically in the bus shelter to pound out a beat, and a diggery-doo player periodically fills the night air with mournful tones.

The quality of entertainment generally is quite high. In addition to the buskers who play for what's dropped in the hat, an "out-to-lunch" weekly summer performance series brings formal live entertainment to the mall. Find a seat on one of the mall's benches and enjoy one of the most entertaining free shows to be found anywhere.

Don't let all the distractions make you forget to shop while you're downtown. Some of Boulder's most popular shoe and clothing shops, cafes, galleries, bookstores, and card and gift shops occupy prime spots along the mall and on adjacent blocks. A stroll along the mall will take you past everything from chain stores like Gap Kids and Banana Republic to only-in-Boulder shops like Peppercorn, which stocks elegant kitchen, bath and bed items; The Printed Page, with charming literary-inspired gifts; El Loro, offering crystals and clogs; and Le Bead Shop, a crystalline mine of beads and do-it-yourself jewelry parts. Rocky Mountain Chocolate Factory seduces with rich whiffs through the open doors, and down the street you work it off on a rented bicycle built for two from University Bikes.

Since the mall was completed in 1976, Pearl Street, both east and west of the mall, has become an increasingly eclectic mix of service and retail businesses plus offices and restaurants. New buildings are

Boulder's Pearl Street Mall is lined with historic buildings that house interesting shops.

PHOTO: DAILY CAMERA/KIRK SPEER

going up all around the downtown, new businesses open almost daily, and sadly, some old favorites have closed down.

East, look for the funky, 1960-ish Crystal Dragon; the traditional Swiss Chalet for quality watches; and H. B. Woodsong's, where you're likely to walk in on an acoustic jam session. There's a fun mix of used bookstores, used clothing shops, and an interesting cluster of craft and gift stores.

The west end is a bibliophile's paradise, from the classy Boulder Bookstore at the end of the mall to the Trident coffeehouse and bookstore. Next door to the Trident is High Crimes (formerly the Rue Morgue) mystery bookstore, with everything from used paperbacks to signed and rare hardcovers. Dozens of top-name mystery writers have spoken and signed their works over punch and cookies here.

The original Dot's Diner, a friendly, '50s-style restaurant in a former gas station, has been replaced by a new complex of housing, parking, and upscale shops that include the West End Gardener, 3rd Street Wine Library, Spruce Confections, and Bedell and Co. Fine Antiques.

You can try your luck at finding on-street parking, but your best bet is the parking structures just off the mall at

14th and Walnut, 11th and Spruce, and 11th and Walnut Streets, and the two new structures north and south of Pearl on 15th. When you park in any of these, ask for validation stickers as you pay for your purchases at downtown stores. Every sticker is good for a half-hour of parking, so you can shop your way to reduced-rate or free parking. Or, like a conscientious Boulderite, you can bike, walk, or take a bus or shuttle and not have to worry about where to store your car. (See Getting Here, Getting Around.)

The Mall itself is city property, managed by the Downtown Management Commission (303-441-4000). Downtown Boulder, Inc. (303-449-3774), acts as a sort of specialized Chamber of Commerce for businesses in the area.

Crossroads Mall
Between 28th and 30th Sts. and
Arapahoe Ave. and Walnut St.
(303) 444-0722

What's going to happen to Crossroads? If you haven't asked or been asked the question, you haven't been in town long. Crossroads, for more than 30 years the region's main shopping center, sits half empty, waiting for the mall's owners, the city, and the owners of the land beneath the mall's empty southern end to decide what's going to happen to it.

With a major new mall threatening from the south and neighboring communities sprouting shopping strips of their own, Crossroads and the city got serious about a makeover. Original grand plans, drawn up with the help of citizens attending public work sessions, included an outdoor plaza with skating rink and amphitheater, multiscreen movie theater, and an additional floor of retail space. Boulder voters in 1998 showed their commitment to the project by giving Crossroads the first ever exemption to the city's 55-foot height limitation, designed to protect views of the mountains. (Yes, there are buildings taller than 55 feet in Boulder, but they were built before the height ordinance was passed.) But after all that, the project didn't happen. A mall anchor vetoed the inclusion of a new department store, and the plan came tumbling down.

Macerich, the corporation that owns the mall, proposed a scaled-down plan and even ritually knocked down a wall to begin the work, scheduled for completion in spring of 2000. Again, the project didn't happen.

The city wants housing included in any redevelopment plan and has been pushing for a conference center on the site. Macerich is now planning to put in a Super Target store on the south end. The Boulder Urban Renewal Authority has advised the City Council to extend Canyon Boulevard and Walnut Street through the site (they now dead-end at Crossroads) and see if developers are interested in developing the site in smaller pieces that include housing. The final solution is yet to be determined.

Meanwhile, mall anchor stores Montgomery Ward and JCPenney have moved out, along with scores of smaller stores, and the only living things in the south end are potted palms and a young couple making the most of the privacy.

The north end of the mall remains open and fairly healthy. Foley's and Sears anchor about 80 smaller stores. Whatever happens at Crossroads in the future, it's generally conceded that it will be a center for Boulder shoppers, not the big dog for the whole county that it once was.

Arapahoe Village/The Village/WaterStreet
Between 28th and Folsom Sts., both sides of Arapahoe Ave. and Canyon Blvd.

In addition to some of the city's most popular retail shops, this complex of somewhat upscale strip malls has developed into an entertainment center, too, with Boulder's greatest concentration of movie houses and some surprisingly good restaurants. The United Artists Village 4 Theatres and Mann's Arapahoe Village Theatres across the street offer a total of eight screens. Memorable restaurants include the Full Moon Grill, Zolo Grill, Viet Hoa Vietnamese cuisine, and the European Cafe. More casual eateries in

Street performers keep Pearl Street Mall shoppers entertained year-round. PHOTO: ROZ BROWN

the area include Le Peep, Red Robin, Noodles & Company, and several yogurt, soup, ice-cream, breakfast, and burger spots. Goodies from Great Harvest Bread, Mountain Man Fruit & Nut Co., and The Brewing Market can fill in any remaining empty spaces.

This busy retail area is where you'll find the original McGuckin Hardware (if they don't have it, you don't need it), Elfriede's Fine Fabrics and Studio Bernina, Wherehouse Music, Video Station (a locally owned video store whose employees seem to have seen every movie ever made and remember the details of each one), the addictively aromatic Ead's News & Smoke Shop, and the upscale Canterbury Oak and Brass furniture. Children's shops clustered near a pleasant child's pocket park include Grand Rabbits toy store, Pour Moi clothing, and Rocky Mountain Kids outdoor gear.

The Marriott Hotel dominates the east end of the Village and offers its own upscale contributions to the shopping, with everything from Essentials Spa to Mustard Seed Gallery and the Buffalo Indian Room (see our Accommodations chapter for more information on the hotel).

The WaterStreet shopping complex, on the north side of Canyon Boulevard between Folsom and 27th, features some of Boulder's most luxurious shops. Christina's Lingerie carries expensive underwear, while The Regiment Shops sell quality men's and women's outerwear. Emerson Green is a men's store that prides itself on its "exceptional men's clothing," while JJ Wells carries equally distinctive women's fashions and accessories. Walters & Hogsett and Meyers Jewelers (see the subsequent "Jewelers" section) offer elegant jewelry.

The little shops in this area are great discoveries. From their names alone, you can guess what fun you'll have at the Colorado Rockies Club, Aspen Eyewear, Time Warp Comics, and the Wild Bird Center. Chain stores include Safeway, Famous Footwear, Wolf Camera, Eastern Mountain Sports, and Pier 1 Imports.

You can reach this area in a variety of ways: the Boulder Creek Path is on the south edge (making walking and biking easy), auto access is a snap (but the parking lots fill up when hit movies are showing), and it's on major bus routes, including the super-convenient Hop.

28th Street and 30th Street
Between Walnut St. and Iris Ave.

These two major north-south streets bracket Crossroads Mall, and a series of strip malls and freestanding stores stretch northward along the two arteries. Because most of them are fronted by parking lots, it's not easy to wander among them. But if you take the trouble, you can find most of Boulder's discount chains such as Target, Kmart, Marshall's, and Ross, and interesting specialty shops strung out along 28th Street.

The Marshall Plaza Shopping Center is home to local outposts of nationally known chains such as Old Navy, Bed, Bath & Beyond, Radio Shack, Office Depot, and Blockbuster Video. Past Crossroads and Target to the north is a huge Whole Foods market (which introduced Boulder shoppers to the concept of valet parking at a grocery store), a six-plex movie theater, Barnes & Noble books, and Vitamin Cottage. The charming building just east of the movie theater is the old Boulder Depot, now available for special events and meetings.

Just past Kmart across Valmont is the tiny Willow Springs shopping center, whose shops include Boulder Soccer and Boulder Ink, one of our city's handful of tattoo salons.

Thirtieth Street merchants include CompUSA, King Soopers, Walgreen's, Office Max, Swalley's Music Studio, Cloth Constructions (designer fabrics and wallpaper), and Concepts (home furnishings and gifts).

Basemar Shopping Center
Baseline Road and Broadway

Wild Oats health food market is the centerpiece of this L-shape strip mall just south of the CU campus. Next door is Le Français, which evokes visions of Left Bank dining with its robust coffee, flaky pastries, and thick soups. The Basemar Cinema, which shows $3 second-run movies, is just down the strip. This center offers a nice mix of little shops and services, including Buffalo Lock and Key, which is quick at matching keys and getting into locked cars. Herb's Quality Meats boasts a wide variety and does a good business in a town sometimes called "The Tofu Capital of Colorado." The Taj restaurant serves a popular Middle Eastern buffet, and Acoma Books has been buying and reselling used scholarly, scientific, technical, and general books since the mid-1970s.

The Meadows Shopping Center
Foothills Parkway and Baseline Road

As Boulder has grown eastward, this strip mall has become busier and busier. More than 50 businesses are now part of this large neighborhood shopping complex, located near several retirement and senior-living facilities. It includes the biggest Safeway in town, along with Photo Finish, Art Cleaners, and Runner's Choice. Take a lunch break at Nick-N-Willy's Pizza or Lee Yuan Chinese restaurant. Michael's Craft Store offers everything from candle wax and rattan by the bundle to baking supplies and picture framing. The Meadows branch library on the south side of the shopping center has a popular meeting room, in addition to the books and other materials of a well-stocked branch.

North Broadway and Community Plaza
Broadway and Alpine Ave., across from Community Hospital

Boulder design group Communication Arts gets credit for the imaginative looping and zigzag rooflines that transformed these 1960s-era shopping malls into trendy mini plazas with a European feel. Pleasant little shops offer flowers, prescription drugs and natural remedies, haircuts, gifts, and more. All the restaurants here have outdoor dining areas—and there are many restaurants here. Moe's Bagels customers rub shoulders with diners at Marie's European cafe. Those enjoying a bowl of Thai noodle soup from the Noodle Company can trade tastes (if they want) with those dining alfresco on sandwiches from the wonderful Ideal Market deli. Ideal is one of Boulder's favorite grocery stores because it combines old-fashioned ambiance with the latest food fashions and friendly clerks. Other great shops include the Boulder Wine Merchant, European Flower Shop, the Ginger and Pickles toy store, Breadworks (free samples), the Stage House Too bookstore, Room to Room furnishings, and the Jacque Michelle boutique.

North Village Mart
Broadway and Quince Street

This is the kind of low-key, small-scale shopping area that any neighborhood would want. You won't find choices galore here, but you'll notice just how lovely and cozy a small neighborhood shopping center can be. The area fits its neighborhood well. Kids arrive from the bike trails to pick up videos, wander into the pet store, and stop for ice cream. Families and friends winding down after work fill the three respectable restaurants, which serve Chinese food, Italian food, and sandwiches. The Nomad Players, a well-regarded community theater group, performs in the quonset just east of the center. North Boulder Market, which anchors this little shopping center, is a good basic grocery store, with one of the better meat departments in town and a more-than-adequate deli. A video outlet, liquor store, florist, and pet supply store round out the shopping opportunities.

Table Mesa Shopping Center
Broadway and Table Mesa Dr.

In addition to a King Soopers and the usual complement of restaurants and various stores, this South Boulder shopping center has many excellent outdoor stores, including The North Face, Neptune Mountaineering, Play It Again Sports, Doc's Ski & Sports (the place to rent skis), and Weaver's Dive Center. Weaver's is for divers, but weavers go to Shuttles, Spindles and Skeins. The Cooking School of the Rockies holds classes, from practical to decadent, recreational to professional, and has a small retail section with gourmet cookware. Next door, Brillig Works Bakery entices with tasty baked goods. Dragonfire Games invites kids and adults to join in the fun of fantasy card games and model painting.

University Hill
Broadway, north and south of College Ave.

Just west of campus and both affectionately and officially called "The Hill," this area caters mainly to the university crowd. The Hill developed in 1906 as a streetcar stop between the Boulder Depot downtown and Chautauqua Park. In 1928, it was the focus of Boulder's first business growth restriction, from homeowners who feared their neighbors would eventually sell out to stores. For that reason, The Hill's retail zone remains quite compact.

The three-block University Hill district is located in central Boulder, bordering the western edge of the University of Colorado.

The district includes 100 businesses and 29 commercial property owners, around the intersection of 13th and College Streets.

Declining sales prompted a facelift in 1997, with street improvements and the addition of trees and artwork and a clock. (As you stroll, keep an eye out for the literary quotations imbedded in the sidewalk.) Unfortunately, the sprucing up has not turned things around, and Hill merchants chipped in for a marketing study, completed in spring 2001.

The plan's recommendations include:

• Creating a marketing fund for such efforts as a Hill business district Web site, specific marketing to the neighborhood and student populations, newsletters and neighborhood forums, collaborative promotions for the university population, and special events such as a Hill Farmers' Market or a foot race.

• More visible patrols by the police, supplementary security patrols, community court for enforcement of nuisance crimes, extending the Blue Light security network, creating weekend maintenance and seasonal clean-up days, and lighting improvements.

• Investigating direct access to the parking lot currently accessed from a side street, installing directional signs to the Hill along Broadway and at College Avenue, and installing gateway landmarks at key entrances to the district at the intersections of Broadway and College Street, and Broadway and 13th Street.

• Adjusting the zoning designation in the district to encourage new development, specifically allowing smaller new restaurants and rethinking height restrictions.

• Recruiting the types of new businesses The Hill wants: sit-down upscale restaurants, a family-friendly movie theater, a bank, an upscale grocery, a hardware store, and activities for those under 21.

- Creating a public/private partnership to market and manage The Hill.

Shops on The Hill are as eclectic as the shoppers, ranging from the elegant and ultra-tweedy men's shop called Kinsley & Co. to tattoo and piercing parlors. Coffee is available approximately every 10 feet, as is fast food of one type and another. The Colorado Bookstore is the largest business on The Hill, its huge glass windows covered over with brick after anti-war riots left them in shards (protestors against the war in Vietnam also closed Highway 36 connecting Boulder to Denver). Across the street is the venerable Jones Drug, and next door, the Pipefitter offers oddments. Art Hardware provides everything for the budding Picasso, and Albums on The Hill has an extensive collection of old and new CDs, tapes, and even vinyl records.

Parking is at a premium on The Hill, but its convenient location on the Hop and Skip routes make it easy to reach from the Pearl Street and Crossroads Malls, as well as from north and south Boulder. Otherwise, it's best to walk or bicycle to this shopping area. You can sometimes find metered spaces on campus, which is a short walk away via a beautiful pedestrian underpass at Broadway and College Avenue that is worth a visit in its own right. If your interest in the Hill runs deeper than shopping, you can pick up a free booklet outlining a self-guided walking tour at the Hill Annex, a small "city hall" for students and visitors in the 1200 block of 13th Street, behind Buchanan's.

Gunbarrel Square
Gunpark Road and Lookout Road, Gunbarrel

It's not extensive, but for the residents of Gunbarrel, who for many years had only a King Soopers grocery and tiny strip mall, the expanded shopping area of Gunbarrel Square is a welcome enhancement. Gunbarrel Square includes the Printed Page, a small but high-quality bookstore with a charming cafe. Other food offerings include Angelo's pizza and subs; House of Chang Chinese restaurant, with a popular lunchtime buffet; a deli; and Serrano's Southwestern grill. Also here are a Mail Box, flower shop, liquor store, even a private elementary school.

East County Shopping Areas

Twin Peaks Mall
Hover Rd. and Colo. Hwy. 119, Longmont
(303) 651–6454

Nearly 10 million shoppers a year visit the 84 stores and 10 eateries at this traditional, regional, enclosed shopping center, which was renovated and expanded in 1997. (The name refers to the view west to two Rocky Mountain peaks.) The big draws presently include JCPenney (the original Penney got his start in Longmont), Sears, and Dillard's department stores. Another major draw is the United Artists 10-screen movie complex.

Twin Peaks features many of the national chain stores: Victoria's Secret, Foot Locker and Gart sporting goods stores, Bath and Body Works, Gymboree children's clothing store, Famous Footwear, and Kay Bee Toys, as well as several jewelry and shoe stores. Woodleys Fine Furniture features locally made items, and Colorful Images is an overstock store full of furniture and novelty items. In addition to such sit-down restaurants as the gut-busting Country Buffet and Chelsey London Pub and Grill, there's a food court that serves up the usual burgers, pizza, and Chinese food.

Like several malls in the area, this one also has a police sub-station.

Lafayette
East on Arapahoe Rd., Baseline Rd., or South Boulder Rd.

Lafayette's main shopping areas are around the intersection of South Boulder Road and Public Road, which is also U.S. 287. To the north, this is an area of small, unique, and charming shops, with the big-box stores just down the road. Antique hunters gravitate to the funky finds at West's Antiques, which is a full block long, and nearby Rayburn Antiques and Matthew's Gifts. Lafayette Florists offers the most bedding plants in the county; a visit is a rite of spring for many Boulder County residents. The Lafayette Flea Market uses sandwich-boarded boosters to draw customers into the rambling series of interconnecting spaces, with everything from antiques to unadulterated junk. Take a trip back a few decades by pulling into the Sonic drive-in on Waneka Parkway for a limeade and a chili dog and run over to the Coal Creek Bowling Center for a game or two. Karen's in the Country restaurant continues the nostalgia theme, serving upscale meals in a farmhouse atmosphere. Country General is still a real country general store, selling farm equipment, dog food, tools, and horse halters despite the rapid suburbanization of the town. You can get a good bite of Mexican food at Efrain's, which serves the hottest green chili around, or La Familia, which is Spanish for "the family," a good name for this homey eatery.

Louisville
East on South Boulder Rd. or Louisville exit off U.S. Hwy. 36

Louisville's quaint and sleepy downtown has been eclipsed of late by the bright lights of the retail strip along McCaslin Boulevard. New big-box retail outlets, fast-food eateries, chain restaurants, a 12-plex theater, and hotels are being joined by clusters of smaller shops. On either side of McCaslin you'll find Home Depot and Eagle Hardware competing across the street from each other, and chain restaurants that include Applebee's, Chili's, and Outback Steak House. The Village Safeway Shopping Center is at South Boulder Road and Centennial; Albertson's grocery is on West Cherry Street. Louisville Plaza, at South Boulder Road off of Colo. 42, has King Soopers and Kmart. The Centennial Center, at McCaslin Boulevard and Cherry Street, is near the movie complex (suffer-

ing from competition from a 24-plex further south in Westminster) and the hotels. In historic downtown, along Main Street, you'll find Wildwood Music and several casual, families-welcome eating places including the Marketplace Bakery, The Blue Parrot restaurant, Joe's Market (for sausage and Italian food), Double Happy Chinese, and Tulien's Vietnamese Restaurant. Thunderbird Barbers, complete with an American flag outside, offers a glimpse of Main Street past, as does the ad for 5-cent Coca-Cola painted on the small brick home of the Louisville Historical Society. Close by, the Old Louisville Inn, at 740 Front Street, features an antique bar and lots of character. Behind a small retail center along South Boulder Road are the real train cars that house Kaddy Shack World Famous Barbecue.

Insiders' Tip
The best parking for the downtown area is in the structures located at 14th and Walnut, 11th and Spruce, and 11th and Walnut Streets. When you're parked in any of these, ask for validation stickers as you pay at downtown stores. Every sticker is good for a half-hour of parking, so you can shop your way to reduced or free parking. In addition, a city-owned garage with wraparound retail is at 15th and Pearl, east of the Pearl Street Mall, and a private structure is one block north at 15th and Spruce Streets.

Specialty Shops

Antiques

Boulder

Carter Home Collection
1779 Valtec Ln., Boulder
(303) 447–0997
This 7,000-square-foot warehouse store, filled with antique furniture and accessories from Europe, is worth the drive east. Trunks, rugs, vintage toys, linens, cupboards, dining sets, art—there's a little of it all here.

Classic Facets
942 Pearl St., Boulder
(303) 938–8851
This unique little shop specializes in rare antiques—diamonds and colored stones, period jewelry from 1700s to 1950s and vintage designer costume jewelry. If you're looking to sell, your stuff better be good—consigners from 30 states and nine countries send items to the exclusive shop; 90 percent of the offerings are rejected.

Sage Gallery
1227 Spruce St., Boulder
(303) 449–6799
After a sojourn in an East Boulder strip mall, Sage is back downtown, just west of the hotel Boulderado. The charming shop offers fine antiques: 18th- and 19th-century furniture, sterling silver, crystal, porcelain, fine art, and Asian antiques are among the specialties.

Lafayette

Cannon Mine Coffee & Antiques
210 S. Public Rd., Lafayette
(303) 665–0625
Have a coffee and pastry and experience first-hand the ambiance created by the antiques sold in this unique shop. Like the chair you're sitting in? Make an offer. It's all for sale.

Lafayette Antiques
611 S. Public Rd., Lafayette
(303) 665–2212
Lafayette Antiques is a multi-dealer shop with collections including furniture, glassware, stoneware, and primitives.

Lafayette Flea Market
130 E. Spaulding St., Lafayette
(303) 665–0433
Good Housekeeping has called this one of the nation's best flea markets. Among the 500,000 items for sale are clothes, glassware, pots and pans, dishes, and antiques. It's open all year, in a clean, well-organized store with friendly salesclerks.

Longmont

Days Gone By Antiques
251 Main St., Longmont
(303) 651–1912

Front Range Flea Market
1420 Nelson Rd., Longmont
(303) 776–6605
This nearly 30,000-square-foot flea market has something for everyone. There is large and small furniture, many usable household goods, decorating items, and even tools. Much of the furniture is new or nearly new. At the same time, antique glassware, old linens, rare furniture, and other collectibles are for sale, making it difficult to spend less than a couple of hours here. Owners call this store an "upscale flea market," and acknowledge what is currently in demand by stocking a large inventory. Each vendor rents a 10-by-10 space so the selection is constantly changing.

Main Street Antique Mall
370 Main St., Longmont
(303) 776–8511

Pacific Auction
1270 Boston Ave., Longmont
(303) 772–7676

Lyons

Left-Hand Trading Company
401 and 405 Main St., Lyons
(303) 823–6311
Lyons Antique Center
4559 Ute Hwy., Lyons
(303) 545–2266

Ralston Brothers Antiques
426 High St., Lyons
(303) 823–6982

Located north of Boulder, Lyons is worth the special trip, whether you're in the market for something specific or just browsing. Lyons Antique Center is a barn-like place with a little bit of everything, including furniture, china, glassware, pottery, jewelry and memorabilia, handled by about a dozen dealers. Left-Hand Trading Company carries general antiques, including those with a Western flair and Indian artifacts. Ralston Brothers, in a historic stone building, specializes in vintage juke boxes, radios, phonographs, light fixtures, toys, and restored furniture.

Nederland

Off Her Rocker Antiques
4 E. First St., Nederland
(303) 258–7976

It's a funky corner shop that feels like a rustic mountain museum. Old wash basins, oak furniture, and nifty used clothes go for bargain prices. On nice days, old rockers bedeck the boardwalk out front, rocking gently in the mountain breeze. The shop is known by watch collectors for its interesting array of old pocket watches in working condition. Local artisans supply such whimsical merchandise as tinkling wind chimes made from flattened antique spoons and forks.

Niwot

Elysian Fields
7915 Niwot Rd., Niwot
(303) 652–1631

Niwot Antiques
136 Second Ave., Niwot
(303) 652–2587

Wise Buys Antiques
190 Second Ave., Niwot
(303) 652–2888

Northeast of Boulder, Niwot has several wonderful antique stores all within a short stroll of each other. Specializing in 18th-century furniture, art, and accessories, Elysian Fields also sells online and conducts auctions. Niwot Antiques is the town's giant. This is a cooperative of more than 40 dealers, many with particular specialties that appeal to collectors. Period antiques, Fiestaware, fine china, art, Oriental rugs, clocks and jewelry are among the treasures found here. Wise Buys offers fireplace mantels, millwork doors, and large pieces of furniture.

Art Galleries

Art Affaire
820 Main St., Louisville
(303) 665–2074

Originals and limited-edition prints by artist Tom Kinkade and others are available here. A computerized print-finding service helps buyers track down the piece they've been looking for.

Art and Soul
1615 Pearl St., Boulder
(303) 544–5803

A unique array of crafts and fine art, this international collection includes sculpture, paintings, fine woodworking, jewelry, and ceramics. It's located just off the east end of the downtown mall.

ArtCycle
1441 Pearl St., Boulder
(303) 449–4950

Formerly located just off the Downtown Mall, this gallery has a new location but the same great concept—consigning the art of sellers who've tired of a piece or are redecorating. The shop carries modern and contemporary art, original and limited-edition prints, sculpture, jewelry, and pop and kinetic art. They also do appraisals and custom framing.

Niwot, northeast of Boulder, is known for its wealth of antiques stores. PHOTO: DAILY CAMERA/DAVID P. GILKEY

Artist's Proof Fine Framing & Gallery
5360 Arapahoe Ave., Boulder
(303) 447-3504

This shop couples fine custom framing, hand-carved matting, and dry mounting with the sale of unusual art. It specializes in interesting sports memorabilia (especially baseball) and original signed black-and-white photographs and other graphic media.

Art Mart
1222 Pearl St., Boulder
(303) 443-8248

This is kind of a crafts supermarket, which bills itself as an "artist outlet store." It overflows with Southwestern objects, including jewelry, pottery, weavings, dream catchers, and all manner of other popular items. The large store also carries clothing, candles, wood inlays, and myriad

weaving, and other items make great gifts or accent pieces for your home. The co-op will also ship purchases anywhere in the continental United States.

Busch Gallery
1426 Pearl St., Boulder
(303) 473-9215

Busch Gallery has two floors of contemporary paintings, ceramics, raku, sculpture, bronzes, and fine jewelry, with space available for community events. Past shows have included oil paintings by Jim Rabby, jewelry by Elisa Browsh, and watercolors by Monika Pate. Recent collections featured African-American art, custom ceramic art tiles, and hand-blown glass art and decorations from Germany.

other crafts, along with a large collection of local and regional photography.

Art Source International
1237 Pearl St., Boulder
(303) 444-4080

This store specializes in antique maps and prints, books, and vintage Colorado photographs. Many are already framed, some are ready for your choice of frame, and all are fascinating. In addition to a great selection of 18th- and 19th-century maps, the gallery displays prints from the same era. Check out the public art just out front—a chess table and two chairs commemorating a Pearl Street Mall frequenter who didn't live to enjoy his dream of playing chess with his grandson on the Mall.

Boulder Arts & Crafts Cooperative
1421 Pearl St., Boulder
(303) 443-3683

This is the biggest and most diverse of the city's several crafts co-ops. It shows the works of more than 150 artists from Colorado and surrounding mountain states, displaying high-quality crafts in all media. Pottery, puppets, jewelry, photographs, weavings, stained glass, clothing, leather wallets stamped with leaves, whimsically painted wood tables and benches, hand-

Limited Edition, Inc.
240 Second Ave., Niwot
(303) 652-2055

Wildlife, Western, and maritime limited-edition prints are the specialty of this shop in downtown Niwot. The prices make it well worth the drive.

Mackin-Katz Gallery of Photography
2041 Broadway, Boulder
(303) 786-7887

This gallery presents several artists but showcases Andy Katz's fine photography, which includes scenes of the California wine country, Poland, Israel, and Vietnam. Andy started showing his work locally in a basement gallery of his own under a cafe and behind a billiards parlor, but this new daylight-filled space is much more conducive to viewing his detailed and delicate photographs.

MacLaren Markowitz Gallery
1011 Pearl St., Boulder
(303) 449-6807

This is a bright gallery, perfect for showing painting, sculpture, jewelry, glasswork, and imports. Featured artists include Doug West, whose acrylics and serigraphs of Western landscapes have become extremely popular, Mary Morrison, and Lisa Jinks. The gallery sometimes puts on Collectors Evenings, which give art lovers an opportunity to meet personally with artists. Poster signings, art talks, and other special events are occasionally on the agenda, too.

Marisol Imports
915 Pearl St., Boulder
(303) 442–3142

West of the Pearl Street Mall, Marisol offers a stunning display of Zapotec and other Mexican rugs, plus Southwestern furniture, Navajo rugs, and crafts. The beautiful but expensive rugs become more affordable at Marisol's annual after-Christmas sale. Pottery, woodcarvings, wrought-iron items, rustic furniture, and unusual knickknacks are also stocked.

Mary Williams Fine Arts
2116 Pearl St., Boulder
(303) 938–1588

This gallery shows old and new American works, including some with strong Western and Native American orientations. Fine prints and graphics on such themes as botanicals, natural history, and architecture from the 17th through 20th centuries abound. There's free on-site parking, a scarce commodity downtown.

The Middle Fish
1500 Pearl St., Boulder
(303) 443–0835

This gallery commemorates the childhood nickname of store owner Malinda Fishman. In one of the new buildings that have sprung up on the east end of the Downtown Mall, The Middle Fish sells unique handcrafted items, including ceramic indoor fountains, garden art, handmade dolls, furniture, lighting, jewelry, and Judaica. Contemporary rather than classical pieces dominate.

Motherland
2028 14th St., Boulder
(303) 543–7903

African art and musical instruments are the featured items in this shop. The art includes masks, wood and ebony carvings, and tapestries and weavings created by artists in Kenya, Zimbabwe, and the Ivory Coast. Musical instruments are imported from Ghana, Ivory Coast, Mali, Morocco, Nigeria, and Togo, and include drums, iron bells, gongs, shakers and rattles, sticks and beaters, and drum-tuning accessories.

Old Tibet
948 Pearl St., Boulder
(303) 440–0323

More than 200 Tibetan Thanka paintings are at the heart of this rich collection of Hindu and Buddhist art and religious items. You will find statues, ceremonial pieces, jewelry, books, singing bowls, bells and cymbals, clothing, music, incense, and beads. The shop is a generous supporter of the struggling country that has attracted the attention and concern of many Boulder citizens.

Ruth Linton & David Haslam Gallery
1217 Spruce St., Boulder
(303) 444–9116

Fine art by Sandra Bierman, YanZhou Xu, William Napier, Elizabeth Black, Robert Venosa, and Ann Herzog Wright are sold next to Pre-Columbian, Grecian, and Egyptian artifacts. Custom framing is available, too.

Smith-Klein Gallery
1116 Pearl St., Boulder
(303) 444–7200

This gallery houses contemporary art including jewelry, hand-blown glass, and folk art animals, by both local and regional artists. A recent show featured a collection of hand-carved Zuni horse fetishes dating from the early 1900s.

Tibet Gallery
1916 13th St., Boulder
(303) 402–0140

Handmade rugs, jewelry, statues, clothing, spiritual gifts, and other arts and crafts of Tibet are sold in this shop next to McGuckin Hardware.

Von Eschen Gallery & Frame Shop/ Wing's Gallery
2660 Canyon Blvd., Boulder
(303) 448–1237, (303) 443–9989

Original art, an eclectic assortment of one-of-a-kind jewelry by local artists, pottery and unusual gifts are available at Wing's Gallery. Von Eschen Gallery & Frame Shop adds limited-edition prints and custom framing.

Arts and Crafts Supplies

Art Hardware
1135 Broadway, Boulder
(303) 444–3063

This is Boulder's top professional (and amateur) artists' supply center, with a full line of art and drafting supplies in a 14,000-square-foot building. The shop also does blue printing, large-format copying for architects and engineers, and custom framing. The store boasts free covered parking for customers, a real rarity on The Hill.

The Dove's Eye
2425 Canyon Blvd., Boulder
(303) 443–6031

This newly remodeled shop is a needle-worker's paradise, selling fabrics, yarns, needles, and stitching accessories. Custom stitching, classes, and unique gifts complete the picture of this special business.

Michael's Arts and Crafts
4800 Baseline Rd., Boulder
(303) 494–2008

Michael's is a bustling warehouse chain store packed with craft items, from dried and plastic flowers to the right kind of muslin and paint sets for creating doll faces. Beads, Styrofoam, jewelry findings, and all sorts of kits appeal to crafters of all ages and skills. It's a big, reasonably priced place where kids and adults like to wander and take classes. There's a framing shop in the back.

Needlepoint of View Gallery, Ltd.
361 Second Ave., Niwot
(303) 652–2177

Area needleworkers say it's worth the drive to this small shop, which offers custom designs, patterns by nationally known designers, and finishing for a prized piece.

Promenade's Le Bead Shop
1970 13th St., Boulder
(303) 440–4807

Just off the Pearl Street Mall, this is a small shop with a huge selection of baubles, bangles, and bright shiny beads. Glass beads in a stunning variety of hues and sizes, antique beads, African trade beads, sequins, rhinestones, sew-ons, studs, jeweler's string, ear wires, posts, clasps, and all the other makings of unique, do-it-yourself jewelry are crammed into Boulder's best beadery. The shop also offers classes, jewelry appraisal by a certified gemologist, and professional pearl stringing.

Insiders' Tip
If you love the idea of handmade items crafted by a grandmother or grandfather, even if they're not your own, plan to stop at the Boulder Senior Services annual Arts & Crafts Fair, normally on a Friday and Saturday early in November. The fair even offers a children's room, with entertainment and a table of $1 to $2 gifts, where children 12 and younger could do their holiday shopping.

Shuttles, Spindles and Skeins
633 S. Broadway, Boulder
(303) 494–1071
This South Boulder shop has walls and walls of yarn in a fantastic array of colors for knitting and weaving. Uncarded wool, silk, flax, and camel hair are all perfect for making doll hair as well as for spinning. You can also find a few handmade items for sale that are truly masterpieces. This small, charming store has a cozy atmosphere that just says "welcome." The staff is very knowledgeable, and the shop offers both craft books for inspiration and classes to show you how to turn the inspiration into action.

Bakeries

Many of our better groceries stock locally produced breads, or you can go straight to the bakeries so you can luxuriate in bread aromas as soon as you open the door. Most have some sort of frequent-buyer program, giving you a free loaf after a dozen or so purchases, and many offer you a chance to sample the wares while you decide which loaf has your name on it.

Breadworks
2644 Broadway, Boulder
(303) 444–5667
This shop bakes 30 varieties of crusty European hearth-baked breads. Focaccia, brownies, cookies, muffins, and scones also come out of the huge brick and tile oven. Monday is half-price day for breads left over from the weekend. Breadworks unlocks the door at 7 A.M. daily. Stop by Ideal Market across the street for butter, find a sunny spot on the grass, and enjoy the bliss.

Brillig Works Bakery
637-G South Broadway in the Table Mesa Shopping Center
(303) 499–5253
The aroma of fresh-baked muffins, scones, cinnamon rolls, and coffee greet shoppers who stop in here. At lunchtime

Brillig Works offers homemade soups, sandwiches, and stews.

Cakes by Karen
2085 30th St., Boulder
(303) 449–6254
The name says only part of it. Photo cakes, custom wedding cakes, birthday cakes, and other sweet goodies certainly are the specialty here, but Cakes by Karen also can fill your need for balloons, party favors, decorating supplies—even a limo.

Great Harvest Bread Company
2525 Arapahoe Ave., Boulder
(303) 442–3062
This is part of a tightly controlled franchise operation that makes rich, chewy, healthful breads and rolls. While other bakeries just put out sample bites, Great Harvest cuts whole slabs and invites you to slather your "taste" with butter and honey.

Just From Scratch
4800 Baseline Rd., Boulder
(303) 494–3635
Pastries, breads, muffins, and coffee cakes—and the espresso and cappuccino to go along—are available in this small shop next to Michael's craft store. Limited seating is available. Pick up a party tray to go.

Karen's Country Kitchen
700 Main St., Louisville
(303) 666–8020
Different Karen, same great smells and tastes. This Karen's is well known in the county for its prize-winning pies, European-style Danish, and countless desserts, all baked fresh daily on the premises.

Le Français
2570 Baseline Rd., in the Base-Mar Shopping Center, Boulder
(303) 499–7429
This traditional bakery offers almost-real French baguettes (French friends say "real" requires French air wafting through

the brick ovens), plus decadent French pastries, both savory and sweet. In addition to take-out baked goods, you can eat in at breakfast, lunch, or dinner. Le Français, which is owned by a French baker, makes the most gorgeous special-occasion cakes.

The Lick Skillet Bakery
5340 Arapahoe Ave., Boulder
(303) 449-7775
It might look like it's part of the neighboring gas station, but folks who live or work in eastern Boulder know that the Lick Skillet is the place to stop for coffee and pastries in the morning. The small shop is popular for raspberry-mousse cake, stuffed focaccia, and wheat-free fruit muffins. In the unlikely event that nothing in the case appeals, they'll even cook you an omelet. Seating is skimpy, so come early.

A Taste of Heaven
1918 Pearl St., Boulder
(303) 448-1047
Elegant desserts, breakfast pastries, and spectacular wedding cakes are the specialties of this bakery on the east end of downtown Boulder. Lunch includes a variety of sandwiches named for local hot spots, and salads that are popular with area businesses and meetings.

Bookstores

Considering the number of bookstores in town, it seems that everyone you see ought to have his or her nose buried in a book. Boulder bookstores were selling coffee and goodies, even meals, long before a corporate somebody stumbled upon the idea.

Acoma Books
2488 Baseline Rd., in the Base-Mar
Shopping Center, Boulder
(303) 494-3309
For 27 years, Acoma has been buying and selling new and used scholarly, scientific, and technical books. Students and profes-sors aren't the only customers, but the shop is conveniently located across the street from the University of Colorado.

Aion Bookshop
1235 Pennsylvania Ave., Boulder
(303) 443-5763
This is a used bookstore with a real antiquarian feeling. The shop rambles through a series of small rooms, which are filled but not crammed, with a fascinating selection of previously owned and previously loved books. The street level features hardbacks, including many of a serious and scholarly nature, as you might expect from a store on University Hill. Downstairs are more popular books, including paperbacks, sci-fi, mysteries, cookbooks, self-help, sports, and such. The selection of science, arts, humanities, and great literature is impressive, as is the knowledge of the folks working there.

Barnes & Noble
2915 Pearl St., Boulder
(303) 444-2501
This may be a big chain store, but it's working to offer a more personal touch that's gaining local respect. The store specializes in popular fiction and nonfiction but has a large sampling of more obscure works, too. People linger in the on-site coffee shop, and the store is the site of regular meetings of locals interested in both the creative and reading aspects of literature. There is also a nice selection of cards, magazines, books on tape, reading lights, and other gifts and accessories.

Beat Book Shop
1713 Pearl St., Boulder
(303) 444-7111
If you want to turn the calendar back a few decades, check out this quirky store, which specializes in literature, poetry, biography, and books on film, sociology, and subculture, all with a distinct retro flair. It offers a commendable selection of first editions, too. The shop also stocks rare records and tapes, some fine art, and used CDs.

The Bookworm
2850 Iris Ave., Boulder
(303) 449-3765

The unprepossessing location of this family-owned and -operated bookstore, tucked into an aging strip mall, does not reflect its status as the largest used bookstore in the county. The stacks and stacks of books just keep going and going and going—400,000 titles in all. There is an extensive mystery section, and there are romances to soften up the hardest pragmatist. Books on tape and videos are a growing collection. The shop also does a mail-order business.

The Boulder Bookstore
1107 Pearl St., Boulder
(303) 447-2074

This is Boulder's local showpiece, named the "Best Bookstore in Boulder" every year since 1987, when the award began. In 1993 the store moved into the historic Buckingham Building, receiving an award of merit from Historic Boulder for "historic preservation and restoration of the second-floor ballroom." The lovely high-ceilinged room with its antique stained-glass windows is the stage for visiting authors; more than 100 are invited to read and chat and autograph their works here each year. Notables have included Barbara Kingsolver, Ram Dass, Amy Tan, Frank McCourt, Whitley Strieber, and Isabel Allende. The 20,000-square-foot, four-story bookstore offers more than 100,000 titles and also has a large selection of magazines, journals, and various book-related items, plus exhibits of works by local artists. The store recently began stocking a small selection of used books, with proceeds going to local charities. It is also a strong supporter of local authors.

The adjacent, but separately owned, Bookend Cafe is connected by an open door and makes a nice stop after browsing through the books.

The Colorado Bookstore
1111 Broadway, Boulder
(303) 442-5051

Located next to the big outdoor clock and the pedestrian underpass on University Hill, this is a classic college bookstore. It sells new textbooks and plenty of used books (they buy and sell) and has a mezzanine devoted to general books. You also can buy CU-Boulder sweatshirts, souvenirs, and school supplies. There's a small post office substation, and copiers, fax machines, prepaid phone cards, photo processing, and other services are available.

Ead's News & Smoke Shop
1715 28th St., Boulder
(303) 442-5900

Also under an outdoor clock, this is actually a mega-newsstand, with Boulder's best selection of magazines and out-of-town newspapers. It also carries an assortment of travel books, popular paperbacks, and adult-only books and magazines, and sells an aromatic selection of cigarettes, cigars, and pipe tobacco (but don't light up until you're outside).

Great Horned Owl Children's Bookstore
1075 S. Boulder Rd., Louisville
(303) 665-6888

Books and gifts for little readers, infant to young adult, are found in this Christopher Plaza shop. There's a daily story hour for kids and resources for parents and teachers. Popular Madame Alexander dolls are also on sale here.

High Crimes Mystery Bookshop
946 Pearl St., Boulder
(303) 443-8346

Formerly Tom and Enid Shantz's Rue Morgue, High Crimes continues the tradition of mysteries and nothing but mysteries. The shop specializes in signed first editions, British imports, and historical mysteries and sells both new and used editions, paperback and hardcover.

Lefthand Book Collective, Inc.
1200 Pearl St., lower level, Boulder
(303) 443-8252

This all-volunteer bookstore is Boulder's resource for progressive books on feminism, national and environmental causes, political thought, gay and lesbian studies, Marxism, and National Liberation. Periodicals cover political, economic, ecological, and Third World issues. They also carry gifts, greeting cards, magazines, and T-shirts.

Lighthouse Bookstore
1201 Pearl St., Boulder
(303) 939–8355

Below street level on the Pearl Street Mall, this store carries Boulder's largest selection of New Age books dealing with spirituality, self-help, religions from around the world, and exploring the inner self. It's well stocked with books, music, candles, Tarot cards, scarves and crystals. Light filtering in from the street-side windows, the aroma of incense, and calming music from the store's New Age and traditional selections create an atmosphere conducive to browsing. The staff is especially helpful here, too.

Logos of Boulder
2525 Arapahoe Ave., Boulder
(303) 449–1919

Since 1971, this has been Boulder's bookstore for historical and contemporary Christian thought. Catering to both Protestant and Catholic readers, the store carries a large and varied selection of Bibles, plus cards, gifts, tapes, and CDs.

The Printed Page
1219 Pearl St., Boulder
(303) 443–8450

Page Two
6565 Gunpark Drive, Boulder
(303) 530–3339

The Pearl Street store carries stationery and gifts, along with a small selection of books, mostly local-interest and children's books. Their Christmas and Hanukkah card selection is one of the best in the city, and there are delightful seasonal gifts tucked in cupboards at the entrance. The Gunbarrel store not only carries a similar inventory but houses a pleasant cafe as

well. Store founder Virginia Patterson, who could pose for pictures as everybody's favorite grandmother, doesn't spend much time in the store anymore, but The Printed Page remains in the family.

Red Letter Second Hand Books
1737 Pearl St., Boulder
(303) 938–1778

This is a readers' store. Step through the front door and you face a forest of books, stacked, spread, and shelved. The shop is jammed and crammed with a selection of used books, including travel, biography, and all sorts of fiction. It offers classics as well as modern works for buying, selling, trading, or simply browsing.

Table Mesa Gifts & Books
645 S. Broadway, Boulder
(303) 499–1269

Table Mesa is a traditional bookstore serving south Boulder, with best sellers, regional books, children's selections, and gift books. They gladly help with special orders and carry greeting cards and gift items.

Time Warp Science Fiction and Comics
1631 28th St., Boulder
(303) 443–4500

This is a word-of-mouth favorite among kids and has been nominated as one of the nation's best comic stores. Regionally, it has garnered "Best of Boulder" and "Best of Denver" awards from the *Boulder Daily Camera* and Denver's *Westword*. Time Warp is known for both mainstream and underground comics.

Trident Booksellers & Cafe
940 Pearl St., Boulder
(303) 443–3133

Trident customers were enjoying a cuppa with their reading when coffee only came in one flavor. Inside, interesting-looking people huddle over tables, apparently engaged in the most existential of conversations. In the summer, the sidewalk tables are similarly filled, usually with a leashed dog or two reclining on the sidewalk. The bookstore has a potpourri of used books, new remainders, cards, and calendars. The sale table just inside the front door always displays interesting books on history, gardening, cooking, travel, spiritual topics, and more.

Word Is Out Women's Bookstore
1731 15th St., Boulder
(303) 449–1415

This section of 15th Street has always had an eclectic collection of stores, so it's only appropriate a bookstore would eventually locate here. Opened in 1997, Word Is Out carries a large selection of books on lesbian and gay issues, women's studies, self-development, poetry, and criticism. There are also mystery and detective books, gifts, greeting cards, tapes, and CDs.

Clothing and Accessories

For Children
Applause
1123 Pearl St. Boulder
(303) 442–7426

This Pearl Street Mall store offers outrageously stylish kids' clothes, endearing baby and toddler duds, and enchanting ballerina and princess get-ups for little girls who like to dress up. It's pricey, but if you're looking for something unique, Applause may have just the thing.

Childish Things
2071 30th St., Boulder
(303) 442–2703

Recycled children's clothing, toys, baby equipment, maternity clothes and accessories, and nursery furniture fill this friendly consignment shop. It's next door to Collage Children's Museum, so you can make shopping here part of an afternoon outing.

Gap Kids
2043 Broadway, Boulder
(303) 473–9891

This chain store one block off the Pearl Street Mall is hard to resist, with its constantly changing, colorful window displays. Just like the regular Gap, this store stocks high-fashion clothes, in this case for newborns through preteens. They offer great sales if you happen to wander in on the right day.

Little Mountain Outdoor Gear for Kids
1136 Spruce St., Boulder
(303) 443–1757

Just around the corner from Gap Kids, this store claims to be the only local outlet specializing exclusively in outdoor clothing gear and accessories for children. If you're a visitor, Little Mountain offers daily rentals on backpacks and baby joggers.

Pockets Children and Maternity Consignment
3103 28th St., Boulder
(303) 444–3554

In addition to clothing for infants and children (sizes up to 6X), this store sells used maternity clothes, toys, baby equipment, nursery furniture, car seats, strollers, and swings. You didn't really want to keep that tent of a shirt with the big bow, did you?

Pour Moi?
2525 Arapahoe Ave., in the Village, Boulder
(303) 442–1723

Girls and women will find a wide assortment of clothing here, from reasonably priced casual items to expensive holiday dresses. They start with clothing for 7-year-olds and continue through teens to women's sizes. Lots of unusual accessories and jewelry are also available.

Rocky Mountain Kids
2525 Arapahoe Ave., Boulder
(303) 447–2267

As you might expect from the name, this store sells fleece and other outdoorsy performance clothing, but it also carries pajamas, holiday outfits, and school clothes. There are clothes for infants through size 12, plus backpacks, baby joggers, and carriers for sale or rent.

For Adults

The best description we've heard of the "Boulder look" is "always ready for a hike." Certainly, casual attire is acceptable just about anywhere in town, for almost any occasion—and when the snow's flying, that philosophy gets kicked up another notch. Boulder abounds with clothiers catering to that outdoorsy look; however, when there's no way around the pantyhose, dressy clothing and office attire are available, too.

Alpaca Connection
1326 Pearl St., Boulder
(303) 447–2047

Natural fiber clothing from around the world, including a large selection of hand-knitted wool sweaters from South America, is sold in this former movie theater on the Downtown Mall. You'll find natural fiber dresses and shirts, too.

Ann Taylor
2070 Broadway, Boulder
(303) 449–3971

This is one of Boulder's best centers for women's career clothing. The clothes are casual but elegant, and you can buy the whole outfit here, from the blouse to the pumps. Great sale racks are filled with a variety of items year-round.

Applause
1123 Pearl St., Boulder
(303) 442–7426

Applause is in a class by itself, with cutting-edge sportswear and dresses. Applause sometimes sells fabulous suits, other times fabulous pants and shirts. The constants are high-quality, moderate-to-expensive clothes to die for, eye-catching shoes and jewelry, and sensational kids' clothes that are almost too adorable to get dirty.

Banana Republic
1147 Pearl St., Boulder
(303) 442–8250

Preparing for a trek to deepest, darkest elsewhere, or just a stroll down the mall? Banana Republic, with its inspiring travel quotes painted around the exterior, has just the durable shorts, skirts, pants, blouses, and other gear to keep you comfortable under a mosquito net or behind a computer.

Boulder Bodywear
Crossroads Mall
(303) 447–9100

If clothes were an element, Boulder Bodywear's stock would be water—flowing, skimming, falling. These clothes are cut for comfort but suitable for uptown.

Chico's
1200 Pearl St., Boulder
(303) 449–3381

"Traveling clothes" is what comes to mind when you step into Chico's small space on the downtown mall. The clothing is simple, unstructured, built for comfort and style, and evocative of places foreign and natural.

Christina's Lingerie
2425 Canyon Blvd., Boulder
(303) 443–2421

When you want to fling it all to passion, consider Chistina's, which offers exquisite lingerie, well-fitting swimsuits, plus a staff that is truly helpful at telling you which styles flatter your figure.

College Corner
1310 College Ave., Boulder
(303) 786–8243

This store on The Hill specializes in CU-Boulder sweatshirts, T-shirts, hats, and other memorabilia. Champion reverse-weave sweatshirts and CU-Boulder baseball caps are especially popular; the hats come in a dozen sizes ranging from kids to huge.

C.P. Shades
2035 Broadway, Boulder
(303) 440–3831

If you want clothing that won't wrinkle (some say it's pre-wrinkled) and that packs like a dream, C.P. Shades is the place to go. It's on the funky side of

Broadway, lined up with delightfully unusual shops like Aria gifts and Get Fleeced (below).

Dragon Fly
1220 Spruce St., Boulder
(303) 447-9777

Imagine a dragonfly hovering, iridescent, over a pond of shifting shadows and you have some idea of what you'll see in the window of this fascinating women's clothing store a block north of the downtown mall. Unique and lovely, the fashions are the sort that cause even a preoccupied passerby to stop for a closer look.

Fresh Produce Sportswear
1136 Pearl St., Boulder
(303) 444-7573

Located on the Pearl Street Mall, this shop spotlights locally manufactured clothing—mostly easy-to-wear knits in colors reminiscent of a bowl of mints. The style is casual, fun, and natural.

Garbarini
943 Pearl St., Boulder
(303) 448-0106

Part of a new row of unique shops built just west of the downtown mall, Garbarini carries fine shoes and clothing for women.

Get Fleeced
2015 Broadway, Boulder
(303) 442-6050

Nothing is as beckoning on a chilly Colorado winter day as a fleece jacket or vest. The material breathes well, wicks perspiration away from your body making it good for active outdoorsy types, and provides plenty of warmth for the weight. Cuddle into your choice from this colorful selection.

Jacque Michelle Apparel and Home Decor
2670 Broadway, Boulder
(303) 786-7628

This might be called a little "everything shop," selling items from T-shirts to locally made hats, cards and arty things, and beautiful seasonal items, many reasonably priced. They will gift-wrap, too.

Jila Designs
2041 Broadway, Boulder
(303) 442-0130

Jila's sells original-design women's clothing, in gorgeous silks and rayons. Another Boulder original, Jila is now offering clothes in some national department stores, such as Nordstrom.

JJ Wells
2460 Canyon Blvd., Boulder
(303) 449-2112

In a new cluster of shops next to McGuckin's Hardware, JJ Wells carries a classic collection of women's clothing—classy pants, earth-toned sweaters, and dresses that make the transition from office to evening outing—by Eileen Fisher, Garfield & Marks, Isda & Co., Zelda, and others. Wardrobe consultants on the staff will help you select just the right accessories, from leather bags to belts to jewelry.

Kinsley & Co.
1155 13th St., Boulder
(303) 442-7260

On The Hill for more than 50 years, this is Boulder's prime men's clothier (it also carries women's fashions for business, evening, and casual). Kinsley carries custom clothing, Barbera and Hugo Boss suits, high-quality accessories.

Knit Wit
2021 Broadway, Boulder
(303) 444-6776

Knit Wit is a cute little store just off the Pearl Street Mall that offers elegant New York and L.A. styles. You can find both casual and dressy clothes and lots of matching accessories.

Meow Meow
1128 13th St., Boulder
(303) 449-7555

Geared toward the college and young professional crowd, Meow Meow offers contemporary dresses and separates from such designers as Betsey Johnson and April Cornell.

The Regiment Shops
2425 Canyon Blvd., Boulder
(303) 443–2713

Traditional, yet updated, tailored business clothes such as Perry Ellis for men and blazer/skirt combinations for women draw Boulder professionals to this shop in the upscale strip mall called WaterStreet.

Robert Schmidt Clothiers
947 Pearl St., Boulder
(303) 444–1213

Like neighboring Garbarini, Robert Schmidt Clothiers is one of the new small specialty shops in a row on the west end of the downtown mall. The collection is for men who care how they look.

Starr's Clothing and Shoe Co.
1538 Pearl St., Boulder
(303) 442–3056

Starr's has reasonably priced, rather sporty attire for men, women, and children. The store's fans in Boulder were relieved that redevelopment on the east end of the downtown mall didn't chase it out of town, just into a new location down the block.

The Studio
2425 Canyon Blvd., Boulder
(303) 786–7827

"Comfortable women's fashions" is The Studio's motto. Boulder-inspired idea here: Go in, try on the mix-and-match sports and party clothes, then order your favorites in exactly the colors and sizes you want.

Talbot's
2700 Arapahoe Ave., Boulder
(303) 449–1556

Women who need professional clothes will find a large selection of suits and blouses with matching accessories in Talbot's large, free-standing store in Arapahoe Village, near the Safeway grocery.

Timbuktu Station
1035 Pearl St., Boulder
(303) 440–6288

Those whose lifestyle includes lots of traveling love this store, which features fun, casual, and professional travel clothes. There are plenty of khaki garments and other attractive, wrinkle-free options to choose from.

Urban Outfitters
938 Pearl St., Boulder
(303) 247–0828

Definitely *not* your dad's (or mother's) clothing store, Urban Outfitters is a jazzy, metallic, neon-colored space with the edgy fashions and accessories that keep the college crowd, and their younger siblings, coming back. The prices please parents and offspring alike.

Weekends
1101 Pearl St., Boulder
(303) 444–4231

For the outdoorswoman or outdoorsman who wants to look very, very good in the wild (or at home in front of the fire), Weekends offers a collection of sturdy trousers, cuddly sweaters, and soft-as-butter flannel shirts, all with irresistible style. In summer, there are shorts and T's, along with jackets for the changeable high-country weather.

Zapa Toes Shoes
2015 10th St., Boulder
(303) 544–6015

This store takes its name from the Spanish word *zapatos*, meaning shoes. They carry designer brands that aren't commonly available in Boulder County, such as Aquatalia, Anne Klein, DKNY, Miu Miu, Isaac Mizrati, etc. With buyers in Italy and New York, this 10th Street shop is determined to be as hip as any store on the Pearl Street Mall.

Consignment and Resale Shops

While there's plenty of good shopping to be done at our traditional retail outlets, some of the best bargains in Boulder show up on the shelves of these consignment and resale shops. They're the kind of places you want to check back with frequently, for you never know what will have just come in, and the best stuff never lasts long.

Boulder Consignment Company
1721 Pearl St., Boulder
(303) 415–0953

This shop specializes in women's casual and vintage clothing, sold on consignment.

The Buffalo Exchange
1717 Walnut St., Boulder
(303) 938–1924

Current and retro vintage clothing is the draw here. If you've got stuff to sell, this place has liberal policies. They buy during all business hours. And rather than taking items on consignment, they buy outright for cash or credit toward a store trade.

Candy's Vintage Clothing and Costumes
4483 N. Broadway, Boulder
(303) 442–6186

Poodle skirts, leather jackets from when bikers were *bikers*, boas, housedresses that somebody's mamma wore, clunky-soled shoes, sleek satin lingerie—a stop at Candy's is like checking out the contents of the closets down the street from Wally and the Beav's house. The shop carries women's and men's clothing from 1900 through the 1980s. There are also costumes for adults and children, vintage home furnishings, and linens and lace.

Clothes Encounters of the Second Kind
1622 Pearl St., Boulder
(303) 449–2232

The area east of the downtown mall has become a real mecca for vintage clothing enthusiasts. This store gets the prize for the best name for a consignment store. The shop specializes in men's and women's apparel from the '70s into the '90s, which may be retro but is certainly not vintage.

Counter Evolution
1628 Pearl St., Boulder
(303) 444–1799

Clothes Encounters spawned a second store nearby that now specializes in true vintage clothing. This shop carries clothing for both men and women mostly from the '20s through the '50s with shoes and accessories to match.

Crazy Amy's Consignment City
1646 Pearl St., Boulder
(303) 443–9042

Formerly Twice Nice, this shop, under new ownership, specializes in casual men's and women's recycled and vintage clothing and some furniture, new and used. Crazy Amy's sells consignment items, paying 50 percent of the price for items that are sold. The Boulder Consignment Company just down the street is an outpost.

Where else are you going to find a feather boa when you need one? The bubble-gum pink Candy's in north Boulder is a great place to find vintage and unusual clothing items that have enjoyed previous use. PHOTO: LINDA CORNETT

No Place Like Home
3550 Arapahoe Ave., Boulder
(303) 440–9011

This is one of the cleanest used-furniture stores you'll ever see, with a nice selection of nearly new items. Those with a sharp eye can find some real bargains, but some of the furniture is surprisingly high-priced considering that it's secondhand. Turnover is rapid, so if you're on the lookout for something in particular, it's best to check fairly frequently. The best stuff borders on the antique; newer, lower-quality offerings are simply used. The store also carries some tableware, framed pictures, and other small objects. If you consign to them, they'll pick up. If you buy, they'll deliver.

Rags to Riches
3120 28th St., Boulder
(303) 400–5758

Newly expanded, Rags to Riches specializes in clothing for teens and women, along with an assortment of housewares. The store accepts consignments most days.

The Ritz
959 Walnut St., Boulder
(303) 443–2850

Around the corner from the Pearl Street Mall, the Ritz inventories a fabulous selection of classic '40s fashions, flouncy prom gowns from the '50s, elegant cocktail attire from various decades, and other unusual and vintage clothing. The store also sells and rents great costumes (Halloween and otherwise), including gorilla suits, creepy creatures from horror films, and masks of current politicians' faces.

Farmers' Markets and Food Co-ops

It's not surprising that health-conscious Boulder boasts more than its share of alternatives to the pre-packed, heavily salted fare preferred by most of the rest of the country. Here are some of our favorite spots for fresh and organic food.

Boulder County Farmers' Market
13th St. between Arapahoe Ave. and Canyon Blvd.
(303) 442–1837

As much of a happening and social event as a shopping opportunity, this market operates from 8 A.M. to 2 P.M. on Saturday and 10 A.M. to 2 P.M. on Wednesday from spring through fall. There's a mouthwatering selection of organically grown vegetables and fruits, and baked goods, as well as herbs, bedding plants, fresh flowers, and crafts. What began as an overflow area on the east side of 13th Street has developed into an alfresco dining experience featuring the best of some of Boulder's best restaurants and bakeries. (See the Attractions chapter for more details.)

Longmont Farmers' Market
Northwest corner of Boulder County Fairgrounds, Hover Rd. and Boston Ave.
(970) 523–0434

As Longmont is still surrounded by farm fields, it makes sense that a farmers' market prospers at the site of the county fairgrounds. Fruits and vegetables are eased out by pumpkins, bales of hay, and gourds as the season progresses. It's open on Tuesday from 3 to 6 P.M. and Saturday from 8 A.M. to 1 P.M.

Mountain Peoples Co-op
30 E. First St., Nederland
(303) 258–7500

This humble food store is a blast from the past. It is a cooperative, and members pay slightly lower prices. The co-op harkens back to the old-time, small-town neighborhood grocery but with a New Age twist. They carry a good selection of some of the tastiest organic and locally grown fruits and vegetables. There are also supplements, grooming supplies, coffee beans, grains, good breads, and other wholesome items and most necessities from toilet paper to Ben & Jerry's ice cream. A deli offers to-go items like burritos, fresh sandwiches, and salads.

Gadgets

The Better Back Store
3034 Walnut St., Boulder
(303) 442–3998

This store is hardly a frivolity to those in discomfort or pain. The inventory is extensive: back-strengthening exercise equipment, ergonomic office furniture, home furniture such as Ekornes Stressless Chairs from Norway and Backsaver recliners, cervical pillows, back cushions, lumbar belts and rolls, seat supports, massage equipment and creams, inversion units and boots, Backsaver snow shovels and other tools, ingenious purses that evenly distribute their weight, and video and cassette tapes. All these gadgets are designed to help you save your back or just to relax, feel good, and even prevent back problems.

McGuckin Hardware
2525 Arapahoe Ave., Boulder
(303) 443–1822

The slogan here is, "If we don't have it, you don't need it." It's just about true. This gigantic hardware superstore carries a do-it-yourselfer's dream of hand- and power-tools and stuff to do with them. You will find wood trim, door and window hardware, lighting fixtures and accessories, electrical and plumbing supplies, and the biggest selection of screws, nuts, bolts, clamps, washers, springs, gaskets, and every other gizmo and widget you can imagine. There are high-quality paint and housewares departments. One department makes keys and sells locks, another has video and audio tapes. Christmas decorations abound during the holiday season, and patio furniture moves in with the warm weather. Gardening tools and supplies, as well as seeds and annual and perennial plants herald summer. McGuckin's also sells sporting equipment, including fishing and hunting supplies, backpacks, and camping equipment, and some outdoor books.

The spring and fall tent sales are three-day extravaganzas that include closeout and special-purchase merchandise at tremendous savings, as well as a blanket 10 percent off everything in the store. What sets McGuckin's apart from the big-box chains is personal service. A veritable army of green-vested salespeople waits to help, advise, guide, and point the way to the department you're looking for.

The Peppercorn
1235 Pearl St., Boulder
(303) 449–5847

If anything stops your stroll down the downtown mall, it's likely to be The Peppercorn's display windows, filled with an ever-changing array of gorgeous glassware, whimsical serving dishes shaped like rabbits or pumpkins or fantastical fish, avarice-inspiring table linens, and things you never knew existed and don't know how you've lived without. You can order by mail, but it's far more fun to personally visit this very pretty, full-to-bursting kitchen store with fine cookware, kitchen gadgets, table linens, a huge assortment of cookbooks, and gourmet foods. Need a mushroom brush? A butter mold? A madeleine pan? A replacement blade for your coffee mill? A spoon rest with a clever design? A set of Calphalon pots? A food processor in Mama Bear, Papa Bear, or Baby Bear sizes? The Peppercorn has them all—and oh-so-much more. Celebrity author-chefs sometimes do book signings and occasionally put on cooking demonstrations here.

The West End Gardener
805 W. Pearl St., Boulder
(303) 938–0607

This is a delightful shop selling top-quality gardening tools, books, fountains, garden signs, wreaths, annuals and bulbs in season, and gifts and goodies for plant-lovers. It makes a putterer want to garden seriously, and a serious gardener strive to make the garden just perfect.

It's xeriscape. Not zero-scape.

It's xeriscape (zer-rih-scape). Not zero-scape. It's beautiful plants that thrive in our dry, windy climate. It's not rocked-over yards or lawns addicted to herbicides, pesticides, and fertilizers. Boulder is a center for xeriscaping. At least a half-dozen books have been published by Boulder-area experts on water-wise gardening. And why not? Water use is critical in a climate that gets less than 17 inches of rain a year. What's more, after wandering Boulder's beautiful open-space trails, many gardeners develop a liking for this natural style. By comparison, the traditional green lawn is, well, boring.

Great area garden stores, filled with bedding plants, perennials and ornamentals include Lafayette Florists, The Flower Bin in Longmont, Sturtz and Copeland, and Fruehauf's. McGuckin Hardware has been voted by readers of Boulder's *Daily Camera* as the best place for garden supplies. It's also a good spot for finding plants if you like the flowers you see around the Village shopping center. (For more on marvelous McGuckin's, read this chapter's "Gadgets" section.) Boulder County has its own plant kingdoms. Most are on the way to Longmont, including the GreenSpot Nursery, The Tree Farm, and TreeHouse Nursery. Mikl and Linda Brawner's Harlequin's Market is little but unique, down to the beautiful display of native and/or xeriscape plants in the Brawners' front yard next door. Wander their display garden and point to whatever gorgeous, thriving plant you like. Then ask Mikl or Linda to guide you to the potted version of the plant—small and inexpensive. For more plant stores, check the Yellow Pages under "Nurseries."

Many local garden centers can offer advice on xeriscaping, a popular alternative to traditional landscaping in environment-conscious Boulder. PHOTO: DAILY CAMERA

If you're shopping for garden space, consider this: 480-square-foot garden plots are available behind the North Boulder Recreation Center. The fee is $45, including water. (Gardeners must provide their own hoses.) Call (303) 441–3400. Or how about a free tree? If you move into a Boulder home with a bare front yard, you can apply to have the city plant a city-owned tree close to the street for you. For information, contact Boulder's Forestry Division at (303) 441–4406.

Now, about those garden books. Here are gems about Boulder area plants and gardens: *Pieces of Light* by Susan Tweit; *The Xeriscape Flower Gardener: A Waterwise Guide for the Rocky Mountain Region* by Jim Knopf; *Gardening in the Mountain West* by Daily Camera columnist Barbara Hyde; *Grow Native: Landscaping With Native and Apt Plants of the Rocky Mountains* by Sam Huddleston and Michael Hussey; *The Shortgrass Prairie* by Ruth Carol Cushman and Stephen R. Jones; *Personal Landscapes* by Jerome Malitz; and *The Undaunted Garden* by Lauren Springer.

Gift Shops

Hangouts
1328 Pearl St., Boulder
(303) 442–2533

Mayan and Brazilian hammocks and hanging chairs in a rainbow of colors give this friendly mall shop its name, but venture inside and you'll also find imported sweaters, tie-dye T-shirts, and odd little trinkets from exotic locales. Stretch out in one of the floor-model hammocks and you won't want to leave the store.

Namaste
840 Pearl St., Boulder
(303) 443–2993

"Gifts that honor the peace within" is the way Namaste describes its inventory. The small shop west of the downtown mall carries music with nary a rough edge, books, incense and candles, and other meditation supplies. Psychic readings are available in the store daily from noon to closing, at $1 per minute.

The Pipefitter
1352 College Ave., Boulder
(303) 442–4200

A throwback to the '60s updated to the present, the Pipefitter carries pipes and smoking accessories, ethnic clothing and T-shirts, jewelry, candles and incense, posters and cards.

High Spirits

The Boulder Wine Merchant
2690 Broadway, in Community Plaza, Boulder
(303) 443–6761

This store is owned by two of the world's great wine experts, Wayne Belding and Sally Mohr. Both master sommeliers, with unerring noses for fine wine, Wayne and Sally and the store's experienced staff take very seriously the business of selecting, analyzing, recommending, and selling wine. Fewer than 30 master sommeliers are active in the United States, and another few dozen have earned the title worldwide. The store sponsors two wine-appreciation classes each year and joins with local restaurants in presenting occasional very special dinners served with very special wines. The whole staff loves to help customers find a match for both palate and pocketbook.

Harvest Wine and Spirits
3075 Arapahoe Ave., Boulder
(303) 447–9832

Harvest offers outstanding selections of imported and domestic wines, billed as the largest selection in the county. There are also microbrews, spirits, and fine cigars. This place is convenient for its location next to the King Soopers grocery store. The friendly, knowledgeable staff is always willing to help.

The Liquor Mart
Corner of 15th St. and Canyon Blvd., Boulder
(303) 449-3374

This is a supermarket-size liquor store, one of the largest in the United States. The variety is staggering, including hard liquor, beer, ale, wine, champagne, mixers, and soft drinks. If you want something exotic, you're as likely to find it here as anywhere in the state. The helpful staff is known for offering informed advice. If that's too much trouble, you can join Club Liquor Mart and receive a monthly selection of wine or a weekly six-pack of beer chosen by the store's staff. Buy a case of wine and get a 15-percent discount; you get 10 percent off when you buy a case of beer or liquor. For such a huge non-specialty store, The Liquor Mart's wine selection is surprising, both in its depth and its breadth. The store hosts frequent special dinners at local restaurants and joins with a local travel agency to sponsor a wine trip to Colorado's own wine country near Grand Junction.

Superior Liquor
100 Superior Pkwy., Superior
(303) 499-6600

At 20,000 square feet, this huge new store has room for a wide variety of liquors, wines, and beers. Regulars can save by joining a Frequent Customer Program and earning rebates. There are weekly specials for all.

Home Furnishings

Artesanias
1420 Pearl St., Boulder
(303) 442-3777

Rustic furniture with the flavor of old Mexico shares this Downtown Mall store with ornamental wrought iron and hand-blown glass, candles, and other accessories. Furniture, including whimsical, brightly painted items from Texas, is the bulk of the stock, with housewares on the side.

Bartlett Interiors
2020 Pearl St., Boulder
(303) 442-5194

It's a toss-up as to whether clients come here more for the stylish decorating advice or for the elegant and unusual upholstered and wood furniture, lamps, and window treatments. The inventory features many dramatic pieces that create a distinctive look. Cheap, it ain't.

Boulder by Design
1711 Pearl St., Boulder
(303) 443-2084

How absolutely Boulder—a furniture and furnishings store with only earth-friendly products. It stocks organic cotton bedding, recycled candles, hemp products like sturdy backpacks, industrial cardboard furniture that can hold up to 1,000 pounds, and much more. The store backs up its philosophy by supporting environmental causes and organizations.

Canterbury Fine Furniture
2480 Canyon Blvd., Boulder
(303) 442-9049

Distinctive American and English 19th- and 20th-century reproductions can be found in this large store. They carry many pieces that have been redesigned for modern living, including roll-top computer desks and hideaway TV cabinets. Although the sign over the door reads "Canterbury Oak and Brass," you'll also find cherry and walnut, rattan and wrought iron.

Concepts
1890 30th St., Boulder
(303) 443-6900

Lean, clean lines, contemporary styling, and affordable prices make Concepts a favorite of college students setting up house in Boulder. The line includes upholstered pieces, dining and bedroom furniture, lamps, and accessories.

Country West Furniture
2525 Arapahoe Ave., Boulder
(303) 443-2030

In the Village Shopping Center next to McGuckin Hardware, this store has been making country, Southwestern, wrought-iron, and mountain-log furniture for more than a decade. In addition to its thoughtful designs, the store takes pride in its furniture's high-quality details such as dovetail drawers and hand-rubbed oil finishes. Country West can also make custom pieces. Armoires, bedroom pieces, dining-room sets, entertainment centers, storage units of oak, pine, cherry, and maple, and a variety of accessories are available.

Danish Furniture
3111 28th St., Boulder
(303) 449-0214

So sleek it's scarcely there, this collection of contemporary wood furniture is imported from abroad. Hard to believe these pieces come from the same trees as the rustic log furniture available elsewhere in town.

Front Range Futons
2125 Pearl St., Boulder
(303) 444-4057

Every college town has at least one futon place, right? The futons here are of various sizes, and the store carries futon frames, futon sofas, and some accessories as well. It is, of course, a popular style of furniture in Boulder, and the price is usually right. The staff friendly and helpful, too.

KRJ Designs
2712 28th St., Boulder
(303) 449-3375

Functional and sleek are the watchwords at this Bluff Plaza shop specializing in desks and other office furniture and home furnishings in leather. Custom desks are available, and there is a broad selection of custom leather goods with a promise of two-week delivery.

Marisol Imports
915 Pearl St., Boulder
(303) 442-3142

The bright showroom features wonderful wood pieces from Mexico, including tables, chairs, and hutches, plus wrought-iron chairs, tables, bar stools, and étagères

that mesh easily with either a country or Southwestern look. Zapotec rugs, pottery, large clay jugs, weavings, pillows, and all manner of harmonious accessories also are stocked. In the summertime, the rustic rockers set outside the shop beckon footsore shoppers.

Out of the Woods
28th St. and Canyon Boulevard, Boulder
(303) 443-8202

Another appealing spot for incoming university students, Out of the Woods is a factory-direct storefront with a reasonably priced line of office furniture—bookcases in every size and dimension, computer desks, file cabinets, chairs. The furniture has been manufactured locally for two decades.

Room to Room
2624 Broadway, Boulder
(303) 473-1950

This small shop tucked into the Community Plaza carries reasonably priced, high-quality furniture and accessories, including everything you need to create a unique bathroom, right down to the soap. The store personnel will provide design services on request.

Techline
1500 Pearl St., Boulder
(303) 440-9656

A purveyor of contemporary furniture, this store is known for its inventory of attractive and functional office and home-business pieces. The showroom also offers professional planning and design consultation.

Timberline Studios
2425 Canyon Blvd., Boulder
(303) 443-3610

Down-filled upholstered pieces, unique accents, a line of dining and bedroom sets—Timberline bills its stock as "eclectic furniture for the Colorado lifestyle." Design consultation is also available.

Unpainted Furniture
2034 Pearl St., Boulder
(303) 443–8229

If you're a do-it-yourselfer, head for this store, which carries Colorado's largest inventory of unfinished hardwood and pine furniture: china and corner cabinets, coffee and end tables, armoires and wardrobes, juvenile furniture, tables and chairs, rockers, chests, dressers, bookcases, and toy boxes. The staff has advice and the finishing materials you'll need, or if you want to spend the extra money and wait a few weeks, they'll do the finishing for you.

Jewelers

In addition to dedicated jewelry stores, you'll find jewelry in the Boulder Arts & Crafts Cooperative and other crafts stores, in the Crossroads Mall, as well as in many of Boulder's art galleries.

Bill Cronin Goldsmith
1235 Alpine Ave., Boulder
(303) 440–4222

Since 1979 this shop north of downtown has been manufacturing high-quality jewelry set with diamonds and other stones. Cronin's specializes in custom goldsmithing, helping local romantics create The Ring to their specifications.

Gatos Designs
2770 Arapahoe Rd., Suite 114, Lafayette
(303) 604–6552

Specializing in platinum jewelry set with diamonds and other fine gems, this shop also offers custom designs, alterations, appraisals, and antique refurbishing. On-site repairs and design work means the piece is back on your hand, neck, or wrist within two to three days.

Hurdle's
1402 Pearl St., Boulder
(303) 443–1084

This is a very traditional jeweler, just what you'd expect to find in a historic downtown like Boulder's. And well it should be, for it was established back in 1947. There's even a little repair booth right in the window, armed with loupes, velvet cushions, and the teeny instruments necessary to perform surgery on delicate watches and jewelry. Hurdle's carries estate and new jewelry of all sorts as well as fine watches, including TAGHeuer from Switzerland.

J. Anderson Jewelry
3183 Walnut St., Boulder
(303) 449–1125

Handmade jewelry is the specialty at Anderson's, which offers custom design and engraving, and experienced watch repair. The store also buys and sells gold and silver.

The Little Jewel
1225 Pearl St., Boulder
(303) 443–3353

On the Pearl Street Mall, the Little Jewel lives up to its name by cramming its tiny dimensions with a lot of pieces in a lot of styles. There's some Southwestern turquoise and silver. There's some Italian gold. There are chains, earrings, bracelets, and wedding sets.

Master Goldsmith
10th and Pearl St., Boulder
(303) 443–3424

Since 1971, Master Goldsmiths has been creating unique and custom-designed jewelry in gold and platinum. Ideal Cut diamonds are imported directly to the store.

Meyers Jewelers
Village Shopping Center, Boulder
(303) 442–2255

Founded in 1960, this store has set up shop in a new home next to McGuckin Hardware. It is known for diamond pieces and wedding sets in contemporary and traditional styles. Among its distinctive, exclusive designs are pendants and earrings depicting the Flatirons and, for CU fans, rings and bracelets of nose-to-tail buffaloes marching along in bands of gold or silver. Meyers Jewelers remains a family business, with talented veterans handling on-site jewelry repair and remounts.

Peter Rosen Jewelry Designer
1216-C Pearl St., Boulder
(303) 443-2852

Since 1980, jewelry designer Peter Rosen has been creating unique pieces, each verified with his signature. The sculpted gold and silver pieces are adorned with precious and semiprecious stones.

Ring Specialty Company
2691 30th St., Boulder
(303) 440-5507

With more than 1,500 pieces on display, selection is no easy task at this custom jewelry store that has been operating since 1944. In addition to wedding sets, rings, bracelets, necklaces, and earrings, you can get stones remounted and repairs on site. Appraisals are also available.

Sierra Small Bird
1108 Spruce St., Boulder
(303) 442-2220

Sierra Small Bird, a member of the Shoshone-Paiute Tribe from Walker River Reservation in Nevada, designs much of the traditional and contemporary jewelry for sale in this shop just off the downtown mall. Also available are jewelry, sculptures, textiles, painting, and baskets by other Native American artists.

Silver Safari
Crossroads Mall, Boulder
(303) 444-6165

Indonesian imports, wood carvings, and other unusual home decor items complement the inexpensive silver necklaces, rings, earrings, and bracelets in this fun shop.

Walters & Hogsett
2425 Canyon Blvd., Boulder
(303) 449-2626

Gold, silver, and gemstones are featured at this highly regarded jewelry store. It stocks fine domestic and imported jewelry, watches, crystal, and silver. In addition to repairs, Walters & Hogsett offers an annual fall special on re-plating silver flatware and hollowware.

Miscellany

Allen Scientific Glass Blowers
1752 55th St., Boulder
(303) 442-2141

The Ph.D. crowd told us that this guide wouldn't be complete without including Ray Allen, called the "God of Scientific Glass." He can make anything out of glass and glass/metal transitions. You know . . . all those things you always wanted for your lab but couldn't find at a really good price.

Blake's Small Car Salvage
2559 Weld County Rd., No. 5, Erie
(303) 665-4312

This junkyard is so darned pretty it was featured on the CBS Evening News. Car parts, fitting everything from a 1959 Anglias to a 1993 Geo Storm, are arranged by country. A Japanese flag flies near the Hondas; a German flag marks the BMWs. Small parts are stored picturesquely in yellow school buses and Chevy vans. The Colorado New Music Association came out here one fall and made, along with other instruments, drums from the hubcaps.

Boulder Early Music Shop
3200 Valmont Rd., Boulder
(303) 449-9231

If you hanker for the sounds of the Renaissance, Medieval, or Baroque hit parade, Boulder Early Music can set you up with the instrument and the sheet music to make it all come alive, again. Recorders are the least of it. Tin whistles and bagpipes, dulcimers, flutes, fifes and psalteries—or kits to build your own, are available here. Wooden thumb rests, a waterproof bag for your viol, tuning forks and postcards of illuminated music from the 10th century are among the accoutrements.

Colorado Baggage
Crossroads Mall, Boulder
(303) 449–8621

Going somewhere? This store has exactly the right bag, tote, suitcase, backpack, overnight kit, money belt, billfold, purse, jewelry case, computer carrier to get your stuff there. Going nowhere? It's a great place to fantasize.

Fascinations Love Shacks & Superstores
2560 28th St., Boulder
(303) 442–7309

A new addition to the 28th Street commercial area, Fascinations is an adult products (ahem) store. The inventory is about what you'd expect but with a more playful, less shadowy corners feel.

Naked Edge Cutlery
Crossroads Mall, Boulder
(303) 938–8839

Everything from the most ladylike of shivs to the perfect knife for the Thanksgiving turkey to a sword perfect for defending someone's honor is available in this shop. There are scissors, too.

Robb's Music
1580 Canyon Blvd., Boulder
(303) 443–8448

Robb's has digital pianos, electronic keyboards, guitars, drums, band instruments, and more. They offer great deals on used instruments and have experts who repair electronic instruments.

Swalley's The Music People
2095 30th St., Boulder
(303) 443–8404

Swalley's is the exclusive home of Baldwin in Boulder and sells sheet music, including that required by local music teachers. They also buy and sell used pianos and have technicians who can come to your home and tune a piano. This is an old-time music store; it's kept the notes flowing since 1960.

Wildwood Music
804 Main St., Louisville
(303) 665–7733

This store specializes in both acoustic and electric guitars including Fender, Martin, Gibson, Paul Reed Smith, Taylor, and Dobro. Wildwood has unbeatable prices.

Nature Stores

Crystal Galleries Ltd.
1302 Pearl St., Boulder
(303) 444–2277

This store features a fine collection of minerals, crystal, fossils, and jewelry made from semiprecious gemstones. The glasswork of René Lalique, plus eggs, spheres, and bookends are all in the inventory.

Nature's Own
Crossroads Mall, Boulder
(303) 444–3536

Unique carved-stone giftware, fossils, minerals, and handcrafted jewelry are found in this shop on the mall's upper level. The huge geodes and carved chair in the shape of a giant hand draw the eyes of most passersby.

Photographic Equipment

Amaranth
2540 Frontier Ave., Boulder
(303) 443–2550

The pros go here for the full-service custom lab, digital imaging and printing and mounting services. They also have a good selection of frames. The service isn't cheap, but it's recognized as high-quality.

Jones Drug & Camera Center
1370 College Ave., Boulder
(303) 443–4420

More than a drugstore, this Hill institution has a very good line of fine cameras, lenses, film, and photo accessories, including filters, bags, books, albums, and frames. In addition to processing film, Jones has a full selection of darkroom supplies and one of the best offerings of black-and-white enlarging paper in the state. The store also sells high-quality used equipment and has a very knowledgeable and helpful staff.

Mike's Camera
2500 Pearl St., Boulder
(303) 443–1715

Boulder's only complete camera shop dedicated exclusively to photographic equipment, related items, and services, Mike's is a local icon. Its services include camera and video repairs, rentals (full spectrum), used camera sales, digital imaging, and photo and video industrial equipment—plus classes on how to use it all. There are also telescopes, picture frames, and bags. The staff is knowledgeable and helpful.

Photo Craft
3550 Arapahoe Rd., Boulder
(303) 442–6410

This shop is another favorite of the professionals, with custom photographic services, including giant photographic color murals and backlits suitable for trade show and store display. It also offers rush service and custom computer imaging services.

Robert Waxman
2520 Arapahoe Ave., in the Arapahoe Village, Boulder
(303) 544–9842

In addition to full photo-finishing services, this chain store offers digital services, photo restoration, classes, con- sultation on photo presentation, and cameras and accessories.

Specialty-Food Shops

The Asian Deli
2829 28th St., Boulder
(303) 541–9377

Need some dried bonito flakes, pickled daikon radishes, lemongrass, or divine curries? This store has them all, plus Asian produce and freshly made Viet-namese spring rolls—cilantro and shrimp enclosed in a delicate rice wrapper.

The Cheese Importer's Warehouse
33 S. Pratt Pkwy., Longmont
(303) 772–4444

The Warehouse is an importer for the Willow River Company and has bargains on wheels of foreign and domestic cheeses and bags of perfect, meltable dark chocolate, all set on industrial-strength shelving in a huge, refrigerated room. A small shop also carries other gourmet foods, coffee, tea, and cookware.

Colorado Craft and Cake Supply
1750 30th St., Suite 12, Boulder
(303) 447–1557

If you are ambitious and want to decorate your own cakes, you can get all the supplies you need here. They sell powdered meringue for frosting and incredible cake decorations.

Herb's Meats & Specialty Foods
2530 Baseline Rd., Boulder
(303) 499–8166

A Boulder institution, this store is just what the name says. Herb's carries the freshest cuts of meat and a large variety of sauces. If you're particular, the perfect leg of lamb or pork roast can be found here.

Mountain Man Nut & Fruit Co.
2525 Arapahoe Ave., Boulder
(303) 546–0920

A locally owned store that carries gourmet candy such as double-dipped malted-milk balls, all kinds of nuts and dried fruits, trail mixes, peach salsa, and dried soups, plus teas, coffees, mustards, and jellies. They do gift baskets too. In the Village Shopping Center, just around the corner from the movie theater, it's a perfect stop if movie popcorn and candy aren't your thing.

The Oriental Food Market
1750 30th St., No. 84, Boulder
(303) 422–7830

This market carries all the ingredients you'll need for all manner of Asian cuisine including Chinese, Japanese, Thai, Indian, Cambodian, Laotian, Vietnamese, Malaysian, Philippine and Indonesian. The small deli serves primarily Indonesian specialties.

Salvaggio's Italian Deli
2655 Pearl St., Boulder
(303) 938–1981
1100 28th St., Boulder
(303) 541–9771

If you're a former Easterner, this deli can satisfy your craving for good, New York–style Italian fare. The store carries Italian cold cuts and cheeses, including fresh, water-packed mozzarella and fresh pastas and sauces.

Scoops
Crossroads, Boulder
(303) 447–2826

Soothe your sweet tooth at this sugar showroom. The store has more than 500 kinds of candy, including chocolate-covered gummy bears, gummy spiders, and many rows of colorful and sweet-filled bins. There is also a section of sugar-free candies. Mugs and tins to store it all in, plus stuffed animals are sold, too.

Whole Foods Market
2905 Pearl Street, Boulder
(303) 402–1494

Ever since it opened just off 28th Street, Whole Foods has been the place to be for shoppers who really love food. Past a huge selection of fruits and vegetables there are fish and meat departments that pride themselves on freshness. Aisles are filled with herbs, foods, cosmetics, and cleaning supplies with an environmental conscience, plus bulk supplies of munchies, cereal, honey, oil, and nut butters. A deli offers browsers samples of crackers, cheeses, meat, and olives. Among the other stores-within-the-store are a bread shop, a pizza shop, and a juice bar. There's a huge selection of prepared foods, from grilled eggplant to corn cakes to barbecued chicken.

Sporting Goods Shops

From one end of town to the other, Boulder is speckled with sporting goods shops, including a number of exceptional mountaineering and climbing stores. You don't have to leave Boulder to find such high-country gear as hiking boots; parkas; alpine and Nordic skis; snowboards; snowshoes; in-line skates; rock-climbing, camping, and backpacking equipment; and clothing and accessories for any terrain or activity. Most stores rent as well as sell clothing and equipment, and some of the best deals are end-of-season closeouts on rental equipment.

Bicycle Village
1681 28th St., Boulder
(303) 440–8525

Mountain bikes, road bikes, comfort bikes, clothing, accessories, car racks, and bikes for rent—Bicycle Village has it all. This is Colorado's largest Schwinn dealer.

Boulder Army Store
1545 Pearl St., Boulder
(303) 442–7616

A Boulder favorite, this store is true to its name and features a full array of such army surplus items as ammo cases, camouflage clothing, combat boots, and canteens. It's a good place to shop for backpacks, nylon climbing rope, hiking boots, sunglasses, hats and gloves of every description, freeze-dried food and water purification systems, solar showers, bandanas, and campfire coffeepots.

The Boulder Outdoor Center
2510 47th St., Boulder
(303) 444–8420

Kayaks and canoes are sold or can be rented here, with instruction available and raft trips scheduled. In winter, the center rents snowshoes and avalanche beacons. In addition to selling new and used equipment, the store offers instruction and accessories and clothing.

Boulder Running Company
28th and Pearl St., Boulder
(303) 786–9255

A free running and walking gait assessment and analysis of your feet ensures that you pick the right footwear. You can check out the results by watching yourself on a video monitor as you try out different pairs.

Boulder Ski Deals
2404 Pearl St., Boulder
(303) 938–8799

This shop sells equipment and clothing for alpine and Nordic skiing and snowboarding. There's a full-service boot and ski repair shop and custom boot fitting. Mostly new but also some traded-in used equipment is available. The store also sells such accessories as hats, gloves, long johns, socks, sunglasses, goggles, and sunscreen. In summer, the shop partially switches over to in-line skating and watersports, including kayaking.

Boulder Sports Recycler
1727 15th St., Boulder
(303) 786–9940

This is a great place to pick up used and close-out skis, in-line skates, and equipment for racquetball, hockey, baseball, golf, camping, football, watersports, biking, tennis, soccer, fishing, and weightlifting. They also sell used sports clothing.

Doc's Ski & Sports
627 S. Broadway, Boulder
(303) 499–0963

Voted one of America's top 50 ski shops by *Snow County Magazine* in 1996, Doc's carries equipment and clothing for skiing, skating, snowboarding, and biking. They also rent equipment and promise overnight repairs for your skis or snowboard. Located in south Boulder, Doc's is a handy stop for skiers and snowboarders heading to the slopes west of Denver.

Eastern Mountain Sports
2550 Arapahoe Ave., Boulder
(303) 442–7566

This is a national chain of East Coast origin that sells North Face clothing and equipment and other top brands, as well as a large number of private-label EMS items. Clothing and equipment are available. It's a great place for fleece items, boots, skis, and good service.

Fleet Feet
1035 Pearl St., Boulder
(303) 939–8000

Specialty shoes for walkers and runners are available here, along with a thorough fitting to make sure they stay comfortable. The shop collects and posts information about area races and fun runs and offers both an analysis of your gait and clinics on how to do it better.

Gart Sports
3320 28th St., Boulder
(303) 449–9021

Gart's offers a wide assortment of sporting goods from tennis and golf equipment to skiing, fishing, and hunting supplies. It's part of a Colorado-owned chain with other stores in Denver and Longmont and elsewhere in the West. It is ideal for gear for team sports, exercise paraphernalia, logo clothing, athletic shoes, and low- to mid-priced sporting goods for skiers and other recreational athletes.

Louisville Cyclery
1032 S. Boulder Rd., Louisville
(303) 665–6343

Road- and mountain-bike specialists help here with sales, rental, custom wheels, professional fittings, and suspension and repair service. They also carry high-quality clothing and gear for the whole family.

Madden Factory Store
2400 Central Ave., Boulder
(303) 442–5828

For all types of day packs, backpacks, and smaller packs, stop here. For some reason, Madden's packs are more popular among the outdoor set in Europe than in the United States, but this local company makes high-quality, sturdy packs of every description that will last for years, and they're all for sale here at factory-outlet prices.

Mountain Sports
821 Pearl St., Boulder
(303) 443–6700

As the name implies, this shop focuses on a variety of alpine activities, including climbing, camping, hiking, snowshoeing, and Nordic skiing. It offers a fine selection of top-quality equipment and apparel, with friendly, very helpful service. The store sponsors periodic slide shows, lectures, and courses. A log book close to the front door enables customers to comment on recent hikes or ski tours they've taken and conditions they've encountered.

Neptune Mountaineering
633 S. Broadway, Boulder
(303) 499–8866

The first among equals for hard-core climbers and mountaineers is this store in Table Mesa Shopping Center. This huge store is owned by Gary Neptune, a prominent U.S. mountaineer who has reached the summit of Mount Everest and other high peaks. Besides ice axes, ropes, and climbing shoes and boots, the store has a good selection of Nordic ski equipment and outdoor clothing. Its book department is one of the best around. Gary's private collection of mountaineering memorabilia, including rarities of immense historic value, is displayed throughout.

The North Face
629-K S. Broadway, Boulder
(303) 499–1731

Located in the Table Mesa Center, this is a national wholesaler/manufacturer that has established one of its handful of retail stores in Boulder. The Berkeley, California–based company sells its tents, packs, sleeping bags, ski jackets, and other products to 800 shops across the country.

Paddle Shop
1727 15th St., Boulder
(303) 786–8799

This shop sells plenty of kayaking equipment but also rents and sells canoes and rafts. They also carry wetsuits and all other related accessories. Kayak instruction and raft trips are available through the shop.

Pro Peleton
2615 13th St., Boulder
(303) 415–1292

A peleton is the large pack of cyclists riding together in a long road race like the Tour de France. On the back side of the

Community Plaza, this high-end shop specializes in serious road and racing bikes and everything you need to embark on heavy-duty cycling.

Rocky Mountain Anglers
1904 Arapaho Ave., Boulder
(303) 447–2400
If the flash of a fighting fish's belly rising from a rushing stream makes your heart beat faster, this shop has what you need. Flies, and the supplies to make them, reels and rods, waders and boots, and fish knives are in stock. There are classes in fly-tying and information on where they're biting, and on what.

Rocky Mountain Racquet Specialists
2425 Canyon Blvd., Boulder
(303) 442–1412
This is where Boulder's major tennis, squash, and racquetball enthusiasts go for the gear and duds. Racquets and balls, of course, are available, but so is name-brand clothing, footwear, and accessories such as eyewear and gloves. This store offers one-day racquet stringing and can also make custom grips. They have abbreviated hours during the winter, so call first.

Rocky Mountain Soccer
2767 Iris Ave., in the Willow Springs Center, Boulder
(303) 938–9166
Soccer is a big deal in Boulder. Apparel and equipment such as shin guards, balls, and cleats are available here. It's a real mecca for soccer-holics and has meeting space available for groups who want to plan events centered around this round-ball sport.

Runners Choice
2460 Canyon Blvd., Boulder
(303) 449–8551
Boulder's oldest running store offers shoes, clothing, and friendly advice for athletes at all levels, but it's not just for runners. You'll find equipment and clothing for walkers and swimmers, too, along with free consultations with a podiatrist.

It's also a good place to find out about competitive and fun runs.

Scuba Joe
3054 28th St., Boulder
(303) 444–7234
Scuba Joe is a dive and snorkel center with an in-store travel agency and convenient basic through instructor classes offered on weeknights or weekends.

Weaver's Dive & Travel Center
637 S. Broadway, Boulder
(720) 304–7557
Weaver's sells dive gear, wetsuits, and swimwear. If you don't know how to dive, they'll teach you and help you get certified. If you dive, you can book a group or individual dive trip to some of the world's top underwater destinations. Weaver's has a full-service travel agency on-site.

University Bicycles
839 Pearl St., Boulder
(303) 444–4196
You can't miss this shop—look for the clever outdoor mural of the bicyclist who appears to be breaking through the exterior wall. This store sells and repairs mountain and road bikes and promises "all the neat stuff you see in bike magazines." It's a handy location to rent a bike, for one or two, for a pedal around downtown.

Yard Sales

Lastly, perhaps some of the best shopping in town is at Boulder's yard and garage sales. Check the classified sections of the local newspapers or just drive around town on summer weekends and keep an eye out for homemade signs on trees and utility poles. Many sales start on Fridays, but Saturdays are the big days—and a few dribble over into Sunday too.

In south Boulder, the bridge across Bear Creek at Table Mesa Drive and the King Soopers entrance is always plastered with yard sale signs around the weekend.

Downtown, the corner of Arapahoe Avenue and Ninth Street is often festooned with garage sale signs. With its transient population of students and upwardly mobile adults, Boulder's yard sales offer everything from skis, bicycles, snowboards, and sailboarding equipment to violins, art, and antiques.

If you're not too picky, dumpsters on The Hill yield a bounty in May when students are moving out and discarding everything that won't fit in a duffel bag.

Festivals and Annual Events

Special events make an evening or weekend sparkle. The following listings are in approximate chronological order. Where possible, they include dates, times, and prices. Other events bloom with serendipity, so planners can't say exactly when and how much until the event draws near. The chapter ends with "Events Central," mentioning groups that track happenings. You can find even more possibilities by checking our Boulder Attractions and Boulder Arts chapters. Keep in mind, volunteers run many of these festivals, and you're welcome to lend a hand.

January

Polar Bear Club Ice Plunge
Boulder Reservoir 51st St., Boulder
(303) 441–3461

Pay around $15 to brave ice-crusted water, dance a jig, screech, then hurry to shore (or stay in as long as you wish). Rescue workers stand by in case anyone gets hypothermia from the morning dip. Plungers say, "It's intensely painful, in a pleasurable sort of way." For spectators, admission to this New Year's Day event is free.

Colorado Mahlerfest
Macky Auditorium (on the CU-Boulder campus) and Boulder Public Library (11th St. and Arapahoe Ave.), Boulder
(303) 447–0513

Mahler fans rave about this one-of-a-kind concertfest during the second week in January. It began in 1988, when enthusiasts played Mahler's Symphony No. 1. Each year, they have played the Bohemian composer's next symphony in line. The celebration also includes lectures and song recitals. Concert ticket prices range from $9 to $25, and there are free public recitals at the Boulder Public Library. In the past the group has also given a free concert at at Lafayette's Rocky Mountain Center for Musical Arts.

Boulder Bach Festival
P.O. Box 1896, Boulder, CO
(303) 494–3159

Only a handful of American festivals play nothing but J. S. Bach. This is one. Local professional musicians and well-known guest artists keep the music lively, playing those hummable tunes you might have thought were modern. The festival is held over the last weekend in January at the downtown Boulder First Presbyterian Church. Additional concerts take place on an irregular schedule from September through May at locations that include the University of Colorado's Grusin Music Hall, University Lutheran Chapel, the Boulder Public Library Auditorium, and Denver's St. John's Cathedral. Ticket prices vary.

National Western Stock Show, Rodeo and Horse Show
I–25 on I–70, Denver
(303) 295–1660

Denver proudly calls itself a "cow town" and proves it during the month of January when the Stock Show comes to town. Since 1906 serious competition combined with showmanship have made this one of the largest stock shows in the world. More than 600,000 people attend. There were nearly 40 performances, including 23 rodeos by the Professional Rodeo Cowboys Association, two Mexican rodeos, two bull riding events, seven horse shows, three Wild West shows, and two evenings of dancing horses. Other events include sheep shearing, mutton busting, barn tours, and a children's petting farm. Recent ticket prices were $7 for adults and $2 for children on weekends; $5 and $1 on weekdays. Rodeo and horse show tickets ranged from $8 to $15, including grounds admission.

Old Town Lafayette Oatmeal Festival
100 S. Public Road, Lafayette
(303) 926–4352

When Lafayette business owners decided to initiate a unique annual festival a few years ago, someone noted that January is "oatmeal month." Not surprisingly, Lafayette now boasts the "world's largest oatmeal breakfast buffet." Quaker Oats was more than happy to participate, and the annual festival now includes a 5K health walk, a health fair, kids' activities, and lots of entertainment. Held on the third Saturday in January, the all-you-can eat breakfast costs $6 for adults, $5 for kids and seniors. Event hours are 8 A.M. until 2 P.M.

February

Chocolate Lover's Fling
Glenn Miller Ballroom (on CU-Boulder campus), Boulder
(303) 449–8623

For the price of a good dinner ($25 to $30), eat all the chocolate you want and benefit a good cause on the Friday or Saturday evening before Valentine's Day at the Chocolate Lover's Fling. Feast your eyes on chocolate TV dinners, armadillos, cabbages, and castles. Boulder's best professional chefs vie with talented amateurs in categories ranging from "Sheer Artistry" to just plain yummy. Enter your creation, or just eat the entries. Profits go to the Boulder County Safehouse, which helps battered families.

March

4-H Carnival
Boulder County Fairgrounds, 9595 Nelson Rd., Longmont
(303) 776–4865

This all-day family event on the second Saturday in March has homemade pies and kid-decorated variety booths. Throw shaving-cream pies and walk through a maze of bright-colored calico walls. You might win a T-shirt by launching a stuffed toy lamb into a cute little pen. Admission is free.

Boulder Bach Festival—Kids for Bach/ Bach for Kids
Boulder Public Library, 11th St. and Arapahoe Ave., Boulder
(303) 494–3159

Children audition by tape to perform in this charming, hour-long program. Musicians range from 6 to 17 years old and play a variety of instruments including piano, violin, and harp. Admission is free.

Bon Temps Ball Mardi Gras Masquerade
UMC Glenn Miller Ballroom, CU-Boulder Campus, Boulder
(303) 449–0858

This is the annual fund-raiser for the Parenting Place, and is typically held in early March. The Parenting Place promotes wholesome caretaker-child relationship through play groups and other activities. The party features dinner, a live and silent auction, live music, and a lot of fun.

April

Conference on World Affairs
CU-Boulder campus, Boulder
(303) 492–2525

International flags festoon the campus during this week-long series of forums held the week after CU-Boulder's spring semester resumes following spring break. The conference has been under new leadership since 1999; director Jim

Palmer has infused new energy to the proceedings and has tried to balance forums by offering more that appeal to college students while still drawing the general public. More than 100 speakers jet to Boulder at their own expense to participate. Call ahead for session topics, or just wander into the University Memorial Center to pick up a schedule and slip into one of the many discussions. Admission is free.

Loyalty Parade
Downtown Lafayette
(303) 665–9993

Get ready for fifes, drums, flags, and equestrian teams. VFW Post 1771 sponsors this state parade, which was founded to counter communism's May Day celebrations. The "Evil Empire" is no more, but Lafayette's parade remains. It starts at 10 A.M. on the Saturday closest to May 1, heading south from Public Road to Waneka Parkway.

Kinetic Conveyance Parade
Pearl Street Mall, Boulder
(303) 444–5600

On the last Saturday in April, more than 50 teams enter wild, wacky, and wonderful kinetic conveyances—that is, non-motorized contraptions designed to race across water and land. Always imaginative and sometimes even functional during the later, challenge portion of the two-pronged competition (see the subsequent May listing), kinetic conveyances make a colorful parade. Panache earns points, so the Floating Elvises in a pink "Cadillac," the deliciously tasteless and terminally politically-incorrect Hooters Guys, and the Mud Sharks have been favorites. The morning starts with a display of the "vehicles" at 9 A.M., followed by a 1 P.M. parade. At the judging booth, contestants attempt undue influence through skits and bribes . . . the more outrageous, the better. The entrance deadline is mid-April; the fee is around $25 per craft and $10 for each team member. Watching the parade is, of course, free.

Puttin' on the Leash
Coors Events Center, CU-Boulder Campus
(303) 442–4030

The annual adoptable animal fashion show and auction fund-raiser for the Boulder Valley Humane Society is held the last weekend in April or the first weekend in May. Auction items have included a trips to Mexico and ski packages. to swim with the dolphins off the coast of the Bahamas. It starts at 6 P.M. at the Coors Events Center on the CU campus. Tickets are around $50 per person.

Taste of the Nation
CU-Boulder's Glenn Miller Ballroom, Boulder
(303) 652–3663 (Community Food Share)

More than 40 of Boulder's finest chefs prepare nibble-sized samples, which evening guests munch with everything from wine and local brewpub beer to mineral water. This April event is one of Boulder's best food festivals. Profits go to Community Food Share, the People's Clinic, International Hunger Relief, and rural Colorado communities. In 2001, tickets were $50 in advance and $55 at the door.

May

Cinco De Mayo Celebration
Clark Centennial Park, Mt. View and Alpine, Longmont
(303) 772–4358

This Mexican cultural celebration offers music, dance, food, singers, and much more. A student talent show features acts related to the Latino culture, including dances and storytelling. A salsa contest offers both restaurants and individuals a chance at prizes. Don't, however, expect margaritas on the side—this is a nonalcoholic celebration to honor families and culture. There is no admission charge. Hours are 9 A.M. to 5 P.M.

Kinetic Conveyance Challenge
Boulder Reservoir, 51st St., Boulder
(303) 444–5600

Around 30,000 people attend this race of non-motorized traveling contraptions. It

The Kinetic Conveyance Challenge combines creativity, spring wackiness, and lots of mud.

PHOTO: DAILY CAMERA

begins at 11 A.M. on the first Saturday in May, but some spectators arrive as early as 6:30 A.M. to get the best spots and enjoy the balloon festival and pancake breakfast. Some conveyances barely make it more than a few yards from shore before sinking. Especially in the early minutes of the race, rescue craft are busy towing the wrecks back to shore. The race consists of a water leg, an overland stretch, and a return across the water. The swiftest contestants finish in 45 minutes, and the lumbering laggards end four hours later. The winners usually have a combination canoe/bicycle thing powered by good-looking legs and shoulders. Entrance fees are roughly $25 for a carload and $5 per pedestrian or cyclist.

Boulder Potters' Guild Show & Sale
CU Armory, 4750 N. Broadway, Boulder
(303) 447–0310

Add some color to your home each spring by purchasing reasonably priced handmade clay tiles, sculpture, mugs, and more. Admission is free and refreshments are plentiful. Hours are Friday, 10 A.M. to 8 P.M., Saturday from 10 A.M. to 5 P.M., and

10 A.M. to 4 P.M. on Sunday. A fall sale is held in November.

Strawberry Festival Antiques Show
Boulder County Fairgrounds, 9595 Nelson Rd., Longmont
(303) 776–1870

This is one of three annual antiques shows hosted by the St. Vrain Historical Society and held in the exhibit hall at the fairgrounds. (The others are the Heritage Festival in July and Pumpkin Pie Days in October.) Antiques and collectibles are available, but those who aren't buying are usually taste-testing the strawberry shortcake sold in the cafeteria. Admission to all three events is $3 to $5 per person.

Boulder Creek Festival and Rubber Duck Race
Boulder Creek, Boulder
(303) 449–3825

This popular rite of spring has been rated the "Best Annual Children's Event" by *Daily Camera* readers. Throughout Memorial Day weekend, craft booths, music and dance, carnival rides, and food stands entertain the throngs who edge their way through the tightly packed festival area all the way from Sixth to 13th Streets and between Canyon Boulevard and Arapahoe Avenue.

On Sunday, more than 4,000 yellow rubber duckies bobble from the Ninth Street and Canyon Boulevard bridge to the Peace Garden at 11th Street and Arapahoe Avenue—all in the name of fun and charity. The race benefits the Boulder Parks and Recreation Department, helping it expand its therapeutic program for children and adults with disabilities. It costs $5 to enter a duck, and prizes range from the trivial to major vacations.

Other activities, such as the kids' Fishing Derby, a sports expo, and a huge art and crafts show help to draw approximately 130,000 people to the Central Park area before the fun ends Monday evening.

Bolder Boulder 10K Race
From 30th and Iris Sts. to Folsom Field, Boulder
(303) 444-RACE

This Memorial Day tradition is rated one of the top road races in the nation and "Boulder's Best Annual Event" by *Daily Camera* readers. It's amazing how much fun it can be to run or walk more than 6 miles. More than 40,000 participants, from the most fleet-footed elite amateur runners in the A wave to first-time walkers in the ZZ, make this one of the nation's largest citizen races. An international field of celebrity runners and top wheelchair athletes make this an important race on the national 10K calendar too. The Bolder Boulder's nonstop party atmosphere is exhilarating. In addition to aid and water stations, entertainment is provided along the route. All runners finish at CU-Boulder's Folsom Field, where thousands of spectators watch world-class professional racers compete after the amateur races are through.

The race fee is about $24, including a commemorative T-shirt and lunch, or $15 without the shirt. Every runner is timed, so you will get your time and ranking calculated in a variety of ways after the race. You can register at local running stores or at race headquarters in the Crossroads Mall. Try to get your application in by early May. (If the race doesn't fill up, you can register on race morning, too, but the price is $10 higher.)

Nearly 40,000 runners make quite a pack, but the race never feels so crowded, for organizers stagger the starting times in

"Paddling ducks" march in the Boulder Creek Festival parade. PHOTO: DAILY CAMERA/JAY QUADRACCI

successive waves to give everyone room. Along the way you'll see belly dancers, including the lady with the sword on her head, and high-stepping grandmas decked out in fringed cowgirl skirts. You'll hear everything from live jazz bands to bagpipers playing rock 'n roll. Don't fear wimping out. In the ZZ wave, the pace is a pleasant amble, and the cheers from the crowd are just as enthusiastic.

The citizens' race starts at 7:20 A.M. at 30th Street and Iris Avenue. The elite professionals, among the fastest in the world, start at 11 A.M. so that citizen racers can watch the pros' final laps in Folsom Field. If you decide to watch, pick a spot anywhere along the course or at Folsom Field. Runners have included wedding parties and guys who leapfrog the whole way. Marines usually sign up for the "M" section and run in formation, entertaining the crowd with military chants along the route. Blind runners and wheelchair racers inspire us all, as do the fleet-footed gazelle types and seniors running with their grandchildren.

June

Artwalk
Pearl St. Mall, Boulder
(303) 444-9116 (Linton-David Haslam Gallery)

The Artwalk is an evening open house featuring downtown galleries. Some serve refreshments, and many give you the opportunity to meet with the artists and artisans whose works they show. Schedules and maps are available at galleries along the Pearl Street Mall. Artwalk takes place the first weekend in June.

Boulder Outdoor Cinema
Boulder Museum of Contemporary Art,
1750 13th St., Boulder
(303) 443-2122

Bring a chair and your own popcorn and enjoy an informal cinema experience in the museum's parking lot. This outdoor walk-in theater screens "B" movies, cult classics, cartoons, and funny short subjects Saturday nights June through August. Prizes are awarded for best costume as it relates to the movie. The film, which starts at dusk, is projected onto an outside wall of the museum. A donation of $5 is requested.

Naropa Summer Institute Performing Arts Series
2130 Arapahoe Ave., Boulder
(303) 444-0202, (800) 603-3117

Naropa brings dancers, musicians, writers, and lecturers from all over the nation. Artists and scholars have included Ram Dass, Maya Angelou, Bernie Siegel, Anne Waldman, Phillip Glass, Cecil Taylor, Meredith Monk, and the Gardzienice Theater Group from Poland. Performances are scheduled extensively during June and July. Admission is as varied as the offerings.

The Colorado Shakespeare Festival
CU-Boulder's Mary Rippon Outdoor Theatre, Boulder
(303) 492-0554

This festival, started in 1958, has presented all the Shakespeare plays. It is now the fifth-largest Shakespeare company in the United States, according to the Shakespeare Theatre Association. The lushly costumed, lavishly acted plays are produced from mid-June through mid-August. A recent season featured three plays, *The Two Gentleman of Verona, King*

Lear, and *As You Like It.* Because the Rippon's amphitheater-style benches are made of stone, the wise theatergoer brings or rents a soft cushion or a stadium chair. After the sun goes down, the evening can turn cool, so toting a sweater, jacket, and even rain gear is smart, too. Tickets range from $14 to $40.

Summer Solstice Festival
Pearl Street Mall, Boulder
(303) 939–8463 (Solstice Institute)

The Solstice Institute hosts this annual gathering to promote sustainable culture and earth-friendly lifestyles. The festival, held at Third and Pearl Streets, features storytellers, dance, and drum presentations. There is also a potluck open house, music, and a silent auction. Admission to this mid-June weekend event is free.

Taste of Louisville
Louisville's shopping districts
(303) 666–5747

Less-than-a-dollar samples from many Louisville eateries are part of this mid-June celebration, which includes 80 participating businesses. The weekend often includes country-dance lessons, face-painting and shuttle buses, which take revelers between this growing city's shopping areas.

Walk and BikeWeek
2018 11th St. to 1739 Broadway, Boulder
(303) 441–3266

BikeWeek was a decade old when the city's alternate modes division added the "Walk" to the title in order to encourage participation by those who don't have a gift for cycling. The annual event is scheduled for the third week in June; Walk or Bike to Work Day is held on the Wednesday of that week. Prizes are offered to those who commute the farthest and to businesses with the most employees who bike or walk to work. More than 30 breakfast stations offer participants a quick bite to eat before they reach the office.

Boulder County Garden Tour
Various gardens throughout Boulder
(303) 666–4435

Local gardeners weed and plant like mad for this late June tour, which benefits the Boulder County Mental Health Foundation and features beautiful gardens at private homes. There are also speakers on gardening topics, a plant sale, and door prizes. Maps and details are available from local garden centers. Tickets are around $15.

July

Colorado Freedom Festival
Central Park and other locations in Boulder
(303) 665–2733

Boulder makes much of multiculturalism throughout the year, but this event—which takes place in Central Park, on the library lawn, and in the library auditorium—is where this commitment is put on display. The festival is essentially one big party celebrating the arts and cultural diversity. The variety of offerings includes dance, art exhibits, a children's talent show, live music performances, a health expo, ethnic food, and more. The festival, often held the weekend preceding the Fourth of July, generally starts early Friday afternoon, runs all day on Saturday and winds down on Sunday.

Fourth of July

An overture of real thunder often ends just before the planned fireworks begin. The public gatherings are grand, but so is a quiet, foothills nook. From a high roost, you can see those giant, bright-colored dandelion puffs all the way from Denver. Once the sun sets, it can get cold. Bring a heavy sweater or blanket. Many other Boulder County communities, such as Longmont, Louisville, and Broomfield, have their own fireworks, often with community picnics and concerts.

Share a patriotic moment at the Fourth of July concert in Chautauqua Park. PHOTO: DAILY CAMERA

Boulder Concert in the Park
Chautauqua Park, Ninth St. and Baseline Rd.,
Boulder
(303) 442–3282

This Fourth of July outdoor concert by the Colorado Music Festival's nationally recognized summer orchestra features pop and sing-along music. Insiders bring picnic baskets and blankets, then linger here to watch distant fireworks. The concert starts at 5 P.M., and admission is free.

Boulder Fireworks
Folsom Field (on CU-Boulder campus),
Boulder
(303) 442–1044

Even without great fireworks, which are launched at dark, this evening extravaganza would be a kick, for the live entertainment is good, and the sing-alongs include popular rock and hokey camp songs. KBCO has sponsored the fireworks in recent years, featuring a rock-n-roll band that plays while families wait for darkness to descend. Admission is free, with a donation requested. It's best to get there early, because the place begins to fill up long before the sun sets.

Louisville Fourth of July Picnic and Fireworks
Downtown Louisville and Coal Creek Golf Course
(303) 666–6565

Enjoy a community picnic, art festival, children's games, and a band concert in Memory Square Park, then "Fireworks on the Links," with the couples on the temporary dance floor swinging.

Nederland Fourth of July Parade and Fireworks
Downtown Nederland and Barker Reservoir
(303) 258–3936

A small-town parade and fireworks put a real old-fashioned spin on this most traditional holiday.

The Colorado Music Festival
1525 Spruce St., Boulder
(303) 449–1397, (303) 449–2413

The festival features a first-rate, full orchestra that plays great classical music at the Chautauqua Auditorium throughout the summer. The CMF season starts with a special children's performance and includes a free Fourth of July outdoor concert. You can get a subscription or single tickets to festival concerts. Insiders often bring a picnic and blanket for a pre-concert dinner on the grassy lawn, and many cluster behind the auditorium and listen to the sounds of brass and strings that waft through the wooden walls. Tickets range from $10 to $35.

CU's Lyric Theatre Festival
CU's Imig Music Building, 18th and Euclid Sts., Boulder
(303) 492–8008

The Lyric Theatre features CU's graduate and undergraduate vocal students from the College of Music. Recent performances by the musical theater group included *The Sound of Music* and *The Mikado*. Tickets are $20, with discounts for children and senior citizens.

Colorado Dance Festival
2590 Walnut St., Boulder
(303) 442–7666

This independent dance group presents classes, workshops, and performances at the university and other spaces throughout Boulder in the summer. Three hundred students join them, with more than 35 performing and teaching artists. Admission varies with each event.

Downtown Boulder ArtFair
Pearl Street Mall
(303) 449–3774

From fine art to fun art, this mid-July event on the Pearl Street Mall features works in all media and styles by 150 artists from across the nation. The fair is held on Saturday from 10 A.M. to 8 P.M. and on Sunday from 10 A.M. to 5 P.M.

Boulder Victorian Fair
1206 Euclid Ave., Boulder
(303) 449–3464

Sponsored by the Boulder Museum of History, this festive day, held at adjacent Beach Park in late July, includes military drill re-enactments, carriage rides, blacksmithing and craft demonstrations, children's games, and entertainment. Colorado foods, quilts, and vintage cars abound. And how about a pie bake-off? There is a costumed vintage women's softball game, gold-panning, and demonstrations of spinning and weaving. Entertainment is provided by a barbershop quartet. An ever-popular Great Boulder Pie Festival includes professional, amateur, and children's categories. Best of all, admission is free.

Ol' Timers and Miners Days
Throughout Nederland
(303) 258–3936

Head up the canyon to enjoy a pancake breakfast, a barbecue, or the festival's Sow-Bellie Lunch. Or join in such contests as the Women's Spike Driving and Men's Hand Mucking competitions. The whole festival harkens back to Nederland's mining history. Admission to this late July event is free.

Chautauqua's Silent Film Series
Ninth St. and Baseline Road
(303) 440–7666

Each year, five or six summer evenings are devoted to silent film classics accompanied by live music. To add to the historic atmosphere, the films are shown inside the cavernous Chautauqua Auditorium in Chautauqua Park. Screenings are Wednesday at 7:30 P.M. Among the films shown in the past are *The Thief of Bagdad*, directed by Raoul Walsh and starring Douglas Fairbanks and Julanne Johnston, and *Behind the Screen*, starring Charlie Chaplin.

RockyGrass Bluegrass Festival
Planet Bluegrass Ranch, Lyons
(303) 823–0848

In a pretty creekside field, internationally known bluegrass fiddlers and banjo pickers entertain campers and picnickers. Bluegrass workshops, late-night campfires, and dips in the St. Vrain River add to the old-time ambiance. In recent years, a three-day pass was $90. Tickets are also available by the day for this weekend event in early August. The producer also presents the famous Telluride Bluegrass Festival in southwestern Colorado.

Boulder County Fair
Boulder County Fairgrounds, 9595 Nelson Rd., Longmont
(303) 772–7170

The whole family will love the goats and rabbits at this down-home country fair, which draws more than 100,000 spectators. Sheep yell "Ma-a!" as 4-H parents do the final, pre-show shearing. The harness horses prance, their braided manes decorated with flowers. At the old-timers' rodeo on the last Friday, see bucking broncos and fancy riding. Admission to the fairgrounds is free, but call ahead to check fees for such events as the rodeo. The fair runs from the first through the second weekend in August.

Rocky Mountain Folks Festival
Planet Bluegrass Ranch, Lyons
(303) 823–0848

Sixties folk legend Arlo Guthrie is among those who have performed at this mid-August festival; others include Bruce Hornsby, Patty Larkin, and Cliff Eberhardt. It's sponsored by Planet Bluegrass, the same folks who host the RockyGrass Bluegrass Festival and the Telluride Bluegrass Festival. These events are organized in a less-than-formal manner, attracting many families who camp in the surrounding area. In recent years a three-day pass was $90.

Old Town Lafayette Antiques & Country Peach Festival
401 S. Public Road, Lafayette
(303) 666–7200

This annual event in early to mid-August features dealers' booths with antiques and crafts all along the Old Town section

The fair comes to town the first week of August each year. PHOTO: ROZ BROWN

of Public Road. It features peach cobbler, peach ice cream, and peach smoothies as well as other food concessions and entertainment. Hours are 9 A.M. to 5 P.M.

September

Louisville Fall Festival and Labor Day Parade
Downtown, Louisville
(303) 666–6565

Louisville's Labor Day parade, one of Colorado's largest, attracts more than 25,000 people. The Saturday and Sunday of Labor Day weekend feature an art fair, carnival, music, and pancake breakfast. The Monday parade includes pets, the King Soopers Shopping Cart Drill Team, marching bands, and antique cars. The parade down Main Street starts at 10 A.M.

Boulder Creek Hometown Fair and Harvest Festival
Municipal Building Lawn, Canyon St. and Broadway, Boulder
(303) 449–3825

Held for the first time in 1998, this Labor Day weekend event is hosted by the same folks who produce the Boulder Creek Festival in May. With old-fashioned flair the event offers a chili cookoff, the Great Zucchini Race, hay rides, a speakers' corner, arts and crafts vendors, food vendors, and a dance hall. Hours are Saturday 10 A.M. to 10 P.M., Sunday 10 A.M. to 9 P.M., and Monday from 10 A.M. to 7 P.M.

Longs Peak Scottish–Irish Highland Festival
Estes Park Fairground, Community Dr., Estes Park
(800) 90–ESTES

You'll find kilts and caboodles of festivities at this festival, the biggest event of Estes Park's year. It's a celebration of Celtic heritage held the first weekend after Labor Day. Naturally bagpipes play a large part in the festival and bagpipers take center stage for the weekend parade. (See our Estes Park chapter for more information.)

Cause for Paws Walk-a-Thon
Boulder County Humane Society
2323 55th St., Boulder
(303) 442–4030

More than 600 people and their dogs participate in the annual event, which helps fund the Humane Society's programs. The mid-September walk meanders a three-mile route through downtown Boulder follows the Boulder Creek Path along a four-mile route and returns along the same route to a People and Pet Fair. The $20 registration fee includes a T-shirt.

Dixieland Swing Festival
Tri-City Elks Lodge
525 Main St., Louisville
(303) 936–3962, (303) 449–5930

Boulder Friends of Jazz host this jammin' festival at Trios Grille in mid-September. BFJ solicits grants from enthusiastic arts-funding agencies and private businesses in order to make this a top-notch affair. Admission is $10.

Golden Aspen Trees
Peak to Peak Hwy. (Colo. Hwy. 72), north of Nederland, and other locations

The greatest fall festival is the natural one—the annual gilding of the aspen. Mother Nature never calls ahead to reserve a day for the best leaf-viewing, so watch local papers for reports of favorable

Insiders' Tip

The weekend after Labor Day is the Longs Peak Scottish-Irish Festival. It's so grand that *USA Today* has listed it as one of the nation's top 10 things to do. See our listings in this chapter and in the Estes Park chapter for more information.

turnings, some time in September or October. The *Daily Camera* runs stories and maps. The aspens east of the Continental Divide generally turn gold, but sometimes pinkish foliage peeks out among the yellow. Often, a whole grove changes at once, for aspen are large, cloned families, connected by their roots. Because "quakies" have loose leaf stems, the shiny leaves really shimmer. The biggest aspen fields are along the Peak to Peak Highway outside of Nederland. Driving is fun. But even better, park at a trailhead and take a stroll. Rocky Mountain National Park boasts several astonishing stands of aspen. The park rangers can direct you to the best. Wherever you hike, the filtered golden light, the tannin scent of fall, and the sound of fluttering aspen leaves are unforgettable.

Walker Ranch Living History
Walker Ranch, Flagstaff Rd. (west of Chautauqua Park), Boulder
(303) 441-3950
The last two weekends in September, blacksmiths pound a ringing "whang" on red-hot iron while the bellows release a throaty sigh. Sunbonnet-clad women prepare victuals at a potbellied stove. They're volunteers, trained by Boulder County Parks and Open Space to live the old-fashioned way for a few days. The ranch is open 10 A.M. to 2 P.M. and has free everything, from watching the horses plow to sampling the homemade bread and hand-churned butter. This gorgeous area frequently has brilliant mountain bluebirds. The ranch is on the left, 7.5 miles west of Chautauqua Park, up Flagstaff Road.

Celebrate Lafayette:
Many Cultures, Many Faces
Old Town Lafayette
(303) 666-9555
Lafayette loves a parade, and this one, held the week after Labor Day, has taken place each year since 1957. It features the Recycled Seniors Umbrella Team, a wild-animal float with real lions and bears and other highlights. The day-long festival

also includes a free pancake breakfast, entertainers, bargain hot-air balloon rides, fun arts and crafts booths, music, and food from local vendors.

Boulder Fall Festival
Pearl Street Mall, Boulder
(303) 449-3774
Loosely styled after a European Oktoberfest, this celebration in late September has become a primo showcase for local and visiting craftsmen. It still includes flowing beer—though now more microbrews than German brews—plus bands, carnival rides, lots of food, and a petting zoo for the kids. It runs 11 A.M. to 10 P.M. on Friday and Saturday and 11 A.M. to 6 P.M. on Sunday.

October

Band Day
Folsom Field, University of Colorado Campus, Folsom and Colorado Ave., Boulder
(303) 492-6584
An autumn regular for more than five decades, Band Day brings stirring high school bands from across the state to compete at Folsom Field. This event is free.

Pumpkin Pie Days Antiques Show
9595 Nelson Rd., Boulder County
Fairgrounds, Longmont
(303) 776-1870
More than 80 dealers display antiques and collectibles at the exhibit hall, where there is plenty of parking and admission is free. This mid-October event was named for celebrations that brought special trains full of visitors to Longmont from 1899 to 1914. The cafe at the exhibit hall serves the pie and other treats. Hours are Saturday from 10 A.M. to 5 P.M. and Sunday from 11 A.M. to 5 P.M.

Boulder County AIDS Project
Boulder Theater, 2118 14th St., Boulder
(303) 543-0025
A costume contest and prizes highlight the annual BCAP Halloween Bash and

Costume Extravaganza. Held the weekend before Halloween, all proceeds benefit BCAP's many programs. The location changes from year to year. Tickets in advance are $15 to $20.

Museum in the Dark
University of Colorado Museum, Broadway and 15th St., Boulder
(303) 492-6892

Bring your flashlight, for tonight the lights are off at the dinosaur museum so that kids can discover the real triceratops head and flying pterodactyl with their own, modern torches. This is an educational (rather than a scary) night, and science volunteers bring live exhibits such as bats and snakes. The idea is to take the spooky out of Halloween but keep the delicious sense of discovery. It's also a great chance to get familiar with this excellent, family-oriented museum, which always has special exhibits. Call ahead to reserve tickets, which usually sell out by party night. Tickets are $5. Museum in the Dark usually happens the Friday before Halloween.

Munchkin Masquerade, Children's Trick or Treat
Daily Camera, **11th and Pearl Sts., Boulder**
(303) 449-3774

On the afternoon of Halloween, approximately 2,000 costumed kids traipse through downtown with their parents plus local performers eager to entertain. The parade runs from 3 to 5 P.M.

November

Souper Bowlder Promotion
Boulder Arts & Crafts Cooperative, 1421 Pearl St., Pearl Street Mall
(303) 443-3683

Hundreds of ceramic soup bowls donated by professional potters sell for $12 each at this benefit for the Boulder County AIDS project and Boulder Shelter for the Homeless. Dried soup mixes from the Women's Bean Project (a workforce of otherwise unemployed women) are also offered.

Boulder Potters' Guild Show and Sale
2108 55th St., Boulder
(303) 447-0310

Here's a chance to purchase tasteful, handcrafted holiday gifts at reasonable prices. This mid-November show and sale runs 10 A.M. to 8 P.M. on Thursday and Friday, 10 A.M. to 5 P.M. on Saturday, and 10 A.M. to 4 P.M. on Sunday. There is no admission fee, and the kids can snack on delicious treats while you browse. This popular show has been held in several different locations in recent years, so call ahead for directions.

Nutcracker Ballet
Macky Auditorium (on CU-Boulder campus), Boulder
(303) 449-1343

The Boulder Philharmonic teams up with the Boulder Ballet for four packed performances of this favorite family ballet during Thanksgiving weekend. Everything's magic when local children play the mice, and rising local stars portray Clara and her Prince. During intermission, kids can peek in the orchestra pit, where friendly musicians demonstrate instruments such as the celesta, which makes those little tinkly bell sounds for the Sugar Plum Fairy. Tickets range from $10 to $60, with discounts for students and children.

Hmong New Year
Lafayette Elementary School, 101 N. Bermont Ave., Lafayette
(303) 665-5046

During this four-day event in late November, coinciding with Thanksgiving weekend, the 700 Hmong who live in Boulder County invite Colorado's Laotian community and others to join this celebration, which includes traditional clothing and food. The needlework is stunning. This event is free.

Boulder Creek Winter Skate
Downtown Boulder
(303) 449-3825

It only lasts a few weeks, but this temporary ice-skating rink, generally in a vacant lot in downtown Boulder, has many fans. Semi-professionals and amateurs, young and old, twirl under the lights, enjoy refreshments, and visit with Santa. The rink is generally open from 10 A.M. until 10 P.M. and group skate rates are available. In recent years the rink has operated for approximately six weeks.

December

Lights of Downtown December Parade
Pearl St. Mall, Boulder
(303) 449-3774

This eclectic parade on the first Friday in December launches Boulder's holiday season. Like many parades throughout the year, the route circumnavigates the pedestrian center. The parade is both sweet and hokey. You'll see everything from Boulder's Girl Scout troops with battery-operated Christmas lights in their hair to the local Polar Bear Club members prancing about the cold streets barefoot and bathing-suited, hopping into a hot tub on wheels whenever they need to warm up again. Eco-elves prance by in curled-toe green slippers, passing out information about recycling; local marching bands play; and gleaming antique cars and fire trucks get festooned with ornaments. The parade starts around 6 P.M.

Louisville Parade of Lights
Downtown Louisville
(303) 666-6565

Garlands swing from Main Street lamps, and choral groups perform by City Hall. There are open houses and hay rides. More than 20 floats join the parade, which starts at 7 P.M. on the first Friday in December.

Artwalk
Pearl Street Mall, Boulder
(303) 444-9116 (Linton-David Haslam Gallery)

On the first weekend in December, grab a gallery guide at any local gallery, then enjoy this tour of Boulder's gorgeous arts and crafts purveyors. This self-guided tour of open galleries is free.

Holiday Festival Concert
Macky Auditorium, CU-Boulder Campus
(303) 492-8008

This early December event is so popular, the auditorium fills up for the dress rehearsal in addition to the actual performance. University of Colorado College of Music students and faculty perform in a festively decorated Macky Auditorium. The program features Christmas favorites and seasonal music from various cultures. There are performances on Friday and Saturday nights and Sunday afternoon. Tickets are $10 for the rehearsal and prices range from $10 to $35 for the actual performance.

Historic Homes for the Holidays
Various Boulder homes
(303) 444-5192

Grand homes deck their halls for the holidays, and everyone is invited to have a look during the first weekend in December. Mapleton Hill Victorians and Romanesque Uni-Hill homes are among those that have been part of the tour. The decorating by the owners and professionals is spectacular. This fund-raiser for Historic Boulder also includes a gift shop and drawings for door prizes. Ticket prices vary; in recent years they were $15 for nonmembers of Historic Boulder and $13.50 for seniors 60 and older.

Celebration of Boulder Ball
Glenn Miller Ballroom, CU-Boulder,
Broadway and Euclid, Boulder
(303) 449-2556

The black-tie holiday ball with silent auction and seated gourmet dinner helps
raise money for the Emergency Family
Assistance Association (EFAA), which
supports Boulder County families in
financial crisis. Tickets are generally
about $100 per person.

Messiah Sing-along
St. John's Episcopal Church, 14th and
Pine Sts., Boulder
(303) 666–9016
Professionals fly in to sing the solos, and
the choir practices for weeks to lead a
rousing rendition of Handel's *Messiah*. But
the passion comes from the regular folks
who fill the pews. Some are practically
pros, while others have never sung before,
but they all join in for the rousing "Hallelujah Chorus," which must be audible
all the way to the heavens. There are two
evening performances and one matinee

the weekend before Christmas Eve. Tickets are around $15.

Events Central

Many other festivals and events occur in
the Boulder area throughout the year.
The *Daily Camera*'s "Friday Magazine" is
loaded with entertainment information
for the upcoming weekend. The chambers
of commerce also have information on
specific local events. Also check out the
choices listed in our Boulder Attractions
chapter. If you're casting about for something to do, call any (or all) of the following organizations: Boulder Chamber of
Commerce (303-442-1044), Boulder
County Fairgrounds (303-678-6235),
CU-Boulder Cultural Events/Concert
Line (303-492-3227), or Chautauqua
Association (303-442-3282).

Attractions

The Top Five

More Museums, Historic Buildings, and Special Places

Business and Science Attractions

Boulder's top five, must-see attractions are detailed here, followed by a smorgasbord of other treats if time and taste permit. Also see our chapters on Boulder Festivals and Annual Events, Kidstuff, Sports, and Neighborhoods and Nearby Communities.

The Top Five

Pearl Street Mall
Pearl St. from 11th to 15th Sts., Boulder

Business people in the 1970s bit their nails as Boulder plunked down more than a million dollars for a pedestrian mall. How on earth would people shop, some wondered, if they couldn't park in front of a store?

Since then, *The Wall Street Journal* has called the Pearl Street Mall one of the nation's most successful pedestrian malls, and it has won national design awards. It's Boulder's people-watching spot, from kids climbing the bronze frog to college-age lovers buying gauzy new clothes to business people grabbing a savory pie at the Empañadas window. Street musicians embroider the air with a saxophone's blue tones, steel-drum calypso, folk guitar, and more. Breathe deeply. The aroma of fresh pretzels might draw you to a kiosk in front of the courthouse; fresh popcorn or stir-fried something might bring you to a pushcart vendor; or a thick, dark river of perfume might sweep you into the Rocky Mountain Chocolate Factory.

In addition to matchless people-watching, the Pearl Street Mall offers abundant free entertainment—though, of course, the jugglers, clowns, and magicians appreciate tips. In the warm months, you can sit to have your portrait painted, your fortune told, or your neck and shoulders massaged; or you might pick a ringside seat in one of the many excellent restaurants with patio tables. Thanks to Boulder's clear skies and mild days, people-watchers often sit out even in winter. Some of Boulder's finest restaurants, galleries, and shops are found on the mall. Discover them as you wander, or check our chapters on Boulder Shopping, Arts, and Restaurants.

Pearl Street's history does not always reflect such a stylish past. It started out Wild West style, with drunks horse-racing down the dirt lane that was the main street. And no proper lady walked a white poodle, for these dogs were popular among the "soiled doves" whose creekside homes advertised, "Men Taken In and Done For." To civilize the street, storekeepers built plank walks, but they didn't match sidewalk height between stores, so shoppers bobbed up and down along the way.

By the 1970s, Pearl Street was drearily, Midwesterny respectable. Aluminum facades hid brick storefronts, cars jammed streets, and "for lease" signs proliferated like mushrooms growing in decay. To halt the decline, planners suggested everything from a covered shopping mall to highrises. Although it seemed so risky to restore the original buildings, tweak the Old West character, and create strolling space with sculptures, trees, and flowers, the mall has been a smash hit. City leaders, however, are not content to let the mall slumber on its success, and began work in 2001 to give the mall a fresh coat of paint, so to speak. Vegetation will be enhanced, new public restrooms built, and a covered

A performer dazzles pedestrians on the Pearl Street Mall. PHOTO: DAILY CAMERA

performance area added in front of the Courthouse. Although some naysayers balked at "fixing what ain't broke," the majority of residents felt improvements would make the mall experience still more enjoyable.

If you're a history buff, stop by the **Hotel Boulderado,** at 2115 13th Street, just north of the mall (303-442-4344). This redbrick hotel, named after Boulder and Colorado, was built in 1909. The city's pride, it features Italianate porch corners, a cherry cantilevered staircase, and an Italian stained-glass ceiling. Robert Frost and Louis Armstrong were among the guests. But the Boulderado suffered decline, too. The glass ceiling crashed in a 1960s snowstorm; kitchen cooks hung bait over vats to drown rats; and vagrants slept in empty rooms. In the 1980s, Boulderado Concept Ltd. restored the grand old hotel. Wander inside. The Catacombs Bar in the basement has live blues, reggae, and jazz most nights of the week, and there's live music

on the mezzanine on Friday evenings; it's reserved for private parties other times.

Another historic area on Pearl Street is the **Boulder Courthouse Square,** between 13th and 14th Streets. The location started as the town's baseball diamond and then was the site of Boulder County's grand Victorian courthouse, which burned down in the 1930s. Local architect Glenn Huntington designed the light-colored stone, art deco courthouse you see today. The lawn, which was extensively redesigned in 1996, is a popular festival spot.

A fountain built in 1935 by the Lions Club began operating again in 1999 after years of disrepair and neglect. It is surrounded by tasteful landscaping and benches, which makes it a wonderful spot to sit and watch Boulder's Summer Concert Band perform Sousa marches on the courthouse plaza.

Just east, at 2032 14th Street, is the **Boulder Theater** (303-786-7030), a turn-of-the-20th-century opera house renovated in the 1930s as the gaudy little sister of the plain blond courthouse. The art deco facade is as lavish as a peacock's tail, and the restored interior has gorgeous, hand-painted, flowery murals. A live music venue for both local and national acts, the former movie house also offers dance, theater, and corporate events and can be rented for private parties. The theater is also home to the weekly *E-Town* live music/talk performances broadcast by National Public Radio to more than 150 cities.

From the Pearl Street Mall, it's an easy walk to **Central Park,** between Canyon and Arapahoe Streets east of Broadway. An art deco band shell built in 1938 and restored in 1996, once again hosts concerts and civic events. A steam locomotive and frequent festivals can be found in Central Park.

On Saturday mornings from early spring through late fall and on Wednesday afternoons in summer, the **Boulder County Farmers' Market** takes place along 13th Street (see the subsequent "Boulder Creek Path" entry for details about this market). On the east side of the street is the **Boulder Museum of Contemporary Art** (see subsequent entry), and the **Boulder Creek Path,** the next must-see attraction, runs along the south side of the park.

Boulder Creek Path
Parallel to Canyon Blvd. and/or Arapahoe Ave. from Four Mile Canyon in Boulder Canyon east to Cherryvale Rd.

Boulder's most popular "architecture" is 12 feet wide, 7.5 miles long, and flat on the ground. This 1980s project lets commuters travel without cars and in the prettiest possible way. The Creek Path dips under 10 major intersections, transforming traffic's roar into a whispered "whoosh." More than a half-dozen wooden pedestrian bridges crisscross the stream, clattering merrily as bicyclists and in-line skaters pass. The bridges are designed to snap to the side and reduce debris if a big flood hits. The whole path was designed with a rising creek in mind. Major flooding is rare, but every few years, some overflow happens. The city's flower plantings along this route are a feast for the eyes.

Each year, nearly 2 million bicyclists, in-line skaters, walkers, runners—you name it—use the Boulder Creek Path. Other non-motor-vehicle routes from all over the city connect so people can really get around without cars. Be alert, however. Some fierce bicyclists and in-line skaters ignore speed signs and can scare the daylights out of walkers. Especially in busy areas near downtown, keep an eye on kids, your dogs, and your own tendency to stray. Choose your chariot—bicycle, feet, in-line skates, or wheelchair—and head to the path.

The **Boulder Public Library**'s main branch (303-441-3100), at 10th Street and Arapahoe Avenue, is a good place to start, and in fact, a stop to admire this gleaming facility is worthwhile, too. About 3,000 folks use it daily. Look for the dramatic glass entry on the Arapahoe Avenue side. Outside are a Pooh-garden, scent garden, and flowers. Inside, the library has approximately 320,000 circulating books, an artists' register showing slides of local artwork, and a computerized media/ browsing system. Books can be delivered to the homebound who can't get to the library, and another service tran-

The popular Boulder Creek Path extends the width of Boulder. PHOTO: DAILY CAMERA/CASEY CASS

scribes text into Braille. Kid-pleasing attractions include a trout habitat, two new multimedia computers with interactive children's software, and storytelling hours. The library auditorium on the Canyon Boulevard side is the site of a free year-round film and concert series. The Learning to Read program provides free, confidential tutoring for everyone from children to adults. There are seven computer terminals with free Internet access, but be prepared to wait as they are extremely popular. The library is open 9 A.M. to 9 P.M. Monday through Thursday, 9 A.M. to 6 P.M. Friday and Saturday, and noon to 6 P.M. Sunday. There are also three branch libraries in Boulder; their hours vary from each other and the main library.

Just west of the library is the **West Boulder Senior Center** at Ninth Street and Arapahoe Avenue. After passing under Ninth Street, be sure to notice the sculpture of Chief Niwot (Niwot means "left hand") on the left. Continue westward to Sixth Street and Canyon Boulevard, where you'll find the **Children's Fishing Pond,** marked by an abstract metal sculpture that looks like leaping fish. On your right is the **Boulder County Justice Center,** with courts for dreary things from speeding tickets to criminal cases, but also where civil marriage ceremonies are performed. Just beyond, west along the Creek Path, the **Xeriscape Demonstration Garden** displays native plants that make environmentally wise gardening choices for Colorado's arid climate, an herb garden, and a "wheel" of lawns comparing bluegrass, two buffalo grasses, fescue, and blends.

Continuing westward, the path opens out to **Eben Fine Park** at Fourth Street, a favorite shady picnic and Frisbee-throwing area, with playgrounds and a congenial family atmosphere. At the park, you'll see a tunnel to the north, or right, under Canyon Boulevard. It leads to **Red Rocks/Settlers Park,** site of the 1858 campsite along Boulder Creek by the gold seekers who became Boulder's first citizens. Historical plaques explain some of Boulder's early history. Near more picnic tables, you'll see a steep trail up to the nearly vertical red rocks, naturally called Red Rocks, and a fine hilltop view of the whole area. Take care should you decide to scramble up the rocks for an even better vista.

Back along the creek path and just west of the park is Boulder's kayak course. Even if you're not into whitewater, it's thrilling to watch kayakers and canoeists test their skills in the rapids during spring and early summer. Inner tube riders crawl into their black doughnut-shaped vessels here too for a bracing ride down to Broadway. Two historic markers along the path tell about the **Switzerland Trail** railroad line and **Farmers' Ditch,** two early landmarks in the development of Boulder County.

For a lovely walk into Boulder Canyon, keep going up the hill and to the west along the Creek Path (watch out for speeding downhill cyclists). After a while, the pavement ends, and the path dips under the canyon road and deposits you at the base of the **Elephant Buttresses** and the **Dome,** two of Boulder's most popular rock-climbing spots. In one vista, you'll see an old water flume and Lycra-clad rock climbers, a perfect combination on the Boulder firmament. Farther along the path, wild roses and purple asters bloom in summer beside the frothy creek, and wild plums and grapes ripen in the fall. The gravel path continues up along the creekside under the rustling cottonwoods

Insiders' Tip

No summer is complete without a stop at Boulder's Farmers' Market. It takes place on Wednesday and Saturday on 13th Street, between Arapahoe Avenue and Canyon Boulevard.

Boulder Falls is a favorite spot for photographs and recreation. PHOTO: DAILY CAMERA/NICO TOUTENHOOFD

and glinting ponderosa pines to **Four Mile Canyon,** about 1.5 miles away. The total distance from Eben Fine Park—the lower bridge at the east end of the park with a boulder marked 0 miles—to the end of the trail is 2.25 miles.

If instead you head east from the Boulder Public Library, you'll soon get to **Central Park** at Broadway. There are small waterfalls, historic railroad cars, a band shell, and sometimes an outdoor sculpture exhibit. The Boulder Museum of Contemporary Art (see subsequent entry) is across the street, east of the park.

On Saturday mornings from spring through fall and Wednesday afternoons during the summer, the **Boulder County Farmers' Market** stretches on both sides of 13th Street between Arapahoe Avenue and Canyon Boulevard. This assembly features a colorful parade of produce, flowers, homegrown and homemade goodies, and weekly cooking demonstrations by local chefs. This beguiling attraction features a changing cornucopia of produce and related wares and has become Colorado's most successful open-air market. Regulars use it as an opportunity to shop, stroll, nibble, and socialize. The location is

perfect, close to the Pearl Street Mall and right next to Central Park. During the market's early weeks, vendors specialize in seedlings that you can take home and plant. At summer's peak, the street's packed with local fresh tomatoes, Western Slope peaches, Rocky Ford cantaloupe and honeydew melons, green beans, lettuce, fresh herbs, and more. Tamales, pirogen, and focaccia give the market a true international ambiance. Fresh and dried flowers, lavender water, hot corn on the cob, honey, and delicacies from goat cheese to smoked trout tempt from many stands. Don't forget sweet ices, lemonade, and fresh-baked pastries—a big colorful crowd. The market opens in mid-April and runs through the end of October. Saturday hours are 8 A.M. to 2 P.M. After June 1, a smaller version is also open Wednesday from 10 A.M. to 2 P.M. until the weather turns cold in the fall. Downtown workers appreciate the lunch menu at the Wednesday market.

The eclectic atmosphere of the farmers' market is a perfect complement to Boulder's unique **Dushanbe Teahouse,** located in the center of all this activity. In 1986, the residents of Boulder's sister city of Dushanbe crated and shipped this elegant teahouse to Colorado. Because there was no unanimity on where it should be built or who should foot the bill, the crates remained warehoused for 11 years. Finally in 1997 the city council agreed (the vote was not unanimous) to spend $800,000 for construction of the teahouse at the 13th Street site. The funding helped bring artisans from Tajikistan to Boulder to complete the intricate assembly. The folks who run the cafe at the Naropa Institute now serve daily meals at the teahouse, which is also the venue for a variety of special community events.

After you enjoy a meal on the teahouse patio you can return immediately to the Creek Path and continue east, past **Boulder High School** and its athletic fields, to a sunny, stone-bench alcove just west of the 17th Street bridge.

Just beyond is **Scott Carpenter Park,** south of Arapahoe Avenue on 30th Street (303-441-3427). Carpenter, a Boulder native who became one of the early astronauts, named his spaceship the Aurora 7 after a local school. The playground has a spacecraft theme, and the park also has an outdoor swimming pool and includes Boulder's state-of-the-art 14,000-square-foot concrete in-ground skatepark for skate boarders and in-line skaters. The park features an exciting street course with rails, curbs, free-flowing forms and bowls, and viewing benches made of old snowboards. The park's sledding hill, which served as the city's landfill many years ago, is one of Boulder's enduring winter meccas.

Farther east, just before Foothills Parkway, you'll pass the **CU-Boulder Research Park.** Landscape designers decided the standard lawn would take too much care, guzzle water, and look boring. So they planted something much better—low-maintenance, drought-tolerant meadows that attract butterflies and birds. The result is so lovely that it's almost too popular.

At the intersection of Arapahoe Avenue and Foothills Parkway is a prairie-

dog town. Prairie dogs get a bad rap as vermin spreaders, but health officials say it's undeserved, and they are appropriate prey for raptors nesting nearby. Still, don't feed them; they are wild animals and should stay that way. Kids love how they stand like little soldiers, then yip before diving underground. Prairie dogs are a remnant of the shortgrass prairie ecosystem and are food for swooping hawks.

You can take the Creek Path northeast from here, to the tent-roofed stands of the **Stazio Ballfields,** at 2445 Stazio Drive (303-441-4410), which are well-lighted and busy well into evening all summer long. Notice that the path veers away from the oldest cottonwood trees. Playing by the creek is fun, but human activity has caused creekside wildlife to decline. By keeping people farther away, critters, such as the red-eyed vireo and yellow warbler, have a better chance. If you ever hear a warbler sing, you'll thank creek planners for giving those birds privacy. As the Creek Path spreads its tentacles, you can take offshoots either to the north or south through residential as well as industrial areas, which is one reason why it is so popular for commuting.

Chautauqua Park
Ninth St. and Baseline Rd., Boulder
(303) 442-3282

At the turn of the 20th century, sites across the nation became gathering spots for summer cultural and educational institutes, all named "Chautauqua" after Chautauqua Lake in upstate New York, where the first such gathering was held. Dozens of Chautauquas once existed, but few remain. Boulder's was one of the rare Western locations. The **Chautauqua Auditorium and Dining Hall** (303-440-3776), built in 1898, and a charming nearby colony of wooden cottages comprise the last original site west of the Mississippi.

Chautauqua's main buildings, decked out in crisp gray, would still be a perfect setting for banjo-strumming gallants in flat-brimmed hats, but summer offerings now draw modern crowds with contemporary interests. There's a nod to the past with July's silent films, accompanied by live piano. The Colorado Chautauqua Association Forum is a lecture series dating from 1898, but today's speakers address topics such as health issues, transportation and world affairs.

The **Colorado Music Festival** (303–449–1397) has a full orchestra of musicians invited here for the summer and features internationally renowned guest artists as well as rising stars with promising futures. The vast majority of classical performances are instrumental, for the wooden auditorium tends to swallow voices. An orchestra or a powerful soloist can make the wonderful barn resonate with great sound. For ticket events, call the Box Office, (303) 440-7666, between May and September.

Chautauqua Park has 58 cottages for rent from June through August, with a minimum four-night stay. They vary in size, but all have a kitchen, bathroom, living area, and one or more bedrooms. For the 2001 season, a four-day stay ranged from $65 to $120 per night depending on the size of the cottage. These fill up fast so make your reservation as soon after November 1 as possible. To rent a cottage for the summer or to learn about the summer programs, call the Chautauqua Association, (303) 442-3282. The Chautauqua Gift Cottage (303- 443-5839) is open daily in the summer only.

Children like the **Chautauqua Park** playground, especially after they discover low-branched trees for playing hide-and-seek. (Only kids can scamper through. Moms and dads have to hunch.) The **Chautauqua Ranger Cottage** (720-564-2000), near the big meadow on the west side of the park, is generally open 10:00 A.M. to 4:00 P.M. daily. Its small garden displays native plants, and the rangers dispense plenty of hiking information. The rangers can answer questions, and they're trained to handle emergencies. They also lead free interpretive hikes that depart from the Ranger Cottage at 8 A.M. Saturday mornings in summer.

Trails lead everywhere. The Boulder Mountain Parks trail system includes everything from short, nearly flat strolls to steep hikes. One of the easiest, and shadiest, is the McClintock Trail, starting southeast of the Chautauqua Auditorium. You can head west on the Chautauqua Trail, cross the big meadow, and watch rock climbers. Or head west and south to the Mesa Trail. It's 3 up-and-down miles to the next major attraction, NCAR (see subsequent entry) and twice that far to the Mesa Trail's southern terminus just off the Eldorado Canyon Road.

National Center for Atmospheric Research
West end of Table Mesa Dr., Boulder
(303) 497–1000

Anyone who has ever gazed at the sky can find something of interest at NCAR (pronounced "en-car"). Founded in 1960 for research on the world's climate, NCAR draws scientists from all over the globe to study our wonderful blanket of air. Interesting displays present the fundamentals of the scientists' fields of expertise. Skywatchers can learn about clouds, air currents, lightning, hail, tornadoes, and

Architect I. M. Pei designed the National Center for Atmospheric Research, which violates, beautifully, Boulder's usual prohibitions against obstructions of the city's scenic backdrop. PHOTO: LINDA CORNETT

Visitors young and old enjoy the hands-on science experiments at the National Center for Atmospheric Research. PHOTO: LINDA CORNETT

other weather phenomena, including global warming. I. M. Pei designed this mesa-top complex, which helped establish his reputation as a world-class architect. "The mountains," said Pei, "gave us scale trouble from the beginning. We had to return to elemental forms. The Rockies humbled us." Local red limestone was mixed into the concrete so it would blend with the Flatirons. The building's angular forms mimic keyhole doors at the Mesa Verde cliff dwellings. This building is considered one of the nation's finest public structures. Two galleries feature community art. The computers in the basement are some of the world's fastest and largest.

The center is open daily for self-guided tours; pick up a brochure in the lobby. Guided walking tours take place at noon

Mondays and Wednesdays all year, and weekdays and Saturdays during the summer. No reservations are needed for the guided tours, but for more information call (303) 497–1174. If you want to bring a school class, scout troop, or any other group, tours must be arranged in advance by calling (303) 497–1173. The Walter Orr Roberts Weather Trail at NCAR is the only one of its kind in the country. Just west of the building, the .4-mile trail is not paved but is wheelchair-accessible. There are signs posted at regular intervals along the trail explaining weather patterns that hikers are then able to observe. In addition, there are many short nature trails near NCAR that are spectacular for more ambitious hikers.

The NCAR is open 8 A.M. to 5 P.M. Monday through Friday, and 10 A.M. to 4 P.M. weekends and holidays. Admission is free. The cafeteria is open to the public on weekdays for lunch.

University of Colorado at Boulder
Intersections of Baseline and Broadway/ Folsom and Colorado/Broadway and College, Boulder
(303) 492–1411

CU-Boulder's 600-acre campus is one of the nation's most beautiful. The buildings are a visual symphony of red tile roofs and warm, native-stone walls that make the entire campus harmonize, and the landscaping is splendid. Norlin Quadrangle is the three-block-long, tree-lined lawn next to Broadway. Nearby are the oldest buildings on campus, including Macky Auditorium, Old Main, Hale Science Building, and the Koenig Alumni Center. Kittredge Pond, near Fleming Law School, and Varsity Pond, just off the intersection of Broadway and College, are "water features" created decades before such amenities got a trendy name. The big old trees, quacking mallards, and basking turtles help time stand still—even among the achingly with-it students all around.

For many, the main draw to the campus is the sports teams, and rabid fans might never get past **Folsom Field** or the **Coors Events Center.** Call (303) 492-8337 for information about Big 12 conference games, or see the Sports chapter for more information. For other folks, the campus is fun for exploring. Maps located throughout the campus pinpoint spots of interest, or call (303) 492-6301 for information about campus visits and tours. An hour-long information briefing followed by a one-hour tour is given at 9:30 A.M. and 1:30 P.M. Monday through Friday and at 10:30 A.M. Saturdays from the lower level of the University Memorial Center in front of Room 235. Go to the main desk for information. University Club. It just south of the **University Memorial Center,** known on campus as "the UMC," at Euclid, just east of Broadway. The **Glenn Miller Lounge and Ballroom** are named after the CU jazz trombone player who popularized Big Band swing. A short walk to the northeast is **Norlin Library,** (303-492-8705) with more than 10 million books, periodicals, manuscripts, government publications, and more—the biggest such collection in the state. CU-Boulder's public art gallery is in the **Sibell-Wolle Fine Arts Building** (303-492-8300). **The Colorado Centennial Foucault Pendulum** (303-492-6952) is at Duane Physical Laboratory, inside Gamow Tower, just south of Gate 2 of Folsom Field. It might seem that the 40-meter pendulum changes direction during the day, but it actually stays steady while the earth rotates underneath it. (At the equator, it would swing the same direction all the time.)

The domed **Fiske Planetarium** on Regent Drive is a campus landmark housing a great theater for star shows and featuring one of the finest stargazing machines in the world. Scientists use it to turn the celestial skies back so that they can compare ancient ruins to an ancient sky. Often, they discover important building features align with star patterns that occurred long ago. Regular visitors can enjoy laser light shows and talks—fun in those leaned-back chairs that coddle your neck while you're staring upward. Star shows are normally scheduled on Friday evenings and some Tuesdays and Saturdays. Adult admission is $4, and children and seniors pay $3 for the evening shows; the fee includes admission to the adjacent **Sommers-Bausch Observatory** afterwards, weather permitting. You can get recorded information on the current week's shows by calling (303) 492-5001. For more detailed information, call (303) 492-5002. At the observatory, the real sky, not a planetarium show, is occasionally open for public viewing. Astronomy students man the telescopes during a special heavenly show, like a spectacular comet, meteor shower, or eclipse; but in recent years, clouds have obscured the most heralded events. Still, you can arrange to visit the observatory if you call ahead, (303) 492-5002.

The **Herbarium** (303-492-3216) houses nearly a half-million dried plant specimens from Colorado and around the world. It is located in the Claire Small building and is open to the public from 9 A.M. to 5 P.M. Monday through Thursday, and 9 A.M. to 3 P.M. on Friday. Hours are curtailed over the summer break.

The **Heritage Center,** a CU-Boulder museum (303-492-6329), is in Old Main, which housed the whole university from 1876 through 1884. This authentic Victorian landmark has been renovated, and the beautiful chapel is an especially cozy area for small performances. The Heritage Center's top floor is noteworthy for its "Space Room" honoring CU-Boulder's 13 astronauts, and for its sensational collection of sports memorabilia. The distinguished alumni gallery in the center includes retired Supreme Court Justice Byron White, Miss America 1958 Marilyn Van Derbur-Atler, Robert Redford (granted an honorary degree), *M*A*S*H* actor Larry Linville, and the 1989 Nobel Prize won by CU-Boulder chemist Tom Cech. An architectural gallery shows the original models for CU, showing its rural Italian design. Hours are 10 A.M. to 4 P.M. Monday through Friday, and 10 A.M. to 2

P.M. on Saturday. Special tours can be arranged, and it's open before and after home football games. Admission is free.

University of Colorado Museum, at Broadway and 15th Street in the Henderson Building (303–492–6892) displays dinosaur fossils that include a triceratops head and a pterodactyl, taxidermy specimens and touchable items for kids, including a sea turtle shell you can try on for size. Established in 1902, the museum has grown to include a diversity of displays, notably in paleontology, anthropology, and botany. Seasonal programs include a "Museum in the Dark" show for kids just before Halloween, and the museum hosts traveling exhibits as. It is open 9 A.M. to 5 P.M. weekdays, 9 A.M. to 4 P.M. Saturday, and 10 A.M. to 4 P.M. Sunday. There are occasionally events that interfere with public hours, so call ahead. Admission is free.

For academic information about CU-Boulder, check the chapter on Boulder Child Care and Education.

More Museums, Historic Buildings, and Special Places

The Arnett-Fullen House
646 Pearl St., Boulder
(303) 444–5192

This fanciful Victorian landmark is a few blocks west of the Pearl Street Mall. Historic Boulder, a nonprofit group based here, sells a walking-tour guidebook and conducts regular summer walking tours. These inexpensive tours include Pearl Street, the Chautauqua Park area, University Hill, and the Whittier and Mapleton Hill neighborhoods. (See our Neighborhoods and Nearby Communities chapter for schedules and rates.) You may also request custom tours, including CU's Norlin Quadrangle. This group also organizes a Christmas house tour and a spring tour of fine local homes in various neighborhoods.

The Arnett-Fullen House is one of the most extreme forms of Gothic gingerbread around, its flamboyance befitting its original owner. Will Arnett was a true 19th-century character. He used $10 gold coins for buttons, built his dream house for twice the $2,000 cost of an average home in those days, and died in 1900 while prospecting for gold in Alaska. No wonder his 1877 turreted Pearl Street home is ornate. Arnett also loved his cast-iron fence, which he had shipped from Pittsburgh for $2,000, a fortune back then. Historic Boulder bought the home in 1993 for $329,000. The first floor of the house is open for viewing from 8:30 A.M. to 4 P.M. weekdays. If you drop in, be sure to notice the walnut-inlaid spiral staircase.

After much wrangling, Historic Boulder bought the garden just west of the Arnett-Fullen House in 1996. Volunteers here restored it to reflect its true Victorian splendor.

Boulder County Fairgrounds
9595 Nelson Rd., Longmont
(303) 441–3927

Anytime you visit, something's happening at the fair. This big, big fairground hosts antiques and craft shows, barrel racing (for non-cowboys, that means racing horses in hairpin turns around barrels), national dog shows, bridge tournaments, circuses, motorcycle shows... the list goes on. Some events attract more than 100,000, and some are small. To reach the fairgrounds, head north to Longmont on Colo. 119. Turn left at Hover Road, whose intersection is marked with big stoplights. Go north on Hover past the Twin Peaks shopping mall to Nelson Road. The fairground is on your right. Call for an event schedule.

Boulder Museum of Contemporary Art
1750 13th St., Boulder
(303) 443–2122

This not-for-profit museum has three exhibition spaces for rotating shows as well as performing arts and mixed media space. Local, national, and international artists and photographers have shown at BMoCA. In the past the museum hosted a very successful outdoor cinema program that attracted many first-time museumgoers. The small museum is open Tuesday through Saturday from 11 A.M. to 5 P.M., and Sunday from noon to 5 P.M. Admission is $4.

Boulder Museum of History
1206 Euclid Ave., Boulder
(303) 449-3464

The three-story, blond-brick Harbeck-Bergheim house, home of the Boulder Museum of History, was built by a New York merchant in 1899 as a summer home. Its most renowned feature is a spectacular 9-foot-tall Tiffany stained-glass window. The museum is an eclectic grandma's attic–type showcase of Boulder County history. Artifacts show how mining, ranching, and everyday life affected Boulder. A costume gallery, one of the largest collections in the state, is on the second floor. The museum and gift shop are open 10 A.M. to 6 P.M. Tuesday through Saturday, and noon to 4 P.M. weekends. Admission is $4 for adults and $2 for children, seniors, and students.

Callahan House
312 Terry St., Longmont
(303) 776-5191

In the early 1900s, a Longmont businessman named T. M. Callahan hired an unemployed Longmont butcher who had gone bankrupt because he refused to pay off the hotel chef with a weekly bottle of bourbon. That butcher, J. C. Penney, went to work for Callahan's chain of "Golden Rule" notion stores, and the Wyoming Golden Rule he and Callahan started became the first store in the Penney chain.

The Callahan home was presented to the city of Longmont in 1938. It is now used for meetings, weddings, showers, receptions, dinners, and other social events. The interior is opulently Victorian, with pink tones, ornately carved wood, swirly plaster moldings, and exquisite light fixtures.

The Victorian (1899) Harbeck-Bergheim mansion is home to the Boulder Museum of History, with exhibits ranging from a proper Victorian parlor to an overview of the scientific advances of the 1930s.
PHOTO: LINDA CORNETT

Callahan House is home to the St. Vrain Historical Society (303–776–1870) the Longmont equivalent to Historic Boulder. The society provides brochures for self-guided tours. These are available at the Longmont Museum or the carriage house behind the Callahan House. Group guided tours can be arranged by appointment. Call ahead for reservations and fees. Terry Street, by the way, is just west of Longmont's Old Main downtown.

Collage Children's Museum
2065 30th St., Boulder
(303) 440–9894

The museum's philosophy is: "I hear, I forget; I see, I remember; I touch, I understand." Therefore, dancing, art, and play are major parts of a visit to this nonprofit hands-on museum, which features changing exhibits and also sponsors community events for children. Past exhibits include *Telling Tales,* which featured 40 original, framed children's book illustrations. A hands-on project called *Art Express* encouraged children to demonstrate their creativity by decorating barrels for Boulder's annual holiday food drive. The museum is open Monday, 10 A.M. to 5 P.M., Wednesday, 2 P.M. to 5 P.M., Thursday, Friday, and Saturday 10 A.M. to 5 P.M.; and Sunday 1 to 5 P.M.; there are extended summer hours. Collage is closed on Tuesday. Story hour is 3:30 to 4:30 P.M. on Wednesdays. Admission is $3.50 per person; $12 per family; and free for members and children younger than 2.

The Leanin' Tree Museum of Western Art
6055 Longbow Dr., Boulder
(303) 530–1442

Landscape paintings, bronze sculptures, and other original art make up one of the nation's largest privately owned Western art collections. The artwork, primarily post–Russell and Remington, are available as a result of Leanin' Tree founder Ed Trumble's 40-year friendship with Western artists. The growing collection keeps expanding into the Leanin' Tree greeting card company's work space.

Since it opened in 1974, the museum has welcomed more than a quarter-million visitors. The gift shop sells greeting cards, framed art, and T-shirts produced at Leanin' Tree. To reach the museum, take the Diagonal Highway (Colo. 119) north to 63rd Street. Turn right on Longbow Drive. The company and museum are the third building on the right. The museum is open 8 A.M. to 4:30 P.M. Monday through Friday and 10 A.M. to 4 P.M. Saturday and Sunday. Admission is free.

Carnegie Branch Library for Local History
1125 Pine St., Boulder
(303) 441–3110

This small, stately marble-columned building was Boulder's original library. Its original interior has been restored and contains local historic materials including books, diaries, oral histories, tapes, genealogical papers, 200,000 photographs, 700,000 documents, and various materials donated by the Boulder Historical Society. If you are researching your house or property, this is the best place to start. Hours are 1 to 9 P.M. Monday, 11 A.M. to 5 P.M. Tuesday and Thursday through Saturday, and extended hours from 9 A.M. to 5 P.M. on Wednesday. Admission is free.

Dougherty Antique Museum
8306 N. 107th St., Longmont
(303) 776–2520

The late Ray Dougherty didn't realize what he was starting when, as a teenager, he bought a reed organ. His wife, Dorothy Dougherty, says the hobby of collecting antique cars, farm equipment, and musical instruments just grew and grew (there's also a stagecoach). The antique autos have starred in many parades. That doesn't happen much anymore, because few have the knack for driving them. After all, you don't just turn the key when a car has a steam engine or needs a hand crank.

A mile south of Longmont on U.S. Highway 287 at the family farm, this exhibit is open from 10 A.M. to 4 P.M. Friday, Saturday, and Sunday from early June

The Carnegie Branch Library for Local History was Boulder's original library. PHOTO: ROZ BROWN

through Labor Day. Admission is $4 for adults, $3 for ages 7 to 12, and free for kids 6 and younger. Large groups are welcome if they call ahead.

Flagstaff Nature Center
Flagstaff Mountain Summit, Boulder
(720) 564-2000

The small log cabin atop Flagstaff Mountain contains interpretive exhibits on Front Range ecology. Its rustic log appearance remains, but the new environmentally sensitive building will have room for more displays and an increased staff. Call the Chautauqua Ranger Cottage at the listed phone number for details on new hours and expanded facilities. Nearby is the landmark Flagstaff Amphitheater, built by the Civilian Conservation Corps, and still the site of evening ranger presentations and, often, weddings. The area affords excellent views of the Boulder Valley and beyond.

To reach the center, follow Baseline Road to Flagstaff Road. The road leading to the large parking lot is well marked and to the right.

Lafayette Miner's Museum
108 E. Simpson St., Lafayette
(303) 666-6686, (303) 665-7030

This refurbished 1890s coal miner's home was moved into town during the 1910 coal strike. The six-room house, maintained by the Louisville Historical Society, displays clothing, tools and other mining equipment and household items of the time. Hours are 2 to 4 P.M. Thursday and Saturday and by appointment. Admission is free.

Longmont Museum
375 Kimbark St., Longmont
(303) 651-8374

This permanent exhibit has earned a national historic award for its Native American beaded buckskin dresses and flint arrows. The museum also displays equipment similar to that used by Major Stephen Long, the namesake of both Longs Peak and Longmont, and his party, who explored the area in the 1820s for the Army. Farming history and large-scale reproductions of early buildings are also on display here. Kidspace includes dress-up, arts and sciences and bubble-blowing. The museum is open 9 A.M. to 5 P.M. Monday through Friday; 10 A.M. to 4 P.M. Saturdays. On Monday, Wednesday and Friday mornings, 9 to 11:30 A.M., and afternoons from 12:30 to 2 P.M. there are staff-supervised discovery programs for children ages two to six. There are extended summer hours. Discovery programs are not available during summer months. Admission is free.

Louisville Historical Museum
1001 Main St., Louisville
(303) 665–9048

Coal mining gave birth to Louisville, and artifacts from the town's early days plus household and personal items fill this small museum. Hours are 10 A.M. to 3 P.M. Tuesday through Thursday, and the first Saturday of each month or by appointment. Admission is free.

Lyons Redstone Museum
340 High St., Lyons
(303) 823–5271

Take a scenic drive from Boulder north to Lyons the town whose sandstone quarries have yielded so much of the building material you see at the University of Colorado and elsewhere in Boulder County. This restored 1881 schoolhouse features displays on the town's history. Hours are 9:30 A.M. to 4:30 P.M. Monday through Saturday; 12:30 to 4:30 P.M. Sunday. Admission is free, but donations are welcome. This museum closes during the winter months.

Old Mill Park
237 Pratt St., Longmont
(303) 776–1870

The oldest log cabin in Boulder County is situated in a privately owned, tree-lined park. A real mill wheel turns at the pond. The park can be reserved through the St. Vrain Historical Society for weddings and meetings. Old Mill Park is open daily to the public for free between 8 A.M. and dusk, except during private events. Call ahead if you want a tour of the furnished interiors.

Tower of Compassion
Missouri St. and S. Pratt Pkwy., Longmont
No phone

This 60-foot-tall pagoda was donated to the city in 1972 by the Kanemoto family, who settled in Longmont in the early 1900s to work in sugar-beet fields. Their family farm later was developed as residences and this city park. The tower was inspired by a family visit to Japan and the Kanemoto's gratitude to the people of Longmont. Its five levels represent love, empathy, understanding, gratitude, and giving selflessly of oneself—all elements of true compassion.

Business and Science Attractions

Celestial Seasonings Tour
4600 Sleepytime Dr., Boulder
(303) 530–5300

Your sinuses will clear as soon as you take a whiff of the 5,000 bales of mint in Celestial Seasoning's peppermint isolation room. Each year, 50,000 people enjoy a 45-minute tour of the nation's largest manufacturer of specialty and herb teas. The tour includes an assembly line where tea gets packed in those pretty little boxes, and there are taste-testing opportunities. Employees' children create safety posters, and the walls are festooned with sayings from the tea boxes. This is a New Age business to its very bones, now with a sleek all-business overlay that belies its counterculture origins in Boulder's haute hippie era.

Free tours are offered Monday through Saturday daily every hour from 10 A.M. to 3 P.M., and on Sunday from 11 A.M. to 3 P.M.. Arrive early to get tickets as tours are given on a first come, first served basis. Children must be 5 or older to go on the factory portion of the tour. Groups of eight or more must make reservations. You can also visit the Tea Shop and Emporium, the herb garden and lunchtime cafe whether or not you take the tour. Shop hours are 9 A.M. to 5 P.M. Monday through Saturday and 11 A.M. to 4 P.M. Sunday. To reach the plant, take the Longmont Diagonal Highway (Colo. 119) to Jay Road. Turn right (east), go a mile to Spine Road, turn left, and continue a half-mile to Sleepytime Drive and Celestial Seasonings. Admission is free.

Eco-Cycle
5030 Pearl St., Boulder
(303) 444-6634

It would be unromantic as well as technically incorrect to describe this as a "trip to the dump," but that's virtually what it is. It is enlightening to see what happens to your recyclables after they leave the curb. Kids love this big, noisy, impressive operation with a magnetic separator, which draws out the steel and leaves aluminum and other nonferrous materials behind. Eco-Cycle is one of the nation's oldest, and still largest, nonprofit recycling companies. Its many honors include a national Excellence Award from the National Recycling Coalition for leadership and environmental protection. After years of indecision, money-woes and the usual political wrangling, Eco-Cycle moved to a newly built facility east of Boulder. Tours, while free, were temporarily discontinued until the new facility is ready for its public debut. Call Eco-Cycle for more information. Tours are offered Tuesday through Friday from 9:30 A.M. to 3:30 P.M. Children must be 10 years or older to participate in the tour. Admission is free.

Insiders' Tip

Get your sinuses cleared in a millisecond by the 5,000 bales of mint in Celestial Seasonings' peppermint isolation room. The free company tour includes a taste test of new teas.

Federal Aviation Administration Tours
2211 17th Ave., Longmont
(303) 651-4315

More than 90 air-traffic controllers watch approximately 40 radarscopes that show the weather and planes moving across nine states. These folks can tell any plane in their area to change routes, altitude and speed because of traffic-on-high or weather. Tours of the facility have been scaled-back in recent years due to personnel cuts within the FAA, so call ahead for an appointment.

Long's Iris Gardens
3240 Broadway, Boulder
(303) 442-2353

For nearly a century, the Long family has chugged an old tractor out to tend their iris fields. The 2,000 varieties range from pretty mongrels to prize-winning queens. You can go to the big yellow farmhouse in early May to mid-June, depending on the year's weather, to buy irises—at 2115 13th Street, just north of the mall or you can pick your own plants. (The Longs will provide supplies so you can dig your own iris clumps.) The delicate scents and the rows of colorful, fluttering petals can make any day better. Digging-season hours are generally 9 A.M. to 5 P.M. daily. An iris clump costs less than $5. The farm is close to town, on Broadway, just south of Iris Avenue (guess how that street got its name). Catalogs come out in April.

Insiders' Tip

Some of Boulder's most
popular stores have
become attractions in
their own right. Boul-
derites often take
out-of-towners to
McGuckin Hardware, The
Peppercorn, and other
distinctive retail
establishments just for
the fun of it. See our
Shopping chapter for
more information.

National Institute of Standards and Technology
325 Broadway, Boulder
(303) 497–1000

Bring your wristwatch. This 90-minute guided tour takes visitors to the nation's timekeeper, the atomic clock. The "leap second" gets added here at this very clock. The Solar Forecasting Center is where visitors can watch researchers study the sun; this is the nation's warning system for solar flares. The tour also includes a demonstration in cryogenics, the study of how extremely low temperatures (–320 degrees F) affect various materials. Guided tours are offered every day at noon.

This is a period building, by the way. Built in the 1950s, it has a crew-cut look, from the sparkling pink travertine walls to the shiny terrazzo floors. The building is open 8 A.M. to 5 P.M. Monday through Friday. Admission is free.

National Oceanic and Atmospheric Administration/David Skaggs Research Center
325 Broadway, Boulder
(303) 497–3333 for tour information

Boulder is nowhere near the beach, but it's a center for incredibly sophisticated weather forecasting and oceanic research, thanks to high-powered scientists and their computers that study world weather. Until March of 1999 scientists were spread out over a half-dozen sites in Boulder. The new $60 million building has nearly 400,000-square feet and 1,000 employees. A real coup was securing the National Weather Service, which relocated to Boulder after 100 years in Denver. The National Institute of Standards and Technology is also on this campus. There are exhibits in the lobby, guided tours, school tours, and a school classroom. Summer tours have been held on Tuesday afternoons at 1 P.M.; the tour schedule typically changes after Labor Day. Call the tour information number for a current schedule.

Kidstuff

Attractions
Classes
Libraries
Museums
Parks
Sports
Summer Camps

"I'm b-o-o-r-r-e-d!!!"

If you have kids, it's an all-too-familiar refrain. But what to do?

Here are ideas for when you get a little bored with your children's boredom. (Also check the chapters on Boulder Festivals and Annual Events, Attractions, and Daytrips.)

Attractions

As You Wish
1938 Pearl St., Boulder
(303) 413–9300

Boulder doesn't have many rainy afternoons, but this a sure bet if you find yourself with a little time on your hands and you want to help your children express their creativity. Kids can pick from ready-to-be-painted pottery in sizes ranging from small enough to hold in your hand to too large to carry. Most children want to paint a miniature animal or a plate they can use for a "personalized dining experience" once they get it home. The pottery is fired after it's painted, meaning it will be a week before the finished piece is available for pickup.

Butterfly Pavilion & Insect Center
6252 W. 104th Ave., Westminster
(303) 469–5441

No matter how many times children visit, they never tire of the Butterfly Pavilion. After touring the display of living insects, visitors enter a greenhouse that's the home of exotic tropical butterflies. The large and colorful butterflies often land on children, producing squeals of delight and a charming sense of awe. In one corner you can watch the last two stages of metamorphosis as butterflies emerge from their chrysalidschrysalides. A gift shop and cafeteria are adjacent to the Pavilion. Admission is $6.95 for adults, $4.95 for seniors, and $3.95 for children.

Up to two children ages 3 and under are admitted free with a paying adult. The Pavilion is open every day from 9 A.M. to 5 P.M. This unique space has proven so popular, a new and improved facility will open on the opposite side of 104th Avenue in 2003. It will include a larger butterfly atrium space and more classrooms.

CU Wizards!
Various locations, CU Campus
(303) 492–6952

Typically on the last Saturday of the month, September through June, the University of Colorado presents its CU Wizards! program. Wizards (actually, there are 10 Mr. and Ms. Wizards) give free morning lectures that pack science lecture halls with laughing, learning kids. This is a great, informal introduction to astronomy, chemistry, biology, and physics for students in grades 5 through 9. Each program lasts about an hour and includes several lively demonstration experiments. The shows begin at 9:30 A.M.

Gateway Park Fun Center
4800 28th St., Boulder
(303) 442–4386

Remodeled and refurbished, the center now has a new building for the video arcade and snack bar; a revamped go-cart area, and driving range; renovated miniature golf courses, and batting cages; and a roller hockey rink and a human maze. Gateway also recently added a new play area for children 7 and younger, including

181

kiddie carts and a kiddie train. There's a fee for each activity, with a discount for children under 7.

Gymboree
3105 28th St., Boulder
(303) 546-0081

For little tykes only, this is a great place for toddlers to play, and the equipment is designed to keep them busy enough that parents have time to chat and possibly meet other new parents. There are regular free introductory sessions. Eight-week sessions are $92, or you can pay by the week.

Laser Storm
700 Ken Pratt Blvd., Longmont
(303) 651-6422

Laser Storm offers laser tag, video games, and other high-tech diversions. Birthday parties are part of the regular schedule, so call ahead to avoid disappointment. If you plan to play laser tag, dress in black for the most enjoyment. Admission is $4.50 per person.

Lois Lafond and the Rockadiles
Boulder
(303) 444-7095

This group packs young fans in wherever they play, entertaining their audiences with funky, high-quality songs with kid-pleasing lyrics. They appear at such events as Halloween parades in the metro area, the Taste of Colorado in Denver, Boulder's Out to Lunch series, and others. Watch for them!

Munson's Family Farm
75th St. and Valmont Rd., Boulder
(303) 443-5330

Before frost hits, you and the kids can tromp into the field and twist a pumpkin off the vine. Choose amongst giants and jack-o'-lantern pumpkins, pie pumpkins, and winter squash, including Delicata, a sweet, buttery-tasting winter squash that the Munsons say they've made famous. Munson's farm stand at this corner is a great place to let the kids help you buy produce all summer.

Pearl Street Mall
On Pearl St. from 11th to 15th Sts., Boulder
(303) 441-4000

The gravel-lined pits and small climb-upon boulders (just west of the courthouse) make the Pearl Street Mall as popular a playground for children as it is for adults. Permanent climbing sculptures in the 14th Street block feature a snail, beaver, and bunny rabbit that never fail to delight toddlers. The well-maintained flower gardens are a visual delight.

Roll-O-Rena
1201 S. Sunset St., Longmont
(303) 651-3720

At this rink they still do the hokey-pokey and schedule open skate and family skate sessions. It's great fun for a birthday party, although parents will probably remember how to skate just about the time the kids get tired. Refreshments are available and the music is lively. Admission is $3 to $5.25, depending on the day and time.

Classes

Boulder Parks and Recreation Program
5660 Sioux Dr., Boulder
(303) 413-7270

This is the largest program in the city, with children's classes in everything from arts and crafts to yoga. They include one-day workshops, multi-week sessions, and options in between. Gymnastics, dancing, and swimming are popular. Or try child/parent pottery classes given at the city's Pottery Lab. A new brochure is published four times a year and is available free at all three of the recreation centers. Don't dawdle with the registration—many of these classes are extremely popular and fill up quickly.

Boulder Rock Club
2829 Mapleton St., Boulder
(303) 447-2804

Great practice for eventually scaling the Flatirons, this club has an indoor rock-climbing wall and a variety of children's programs. They start with RockKids—10 hours of climbing time for children ages 5 to 9 (available individually or for four lessons). Youth Certification (ages 12 to 17) and Junior Team (ages 10 to 19) programs have multi-day sessions at various levels.

Boulder Suzuki Strings
Boulder
(303) 499–2807

This group specializes in string instrument instruction for kids from age 4 through high school. Boulder Suzuki Strings offers private and group lessons, note reading, performances, recitals, and workshops.

The Cooking School of the Rockies
Broadway and Table Mesa Dr., Boulder
(303) 494–7988

A parent/child Gingerbread House Baking Class is held on four Sundays during November and December. There is also a Cookies 'n Kids class on a Saturday in early December.

Dance West
1637 Pearl St., Boulder
(303) 545–2252

Dance West offers ballet, jazz, African, hip-hop, techno tap, Latin, modern, and family dancing for youngsters of all ages. There are summer camps and lots of great discount rates.

Flatirons Martial Arts
4770 Pearl St., Boulder
(303) 442–4311

Flatirons Martial Arts specializes in teaching youngsters age 5 and up the skills and self-discipline of karate and other martial arts. The motto here is "the art of peaceful confidence."

Northern Colorado Fencers
1949 33rd St., Boulder
(303) 443–6557

Northern Colorado Fencers boasts nationally and internationally ranked fencers who give high-quality instruction

The Peanut Butter Players theater company features kids ages 5 to 18. PHOTO: ROZ BROWN

to children; lessons include respect for the rules and safety.

The Peanut Butter Players
2475 Mapleton Ave., Boulder
(303) 786–8727

Voted the "Best of Boulder in Kids' Entertainment" by *Daily Camera* readers, this children as theater company delights audiences with musicals several times a year. For a modest fee you can enroll your child, but be prepared for an extensive rehearsal schedule—the director expects a professional performance and makes kids toe the line. Regardless of his or her experience, every child gets a speaking part, even if it's only one line. Summer programs are on a grand scale.

The Studio for Performing Arts
2010 14th St., Boulder
(303) 442–1908

The Studio for Performing Arts offers classes in dance, acting, music, directing, and filmmaking. There are after-school programs, and students put on an annual summer musical performance. Students have performed *Music Man, Into the Woods,* and *Darn Yankees.*

Libraries

Boulder Public Library—Main Branch
1000 Canyon Blvd. at Ninth St., between Canyon Blvd. and Arapahoe St., Boulder
(303) 441–3100

Most Boulder-area libraries offer abundant reading nooks, computers, and storytelling times. This is the city's crown jewel, an eye-popper with an outstanding selection of books, publications, videos, and other materials. The espresso shop on the second floor offers a view of the creek that is stunning anytime of year. The main library is open 9 A.M. to 9 P.M., Monday through Thursday; 9 A.M. to 6 P.M., Friday and Saturday; and from noon to 6 P.M. on Sunday.

The Meadows Branch Library, which serves residents of southeast Boulder, has a nice children's section.
PHOTO: ROZ BROWN

Boulder Public Library—George Reynolds Branch
3595 Table Mesa Dr., Boulder
(303) 441-3120

A branch library serving south Boulder, it offers easy access and an extensive video- and audio-tape section. It's open from 9 A.M. to 9 P.M. Monday through Thursday; 9 A.M. to 6 P.M. on Friday and Saturday; and from 1 to 5 P.M. on Sunday.

Boulder Public Library—Meadows Branch
4800 Baseline Rd. at Foothills Pkwy., Boulder
(303) 441-4390

This is the newest branch library, serving residents who live east of downtown. Adjacent to the Meadows Shopping Center, it features a nice children's section, and with fewer patrons the staff always has time to help. The library is open from 9 A.M. to 9 P.M., Monday through Thursday; 9 A.M. to 6 P.M., Friday and Saturday; and from 1 to 5 P.M. on Sunday.

Lafayette Public Library
775 W. Baseline Rd., Lafayette
(303) 665-5200

This new and contemporary 30,000-square-foot library opened in October 1997 and is 10 times the size of the original library. The large and knowledgeable staff can help you access books, audio books, computer programs, and the Internet. Lafayette's library is open Monday through Thursday, 10 A.M. to 9 P.M.; Friday and Saturday, 10 A.M. to 5 P.M.; and on Sunday from 1 to 5 P.M.

Longmont Public Library
409 Fourth Ave., Longmont
(303) 651-8470

Longmont's library was built in 1993 on the site of the original Carnegie Library. The new library contains a children's section and a separate teen section. There is a large CD, video-, and audio-tape section; periodicals and easy parking are other pluses. This library is open Monday through Thursday, 10 A.M. to 9 P.M.; Friday and Saturday, 9 A.M. to 5 P.M.; and

Sunday, 1 to 5 P.M. The library alters its hours during the summer months.

Louisville Public Library
950 Spruce St., Louisville
(303) 666-6037

Louisville's library has a long history, dating back to 1923, when the Chinook Campfire Girls made it their project to collect books that would eventually be housed in the town's library. It wasn't until 1980 that the library had a permanent home, and just 10 years later the collection moved again. It hasn't seemed to bother residents, who visit so often the library has one of the highest circulation statistics for a library of its size in the state. There are children's and young adult sections plus the usual audio and visual offerings. The library is open Monday through Thursday, 10 A.M. to 8 P.M.; Friday and Saturday, 10 A.M. to 6 P.M.; and Sunday from 1 P.M. to 5 P.M.

Museums

Boulder Collage Children's Museum
2065 30th St., Boulder
(303) 440-9894

The motto here is, "I hear, I forget; I see, I remember; I touch, I understand." Collage is a hands-on, interactive museum for children 9 months to 9 years old. Past exhibits featured an interactive computer, dancing with colored shadows, and the "Dragons of the Dump," with "recycled" dragons created by kids. If you're not a member there's a nominal admission fee. Collage is open Monday and Wednesday through Saturday, 10 A.M. to 5 P.M.; Sunday from 1 P.M. to 5 P.M. It is closed on Tuesday.

Denver Children's Museum
2121 Children's Museum Dr. (just off I-25), Denver
(303) 433-7433

If you're up for a drive or heading in that direction anyway, this is the biggest, most comprehensive children's museum around.

It features a stunning variety of laboratories, interactive displays, a miniature grocery store where youngsters can shop or act as cashiers, and a terrific toddler area. You'll find this museum open from Tuesday through Friday, 9 A.M. to 4 P.M., and from 10 A.M. to 5 P.M. on Saturday and Sunday. Admission is $3.50 for ages 1 to 2; $6.50 for ages 3 to 59; and $3.50 for those 60 and older.

KIDSPACE at the Longmont Museum
375 Kimbark St., Longmont
(303) 651–8374

This museum specializes in self-structured, hands-on science, history, and art activities. Permanent features are a puppet area, pioneer dress-up theater, and reading area; rotating activities include a water table, an electronic board, and "Tub-O'Bubbles," where kids can create giant soap bubbles with wands. There is no admission fee, but donations are always appreciated. It is open Monday through Friday, 9 A.M. to 5 P.M., and Saturday from 10 A.M. to 4 P.M. The museum is closed on Sundays and holidays. A nominal fee is charged for KIDSPACE special events.

University of Colorado Museum
Broadway and 15th St., Boulder
(303) 492–6892

The CU museum has a kids' corner and numerous kids' activities and special events. This place is definitely one of Boulder's best-kept secrets. Find the real triceratops head, and try on the sea-turtle shell. This museum is open from 9 A.M. to 5 P.M. Monday through Friday; Saturday from 9 A.M. to 4 P.M.; and Sunday from 10 A.M. to 4 P.M. Admission is free.

WOW! (World of Wonder) Children's Museum
1075 South Boulder Rd., Louisville
(303) 604–2424

Call it a positive feature of the population growth in eastern Boulder County—a new children's museum! WOW is designed for toddlers and school-age children and their families. It offers a variety of interactive and informative educational and cre-

ative exhibits and programs that stimulate learning. A very clever pirate ship, for instance, turns out to be a dress-up room. Opened in 1996, the museum features both permanent and traveling exhibits. There are three party rooms, a snack area, and a gift shop. This museum is open from 9 A.M. to 5 P.M. Monday through Friday; 10 A.M. to 6 P.M. Saturday; and on Sunday from noon until 4 P.M. Parents are admitted free, while children pay $6 for all-day admission. There are also frequent-visitor cards, memberships, and group rates.

Parks

Cave Park (Arapahoe Ridge Park)
1220 Eisenhower Dr., Boulder
(303) 413–7200

Cave Park, also known as Arapahoe Ridge Park, offers the best and most creative array of playground equipment around. It's next door to Eisenhower Elementary-but large enough for everyone.

Chautauqua Park
Ninth St. and Baseline Rd., Boulder
(303) 441–3440

Chautauqua Park boasts a great expanse of lawn, away from traffic, as well as recently installed playground equipment, including a child-size playhouse. The huge grassy area is great for kids and Frisbee-chasing dogs. In summer months the Chautauqua Dining Hall is the perfect place to grab a bite to eat; it has convenient restrooms, too.

Scott Carpenter Park
30th and Arapahoe Sts., Boulder
(303) 441–3427

Rated "Boulder's Best Park" by *Daily Camera* readers, this park was named after a local astronaut and features a climbing apparatus resembling a rocket ship. The playground was completely refurbished in 1998 with new equipment that adheres to the "space" theme. The Boulder Skatepark is also here. Open to kids 8 years old and older, it lets skateboarders test their skills

Kids can climb a rocket ship at Scott Carpenter Park. PHOTO: DAILY CAMERA/K.SCHULENBERG

on the 10-foot vertical half-pipe, or play it safe on the 6-foot or 4-foot mini-ramps and street course. Admission is free; helmets and pads are required and can be rented for a small fee. In winter, the park is Boulder's most popular sledding area. After a winter storm, the sledding hill is small enough to be manageable but big enough to be exciting.

Insiders' Tip

Grab some wheels and head to the Boulder Creek Path. Don't have wheels? In-line skates or bikes can be rented at many bike shops.

Sports

Biking

If your child lacks a bike, isn't it time to buy one? "Pl-e-a-s-e? Pretty please?" The bike trails in Boulder are so wonderful, wheels can be the highlight of a child's vacation or life in Boulder. But make sure children wear helmets. In fact, set a good example and wear one yourself, and ride with the kids until you're sure they understand trail safety and bicycling rules. Although most riders are polite and considerate of children, paths can get crowded, and a few rude racers are ruthless.

Boulder Creek Path and its tributaries are perfect for bicycling and in-line skating (also see "Hiking"). Many places nearby rent in-line skates and bikes.

Boulder Bikesmith
2432 Arapahoe Ave., Boulder
(303) 443–1132

Should your child's two-wheeler "bite the dust" on Boulder's bikepath, head for this shop, adjacent to the Boulder Creek Path. Trained experts on staff can help with bike service, the sale of new or used bicycles, and, as a last resort, in-line skate rental.

University Bicycles
839 Pearl St., Boulder
(303) 444–4196

This is a great downtown location from which you can rent kids' bikes, bike trailers, tandem bikes, and trail-a-bikes, a new style of hybrid tandem with an adult-size bike in front and a kid-size one in the rear. One way or another, you can get the whole family on wheels.

Hiking

For more information on trails in the area, see our Sports chapter.

Boulder Creek Path
Broadway and Canyon Blvd., Boulder
(303) 441–3090

A stroll along the path—keeping mindful of fast-moving cyclists and in-line skaters, please—can take on exploratory aspects with small detours down the creek along the way, to the murky but well-intentioned trout-viewing windows near the Regal Harvest House Bridge, or to the duck-pond overlook between Ninth Street and the Justice Center. Freelance musicians might be playing in the park between Broadway and 13th Street. Be sure to read the interpretive signs along the way.

City Parks and Administration/Open Space and Mountain Parks
3198 Broadway, Boulder
(303) 413–7200 or (303) 441–4142;
(303) 441–3440 (Open Space)

After the paved Creek Path, a logical next step might be some of the area's easiest unpaved trails. Short-legged, short-burst-of-energy little hikers often do best with modest walks along relatively flat trails. From the Bobolink trailhead at Baseline and Cherryvale Roads, it's just a little more than .75-mile to the East Boulder Community Center, and about 1.3 miles to South Boulder Road. The Baseline-EBCC section features a series of interpretive signs on grasslands, wetlands, and river ecology.

The Teller Farm Trail runs 2.2 miles through a picturesque rural area between Arapahoe (the signed trailhead is off a dirt road between 75th and 95th Streets) and Valmont Road (the trailhead is near 95th Street). Partway along the trail is a small lake (fishing permitted). The nearby White Rocks Trail, whose trailhead is also near Valmont Road and 95th Street, is about 4 miles long, and its first stretch is really flat. A $7 map is available from the parks department.

With older children who have more stamina, the options multiply. Red Rocks is a good place to start. This short, steep trail, accessible from a well-marked trailhead at the mouth of Boulder Canyon, makes a suitable first challenge with some optional rock scrambling on top. Trails in the Boulder Mountain Parks; Walker Ranch, way up Flagstaff Road; the Rabbit Mountain open space near Lyons; Brainard Lake and the Indian Peaks Wilderness west of Ward; and Rocky Mountain National Park are among the abundant nearby options for various levels of stamina and interest. (See our Parks and Recreation chapter and our Rocky Mountain National Park overview.) If it's windy, a trail right against the foothills can provide some shelter from big gusts. If it's snowy, choose a flat one. If it's hot, find a creek with shade, or drive up to the mountains. Remember to watch little ones closely near any creeks with fast-moving waters.

Walden and Sawhill Ponds
75th St. between Jay St. and Valmont Rd., Boulder
(303) 441-3964
This is a beguiling 113-acre complex of ponds reclaimed from old gravel pits—an example of nature's ability to heal a scarred landscape. The ponds, with their aquatic vegetation and fish, have become an attractive habitat and breeding area for waterfowl, painted turtles, muskrats, and other fauna. Two miles of ultra-gentle trails, picnic areas, and fishing areas make these ponds a fine family destination.

Ice Skating

Aspen Lodge
6120 Colorado Hwy. 7, Estes Park
(970) 586-8133
During the winter this lodge offers outdoor ice skating from 8 A.M. to 9 P.M. The lodge charges $3 for both skating and skate rentals for adults and children.

CU Ice Arena and Skate Shop
CU campus, Broadway and College, Boulder
(303) 492-7255
CU-Boulder's indoor ice-skating rink is free to students and members, otherwise the cost is less than $5, plus $1 for skates. You must be a guest of a student or member to use this facility. Recreational skating hours vary from day to day.

Gold Lake Mountain Resort
3371 Gold Lake Rd., Ward
(303) 459-3544
At Gold Lake one-day packages include not only ice skating but also a brunch, use of the hot tubs, and the chance to do other winter sports including snowshoeing and cross-country skiing. Rental equipment is available. Packages start at $65.

Skiing

Eldora Mountain Resort
2861 Eldora Ski Rd., Nederland
(303) 440-8700
This resort is tailor-made for family skiing with easy and challenging downhill trails plus lots of ski and snowboarding instructors. This is an excellent learning environment for children. Lessons are available for kids 4 and older. In conjunction with the Mom's Monday, a series of

women-only classes on Monday afternoons, Little MAC (an acronym for Monday Afternoon Club) provides two-hour lessons and rental equipment for 4- to 6-year-olds. The Nordic Center is adjacent to the downhill ski areas. In addition to beautiful, wind-sheltered trails, it offers cross-country skiing lessons. Instructors set up the kids' lessons so everything's a game, and because there's so much movement, children tend to stay warmer than they do during downhill skiing.

Swimming and Sailing

Boulder Recreation Centers

At the East, North, and South Boulder Recreation Centers, adult city residents pay $5; senior citizens 60 and older pay $3; and children and teens under the age of 18 pay $2.25 per visit. Punch cards purchased in advance will reduce the fee for those who plan to visit regularly. There are also annual passes and a corporate pass program.

East Boulder Recreation Center
5660 Sioux Dr., Boulder
(303) 441-4400

The "Lazy River" is very popular with small children, and the tall water slide can surprise even the most adult adult. Lap lanes are also available. This center is open Monday through Thursday from 5:30 A.M. to 9:30 P.M.; Friday from 5:30 A.M. to 9 P.M.; Saturday from 7:30 A.M. to 7 P.M.; and Sunday from 8:30 A.M. to 8:30 P.M.

North Boulder Recreation Center
3170 Broadway, Boulder
(303) 413-7260

This is the city's oldest recreation facility. Its family swim on Sunday afternoon is inexpensive and often a lifesaver for parents or children who find themselves winter-weary and/or housebound. This center is open Monday through Thursday from 6 A.M. to 9 P.M.; Friday from 6 A.M. to 6:30 P.M.; Saturday from 6:30 A.M. to 5 P.M.; and Sunday from 8 A.M. to 5 P.M. The North Recreation Center started a new program in the fall of 1997 for kids 9 through 14. Called

"Boulder Nites," it allows kids to participate in a variety of activities from 7 to 11 P.M., after parents have registered their children and paid the $8 fee. The Center promises a safe, secure environment with a police officer on the premises. The popular program offers swimming, laser-tag games, blackout wallyball, alien art, dancing, swimming and diving contests, and other activities. Note: the North Center is closed until the spring of 2003 for extensive remodeling.

South Boulder Recreation Center
1360 Gillaspie Dr., Boulder
(303) 441-3448

The South Center was renovated in 1998 to include a new lap pool, new locker rooms, an improved weight room, and an elevator. Young runners can take several mostly traffic-free jogging routes from here. This center is open Monday through Thursday from 6 A.M. to 9:30 P.M.; Friday from 6 A.M. to 9 P.M.; Saturday from 6:30 A.M. to 5 P.M.; and Sunday from 8 A.M. to 9 P.M.

Boulder Reservoir
5100 N. 51st St., Boulder
(303) 441-3461 or (303) 441-3468

This is a summer-only magnet for families (see our Parks and Recreation Centers chapter). Highlights are a sand beach and rentals of non-powered watercraft including canoes, rowboats, paddleboats, and Sunfish. The reservoir is open from 6 A.M. until dusk for sailboarding, sailing, and waterskiing. Swimmers are admitted from 9:30 A.M. until 6:30 P.M. Daily admission at the reservoir is $5 for adults; $2.50 for kids 4 through 18; $2.75 for seniors;

Insiders' Tip
The local recreation centers, which are open to the public for a fee, have great swimming pools, "lazy rivers," and wading areas.

children under 4 get in free. Money-saving resident and nonresidents passes are available.

Broomfield Recreation Center
280 Lamar St., Broomfield
(303) 469–5351

With a six-lane pool and typical amenities, this outdoor aquatics park is a real summertime treat. It is open Monday and Wednesday 5:30 A.M. until 10 P.M., Tuesday and Thursday 8 A.M. to 10 P.M., Friday 5:30 A.M. to 7 P.M., Saturday 8 A.M. to 8 P.M., and Sunday from 6 A.M. until 8 P.M. Admission for adults is $3; seniors pay $2.50; kids are charged $2 per visit. Annual passes are available.

Lafayette Bob L. Burger Recreation Center
111 W. Baseline Rd., Lafayette
(303) 665–0469

This center has it all—a huge water slide, a "lazy river," and a children's pool. Even when their fingertips look like prunes and their lips are blue, children beg to stay "just a little longer." This center is open from 6 A.M. until 10 P.M., weekdays, 8 A.M. until 6 P.M. on Saturday, and 10 A.M. until 6 P.M. on

Sunday. The admission fee for adults is $4; seniors pay $2 as do children ages 3 to 12; the charge for kids 13 to 18 is $2.50.

Louisville Recreation Center
749 Main St., Louisville
(303) 666–7400

This center's six-lane pool allows adults to swim while kids frolic in the children's pool, which features an impressive water slide. Louisville's center is open Monday through Friday 6 A.M. to 10 P.M., Saturday 7 A.M. to 7 P.M., and Sunday from 9 A.M. until 8 P.M. Adults pay $5 per visit; seniors pay $2.75; kids ages 13 to 17 pay $3.50; and those under 14 pay $2.75.

Scott Carpenter Pool
30th and Arapahoe Sts., Boulder
(303) 441–3427

This is Boulder's largest public swimming pool, open in summer only, with three wide lap lanes, a 151-foot water slide, a snack bar, a toddler pool, and plenty of space to sunbathe. The pool is open for adult lap swimming from 11 A.M. to 1 P.M. daily. Open swim is from 1 P.M. to 5 P.M. weekdays, 1 P.M. to 6 P.M. on Saturday and

Centrally located Spruce Pool is a family favorite. PHOTO: ROZ BROWN

Sunday. Single-entry admission is $4.25 for adults; $2.50 for seniors 60 and older; and $2 for teens and children 18 and younger. A punch card or an annual pass will reduce the fee. Swimming lessons are offered weekday mornings.

Spruce Pool
2102 Spruce St., Boulder
(303) 441–3426
Boulder's oldest public swimming pool, this central Boulder gem was once called the Hygienic Swimming Pool. Open during summer months only, it has a colorful mural, water slide, and grassy sunbathing spot that make it a family favorite. The pool is open from 6 A.M. to 7 P.M. for adult lap swim. Open swim is from 1 P.M. to 5 P.M. weekdays and from 1 P.M. to 6 P.M. on Saturday and Sunday. Single-entry admission is $4.25 for adults; $2.50 for seniors 60 and older; and $2 for teens and children 18 and younger. A punch card or an annual pass will reduce the fee. Swimming lessons are offered weekday mornings.

Viele Lake
1360 Gillaspie Dr., Boulder
(303) 441–3448
Complete with canoes, paddleboats, and lots of Canada geese, this man-made lake is a central feature of this south Boulder neighborhood. For students who attend the nearby Fairview High School, it's a nice place to take a break. There's no swimming allowed.

Waneka Lake
1600 Carla Dr., Lafayette
(303) 665–0469
Lafayette's answer to the Boulder Reservoir, this lake is open Memorial Day to Labor Day. It has a great deal on canoe rentals, and a pretty area where the herons hang out. Canoe rental on weekdays during summer months is $3 but increases to $4 on weekends and holidays. The lake is typically open for boat rentals from 1 to 8 P.M. and from 10 A.M. until 7 P.M. on weekends and holidays. No swimming is allowed.

Team Sports

High school and college sports abound in Boulder, and pro teams are no farther away than Denver. See our Boulder Participatory, Spectator, and Professional Sports chapter for further information.

Boulder Junior Soccer
2400 Central Ave., Boulder
(303) 443–1618
Soccer is a great way for youngsters to learn cooperation and team spirit and for newcomers to make friends. This is the biggest program around, with spring and fall seasons for schoolchildren as young as kindergartners. Boulder Barrage is for strong older players.

YMCA
2850 Mapleton Ave., Boulder
(303) 442–2778
The "Y" has baseball programs in spring and summer; basketball in winter and spring; and soccer, volleyball, flag football, and in-line hockey in fall. Children are grouped according to age. Girls will find as many activities and as enthusiastic coaches as the boys.

Summer Camps

A week or more out of the house can go a long way toward relieving the tedium of a bored child's summer. Overnight camps, day camps, and camps that provide both options abound in the Boulder area. Camps are great for learning about everything from computers to archery, outdoor skills to swimming. Area newspapers publish special camp issues in spring.

Boulder Conservatory Theater
5001 E. Pennsylvania, Boulder
(303) 444–1885 or (303) 664–9064
The Boulder Conservatory Theater has offered two-week intensive summer theater programs for 18 years. Daily classes are offered in acting technique, Shakespeare, voice, speech and dialects, singing,

Boulder is a soccer town, and supportive parents share the excitement with their children every weekend during the summer and fall. PHOTO: LINDA CORNETT

dance, stage combat, and musical theater. The major conservatory is for students in high school, but there are also programs for students as young as five.

Boulder County Force
2769 Iris St., Ste. 115, Boulder
(303) 443–8877 or (303) 651–6036

It has been one of Boulder's premier soccer camps for more than 21 years. Force recently added an exclusive program for girls ages 6 through 9.

Boulder Parks and Recreation
5660 Sioux Dr., Boulder
(303) 441–4401

Boulder Parks and Recreation offers many day-camp-type options, from playground programs to a Teen Adventure Program with kayaking and overnight camping, plus programs for people with disabilities.

Boulder Valley Community School Program
805 Gillaspie Dr., Boulder
(303) 499–1125

Run by the school district, this program offers all kinds of classes at various locations around town. Past offerings have included basketball camps for boys and girls, and lessons in single-track mountain biking, and cartooning.

Colorado Mountain Ranch (Trojan Ranch)
10063 Gold Hill Rd., Boulder
(303) 442–4557

The Walkers' family-run mountain ranch, also known as Trojan Ranch, is more than 50 years old. The camp offers both week-long overnight sessions and day sessions, both featuring Western riding, swimming in a heated pool, Indian lore, archery, gymnastics, drama, and confidence-building outdoor adventures.

The Front Range Natural Science School
Thorne Ecological Institute, 5398 Manhattan
Circle, Boulder
(303) 499–3647

This children's environmental education program gets high marks for offering classes that include lots of outdoor explo-ration. Classes are offered year-round, but the summer program is the biggest.

Highlands Presbyterian Camp
P.O. Box 66, Allenspark, CO 80510
(303) 747–2888

This Christian camp in a mountain set-ting is open to campers of all faiths. Pop-ular with elementary and middle-school students, it offers co-ed and day camps for everyone from children entering first grade to senior citizens. Specialty camps include horse camps; music, art and drama camps; backpacking camps; and grandparent/grandchild camps. Tradi-tional camps feature horseback riding, mountain biking, archery, canoeing, crafts, hiking, and sports.

Mad Science Summer Camps
7100 W. Grandview Ave., Boulder
(303) 403–0432

Since 1996 students ages 6 to 12 have been entertained and educated with hands-on activities based on "mad sci-ence" daily themes. Concepts explored include vortex generators, cool chemical reactions, slippery slime, light shows, and more.   There are both half-day and full-day programs.

Peak Arts Academy
2590 Walnut St., Boulder
(303) 449–9291

The Academy is the official school of the Boulder Philharmonic and the Boulder Ballet. There are camps for music, theater, dance, and art for ages 3 through adult. Musical instrument camps focus on strings, piano, and winds. The Academy also offers campers the opportunity to work with the Colorado Shakespeare Fes-tival at Mary Rippon Theater on the CU campus.

Rainbow Valley Farm
10870 N. 49th St., Longmont
(303) 651–7222

Rainbow Valley is a low-key farm school where kids can help gather eggs and han-dle the sheep. It's quite a drive from Boul-der each day, but city kids have nothing but good things to say about the experi-ence.

Renaissance Adventure Quest Day Camp
At Calwood Ranch, Jameston
(303) 786–9216

These camps, which focus on active out-door Renaissance-theme theater games have been offered to children ages 6 to 16 since 1995. Participants are the heroes of a mythic quest to solve mysteries and rid-dles, brainstorm creative solutions to puzzling dilemmas, swashbuckle with foam swords, and negotiate peace treaties.

Science Discovery Summer Camp
CU Campus, Regent Dr., Boulder
(303) 492–7188

This camp is co-sponsored by CU-Boulder's Science Discovery Program and Experien-tial Learning Associates. The well-regarded program provides five- or six-day environ-ment-oriented experiences that include excursions to Colorado wonders such as the Great Sand Dunes and Dinosaur National Monuments and Cortez Cultural Center. The program is so popular partici-pants are chosen by a lottery system. There

Children dress as candy canes for the Lights of December Parade. PHOTO: DAILY CAMERA/CLIFF GRASSMICK

are local programs and overnight options. Activities include hiking, paleontology, river rafting, and mountain biking.

University Of Colorado Basketball School
Folsom Stadium, Colorado Ave., Boulder
(303) 492–6877, (303) 492–6086

Girls and boys of all ages flock to these camps to work with the head coaches of both the CU women's and men's basketball programs. Coaches Ceal Berry and Ricardo Patton and their staff and players hold day and overnight camps, most of them three days long, on the CU campus. There are different levels for children as young as 6, as well as elite camps for 15- to 18-year-olds with varsity experience.

University of Colorado Volleyball Camps
Folsom Stadium, Colorado Ave., Boulder
(303) 492–6141

This camp gives boys and girls, grades 3 through 6, the fundamentals needed to play the game of volleyball. This half-day camp is offered one week every summer.

YMCA of Boulder Valley
2850 Mapleton Ave., Boulder
(303) 442–2778

The Y offers an extensive variety of camps: nature, sports, teen adventures, teen leadership, "Y-Riders" bicycling, fine arts, making memories, and mountain camp. All are licensed and staffed by professionals. In addition, the Y runs excursions to Denver-area fun spots such as Water World, and staffs daylong summer camps at many schools.

Daytrips and Weekend Getaways

Denver

Colorado Springs

Cripple Creek

The Gambling Towns:
Black Hawk and
Central City

Ski Country (Both
Summer and
Winter)

From the mountains to the plains, the area around Boulder offers a wealth of possible daytrip activities, from cultural attractions and historic sites to outdoor recreation, shopping, dining, and just enjoying the beautiful scenery. Among the places covered in this chapter are the Air Force Academy in Colorado Springs, the gambling casinos of Central City and Black Hawk, the ski resorts of Summit County and Winter Park, and the museums and other attractions of Denver. We've provided some history and vital information about each, along with details on special events, dining, and shopping opportunities. Among the popular activities in the mountains are skiing, Alpine-sliding, and sleigh-, hay-, and horseback riding. Athletes with disabilities can learn to ski, rock climb, and take on other challenges at Winter Park, site of the National Sports Center for the Disabled. For hiking, backpacking, bicycling, and cross-country skiing (and other participatory sports) also see our Sports chapter.

Denver's Zoo, with its Tropical Discovery exhibit, and the Denver Botanic Gardens will cheer you with lush greenery and tropical creatures even during the cold winter months. Drive up Pikes Peak in the summer and you can say you've been on top of one of Colorado's "Fourteeners"—the 54 mountains in the state that reach 14,000 feet or higher. Or take a leisurely sail across scenic Lake Dillon or Grand Lake.

Whatever your inclination, the area offers activities that are fun, challenging, inspirational, educational—or perhaps all of the above.

Accommodations

Price-Code Key

Accommodation listings include dollar signs ranging from one to five ($-$$$$$) indicating the price range for a one-night stay, double occupancy, during the summer season.

$	$55 or less
$$	$56 to $75
$$$	$76 to $100
$$$$	$101 to $125
$$$$$	$126 or more

Restaurants

Price-Code Key

Restaurants are listed with dollar signs ranging from one to five ($-$$$$$) indicating the average cost of dinner for two, excluding appetizer, alcoholic beverages, dessert, tax, and tip.

$	$20 or less
$$	$21 to $40
$$$	$41 to $60
$$$$	$61 to $100
$$$$$	$101 or more

Denver

Believe it or not, Denver actually has some attractions that Boulder doesn't, though Boulderites hate to admit it. Driving time between Boulder and sprawling Greater Denver can vary depending on which part of the city you visit. All the attractions listed here are in the center-city area and an hour's drive or less from Boulder. It's fun to spend a day in the "big city" visiting museums, shops, restaurants, or galleries, or going to the Colorado Symphony or a show.

Some of Denver's top attractions are the Denver Botanic Gardens, the Denver Zoo, the Museum of Natural History, the elegant Brown Palace hotel (which serves high tea), and the Black American West Museum and Heritage Center. There's also good shopping on Larimer Street, the 16th Street Mall, Cherry Creek at the Tabor Center, and the lavish, new Park Meadows Mall—and lots of good restaurants, too.

If you're a parent looking for fun activities to do with your children, make sure you see the following "Denver for Kids and the Young at Heart" section. For the complete Insiders' scoop on Denver, check out the *Insiders' Guide to Denver*.

Getting There

Take U.S. Highway 36 from Boulder to the I-25 exit. The new, improved I-25, with six lanes in some places, can be a bit intimidating for non-city drivers. It helps to have someone else along for navigation. Once on I-25, stay to the middle/right, because some of the far right lanes are "exit only" to such places as Denver International Airport or Limon in eastern Colorado. Follow I-25 for a few miles as it nears downtown Denver and watch for the sign for the Speer Boulevard S. exit, which comes up quickly after the sign (not to be confused with the Speer Boulevard N. exit). Take the exit and head for the tall buildings over Speer Boulevard. There are signs for the Denver Art Museum on Speer past Colfax Avenue.

Or avoid the hassle of traffic and parking and take the RTD bus, which leaves from the RTD station in Boulder at 14th and Walnut Streets (and other stops along Broadway). The bus goes to the Market Street station in downtown Denver, right at the 16th Street Mall. There are numerous trips daily. In Denver, a free shuttle takes riders up and down the 16th Street pedestrian mall. The far end of the mall (and the shuttle stop) is only a few blocks from the State Capitol and art museum. For RTD route and schedule information, call (303) 299-6000. A one-way ticket to Denver is $3. Tickets can be purchased on the bus, but you must have exact change.

In Denver, the Gray Line (303-289-2841) stops every half-hour at or near Denver's cultural attractions and sights downtown. It runs daily from 8:30 A.M. to 5:30 P.M., from early May until early September. A pass—$16 for adults, $8 for children under 12—allows riders to get on and off as often as they like. Buy tickets when you board the bus.

To get to the Denver Zoo and the Denver Museum of Natural History by car, I-25 to I-70 eastbound. Follow I-70 to the Colorado Boulevard exit, then proceed south on Colorado Boulevard for 2 miles to 23rd Avenue and turn right. The zoo is on 23rd Avenue between Colorado Boulevard and York Street (look for signs). The

Insiders' Tip

Those planning a daytrip to Denver from Boulder or elsewhere should wait until the morning rush hour is over—usually around 9 A.M. Likewise, time your return for either before 3 P.M. or after dinner—unless you want to get caught in the traffic jam on I-25.

museum is nearby in City Park at Colorado Boulevard and Montview.

To get to the museum from downtown Denver by car, go east on 17th Street (which eventually becomes E. 17th Avenue) and turn left (north) on Colorado Boulevard. Look for signs for the museum and the zoo.

For the Denver Botanic Gardens, from downtown take 14th Street east to York Street, turn right (south) on York and go four blocks; free parking is on the left, and the gardens are on the right.

To reach the Black American West Museum and Heritage Center, go northeast on Stout Street (a block over from California Street) from downtown Denver out to 31st Street.

Attractions

Black American West Museum and Heritage Center
3091 California St., Denver
(303) 292–2566

Black Americans played an important role in the settling of the West; documentation at this unique museum shows that roughly a third of the West's cowboys were black. There were also many black businessmen, miners, pioneer doctors, politicians, soldiers, and teachers—a fact that historians have generally overlooked. At this museum, numerous photos and displays explain the role of black Americans as early settlers in Denver and Colorado. Every six months there's a changing exhibit with such subjects as the history of jazz in Denver or black churches in Denver. Summer hours are from 10 A.M. to 5 P.M. daily; winter hours are 10 A.M. to 2 P.M. Wednesday through Friday and weekends from noon to 5 P.M. Admission is $6 for adults, $5.50 for seniors, and $4 for children 5 to 12; children 4 and younger are free.

Denver Art Museum
100 W. 14th Ave., Denver
(720) 865–5001

The Denver Art Museum has one of the best and most extensive collections of Native American crafts in the United States plus works of Picasso, Georges Braque, Matisse, Frederic Remington, Winslow Homer, Thomas Hart Benton, and many others. You'll find a cafe and restaurant and gift shop here as well. The museum is near the State Capitol. Look for the distinctive castle-like silhouette of cutout geometric shapes. Hours are 10 A.M. to 5 P.M. Tuesday through Saturday (until 9 P.M. on Wednesday) and noon to 5 P.M. Sunday (closed Mondays and major holidays). Admission is $6 for adults, $4.50 for seniors and students 13 to 18; free for museum members and children younger than 12. Admission is free for everyone on Saturday.

Denver Botanic Gardens
1005 York St., Denver
(303) 331–4000

Enjoy 23 outdoor acres full of beautiful flowers, trees, and shrubs, including a Japanese garden and an alpine rock garden, just 10 minutes east of downtown Denver. You'll find an indoor conservatory with special tropical and orchid areas plus a library and gift shop, too. There's increasing focus on Japanese-style designs, native prairie areas, and rock gardens. The curator of the Rock Alpine garden, Panayoti Kelaidis, is a Boulder native who has gained a national reputation for his daring eye and superb plant knowledge. For anyone who wants to learn what grows beautifully in this climate, the Botanic Gardens is a required stop. Although most visitors choose to see the brilliant summer flowers, winter, Colorado's longest season, is a good time to visit—especially to experience the 50-foot-tall tropical forest. For anyone with the winter blues, this lung-full of Hawaii is a sure, if temporary, cure. Hours are 9 A.M. to 8 P.M. Saturday through Tuesday; 9 A.M. to 5 P.M. Wednesday through Friday. Admission is $6.50 for adults, $4.50 for students and children ages 6 to 15, and $4 for seniors older than 65. Children ages 5 and younger are free.

The Denver Botanic Gardens are a short drive from Boulder. PHOTO: DAILY CAMERA/JAY QUADRACCI

**Denver Museum of Natural History and
IMAX Theater
2001 Colorado Blvd., Denver
(303) 370–6357;
(303) 322–7009 (reservations);
(303) 370–8257 (hearing-impaired TDD)**

Besides dinosaurs, the museum features exhibits of Colorado's birds and animals and a fantastic collection of other natural history exhibits and dioramas. From time to time the museum also hosts spectacular world-traveling exhibitions such as "Ramses II" and "Aztec." *Prehistoric Journey,* an award-winning dinosaur exhibit popular with kids, is a permanent attraction that includes walk-through "enviro-ramas." The museum is open daily from 9 A.M. to 5 P.M. and until 9 P.M. on Fridays. The museum's IMAX Theater, with its four-story screen, shows educational and entertaining movies. Shows start daily at 1 P.M. call for the schedule. Admission to the museum is $6 for adults, $4.50 for children ages 3 to 12 and seniors older than 60. IMAX shows cost $6 for adults, and $4.50 for children ages 4 through 12 and seniors older than 60. There are also combination museum and IMAX tickets available.

**Denver Zoo
2300 Steele St., Denver
(303) 376–4800**

The tropical *Discovery* and *Primate Panorama* exhibits are the zoo's newest attractions. The Primate exhibit re-creates an African village, complete with thatched roofs, and has 29 species of primates from around the world. The gorilla enclosure is one of the largest outdoor gorilla yards in any zoo and is home to Kounda, the largest known gorilla in captivity, weighing 600 pounds. The zoo is in the process of updating Bird World and adding additional parking. Zoo hours are 9 A.M. to 6 P.M. daily in summer, 8 A.M. to 5 P.M. daily in winter. Some exhibits close earlier. Admission is $9 for adults; $7 for seniors (62 and older) and $5 for children ages 4 to 12; free for children 3 and younger. Call for free days for Colorado residents. The zoo's cafeteria serves light meals and snacks.

Restaurants

On the 1400 block of Larimer Street and along the 16th Street Mall, a potpourri of restaurants offer ethnic foods, sidewalk cafes, and lots of ambiance. See the price-code key at the beginning of this chapter. The following are some favorites:

Josephina's
1433 Larimer St., Denver
(303) 623–0166
$$$

A lively, colorful Italian restaurant, Josephina's has been pleasing diners for years with its antipasto, pizza, lasagna, eggplant parmesan, and other Italian favorites. Josephina's is open daily for lunch and dinner.

The Little Russian Cafe
1424 H Larimer Sq., Denver
(303) 595–8600
$–$$

The Little Russian serves such hearty peasant fare as dumplings, stuffed cabbage, borscht, and apple strudel. It also offers a great selection of unusual flavored vodka drinks. The cafe is open daily for dinner only.

McCormick's Fish House & Bar
1659 Wazee St., Denver
(303) 825–1107
$$

McCormick's serves all types of American food plus seafood, which is their specialty. The popular eatery serves breakfast, lunch, and dinner daily, with a special weekend brunch on Saturday and Sunday.

Racine's
850 Bannock St., Denver
(303) 595–0418
$$

About four or five blocks from the Denver Art Museum (at 13th and Bannock Streets), Racine's is a great spot for dessert or an inexpensive meal. The restaurant has its own in-house bakery and is known for its great brownies, carrot cake, and muffins. Besides sweets, a wide range of meal offerings includes pastas, Mexican entrees, and sandwiches. Friendly and inexpensive, with a comfortable but interesting ambiance, Racine's offers something for everyone, serving breakfast, lunch, and dinner daily. It also has an attractive bar that is a fine place for an after-the-show drink or dessert.

Wazee Supper Club
1600 15th St., Denver
(303) 623–9518
$$$

This is a classic LoDo institution serving up burgers, wonderful pizza, a large beer selection, and plenty of neighborhood character for more than two decades. It's open daily for lunch and dinner.

The Wynkoop Brewing Co.
1634 18th St., Denver
(303) 297–2700
$–$$

A few blocks from Larimer Square, the Wynkoop provides an interesting dining and drinking experience. This was Denver's first brewpub, founded in 1988, and it's housed in a historic 19th-century

> **Insiders' Tip**
> Among the Denver Art Museum's newest galleries are ones that focus on Art of the American West, and European and American Art.

building. Though the Wynkoop can be a bit noisy, crowded, and smoky, the choice of ales and pub fare at reasonable prices and the lively atmosphere more than compensate. It's open daily for lunch and dinner.

Accommodations

Since Boulder is so close to Denver, most people just make it a daytrip. But should you decide to have a little Denver holiday, many downtown hotels offer special weekend-getaway packages. Call the Colorado Hotel and Lodging Association reservations service line at (303) 297–8335 for information. See the price-code key at the beginning of this chapter.

The Brown Palace
321 17th St., Denver
(303) 297–3111
$$$$$

The Brown Palace is Denver's most famous hotel. It is quite elegant but expensive, starting at $225 for a standard room, $265 for a superior room, and $375 for a deluxe room per night, single or double occupancy. Suites range from $350 to $925. The hotel has three restaurants: Elyngton's and The Ship Tavern are casual; The Palace Arms is an acclaimed formal dining room. Churchill's, a cigar lounge, serves cocktails. Drinks are also available in the lobby and The Ship Tavern, and lunch and afternoon tea are served in the beautiful Victorian-style lobby.

The Queen Anne Inn
2147 Tremont Pl., Denver
(303) 296–6666
$$$

Just north of downtown in a historic neighborhood, the Queen Ann occupies two adjacent Victorian buildings, built in 1879 and 1886 in the Queen Anne–style of architecture. Single rooms are in the $95 to $175 range, which includes breakfast. There are 14 rooms, all with private baths. The inn is popular with honeymooners and for weddings.

Shopping

Denver has a number of popular shopping areas, some within walking distance of each other and others not. Downtown in the historic district are Larimer and Writer Squares. Farther afield are Cherry Creek and the new Park Meadows shopping center.

Cherry Creek Shopping Center
3000 E. First Ave., Denver
(303) 388–3900

With some 160 specialty stores—mostly high-end—Cherry Creek attracts 16 million visitors annually. Stores include Ann Taylor, Lord & Taylor, Saks Fifth Avenue, Abercrombie & Fitch, Nieman Marcus, and Foley's, among others. The center expanded in 1998, adding 30 new stores including Tiffany & Co., Z Gallerie, Eddie Bauer, and the Banana Republic. North of the mall are several blocks of trendy establishments including art galleries and restaurants. The Tattered Cover Book Store (2955 E. First Ave.) is nationally known and has three huge floors of books, easy chairs for reading, and a nice restaurant on the top floor with great city and mountain views.

Larimer and Writer Squares
15th and Larimer Sts., Denver
(no main number)

Historic Larimer Square, at Larimer and 15th Streets, is packed full of upscale clothing boutiques, art galleries, cafes, and other shops, as is Writer Square just across 15th Street. Looking for antique and estate jewelry? Victoriana, an interesting shop on Writer Square, is worth a visit. Find unusual artistic greeting cards at Avant-Card. Ann Taylor, the popular women's clothing and accessory shop, is also in Larimer Square (1421 Larimer).

Park Meadows Shopping Center
8401 Park Meadows Center Dr., Littleton
(303) 792–2533

The Park Meadows Shopping Center is in Douglas County (and not actually Denver proper). One of the big draws is Nordstrom, one of only two in Colorado. There's also Denver's first Dillard's department store. Other popular shops are Crate and Barrel and Restoration Hardware, with all types of gourmet kitchen and unusual decorating items. Park Meadows' entertainment section has four virtual theaters at a complex called Starport, where you can do things like virtual hang gliding. There are also movie theaters and a massive food-court area. For those who prefer finer dining, there's the California Cafe with upscale, nouvelle cuisine; Bella Restaurante for Italian food; and Alcatraz Brewing Co., a brewpub.

The 16th Street Mall
16th St. between Market and Colfax, Denver
(no phone)

There are lots of inexpensive souvenir-type shops along the 16th Street Mall. It's fun to walk up 16th Street or take the shuttle. This is the place for a quick cup of coffee, finding a tacky Denver souvenir, or people-watching, but not serious shopping.

The Tabor Center
1201 16th St., Denver
(no main number)

The greenhouse-like Tabor Center at the 16th Street Mall's north end (1201 16th Street) houses such fun places as The Kite Store, Flag World, African House (arts and handicrafts), It's Your Move (game store), and American Sports Classics (sports memorabilia)—plus miscellaneous clothing and other shops.

Denver for Kids and the Young at Heart

Attractions
On the Road to Denver

The Arvada Center for the Arts and Humanities
6901 Wadsworth Blvd., Denver
(303) 431–3939

The Arvada Center offers participatory fairy-tale theater for children many week-

day mornings and some Saturdays. Kids are often invited to come on stage to join the acting. Tickets cost around $4 during the week and $5 on Saturdays; summer shows are $5. The evening adult dramas and concerts, which cost from $20 to $26, are excellent, and the free museum has art and cultural displays.

The Butterfly Pavilion & Insect Center
6252 W. 104th Ave., Westminster
(303) 469–5441

This amazing place is about 20 minutes south of Boulder on the Church Ranch Boulevard exit off U.S. 36 to Denver. Half of the center is a fascinating display of living insects, the other part is a greenhouse for exotic tropical butterflies. At the insect center, visitors can handle a live tarantula, see scorpions that glow in the dark and learn about exotic cockroaches of the world. In the Butterfly Pavilion, 70-percent humidity and lush tropical foliage simulate the Costa Rican rain forest and butterflies flit around freely, hitchhiking on visitors.

There's also a nifty gift shop full of butterfly-themed items, plus a cafeteria. The center was created by the Rocky Mountain Butterfly Consortium and is a nonprofit organization. Its purchase of the insects from various tropical countries helps create a viable industry for sustaining tropical forests. The Butterfly Pavilion purchases butterfly chrysalises and hatches its own butterflies. Those who visit in the morning can see these beauties emerging from their chrysalids and cocoons. Outside, the facility has gardens of native wildflowers and prairie grass planted to attract local butterflies, so it's a great place for gardening ideas, too. Open daily 9 A.M. to 5 P.M.; admission is $6.95 for adults, $4.95 for seniors, and $3.95 for children. Two children ages 3 and under are admitted free with a paying adult.

Casa Bonita
6715 W. Colfax Ave., Denver
(303) 232–5115

For sheer kitsch value, Casa Bonita is an experience not to be missed. It's the

Insiders' Tip

Water World gives you
the most splash for
your money, and it's
only 20 minutes from
Boulder.

favorite dining experience of many youngsters. The Mexican food is passable, the donut-sweet sopapillas are tasty, but the main draw is the entertainment. At the indoor lagoon, a dramatic troupe presents plays that usually end with heavily costumed actors splash-landing in the pool. A dark cave maze is popular for hide-and-seek, and troubadours wander among the tables singing "Happy Birthday" when requested. The experience is hokey beyond belief and adored by children. A meal generally costs less than $10; children 12 and younger eat for less than $5. Casa Bonita is open 11 A.M. to 9:30 P.M. Sunday through Thursday, and 11 A.M. to 10 P.M. Friday and Saturday.

Hyland Hills Water World
1800 W. 89th Ave., Federal Heights
(303) 427–7873

The 64 acres of water rides and 40 attractions make Water World America's largest family water park. *USA Today* rated its Voyage to the Center of the Earth one of America's top-10 attractions. To get here, take U.S. 36 to the Pecos exit, close to Denver. Turn north (left) and drive until you see those blue canopies on the hilltop. Water World offers several safe introductions to whitewater rafting. For those missing surf, Water World's big wave pools make plenty. Add an entertaining wading area for tots and grade-schoolers, plus many theme rides, and you've got wet for kids of all ages. Beach Boys music bops from the loudspeakers. A day of splashing costs $24.95 for adults and $20.95 for children ages 4 to 12. Seniors (60 and older) and tots (3 and younger)

are free; half-day rates are offered. Water World is open daily in the summer from 10 A.M. to 6 P.M., weather permitting, and accepts major credit cards but no personal checks.

Lakeside Amusement Park
4601 Sheridan Ave., Denver
(303) 477–1621

Lakeside opened in 1908. The miniature train still circles the lake, powered by a 1903 steam engine. That tortuous white skeleton is the 90-foot-tall Cyclone; a ride on this roller coaster seems like 3,000 knuckle-white lifetimes but actually takes only 2.5 minutes. The Cyclone's rated one of the top-five roller coasters by American Coaster Enthusiasts and is one of the few wooden roller coasters left in the country. During the week Lakeside opens at 1 P.M. for kiddie rides, and the major rides are open from 6 P.M. to 11 P.M. On weekends the whole park is open from noon to 11 P.M., from May through Labor Day. Unlimited rides cost $11.25 during the week and $14.75 on weekends. But if you're just riding the bench, it's $3 (children 2 and younger are free).

Downtown Denver

Denver Art Museum
100 W. 14th Ave., Denver
(720) 865–5001

From the fantasy fortress facade outside to the hands-on displays, kids' corner, and videotape nooks inside, kids will particularly enjoy this museum. Count on spending an hour, maybe 90 minutes, with the kids in tow. The museum is open Tuesday through Saturday from 10 A.M. to 5 P.M. and Sunday from noon to 5 P.M. (closed Monday). The entrance fee is $6.50 for adults, $4.50 for students and seniors; free for kids younger than 5, and free for everyone on Saturdays.

The Denver Mint
320 W. Colfax Ave., Denver
(303) 405–4761

Any kid who likes money will love the Denver Mint, between Delaware and

Cherokee Streets (tour entrance on Cherokee). It began when Coloradans made their own money. In those days, real U.S. currency was hard to find this far west, and locals tired of weighing gold dust to exchange for food. Later, this private enterprise became an official U.S. mint. Teeth-rattlingly loud machines stamp coins from sheet metals. People hush as they pass a safe displaying 27.5 pounds of gold in six 400 troy-ounce gold bars. The bars are surprisingly small, like $3 bars of good chocolate in shiny yellow wrappers. They're a fraction of Denver's gold, which is one of three stashes nationwide (West Point and Fort Knox are the other two). Twenty-minute tours take place weekdays from 8 A.M. to 3 P.M. (9 A.M. on the last Wednesday of the month) on a first come, first served basis. Tours are free, but slots fill quickly during the summer, so it's best to get your ticket by midmorning. The coin sales area operates during the same hours as the tours and is accessible only by taking the tour. The mint is closed on weekends and holidays.

The Molly Brown House
1340 Pennsylvania St., Denver
(303) 832–4092
Rent the movie *The Unsinkable Molly Brown*, starring Debbie Reynolds, then tour this landmark. It's just a few blocks from Denver's gold-domed Capitol building. Molly Brown was a diamond-in-the-rough whose husband made a gold strike. Denver society snubbed Molly, but she became a heroine when the Titanic sank in the freezing North Atlantic. Molly was onboard that fateful day, and she saved many by pulling them into her lifeboat. Her mansion is 10,000 square feet of Victoriana. It's open from 10 A.M. to 4 P.M. Monday through Saturday and noon to 4 P.M. Sunday (closed Monday from September through May). The history-filled 45-minute guided tour is $6.50 for adults, $4.50 for seniors 65 and older, and $2.50 for children ages 6 through 12. The last tour is at 3:30 P.M. (See this chapter's Close-up for more information about Molly Brown.)

West of Downtown, Near I–25

Children's Museum
2121 Children's Museum Dr., Denver
(303) 433–7433
Near the Elitch Gardens Amusement Park (see below) is a square green building that appears to be wearing a burgundy pyramid cap. This is the Children's Museum, which offers hands-on exhibits such as a science lab and a Wild Oats Community Market where kids can play shopping. The museum is open daily from 9 A.M. to 4 P.M. and is closed Mondays in September through May. Entry fee is $6.50 for ages 2 to 59 and $3.50 for adults 60 and older. Children under 1 are admitted free. Call for show and schedule information for the Children's Theatre.

Coors Field
20th and Blake Sts., Denver
(303) 292–0200
Home to the Colorado Rockies, this 50,000-seat stadium is extraordinarily detailed, down to 40 plate-size blue columbines on the exterior. (Columbines are Colorado's state flower.) A ball game with kids is delightful here. They'll love the hot dogs, pizza, sodas, and snacks. You can find Rocky Mountain Oysters for sale, too. (Those are fried bull testicles, in case you're munching one right now and wondering what you just ate.) Rockies Larry Walker, Todd Walker, and Jeff Cirillo often hit home runs, and the mascot, Dinger the Purple Dinosaur, is always performing antics somewhere. Obviously, baseball is not just for kids. We know people who take first dates to the ball game. If the chemistry's dynamite, there's plenty of time for getting acquainted. If things just don't click, they can get very, very interested in the game. You get the idea. The Rockies still have the "Rockpile," where you can come on game day and buy tickets for kids or seniors at $1 each or for adults for $4. Tickets in advance are generally $5 to $37; call (303) ROCKIES. From I-25, take the Park Avenue W. Exit to reach the stadium. (See our Sports chapter for more information on the Rockies.)

Unsinkable Molly Brown and Her Revived House

A visit to the Molly Brown House is more than a trip into Denver's past. Brown was one of the survivors of the *Titanic,* and a small museum on site tells the story. "Typical Brown luck, we're unsinkable," she proclaimed, after rescue. She had traveled to Europe on the *Titanic*'s sister ship, the *Olympic,* and spent part of the winter in Egypt with the Astors, who encouraged her to book first-class return passage on the *Titanic's* maiden voyage. The *Titanic* was the largest ocean liner of its time and was considered to be unsinkable. Its anchor had 1,050 feet of chain. The ship had a gym equipped with stationary weights, a bicycle, a rowing machine, and an electric camel ride.

On April 14, 1912, at 11:40 P.M., the crew of the *Titanic* spotted an iceberg, which was unavoidable because the ship was too big to maneuver quickly. The ship broadsided the iceberg, broke in two and at 2:20 A.M. sank to the bottom of the freezing North Atlantic, taking most of its 2,228 passengers—only 705 survived, among them Brown. Most of the survivors were women and children because Victorian ethics demanded that they be saved first. Brown assisted in the rescue efforts in the lifeboat and made the women sing so they would stop crying. After they were rescued she raised more than $10,000 for the survivors. She also submitted an insurance claim against the shipping company for more than $27,000, including a necklace valued at $20,000 and three-dozen gloves at $50.

The Molly Brown House in Denver is a worthwhile stop.

PHOTO: JEFF BLACK

Molly's real name was Margaret "Maggie" Brown. The name "Molly" was the invention of the 1960s Broadway musical based on her life. According to a guide at the Molly Brown House, the movie version starring Debbie Reynolds—though entertaining—is not very accurate. Brown was born to a Hannibal, Missouri, ditch digger and his wife in 1867. She said Mark Twain inspired her to go west. She went to Leadville, Colorado, and worked as a seamstress at the Daniel and Fisher department store. There, she met her husband-to-be, James Joseph (J. J.) Brown, who was from Pennsylvania and working for the Ibex Mining Company. After the 1893 silver crash, J. J. found gold in the Little Johnnie mine and became a millionaire. The Browns then moved to Denver, where Molly was considered by Denver society to have three strikes against her: she was Catholic, Irish, and nouveau riche. Nevertheless, the Brown home soon became the focus of Denver society.

She and her husband never got along well, partially due to Molly's unorthodox but charitable behavior. She told impoverished Native Americans to set up their tents on her front lawn after they were driven off the State Capitol grounds. That was the final straw for her husband, who then moved out. Molly continued to live an extravagant life, traveling and circulating in the high society of Denver, Newport, and Europe. But she also spent much of her time and money supporting various causes, including women's suffrage, local Catholic charities, and the reform of maritime law. She received the French Legion of Honor, with Sarah Bernhardt, for her efforts during World War I. During the 1920s Molly lived at the Brown Palace Hotel, and her lovely home became a boarding house. She died in 1932.

The home fell into ruin, but in 1970 its acquisition and restoration became the first project of Historic Denver, which was created for this purpose. The dark red stone mansion is a late Victorian Queen Anne–style home, with Romanesque touches. The neighborhood was considered to be upper-middle class when the Browns resided there. Nearby Grant Street was millionaire's row, where cattle barons and railroad magnates lived in rambling mansions.

The Molly Brown house is filled with antiques, many of which are the family's original furniture dredged up from various Denver sources, including thrift shops. The beautiful stained-glass windows and golden oak woodwork are original. More than a half-million dollars in private funds have been raised to restore the Molly Brown House, which is well worth a visit. Tour guides wear white Victorian dresses and carry white lace parasols. There's a great gift shop in the old carriage house with a room devoted to the *Titanic*. The Molly Brown House Museum and Gift Shop, 1340 Pennsylvania Street, Denver (303–832–4092) is open Monday through Saturday from 10 A.M. to 4 P.M. and Sunday from noon to 4 P.M. (closed Mondays from September through May). The last tour is at 3:30 P.M. Admission for adults is $6; seniors 65 and older, $3.50; children ages 6 through 12, $2. It's three blocks east of the State Capitol and one and a half blocks south of Colfax Avenue.

Forney Transportation Museum
4303 Brighton Blvd., Denver
(303) 297–1113

The Forney collection consists of antique cars, buggies, and trains including *Big Boy*, the largest steam engine in the world. The famous pilot, Amelia Earhart, drove the Gold Bug Kissel roadster. The museum is open 9 A.M. to 5 P.M. Monday through Saturday and is closed on Sunday. Admission is $6 for adults, $5 for seniors, $4 for children 12 to 18, and $3 for children 6 to 11. Children younger than 6 are admitted free.

Invesco Field at Mile High
1701 Bryant St., Denver
(303) 458–4848

At Mile High, which is what loyal fans insist on calling this stadium, despite the name change, sports events are a special occasion, with or without kids. This is where the Broncos battle other National Football League teams, and often practically every seat in the stadium is occupied. That's part of the reason voters in 1998 agreed to pay additional taxes in order to build the Broncos the new, modernized stadium which opened in August 2001. (See our Sports chapter for more information.)

The Colorado Avalanche won the National Hockey League's Stanley Cup in 1996 and 2001.

PHOTO: DAILY CAMERA

Pepsi Center
1000 Chopper Circle, Denver
(303) 405-8555, (303) 405-8546

The Pepsi Center, located in Denver's central downtown area, officially opened on October 1, 1999. The new arena replaces McNicholls Sports Arena, which was demolished in the fall of '99. The Pepsi Center is home to about 160 sporting and entertainment events, including the National Basketball Association's Denver Nuggets and the Colorado Avalanche of the National Hockey League. Pepsi Center features include two dramatic, six-story atrium entranceways; views of the Central Platte Valley, downtown Denver, and the Rocky Mountains; a 236-seat club-level restaurant; 95 fully furnished luxury suites; and plenty of parking. The center is easy to reach off I-25; exit South Speer Boulevard to Auraria Parkway.

Six Flags Elitch Gardens Amusement Park
2000 Elitch Circle (off Speer Blvd.), Denver
(303) 595-4386

This is Denver's oldest and grandest amusement park, in a brand-new location near lower downtown Denver. Families can enjoy the live restaurant entertainment and the progression from kiddie rides to hair-raising ones. The new location lacks the 100-year-old trees and turn-of-the-20th-century elegance of the former site, but with 67 acres, it's more than twice the size of the old park. The 1925 carousel with wooden horses is there. Twister, the famous wooden roller coaster, has been rebuilt, which relieves most parents, because although the old roller coaster was safe, sometimes you wanted to take a hammer on the ride and whack in a few extra nails. Like the old Twister, the new one is listed as one of the top 10 in the country by American Coaster Enthusiasts. The landscaping includes formal gardens, shaded areas, and several thousand young trees. Elitch's is open 10 A.M. to 10 P.M. daily. Unlimited ride admission is $32.99 for anyone 48 inches or taller, and $16.49 for those 48 inches and shorter. It's free for kids 2 and younger or adults 70 or older. Elitch Gardens is easy to find. To get there, take I-25 to Speer Boulevard S. and head for the roller coasters.

East of Downtown

In Denver, you'll find many child-pleasing attractions about 10 minutes east of downtown. We've discussed the addresses, hours, and fees of these in the previous section on Denver Attractions. Here's a look at them from a kid's point of view. Please refer to the individual listings on these attractions above for details.

With 23 lovingly landscaped acres, the **Denver Botanic Gardens** has room for serious gardeners and kids who need to frolic. At the **Denver Zoo,** the Tropical Discovery and the Primate Panorama exhibits are full of animals that would need overcoats out in a Colorado December. The polar bears and sea lions make any summer day seem cooler. They're most fun to watch from underwater portholes.

Next to the zoo is the huge **Museum of Natural History.** Just follow the crowd toward the Hall of Life and the wonderful mineral displays. They include twinkling gems, gold-filled boulders, and a quirky series of statuettes, all made of different colored stones. We grown-ups talk the kids into lingering in the Explore Colorado Hall, which has beautiful renditions of Colorado's prairie and alpine forest. Changing exhibits always pack in people.

While at the museum, enjoy the **IMAX Theater,** with 30 speakers to help the sound track thunder into your solar plexus while you watch cliff-hangers about sharks, volcanoes, and other wonders.

Shopping and Dining in Denver with Your Kids

Denver's premier shopping area is east on Speer Boulevard at Cherry Creek. Here you will find a variety of shops and fast-food restaurants. Some specific ones are listed below. With kids, downtown shopping is most fun around the Tabor Center, Larimer Square, and LoDo (pronounced low-dough), as lower downtown is known. It's not hard to find places to eat with kids. Most shopping areas have casual eateries.

Healthy Habits
865 S. Colorado Blvd., Denver
(303) 733-2105

There's a salad bar with 70 items, a pasta and soup bar, plus pizza and a bakery here in a comfortable, casual atmosphere.

The Tabor Center
1201 16th St., Denver
(303) 572-6865

The food court in the Tabor Center, downtown by Larimer Square, offers pizza, Mexican food, a Vietnamese Kitchen, Panda Express, and many other choices.

Tattered Cover Book Store
2955 E. First Ave., Denver
(303) 322-7727
1628 16th St., Denver
(303) 436-1070

This is Denver's biggest bookstore, and the lower level has a comfortable reading sofa where older kids can peruse books while you browse. If you're double-teaming your kids, one of you can read with them while the other shops. There is also a new Tattered Cover in lower downtown housed in a rambling old warehouse across from Union Station.

Union Station Gift Shop
170a Wynkoop St., Denver
(303) 534–1012

The gift shop at the train station provides a chance to look at Union Station and real railroad paraphernalia. It's open daily from 7:30 A.M. until the train comes in an hour or two later, then closes until the next train arrives.

Warner Bros. Studio Store
3000 E. First Ave., Denver
(303) 321–7747

Look on the second floor of the Cherry Creek Shopping Center for this store with Tweety Bird, Bugs Bunny, and other Looney Tunes cartoon characters emblazoned on toys and other products.

The Wizard's Chest
230 Fillmore St., Denver
(303) 321–4304

Find all types of magic tricks and toys at this entertaining shop in Cherry Creek.

Family Accommodations

Denver International Youth Hostel
630 E. 16th Ave., Denver
(303) 832–9996
$

The ultimate bargain accommodation, the youth hostel requires guests to pitch in and do a chore or two here as part of the deal. Like other youth hostels, the doors are locked during the day. Check-in time is between 8 and 10 A.M. and 5 and 10 P.M. There are about 30 beds total distributed among various dormitory-style rooms, plus kitchen and bathroom facilities. No frills, but clean and basic accommodations, and you're guaranteed to meet the other guests.

Holiday Chalet
1820 E. Colfax Ave., Denver
(303) 321–9975
$$$–$$$$

Originally the home of the Bohm family and built in 1896, this immaculate and friendly hostelry is ideal for families and even accepts pets for $5 per day. It has a unique, historic charm with stained-glass windows and a crystal chandelier to add to the ambiance. The 10 rooms/suites are all sunny and have their own personality with various nooks and crannies. Though Colfax Avenue is a bit noisy, the thick walls of the old mansion provide a quiet refuge. The rooms are three different sizes and each has a TV, VCR, kitchen, and bathroom.

Loew's Giorgio Hotel
4150 E. Mississippi, Denver
(303) 782–9300
$$$–$$$$

Kids might enjoy the looming *Star Wars* quality of this ultramodern hotel, which has a surprising northern Italian country-villa interior decor. The large property has 180 rooms and 20 suites, and the price includes complimentary continental breakfast and access to a fine Sporting Club. Though the hotel caters more to a business clientele, it offers weekend packages for families.

Melbourne International Hostel
607 22nd St., Denver
(303) 292–6386
$

For those seeking a private room at bargain prices, here's the place. Rooms have a refrigerator and some have private baths. Dorm rooms are also available. The hostel has a convenient downtown location and is clean and basic—definitely for the more adventurous and outgoing traveler or family. Check-in is from 7 A.M. to midnight, but those checking in after 7 P.M. should call first.

Colorado Springs

Getting There

Just two hours south of Boulder is Colorado Springs. To get there, take I–25 through Denver, and keep going south through the rolling foothills until you're at the foot of Pikes Peak mountain—and

Colorado Springs. Try to avoid Denver rush hour, which can add a half-hour to the trip. If you squeak through Denver on weekends or when the traffic is lightest, some commuters who nudge the speed limit a bit say you can slip into town in less than two hours.

Top attractions in Colorado Springs are the United States Air Force Academy, Cave of the Winds, the Cheyenne Mountain Zoo, Garden of the Gods, and the Broadmoor Hotel. For quick, up-to-date information on the area, call the Colorado Springs Visitor Center at (719) 635-7506 or (800) DOVISIT.

We'll tell you about these many special attractions next. But first, some perspectives from the past.

History

Before 1900, the Denver Rio Grande railroad wanted to establish communities near the remote Colorado foothills in order to profit from buying and selling goods along its train route. In 1871, it backed the Fountain Colony, with 150 buildings and 800 residents. The promoter, Gen. William Jackson Palmer, wanted a genteel, well-bred crowd, so he advertised "villa sites" to wealthy English compatriots. Thus began a community that would grow into Colorado's second-largest city, Colorado Springs, with nearly a half-million people.

One Englander said the brand-new community was a "very high-toned sort of new town" run by a "very tony company on teetotal lines." It was a tourist attraction and resort health spa for wealthy tuberculars.

Colorado Springs has gracefully reached much of its potential. But 100 years ago, early settlers who had been assured they were moving to tree-lined avenues and fenced English farmlands got a big surprise when they saw the windswept plain. One irate Englishman, stepping out of his train in a March snowstorm, huffed in a furious, highbrowed Edwardian "haccent," "And h'is this the H'italian climate of H'america?"

The resort town diversified into many other businesses. Tourism, defense, and high-tech are big employers. North American Air Defense Command (NORAD) is dug deep into hollowed-out Cheyenne Mountain. South of town is Fort Carson, an active Army base. Colorado Springs is the site of the Winter Olympic Training Center and excellent colleges such as the Air Force Academy, Colorado College, and the University of Colorado at Colorado Springs.

Colorado Springs and Boulder share similar aspirations of being well-planned, beautiful, wealthy utopian communities. But if you could imagine social and political outlook as the pendulum of a great clock, then Boulder's liberal tendencies would pull the pendulum left, while the conservative outlook of Colorado Springs would swing the pendulum far to the right. This typecasting isn't set in stone. But it's a fair comparison that has stood the test of time. For instance, Boulder opposed Amendment 2, which denied "special rights" for gays; Boulder residents viewed the amendment as a hate vote against homosexuals. A Colorado Springs group called Coloradans for Family Values initiated that amendment. While many of the positions they take earn praise because they focus attention on family responsibility, this coalition also has raised concerns because of its hostility toward homosexuals and its growing demand to include Christian doctrine in public schools.

Attractions

Air Force Academy
I-25, Exit 156B
(719) 333-2025

Colorado's leading human-made attraction is the Air Force Academy at the base of Rampart Range. Under normal circumstances the visitors center is open 9 A.M. to 6 P.M. daily in the summertime, and it closes an hour earlier the rest of the year. But in the wake of the September 11, 2001, tragedy, the academy was closed to visitors until further notice. Call for current information.

Four thousand cadets train at the academy to become astronauts, pilots, engineers, scientists, and tactical leaders. The campus includes 143 acres of athletic fields, a 2,500-seat ice rink, and a 6,000-seat basketball arena. What's more, the setting is memorable. More than 18,000 acres of the campus are a wilderness refuge, thick with Colorado's scrubby native oak, Gambel's oak, pine trees, and other native plants.

When the campus was established in 1954, 340 architectural firms competed to design the buildings. The Chicago firm Skidmore, Owings and Merrill Architects and Engineers won. Their modern ideas stunned Congress. The chapel was described as an "accordion." That seems funny today, when most people consider that chapel a masterpiece. Overall, the buildings are as crisp as their crew-cut era. But their futuristic tone might make them appropriate for Star Trek's Star Fleet Academy, too.

The visitor center displays space suits of graduates and shows free 14-minute informational movies every half-hour. Cadets lead a free campus tour.

The crown jewel is the chapel, with 17 gleaming aluminum spires that rise 99 feet into the clear blue sky. Ribbons of stained glass separate each spire and create a rainbow of color inside. The arrangement inside says something about the '60s world view of American religion. The Protestant chapel on the main floor seats 1,200. The Catholic chapel, seating 500, is on the lower level, and in the back is a 100-seat Jewish worship area, with a nondenominational area behind. Generally, chapel hours are 9 A.M. to 5 P.M. Monday through Saturday and 1 to 5 P.M. Sunday (in summer, chapel hours are extended to 6 P.M. daily). There are weekly Protestant, Catholic, Jewish, Islamic, and Buddhist services. But the chapel occasionally closes for special services, such as funerals and weddings—and there are a lot of cadet weddings. For an up-to-date schedule, call (719) 333-4515.

Cave of the Winds
U.S. Hwy. 24 W., Manitou Springs
(719) 685-5444

Just west of Colorado Springs, of these caves are open 9 A.M. to 9 P.M. daily in summer; 10 A.M. to 5 P.M. the rest of the year. More than 200,000 people a year choose the standard 45-minute guided tour, which costs $15 for adults and $8 for kids older than 6. Or, dress in clothing you won't mind getting muddy, bring a flashlight, and join the Explorers Trip, where an experienced guide goes climbing and crawling with you into danker, darker, mysterious places. The Explorers Trip lasts three to four hours, costs $80, requires reservations and a $20 per person deposit and depends on a strong confidence that you won't get claustrophobic.

For those who get flutter-nerved just thinking of that Explorers Trip, relax. The regular tour probes caves just deep and narrow enough to feel a little creepy sometimes, but they're perfectly safe. In some areas, tour-goers walk single file, but most corridors open into large cave rooms wondrously lit to show off the stalactites hanging from the ceiling and the stalagmites growing, century by century, from the floor. Hokey lighted areas get dumb names from the guides. In one spot, the crusty gray rock has been rubbed smooth by the oil from millions of human hands, revealing a honeyed glow like alabaster.

Cheyenne Mountain Operational Center (NORAD—North American Air Defense Command)
1 NORAD Rd., Stes. 101-215,
Alpha Cheyenne Mountain Air Station
(719) 474-2238, (719) 474-2239

Following the September 11, 2001 tragedy, NORAD was closed to visitors until further notice. Call for current information.

When the facility is open to the public, tours often fill six months ahead of time, so call early for reservations are required. A bus takes visitors to the mountaintop auditorium for a briefing, slide show, and explanation of the mission of Cheyenne Mountain. Then visitors ride a bus through a tunnel to the NORAD Command Center—the entire complex is underground. Inside the facility visitors can walk around in a restricted area. Visitors also see an industrial area with reservoirs and turbines that power the facility. For obvious reasons, this is a high-security tour and you'll be asked for a photo I.D. and Social Security number.

Cheyenne Mountain Zoo
4250 Cheyenne Mountain Zoo Rd., Colorado Springs
(719) 475-9555

West of the Broadmoor Hotel, this is one of the largest privately owned zoos in the nation. It started in 1938 as Spencer Penrose's own collection and grew from there (Penrose built the Broadmoor Hotel). More than 145 species are at the 75-acre zoo. Perhaps the 6,800-foot altitude invigorates the animals. Maybe it's the generally spacious pens. Whatever, the zoo is known for producing babies, including endangered species, such as tiny, golden tamarind monkeys, black rhinos, red pandas, snow leopards, and Andean condors. The most popular animal is the African elephant, followed by the orangutans in their large climbing area. The zoo's open from 9 A.M. to 5 P.M. daily in the summer and to 4 P.M. the rest of the year. Admission is $10 for adults; $8 for ages 12 to 17 and 64 and older; $5 for children ages 3 to

11. The entrance fee also gives you access to the Will Rogers Shrine of the Sun and beautiful vistas. From I-25, take exit 138 west to the Broadmoor, then turn right and follow the signs.

Garden of the Gods
I-25, Exit 146, Colorado Springs
(719) 635-7506, (800) 368-4748

This drive-through garden has 2.5 square miles of eroded red rocks that are remnants of ancient mountain ranges. The highest rock is 350 feet high, and the strange natural "sculptures" include formations known as Kissing Camels and Balancing Rock. To reach these spectacular natural formations take exit 146 and continue west until it dead-ends. Then take a left on 30th Street. The park is open 5 A.M. until 11 P.M. daily May through October, and 5 A.M. to 9 P.M. November through April. The visitor center is open 8 A.M. to 8 P.M. in the summer, with shorter winter hours.

Pikes Peak Cog Railway
515 Ruxton Ave., Manitou Springs
(719) 685-5401

Since 1891, the bright-red train cars have made the three-hour round-trip by following Ruxton Creek through the aspen and Englemann spruce forests of Pikes Peak. In addition to wheels and tracks, a cog train has a center cog gear that pulls the train up the mountain, useful against slipping in steep spots. To get there, take U.S. 24 to the Manitou exit. Go west on Manitou Avenue to Ruxton Avenue and turn left. In summer trains depart daily every hour and 20 minutes, with the first at 8 A.M. and the last at 5:20 P.M. Tickets cost $24.50 for adults; $13 for children ages 5 to 11 (July 1 to August 15: $25.50 and $13.50). Younger children ride free if they sit on your lap.

The Pikes Peak Highway
2 miles west of Colorado Springs on U.S. Hwy. 24

This scenic drive is generally open May through November. It's a long, slow way up, with many hairpin turns to the peak of Pikes, one of Colorado's highest mountains. At 11,578 feet, trees shrink to ground-huggers that might take 100 years to grow an inch. Here, you might spy yellow-bellied marmots. The 14,110-foot Pikes Peak is a boulder-strewn, windswept summit. Take a jacket, even if the temperature in Colorado Springs is more than 90 degrees. And stop at the Summit House, which has been selling delicious donuts and hot chocolate since the turn of the last century.

Santa's Workshop
U.S. Hwy. 24, 10 miles west of Colorado Springs
(719) 684-9432

If you thought the North Pole was a few thousand miles away, here are new directions. This outpost, just 10 miles west of Colorado Springs, is open in the summer from 9:30 A.M. to 6 P.M. daily. Weather permitting, it's open in the fall from 10 A.M. to 5 P.M., except for Wednesdays and Thursdays. Generally, it stays open through Christmas Eve. This sweet little amusement park has 24 safe rides for little kids, a full-size Ferris wheel (the 7,500-foot altitude makes it the highest wheel in the world), and a colorful cottage in which Santa Claus waits in his rocking chair. Kids can have their picture taken with a truly plump Santa, whose curly white beard is real. In summer, he often wears knickers with suspenders and a colorful shirt, or red trousers and boots with a colorful shirt. When it gets cold, Santa dons his red jacket. The cost for unlimited rides here is $12.95 per person; $5.50 for seniors; and free for kids younger than 2.

The Winter Olympic Training Center
1 Olympic Plaza, I-25 Uintah Exit 143
(719) 578-4618

You may see Olympians—such as Amy Van Dyken, four-time gold medal swimmer, and John McCready, a member of the men's gymnastic team—training at the two sports centers here. Free tours are offered daily every hour on the hour from 9 A.M. to 5 P.M. (during summer, they're every half-hour). Sunday tours are 10 A.M. to 5 P.M. Groups of eight or more are asked to make group reservations. Otherwise you can just show up and take the tour, which includes a 15-minute film on the Olympics or the Olympic movement. The best times to see athletes training are on the 9 A.M. and the 4 P.M. tours. The center is closed Thanksgiving, Christmas Eve, Christmas, New Year's Day, and Easter.

Restaurants

The Broadmoor Hotel's many fine restaurants are described in the hotel entry in next section on Accommodations. Other Colorado Springs choices are listed below. See the price-code key at the beginning of this chapter.

Anthony's
1919 E. Boulder Ave., Colorado Springs
(719) 471-3654
$$

The pasta is made fresh on the premises. You'll be tempted by the veal marsala and seafood pasta. Anthony's is open for lunch and dinner daily.

The Dale Street Cafe
115 E. Dale St., Colorado Springs
(719) 578-9898
$

A former Victorian home, this charming cafe offers Southern French and Northern Italian cooking, including homemade pizzas, pastas, soups, salads, and desserts. There are also grilled items and two fresh fish specials daily. Dale Street is open daily for lunch and dinner.

Giuseppe's Depot
10 S. Sierra Madre St., Colorado Springs
(719) 635-3111
$

Kids especially like Giuseppe's, an old railroad station that has been converted into a restaurant. You can see freight trains go by, and there's a view of the mountain range, too. Ribs, steak, chicken, spaghetti, pizza, and a children's menu are available. The restaurant serves lunch and dinner daily.

La Casita
1331 S. Nevada Ave., Colorado Springs
(719) 633–9616
$

Right next to I-25, this pink stucco restaurant has great personality, down to the black velvet paintings, metalwork frames, and murals of tropical birds. Beer-soaked barracho beans, known as drunken beans, are a house specialty. Try the chicken or beef fajitas. La Casita serves breakfast, lunch, and dinner daily.

The Peppertree
888 W. Moreno Ave., Colorado Springs
(719) 471–4888
$$

Here, the chef will prepare a pepper steak flamed with brandy right at your table—or steak Diane, Chateaubriand, or veal sweetbreads. The cuisine is continental and excellent. The atmosphere is very romantic, on top of a hill with a view of the city. Peppertree is open daily for dinner only.

Manitou Springs Restaurants

This cute community just west of Colorado Springs offers lots of good restaurants.

The Briarhurst Manor Inn
404 Manitou Ave., Manitou Springs
(719) 685–1864
$$

Chef-owned and operated, this inn occupies the landmark home of the founder of Manitou Springs. Built in 1878, the mansion has seven different dining areas. The varied menu offers rack of lamb, Chateaubriand, and trout. The steak tartare and alligator pears (an avocado stuffed with crabmeat and served with a special sauce) are great appetizers. The Briarhurst is open nightly for dinner.

The Craftwood Inn
404 El Paso Blvd., Manitou Springs
(719) 685–9000
$$$

This inn is another mansion, built in 1908. Regional Colorado cuisine is served, including venison, antelope, and wild boar. Ostrich and buffalo are also on the menu, plus vegetarian entrees, seafood, and other meats. The seven vegetables served with the meal are cooked separately to perfection then combined in a colorful medley. Entrees usually are served with wild rice or quinoa. There's a unique wine list along with views of Pikes Peak and a very romantic atmosphere. The Craftwood Inn is open nightly for dinner.

The Mission Bell Inn
178 Crystal Park Rd., Manitou Springs
(719) 685–9089
$

Come here for good Mexican food. The specialty is green chile with pork. Burritos come stuffed with green chile, and flautas are rolled with beef and onions then baked with red chile.

Accommodations

Many Colorado Springs accommodations are also attractions. Read this section, even if you're not planning to stay overnight. These places take Visa and MasterCard. See the price-code key at the beginning of this chapter.

The Broadmoor Hotel
1 Lake Ave., Colorado Springs
(719) 634–7711, (800) 634–7711
$$$$$

For Old World elegance, check into the Broadmoor Hotel. With more than 3,000 acres of delights, the Broadmoor, built in 1918, has 700 rooms in four different buildings. The exterior is Italian Renaissance. Authentic Chinese lion statues guard the entry. The renovated interiors have rich hunter green and burgundy decor. Although freshly decorated, the atmosphere feels straight from the Kennedy Camelot era. You might imagine Jackie, in a Chanel suit and pillbox hat, pulling on white gloves as she heads toward the Broadmoor's shops. A beautiful new addition is a bridge across the lake that connects the main hotel with the Broadmoor West building for the convenience of the guests. Paddleboats can still glide under it, followed by the Broadmoor's famous white and black swans.

Three 18-hole championship golf courses, 12 tennis courts, a 90,000-square-foot golf/tennis clubhouse and spa, bicycle rentals, horseback riding, fly fishing, and hot-air balloon rides are all here. The children's program is famous, and hiking trails are right out the door.

Nine restaurants make the dining choices exquisitely difficult. The fanciest is the Penrose Room, with views of both city and mountains. This Edwardian salon offers such continental cuisine as Chateaubriand served on silver place settings by tuxedo-clad waiters. The average price of dinner with wine and dessert is $170 for a couple. Charles Court is casual and contemporary, with one of the best wine lists in the country. Dinner for two here is around $150. Some specialties include baked double Colorado lamb chops with goat cheese and mustard seed crust; Prince Edward Sound grilled salmon; seared Colorado native bass; elk with lingonberry compote; and black-diamond rattlesnake quesadillas. The Tavern offers traditional fresh seafood, prime rib, and pasta, as well as an assortment of entrees cooked on the wood-burning open grill over pine, applewood, mesquite, and other flavor-enhancing woods. The average price for two is around $100. A baby-sitting service provides caregivers that come to the room. But if you wish to take them along, kids prefer Julie's sidewalk cafe, which serves sandwiches, salads, and ice cream.

Twenty-five specialty shops include Ralph Lauren, for women; Broadmoor Kids' Shop for infant and toddler wear; a year-round Christmas store; Cheyenne Gourmet for cooking enthusiasts; the Signature Shop for souvenirs; and the Espresso/Newsstand. The Golf Pro Shop and Tennis Shop are very popular.

During the summer, the average price for two people staying overnight is $325 for a regular room, with discount rates in the quieter seasons. For $2,415 you can have a night in the Penrose Suite. The sixth-floor suite features a parlor, sunporch, 20-seat dining room, and three bedrooms. Julie Penrose, wife of the Broadmoor's builder, Spencer Penrose, lived here in her later years. The furnishings include antiques she collected.

At Christmas, a package deal includes a room, dinner, and a show called *Colorado Christmas,* with carols sung by talent from Nashville's Opryland. There's also a movie theater on the grounds with first-run movies.

To get here, take exit 138 off I-25. This is the Circle Avenue exit. Go right (west). Circle Avenue changes into Lake Avenue, and at the end is the Broadmoor.

The Room at the Inn
618 N. Nevada, Colorado Springs
(719) 442-1896, (800) 579-4621
$$$-$$$$$

This is an 1896 Victorian bed and breakfast in the elegant historic district. The eight available rooms range in price from $90 to $160. All have queen-size beds, hardwood floors, and oriental rugs. A full breakfast and afternoon tea are served. To reach the Inn take exit 143 (Uintah Street). There are phones in each room, but the only TV is located in a common area. Pets are not allowed and children must be 12 or older.

Cripple Creek

About 50 miles southwest of Colorado Springs is the gaming town of Cripple Creek, with gambling, melodrama, and more. If you decide to go there, then find you want some peace and quiet to contrast with the hubbub, check out these two places. See our price-code key at the beginning of this chapter.

Accommodations

Hospitality House Travel Park
600 N. B St., Cripple Creek
(719) 689–2513, (800) 500–2513
$–$$

Owners Stephen and Bonnie Mackin say you can come here and get well—the place used to be a hospital. It has been renovated, then furnished with period furniture and modern amenities such as TVs. The property also has a hot tub, areas for volleyball and horseshoes. It's very relaxed and has a Victorian feel. There are 50 spots with full hookups for RVs, along with tent spaces. Camping costs around $18; rooms run around $70 with a private bath.

The Victor Hotel
Fourth and Victor Sts., Victor
(719) 689–3553, (800) 748–0870
$$$

If you want to stay near Cripple Creek, consider The Victor Hotel. This award-winning Victorian hotel was built in 1899 and includes a new wing. It currently has more than 30 rooms, which generally cost around $99 a night for two people. Take U.S. 24 southwest of Colorado Springs to Colo. 67 and proceed about 18 miles.

The Gambling Towns: Black Hawk and Central City

Getting There

About an hour southwest of Boulder, on scenic Peak to Peak Highway, you enter tiny Gilpin County. The easiest route is to take Canyon Boulevard west to Nederland, then head south from Nederland on Colorado Highway 119. Enjoy the aspens and great mountain views. Pretty soon, you'll reach the biggest towns in the county—Black Hawk and Central City. These are Boulder's closest gambling centers, with colorful extras such as brightly

> ## Insiders' Tip
>
> Those going to Cripple Creek (near Colorado Springs) should go a bit farther to the charming town of Victor—at the end of the same road (Colo. Highway 67). It's only another 6 miles and Victor is where most of the mining in the area took place. It retains the historic character of the times more than Cripple Creek with its many casinos. Stroll around the small downtown area and enjoy the antique shops—and don't miss the handmade broom and wax shop.

painted buildings, historic cemeteries, nearby ghost towns, and one of the finest musical theaters in the west—the Central City Opera.

Those coming from Boulder might want to consider taking the Boulder County Express (303–829–1966)—an especially good way to travel if you're thinking of drinking while you're up in the mountains. Groups or individuals can go anytime at a cost of $22 per person round-trip; seniors and groups of 10 or more pay $17 each. All round-trips include casino packages for Colorado Central Station in Black Hawk. These packages consist of $10 in cash, blackjack money, free drink coupons, and other extras—making the shuttle trip virtually free. There are daily shuttles normally leaving at 8:30 A.M. from Boulder, as well as shuttles on demand. Group charters of any size can be arranged in advance. Individuals or small groups should call for a reservation the night before or early on the morning of the trip. Colorado Central Station casino (listed below) offers transportation from Golden and Denver as does Ace Express (888-223-2877).

Love, Hate, or Whatever

Depending on your preferences, you'll either love these gambling towns or hate them. If you love them, you'll enjoy the easy entertainment in a beautiful mountain setting, with quaint touches of mining and mountain history.

But you may hate gambling, seeking, instead, a quaint mountain setting with a bric-a-brac of small mom and pop stores owned by third-generation mountain families. This section will describe what the mountain towns offer gamblers. Then it explains what Gilpin County has for those who want something in place of, or in addition to, the one-armed bandits. But first, to understand how legalized gambling has changed the area, consider its history.

History

Placer mining revealed gold south of Boulder, and dozens of mountain towns boomed. Central City and Black Hawk were among them. Up here, the Wild West was not so awfully woolly. Public drunkenness was the biggest crime problem (as it is again today), and miners felt comfortable sleeping in unlocked cabins with their gold dust under their pillows. One congregational preacher reported that, rather than being rude and wicked, a few Central City residents were well-educated and cultivated enough to be among the more pleasant families that "demand and appreciate good preaching."

The pros of a boomtown were showing when Central City built the Teller House Hotel in 1872, one of the most lavish hotels west of the Mississippi at that time. It had a luxurious bar and a tall diamond-dust mirror that was carried over precarious mountain roads by an oxen team. The Teller House drew Mae West and Mark Twain. Sarah Bernhardt and Edwin Booth appeared at the opera house in the 1880s. But the mining operations that fueled these fancy places were not so attractive. Mining sluices ruined the countryside. Trees were toppled to build peaked-roof houses on the sloping hills, leaving the mountains barren for decades.

By the end of World War II, the mother lodes were barren and most Gilpin County mining centers were ghost towns. A few, however, experienced a new boom. "We still get the gold," quipped Central City's mayor in the 1950s. "We get it from some 450,000 tourists a year."

Historian Robert G. Anthearn, author of *The Coloradans,* scorned Central City when he wrote in 1976 that it had become a "classical example of fakery in the world of tourist traps." He lamented, "That once charming little town was turned into the Coney Island of the Rockies."

Well, it was tawdry, but it didn't have gambling then. Before gambling, the colorful little hillside homes sheltered grizzled miners and third-generation families. The area limped downhill on fading tourism. Buildings were condemned, and many residents commuted to Boulder or Denver for work.

Colorado residents voted for gambling in 1990. The measure passed, with limitations. Bets had to stay low, and gambling would be legal in only three places—Black Hawk, Central City, and Cripple Creek. Interestingly, the measure was written so that even if one of the towns hated gambling, the state vote could impose it on them. (Since then, the law has been changed so that a town must want gambling before a state vote can bring it into the gaming community. So far, Coloradans have not voted for more gambling.)

Gilpin County voters went along with the state's gambling fever in 1990, hoping to save their towns. Many believed gambling would bring renewed tourism to the little shops and help restore the historic buildings. What they've discovered is that maintaining a community alongside a gambling center is a learning process.

Businesses that tried to stick a slot machine next to their gift items couldn't compete with national casino chains that put slot machines wall-to-wall. Expenses such as buying slot machines and paying gambling taxes required deep pockets for getting started, and many local businesses went under. People who owned buildings in easy-to-reach areas made good money by selling. Those who lived out of the way had a harder time selling, even though their regular livelihood was being smothered. So, with some people making fortunes and others losing modest savings, many of the area's pre-gambling residents left. Meanwhile, residents who stayed discovered that gambling profits did not just stay in their towns. The money went to state taxes and out-of-state investors.

As old-timers left, authentic charm left too. Local services dwindled. In Central City and Black Hawk today, don't count on buying gasoline (you can buy gas at the KOA campground on Colorado Highway 46, about 6 miles north, back toward Nederland). And those buildings that locals hoped would be restored often were gutted, with only the facade, or a copy of the facade, remaining.

People who view gambling more positively point out another set of facts. Many old buildings were beyond repair, and re-creating them has given the town a fresh, glitzy kind of charm. Those gutted interiors had been changed many times in the past already. Streets and utilities are in better repair, and the towns are prettier for walking. As for services, there weren't any basic services in Central City at the time gambling came in. Black Hawk had a little grocery store and two gas stations, which are gone. But a small grocery, Annie Oakley's, on Main Street, is now in Central City, and there's another small grocery in the Wild Card Casino on Main Street in Black Hawk. Some people who commuted to Denver for jobs at the supermarkets now can earn more in casinos. Some casinos sponsor local athletic teams and provide matching grants to local schools. Some residents who were struggling

before now have nice new homes out of town. Shops can open and close almost weekly, according to Doug Dorsey, chairman of the board of the Black Hawk/Central City Chamber of Commerce, so it's hard to keep track of the businesses in town. Therefore some shops listed in this book may no longer exist, but new ones may have taken their places.

Without gambling, rural parts of Central City and Black Hawk might have faded into ghost towns. And after the newness of gambling wears off, perhaps diversity will return. Right now, the hunger to build yet another slot palace fuels development. Black Hawk has captured 53 percent of all the gaming revenues in the state. Central City and Cripple Creek fight for the remaining revenues. Central City has been blighted with the "extra-mile" syndrome: People either don't realize it's a mile away from Black Hawk or don't want to drive the extra mile. They see all the casinos in Black Hawk and think they've arrived at both destinations.

Central City has a lot more to offer than just casinos—richer history, the opera house, and the Gilpin History Museum, which gives visitors a good grasp of the city's colorful past. (See listings below.) Be sure to visit the museum, especially if the kids are along, to learn about the area's mining history—it's only a block from the gaming area. A free valet parking system in Central City has solved the city's former parking problems.

A Gambler's View of Black Hawk/Central City

Colorado's limited stakes tend to keep the focus on fun. Bets are $5 and less. Only poker, blackjack, and platoons of one-armed bandits are allowed at the nearly 40 parlors, and the maximum hours are 8 A.M. to 2 A.M.

Try setting aside some money—anywhere from $1 to $100—and see how long you can play before you lose it. One friend sets the limit at $20 for a night. Another goes for $50. They both recall times when they have played into the wee hours and managed to take home more than they brought, then other days when they have lost all their change in the first half-hour.

Slot machines gulp quarters everywhere. Some casinos offer good deals on food and entertainment. Central City and Black Hawk are less than a mile apart, linked by shuttle buses and plenty of on-the-street attendants. Altogether, the two towns have only six main streets, so it's easy to poke around. In general, Black Hawk gamblers seem more serious, drinking and looking intently at their cards, while Central City is a little more lighthearted. As one gambler puts it, you wander until you find where your luck seems best.

While we hate to end with a caution, here goes. For most people, gambling is just plain fun. But Daniel Minerva, Ph.D., a psychologist at Boulder's Addiction Exchange (303–442–3110), notes that the problem of gambling addiction is growing. About six gamblers a year sought his help before 1990. Since legalized gambling, he now works with 30 to 40 people each year who gamble so much they have stopped working, lost their money, and started lying. If this happens to you, be one of the lucky ones who seek help. Gambler's Anonymous (303–754–7119) in Denver is another source of assistance.

Casinos

Bullwhackers Casino
101 Gregory St., Black Hawk
(303) 271–2733
Silver Hawk
100 Chase St., Black Hawk
(303) 271–2933, (800) GamBULL

Under the same ownership, the Bullwhackers and Silver Hawk casinos could be described as fancy in a cheesy sort of way. Bullwhackers offers transportation to and from Denver and Westminster (the RTD Park and Ride at Wadsworth, and the Boulder Turnpike, which is Colo. 36).

Colorado Central Station Colo.
Hwy. 119, Black Hawk
(303) 279–3000

The game of Hold'em 88 was invented here. Now being offered in at least a half-dozen casinos, Hold'em 88 is a simpler version of Texas Hold'em, the most popular form of poker played at casinos. In Colorado, where $5 is the maximum amount allowable for any single bet, the Hold'em 88 player can lose no more than $10 on a single game. In Texas Hold'em, which has four betting rounds and up to five raises per round, a single game can cost a player more than $100. Set in an authentic railroad depot, this casino boasts at least 10 tables of blackjack and seven poker tables, along with 600 slot machines.

The Gilpin Hotel Casino
111 Main St., Black Hawk
(303) 582–1133

At the Gilpin, the eight poker tables play Texas Hold'em, Hold'em 88, Omaha, and occasionally Stud. There's also off-track betting for dog and horse races. The Gilpin Hotel started slot machine tournaments in Colorado, and they still have the biggest. This historic building has the original Victorian-style facade from 1869. It's brickwork adorned with ornate hardwood. The Mineshaft Bar has been a locals hangout for 100 years. It's full of memorabilia and offers nightly live entertainment that sometimes includes karaoke singing. There's free valet parking across the street. Lucille Malone's restaurant is named after the hotel's resident ghost. After Lucille's fiance died in a wagon accident, the distraught schoolteacher hurled herself off a balcony. Locals say she's been hanging around ever since.

Harveys Casino Hotel
321 Gregory St., Central City
(800) 924–6646

Harveys is one of the newest casinos in this area and offers one of the largest selections of slots, video poker, video keno, live poker, and live blackjack in the state. It it has earned the only three-diamond rating for a casino/hotel property in Colorado. Enjoy the ribs and steaks at Tony Roma's, one of two dining options here.

Otto's and the Rohling Inn
260 and 160 Gregory St., Black Hawk
(303) 582–0150
Owners Kay and Bill Lorenz have expanded their operations into two gambling houses with Otto's and the Rohling Inn. There's free parking with validation, and blackjack as well as slot machines. The Lorenzes also operate the Black Forest Inn next door, which is a highly rated German restaurant serving diners for more than 35 years.

Black Hawk/Central City When You're Not Gambling

Some gambling friends complain that Black Hawk and Central City get boring after you've spent all your pocket change and are waiting for your friends to lose theirs. After all, this isn't Vegas. Some slot parlors don't even have a TV ballgame. Fortunately, many casinos are catching on. Some places offer sports television and good restaurants, and if you step away from the casinos, you'll find other reasons to see these mountain towns.

Cemeteries
West on Eureka St., Central City
Ten cemeteries let you glimpse more mining-era history. Was the idea that Woodcutters, Masons, and Catholics would go to separate heavens? Judging from the separated plots, it looks that way. Actually, in those days, not everyone could afford a burial. So people were buried in plots bought by their fraternity, charity or lodge. Children's tombstones bear witness to the worldwide flu epidemic of 1919, plus smallpox and other diseases that wiped out whole families.

Central City Opera House
Eureka St. (just west of Main and the Teller House), Central City
Tickets and information:
Central City Opera House Association
621 17th St., Ste. 1625, Denver
(303) 292–6700, (800) 851–8175
Central City Opera is a beautiful, historic opera house built in 1878. The summer troupe is one of the oldest opera companies in the country, with a distinguished national reputation. All performances are in English, well-sung and wonderfully acted. Everyone stays in historic Victorian character, including the uniformed ushers, who ring brass hand bells when it's time to take your seat. The theater is beautifully decorated, right down to the handpainted murals of Pegasus and cafe chairs engraved with the names of famous benefactors. Every seat is good. You're close enough that the actors and actresses come across as real people who feel life so strongly, they've just got to sing about it. See our entry on the Central City Opera in the Boulder Arts chapter for details.

When opera doesn't fit your schedule, sign up for a Festival Extra (303–292–6700). There are various choices: at Salon Recitals on weekends, opera stars do short recitals during a gourmet brunch at the Teller House Hotel, next to the opera house, at 11:45 A.M. Tickets cost around $25. For Opera a la Carte, famous opera

Insiders' Tip
You can still find two funky little places to pan gold, Vick's Gold Panning and The Old Timer Panning (across from the Gold Dust Lodge), about 2 to 5 miles from Black Hawk on Colorado Highway 119. They don't have phones, so just drive down to see if they're open.

scenes are fully staged at Williams Stables, across the street; tickets cost $8 ($5 for subscribers). *Face on the Barroom Floor* is a 30-minute cabaret opera recounting the Teller House's famous legend. It is also performed at Williams Stables; tickets are $8 ($5 for subscribers). Seating is general admission.

Gilpin History Museum
228 E. High St., Central City
(303) 582–5283

Housed in the first stone schoolhouse west of the Mississippi, the museum displays about 10,000 artifacts arranged in period rooms such as a Victorian parlor and kitchen. Business memorabilia dating from mining days are here, including items from the doctor's office, the law office, bank, and more. A general store and hand-drawn fire-fighting equipment are on display, plus an early schoolroom from Russell Gulch. There's also a carriage display, doll collection, and mining tools. It's open daily Memorial Day to Labor Day from 11 A.M. to 4 P.M. and costs $4 for adults and $2 for children 12 and younger.

Nevadaville Ghost Town
1 mile north of Central City

A mile above Central City is a real live— well, maybe not live— ghost town. In the 1800s, 4,000 people lived here, operating 20 quartz mills, and several stores and hotels. Few historic structures still stand. But nothing's left of many other Gilpin County boomtowns. Lost cities include Deadwood Diggings, Dogtown, Eureka, Gambell Gulch, Gold Dirt, Glory Hole, Hoosier City, Quincy, Springfield, Trail's End, and Wide Awake.

St. James Methodist Church
123 Eureka St., Central City
(303) 582–5882

Founded in 1859, this is the state's oldest church building. The stone structure was erected by Cornish masons in 1871. The stained glass is lovely; the pipe organ was installed in 1899: The church seats 350,

and it's active today. It's open for free tours 11 A.M. to 4 P.M. daily in the summer.

Teller House
120 Eureka St., Central City
(303) 582–9608

That, part of local legend, is painted in the Teller House, right next to the opera. You may expect a colossal face. Well, it's not big, but it's pretty. So are the eight *Muses of Central City*, originally painted in 1883. Five decades later, a restorer added jokes. You might notice a male figure with two left feet, a swan's head twisted backward and Venus's left nipple on the apple she holds. Gambling at the Teller House ended in 2000 and the historic house and museum is now open for self-guided tours, from 10 A.M. to 4 P.M. daily May through August.

The Thomas House
209 Eureka St., Central City
(303) 582–5283

This is an 1870 Greek-Revival Victorian house. It's mostly yellow with white trim. However, Marsha Thomas was a free thinker, and on a trip back East she bought a gallon of salmon paint for the porch. During every world war, the government ordered gold mining to stop in an effort to stabilize the economy, so in World War I Central City took a dive. Ben Thomas, vice president of the local mercantile store, no longer had any business. In 1917, the Thomases locked the house and relocated to Denver. Marsha visited for summer operas, but they never moved back. All the furnishings—from spices to fine art to the 13 different varieties of clocks—are intact from 1917. The corset of 4-foot, 11-inch Marsha hangs beside the long johns of 6-foot-plus-tall Ben. Because Marsha was so short, Ben cut the legs off the kitchen's wood-burning stove so it would match her height. The house is open 11 A.M. to 4 P.M. Friday through Monday in summer only, with $4 admission for adults. (If you tour the Gilpin History Museum, too, the total cost is only $5 for both.)

Restaurants

Many of the casinos feature only fast food—there's a Burger King in Colorado Central Station. But Jazz Alley across the street offers sit-down dining. Many of the casinos offer very inexpensive buffets, too. For fine dining, it's wise to get a reservation. Below are a few recommended restaurants. See the price-code key at the beginning of this chapter.

Fitzgerald's Shamrock Cafe
101 Main St., Black Hawk
(303) 582–3203
$$

This very green Irish-themed restaurant with comfortable booths and tables serves just about everything from corned beef and "shamrock stuffed potatoes" to salads, steaks, prime rib, hamburgers, pork chops, meat loaf, salmon, and pasta. It's open daily for breakfast, lunch, and dinner.

Jazz Alley
321 Main St., Black Hawk
(303) 582–1125
$

Jazz Alley has been through several incarnations in recent years and currently offers Chinese food for lunch and dinner daily.

Madeline's
The Teller House, 120 Eureka St., Central City
(303) 582–9608
$

Next to the Opera House, this restaurant in the historic former hotel opens into the historic Face Bar. Light fare such as burgers, sandwiches, soups, and salads are available. Madeline's serves lunch and dinner daily from May through August.

Accommodations

See our price-key code at the beginning of this chapter.

The Gold Dust Lodge
Colo. Hwy. 119, Black Hawk
(303) 582–5415
$$

On the main highway in Black Hawk, this lodge offers 25 nicely decorated, comfortable rooms in a convenient location.

Harveys Wagon Wheel Hotel and Casino
321 Gregory St., Central City
(303) 582–0800, (800) 924–6646
$$–$$$$$

One of Central City's newer casino/hotels, it has 118 rooms, giving a big boost to the accommodations options in this little county. It's the only casino/hotel in Central City. Tony Roma's is the on-site restaurant.

Primrose Inn
310 E. First High St., Central City
(303) 582–5808
$$

Jan Ward runs this cute bed and breakfast right next to the Gilpin History Museum, on the northeast side of Central City. Currently open only in the summer, the yellow-and-white Victorian sits high on the hill. Burgundy brocade wallpaper, lace curtains, a brass bed, and a 7-foot-tall antique mirror decorate one room. Breakfast is included with the room price.

Ski Country (Both Summer and Winter)

Winter Park and Summit County offer some of the nation's best skiing and summer recreation. Both are within a two-hour drive of Boulder. The individual ski areas, resorts, and towns are listed below with separate contact numbers for each. There are also separate listings for getting there, attractions, restaurants, accommodations, and recreation.

Please note that we list prices for accommodations instead of using the price-code key in the Ski Country section. That's because rates are rarely less than $100 per night, especially during ski season, and go can as high as $850 per night at the most luxurious condominium complexes.

Winter Park

The town of Winter Park, 2 miles north of the Winter Park ski area, offers numerous restaurants and lodging places. It's set in a beautiful valley surrounded by high peaks. Continuing northwest on U.S. 40 brings you to the small towns of Fraser and Tabernash. Fraser often reports the coldest temperatures in the country, so some Coloradans call it "Freezer." But it's a beautiful area with broad open meadows and spectacular views. If you look up toward the Continental Divide to the east, you might be able to spot the jutting rock formation known as the Devil's Thumb, north of Fraser, for which the nearby cross-country ski resort was named. Continuing north will eventually bring you to the town of Granby and to the intersection with U.S. 34, which leads to Grand Lake, on the western boundary of Rocky Mountain National Park. (See our chapter on Grand Lake.)

Getting There

Winter Park is 70 miles west of Denver. From Boulder, drive south on Broadway (Colo. 93) toward Golden and, at the new Golden bypass, follow the signs for I-70 W. Or you can take U.S. 6 up Clear Creek Canyon, which follows the old Colorado Central Railroad bed and deposits you right on I-70 headed west. Follow I-70 and exit onto U.S. 40 W. at Empire and continue over Berthoud Pass, which is well-maintained all winter. There are two entrances to the ski area: Mary Jane offers expert skiing with challenging mogul runs; the main Winter Park base is better

for beginners and intermediates. The town of Winter Park is 2 miles farther on U.S. 40. Fraser is 3 miles past Winter Park.

The Ski Train
Union Station, 17th and Wynkoop Sts., Denver
(303) 296-I-SKI

During winter, the Ski Train provides another, more interesting way to get to Winter Park. It requires going into Denver, making the trip a bit longer than driving directly, but you won't have to deal with traffic or icy mountain roads. The Ski Train departs from Denver's Union Station at 7:15 A.M. and takes skiers within walking distance of the lifts. It goes through some 30 tunnels, including the 6.2-mile-long Moffat Tunnel, drilled a mile below the Continental Divide—a nifty ride and worth experiencing, especially with children. The Ski Train leaves Winter Park at 4:15 P.M., just after the lifts close. The trip takes two hours each way. The adult Coach Car fare is usually $35 for a same-day round-trip. It increases to $45 for a round-trip on Saturdays during the months of February, March, and April. The same trip is $70 in the Club Car including continental breakfast and après-ski refreshments. Discounted lift tickets are available on the train. The Ski Train runs Saturdays and Sundays from mid-December until late March plus additional days during Christmas–New Year's week and on Fridays in March.

Downhill Skiing

In winter, skiing and snowboarding, of course, are the main attractions at Winter Park.

Winter Park: The Resort and Area
677 Winter Park Dr.
(970) 726-5514, (303) 892-0961

Winter Park operates on U.S. Forest Service land, as do most Western American ski areas, but it is unique in that the city of Denver owns its assets, which are run by a nonprofit corporation. It is Colorado's fifth-largest ski area in terms of skier visits. Skiers and snowboarders can move among four interlinked mountains: the original Winter Park, Mary Jane, Vasquez Ridge, and Parsenn Bowl. Twenty lifts, including seven high-speed express quads, access 1,414 acres of skiable terrain. Children's programs are exemplary, including daycare for youngsters ages 2 months to 5 years and ski instruction for 3-year-olds to teens.

In recent years, price for a one-day lift ticket was just under $60 for adults. Discounted tickets are available at Front Range grocery stores and ski shops. The best deal for frequent skiers is the Value Card. It offers adult skiers a 44-percent discount off lift-ticket window rates, two discounted buddy passes, and discounts to the Denver Zoo, the Denver Botanic Gardens, and the Ski Train.

If you don't know how to ski or snowboard, January is a good month to learn. Winter Park offers instruction ranging from $25 to $40 per lesson. Discovery Park, a mid-mountain learning area slope with its own slow-moving chairlift, is like a ski area within a ski area, where novices can practice comfortably.

Winter Park is also well-known for its disabled skiers program and is the site of the National Sports Center for the Disabled located at 677 Winter Park Drive (970-726-1540). Founded in 1970, the center has 39 full-time employees, including instructors and coaches, and 1,000 volunteers who work with people with many different types of disabilities—cerebral palsy sufferers, amputees, paraplegics, and others—and provide nearly 11,000 private, customized lessons each winter. The center has expanded its scope to include snowboarding and snowshoeing lessons as well as a substantial program of adaptive summer sports.

Cross-Country Skiing

Devil's Thumb Cross-Country Center
3530 County Rd. 83, Tabernash
(970) 726-5632

This center offers 105 kilometers of great groomed trails for beginners to advanced cross-country skiers. There are flat trails for beginners and smooth wide lanes for ski-skaters plus lovely rolling meadows and some steep downhills for thrills. In recent years a trail pass was $12 for adults; $10 for children ages 7 to 12 and seniors 60 and older; free for children younger than 6.

Snow Mountain Ranch
1101 County Rd. 53, Granby
(970) 887-2152, (303) 443-4743

In addition to various winter activities for kids and families, Snow Mountain has 100 kilometers of groomed trails, including 3 kilometers illuminated for night skiing. A pass is $5 per day, per family.

Other Winter Activities

Dashing Through the Snow
1400 County Rd. 5, Tabernash
(970) 726-5376

This group runs one of Colorado's longest sleigh trails—3 miles—to a secluded and delightful backcountry cabin, where a six-course gourmet feast with a choice of chicken or rib-eye steak is served, with live entertainment as a bonus. The price is $60 for adults; $45 for children; free for those under the age of 3. Bonfire/hot chocolate rides are available as well. (Sleigh rides become carriage rides in summer.)

Dinner at the Barn
County Rd. 8, Winter Park
(970) 726-4923

One of two dinner sleigh rides available in the area, Dinner at the Barn combines a ride through the woods and meadows of an 80-acre ranch with a gourmet dinner served by kerosene lantern light, with Western-style entertainment following. In summer, horse-drawn wagons replace sleighs. Advance reservations are required. Cost is approximately $50 for adults; $30 for ages 4 to 12; and free for ages 3 and younger.

Dogsled Rides of Winter Park
King Crossings Rd. at the Railroad Crossing
(970) 726-8326

Dogsled teams take riders through 1,000 acres of pristine backcountry. Sleds pulled by 8- to 10-dog teams—all purebred

Siberian huskies—can attain 30 miles per hour on downhill stretches. The cost for a one-hour ride varies at different times of winter, but figure on more than $250 for two people; reservations are required.

Jim's Sleigh Rides
77849 U.S. Hwy. 40, Winter Park
(970) 726–9247, (970) 726–0944

These sleighs take 20 guests on a horse-drawn ride past the historic Cozzens Ranch beside the Fraser River. The 70-minute ride includes a bonfire stop with refreshments. The cost—$25 for adults; $15 for ages 3 to 12; free for children 2 and younger—is the same for summer hayrides.

Snowcat Tours
Departures from the Balcony House, at the base of Winter Park
(970) 726–5514, (303) 892–0961

Nonskiers can enjoy the ambiance of the slopes by taking a two-hour mountain tour. They have frequent departures. The cost is $30 for adults, $25 for children and seniors.

Winter Park Ice-Skating Rink
Cooper Creek Sq., Winter Park
(970) 726–4118

Bring the whole family and enjoy free ice skating here; skate rentals are available nearby at the Ski Broker and SportsStalker. Call the Winter Park/Fraser Valley Chamber of Commerce (303–422–0666 or 970–726–4118), for information on snowmobile tours and rentals and other winter diversions.

Summer Activities, Events, and Attractions

Alpine Slide, Zephyr Express, and Other Winter Park Attractions
Winter Park Resort, 677 Winter Park Dr.
(970) 726–5514, (303) 892–0961

The Alpine Slide is Colorado's longest, and a big summer attraction for young and old.

With special bike mounts, Winter Park's Zephyr Express chairlift takes mountain bikers to the top, where they can ride 45 miles of steep, exciting single-track trails and gentler jeep roads. Rental bikes are available.

Also at the resort you'll find miniature golf, a human maze, a climbing wall, a zip line, mountain scooters, and chairlift rides to the top of the mountain. In recent years, fees started at $10 for adults; $8 for children ages 6 to 13 and seniors ages 62 to 69. Full-day park passes for all activities were $43, and morning or afternoon half-day passes were $30. Passes for anyone younger than 5 or older than 70 are free. Summer hours are 10 A.M. to 6 P.M. (5 P.M. in September, weather permitting).

Arapahoe National Forest Ranger District Office
(970) 887–4100

Visitors to the national forest will enjoy fishing, hiking, horseback riding, jeeping, and rafting. The Winter Park Chamber of Commerce (970–726–4118) has information about outfitters.

Bicycling
Winter Park Chamber of Commerce Visitor Center
78841 U.S. Hwy. 40, Winter Park
(970) 726–4118

Bicycling is a popular participant sport and Winter Park accommodates cyclists with 600 miles of marked, mapped, and maintained trails. There are 10 bike shops in the Fraser Valley. Free town rides are held every Thursday evening and free women-only rides take place on Wednesdays throughout summer. Bikers meet at Beaver's Bike Shop to begin the rides. Area bike trail maps are available at local bike stores or at the Chamber of Commerce Visitor Center. It is open from 8 A.M. to 5 P.M. daily.

The High Country Stampede Rodeo
John Work Arena, one mile west of Fraser
(303) 422–0666, (970) 726–4118

The rodeo takes place every Saturday evening from early July to late August. The junior rodeo gets underway at 5:30 P.M., followed by the pros. Bull riding, bronc busting, barrel racing, and other popular events are held. In recent years admission was $10 for adults and $6 for children. A low-cost barbecue dinner is also available.

The Pole Creek Golf Club
6827 County Rd. 5, Tabernash
(970) 726–8847

Golf Digest named this the best public course in Colorado. It offers golfers 18 holes of gorgeous greens. In recent years greens fees were $80 and $50 (for high and low seasons, respectively). Golf carts, which are optional, are $12.50 per rider.

Winter Park Resort Mountain Bike Race Series
239 Winter Park Dr., Competition Center
(970) 726–1589

The resort hosts this annual series, which composed of five events with different formats, including hill climb, circuit racing, and point-to-point racing. It's held from early June to early August. Two hundred and fifty competitors age 8 and older take part in each event. The entry fee is $25 in advance or $35 on race day.

Winter Park Resort Music Festivals
Winter Park Resort, 677 Winter Park Dr.
(970) 726–5514, (303) 892–0961

Winter Park also hosts two major music events in July: The KBCO World Class Rock Festival and The Winter Park Jazz Festival featuring nationally known bands.

Restaurants

The price-code key for restaurants appears at the beginning of this chapter.

Carver's
93 Cooper Creek, Winter Park
(970) 726–8202
$

Tucked into a log cabin behind Cooper Creek Square, Carver's offers excellent baked goods and an eclectic menu that includes burgers and pasta, sandwiches, and lots of vegetarian fare, all moderately priced. Breakfast and lunch are served daily, and dinner is served Thursday through Sunday.

Crooked Creek Saloon & Eatery
401 Zerex Ave., Fraser
(970) 726–9250
$

This is a family-style Mexican and American restaurant that is best known for giant burgers and fiery wings. There are also steaks and pasta. It's open daily for lunch and dinner with the bar open until 2 A.M.

Gasthaus Eichler
78786 U.S. Hwy. 40, Winter Park
(970) 726–5133
$$

This place is noted for Austrian and German specialties. Try the veal dumplings, bratwurst, or goulash. It serves breakfast to overnight guests only, and lunch and dinner to the public. Reservations are suggested.

Hernando's Pizza and Pasta Pub
78199 U.S. Hwy. 40, Winter Park
(970) 726–5409
$

This is a local favorite for homemade pastas, including delicious lasagna, as well as good pizza and a summer beer garden. Hernando's is open for lunch and dinner during the summer, dinner only during the winter months.

The Shed
78672 U.S. Hwy. 40, Winter Park
(970) 726–9912
$

This is a longtime Winter Park favorite, now serving hearty breakfasts and Southwestern-style dinners. The weekend buffet is popular with hungry skiers. It's closed on both Tuesday and Wednesday.

Winter Park: The Resort and Area
677 Winter Park Dr.
(970) 726–5514, (303) 892–0961
$–$$$

The Winter Park ski area has dining options both at the base and on the mountain. The Coffee and Tea Market in Winter Park's Balcony House is open for breakfast and lunch, and the nearby West Portal Station day lodge has self-service snack and lunch service as well as the Derailer Bar. The Mary Jane Center features a cafeteria, a sit-down restaurant called The Club Car, and Pepperoni's Pizza and Sports Bar. The beautiful and monumental Lodge at Sunspot, at the top of the Zephyr Express chairlift, offers snacks and lunches at The Provisioner, a self-serve facility; table service is available in the Dining Room, which is also open for dinner Thursday, Friday, and Saturday evenings in winter, with access via gondola. Reservations are recommended. Other on-mountain eating facilities include Snoasis, mid-mountain at Winter Park; and Lunch Rock and Sundance Cafe, snack bars atop Mary Jane and Vasquez Ridge respectively.

Accommodations

Reservations are necessary in this popular area for most accommodations. You can make them through Winter Park Central Reservations (800-729-5839 or 970-726-5587) or by calling individual properties.

Devil's Thumb Ranch Resort
3530 County Rd. 83, Tabernash
(970) 726-8231, (800) 933-4339

This is a quiet, beautifully-located retreat ski lodge open year-round. It is equally nice for cross-country skiing in winter and horseback riding, hiking, fly fishing, and mountain biking in summer. Cabin rentals are consistent for both summer and winter months. Three miles north of Fraser (before the bridge entering Tabernash), turn east (right) off U.S. Highway 40 onto County Road 83; after another 3 miles take the right fork in the road. Cabins rent for $130 to $150 for two people, both summer and winter.

Gasthaus Eichler
78786 U.S. Hwy. 40, Winter Park
(970) 726-5133, (800) 543-3899

This small, European-style hotel offers rooms that are warm and cozy, with all of the modern conveniences. The down comforters and lace curtains add to the European flavor. The restaurant serves authentic German cuisine, and the guest list often includes many from Europe, creating a lively, international atmosphere. Rates start at around $95 without meals and $115 with meals.

The Grand Victorian
78542 Fraser Valley Pkwy., Winter Park
(970) 726-5881, (800) 204-1170

This is the first among equals when it comes to Winter Park's growing selection of charming bed-and-breakfast inns. Secluded in a grove of lodgepole pines, this romantic neo-Victorian offers lodging in three sumptuous fireplace suites. The rates include a gourmet breakfast and afternoon drinks and hors d'oeuvres. Suites go for about $100 to $145 in summer and $155 to $235 in winter.

Idlewild Lodge
398 Ski Idlewild Rd., Winter Park
(970) 726-8352

In a great downtown Winter Park location, Idlewild is open year-round. A double room costs $175 per night and includes a full buffet breakfast and dinner for two in winter. Summer rates are the same and include three meals plus horseback riding, hayrides, evening entertainment, and a children's recreation program. Idlewild is an alcohol- and smoke-free environment (no firearms allowed, either) geared toward family vacations.

The Iron Horse Retreat
2527 Winter Park Dr., Winter Park
(303) 573-1545, (970) 726-8851

This is the resort's only ski-in, ski-out property. It has 130 rooms, all with full amenities, including fireplaces. A full-service restaurant with room service, and heated indoor and outdoor pools are other pluses. In addition to winter ski packages, golf packages are offered during summer months. The attractive condos range from $90 to $175 for two during summer and $115 to $600 in winter.

Super 8 Motel
78665 U.S. Hwy. 40, Winter Park
(970) 726–8088, (888) 726–8088

Right in town, the new Super 8 has 60 rooms, all with two queen-size beds and some with refrigerators. Rooms run to around $138 during winter and $70 in summer. Room rates here increase dramatically during the ski season and on certain festival weekends.

Summit County

The four Summit County ski areas of Breckenridge, Copper Mountain, and Keystone, and Arapahoe Basin collectively attract more skiers and snowboarders than any other ski destination in North America. They offer an incredible range of great terrain. During summer, Summit County offers hiking and backpacking in the Arapahoe National Forest; fishing and boating on Lake Dillon; whitewater rafting on the Blue River; and an excellent network of bike trails and several good golf courses, as well as a calendar full of special events and festivals. Forest information is available from the Dillon Ranger District Office (970–468–5400).

The Summit County towns of Breckenridge, Dillon, Silverthorne, and Frisco—and the resort developments of Keystone and Copper Mountain—also offer outstanding restaurants and accommodations, all in proximity to the Greater Denver area and Boulder.

Getting There

Road condition or traffic slowdowns excepted, all Summit County ski areas are less than a two-hour drive from Boulder. Drive south on Broadway (Colo. 93) toward Golden and, at the Golden bypass, follow the signs for I–70 W. Or take U.S. 6 up Clear Creek Canyon directly to I–70 W. Follow I–70 to the Eisenhower Tunnel. For Arapahoe Basin, exit at U.S. 6 west over Loveland Pass. For all the other resorts, proceed through the tunnel. Keystone is reached by taking the first exit after the tunnel, which is U.S. 6 east. For Breckenridge, take the Frisco exit and drive south on Colo. 9 for

about 9 miles. Copper Mountain is directly off I–70, at exit 195, just before the highway climbs up to Vail Pass.

Breckenridge

Breckenridge, the town, is the oldest and largest of the Summit County communities and home to the Breckenridge Ski Resort. The town was founded in 1859 when gold was discovered in the area. It remains a picturesque and historic renovated mining town. The main street is still lined with some of the handsome Victorian homes that housed the first prosperous citizens, along with numerous restaurants, cafes, shops, and art galleries. Every summer the National Festival of Music at Breckenridge mounts a two-month season of classical music.

Downhill Skiing
Breckenridge Ski Resort
1599 C Summit County Rd. 3, Breckenridge
(303) 573–7350

Breckenridge, the ski area, is huge and wide-ranging. Peak 8 is the original ski area, with a complex network of interlaced trails for all ability levels. It also offers access to high, above-the-treeline bowls and chutes as well as Peak 7, a steep mountain that is patrolled but not groomed and has no lift service—extreme terrain by anyone's standards. Peak 9 offers the greatest concentration of beginner and novice terrain and access to Peak 10, fabled for moguls, steeps, and open glades. You can ski from mountain to mountain and back again, crisscrossing Breck's 1,600-acre playground via different routes each time. There are excellent children's facilities at both the Peak 8 and Peak 9 bases. Breckenridge has long welcomed snowboarders with a half-pipe, terrain features, and just plain good riding.

Breckenridge has 135 trails on 2,031 acres with 20 lifts. In recent years, at-the-window tickets were just under $60 for adults (one-day passes), with discount tickets available at King Soopers, Safeway, and Albertson's supermarkets, Total and Diamond Shamrock gas stations, and Gart Sports. Children's lift tickets (ages 5

Summit County ski areas, including Copper Mountain, offer lessons for skiers of all ages.

PHOTO: BEN BLANKENBURG/COPPER MOUNTAIN RESORT

to 12) are about $25. The purchase of multiday passes can save a skier $7 to $10 dollars per day, depending on the number of days purchased.

Cross-Country Skiing

The Breckenridge Nordic Center
1200 Ski Hill Rd., Breckenridge
(970) 453–6855

The Breckenridge Center has more than 23 kilometers of groomed track set in the valleys below Peaks 7 and 8. The Breckenridge and Frisco (see below) Nordic Centers are under the same management and share an interchangeable trail pass. Both offer instruction and rentals of cross-country skis and snowshoes.

Other Winter Activities

Breckenridge Recreation Center
880 Airport Rd., just off Colo. Hwy. 9,
Breckenridge
(970) 453–1734

This outstanding facility offers indoor lap and recreational pools, a kiddie foun-

tain, tennis and racquetball courts, a running track, fitness facilities, a climbing wall, and a variety of programs. There are also outdoor tennis, basketball, and volleyball courts; a skateboard park; and a playground. It is open 6 A.M. to 10 P.M. on weekdays, 7 A.M. to 10 P.M. Saturdays, and 8 A.M. to 10 P.M. on Sundays. Nonresident adults pay $10; youths 13 to 17 and seniors 60 and older, $6; children ages 3 to 12, $5; and toddlers under 3 get in free.

Ice Skating at Maggie Pond
Village of Breckenridge, 535 S. Park Ave.,
Breckenridge
(970) 453–2000

There's ice skating on Maggie Pond at the village of Breckenridge, behind the Bell Tower Mall. Cost is $8 for adults and $5 for children.

Sleigh Rides/Snowmobiling/Dogsled Rides
Breckenridge Guest Services and Activity Center
150 W. Adams St., Breckenridge
(970) 453–2918

Skiing is the No. 1 activity in winter in Summit County, but other options, snow-related and otherwise, abound. Winter sleigh rides, snowmobiling, dogsled rides, and other activities can be arranged by the Breckenridge Activity Center. In addition to making reservations, it can provide information on prices, hours, and availability of off-slope activities. Or contact Tiger Run (800-318-1FUN), one of the nation's top snowmobile tour operators, or Good Times (800-477-0144), which can arrange snowmobile tours, sleigh rides, and dogsledding trips.

Summer Activities, Events, and Attractions

The Breckenridge Golf Club
200 Clubhouse Dr., Breckenridge
(970) 453-9104

This club offers outstanding golf at America's only Jack Nicklaus–designed municipal course. High-season greens and cart fees are about $100 for 18 holes.

Breckenridge Stables
1799 Ski Hill Rd. (above the Super Slide on Peak 8), Breckenridge
(970) 453-4438

This stable offers rides over the Ten Mile Range and prides itself on its gentle horses. A 90-minute ride is $40, half-price for children 6 and younger.

National Festival of Music at Breckenridge
150 W. Adams St., Breckenridge
(970) 453-2918

This festival usually begins in early August and continues through September with classical, jazz, and modern music. Visitors are invited to enjoy free, open rehearsals. Concerts are held at the Riverwalk Center, an elegant 750-seat multipurpose facility.

Summit County Historical Society
309 N. Main St., Breckenridge
(970) 453-9022

The society conducts a variety of walking tours, mainly in summer but also in winter on request.

Washington Gold Mine/Lomax Placer Gulch
137 S. Main St., Breckenridge
(970) 453-5579

Ninety-minute tours of Breckenridge's mines are offered Monday through Saturday at 1 P.M. and 3 P.M. The price is $5 for adults, free for children. For directions, call the Breckenridge Guest Services and Activity Center at the number listed.

Restaurants

The price-code key for restaurants appears at the beginning of this chapter.

Blue Moose Restaurant
540 S. Main St., Breckenridge
(970) 453-4859
$$

The Blue Moose offers a casual atmosphere with a wide range of American-style food served at breakfast and lunch.

The Cafe Alpine
106 Adams St., Breckenridge
$

The charming Victorian setting complements the eclectic menu, which includes steak and seafood. The Alpine is open for lunch and dinner during the summer, for dinner only during winter months.

Mi Casa Mexican Restaurant & Cantina
600 S. Park Ave., Breckenridge
(970) 453-2071
$

Mi Casa has traditional Mexican specialties served at lunch and dinner. Specials also include Mexican-style pork chops and steak.

Mountain Sage Cafe & Gold Pan Saloon
105 N. Main St., Breckenridge
(970) 453-5499 or (970) 547-4628
$

Enjoy a Tex-Mex breakfast, or cheap pizza and bar food later in the day. There are also burgers, veggie wraps, and steaks.

The classic sights of summer in Summit County are often seen on horseback. PHOTO: SKI THE SUMMIT/BOB WINSETT

Pierre's River Walk Café
1375 Main St., Breckenridge
(970) 453–0989
$$$

Pierre's is a fine French restaurant with lovely atmosphere and outdoor dining available in summer for lunch and dinner. It is closed on Monday during the winter months.

The St. Bernard Inn
103 S. Main St., Breckenridge
(970) 453–2572
$

The St. Bernard specializes in classic Northern Italian food and also offers contemporary cuisine. The inn is open for lunch and dinner; there's a lounge, too.

Accommodations

With lodging for nearly 25,000 visitors, Breckenridge ranks as one of Colorado's major resort towns, offering all types of overnight options in many price ranges. Call the Breckenridge Resort Chamber of Commerce Central Reservations (970–453–2918 or 800–221–1091), for information or reservations at the town's many condominiums, bed and breakfasts, and other accommodations.

Beaver Run Resort
620 Village Rd., Breckenridge
(970) 453–6000

A ski-in/ski-out establishment on Peak 9, this is Breckenridge's largest property, with lodging ranging from hotel rooms to three-bedroom suites. The fully equipped resort has indoor and outdoor swimming pools, hot tubs, fitness facilities, shops, restaurants, and even an indoor miniature golf course. Winter rates begin at $300 per night, summer rates at $135.

Great Divide Lodge
550 Village Rd., Breckenridge
(970) 453–4500

Formerly the Hilton, the lodge offers full hotel services, including complementary van service. Rooms have two queen-size beds, a king-size bed, or a king-size bed with a sleeper sofa. An on-site restaurant provides room service, and a lounge, indoor swimming pool, workout room, sauna and hot tub are on the premises. Prices for rooms begin at $225 per night in winter and $160 in summer.

William's House Bed & Breakfast
303 N. Main St., Breckenridge
(970) 453–2975, (800) 795–2975

This is a lovely 19th-century home in classic Victorian style. The house has a Jacuzzi, fireplace, and sitting area. Rates are from $89 to $325, for rooms or the cottage, depending upon the season. Five rooms with fireplaces are in a new building, The Barn Above the River, overlooking the Blue River. Some rooms are wheelchair-accessible.

Copper Mountain

Copper Mountain is a self-contained resort that was constructed a quarter of a century ago and has since won kudos for its outstanding trail and slope design as well as its compact and congenial village. It has the distinction of being the site of Club Med's first and only North American ski village.

Downhill Skiing

Copper Mountain Resort
209 Ten Mile Circle, Copper Mountain,
(U.S. I–70, Exit 195)
(970) 968–2882, (800) 458–8386

Copper Mountain, which celebrated its 50th anniversary in 1997, is treasured for its well-laid-out terrain and congenial ambiance. Copper Mountain is famous for its logical layout. As you are looking at the mountain, with I-70 at your back, most of the easy terrain is in the middle, most of the intermediate runs are in the middle or on the right, and most of the challenging turf is to the left. Copper Peak, 12,441 feet, is (after Araphahoe Basin) Colorado's second-highest lift-served summit. Spaulding Bowl, Union Bowl, and Resolution Bowl have long been favorites with powder-loving skiers and snowboarders, but in 1995-96, the area built the first of two lifts in Copper Bowl and catapulted into the top rank of

Summit County ski areas. All the bowls are steep snow pockets, treasured by advanced skiers and riders.

Copper Mountain now boasts 21 lifts (including three high-speed express chairlifts), 2,601 vertical feet, and 2,433 acres of skiable terrain—the most in Summit County. If you start at the village center you have the choice of two high-speed express lifts, American Flyer or American Eagle, that shuttle skiers toward Copper Peak and Union Peak, respectively. These two summits, the snow-kissed slopes cascading down on all sides and the valley between them offer a sensational array of ski and snowboard terrain for all ability levels. The Union Creek area, with a separate day lodge, is one of Colorado's best novice areas. If you're a new skier who needs practice, you can ride the K and L lifts and ski nearly 1,000 vertical feet of gentle terrain free of charge during part of the ski season.

Copper's well-regarded daycare facility is in the Mountain Plaza Building. The children's ski school, which offers ski lessons for kids age 3 and up as well as snowboarding instruction for older children, is headquartered in its own building, with ski school desk, kids' equipment rentals, and food service under one roof.

At-the-window, one-day tickets cost about $55 for adults and $22 for children ages 6 through 14; kids 5 and younger and seniors 70 and older are admitted free. Discount tickets are available at King Soopers, Safeway, Albertson's, Diamond Shamrock, Total, Christie Sports, and other locations. The Copper Card, which costs $18 to $40, depending on when it's purchased, enables you to buy up to four lift tickets discounted to the lowest available price every time you visit. It also offers additional discounts on food at the resort and on goods and services at Copper and elsewhere in Summit County. You can obtain more information from the resort or call the Copper Mountain Chamber of Commerce at (970) 968–6477.

A snowboarder gets some air at Copper Mountain. PHOTO: COPPER MOUNTAIN RESORT/TODD POWELL

Cross-Country Skiing

Twenty-five kilometers of machine-set tracks and skating lanes start at Union Creek and wind through the wooded valleys of the Arapahoe National Forest.

Summer Activities, Events, and Attractions

During the summer months, Copper Mountain offers golf, horseback riding, mountain biking, paddleboat rides, tennis, and free scenic chairlift rides. Over Labor Day weekend, the resort hosts Michael Martin Murphey's WestFest—three days of country-western music, crafts, and food. Call (970) 968-2882 or (800) 458-8386 for details.

Copper Creek Golf Course
104 Wheeler Pl., Copper Mountain
(970) 968-2339, (800) 458-8386

At 9,650 feet, this is the highest-altitude 18-hole championship golf course in America. It is said that balls will fly 15 percent to 20 percent farther here than at sea level. Greens fees are $44 for 9 holes, $79 for 18. Golf packages are available. Clubs can be rented for $25 for 9 holes or $40 for 18.

The Wheeler-Dillon Pack Trail
Copper Mountain Stables
355 Beeler Pl., Copper Mountain
(970) 968-2232

This trail begins across the highway from Copper Mountain and climbs steeply into the rugged Gore Range. It offers a challenge for hikers, backpackers, and horseback riders. Pack trips can be arranged through the stable.

Restaurants

The price-code key for restaurants appears at the beginning of this chapter.

Beachside Pizza and Pasta
U.S. I-70, in the Copper Junction Bldg.
(970) 968-2882
$

This eatery is at the base of the American Eagle lift. Lunch and dinner are served during the winter months, but the restaurant is typically closed during summer months.

Molly B's
U.S. I-70, in the East Village at Copper Station (970) 968-2882
$

This new restaurant is getting great reviews for its American cuisine. Open for breakfast, lunch, and dinner year-round.

Salsa Mountain Cantina
Snowbridge Square, Copper Mountain
(970) 968-6394
$

Traditional Mexican fare, plus hamburgers and daily specials that include lasagna and seafood, are served here. It's open daily for lunch, Wednesday through Sunday for dinner.

Accommodations

Club Med
50 Beeler Pl., Copper Mountain
(800) CLUB-MED
$$$$$

Geared for week-long ski vacations, this adults-only all-inclusive facility costs about $1099 per week. There are extra fees for membership and initiation. Club Med offers a basic room without a television or telephone. There are two restaurants on-site, a workout room, and planned activities for first-time skiers.

Copper Mountain Resort
209 Ten Mile Circle, Copper Mountain
(970) 968-2882, (800) 458-8386
$$$$-$$$$$

With the exception of Club Med, all of the overnight lodging at Copper Mountain is in condominiums. Units range from compact studios to luxurious four-bedroom townhomes. Depending on the season, the price for a single room can range from $125 to $275, while a four-bedroom townhome would run $750 to $1,400 per night. Multiday packages, including excellent family values, are available. All resort guests have free access to the excellent Copper Mountain Racquet & Athletic Club.

Keystone

The town of Keystone is the site of two ski resorts: Keystone and its sister, Arapahoe Basin.

Downhill Skiing

Arapahoe Basin Ski Area
U.S. Hwy. 6, Keystone
(970) 496–7077

Arapahoe Basin is America's highest ski area, with a base altitude of 10,800 feet and a summit elevation of 12,450 feet. Rugged terrain, fabled steeps, open bowls, and high, tree-free snowfields make it paradise for advanced and expert skiers and snowboarders. The lifts can run into summer (in 1995, A-Basin finally closed on August 10).

Both A-basin and Keystone have childcare facilities. Arapahoe Basin's nursery accepts children as young as 18 months. It offers ski lessons from age 3 and snowboarding lessons from age 8.

A-Basin has 61 trails with 490 skiable acres and five lifts. Fifteen percent of the trails are beginner, 45 percent are intermediate, and 40 percent expert. A one-day pass is $44 for an adult, $15 for a child. Tickets can be purchased in advance at King Soopers, Safeway, and Christie Sports.

Keystone Resort
U.S. Hwy. 6, Keystone
(800) 842–7415

Keystone is a self-contained resort with skiing on three contiguous mountains: Keystone Mountain, primarily for novice and intermediate skiers; North Peak, with its excellent mogul runs; and The Outback and The Outback Bowl, with powder-holding glades and steeps. Thanks to a huge and efficient snow-making system, Keystone is traditionally the first Colorado ski area to open for the season. Mid-October openings are not uncommon, and Halloween skiing is a tradition. In the 2000-2001 season, Keystone also welcomed snowboarders to a sensational snowboarding park in Packsaddle Bowl. It's the only Summit County area (and one of the few in Colorado) to offer night ski-ing and snowboarding, nightly until 9 P.M. during most of the season.

Keystone has 91 trails and 21 lifts and offers great deals on night skiing. A single-day ticket is about $57, while a multiday pass runs around $49 per day. Children ages 5 to 14 ski for $25 per day. Discounts are offered to seniors ages 65 to 69, and those over 70 ski free. On the Front Range tickets are available at King Soopers, Safeway, and Albertson's. Keystone's childcare center, which remains open in the evening during night skiing, takes babies as young as 2 months, and parents may use complimentary pagers to stay in touch with the center. Skiing lessons are offered to kids age 3 and up; snowboarding instruction begins at age 8.

Cross-Country Skiing

Alpine Institute
U.S. Hwy. 6, Keystone
(970) 496–4275

The Alpine Institute is near the stables on Soda Ridge Road about a mile west of the main lodge. Directed by ebullient former Olympian Jana Hlavaty, it offers outstanding instruction programs and guided ski tours. Nearly 35 kilometers of prepared trails lace through the Snake River Valley and high on the mountain, accessible from North Peak.

Other Winter Activities

Ice Skating on Keystone Lake
Keystone Resort, U.S. Hwy. 6, Keystone
(970) 496–7103

Keystone Lake is the largest maintained natural-ice surface in the country. For rink use and rentals the cost is $10 for adults; $8.50 for ages 13 to 17; $5 for ages 5 to 12; and $1 for those 4 and younger.

Summer Activities

Keystone Golf Course
Off U.S. Hwy. 6, Keystone
(970) 496–4386 (Keystone Resort Activity Desk)

Designed by Robert Trent Jones Jr., this golf course is known for both scenery and challenge. After exiting onto U.S. 6, look for signs to the golf course (take Soda Ridge Road to the end, then go left on Keystone Ranch Road). The Activity Desk takes tee-time reservations. Greens fees are about $125 per person, including cart. Keystone lodging guests pay $120 per round, and golf packages are available.

Restaurants

Alpenglow Stube
U.S. Hwy. 6, Keystone
(970) 496–4386
$$$$$

In The Outpost at the top of Keystone's North Peak, this restaurant serves elegant, Bavarian-influenced contemporary cuisine for lunch and dinner. Lunch is served only during ski season, dinner is served year-round, and reservations are required. The fixed-price meals include appetizer and dessert.

Der Fondue Chessel
U.S. Hwy. 6, Keystone
(970) 496–4386
$$$$

Der Fondue Chessel, in The Outpost, is a self-serve restaurant offering Swiss specialties. It serves dinner only, to the oompah of live entertainment. For both options at The Outpost, you can ski in during the day, and in the evening, you ride out on the enclosed gondola from the top of Keystone Mountain. Der Fondue typically closes for a month when the ski season ends, from approximately mid-May to mid-June. Call ahead to make sure the restaurant is open on summer evenings.

Keystone Ranch
U.S. Hwy. 6, Keystone
(970) 496–4386
$$$$$

Down in the valley, the elegantly rustic ranch has garnered accolades for its six-course dinners and an outstanding wine list. Only dinner is served and a reservation is recommended. The fixed-price meals include appetizer and dessert. There is year-round dining here, but only

on certain evenings, so call ahead for information.

Ski Tip Lodge
U.S. Hwy. 6, Keystone
(970) 496–4386
$$$$

Once a stagecoach stop and Summit County's original ski lodge, this lodging spot is reminiscent of an Old New England Inn. Its quaint and charming restaurant serves excellent American and continental cuisine. Breakfast is served to overnight guests only; the restaurant is open to the public for dinner year-round.

Accommodations

A new pedestrian village at the base of the River Run gondola now offers additional lodging options at the Keystone Resort. The new properties can accommodate about 1,500 more visitors.

Keystone Inn
23044 U.S. Hwy. 6, Keystone
(970) 468–1334
$$$$$

The inn offers rooms with two double beds or one king, as well as a few one-bedroom suites. There are also two suites with spas. The restaurant offers room service, and other amenities include laundry service, ski lockers, and three hot tubs. The inn is within walking distance of the ski lift. Double rooms start at $175 a night and studio condos start at $150.

Keystone Lodge
U.S. Hwy. 6, Keystone
(800) 222–0188
$$$$–$$$$$

The original Keystone development centered around Keystone Lake and the surrounding woods. The lodge offers luxurious mountain- and lake-view rooms for around $160 per night in low season to $220 in winter high season, double occupancy. Keystone also offers nearby condominium and private home rentals of various sizes, styles, and prices. As a rule of thumb, figure on paying from

$100 nightly in low season for a one-bed-room unit to $800 in high season, and $500 to $1,000 for a two-bedroom.

Frisco, Dillon, and Silverthorne

Frisco and Dillon were once mining towns, though the original Dillon is now at the bottom of Lake Dillon, a reservoir, and what you see was either moved before it was filled or rebuilt since then. The reservoir was filled between 1960 and '65. Silverthorne has become known as a major outlet shopping center, with more than 80 manufacturers' outlets. All three now have numerous stores, restaurants, and accommodations (including condos) convenient to all the Summit County ski areas.

Cross-Country Skiing

The Frisco Nordic Center
18454 Colo. Hwy. 9, Frisco
(970) 668–0866

The Frisco Center has 35 kilometers of trails groomed daily, with much of the system also offering great views of Lake Dillon and a particularly congenial log day lodge. The Breckenridge and Frisco Nordic Centers are under the same management and share an interchangeable trail pass. Both offer instruction and rentals of cross-country skis and snowshoes.

White River National Forest
Dillon Ranger District, 680 Blue River Pkwy., Silverthorne
(970) 468–5400

Several Nordic routes are accessible from the road to Montezuma or directly from this old mining camp. Peru Creek is a good trail for novices, while the routes to the St. John and the Wild Irishman Mine trails are popular with intermediate skiers and snowshoers. All are open to the public free of charge.

Summer Activities

Biking
Summit County Chamber of Commerce and Frisco Visitors' Center
(970) 668–2051
Dillon Visitors' Center
(970) 262–0817

Mountain biking is king all over Colorado, but in Summit County, riding along the paved Blue River Bikeway connecting Breckenridge and Frisco is a milder option. The route parallels Colo. 9, winding through meadows and forests. If you can handle the uphill, take the paved Ten Mile Canyon National Recreation Trail from Frisco up to Copper Mountain, or put your bike on a free Summit Stage bus and coast down. From Copper Mountain, you can also continue on the Vail Pass Bikeway, a 20-mile route (one-way) that climbs over 10,600-foot Vail Pass and down into Vail Village. These are beautiful rides anytime but especially in early fall when the aspen trees are turning gold. For trail maps contact either of the above telephone numbers.

Boating on Lake Dillon
300 Marina Dr., Dillon
(970) 468–5100

This is a 3,000-acre reservoir offering opportunities and charters for all types of boating, including fishing and sailboats. The Dillon Marina is open from the end of May through October.

Restaurants

The Arapahoe Cafe
626 Lake Dillon Dr., Dillon
(970) 468–0873
$

Breakfast, lunch, and dinner are served daily in a cozy log cabin. Early in the day you'll find omelets, hamburgers, and salads, and by evening steak, seafood, and pasta.

The Mint
341 Blue River Pkwy., Silverthorne
(970) 468–5247
$

This restaurant is in one of Summit County's oldest buildings (one of those rescued from the bottom of the lake) and is a good family-dining spot. You cook your own steak or chicken on the grill.

Old Dillon Inn
Colo. Hwy. 9 in Silverthorne, north of I–70
(970) 468–2791
$

For a great margarita—though you'll have to fight the crowds—go to the Dillon Inn. The restaurant serves primarily Mexican food at the dinner hour only and has a 19th-century bar and lively music.

The Snake River Saloon
23074 U.S. Hwy. 6, Dillon
(970) 468–2788
$–$$

Open daily for dinner only, this is a popular spot for après-ski, with steak and seafood and not-to-miss late-night entertainment on weekends.

Accommodations

Chateaux d'Mont
0175 County Rd. 8, Dillon
(888) 222–9298
$$$$$

Close to the Keystone Resort, the Chateaux costs $700 to $900 per night for a truly deluxe two- or three-bedroom condo within walking distance of the lifts and featuring a private hot tub on a glass-enclosed balcony. Amenities include a welcome grocery package, fresh flowers, plush terry-cloth robes, nightly turndown, complimentary newspaper, and concierge service.

The Boulder Ballet performs two different ballets each season. PHOTO: JUDITH PHILLIPS PHOTOGRAPH

Arts

Dance
Film
Music
Theater
Visual Arts

Despite its small-city size, Boulder offers a big-city arts scene, ranging from local artists with national reputations to the summer Colorado Music Festival with musicians from around the world. The internationally renowned Colorado Dance Festival and the Colorado Shakespeare Festival also attract top talent. The Boulder Museum of Contemporary Art (BMoCA) and the University of Colorado galleries show work by both locally and nationally known artists. In addition to exhibitions, BMoCA and Naropa University (see our chapter on Education) sponsor innovative arts events and community theater; dance and music groups provide a varied mix of entertainment.

Proximity to Denver expands the arts horizon with the Denver Art Museum, Colorado Symphony, Denver Center Theatre Company, and a number of small theater companies. Even closer, the Arvada Center for the Arts and Humanities offers theater, music, dance, and visual art by Colorado's best and nationally known artists. The nearby communities of Longmont, Louisville, Lafayette, Lyons, Central City, Golden, and Nederland offer their own historical museums, music and theater groups, and art exhibitions as well.

Below are the highlights of the area's arts offerings. Note that we have listed museums in our Boulder Attractions chapter. You may notice that many of the groups have the same address. That's the Dairy Center for the Arts, a 40,000-square-foot space that used to house the Watts-Hardy Dairy. The empty building was purchased as a home for small arts groups, and today about 15 such groups make their home there.

Dance

Boulder Ballet
Dairy Center for the Arts, 2590 Walnut St., Boulder
(303) 442-6944
Founded in 1981, the Boulder Ballet is Boulder County's only classical ballet company. Boulder Ballet is a company of local professionals and amateurs and visiting professionals. The ballet collaborates annually with the Boulder Philharmonic Orchestra to present two full-length productions—*The Nutcracker* ballet, a winter tradition so popular the two performances sell out every year, and spring performances (*Romeo and Juliet* and *Swan Lake* in 2001).

As a member of the Peak Association of the Arts, the Boulder Ballet also provides ballet instruction through the PeakArts educational wing, the Boulder Arts Academy. In addition, the Ballet tours Boulder County schools presenting "Steps in Time," an interactive educational program for young people.

Performances are held in a variety of places, including Denver's Boettcher Hall and Macky Auditorium in Boulder.

Boulder Jazz Dance Workshop
CU-Boulder campus
(303) 449-0399
Founded in 1978 by Lara Branen, then a graduate student at CU-Boulder, this two-week August workshop includes public performances. This now-independent group returns to Boulder each year, where CU-Boulder's Theatre and Dance Department lends its facilities. The workshop is open to the public, offering classes in jazz dance, hip hop, jazz funk, and modern dance, as well as ballet barre, a mat class

241

based on the principles of Joseph Pilates, and special classes emphasizing partnering and turns for students 16 and older.

Following the workshop (the first two weeks in August), there are performances by students, faculty, and the company in residence, Interweave Dance Theatre of Boulder, which is composed of some 30 dancers. Thirty to 40 percent of the workshop participants come from other states and countries, including Mexico, Italy, and elsewhere. Participants can receive up to two college credits at CU, and housing is available. Sign up early—the program fills very quickly.

Cleo Parker Robinson Dance
119 Park Ave. W., Denver
(303) 295–1759

This 31-year-old dance company–cum-school and theater is dedicated to providing cross-cultural, African-centered performances and classes. Its fall and holiday performances are at the Denver Center for the Performing Arts. Jazz and modern-dance aficionados will relish this internationally renowned group. Well-known performers from around the world visit the school and theater, and the ensemble goes on extended tours. An annual July event is the International Summer Dance Institute, which hosts great master instructors from all over the world. The instructors teach all types of dance, music, theater, storytelling, and cultural rituals to children and adults. The company also operates the Season of Schools program that introduces more than 50,000 students in Denver metro schools to dance. One of Denver's greatest holiday traditions is the annual December concert, "Granny Dances to a Holiday Drum." There's usually an annual spring performance as well. The school also runs Project Self-Discovery, an outreach program for at-risk youth. Call for information and current schedules for these excellent performances, classes, and workshops.

Colorado Ballet
1036 14th St. (ticket office); 1278 Lincoln St. (administrative office), Denver
(303) 98–MUSIC (tickets)

Born from a ballet school in Denver, the Colorado Ballet was established in 1961, making it one of Colorado's oldest arts institutions. The company now includes 30 professional dancers from around the world and 25 apprentice dancers. In 1997, Colorado Ballet II was created to provide uppel-level students at the company's Colorado Academy of Ballet an opportunity to gain performance experience.

The Colorado Ballet performs such classics as *La Sylphide* and *The Nutcracker* each Christmas season, but also offers more innovative works such as those of

George Balanchine. The 2001 season included *Dracula, Where the Wild Things Are,* and *A Midsummer Night's Dream.* The performance season is from October through May. Series tickets are available.

Colorado Dance Festival
2590 Walnut St.
(303) 442–7666

Now the third-largest dance festival in the nation, the Boulder-based Colorado Dance Festival (CDF) is partially funded by the National Endowment for the Arts. CDF has earned international recognition with its innovative programs and renowned performers, including such top names as Trisha Brown and the late, great tap dancer Honi Coles. The CDF also founded the Boulder-based International Tap Association (303–443–7989).

In 2001, the festival's 19th season, more than 400 dancers from around the globe gathered for intensive training with a faculty of 40 from five continents. The program has something for beginners to experienced professionals.

Performances for the 2001 season included the "defiant physicality" of Doug Varone and Dancers; Martha @ The Dairy, an homage to Martha Graham featuring Richard Move; and the hip-hop-infused Illadelph Legends, featuring Rennie Harris PureMovement.

In addition to performances and classes, CDF continues with its energetic Youth Dance Project, which gives young dancers ages 12 to 18 a chance to study with renowned professional dancers; the lecture-demonstration Informances; and the Family Series of matinee performances that give the audience a chance to take a turn onstage.

Community Dance Collective
2020B 21st St., Boulder
(303) 447–2566

The collective offers rehearsal space and classes, as well as performances in folk, ballet, modern dance, and jazz for all ages. The organization is the oldest nonprofit dance group in Boulder. Call for a schedule.

Frequent Flyers Productions
Dairy Center for the Arts, 2590 Walnut St., Boulder
(303) 444–5569

If dance sometimes resembles floating, flying, and swooping through air, Frequent Flyers Productions really makes it so. The company uses trapezes to set dancers free of gravity. It all began in 1988 with a chilling performance inspired by Anne Rice's vampire novels. Now, the company offers workshops and classes for adventurous folks 10 and older, along with periodic performances (the vampire program has become a Boulder staple at Halloween, drawing a repeat audience with many in full white-faced, fanged, black-clad regalia).

Steven Homsher and Valerie Morris fly frequently as members of the airborne dance company Frequent Flyers. The group uses trapezes, bungees, stilts, and whatever else occurs to them to take dance off the ground. PHOTO: FREQUENT FLYERS

The company's third annual Aerial Dance Festival, held in 2001, brought together aerial artists from around the world for a week of performance, experimentation, teaching, and discussion. Faculty demonstrated their talents on the trapeze, stilts, ropes, and harness and bungies. The company also uses the Boulder Rock Club's climbing wall (see Sports chapter) for its performances.

The Naropa University Performing Arts Series
2130 Arapahoe Ave., Boulder
(303) 546–3538,
(303) 786–7030 (ticket office)

A private, nonsectarian liberal arts college with roots in Buddhism, Naropa opened its doors in 1974. It concentrates mainly on avant-garde and new dance, offering classes, workshops, and performances. A spring cultural festival combines dance with music, costume, food, films, and storytelling from around the world. Call the ticket office for other events and classes.

Postoley Dance Ensemble
2020B 21st St., Boulder
(303) 499–6363

This newly formed company teaches and performs ethnic dances of Eastern Europe under the direction of artist-in-residence Konstyantyn Butsura from the Ukraine. Rehearsals are open and free. They are held Thursdays at 7:15 P.M. at the Community Dance Collective space. The group performs at events around the region.

University of Colorado Department of Theatre and Dance
CU-Boulder campus
(303) 492–7355, (303) 492–8181 (tickets)

Throughout the school year this talent-filled university department presents a number of innovative performances including ballet, modern, African-American, and other dance forms. In the summer, all resources are focused on the Colorado Shakespeare Festival (details below, under "Theater"). There are student perform-

ances all year-round, with the main one presented in late fall; a faculty performance takes place in late spring. Call for a current schedule.

Film

In addition to the special film series listed below, Boulder has some 20 commercial movie theaters, among them United Artists and Mann Theater complexes, Flatirons Theatre on University Hill, and the Basemar Cinema Saver Theatres—the best bargain of all. A 12-plex of theaters at the Louisville exit off of U.S. Highway 36 gives moviegoers an even bigger selection, and a 24-plex farther south off Highway 36 offers stadium seating and butter-your-own popcorn. In the summer, the Almost Free Outdoor Cinema unrolls a screen and turns the parking lot behind BMoCA into an open-air theater featuring everything from classic films like *Yellow Submarine* to the campy *Monty Python's Meaning of Life*. Every Saturday night between early June and early September, fans bring blankets, lawn chairs, even couches and coffee tables, and fill in the time during reel changes with costume and trivia contests.

Boulder Public Library Film Program
Main Branch Auditorium, Ninth St. and Canyon Blvd., Boulder
(303) 441–3197

Since 1974, this free film program has offered everything from Asian anime and the French classic *Diabolique* to documentaries and series on such topics as Depression Era Musical Comedies. The library also shows mainstream Hollywood movies. Call for information, or visit the library to pick up the latest schedule. Movies are shown in the library's comfy, cozy auditorium.

Chautauqua Summer Film Festival
Ninth St. and Baseline Rd., Boulder
(303) 440–7666

Moviegoers of all ages will feel like kids at summer camp inside Chautauqua's barn-like auditorium. This summer-only program shows historic silent films from the 1920s and earlier, such Charlie Chaplin's *The Kid* and Marion Davies in *The Patsy*, many with live piano accompaniment by Hank Troy. Prices are $5 for adults and $4 for children (younger than 12), $7 and $5 for films with piano accompaniment. There are special prices for film series.

International Film Series
Muenzinger Auditorium, Muenzinger Plaza, CU-Boulder campus (west of Folsom Stadium near the corner of Colorado Ave. and 18th St.)
(303) 492–1531

Connected with the CU-based Rocky Mountain Film Center, this series is the West's longest-running continuous forum for international and art-film screenings and has entertained university and Boulder audiences for more than 50 years. The First Person Cinema is affiliated with the RMFC and features visiting artists throughout the academic year. It includes avant-garde works by independent and personal filmmakers such as Stan Brakhage, Fred Worden, and Caroline Leaf, as well as wonderful, entertaining films from all over the world that aren't available in mall theaters or video stores. The spacious, steeply sloping Muenzinger Auditorium offers every moviegoer a perfect view for the right price—$4 ($3 for CU students). The 24-hour hotline above lists each week's events.

University of Colorado Program Council Film Series
Forum Rm. in the UMC, and Chem. 140 in the Chemistry Bldg. (next building over from UMC), 16th St. and E. Euclid Ave., CU-Boulder campus
(303) 492–5458

These free and bargain-priced films offer some of the best entertainment around. Catch up on first-run movies you might have missed at the local theater last year. A high-tech Dolby stereo cinema sound processor makes the sound system in the university's Chemistry 140 auditorium one of Boulder's best. Pick up a film schedule at the University Memorial Center

> ## Insiders' Tip
> Among the best local entertainment values are CU-Boulder's Program Council Films and the more art-oriented International Film Series. Both are held on campus. The Program Council features recent first-run movies; the International Film Series has excellent award winners from all over the world that you'll have a hard time finding at a regular theater. Look for a free schedule in the Boulder Public Library and at area bookstores. See the listing in this chapter for more information.

(UMC), Boulder Public Libraries, city recreation centers, and local supermarkets. The screen is dark during the summer.

Music

Ars Nova Singers
(303) 499–3165

This group of 40 a capella singers presents music from the Renaissance and 20th and 21st centuries, including works by Colorado's finest composers, and performs in churches in Boulder and Denver. Founded in 1985, Ars Nova was one of the first choirs from Colorado funded by the National Endowment for the Arts and the only one to receive funding for three consecutive years. In 1998, the choir performed its first international tour, and it was later invited to perform at the statewide memorial service for the victims of the Columbine High School shootings, also attended by Vice-President Al Gore. Ars Nova presents annual Christmas concerts in Boulder and Denver at area churches. The ensemble has performed the complete *Responsoria* by Renaissance composer Carlo Gesualdo, Gyorgy Ligeti's *Lux Aeterna,* Charles Ives's cantata *The Celestial Country,* and many experimental and avant-garde choral works. The Ars Nova Singers have been heard in radio broadcasts throughout the United States, Canada, South America, and Europe. The group has released six CDs. Ticket prices are $10, $8 for students and seniors 60 and older.

Artist Series
Macky Auditorium, Grusin Music Hall, and Imig Music Building, CU-Boulder campus
(303) 492–8008

The University of Colorado-Boulder's Artist Series has been going strong for some 65 years, with a full season of varied performances. Recent highlights included Christopher Parkening and Jubilant Sykes, the Parsons Dance Company, and Samul Nori. The Takacs String Quartet, composed of the series' Hungarian artists-in-residence, also performs. The Artist Series is held in the university's Macky Auditorium, Grusin Music Hall, and the Music Theatre in Imig Music Building, and includes performance art, jazz, classics, dance, folk, and ethnic performances. Tickets prices range from $10 to $32.

Arvada Center for the Arts and Humanities
6901 Wadsworth Blvd., Arvada
(303) 431–3939

About a 30-minute drive south of Boulder, the 25-year-old Arvada Center is a sophisticated venue for music of all types, from popular to classical, with nationally known groups and performers. During performances, the upper gallery is open so that audience members may view the work of nationally known artists and craftspeople. Summer concerts are in an outdoor amphitheater. The 2001 season included performances by such varied artists as

Lavay Smith & Her Red Hot Skillet Lickers, Arvada Center Chorale with the National Repertory Orchestra, and Herman's Hermits starring Peter Noone. Tickets run from $8 to $24. The center also offers year-round theater, concerts, and dance performances, a historical museum, and classes in ceramics, dance, writing, acting, visual arts, and more.

Boulder Bach Festival
(303) 494–3159

It began in 1981 as a one-weekend festival; now the Boulder Bach Festival has evolved into a year-round series of concerts highlighting the famous composer's work. The annual three-day Bach Festival is in January. Lecture series, master classes, youth competitions, and an enrichment program for local elementary schools round out the offerings. The very unstuffy company puts on a lively New Year's Eve performance with a champagne reception. There are also children's concerts in March and May, and a fall concert in the 100-year-old Ryssby Church west of Longmont.

Boulder Philharmonic Orchestra
2590 Walnut St., Boulder
(303) 449–1343

The orchestra, under the direction of Music Director Theodore Kuchar, celebrated its 42nd season in 2001. The year's guest performers were Jessye Norman, Lynn Harrel, and Peter Donohoe. In past seasons, the list has included Yo-Yo Ma, Itzhak Perlman, Mstislav Rostropovich, Anne Sophie Mutter, and Sarah Chang. The Sinfonia of Boulder, the state's only professional chamber orchestra, is composed of members of the Boulder Philharmonic led by Phil conductor Theodore Kuchar. The group is performing all of Mozart's symphonies in a three-year series. The Phil also holds an annual Symphony Ball in the spring, sponsored by the volunteer fund-raising organization Club Phil, one of the orchestra's greatest assets. The Boulder Arts Academy, with instructors from the Boulder Philharmonic and some 700 students, offers group classes and private lessons and has large ensembles. Recently the Boulder Arts Academy collaborated with the Boulder Ballet and offered ballet as well as music classes.

Central City Opera
Eureka St., Central City
(303) 292–6700, (800) 851–8175

One of Colorado's favorite outings, the Central City Opera features operatic works sung in English in this old mining town, now a glitzy gambling haven. This summer troupe is one of the oldest opera companies in the country, with a distinguished national reputation. The CCO also offers daytime cabaret opera and special youth performances. The opera house was built in 1878 in an effort to bring culture to the formerly rough and rowdy mining town. Performances are frequently sold out, so call ahead for reservations for the summer-only program. In 2001, Central City Opera became the first American opera company to stage Benjamin Britten's regal, romantic *Gloriana*. First performed in 1953 for the coronation of Elizabeth II, Britten's compelling portrait of Elizabeth I was joined by the regional premiere of Mark Adamo's *Little Women* and a revival of Giacomo Puccini's *La Boheme* for Central City Opera's 69th season.

Reserved parking is available, and a shuttle bus takes operagoers from the parking area (a half-mile away) right to the opera house's front door. The bus leaves about every 10 minutes during the two hours before and after the opera, so there's plenty of time for a meal, gambling or sightseeing in Central City. Tickets range from $39 to $69, $10 to $70 for special events—the grand ball is $190 and reportedly worth every cent. (Please see the Close-up in this chapter for more information.)

Chautauqua Summer Festival Concerts
Main Office, South of Ninth St. and Baseline Rd., Boulder
(303) 440–7666 (summer only),
(303) 545–6924, ext. 18

Summer in Boulder wouldn't truly be summer without Chautauqua, which features a series of popular-music concerts and performances in addition to the classical Colorado Music Festival (see our subsequent listing and Close-up in this chapter). This historic music venue has been an institution since 1898, when Boulder's Chautauqua first opened as part of a national movement that brought the arts to numerous summer camps around the country. Today, many concertgoers enjoy dinner on the lovely old veranda of the picturesque Chautauqua Dining Hall or bring a picnic to enjoy under the shady trees on the green. The Summer Festival Concerts have featured such groups and performers as Rosanne Cash, Los Lobos, Peter Kater, Michelle Shocked, Richard Thompson, Joan Armatrading, Laurie Anderson, The Persuasions, and the delicately named Mother Folkers. Some folks picnic into the night and enjoy the music (for free) from outside the concert hall. Dance fans can see performances by Cleo Parker Robinson and Danielle Helander. Chautauqua makes it a point to feature quirky performances such as the Reduced Shakespeare Company, "the Bad Boys of Abridgement," and The Barbershoppers, a large barbershop chorus. Among the many others who have appeared here are Karla Bonoff, Spaulding Gray, and Hunter S. Thompson. The Boulder Folk and Bluegrass Festival is also held at Chautauqua.

Colorado Children's Chorale
910 15th St., Denver
(303) 830–8497 (Ticketmaster),
(303) 892–5600 (info)

Children from all over the Denver metro area audition to get into one of the five chorales. The CCC presents popular and traditional music such as *Carmina Burana* and special compositions written for the chorale by resident composers. There are annual U.S. and international tours by the group. A December Christmas concert features traditional holiday music, and there's a special spring concert in May. Tickets range from $6 to $25. The chorale has recorded three tapes, available by calling (303) 892-5600.

Central City Opera

Central City's historic opera building, just west of Main and Eureka streets, was built in 1878. The first-rate, sung-in-English performances have entertained even lukewarm opera fans since 1932. Everyone stays in historic Victorian character, including the uniformed ushers, who form a chorus and sing a tune out in the street about a half-hour before the show. Then they ring brass hand bells every 10 minutes or so announcing that the opera will soon begin.

With hand-painted murals of Pegasus and cafe chairs engraved with the names of famous benefactors, the Victorian theater is a treat. You're close enough that the performers come across as real people who feel life so strongly, they've just got to sing about it.

Literally, every seat is good, thanks to the recent installation of new, roomier theater-style and continental seating in front of the orchestra. The seat renovation project reduced the theater's seating by 27 percent, making it even more likely that shows will sell out. Get your tickets as early as possible, since some operas sell out weeks or months in advance. (Although on some nights, you can buy tickets at the door.)

Since Colorado voters approved limited stakes gambling in Central City and Black Hawk, getting to the opera is a little more complicated because parking in the area is limited. You can pay $5 for a reserved spot in the opera house parking lot when you order tickets in advance. Or try the bus from Denver and Lakewood for every performance; on Fridays there's a bus from Boulder. Cost is $15 for adults, $13 for seniors 62 and older.

Built in 1878, the Central City Opera House features a restored interior with beautiful trompe l'oeil murals by John C. Massman. PHOTO: MARY KIRYLUK

The season kicks off with Opera Pops "Picnic Without Ants" (picnickers $30; patrons $60) in Denver at the Marriott City Center. The price includes an evening of opera pops and an indoor, gourmet picnic.

For something a little more elegant, there is the Opening Night Yellow Rose Ball ($190 per person, including the opera) at The Teller House, beside Central City's Opera Building. The eclectic celebration includes presentation of the Central City Flower Girls, a waltz on Eureka Street, ringing bells, a dynamite blast, and a sit-down dinner, followed by an opera performance.

Weekend Opera Lovers' Dinners were created specifically for opera patrons who prefer to avoid the casino atmosphere. They begin at 6 P.M. and are held in a private banquet room in the Teller House. The four-course buffet with dessert, wine, and soft music, costs $30 per person and is offered on selected Friday and Saturday evenings; the price of the opera ticket is extra. Reservations are required; call (303) 292–6700.

If you are on a budget, bring your own picnic dinner, and enjoy it in the little park between the Teller House and the Opera House. It takes about an hour to drive from Boulder to the Opera House parking lot. Try to reach it at least an hour early. This way, a brief traffic jam won't spell trouble, and there will be time for a beverage stop or a stroll around town to enjoy the lovely Victorian houses. Be sure you arrive at the opera house at least 10 minutes before the show. If you're late, you'll be allowed to enter only between acts.

There are also a number of options for those who would like just an opera appetizer and not the full course. At weekend Salon Recitals, opera stars perform short recitals during a gourmet brunch at the Teller House Hotel, next to the opera house. Tickets cost around $25. Opera a la Carte offers fully staged scenes from famous operas Wednesdays and Fridays at 1:15 pm at a cost of just $8 ($5 for subscribers). *Face on the Barroom Floor* is a 30-minute cabaret opera recounting the Teller House's famous legend. These performances are at 1:15 P.M. Saturday and Sunday at Williams Stables, right across the street, and cost $8 ($5 for subscribers).

Or ask for the *Opera Lovers' Guide* from the theater for information on places to eat, lodging and background information. The guide is free.

Colorado Music Festival
1525 Spruce St., Suite 101, Boulder
(303) 449–1397 (year round),
(303) 449–2413 (summer tickets)

From late June through mid-August each year, classical musicians from around the country and world come to Boulder to participate in the Colorado Music Festival at Boulder's historic Chautauqua. Founded in 1976, the series is organized around themes such as "Renaissance to Gen X," "American Music," "Romantic Refresher," and "Baroque to Bel Canto." There are several children's and family concerts, too. A Boulder Fourth of July tradition is the Colorado Music Festival's free concert on the Chautauqua lawn, highlighted with foot-thumping John Philip Sousa marches. The festival's new music director, Michael Christie, is just one year older than the festival founded by Giora Bernstein, who retired a year ago. Season tickets are available in advance, or concertgoers can pay at the door.

Colorado Symphony
821 17th St., Suite 700 (admin. office);
Boettcher Hall, Performing Arts Complex,
14th and Lawrence Sts., Denver
(303) 98–MUSIC

Many Boulderites gladly make the trek to Denver to enjoy the Colorado Symphony at Denver's delightful Boettcher Hall. The director is Marin Alsop, the highest-placed female conductor in the world, who has been with the CSO for three years. Choices include a regular concert series and special holiday concerts, plus Family, Masterworks and Popular Classics, and Pops concert series. The Colorado Christmas concert features the Colorado Children's Chorale and Colorado Symphony Chorus. A New Years' Eve Celebration features a post-concert dinner dance in Boettcher and the Pavilion of the Performing Arts complex. Past highlights include an evening of Copland with pianist mezzo-soprano Marietta Simpson, and a program of percussion with Colin Currie.

Family concerts are held in February with such offerings as a Symphony Safari at the Denver Zoo, and an exploration of "What Is Music?" at the Museum of Natural History.

Summer in Boulder Means Chautauqua

"Chautauqua" is a Native American word that means "two moccasins tied together." It's also the name of a lake in New York state that was the birthplace of a late 19th- and early 20th-century national movement. During this period, summer camps/retreats called Chautauquas, where people went for cultural or spiritual renewal, popped up across the country. At the turn of the 20th century there were 12,000 Chautauquas in the United States. Today there are only three. One of them is in Boulder.

While others around the country focused on religion, Boulder's Chautauqua always focused on arts and entertainment. Boulder hosted such famous guests as statesman William Jennings Bryant and musician John Philip Sousa. Boulder's Chautauqua has a lovely park setting on the edge of Boulder's Mountain Park system and is a designated national historic district, jointly run by the National Park Service and the City of Boulder. According to *Inside Performance Magazine,* performing artists voted Boulder's Chautauqua Auditorium one of the top 10 halls in the United States in which they love to perform.

Flowers and Flatirons frame Chautauqua Auditorium. PHOTO: DAILY CAMERA/LOURIE ZIPF

In the past, the Pops series has featured Yo-Yo Ma, a three-day Jazz in America series with guest Dr. Billy Taylor, the Lincoln Center Jazz Orchestra with Wynton Marsalis, pianist Fabio Bidini, and Hot Latin Nights with Doc Severinson as conductor and on trumpet.

Family series tickets cost $10 for adults and $7 for children and are sold through the Denver Center for the Performing Arts. Single tickets may be purchased in person, at the Denver Center Box Office at 14th and Curtis Streets, Monday through Saturday from 10 A.M. to 6 P.M., online at www.denvercenter.org, or by phone during regular business hours at (303) 893-4100. A $3 charge per ticket is assessed on purchases made by phone or through the Internet. No fee is charged on orders placed in person.

Fiddler's Green
6350 Greenwood Plaza Blvd., Englewood
(303) 220-7000

About an hour's drive from Boulder, Fiddler's Green, a popular outdoor concert hall on Denver's south side, offers nationally known groups that aren't likely to visit Boulder. Enjoy these summer-only concerts either from reserved seats or while picnicking on the lawn. Tickets are available at the box office or by calling Ticketmaster at (303) 830-8497.

Public Library Concert Series
1000 Canyon Blvd., Boulder
(303) 441-3100

This free series at the Boulder Public Library Auditorium (Canyon Boulevard entrance) offers music lovers a wealth of listening, from Bach to ragtime. Piano and harp soloists, string quartets, members of the Boulder Philharmonic, and local musicians are among the varied performers.

Red Rocks
Morrison St., Morrison
(303) 640-7334 (recorded information and events)

Celebrating its 60th anniversary this season, this spectacular natural-rock open-air

amphitheater is the venue for most top performers who come to the Denver area. The 2001 season included performances by Chris Daniels Band, Big Bad Voodoo Daddy, and Arturo Sandoval. Red Rocks information and tickets are available through Ticketmaster at (303) 830-8497. Check local newspapers for a rundown of the performers appearing at Red Rocks or call the number listed above. Tickets range from $25 to $40 and are available with no service charge at the Pepsi Center and the Denver Performing Arts Complex in downtown Denver (cash only and in person).

Theater

Arvada Center for the Arts and Humanities
6901 Wadsworth Blvd., Arvada
(303) 431-3939

The Arvada Center opened its stage doors in 1976 and has been an equity theater since 1992, bringing professional talent into an intimate setting. The indoor theater seats 500, and the ticket prices range from $12 to $28, with discounts for seniors and students. Shows run Tuesday through Sunday with matinees. The Arvada Center also has a huge education program offering more than 100 classes for both children and adults in everything from acting, performing arts, and music to ceramics and the humanities.

Boulder's Dinner Theatre
5501 Arapahoe Ave., Boulder
(303) 449–6000

From *Paint Your Wagon* to *South Pacific*, Boulder's Dinner Theatre is the only local venue for popular musicals. It has won a number of awards for its professional performances with excellent sets and staging. The theater offers cocktails and a choice of delicious dinners (the prime rib is great!) served by its talented singers and performers. Tickets cost $35 to $46.50 per person and are discounted for seniors and children for some performances.

The Boulder Repertory Company
Boulder Public Library, 1000 Canyon Blvd., Boulder
(303) 449–7258

The Boulder Repertory Company presents three meaty shows a year. Lacking a home of its own, this company has performed in approximately 11 different locations. The performances are usually in the Boulder Public Library auditorium and occasionally in Denver. The Boulder Rep's fine productions are worth seeing. Artistic director Frank Georgianna launched TBRC in 1975, and it has become one of Boulder's most respected companies. Georgianna was a director and actor at the Denver Center Theatre from 1985 to 1994.

Colorado Shakespeare Festival
Mary Rippon Theatre, CU-Boulder campus
(303) 492–0554

Film actor Val Kilmer took part in these Shakespeare productions one year, and other top performers, such as TV star Jimmy Smits, have likewise been attracted to this highly regarded annual summer festival. Held at the outdoor Mary Rippon Theatre, this is another local institution. It includes both traditional and modern renditions of the bard's work. The 2001 season offered *Two Gentlemen of Verona, King Lear, As You Like It,* and *Queen Margare,* a "Shakespearean" play adapted by Robert Potter. Theatergoers can order a box dinner and dine on the green before

the show. Be sure to fit in a stroll through the Shakespeare Gardens, planted each year with herbs, flowers, and even vegetables mentioned in the summer's plays. There are evening and Sunday matinee performances. Single tickets are $16 to $40 (smart fans get in free by volunteering as ushers).

Denver Center Theatre Company
1050 13th St., Denver
(303) 893–4100

The Denver Center for the Performing Arts attracts big Broadway shows with national touring companies, but the Denver Center Theatre Company, now in its 29th season, is the local theater company that performs at the center. Featuring a varied menu of entertainment ranging from works by Dickens and Shakespeare to the life of Janis Joplin, the company has received many awards, including, in 1998, the Tony Award for Outstanding Regional Theater.

Longmont Theatre Company Performing Arts Center
513 Main St., Longmont
(303) 772–5200

A short drive from Boulder via the Longmont Diagonal Highway (Colo. 119), the Longmont Theatre Company, founded in 1959, offers musicals, drama, comedy, children's performances, a Christmas show, and a Shakespeare Festival. Call for a current schedule of performances. The 2001 season included *Cyrano de Bergerac, Cabaret,* and *Witness for the Prosecution.* Tickets run $10 to $12 and are available by phone or at the box office 90 minutes before a performance.

Naropa University Performing Arts Center
2130 Arapahoe Ave., Boulder
(303) 546–3538

Not limited to theater per se, Naropa has speakers, poetry readings, and various performances. There are student-run shows, inter-arts faculty concerts (including music, art, dance, and theater), faculty and student readings every semester, and annual Balinese and African concerts. The university offers workshops, dance performances, and art exhibits, too. Call for a schedule of events.

Nomad Playhouse
1410 Quince St., Boulder
(303) 786–9808

Since 1951, Nomad has been providing community theater in a quonset hut "Just a little off Broadway"—Boulder's Broadway, that is. The theater was completely renovated in 1998. Former Boulderites, Joan Van Ark of *Knot's Landing* and Larry Linville of *M*A*S*H* both got their acting start with the Nomad, which hosts some excellent serious and not-so-serious drama.

Opera Colorado
695 S. Colorado Blvd., Denver
(303) 98–MUSIC

Opera Colorado's season consists of three operas presented in March, April, and May. The 2001 season included *Turandot, Orpheus,* and *Eurydice and Ariadne auf Naxos.* Some tickets are available at the door if the show is not sold out.

Peanut Butter Players
2475 Mapleton Ave., Boulder
(303) 786–8PBP

Based in the Toadstool Playhouse, one of Boulder's funky landmark buildings, this theater company of local youngsters ages 5 to 18 offers year-round performances. The luncheon theater here is just like adult dinner theater, except the performance is at lunchtime and the performers are a lot shorter. There are classes during the school year and a day camp in summer that teach such things as music, puppetry, pantomime, dance, makeup, voice dialects, clowning, and theater crafts. Each summer PBP puts on a major production at Boulder High School with about 250 children ($6 for adults, $4 for children). The 2001 production, *Peter Pandemonium,* even had parts for parents.

Actresses Alicia King and Ronni Stark ponder the mother-daughter relationship during Boulder's Dinner Theatre's production of Gypsy, *while the audience, seated at tables, finishes off dessert.*
PHOTO: BOULDER'S DINNER THEATRE

University of Colorado Department of Theatre and Dance
CU-Boulder campus
(303) 492–7355

Considered by local critics to present the most consistently good and reliable performances, the CU-Boulder Theatre Department won the 1993 Denver Drama Critics Circle award for Best Season for a Company. Throughout the school year, this university department holds numerous performances at campus theaters. The 2001 season included Sam Shepard's

Curse of the Starving Class. The department also offers performances by students in the master of fine arts degree program, and student dance performances. Call for more information or a complete schedule.

Upstart Crow Guild Theatre
Dairy Center for the Arts, 1590 Walnut St., Boulder
(303) 442–1415

Performing since 1979, this ensemble presents classical plays in their complete and uncut versions, as well as more current productions. The 2001 season includes *Oedipus the King, The Devil's Disciple,* and *King Lear.* Individual tickets are $12 to $15. Thursdays feature "name your price" performances—drop an envelope in the collection box as you leave with as much or as little as you like.

Visual Arts

Admission to the following galleries and shops is free unless otherwise noted.

ArtCycle
141 Pearl St., just off the Downtown Mall at 15th St., Boulder
(303) 449–4950

Featuring recycled art at its best, this store offers a high-quality selection of pre-owned art in all media and price ranges by successful local and nationally known artists. There are paintings, limited-edition prints, sculptures, photographs, and more. ArtCycle takes new consignments all the time and also offers custom framing. It is open 10 A.M. to 6 P.M. Monday through Saturday, and noon to 6 P.M. Sunday.

Arvada Center for the Arts and Humanities
6901 Wadsworth Blvd., Arvada
(303) 431–3080

The Arvada Center hosts 12 to 15 art exhibits a year. Nationally known artists and Colorado's best artists and craftspeople show their work in the excellent gallery. There is also a permanent historical exhibit on the area's early days. The gallery is open 9 A.M. to 5 P.M. Monday through Saturday, 1 to 5 P.M. Sunday.

Boulder Arts & Crafts Cooperative
1421 Pearl St., Boulder
(303) 443–3683

The co-op has 45 members and shows the work of more than 150 artists, including nationally known artists and participating members and consignees from Colorado and surrounding mountain states. Nowhere else in the area will you find such a concentrated collection of top-quality pottery, puppets, jewelry, photographs, fiber art, stained glass, woodwork, and other items. The co-op has an extensive and spectacular selection of jewelry made precious metals, as well as contemporary fashion jewelry. There are handcrafted clothes that are works of art on hangers, whimsical painted wooden furniture, too. Opened in 1971, the member-directed co-op celebrated its 30th year in 2001. A Visiting Artist Series brings the work of outside talent to exhibit in the gallery from late May through early November. There is also a series of shows that benefit local nonprofit organizations. The co-op is open daily 10 A.M. to 6 P.M. every day, 10 A.M. to 9 P.M. during the summer.

Boulder Public Library
1000 Canyon Blvd., Boulder
(303) 441–4397

Besides the library's permanent art collection in both wings, there are ongoing exhibitions by contemporary regional artists in various media in an area called The Exhibit Space (entrance on Canyon Boulevard). With a ceiling height of 11 feet, 10 inches, and 160 linear feet of exhibition walls, it's one of the largest display spaces in Boulder. Most artists represented are well-known Colorado painters and sculptors, though some national traveling exhibits are also displayed. Another worthwhile stop is at the display cases on the bridge, where all types of

Watching the bustle of the Downtown Boulder Mall with bronze languidness, the sculpture titled Hearts on a Swing *reminds the crowd to slow down and enjoy.* PHOTO: LINDA CORNETT

interesting exhibits are shown monthly. The Boulder Public Library Meadows Branch, 4800 Baseline Road (303–441–4390), also has a display space, featuring such items as raku pottery and Hawaiian leis and ceremonial capes made of feathers. If you're interested in historic photographs, check out the Carnegie Library, 1125 Pine Street (303–441–3110), which has digitized about 7,000 of its best photographs so people can view them on a computer screen without touching and possibly damaging them. The library is open 9 A.M. to 9 P.M. Monday through Thursday, 9 A.M. to 6 P.M. Friday and Saturday, and noon to 6 P.M. Sunday.

Boulder Stained Glass Studios
1920 Arapahoe Ave., Boulder
(303) 449–9030

Specializing in glasswork in Boulder for more than 25 years, the studio specializes in custom design and fabrication, and both architectural and period work. The general approach is architectural, though there's a selection of beautiful glass items, including blown-glass vases, jewelry, clocks, and imaginative pieces by various Colorado artists. The studio is known for its high-quality contemporary and period leaded, etched, and beveled stained glass. It primarily promotes glass crafts by Colorado artisans. The studio is open 9 A.M. to 5:30 P.M. Monday through Friday and by appointment.

CU Art Galleries
Sibell-Wolle Fine Arts Bldg. (east of UMC at Broadway and Euclid), CU-Boulder campus
(303) 492–8300

At CU Art Galleries, the large group shows of student work are especially fun and zany—a little bit of New York in Boulder. The gallery also hosts exhibitions by nationally known artists, and there are 5,000 pieces in its permanent collection. Be sure to check out the Sibell-Wolle galleries, which in addition to student work, also regularly feature impressive work by national and international artists. In summer the galleries are open 8 A.M. to 5 P.M. Monday through Friday, 8 A.M. to 8 P.M. Tuesday, and noon to 5 P.M. Saturday; call for winter hours. Closed Sunday year-round.

Denver Art Museum
100 W. 14th Ave., Denver
(303) 640–4433 (hotline)

Whether you like the architectural style or not, the Denver Art Museum has perhaps the most unusual profile of any building in Denver. With its silhouette of see-through geometric shapes, this modern six-story castle of art resembles a giant paper cutout. Inside is one of the best and most extensive collections of Native American crafts in the United States, and an internationally acclaimed pre-Columbian art collection. You can also enjoy works by Picasso, Georges Braque, Matisse, Frederic Remington, Winslow Homer, and Thomas Hart Benton, and two beautiful paintings by Monet: *Waterloo Bridge* and *The Water Lily Pond*. The lower level is dedicated to educational programs, with studios, a lecture room, classrooms, and a reception area.

The museum is currently in the midst of a $62.5 million, 146,000-square-foot expansion to make room for its growing collections.

An underground concourse connects the museum with the public library. Call (303) 640–KIDS for information on family and children's classes and programs; call (303) 640–ARTS for details on adult classes. In addition, there are free walk-in programs for parents and kids on Saturdays, and teacher training. The museum is open 10 A.M. to 5 P.M. Tuesday through Saturday (Wednesday until 9 P.M.), and noon to 5 P.M. Sunday. Admission is $6 for adults; $4.50 for seniors and students 13 to 18; free to members and children younger than 12; and free to Colorado residents on Saturday.

Fiske Planetarium
Regent Dr., CU-Boulder campus
(303) 492–5001 (star shows), (303) 492–5002 (administration and information)

Stargazers and sci-fi fans will enjoy the small gallery outside the planetarium's star-show auditorium, which often displays astronomical or futuristic artwork. Take the kids and take it all in—art exhibit and a star show, workshop, or lab. The planetarium is open 8 A.M. to 5 P.M. Monday through Friday and offers public shows on Friday evenings and some Tuesdays and Saturdays. A tour of the gallery is free; star shows are $3 for kids and seniors, $4 for adults; laser shows are $5.

The Leanin' Tree Museum of Western Art
6055 Longbow Dr., Boulder
(303) 530–1442

This museum houses the nation's largest privately owned Western art collection. The works, primarily post-Russell and Remington, include paintings and sculpture. The collection is a result of Leanin' Tree founder Ed Trumble's 40-year friendship with Western artists. Admission is free; the museum is open 8 A.M. to 4:30 P.M. weekdays, 10 A.M. to 4 P.M. Saturday and Sunday. For more information, see our Attractions chapter.

Mackin-Katz Gallery of Fine Art
2041 Broadway, Boulder
(303) 786–7887

Described by *Town & Country* magazine as having world-class flair, this gallery features the work of Boulder-based photographer Andy Katz and other internationally shown artists, including painters, photographers, potters, furniture makers, and glasswork artists. Katz's black-and-white and color photography captures images from around the world, including vanishing Jewish societies, the scenery and people of France, Costa Rica and Japan, and a tour of sunny California wineries. His work is also exhibited in museums and galleries throughout the world. The gallery is open seven days a week and by appointment.

In Colorado, Supporting the Arts is More than "Bearable"

Boy, that polar bear gets around. If you haven't seen him yet, keep your eyes open. He's sure to pop up somewhere where people are enjoying a concert, learning about an ancient civilization, cogitating over a piece of art, or experiencing an evening of theater.

The bear, dubbed Popsicle, is a symbol of the unique six-county tax that Colorado citizens have levied on themselves to pay for scientific and cultural facilities and organizations.

When federal and state funding for such organizations dried up, Metro Denver residents voted in 1988 to create a Scientific and Cultural Facilities District (SCFD) funded by a one-cent sales tax on every $10 spent in the metro area. That amounts to about $30 million a year to help support everything from "arts to zoo."

Funding is handed out to three tiers of recipients. The big four at the top of the funding heap are the Denver Zoo, the Denver Botanic Gardens, the Denver Art Museum, and the Denver Museum of Nature and Science. Next come large organizations that have annual budgets of more than $850,000 (Chautauqua Park and the Butterfly Pavilion in Broomfield are in this group).

More than 300 small groups make up the base of the pyramid, applying for grants each year. In Boulder County, the list includes Ars Nova Chamber Singers, Boulder Museum of Contemporary Art, Collage Children's Museum, E-Town (see the Nightlife chapter), Nomad Players, Boulder Friends of Jazz, Wild Bear Science School, Upstart Crow Guild Theatre . . . the list goes on and on.

SCFD funding also supports special arts programs at public schools, where funding for the arts has grown tighter. The tax also has paid for art education classes for young people incarcerated at Lookout Mountain Youth Services Center.

As a thank you to the community, the SCFD-funded organizations provide more than 2 million free admissions a year to various events and facilities for residents who couldn't otherwise afford to go. The public response has been enthusiastic. In 1994, voters extended the tax until 2006, and it's likely it will be extended again before it expires; after all, 8 million people attend SCFD organization events every year.

MacLaren Markowitz Gallery
1011 Pearl St., Boulder
(303) 449-6807

Featuring the works of some of the area's most popular fine artists, MacLaren/Markowitz Gallery has a history of exhibiting top-quality contemporary art in Boulder. Lyrical landscapes by Doug West, and the colorful Hispanic-flavored art of Tony Ortega are some of the standard favorites at this attractive downtown gallery. Other popular artists include sculptor Bill Worrell, and painters Merrill Mahaffey, Lindsey Leavell, Randy Pijoan, Julia Jordan, and Pam Furumo (who also works in pastels). The gallery is open 10 A.M. to 5:30 P.M. Monday through Wednesday; 10 A.M. to 9 P.M. Thursday, Friday and Saturday; and noon to 5 P.M. Sunday. Winter hours are abbreviated, so call before going.

Western architecture buffs will love the Boulder Museum of History, which provides exhibits showing the history of Boulder's neighborhoods and gives detailed information on how to tour Boulder, offering several routes and various recommended walks. Be sure to ask about Boulder's two world-class landmarks: the National Center for Atmospheric Research for its building, and the University of Colorado for its landscaping.

Mary Williams Fine Arts
2116 Pearl St., Boulder
(303) 938–1588

This gallery specializes in antique prints and original art from the 19th and 20th centuries. You'll find fine prints and graphics with botanical, natural history, and architectural themes. If you want a John James Audubon, a Currier and Ives, or an Edward S. Curtis on your walls, here's where you'll find one.

Mustard Seed Gallery
Marriott Plaza, 2660 Canyon Blvd., Boulder
(303) 447–8626

Mustard Seed, in business for almost 30 years, has long been a favorite local source for traditional and contemporary paintings, pottery, prints, art glass, jewelry, photography, and fine crafts. Mustard Seed is a partnership gallery run by seven artists, and there is a different show each month by members and others. Gallery hours are 10 A.M. to 6 P.M. Monday through Saturday, noon to 4 P.M. Sunday.

Ruth Linton & David Haslam Gallery
1217 Spruce St., Boulder
(303) 444–9116

This gallery features fine art from national and regional artists, including classic Impressionistic and realistic works. There's a good selection of oils, pastels, watercolors, and fine bronzes, plus jewelry and photography in this attractive gallery a block off the downtown Pearl Street Mall. The frame shop staff also provides conservation framing to museum standards.

The gallery is open 11 A.M. to 5 P.M. Monday through Thursday, 11 A.M. to 9 P.M. Friday and Saturday, 1 to 5 P.M. Sunday. In summer it's open until 9 P.M. daily except Sunday.

Smith-Klein Gallery
1116 Pearl St., Boulder
(303) 444–7200

This contemporary space offers an extensive collection of old and new jewelry, statues, hand-blown art glass, and traditional and contemporary paintings. It also features work by contemporary Native American artists. Smith-Klein is open daily.

Von Eschen Gallery
2660 Canyon Blvd., Boulder
(303) 443–9989

If you're a fan of Western and wildlife art, this is the place to go. There are paintings in all media, bronze sculptures, wood carvings, and limited-edition prints. The gallery offers signed and numbered lithographs by such well-known artists as Robert Bateman and Bev Doolittle. Bateman's vivid portrayals of nature have earned national recognition, as have Doolittle's mystifying dual-image watercolors. A new addition is American Indian jewelry and pottery. They also do picture framing. Gallery hours are 9:30 A.M. to 5:30 P.M. Monday through Friday, and Saturday 10 A.M. to 4 P.M.

Parks and Recreation Centers

Parks
Recreational Facilities
Other Recreation Options

From the Boulder Creek Path and mountain parks to the reservoir and recreation centers, our city is rich with recreational facilities, both indoor and out, public and private. Boulder offers a total of 54 urban parks and 37,000 acres of open space and mountain parks, a 1-acre reservoir, a golf course, two outdoor pools, three athletic complexes, a 7.5-mile linear creek-side park, three recreation centers, and an extensive program of classes and activities. Following is a description of some of Boulder's most popular parks and their special features. Details on additional outdoor recreational activities can be found in our Sports chapter.

Parks

City Parks

Boulder Creek Path
Parallel to Canyon Blvd. and/or Arapahoe
Ave. from Four Mile Canyon in Boulder
Canyon east to Cherryvale Rd.
(approximately 7.5 miles)

Certainly the most popular and accessible park and the best way to see Boulder is the Boulder Creek Path, which cuts through the heart of the city, following the creek's tumbling path down Boulder Canyon and out to the eastern plains. The Creek Path hugs Canyon Boulevard down to Broadway then veers off south under Arapahoe Avenue. It meanders back under Arapahoe after 30th Street. For a close-up look at what goes on inside the creek, from mountains to plains, stop off at the Boulder Public Library and check out the creek fish tank, complete with colorful rainbow trout. You can also take a peek under the water at the observatory on the creek near Folsom Avenue.

Bicyclists, walkers, and in-line skaters crowd this scenic path, shaded by some of Boulder's oldest cottonwoods and willows. The path branches off into various other routes and is accessible at sidewalk intersections throughout its length. Many Boulderites use the Creek Path to commute across town, so be sure to stay to the right or you might be run down by those on wheels. Stop and enjoy the scenery or have lunch at one of the many benches.

The creek itself provides recreation, too. There's a kayak course near the mouth of the canyon, catch-and-release fishing, and in the summer tubers bob from Eben Fine Park to Central Park. The water is too shallow and swift for swimming, but waders brave the chilly flow to reach a mid-creek perch on a rock.

While you're enjoying the rushing water, keep in mind that in the 1970s the Corps of Engineers suggested that Boulder might want to cut channels in the creek to reduce flood danger. Boulder, typically, took another path, bringing in huge boulders to re-create the creek's natural profile of burbling rapids and quiet pools for resting fish. The city is gradually buying property along the path of the creek to allow the inevitable flood waters to spread with a minimum of destruction.

The Boulder Creek Path is described in detail in the Boulder Attractions chapter.

Central Park
Broadway and Canyon Blvd., Boulder
No phone

Arid Boulder has a love affair with the mountain creek that runs through it, but the town is well aware that water can be treacherous. The Boulder Creek Path serves both as a park and a clear area for the inevitable major flood. A row of sandbags atop a retaining wall is testimony to the creek's annual spring spillover. PHOTO: LINDA CORNETT

There's always something going on in this pretty park in the heart of downtown, with its historic passenger train, creekside picnic tables and lawns, bandshell, and plentiful green grass for lounging and watching the passing crowds. Right on the Boulder Creek Path and across from the Boulder Museum of Contemporary Art and the Boulder-Dushanbe Teahouse, the park is also adjacent to the Saturday and Wednesday Farmers' Market along 13th Street.

Eben Fine Park
Third St. and Arapahoe Ave., Boulder
(303) 413–7200

Green grass, rushing cool water, lofty trees, creekside picnic tables and grills, a covered shelter, and playground equipment make this mouth-of-the-canyon park a popular retreat from the heat. The Boulder Creek Path passes by on its way up the canyon.

The rustic shelter, with generous picnic tables and its own grill, can be rented for parties. Call the number listed above.

Foothills Community Park
Eighth and Cherry Sts., Boulder
No phone

This 69-acre site was purchased in 1985 with money from a voter-approved bond issue. The south portion of the park between Locust and Cherry Streets opened in 2001. It has two playgrounds, two outdoor hockey rinks, and open, grassy areas for sledding, Frisbee, ball playing, and just running around. The park is also linked to Open Space trails and to the Foothills Community Gardens, one of three community gardens in Boulder. A second phase of the project, which will double the size of the park, has been postponed indefinitely due to lack of funds.

Salberg Shelter
19th and Elder Sts., Boulder
(303) 413–7200

This small park in the north-central part of town has a crafts building, playground, and everyone's favorite—a giant, stationary human-propelled barrel. Kids and adults can feel like pet mice in exercise wheels as they run inside the barrel, making it spin. The shelter, with restrooms, a lighted stage, tables and chairs, and a grill, can be rented year-round by calling the Parks and Recreation Department at the listed number.

Scott Carpenter Park
Arapahoe Ave. and 30th St., Boulder
(303) 441–3427 (pool)

Named for Boulder's own astronaut, this is a favorite warm-weather spot for kids, with its outdoor pool and playground featuring a rocket jungle gym commemorating the feats of its namesake. Open swim is from 1 to 5 P.M. Monday through Friday, 1 to 6 P.M. Saturday and Sunday between Memorial Day weekend and Labor Day. Admission for residents on a per-visit basis is $4.25 for adults, $2.50 for seniors 60 and older, and $2 for kids and teens under age 19. Season passes are available; a single adult resident pays $115, a nonresident adult $144; a family of four pays $150 if they live in Boulder and $188 if they are nonresidents.

Skatepark
30th St. and Arapahoe Ave., Boulder
No phone

Next door to Scott Carpenter Park is a newly designed street-course for skateboarders, in-line skaters, and BMX bicyclists. The unsupervised park is free and open dawn to dusk. There are rails, curbs, bowls, and free forms to challenge the most daring air-eater. It's skate-at-your-own-risk; helmets and pads are strongly recommended. The park was designed by nationally known skateboarder and skatepark designer Michael McIntyre with advice from Boulder area skateboarders. The Boulder YMCA (303–442–2778), which operates the skatepark, is organizing a Skatepark Advisory Committee and is recruiting volunteers to staff the park. From 3:30 to 5 P.M. Wednesdays and 10 to 11 A.M. on Saturdays, the park is reserved for Little Dudes—kids 12 and younger. BMX bikes have the run of the facility 7 to 10 A.M. daily. And Graffiti artists are wel-

Boulder's YMCA spearheaded the effort to provide the city's skateboarders with a place where they could practice their swooping skills safely. Boulder Skatepark is next to Scott Carpenter Park on 30th Street, where a graffiti wall has been erected to allow taggers to practice their art legally. PHOTO: LINDA CORNETT

come to demonstrate their abilities on a graffiti wall just north of the Skatepark.

Spruce Pool
2102 Spruce St., Boulder
(303) 441–3426

This outdoor pool is a particular favorite of summer lap swimmers, who stop by before and after work or over the lunch hour for a wet workout. Open swims are from 1 to 5 P.M. Monday through Friday and 1 to 6 P.M. Saturday and Sunday from mid-June to early September. In addition to lap lanes, there is a separate kiddie pool and a great slide. Sunbathers can stretch out on a grassy hill that borders the pool. Red Cross–certified swim lessons are available. Fees for residents and nonresi-

dents are the same as for the Scott Carpenter Park pool, listed previously.

Dog Parks

Airport and Valmont Rds.;
5660 Sioux Dr.; and
Howard Heuston Park, 34th St. and Iris Ave., Boulder
No phone

Boulder residents love their dogs, and they love their parks. The two passions have been combined with the creation of two fenced parks just for dogs and their owners. The parks are open daily from dawn to dusk and are surrounded by four-foot chain link fences so dogs can safely run off-leash. A 3.5-acre park at Valmont and Airport Roads in northeast Boulder is on a portion of the otherwise undeveloped Valmont City Park. Water spigots are available for thirsty pooches. The second park is on 1.5 acres in an undeveloped portion of the East Boulder Community Park, next to the East Boulder Community Center at 5660 Sioux Drive. This park gives dogs access to a portion of a pond. Only licensed and unaggressive dogs may visit the parks. In addition, there is an unfenced dog exercise area at Howard Heuston Park at 34th Street and Iris Avenue. Dogs visiting this park must respond to voice commands.

Mountain Parks and Open Space

Way back in 1898, long before Colorado's Front Range became one of the fastest developing regions in the country, Boulder's prescient citizens bought their first piece of land for preservation. In the years since, the city has bought up a sweep of mountain backdrop and a ring of high plains prairie that shapes the city, protects it from encroachment by its fast-growing neighbors, preserves precious ecosystems, and gives residents a refuge for passive recreation and contemplation. That 37,000 acres of open space and mountain parks land is the envy of other cities that are just now recognizing the value of undeveloped land.

An excellent introduction to the mountain parks is the drive up Flagstaff Mountain. The hairpin-turn, two-lane drive offers spectacular panoramas along the way, as well as pull-offs, trails, and picnic spots. Keep your eyes on the road and let your passengers describe the human flies climbing on the rock formations. To get there, take Baseline Road west, follow its curve to the right and up Flagstaff Mountain. (The elegant Flagstaff House restaurant along the way is open for dinner only.)

A glut of visitors from other cities in the region has put a strain on the popular area. To reduce that number, and recoup some of the cost of maintaining the area, the city requires cars not registered in Boulder County to pay for parking both on Flagstaff Mountain and in Gregory Canyon (the area below Flagstaff). Annual permits are $15; daily permits are $3 and may be purchased at six self-service stations along Flagstaff Road. Be warned: rangers do patrol the lots and ticket cars without permits.

More than 120 miles of hiking trails lace the mountain backdrop and the plains below. Popular mountain trailheads begin at Chautauqua Park, Flagstaff Mountain, the National Center for Atmospheric Research, and Eldorado Springs. You can hike to Bear Peak, Green Mountain, Mount Sanitas, and to the Devil's Thumb—all of which are popular, substantial hikes taking from several hours to most of the day, depending upon your level of fitness. (Some specific locations and suggested hikes are described under "Hiking" in the Sports chapter.)

Among the flat, popular trailheads are: Bobolink, a favorite of dog walkers offering a shady stroll along South Boulder Creek, located at Cherryvale and Baseline Roads; Boulder Valley Ranch, a long prairie path popular with horseback riders, past one of the working ranches leased from the city, located a mile east of Highway 36 on Longhorn Road; and Doudy

Draw Trailhead, a meandering trail through ponderosa pine and the South Boulder Creek riparian corridor, past historic homesites (and a great place to find bear sign or even spot a black bear), located 1.8 miles west of Highway 93 on Eldorado Springs Drive.

Trail maps are available from the Open Space and Mountain Parks Department (303-441-3440); Boulder Chamber of Commerce, 2440 Pearl Street (303-442-1044), and Boulder Map Gallery, 1708 13th Street (303-444-1406).

Rangers and naturalists offer a series of free hikes and educational programs on topics ranging from the truth about rattlesnakes to where to find (but don't disturb) wild irises to the best spots for bass fishing. They even offer an evaluation of canine citizenship to help owners determine if their dogs are well-trained enough to handle the distractions of a hike off-leash, where allowed.

Boulder residents love their dogs, and their dogs love their dog parks—like this one next to the East Boulder Recreation Center. PHOTO: LINDA CORNETT

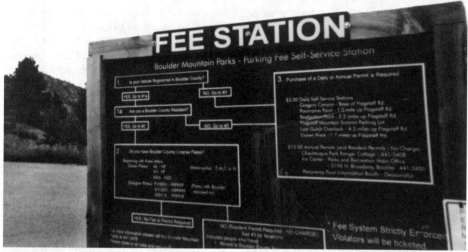

Boulder's open space and parks are so popular with residents and neighboring communities that out-of-towners must pay a fee to park in some areas, including Flagstaff Mountain. PHOTO: LINDA CORNETT

Chautauqua Park
Ninth St. and Baseline Rd., Boulder
(303) 441-3408 (Rangers' Cottage)

At the base of the Flatirons, Boulder's first park opened as a summer camp and retreat for visitors from Texas in 1898 and was originally called Texado Park. Perched on a hill overlooking the city, the park features a sweeping grassy area below the camp's cottages (some for rent and some owner-occupied) and communal buildings; it invites casual summer sports such as Frisbee throwing and badminton. An auditorium hosts a summer concert series and popular movie series. Many concertgoers bring their own picnics to enjoy under the shady cottonwoods. A dining room serves meals year-round. There are two playgrounds and several hiking trails into the foothills.

State Parks

Eldorado Canyon State Park
Colo. Hwy. 170, Eldorado Springs
(303) 494-3943

One of the best rock-climbing areas in the United States, this canyon is lined with spectacular rock walls rising to 1,500 feet, the patient work of South Boulder Creek. It's a great place to watch some world-class rock climbing on the 500 routes or to do a bit of hiking, biking, or fishing. In the early 1900s, daredevil Ivy Baldwin made unique use of the towering canyon walls, walking a high wire from the Bastille to the aptly named Wind Tower. Ike and Mamie Eisenhower reportedly honeymooned in the canyon, when it was operated as a private resort. The park is open until dusk. The entrance fee is $1 for walk-ins, $4 per vehicle, and $40 for an annual state parks pass ($10 for those 62 and older or with a permanent disability). Check the maps at the park entrance and ranger station for information on the length and level of difficulty of the various trails.

On the way to the park you'll pass Eldorado Artesian Springs (303-499-1316, ext. 20), a privately owned historic resort (see our History chapter). The thermal pools and snack bar are open from 10

A.M. to 6 P.M. daily from Memorial Day through Labor Day. Cost per day is $5 for adults, $3 for kids ages 3 through 12 and for seniors 60 and older; children younger than 3 are admitted free.

The park is 8 miles south of Boulder. Take Colorado Highway 93 to Colorado Highway 170 and head west.

Recreational Facilities

Boulder Recreation Centers

The City of Boulder operates three excellent recreation centers. Daily admission for adults is $5; children ages 4 to 18, $2.25; seniors over 60, $3. Admission is reduced by purchasing a punch card, for which prices vary by age group, number of punches, and residency. There is also an annual pass, costing about $400 for a single resident adult and varying based on age and residency. The centers are open daily; call for specific hours of operation. Reservations must be made two days in advance for the handball, racquetball, and tennis courts. Players on indoor courts pay the drop-in fee; outdoor courts rent for $8 per court. Childcare is available for children 6 months to 5 years for $2.50 for the first hour, $1.25 per hour after that; call each center for childcare schedules. Childcare space is limited, so it's smart to call first.

East Boulder Recreation Center
3660 Sioux Dr., Boulder
(303) 441-4400, (303) 441-4150 (senior center)

Boulder's newest recreation center combines a senior center and recreation center. The Senior Center wing includes a cafeteria, a common area, an arts-and-crafts room, and computers with Internet access for public use. The recreation facility features a 25-yard indoor lap pool and leisure pool with water slide and children's play area; gymnasium with adjustable basketball hoops; extensive weight rooms with free and body-master weights, rowing machines, and stationary cycles; a climbing wall; an aerobics room; and a dance studio. Outdoors you'll find tennis, basketball, and racquetball courts, as well as a wheelchair-accessible playground. Kayakers make use of the pond.

The long, lovely slope leading to Bluebell Canyon near Chautauqua lures hikers, backpackers, nature classes, and picnickers to explore its charm. PHOTO: LINDA CORNETT

Kids love the water slide at the East Boulder Recreation Center. PHOTO: ROZ BROWN

North Boulder Recreation Center
3170 N. Broadway, Boulder
(303) 441–3444

The heavily used center will be closed for a major overhaul until spring 2003. Built in 1973, the center is due for updated facilities. The revamped center will have a leisure pond with a twisting body slide; a separate 25-yard lap pool with a ramp for swimmers with disabilities; an expanded weight room and yoga center; a children's garden; an enhanced gymnastics center with a foam pit, vaulting space, and area for "air tumbling"; expanded locker rooms; and a new family locker room.

South Boulder Recreation Center
1360 Gillaspie Dr., Boulder
(303) 441–3448

This center has a pool with a wheelchair ramp, a hot tub, a sauna, locker rooms, showers, classrooms, a gymnasium, an expanded weight room, a racquetball/handball court, outdoor sand volleyball

courts, and four outdoor tennis courts. On Sundays, a huge inflatable pyramid is put in the pool for kids to play on. Neighboring Viele Lake offers canoeing and paddleboating, as well as a fitness course around the lake.

Other Recreation Options

Boulder Reservoir
5100 51st St., off north side of the Diagonal Hwy., Boulder
(303) 441–3456 (boathouse)
(303) 441–3468 (gate)

For those craving a beach, this is the closest thing to it in Boulder County. Tons and tons of sand were trucked in to create the beaches for the reservoir, and more is added periodically. Swimmers, sailors, sailboarders, canoeists, kayakers, and water-skiers make this a busy place on summer weekends. Various watercraft are for rent, including sailboats and Windsurfers; call the boathouse for rates. Grills and picnic tables provide a nice spot for summer barbecues on the swimming beach. The reservoir hosts sailboat races, volleyball tournaments, and a national in-line skating competition. The chilly reservoir is also the scene of the annual Polar Bear Dip on New Year's Day (see our Boulder Festivals and Annual Events chapter) and the Kinetic Conveyance race, in which bizarrely garbed contestants try to muscle homemade vehicles over water, prairie, and mud. Waterskiing, sailboat, and sailboard classes are available. One-day summer admission to The Rez is $5 for adults 19 and older; $2.50 for children and teens 4 to 18; $3 seniors ages 60 to 64; and free for seniors 65 and older and children younger than 4. Season passes are available; call the gate for information. The one-acre reservoir is open year-round, but services are provided weekends only in the spring (Memorial Day weekend to the second Monday in June) and fall (third Monday in August to Labor Day weekend), seven days a week during the months in between. There is no admission charge during the rest of the year.

Boulder Reservoir is 1.5 miles north of Jay Road via the Diagonal Highway (Colo. 119).

Mapleton Center Therapy Pool
311 Mapleton Ave., Boulder
(303) 441-0436

If a bathtub-style dip is more your style, try out the therapy pool at the Mapleton Center of Boulder Community Hospital. The indoor pool is kept at a balmy 94 degrees. It is used by patients at the rehab hospital but is also open to the public for open swim—call (303) 441-0542 for hours—and lessons for children through adults. Drop-in fees are $6 for ages 13 to 59, and $4 for adults over 60; punch cards are available. Children under 12 are not allowed in the open swim, but swim classes are offered for kids and adults.

YMCA of Boulder Valley
2850 Mapleton Ave., Boulder;
4990 Moorhead Ave., Boulder;
95th St. and Arapahoe Ave., Lafayette
(303) 442-2778

There are three Y facilities in Boulder County, offering everything from an indoor running track to an outdoor swimming pool to the county's only public indoor ice-skating rink. The main facility is in Boulder at 2850 Mapleton Avenue. It offers a full range of facilities and classes, including racquetball/handball courts; a 25-yard indoor pool; a full gym; indoor running track; Jacuzzi, Cybex, Nautilus, and Hydrogym equipment; an aerobics studio; a picnic area and playground; a nursery and childcare facility; and single-sex saunas. Admission for nonmembers is $10 for teens and adults; $5 for kids younger than 13. Adult membership is $50 to join and $38 per month; family membership is $50 to join and $53 per month.

The Hi-Mar Center at 4990 Moorhead Avenue in South Boulder is open summers only, with an outdoor pool, picnic tables, playground, tennis courts, and space for in-line skating or hockey. Hi-Mar is open Memorial Day to Labor Day. Call (303) 499-7016 for more information during the summer.

The Arapahoe Center is a new 55,000-square-foot facility located near the intersection of 95th Street and Arapahoe Avenue. This Y includes a full gymnasium, locker rooms, an indoor track, free weights, an in-line skating rink, aerobic space, and the only public indoor ice arena in Boulder County. The drop-in fee is $10 for adults and $5 for children for use of all the facilities. Call (303) 664-5455 for more information.

Sports

Participatory Sports

Spectator Sports

Many people move to Boulder specifically for what's contained in this chapter: bicycling, hiking, camping, skiing, rock climbing, running, and other outdoor sports. Boulder has been called "the sports town" by Outside magazine, and you'll share the trails, parks and facilities with some of the nation's and world's best athletes, who come here to train.

Non-Olympians also abound, and you'll find them poking around in sporting goods shops and at meetings of the various clubs and organizations for bicycling, skiing, rock climbing, and hiking listed in this chapter.

If you're a spectator rather than a participant, you'll be in the minority, but you'll have plenty of exciting games to watch. Football fans cheer for CU-Boulder's Buffaloes, who are members of the NCAA Division I Big 12 Conference and former national football champions, and the National Football League's Denver Broncos. If you like basketball, you can follow CU's women and men Buffaloes, as well as the National Basketball Association's Denver Nuggets. Other sports teams in our area include the Colorado Rockies Major League Baseball team, the Colorado Avalanche National Hockey League team (formerly Quebec's Nordiques, the Avalanche have firmly endeared themselves to Coloradans by winning the 1996 and 2001 Stanley Cup), and various college teams. The Rockies and Avalanche are both based in Denver.

Participatory Sports

Bicycling

Boulder provides more than 90 miles of bikeways, from marked on-street bike lanes to separate paths reserved for non-motorized travel, including cycling, in-line skating, walking, skateboarding, and running. Bicyclists are very active in lobbying for their facilities (in fact, several members of the City Council ride their bikes to and from council meetings). The city sponsors a 15- or 24-mile bicycle-around-the-city event to encourage citizens to get acquainted with the city's bicycle accommodations. Local organizations include Boulder Bicycle Commuters (303–499–7466), Boulder Off-Road Alliance (303–447–9378), and Bicycle Colorado (303–530–0051).

Rentals and Information

A delightful symbiosis has developed between the city of Boulder and New Vista High School. Donated bikes are taken to the school, where students learn to repair and paint them. The bright green bikes are then left at locations around town for use by anyone for free. Just leave the bike in a fairly public place when you're done with it.

Bikes can also be rented at various shops around town, including Doc's Ski and Sports, 627 S. Broadway, south Boulder (303–499–0963); University Bicycles, 839 Pearl Street, downtown (303–444–4196); Boulder Bikesmith, 2432 Arapahoe Ave., Arapahoe Village Shopping Center (303–443–1132); and Louisville Cyclery, 1032 S. Boulder Rd., Louisville (303–665–6343). Average rates are $12 to $16 for four hours (city or mountain bike); $16 to $21 per full day; and $35 to $50 per weekend.

Bike paths weave all around and through Boulder, and a map is a good bet if you don't want to get lost. The transportation department's Bicycle and Pedestrian Map is available free from Go Boulder, the city's alternative transportation program, 1739 Broadway, second floor, (303–441–3266); the Boulder Cham-

Boulder bicyclists are a hardy bunch, always looking for a destination that's uphill. Fortunately, the geography cooperates. PHOTO: LINDA CORNETT

ber of Commerce, 2440 Pearl Street (303-442-1044); and also at the bicycle shops listed above. Other resources for bicycling information are the University of Colorado Bike Office (303-492-2322), and the local clubs for cycling enthusiasts listed above.

Bicyclists are treated as vehicles and must obey the same traffic laws as cars. That means no riding on sidewalks, yielding to pedestrians, obeying traffic signals, and riding on the right side of the road. You must have a rear reflector and a front light when riding after dark. The county Sheriff's Office has gotten very serious about enforcing rules against bicyclists riding abreast and blocking traffic lanes. A helmet isn't required but is highly encouraged.

Boulder's Bike Paths

The city's plentiful bike paths are the obvious place to start pedaling.

Bear Creek Greenway
Northeast corner, Broadway and
Table Mesa Drive

South Boulderites can enjoy a beautiful bike path that heads northeast from Martin Park, on the corner of Broadway and Table Mesa Drive. Access the path at the far northeast end of the park. Called the Bear Creek Greenway, the path winds along Bear Creek under highways and eventually over Foothills Parkway, where cyclists have the choice of heading farther east on the Centennial Bike Path or heading north across Arapahoe Avenue and connecting with the Boulder Creek Path.

Boulder Creek Path
Various locations

Cruise right onto the very popular Boulder Creek Path, the backbone of the city's bike path network. The path, which also accommodates pedestrians and in-line skaters, is most easily accessed at Central Park (Broadway and Canyon); Eben Fine Park (Fourth and Arapahoe); the Regal Harvest House Hotel (1345 28th Street, just south of Arapahoe); or Scott Carpenter Park (30th Street south of Arapahoe Avenue). Most major intersections crossing Arapahoe Avenue have a sidewalk ramp onto the bike path.

Head east or west—both directions offer a great ride and scenery. Going west, the paved section ends about a half-mile into Boulder Canyon, and a wide packed-gravel path continues a little more than 2 miles (from Eben Fine Park) up to Four Mile Canyon, where the Creek Path ends. It's not a steep or difficult ride to the end of the path, but those new to Boulder's elevation might be a bit breathless as the trail gradually climbs the canyon, paralleling the highway. It's best ridden on a mountain bike, but skinny tires can make it, too, with care on the gravel and "curbs" at the bridges.

For those who prefer no hills, ride east, where the Creek Path sweeps out onto the plains past 30th Street and CU-Boulder's Research Park for a panoramic view of the Front Range, past duck ponds, cottonwoods, and prairie dog towns. See the Boulder Attractions chapter for a detailed description of the path.

Paved Roads (Skinny Tires)

Around Boulder

Flagstaff Mountain

Macho cyclists can tackle Flagstaff Mountain—a real muscle-buster right in town, due west on Baseline Road. You'll be hunched over the handlebars on the way up, but the zoom down provides some beautiful vistas of the Boulder Valley, and the Chautauqua Dining Hall (303-440-3776) waits at the bottom of the hill.

Beyond Boulder

Jamestown

For a good mountain ride, head for Jamestown (17 miles from Broadway and Canyon). Take Broadway up Lefthand Canyon (8 miles north of town) and then, after 6 miles, up James Canyon Drive. (Look for mile markers in the canyon.) The picturesque Jamestown Mercantile Cafe (303-442-5847) offers breakfast, lunch, and snacks.

Louisville

To reach Louisville (12 miles from Broadway and Canyon), go south on the bike path along the east side of Broadway to Marshall—south of Boulder—through Marshall and over Colo. 170. Cross U.S. 36, make a right on Dillon Road, a left on

96th Street, then look for nearby Main Street and Karen's Country Kitchen (303-666-8020).

Lyons

The very popular ride to Lyons is a little hilly. To reach Lyons (16 miles from Broadway and Canyon), ride north on Broadway (U.S. 36), which has a wide shoulder part of the way, all the way to Lyons, and turn left at the railroad track. Andrea's (303-823-5000) is a dandy breakfast or lunch spot (closed Wednesdays).

Nederland

The 17 miles up Boulder Canyon to Nederlands is a strenuous ride. Be cautious—the curving canyon road with its narrow shoulder and speeding cars can be quite hazardous for cyclists. Choose less busy times such as midweek and midday for this ride.

Niwot

The ride to Niwot is relatively flat and pastoral, winding past ponds and pleasant countryside (16 miles from Broadway and Canyon). Go north on Broadway to Nelson Road and turn right (for a shorter ride turn right on Neva Road before Nelson). Follow Nelson Road to Colo. 73, turn right and go to Niwot Road and turn left; proceed into Niwot. Daniel's Bistro (303-652-0747) offers a tasty brunch on Saturdays from 10 A.M. to 2 P.M.

Ward

The truly tough can ride all the way up Left Hand Canyon to Ward (23 miles one way from Broadway and Canyon)—all steady climbing from the start of Left Hand Canyon. If you can make it over the

> ## Insiders' Tip
> Boulder's Creek Path is a great place for in-line skating—and the farther east, the flatter the path.

final hill out of Ward to the Peak to Peak Highway (Colo. 72), great meals, home-made pie, and local ambiance await you at the Mill Site Inn (303-459-3308), just north of Ward.

Unpaved Roads (Fat Tires)

Bicycles aren't allowed off-trail on publicly owned lands around Boulder, but there are 120 miles of trails in the city's open space and mountain parks and another 80 miles of trails on county open space, many of them open to bicyclists.

The Boulder Offroad Alliance, a citizen's nonprofit organization formed in 1991 to provide "a positive voice for Mountain Biking," hosts social rides two or three times a week during the summer and encourages riders to volunteer time for trail maintenance. Call (303) 667-2467 for more information.

A few suggested off-road mountain bike trails follow.

Around Boulder

Community Ditch Trail

The Community Ditch Trail is a 4-mile dirt service road of moderate difficulty that travels through grasslands, mesas, and land with evidence of early farming and mining activity. Taken from the Marshall Mesa Trailhead, this ride is a huff and a puff up the mesa, but riders will be rewarded with spectacular views of the mountains and a delightful flat ride along the flower-lined (in spring) mesa and the Community Ditch, which in warm weather invites a swim.

You'll find the trail south of Boulder, at the Doudy Draw Trailhead on the south side of Colo. 170, 1.7 miles west of Colo. 93, or at the Marshall Mesa Trailhead, 0.9 mile east of Colo. 93 on the south side of Marshall Road.

Cross Colo. 93 (Broadway) and continue along the ditch winding back among the cottonwoods. To make a nice loop back to Boulder, head for the Doudy Draw Trailhead at the junction of Community Ditch Bridge. At Doudy Draw Trailhead you can choose between a side

trip into Eldorado Springs (turn left on the paved highway) or turn right to return to Colo. 93 to Boulder or the Marshall Mesa Trailhead. Eldorado Springs (about 2 miles) provides a chance to refuel with spring water, swim (in the summer) at Eldorado Springs Resort, graze at the snack bar, or gaze at the daring rock climbers in the state park (303-494-3943) climbing the impressive Bastille and other formations. To return to Boulder or the Marshall Mesa Trailhead, ride back out to Colo. 93 on the Eldorado Springs road, crossing at the light and continuing straight into the tiny settlement of Marshall. The trailhead is just a little farther east on Marshall Road. If you choose the reverse direction, starting at the Doudy Draw Trailhead, go left (east) at the junction of Community Ditch Bridge and the dirt road you're on. The trail crosses Colo. 93 and goes to the Marshall Reservoir inlet and up a steep hill to the Marshall Mesa Trailhead.

East Boulder Trail

Access Teller Farm S. Trailhead, on Arapahoe Rd., 1 mile east of 75th St.

The 7-mile East Boulder Trail has a difficulty ranking of moderate. A 2.2-mile level section of the trail goes through a wildlife preserve and past Teller Lake. Then, a 2.7-mile section climbs a mesa on dirt trails and service roads to the Gunbarrel Farm. The Gunbarrel Farm section travels along a dirt service road with moderate grades and turns east at 1.2 miles into the White Rocks area.

Greenbelt Plateau Trail

This gentle trail rolls across a mesa top through open grasslands with beautiful views of the foothills. At 1.3 miles, bicyclists may choose to take the dirt path to Community Ditch Trail or continue on the service road to Colo. 93.

This trail is ranked as easy and covers 1.6 miles on gravel surface road. The Greenbelt Plateau Trail is south of Boulder, on the north side of Colo. 128, just east of Colo. 93.

In the Mountains

Most mountain biking in the local high country requires an outstanding pair of lungs and legs, since it's mostly uphill and at high altitudes.

Gold Hill

For a ride right out of town, go west on Mapleton Avenue, which becomes unpaved in Sunshine Canyon and continues to the historic mining town of Gold Hill, about 10 miles uphill. From there you can continue to Nederland and return down Boulder Canyon. Or, start the ride at the mouth of Boulder Canyon along the Creek Path, which ends in 2 miles at Four Mile Canyon (County Road 118). Then, proceed up Four Mile Canyon and turn right at the sign for Gold Hill—also about 10 miles uphill from the mouth of Four Mile Canyon.

Rollins Pass

For those in really top shape, try Rollins Pass, one of Colorado's premier mountain biking (and four-wheel-drive) routes. This former railroad bed crosses the Continental Divide. Cars used to be able to make this exciting drive over rickety railroad trestles perched above thousand-foot drops, until the Needle's Eye tunnel caved in. Today, the tunnel, 1.5 miles from the Divide, is the end of the road for vehicles, but mountain bikers and hikers can bypass the tunnel and continue on the roadbed over the pass and all the way down the other side to Winter Park, if desired. To reach Rollins Pass Road, drive west up Boulder Canyon (Colo. 119) to Nederland, then south on Colo. 72 to Rollinsville. Turn right (west) on the dirt road marked with signs to Tolland and East Portal and drive 8.5 miles to the East Portal and Moffat Tunnel. The Rollins Pass road begins there, as marked. Bicycling over the pass is an all-day affair requiring another vehicle on the Winter Park side and lodging reservations or plans—not to mention advanced physical fitness.

Sourdough Trail

Accessible from the Peak to Peak Highway (Colo. 72) west of Nederland, the Sourdough Trail is 17.5 miles long but has different segments at various trailheads. The

A mountain biker hops down a mountain trail near Boulder. PHOTO: JAMES KEIVON

trail was constructed with help from the Colorado Mountain Club mainly for ski touring and mountain biking, and features pleasant rolling terrain through the pines. From Camp Dick Campground to Beaver Reservoir is 2.3 miles. From Beaver Reservoir to Brainard Road it's 7.4 miles, and from Brainard Road to Rainbow Lakes Road, 7.8 miles. All access to the various connections to the Sourdough Trail is via the Peak to Peak Highway. Camp Dick Campground is on Middle St. Vrain Road, 5.8 miles north of Ward and 0.5 miles west of Peaceful Valley. One Sourdough Trailhead is on the left-hand side of County Road 96 just east of Beaver Reservoir, 2.5 miles north of Ward and 2 miles west on County Road 96. The Red Rock Trailhead is on the right-hand side of County Road 102, just east of Red Rock Lake, 2.5 miles west on Brainard Lake Road. Another Sourdough Trailhead is on the right-hand side of Rainbow Lakes Road (County Road 116), 4.7 miles south of Ward (7 miles north of Nederland) and 0.4 miles west on County Road 116.

Switzerland Trail

The historic Switzerland Trail, a former single-gauge railroad track, makes for some scenic riding with spectacular mountain views and reasonable climbing grades. Most riders start at the town of Sunset and go south toward Bald and Sugarloaf Mountains. To reach Sunset, head up Four Mile Canyon (see "Gold Hill," above), and stay on County Road 118 past Salina and Wallstreet until you reach Sunset, 17 miles from Boulder. Go right to reach Gold Hill or left to Glacier Lake.

Camping

Camping beneath the pines in the cool, clear air of the high country—and perhaps near a gleaming mountain lake or stream—is one of the Rockies' greatest joys. The U.S. Forest Service, state of Colorado, and city of Boulder maintain many such sites. (For information on camping in Rocky Mountain National Park, please see that chapter later in this book.)

Boulder County

Roosevelt National Forest

The following campgrounds are within the national forest. For information about federal regulations within Roosevelt, call (303) 444-6600. Call toll-free (877) 444-6777, for reservations.

Golden Gate Canyon State Park
10 miles south of Nederland on Colo. Hwy. 72, 2 miles east on Gap Rd.
(303) 582-3707
Golden Gate offers many miles of hiking plus backpacking, fishing, and camping at 7,900- to 10,500-foot elevations. You'll find 155 sites, including some in the backcountry. Fees are $14 per night for RV or motor-home sites with electricity, $10 for drive-in tent sites with showers, $6 for walk-in hut and tent sites. There's a one-time reservation fee. Golden Gate is open year-round, weather permitting. A day pass costs $4. For reservations, call (303) 582-3707.

The park's north entrance is 10 miles south of Nederland on Colo. 72 and 2 miles east on Gap Road. For the south entrance drive 3 more miles, then 4 miles east on Colo. 46.

Kelly Dahl
3 miles south of Nederland on Colo. Hwy. 119
This campground offers a scenic view of the Continental Divide and limited hiking. There is a small playground, but no electrical hookups, dump stations, or showers. There are 46 sites at an elevation of 8,600 feet. The season lasts from late April or early May through October 31 or the first snow, whichever comes first. The fee is $12 with water ($6 without).

Olive Ridge Campground
15 miles south of Estes Park, or 1.5 miles north of Allenspark, on Colo. Hwy. 7
Nestled close to lush Rocky Mountain National Park, this campground offers access to the park as well as horse rentals at nearby stables. There are 56 sites at an elevation of 8,400 feet. The season is mid-

May through mid-October. Half the sites can be reserved; there's a $8.65 reservation fee. Site fees are $12 to $15, $6 for a second vehicle.

Pawnee Campground
5 miles west of Colo. Hwys. 119/72 on County Rd. 102 (at Brainard Lake)

This extremely popular (and heavily used) campground offers beautiful views, fishing, and nonmotorized boating with access to the wilderness area. The 55 sites lie at an elevation of 10,400 feet, and the brief season lasts from July 1 through mid-September. Half of the sites may be reserved, the rest are first come, first served. There is a $8.65 reservation fee. The site fee is $12, $6 for a second vehicle.

Peaceful Valley and Camp Dick
15 miles west of Lyons on Colo. Hwy. 7, left at the junction with Colo. Hwy. 72, 6 miles farther

Peaceful Valley is a pleasant, pine-shaded campground with 18 sites at an elevation of 8,500 feet. The season is mid-May through mid-October. Half of the 17 sites may be reserved for a reservation fee of $8.65. Site fee is $12 ($6 with no water).

To reach Camp Dick campground, located a mile west of Peaceful Valley, follow the dirt road to the 46 sites at an elevation of 8,600 feet. Nineteen sites may be reserved for a reservation fee of $8.65. Horses are available for rental nearby. The season is from late Memorial Day through mid-September. The fee is $12 to $15, $6 for a second vehicle.

Rainbow Lakes
6.5 miles north of Nederland off Colo. Hwy. 72

Rainbow Lakes campground is set near several small but lovely lakes. There is no available running water, but good fishing is nearby in the Indian Peaks Wilderness Area. There are 18 sites at an altitude of 10,000 feet, available on a first come, first served basis. The season runs from late mid-June through mid-October, or the first snow. The fee is $6, $3 for a second vehicle.

City of Boulder Open Space and Mountain Parks

Buckingham Campground
12 miles northwest of Nederland
(303) 441-3440

The campground is at an elevation of 10,160 feet and is accessible to Indian Peaks Wilderness. Buckingham's eight sites, available on a first come, first served basis, are heavily used. Camping is allowed only in the designated sites, as the surrounding vegetation is easily damaged. The season runs from early June until snow season. No ground fires or charcoal fires are permitted; only gas grills or camp stoves may be used for cooking. No reservations are required, and there's no fee charged for camping, but no water is available.

Buckingham Campground is at the Fourth of July Trailhead, 12 miles northwest of Nederland. Take County Road 107 west through Eldora to County Road 130 (a rough road) and proceed to its end.

Climbing

Boulder is internationally known for its great rock climbing areas, particularly the Flatirons and Eldorado Canyon in the state park (see our Boulder Parks and Recreation Centers chapter for more information on these parks). With proper equipment and training, rock climbing can be a relatively safe sport, and rock jocks dancing up the cliffs at Eldorado Canyon might even make it look easy. Tempted as they might be, however, those without proper training and equipment should stay on the ground. Every year Colorado witnesses several fatalities involving inexperienced scramblers without equipment—especially around the Flatirons and Boulder Falls (in the Boulder Canyon). The book *Flatiron Classics* by Gerry Roach, a famous local mountaineer and climber, has detailed route information for experienced climbers who want to climb the Flatirons and other popular routes. *Rock Climbing Colorado* by Stewart M. Green is a very thorough book that covers the whole state, describing 1,500 routes.

Camping and Backcountry Travel

Various wilderness areas and national forests have their own sets of use regulations, but the following general guidelines apply to all areas. Remember: Even when we are careful, our presence and actions have an impact on the natural world. As our human population grows, negative impacts become more and more severe.

Backcountry Travel

Travel quietly and in small groups. Avoid disturbing others.

Spread out impact by exploring less heavily visited areas.

Leave your pets at home to keep from bothering wildlife and other visitors.

Stay on maintained trails whenever possible. Do not take shortcuts; doing so destroys vegetation and causes erosion.

Be especially careful when trails are muddy, and minimize horse use when trails are wet.

On narrow trails, walk single file rather than several abreast, and try to avoid congregating in large groups in sensitive areas.

Don't pick wildflowers or dig up plants; it's illegal in all parks, and permission is needed on private land. Be judicious in picking fruit so that you leave enough for wildlife.

Comply with signs regarding vehicles and mountain bikes, which are prohibited on many trails because of erosion problems. Refrain from using bikes on muddy slopes, where deep ruts develop quickly, and yield to other trail users.

If you are photographing or observing wild animals and they become nervous, you are too close. Back away.

Give right of way to horses, keeping to the downhill side. The same rule applies to all large mammals, who will become stressed if you remain above them.

Avoid disturbing nesting birds, and comply with closures designed to protect plants and animals.

Leave gates as you find them unless signs instruct otherwise.

Campsite Selection

In heavily visited areas, use existing campsites to confine impact to a small area.

In less-visited areas, choose a site well away from streams and lakes and out of sight of other users. Eliminate all traces of your camp.

Carry out all trash. Do not bury it.

If you must use soap for washing or bathing, use biodegradable products, stay at least 150 feet from any water sources, and pour the water into absorbent ground.

Stoves and Fires

Use a gas stove for all cooking. Wood is scarce in the high country and an essential part of the ecosystem. Gas is quicker, cleaner and won't leave a scar of charred and sterilized soil.

Chautauqua Park is the starting point for many trails through Boulder's open space. PHOTO: DAILY CAMERA

Campfires are becoming controversial. If you absolutely must build a fire, use only dead and down wood. Use existing fire rings and keep the fire very small. Use only as much wood as will burn completely.

Never leave fires unattended, even for a moment. When you leave, make certain that the fire is dead and cold. Clean out fire rings so they will be ready for the next visitor.

Sanitation

Bury human waste in a small cat-hole about 6 inches deep and dug in organic soil (not just leaves or rocks) away from heavy-use areas and at least 150 feet from any water.

Soiled toilet paper, diapers, and sanitary napkins should be carried out.

Place all trash in trash cans. In Colorado's climate, organic wastes such as orange peels, egg shells, and paper can take more than 100 years to decompose if left outside.

If you feel like doing a good deed, carry out litter left by others.

This safety and environmental information comes from the American Medical Association's *Encyclopedia of Medicine, A Roadside Guide to Rocky Mountain National Park* by Beatrice Elizabeth Willard and Susan Quimby Foster, *A Climbing Guide to Colorado's Fourteeners* by Walter Borneman and Lyndon Lampert and the *Boulder County Nature Almanac* by Ruth Carol Cushman, Stephen Jones and Jim Knopf. The latter three are excellent resources for detailed information on these areas of Colorado.

Those interested in learning to climb have many options, some of which we've listed below.

The Boulder Rock Club and Rock School
2829 Mapleton Ave., Boulder
(303) 447–2804, (800) 836–4008

The Boulder Rock Club and Rock School has an indoor climbing wall and offers instruction. A full range of lessons and outdoor clinics are available, as is rental equipment. The club's building has 10,000 square feet of climbing surface, 35-foot lead walls, and a 2,000-square-foot bouldering cave.

Colorado Mountain Club
900 Baseline Rd., Boulder
(303) 554–7688

The CMC, as it is known, offers mountaineering classes that will take you from rank beginner to advanced mountaineer. Learn all the basics of rock climbing and mountaineering in these courses. CMC also offers advanced mountaineering courses, as well as many scheduled trips both locally and internationally. Many of the classes and outings are free, and the prices of others are very reasonable.

East Boulder Recreation Center
5660 Sioux Dr., Boulder
(303) 441–4401

The city offers rock-climbing and mountaineering courses for adults, teens, and children as part of its Adventure Program. There's a climbing wall at the East Boulder Community Center.

Neptune Mountaineering
633 Unit-A, S. Broadway, Table Mesa Center, Boulder
(303) 499–8866

Another excellent resource for climbing and mountaineering information, books, and equipment (though no instruction is offered) is this shop owned by Gary Neptune, a prominent U.S. mountaineer who has stood on the top of Mount Everest and many other peaks worldwide. The shop hosts talks by adventurers and authors fresh from conquering peaks around the world, free or for a minimal fee. The museum located in the shop includes boots and crampons from Sir Edmund Hillary's first ascent of Mount Everest, a Russian oxygen bottle brought back from Everest, and antique ice axes, alpenstocks, pitons, and carabiners dating back 100 years. It's the most extensive collection of its kind in the country.

Fishing

Many lakes and streams in the area offer good fishing for both warm- and cold-water species. The Fish Observatory on the Boulder Creek Path just behind the Regal Harvest House Hotel at 1345 28th Street is a fun place to see the local species of Boulder Creek. There are windows built below water level for viewing. Look for brown, brook, and cutthroat trout. The Boulder Public Library at Ninth Street and Arapahoe Avenue also offers a living stream habitat display showing the fish and plant life found at various levels of the creek.

Some easy-to-reach area streams that offer good trout fishing include the Middle and South forks of St. Vrain Creek; Left Hand Creek between Left Hand Reservoir and Buckingham Park; North Boulder Creek between Colo. 72 and Boulder Falls; Middle Boulder Creek from its headwaters to 28th Street (with special restrictions in city limits); and South Boulder Creek from its headwaters to Baseline Road (with special restrictions between Walker Ranch and South Boulder Road). Golden Gate State Park is a good place to take kids fishing, and also offers camping and numerous hiking trails (see details under Hiking). Some favorite spots in and around Boulder are Wonderland and Thunderbird Lakes, Walden Pond (there's a special area for seniors and people with disabilities), and Sawhill Pond. You'll get a detailed map and information on these areas when you buy your fishing license at one of the locations listed below under "Licenses."

The Colorado Division of Wildlife (303–291–7534) offers a weekly fishing conditions report that lists areas that have been recently stocked, and reports of where they're biting and where they're not.

Barker Reservoir
17 miles up Boulder Canyon, on Canyon Blvd., Nederland

Barker Reservoir in Nederland attracts many anglers at its western end, where Boulder Creek empties into this scenic reservoir on the east side of Nederland. Anglers can catch some of the stocked rainbow trout, about a foot long. The water level fluctuates quite a bit, depending on the season and downstream water needs. No boats of any kind are allowed on this reservoir, which is owned by the Public Service Company of Colorado and supplies some of the drinking and irrigation water to towns below.

Boulder Reservoir
5100 N. 51st St., 1 mile north of Jay Rd., Boulder
(303) 441-3461 or (303) 441-3468

Out on the eastern plains, with a nice mountain vista, Boulder Reservoir is loaded with crappie, catfish, and largemouth bass. It's open year-round. The best place for bank fishing is the deep water near the dam embankment at the eastern end. Boating is prohibited on weekends unless you are a Boulder resident. Please see the subsequent listing under "Swimming" for admission fees. Drive toward Longmont on Colo. 119 to reach 51st Street.

Brainard and Red Rocks Lakes
5 miles up Colo. Hwy. 119, Ward

These beautiful mountain lakes attract many anglers looking for rainbow trout, brookies, and brown trout. Fishing is permitted with flies and lures only. To reach these lakes, drive up Boulder Canyon to Nederland and head north on Colo. 72; the turnoff is just past Ward, 200 yards on the left. Or, drive up Left Hand Canyon north of Boulder past the Greenbriar Inn. Turn left (west) and proceed up the canyon through Ward and on to Colo. 72. Turn right and look immediately to the left for the Brainard turnoff. Brainard Lake is 5 miles up County Road 102.

Diamond Lake/Indian Peaks

For those who desire more solitude (which you won't find at Brainard Lake), hike up to beautiful Diamond Lake, from the Fourth of July Trailhead. To reach Fourth of July Trailhead, travel west from Nederland for about 7 miles on County Road 107—you'll pass through the rustic town of Eldora—then continue up County Road 130 (a rough, dirt road) for about 5 miles. It's about a 2.5-mile hike up to Diamond Lake from the trailhead.

Gross Reservoir
Flagstaff Rd.

Gross Reservoir is another favorite of local fishermen looking to hook trout and bass. To reach it, drive west on Baseline Road, which becomes Flagstaff Road as it twists and turns up Flagstaff Mountain above Boulder. The reservoir is a few miles from the top of the road.

Licenses

Required fishing licenses cost $40.25 for nonresidents, $20.25 for residents, $10.25 for seniors, and $1 for kids under 16 and are good for one calendar year. Five-day and one-day licenses are also available for

---

Insiders' Tip

Want to learn a new sport or have an adventure? The City of Boulder Parks and Recreation Department offers everything from kayaking and rock climbing to tango lessons. Call (303) 441-7200.

$18.25 and $5.25 for everyone. They are available—along with maps—at McGuckin Hardware, 2525 Arapahoe Avenue in Boulder (303-443-1822) and at Ace Hardware Store, 20 Lakeview Drive, in Nederland's shopping center (303-258-3132) in the shopping center. For more information contact the City of Boulder Open Space Department (303-441-3440); Boulder County Parks and Open Space (303-441-3950); or the Colorado Division of Wildlife (303-297-1192).

Fitness Centers

Boulder has numerous private health clubs and fitness centers, many of which are open to nonmembers.

Boulder Rock Club
2829 Mapleton Ave., Boulder
(303) 447-2804

Boulder Rock Club offers all types of indoor climbing walls for rock climbers (including bouldering, top-roping, and lead-climbing) for $14 a day. Lessons (indoor and out), clinics, and rental equipment are available here. The Boulder Rock Club's Mapleton Avenue facility is open all year.

Flatiron Athletic Club
505 Thunderbird Dr., Boulder
(303) 499-6590

Flatiron offers an enormous array of classes and equipment. For $10 you can enjoy all the facilities for the day, including a lap pool and coed hot tub; tennis courts; saunas; a steam room; handball, squash, and racquetball courts; volleyball; aerobics classes; an indoor running track; and a complete weight room. There are also Pilates and spinning equipment and classes, and massage therapy.

Front Range Boxing
3146 28th St., Boulder
(303) 546-9747

Front Range offers a relaxed atmosphere where you can work one-on-one with a trainer to master that quick jab, or just

get a workout with the punching bag. Nonmembers can drop in for $15 (the trainer is extra).

The Pilates Center
4800 Baseline Rd., The Meadows, Boulder
(303) 494-3400

Sisters Amy Alpers and Rachel Segel founded this pilates center and teacher training certification school in 1990. Nonmembers are welcome to stop in for an evaluation lesson, a mat class, private lessons, and group classes. Fees vary.

Pulse Fitness Center
1375 Walnut St., Boulder
(303) 447-8545

Nonmembers pay $12 for a day of working out with free weights and Nautilus equipment, attending step and aerobics classes, and finishing up with physical therapy or a massage. Guests who come in with a member pay $10.

RallySport
2727 29th St., Boulder
(303) 449-4800

In addition to its local members, RallySport is open to members of other clubs affiliated with IRSHA, the International Racquet, Health and Sports Association, for a fee of $10 a day. This club has a full range of facilities including racquetball, squash, handball, tennis, volleyball, and wallyball courts plus all types of classes, weight-training equipment, and indoor and outdoor pools. There's a well-run childcare facility on-site.

24-Hour Fitness Center
2950 Baseline Rd., Boulder
(303) 443-2639
1375 Walnut St., Boulder
(303) 447-8545

For $10 nonmembers can have full run of the center's Nautilus equipment, free weights, step classes, low- and high-impact aerobics classes, and group cycling. There are lap pools and basketball courts, yoga and boxing lessons, and certified personal trainers are on staff. Guests can come in 7 A.M. to 10 P.M., but as the name suggests, members can work up a sweat 24 hours a day.

Golf

Golfers have a reasonable selection of public courses to choose from in Boulder and the surrounding area. Most of the courses listed here have driving ranges, equipment rentals, snack bars, pro shops, and lessons.

Coal Creek Golf Course
585 W. Dillon Rd., Louisville
(303) 666–7888

Coal Creek has 9- and 18-hole courses, a driving range, a snack bar and lounge, golf accessories and rentals, and a lovely view of the Front Range of the Rockies. Greens fees for residents are $14 and $20 ($16 and $27 weekends and holidays) for 9 and 18 holes; for nonresidents, fees are $18 and $27 ($20 and $32 on weekends). The pars are 36 and 72 for 9 and 18 holes. Carts are $10 and $20 but generally are not necessary.

Eagle Golf Club
1200 Club House Dr., Broomfield
(303) 466–3322

Eagle has an 18-hole course, driving range, putting green, bar, golf accessories, and rentals. Greens fees for nonresidents are $20 to walk, $28 with a cart; $30 and $40 on weekends. Residents play for $17, $25 with cart. The par is 35 or 36 (depending upon which tees you're playing from) on the 9-hole layout and 71 on the 18-hole course.

Flatirons Golf Course
5706 Arapahoe Ave., Boulder
(303) 442–7851

The city of Boulder operates the Flatirons Golf Course. Nonresident player fees are $16.50 for 9 holes, $25.50 for 18. Boulder residents can buy a discount card for $10 and save $4 every time they play. Par is 35 and 70. There's a driving range, and golf carts available for rent.

Golf Haystack
5877 Niwot Rd., Boulder
(303) 530–1400

The course of choice of "duffers" (according to one local, who includes himself in that category), Haystack is excellent for beginners, and there's no need to reserve a tee time—just show up. The easy nine-hole course is par 32, and greens fees are $15 on weekdays (Monday through Thursday) and $16 on weekends and holidays. No motorized carts are available, only pull-carts. There is an excellent driving range with cover, so rain doesn't halt play.

Indian Peaks Golf Course
2300 Indian Peaks Tr., Lafayette
(303) 666–4706

Indian Peaks offers 9 and 18 holes, a driving range, a snack bar and lounge, and golf accessories and equipment rentals. Nonresident fees are $21 and $38 every day. Residents pay $19 and $32. The par is 36 or 72, and golf carts cost $16 or $24.

Lake Valley Golf Club
County Rd. 34, north of Boulder
(303) 444–2114

Also in Boulder, this is an 18-hole championship course. Par is 70. After paying the annual dues, members never pay greens fees. Nonmembers pay $28 weekdays for 9 holes, including a cart and practice balls, or $45 for 18. On weekends and holidays, nonmembers pay $33 for 9 holes with a cart and practice balls, $50 for 18 holes.

Sunset Golf Course
1900 Longs Peak Ave., Longmont
(303) 776–3122

Sunset has both 9- and 18-hole options, a pro shop, instruction, and rentals. Fees for Longmont residents are $11 for 9 holes and $16 for 18 holes (nonresidents pay $12 and $17). Junior and senior weekday rates are $8 and $11 and are the same on weekends after 2 P.M. ($10 and $13 for nonresidents). Par is 34 and 68 for 9 and

18 holes respectively. Golf carts rent for $14 and $22 but are not usually necessary on this layout, which is a pleasure to walk.

Twin Peaks Golf Course
1200 Cornell Dr., Longmont
(303) 772–1722

Twin Peaks offers 9 and 18 holes, a driving range, a pro shop, a snack bar, and a restaurant. Instruction and rentals are available. Residents pay $14 for 9 holes on weekdays and $20 for 18 holes, $15 and $22 on weekends. Nonresidents pay $16 and $22 on weekdays, $17 and $24 on weekends. The par is 35 for both the front and back nines. Golf carts ($14 and $22) are generally not necessary because it's so flat.

Hiking and Backpacking

If recreation is Boulder's raison d'etre, then hiking is, perhaps, the biggest raison. Most people moved to Boulder to be near the mountains, and in Boulder trails are literally just out your back door. On the toughest trails and even mountaintops you'll also see lean runners in flimsy nylon shorts and singlets, equipped with only water bottles.

There are so many places to hike around here, it's hard to know where to begin. But in town, the logical place to start is the mountain parks. Again, for serious hikers, a map is the best bet for choosing the scenic destination, distance, and degree of difficulty accordingly. Maps of open space and mountain parks trails are available at most sporting goods stores. Eldorado Canyon State Park, south of Boulder (see the Boulder Parks and Recreation Centers chapter), also has spectacular scenery and good hiking trails. See this chapter's "In the Mountains" (to follow) and "Camping" (previous) sections for information on overnight getaways in the wild. For more information on city of Boulder mountain parks call (303) 441–3440 or visit the website at www.ci.boulder.co.us/openspace.

Hiking in Boulder
Bear Peak
NCAR Trailhead

For a fairly strenuous hike of four to six hours—or more (depending on your conditioning)—climb Bear Peak (8,461 feet). It's 7 miles round-trip with an elevation gain of 2,200 feet and many steep sections of trail. But the view from the top is worth it, and if you're there in the early fall, you'll see tens of thousands of ladybugs clinging to the rocks at the summit, where, amazingly enough, they winter in the rock crevices. Don't disturb them as they prepare for their hibernation. They will emerge in spring to mate and lay eggs. There are several routes up Bear Peak. One good way is from the NCAR Trailhead (described below) to the Mesa Trail (past the large water tank on the hill and then down the hill). Turn left on the Mesa Trail, which descends and joins Bear Canyon Road below. Turn right on the road and look for the Fern Canyon Trail sign, and follow that trail to the summit of Bear Peak. This is the shortest, but steepest, route. Another alternative is the earlier trail turnoff via Bear Canyon, which affords great views to the west. Just below the summit on the Bear Canyon Trail, a sign points to the Fern Canyon Trail to the northeast. Toward the top, the trail becomes quite steep, and some rock scrambling brings hikers to the summit. A nice loop can be made by going up one trail and down the other.

Gregory Canyon
West on Baseline Rd. (base of Flagstaff Mtn.)

Several fine hikes start in Gregory Canyon at the base of Flagstaff Mountain, where Baseline Road becomes Flagstaff Road. Catch the Flagstaff Mountain Trail (3 miles round-trip, 1,100 feet elevation gain) at the mouth of the dirt road into Gregory Canyon, across from the curving Armstrong Bridge. The trail zigzags back and forth across the paved road to the summit of the mountain. Continue upward, past a fork that leads down to Panorama Point. A small parking lot on the south side of the road from the trail marks a popular bouldering (rock-climbing) area that includes Monkey Wall, Crown Rock, Alamo Rock, Tree Slab, and Pebbles. Though many folks drive up, the hike provides a close-up of rock climbers, wildflowers, native shrubs, and wildlife. Flagstaff Summit Nature Center is open weekends in summer from 10 A.M. to 4 P.M. Once you reach the top, look for Boy Scout Trail, which leads a short distance west to May's Point and Artist's Point with fantastic views of the Continental Divide. Another trail at Flagstaff summit called Rangeview leads down to Realization Point, also with spectacular views of the Divide, North and South Arapaho peaks, Mount Audubon, Mount Meeker, and Longs Peak.

Mallory Cave
NCAR Trailhead

There are various options for longer hikes at the NCAR Trailhead (see below)—including a connection to Bear Canyon and the Mesa Trail. For an interesting longer hike (3.2 miles round-trip), look for the Mallory Cave Trail just south of the NCAR Mesa Trail junction and north of Bear Canyon. Please observe the trail closures, which are allowing revegetation as well as protecting endangered wildlife nesting areas. Mallory Cave is a nesting site for the bats that you may see sweeping over this area at dusk, scooping up a tummyful of insects. This trail weaves through a forest of ponderosa pines, leading to a meadow of yucca and low shrubs. Follow the small trail to a huge lichen-covered boulder at the entrance to a stone "staircase" between the rock slabs. Look for a sign at the fork indicating a left turn for the cave, which has been notoriously hard to find for many hikers. The final approach is a shimmy up a 50-foot, 40-degree-angle rock chimney with plenty of hand- and footholds but challenging nonetheless. The cave is shallow, but the vista is grand. At the age of 18, E. C. Mallory rediscovered this cave, which was known by locals but never recorded. Mal-

lory later graduated from the University of Colorado and worked as a miner and eventually a chemist for the USGS. For many years he kept the cave a secret.

National Center for Atmospheric Research
1850 Table Mesa Dr., Boulder

For a really short hike, but one with a great view, stroll out behind the National Center for Atmospheric Research (NCAR—pronounced "en-car"), at the west end of Table Mesa Drive (see our Attractions and Overview chapters for details on the research center). The Walter Orr Roberts Nature Trail (0.4 miles round-trip), named for NCAR's founder, is perfect for those with limited time or who don't want to walk much. It's also wheelchair-accessible. The drive up the NCAR mesa is beautiful, and you're sure to spot some grazing deer along the way. The nature trail is a pleasant ramble along the mesa top offering great views and a fine introduction to the local flora, fauna, and terrain.

The NCAR building, known as the Mesa Laboratory, was designed by the internationally acclaimed architect I. M. Pei (who also designed new sections of the Louvre in Paris and the National Gallery in Washington, D.C.). It's made of Lyons sandstone mixed with concrete to tint it pink and blend with the Flatirons rock formations. The design is reminiscent of Anasazi ruins like those of Mesa Verde in Southwestern Colorado. If it looks familiar, you may be remembering Woody Allen's comedy, *Sleeper,* which was filmed partially at NCAR.

Royal Arch, Enchanted Mesa, McClintock
Nature Trail via Mesa Trail
Ninth St. and Baseline Rd. (Chautauqua Park)

The Mesa Trail—also a popular running trail—begins just below the Bluebell Shelter at Chautauqua Park and leads 6 miles south to Eldorado Springs, with close-up views of the Flatirons and Front Range and sweeping vistas of the plains. The steep, strenuous 3-mile (round-trip) hike to the Royal Arch from Chautauqua is a local favorite. Access it south of Bluebell Shelter at the end of Bluebell Road in Chautauqua Park. The trail quickly climbs almost 1,500 feet on the slopes of Green Mountain to the natural sandstone arch, which offers superb vistas.

An easier trail, and one suited for young children or tired adults, is the McClintock Nature Trail (2.5 miles round trip) at Enchanted Mesa. Begin at the picnic shelter next to Chautauqua Auditorium in Chautauqua Park and descend to cross Bluebell Creek and arrive at a fork. Take the right branch that climbs to intersect the Enchanted Mesa Road at an old apple tree. Cross the road and continue uphill along the creek. Look for interesting interpretive signs on the area's natural history. The trail then reaches the Mesa Trail, where you turn left (south) and continue a third of a mile to a large trail intersection. Take the left fork, passing a covered reservoir to reach the Enchanted Mesa Road, which is closed to traffic. Pines and wildflowers invite a picnic on the mesa top, and this gentle trail also makes a nice moonlight hike. Enchanted Mesa Road intersects McClintock Trail at Bluebell Creek, and this makes a return loop to Chautauqua, downhill all the way back.

Hiking in the Mountains

Called the Snowy Range by the area's first settlers, the spectacular snow-covered mountains just west of Boulder—among them, skyscraping Mount Audubon, North and South Arapaho Peaks, Mount Toll, and others—are part of the Indian Peaks Wilderness Area. Many soar above 12,000 feet and several above 13,000 feet. This 73,391-acre area west of Boulder contains some of Colorado's best scenery and highest peaks. The wilderness area, so designated in 1978, encompasses parts of Arapaho and Roosevelt National Forests. Indian Peaks shares a boundary with Rocky Mountain National Park to the north and Rollins Pass to the south.

Brainard Lake
Past Ward on Colo. Hwy. 72

The U.S. Forest Service trails throughout the Indian Peaks Wilderness Area are interchangeable as hiking, backpacking, and cross-country skiing trails. Some of our favorites are in the Brainard Lake area, just past Ward on Colo. 72. Drive up Boulder Canyon to Nederland and head north on Colo. 72; the turnoff is 200 yards past Ward on the left. Or, drive up Left Hand Canyon, north of Boulder past the Greenbriar Inn. Turn left (west) and proceed up the canyon through Ward and on to Colo. 72. Turn right and look immediately to the left for the Brainard turnoff. Brainard Lake is 5 miles up County Road 102.

Two popular hikes at Brainard Lake are Mount Audubon (13,223 feet, 8 miles round-trip, and 2,750 feet of elevation gain), an arduous all-day climb, or much easier Long Lake, a 3-mile loop around the lake. Once at Brainard Lake, drive past the lake and look for the Long Lake and Mitchell Lake parking areas for these trailheads. The Long Lake Trail is a level stroll around this beautiful lake with spectacular views, colorful wildflowers, and wheelchair accessibility. Hikes from this area to Mitchell Lake (1 mile, one way), Blue Lake (2.5 miles, one way), and 12,550-foot Pawnee Pass via Lake Isabelle (4.3 miles, one way) are all spectacular and easy to follow (though not all are easy to ascend) on the well-marked trails. Due to the area's great popularity and heavy use, there is now a $3 per vehicle charge, good for five days; or an annual pass is available for $15. The fee goes toward protecting the area.

Diamond Lake, North and South Arapaho Peaks, and Arapaho Pass
Fourth of July Trailhead

This trailhead leads to spectacular hikes to Diamond Lake, South Arapaho Peak, Arapaho Pass, Fourth of July Mine, and Dorothy Lake. Fourth of July Trailhead is just north of Hessie (see below) via the same road through the town of Eldora. To reach these trailheads from Boulder, drive to Nederland via Boulder Canyon. From the southwest end of Nederland, follow Colo. 72 to the town of Eldora, where County Road 130 begins at the west end of town. Follow this dirt road to the Hessie fork and take the right branch, which is a very rocky and bumpy 5-mile ride to Buckingham Campground (also called Fourth of July Campground). From the campground, take the right fork up to the parking lot at the trailhead. From the trailhead (10,121 feet) it's a 3-mile climb to Arapaho Pass at 12,061 feet. One mile from the trailhead is a turnoff to Diamond Lake, another 1.3 miles away at 10,960 feet. The Diamond Lake Trail dips down the valley and crosses the North Fork of Middle Boulder Creek. The trail crosses several small streams and continues upward to a big, wet meadow full of wildflowers. A trail junction sign directs hikers to the left for Devil's Thumb Trail and Jasper Lake, but continue going straight for Diamond Lake, which sparkles like the gem for which it was named. By continuing on the Fourth of July Trail (instead of taking the Diamond Lake Trail), hikers reach the Fourth of July Mine at 1.5 miles, a worthwhile destination in itself, with interesting old mining equipment and a great view of Arapaho Pass on the Continental Divide. At the mine, there's the option of turning right and continuing up the Arapaho Glacier Trail to the glacier overlook and on up South Arapaho Peak (13,397 feet and 3.5 miles one way from the start of the trail). North Arapaho Peak (13,502) is another .75 miles along a connecting ridge with some exposure.

These peaks should be attempted only by strong, experienced climbers with proper equipment. It's also important to get an early start to avoid the regular afternoon lightning storms. (The rule of thumb in summer is to be off a peak and headed back down by noon.) By continuing straight up the trail at Fourth of July Mine, hikers can reach Arapaho Pass in another 1.5 miles along a barren, rocky old wagon road. Listen for the whistles of marmots and pikas along the way, and look for these appealing, high-altitude critters. Marmots are similar to ground-

Insiders' Tip

Even people who have no intention of ever climbing a rock wall themselves might enjoy watching others do so. A short drive or walk up Boulder Canyon (on foot up the Creek Path from Eben Fine Park, it's less than a mile) takes you to the Elephant Buttresses and the Dome (just past where the Creek Path goes under Canyon Boulevard), two of Boulder's most popular rock-climbing spots. On the Dome, watch climbers tackle a route called the "Disappearing Crack"—you'll see why. A bench along the creek invites spectators.

hogs, and pikas are guinea pig–size creatures related to rabbits, not rodents. Arapaho Pass is usually extremely windy, but the view is sublime, looking over the Continental Divide down the western slope to Caribou Lake and Coyote Park. Another short jaunt of .5 miles to the left leads to scenic, snowfield-crowned Dorothy Lake, at a chill 12,061 feet with usually an iceberg or two. Take care to avoid trampling the tiny tundra flowers around the lake—rock hopping is best.

Hessie and Fourth of July Trailheads
County Rd. 130

South of the Brainard Lake area in the Arapaho Peaks area you'll find two very popular trailheads: Hessie and Fourth of July, 8 and 12 miles, respectively, west of Nederland. To reach these trailheads from Boul-

Mountain Safety and Environment

Colorado's Rocky Mountains can take the unwary and unprepared by surprise. Remember: Going above or near timberline is the same as visiting the Arctic regions of the world. Mountain weather can change from a warm, sunny day to hail, snow, thunder, and lightning in minutes. It can snow at any time of the year. Summer daytime temperatures in Rocky Mountain National Park on Trail Ridge, Fall River, and West Slope roads average in the 50s (10 C). The record high temperature in the alpine tundra is 63 (17 C). Wind chill can make these temperatures seem much lower—and it's usually windy in the mountains.

Visiting the high mountains can be a safe and extremely rewarding experience, as long as people are prepared and aware of the following dangers. As usual, prevention is the best way to make your trip safe and enjoyable.

1. Hypothermia. More of a threat to backpackers, day hikers, and skiers, hypothermia occurs from prolonged exposure to the cold and a resulting drop in body temperature. It's more common among elderly people. Symptoms include a slowed heart rate, puffiness, pale skin, lethargy, and confusion. In severe cases, breathing slows and intravenous liquids are required. Hypothermia is a killer and has claimed many victims in the mountains. Always bring a hat, rain and wind gear, and extra warm clothing (layers are best) when going into the mountains. Staying well-hydrated by drinking liquids frequently also helps to prevent hypothermia. Keep a hat on if it's chilly—most body heat is lost from the head.

2. Dehydration. Colorado's dry climate, combined with exertion at high altitudes, can cause dehydration: a drop in the body's water level and often a drop in the body's level of salt. Symptoms include severe thirst, dry lips, increased heart and breathing rates, dizziness, and confusion. The skin is dry and stiff. There's little urination, and what is passed is dark. Salt loss causes headaches, cramps (often in the legs), lethargy, and pallor. Drink liquids frequently in the mountains. If you're feeling thirsty, your body's telling you that you're already about a quart low on water. Take salty snacks such as pretzels, chips, and crackers. Rehydration drinks, such as Gatorade, are also good aids to take along.

3. Lightning. Lightning is much more dangerous above timberline. Every year lightning claims a number of lives in Colorado's high country. If a storm develops, stay off ridges and peaks. Keep away from trees, boulders, isolated buildings, and metal objects. The safest place is in your car. A tingling sensation at the base of the neck or scalp and hair standing on end with static electricity are both signs that lightning is about to strike near you. Move rapidly to your car. Do not stand still, no matter what. If you are unable to return to your car, squat and wrap your arms around your knees, keeping your head low. Do not lie or sit on the ground (because if lightning strikes you or the ground and travels through your body, you want it to have a way out—an open circuit).

To estimate your distance from a lightning strike, count the seconds between the flash and the accompanying thunder and divide by five to get the distance in miles. It takes five seconds for the sound to travel a mile.

4. Altitude sickness. Symptoms include headache, dizziness, nausea, shortness of breath, and impaired mental abilities. Breathing into a paper or plastic bag for five minutes reduces these symptoms. In severe cases, fluid can build up in the lungs, causing breathlessness, heavy coughing, and heavy phlegm. If untreated, these symptoms can lead to seizures, hallucinations, coma, brain damage, and death. There is 40 percent less oxygen in the air above 8,000 feet (2,438 meters) than at sea level. To avoid altitude sickness, refrain from strenuous activity for the first few days at high altitude. Move slowly above timberline, eat lightly, and drink fluids frequently. Alcoholic beverages may aggravate the symptoms. Move to a lower elevation if symptoms persist. People with respiratory or heart problems should check with a physician before going to high elevations.

5. Sunburn. Sunburn is much more severe at high altitudes because the reduced atmosphere is less able to filter out the sun's harmful ultraviolet radiation. With 5 percent more ultraviolet light per 1,000 feet, Colorado has 25 percent more damaging sun rays than Florida's beaches. Skiers and other winter sports enthusiasts need to be especially careful, because reflection from snow can cause severe sunburn. Skiers have been known to get sunburned inside their nostrils. In summer, to avoid burning, wear a long-sleeved shirt and a brimmed hat. Use sunscreen with at least a 15 SPF (sun protection factor) rating year-round.

6. Dangerous currents and floods. Though they look shallow and serene, mountain streams have strong currents, slippery rocks, and cold temperatures that have been contributing factors in many drownings. Be especially careful when fishing or allowing children to play near streams. Sudden rains can raise stream levels rapidly and even cause flash floods. If rain continues, move to higher ground.

7. Giardia. Don't drink water from streams and lakes. Tempting though it might be, many mountain streams and lakes contain bacteria and a microscopic organism called Giardia lamblia, which can cause long-term intestinal problems. The organism is transmitted into water by cysts in human, domestic animal, and wildlife feces. Dogs and cats can catch and transmit Giardia. Symptoms of Giardia include violent diarrhea, gas, cramps, loss of appetite, and nausea. Carry your own water bottle filled with tap water. Campers and hikers should boil all stream or lake water for 10 or more minutes, use water-purification kits or the now-popular (and expensive) microfilters (portable pumps that filter water). A microfilter must filter down to four microns to filter out Giardia.

8. Ticks. Not usually a problem in the higher mountains, wood ticks appear in the spring after vegetation begins to leaf in the Lower and Upper Montane zones—the areas below 9,500 feet (2,896 meters). They can appear as early as February in forested and shrubby areas and remain active into late summer. They are rare in the subalpine zone and above the tree line (above 9,500 feet). Applying insect repellent and wearing long pants and long-sleeved shirts help prevent tick bites. The best precaution is to check frequently for ticks on your clothing, hair, and body, because it takes several hours for a tick to attach. After being outdoors, undress in a shower or tub or on a ground cloth outside your tent. Inspect clothing carefully before putting it back on. Destroy ticks, but do not crunch them with your fingers.

Wood ticks can transmit Colorado tick fever and the more serious (but fairly uncommon) Rocky Mountain fever. Consult a physician if you have localized swelling, a rash, enlarged lymph glands or a fever in the days or weeks after a tick bite. Lyme disease is uncommon in Colorado, but it does occur from non-native ticks that somehow hitch a ride into the state.

To remove an attached tick, disinfect the area. Grasp the tick firmly with tweezers close to its head. Gently remove it by pulling it upward and out from the skin. Never twist or jerk on it. Putting nail polish, cooking oil, or petroleum jelly on the tick can make it release its grip more easily.

der, drive to Nederland via Boulder Canyon. From the southwest end of Nederland, follow Colo. 72 to the town of Eldora, where County Road 130 begins at the west end of town. So popular are these trails—and with good reason—that it's hard to find a parking place on weekends, so weekday hiking is recommended. The left fork leads to the old town site of Hessie, 1.5 miles west of Eldora, now just an old cabin or two. The short road to Hessie (and the trailhead) is usually underwater and not passable by ordinary passenger cars. So park where permitted along the road. Observe the "No Parking" signs, because they're strictly enforced, and cars are towed. Reach the Fourth of July Trailhead via the right fork of County Road 130.

Lost Lake
Hessie Trailhead

The 4-mile round-trip hike to Lost Lake is especially nice in the fall with the changing aspen leaves. The trail is a gravely road that climbs through aspen groves. When it sort of levels out for a bit, listen for the roar of water, take a short detour to the left (not marked), and look for a gorgeous series of cascades culminating in a thundering waterfall. Continue on the trail to a junction sign at a bridge. Don't take the Devil's Thumb Bypass Trail; instead, cross the bridge and continue up the left-hand side of the creek past another beautiful falls. The trail leads to Woodland Flats, a large, open meadow with fine views of Devil's Thumb and the mountains. Don't miss the sign at this point for Lost Lake to the left; it's another 0.5 miles up to this pretty, wildflower-lined lake and the site of much early mining activity. Reach the Fourth of July Trailhead via the right fork of County Road 130.

Backpacking

Hiking trails are interchangeable as backpacking trails, but backpackers will need permits to stay overnight in the Indian Peaks Wilderness Area, which includes many of the trails described above. Certain trails are also off-limits for backpacking,

so check with the District Ranger Office (see subsequent information) before heading for the hills. The following are various trails in the Indian Peaks area and elsewhere that offer access to good backpacking destinations. Also see the preceding "Camping" section for more details. Information on the Indian Peaks Wilderness is available from the U.S. Forest Service Boulder Ranger District (see below under "Permits"). Entire books have been written just on Boulder-area hiking and backpacking trails with detailed descriptions and interesting historical notes; look for them at local mountain sporting goods shops. An especially good book is *Boulder Hiking Trails* by Ruth Carol Cushman and Glenn Cushman. Another good one is *50 Front Range Hiking Trails* (including Rocky Mountain National Park and the Indian Peaks Wilderness Area) by Richard DuMais. Hikes in Rocky Mountain National Park are described in the chapter on the park in this book.

Golden Gate Canyon State Park
10 miles south of Nederland on Colo. Hwy. 72
(303) 582–3707

This 14,000-acre state park offers many miles of hiking plus backpacking, fishing, and 155 camping sites at lower altitudes than the Indian Peaks Wilderness Area. It's a lovely spot in the fall with the changing colors. Don't forget your camera when you visit Panorama Point, which offers a view of 100 miles along the Continental Divide. (See admission fees in the preceding "Camping" section.)

Indian Peaks Wilderness

There are numerous backpacking options in the Indian Peaks Wilderness. The Arapaho Pass Area begins at the Fourth of July Trailhead (see above under "Hiking in the Mountains") and offers many choices on both sides of the Continental Divide. The trail climbs 3 miles to the 11,900-foot pass and drops down on the other side to Caribou Lake, where it continues southwest over Caribou Pass to Columbine Lake. To reach Fourth of July

Trailhead, travel west from Nederland on Colo. 72 to the town of Eldora. County Road 130 begins at the west end of the town of Eldora. The Fourth of July Trailhead is 5 miles farther (take the right fork at the Hessie intersection).

Pawnee Pass (Indian Peaks)

The climb to Pawnee Pass (12,541 feet) starts at Brainard Lake on the extremely popular Isabelle Lake Trailhead, on the right side of Long Lake, but the crowds thin as the going gets rougher and higher. This 4.5-mile hike is quite steep for the last 2 miles. An interesting backpacking loop leads over the pass to Monarch Lake and returns to the east side of the Divide over Arapaho Pass—you'll need two cars or a drop-off and pickup arrangement to complete this one.

Permits and Regulations

You must have a permit to backpack anywhere in the Indian Peaks Wilderness Area from June 1 to Sept. 15. Permits and detailed maps and routes are available at the Boulder District Ranger Station of the U.S. Forest Service, 2140 Yarmouth Ave. at Highway 36 (303-444-6600; recorded information line: (303-541-2519). Permits are not required for individual backpackers, but are required for organized groups. Backpacking group size is limited to 12; permits cost $5 for up to 14 nights. Dogs are allowed in Indian Peaks (but not Rocky Mountain National Park) but must be on a 6-foot (maximum), hand-held leash at all times. (There's a $50 fine for violation of the leash law.) It's important to observe this regulation because the great number of hikers with dogs has caused considerable disturbance to wildlife and other hikers, particularly in recent years. Back- packing permits for Indian Peaks are available on weekends (when the Boulder District Ranger Station is closed) at Nederland's Ace Hardware, 20 Lakeview Drive (in the shopping center). National forest maps of Indian Peaks cost $4 ($6 for waterproof) and are also sold at area climbing, hardware, and sporting goods stores.

Horseback Riding

What could be more Western than riding a horse? Most stables are out of town a bit, on the plains or in the mountains.

Bradley-Beggs Stables
1375 N. 111th Ave., Lafayette
(303) 665–9247

Bradley-Beggs Stables offers guided rides, lessons, and birthday parties and company picnics year-round, at your place or theirs. The hourly rate is $20 per person in the Bradley-Beggs corrals. Trail rides in the flatlands east of Lafayette are $30 each. Lessons cost $30 per person for a 90-minute group (three or more) lesson, $35 for a semiprivate lesson (two people), and $40 for a private lesson.

The Lazy H Guest Ranch
Colo. Hwy. 7, about a mile south of Allenspark
(303) 447–1388

Lazy H offers a full dude-ranch program in June, July, and August, and hourly rides in May, September, and October. The cost

> **Insiders' Tip**
> Though Fido might love to hike, check regulations at the trailheads. Dogs must be on leashes at all times in the Indian Peaks Wilderness Area, with a $50 fine for violators. When skiing or snowshoeing in winter, take only dogs that truly respond to voice control. Out-of-control dogs on ski trails—especially the downhills—endanger both dogs and skiers.

is $1,185 for a weeklong dude-ranch vacation (including horseback riding, meals, and children's program); rides are $18 an hour per person (children and adults).

Peaceful Valley Lodge and Guest Ranch
Peak to Peak Hwy. (Colo. Hwy. 72), 8 miles
north of Ward
(303) 747-2881

Peaceful Valley offers nonguest pack trips, breakfast rides, and guided trail rides from mid-May through mid-October, based on availability. Hourly rides cost $20 per person. All-inclusive six-day packages run $1,350 to $1,650 for an adult, less for kids. A three-day package is $750 to $1,650.

Hunting

To be honest, Boulder County isn't going to be your best bet for hunting. Most of the open land around Boulder is city or county open space, where hunting is not allowed, and in fact, even killing a rattlesnake can get you in big trouble. Locations, seasons, and regulations for hunting particular animals are complicated (too much so to outline here), so it's necessary to get the appropriate information for hunting elk, deer, bear, mountain lion, grouse, rabbit, squirrel, etc. Pamphlets and information are available wherever hunting licenses are sold, such as McGuckin Hardware, 2525 Arapahoe Avenue (303-443-1822); Kmart (small game licenses only), 3325 28th Street (303-443-7850); and, of course, the Colorado Division of Wildlife, 6060 Broadway in Denver (303-291-7227); call (303) 291-7530 for hunter education and (303) 291-7529 for big-game information.

Just to give you an idea of costs, hunting licenses for Colorado residents cost $20.25 for deer and $30.25 for elk; for nonresidents, licenses cost $270.25 for deer and antelope, and $450.25 for elk. A youth hunting tag is $100. (Twenty-five cents per license sold goes to search-and-rescue services provided, if necessary, by the state.) Fees may increase pending legislation.

In-line Skating

The Boulder Creek Path is the most popular spot for in-line skating, but any of the city's bike paths are good (check our previous "Bicycling" section). Rates to rent in-line skates are around $5 an hour and $15 to $20 a day. You can rent in-line skating equipment at the following shops:

The Bikesmith
2432 Arapahoe Ave., Boulder
(303) 443-1132

Look for this bike shop in the Arapahoe Village Shopping Center. All types of bicycling and in-line skating equipment are sold and rented.

Cutting Edge Sports
2516 Broadway, Boulder
(303) 413-0228
1387 S. Boulder Rd., Louisville
(303) 666-4550

Cutting Edge specializes in sales, rental, and service on all kinds of bikes, skis, and skates.

Kayaking, Canoeing, and Rafting

Canoeing and kayaking are mainly done at Boulder Reservoir and Boulder Creek, although the pond at the East Boulder Recreation Center draws an occasional craft. Boulder kayakers practice at a course set up on Boulder Creek (in memory of an avid kayaker). For extended river trips, they head to the Arkansas River near Buena Vista (a few hours' drive from Boulder), or over to Utah and other states. If you want to take a longer paddling trip, you'll have to travel elsewhere.

Acquired Tastes Inc.
(303) 443-4120, (800) 888-8582

This reputable Boulder guide service specializes in whitewater excursions on the Arkansas River, with one-, two- and three-day trips available from mid-May through August.

Two kayakers try out the waters of Boulder Creek. PHOTO: LINDA CORNETT

Boulder Outdoor Center
2510 N. 47th St., Boulder
(303) 444–8420

An excellent, professional operation dedicated to river preservation, this shop also sells and rents all of the necessary equipment for river outings. Boulder Outdoor Center offers raft trips and resort package trips that include kayaking and canoeing instruction.

Paragliding

A silent glider ride over the Front Range is an experience of a lifetime. For those who want nothing to stand between them and the great blue sky—other than a chute of sheer nylon—there's paragliding. Local instructors include:

Fly Away Paragliding
Golden
(303) 642–0849

Owner Bill Lawrence, who has competed in two national championships, is a tandem-rated instructor and has been flying for seven years. He originally trained in Switzerland. He runs trips out-of-state but mostly works out of Boulder. His company specializes in pilot training and small classes.

Rugby

Rugby aficionados can contact the 30-year-old Boulder Rugby Club at the BRFC Hotline (303–575–5698) for information about practices and games.

Running

Anywhere you look in Boulder, you'll see people running. Runners choose just about any location: the Boulder Creek Path (see our Parks chapter), quiet streets through town, the Mesa Trail (see the "Hiking" section in this chapter), various open space trails, and even mountains. For more information contact the following shops and clubs:

The Boulder Road Runners
P.O. Box 1866, Boulder, CO 80306

This group offers organized runs and programs for runners of all ages and abilities. For serious runners there are training and running groups and speed workouts; for information, call president Rich Castro at (303) 492-8776.

Boulder Running Company
2775 Pearl St. (at 28th St.), Boulder
(303) 786-9255

This running store offers a great selection of running shoes, clothing, and other accessories. Talk to the staff about local runs.

Runners Choice
2460 Canyon Blvd. (Village Center near McGuckin's), Boulder
(303) 449-8551

A longtime Boulder running shop, Runners Choice has helpful staffers who will fit you with shoes or provide information on local runs.

Sailing, Sailboarding, and Powerboating

With Boulder's capricious chinooks and occasional gale-force winds, sailing and sailboarding can be exciting experiences here. The mountains may be our most popular attraction, but water-lovers can find plenty of places to catch a wave.

Boulder Reservoir
51st St., 1.5 miles north of Jay Rd. via the Diagonal Hwy. (Colo. Hwy. 119)
(303) 441-3456 (boathouse)

In the summer, sailboats and sailboards can be rented at Boulder Reservoir through the City of Boulder–operated boathouse. The city also offers instruction at the reservoir. Classes are offered in sailing as well as sailboarding. Daily admission with a sailboard or sailboat (weekdays only) is $15 for city residents, $25 for nonresidents. On weekends, the cost is $20 and $30. McGuckin Hardware sponsors a wind-conditions hotline at (303) 581-WIND.

Powerboats also are permitted at Boulder Reservoir (303-441-3468, administrative office). Admission on weekdays only is $35 for residents and $60 for nonresidents (it's also necessary to have $300,000 watercraft liability insurance). For boats with 49 horsepower or less, admission is $15 for residents and $25 for nonresidents (the same insurance coverage is required). No daily passes are sold for weekend powerboating; you'll have to purchase a season permit. These cost $325 for city residents, $425 for county residents, and $750 for out-of-county residents (for boats with more than 49 horsepower). For boats with less than 49 horsepower, the pass costs $65 for city residents, $100 for county residents, and $105 for out-of-county residents. Season passes allow holders to boat on the reservoir seven days a week.

Union Reservoir
461 Weld County Rd. 26, Longmont
(303) 772-1265

Another popular sailing spot (only wakeless boating allowed) is Union Reservoir. From Boulder, take the Diagonal Highway (Colo. 119) east to Weld County Road 1, and follow the signs. Or, from Longmont take Ninth Avenue east to County Line Road, turn right and follow the signs. The gate fee is $5 on weekends and $4 on weekdays for a car or a trailered boat.

Skiing

Since skiing, in all its variations, is so popular with Colorado residents and visitors, we've presented information on the sport

Take Pictures, Leave the Plants

Hiking one of the many trails that meander through city of Boulder open space and mountain parks land, you may be tempted by a field of brilliant gold or purple or orange flowers. What could it hurt to pick just one, a souvenir of a lovely day?

If you were the only visitor to these urban natural areas, it probably wouldn't matter much. But there are an estimated 3 million others a year right behind you. If everyone took just one flower or pebble or leaf or water-buffed bit of wood, it wouldn't take long for open space to be down to bare dirt.

The seeds from that one flower are the hope of next year's crop. That handful of blackberries should be part of a hungry bear's lunch.

But, there's no harm in looking. The Open Space and Mountain Parks Department will even provide you with a colorful booklet to help you track the summer in wildflowers.

As early as February, look along Flagstaff Trail for fragrant yellow Oregon grape holding the hillside in place. Tiny purple pasqueflowers can be found along McClintock and Gregory Canyon Trails.

By April, wild geranium will be scattering color on meadows and hillsides, and stately wild iris will invite your admiration on Big Bluestem and Mesa Trails.

May brings the bright yellow brush of arnica, filling meadows and Douglas fir groves, and versatile yucca will send up its spires on Hogback Ridge and Red Rocks Trails.

By June, Colorado's state flower, the purple and white columbine, can be found in aspen forests. Look for brilliant gaillardia moths hiding in plain sight on the red and yellow blanketflowers on Marshall Mesa and Big Bluestem.

The misnamed western wallflower, with a single stalk sprouting petals of red, yellow, orange, and pink, bides its time until July; look in ponderosa pine forests and meadows along the Tenderfoot Trail.

That's just a sampler of the beautiful wildflowers to be found every year, as long as we remember to leave them where we find them.

in several places in this book. For a brief review, see the subsequent sections. For more information—prices, related activities, lodging—on Ski Country, see our Attractions and Daytrips and Weekend Getaways chapters.

Downhill Skiing

Eldora Mountain Resort
2861 Eldora Ski Rd., Nederland
(303) 440–8700

It's not Vail or Aspen, but it's only 21 miles from Boulder and there are no mountain passes or giant ski-traffic jams to slow you down. Eldora is a great little ski area right in Boulder County. It has 12 lifts: two quads, two triple, four double, and four surface. With a top elevation of 10,600 feet, Eldora has 1,400 feet of vertical gain—and beautiful views from the top. You'll probably get more skiing in and less standing in lift lines at Eldora than at the bigger resorts. There's a ski school, rentals, a lodge, races, leagues, Nordic and telemark trails, and even an RTD bus from Boulder that makes numerous daily trips right to the resort.

Other Ski Areas

Keystone, Arapahoe Basin, Breckenridge, Copper Mountain, and Winter Park are within a two-hour drive of Boulder (see the "Ski Country" section of our Daytrips and Weekend Getaways chapter). For information on these and other Colorado ski areas, call Colorado Ski Country USA, Monday through Friday, (303) 825-SNOW (recorded information) or (303) 837-0793 (administrative office). Discount lift tickets to the aforementioned areas are available at King Soopers and Safeway, among other places.

Rocky Mountain Skiing by Claire Walter (this book's former co-author and contributing editor for *Skiing* magazine) is a great resource book for the entire Rocky Mountain region and is available at local bookstores.

Cross-Country Skiing

Before you head to the mountains, you can warm up and practice right in Boulder. The Boulder Nordic Club, in coopera-tion with the Boulder Parks and Recreation Department, sets a nice track around North Boulder Park (Ninth and Dellwood Streets), whenever there's enough snow on the ground. Skiing at the park is free. The Boulder Nordic Club is full of very serious skiers, most of whom compete in the various citizens' races throughout Colorado and beyond. BNC provides information on local skiing conditions at 303-441-4060 ext. 603.

Farther away—but still just an hour's drive into the mountains—lie our favorite spots in the Brainard Lake area: East Portal from Rollinsville (see directions to Rollins Pass Road in this chapter's "Biking" section), and the Hessie and Fourth of July roads at the west end of the town of Eldora and Peaceful Valley (north of Nederland and Ward on Colo. 72; see the previous "Hiking" section for more directions to these areas).

The Colorado Mountain Club (303-279-3080) and Flatirons Ski Club (303-449-8335) operate weekly scheduled trips that are open to the public. (Membership is eventually expected if you take a number of the trips.) They both provide a great way to meet other skiers and explore local ski trails for those new to the area. Ski rentals, books, maps, and trail information are

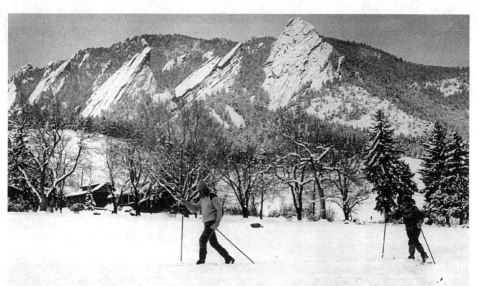

Cross-country skiers enjoy new snow in Chautauqua Park. PHOTO: DAILY CAMERA

available at Mountain Sports (303–443–6770), Eastern Mountain Sports (303–442–7566), Neptune Mountaineering (303–499–8866), and Doc's Ski & Sports (303–499–0963). Please refer to this book's Shopping chapter for addresses and other details on these shops.

Excellent sources for local cross-country skiing are *Peak to Peak Ski Trails of the Colorado Front Range* by Harlan N. Barton and *Backcountry Skiing* by Brian Litz.

Brainard Lake

Many national forest summer hiking trails are used for cross-country skiing in the winter. For absolute beginners who want no hills or spills, the Brainard Lake Road offers nearly level terrain to the lake with no surprises and great scenery. Just follow the road up past the closure—2.2 miles to the lake.

Left Hand Reservoir at Brainard Lake is more challenging, but the wide trail offers plenty of margin for error. Begin on the south side of the Brainard Road below the gate closure and follow the trail signs up a roadbed about 2 miles to the reservoir. There are thrilling downhill runs back on the wide trail.

The Colorado Mountain Club South Trail begins on the south side of Brainard Road 50 yards west of the closure gate and is a bit longer and narrower through wooded areas. Climb a short hill and ski the rolling 2.5 miles to Brainard Lake.

For intermediate to advanced skiers comfortable on narrow, steep hills and turns, there's the Waldrop North Trail, about 5.5 miles round-trip, accessible just north of the closure.

Buchanan Pass Trail begins at the curve on Colo. 72 (5.8 miles north of Ward) at Peaceful Valley. Follow the trail on the north side of the creek west of Camp Dick campground. An 11-mile loop can be made by returning on the Middle St. Vrain four-wheel-drive road (some snowmobiles), but you can ski whatever distance you like.

The Sourdough Trail is 17.5 miles long, but has different segments at various trailheads. From Camp Dick Camp-ground to Beaver Reservoir, it's 2.3 miles. From Beaver Reservoir to Brainard Road, it's 7.4 miles, and from Brainard Road to Rainbow Lakes Road, 7.8 miles. The trail was built mainly for ski touring and mountain biking, and is pleasant rolling terrain though the pines. All accesses to the various connections to the Sourdough Trail are on the Peak to Peak Highway (Colo. 72), west of Nederland. Camp Dick Campground is on Middle St. Vrain Road, 5.8 miles north of Ward and .5 miles west of Peaceful Valley. One Sourdough Trail-head is on the left-hand side of County Road 96 just east of Beaver Reservoir, 2.5 miles north of Ward and 2 miles west on County Road 96. Another Sourdough Trailhead is on the right side of Rainbow Lakes Road (County Road 116), 4.7 miles south of Ward (7 miles north of Nederland) and .4 miles west on County Road 116. The Red Rock Trailhead is on the right side of County Road 102, just east of Red Rock Lake, 2.5 miles west on Brainard Lake Road.

Eldora Mountain Resort Nordic Center
2861 Eldora Ski Rd., Nederland
(303) 440–8700

Eldora Mountain Resort's Nordic Center is one of Colorado's largest and most popular cross-country centers, with 45 kilometers of marked and groomed trails. There's a cozy log cabin lodge with refreshments, rentals, and lessons. At Eldora, there's also access to the free national forest Jenny Creek Trail. Climb up the Ho-Hum downhill run next to the Little Hawk lift, turn right and look for the trail signs. The trail weaves up and down through the woods and then descends on a narrow trail (which is bad when icy) to the Jenny Creek Road. You can turn around here or follow the creekbed, eventually leading up to Yankee Doodle Lake (9 miles round-trip from the Eldora parking lot). Or, at the Jenny Creek Road, take another trail to the right, the Guinn Mountain Trail, which leads up a steep, difficult climb to the distant Guinn Mountain cabin (10.5 miles round trip), operated by the Colorado

Mountain Club. Skiers can bring camping gear to spend the night; call the subsequently listed CMC number for information.

Snowboarding

All of Colorado's ski areas except Aspen Mountain allow snowboarding, rent the equipment, and offer lessons. Snowboards are now generally available for rent at skiing and mountaineering equipment shops, and a whole new genre of snowboard (and skateboard) specialty shops have sprung up to accommodate the growing popularity of this sport. One-day snowboard rentals cost around $20 for the board, boots, and bindings on the weekend and $15 during the week. Ask about high-performance equipment. Some shops that rent and demo snowboards include:

Boulder Outdoor Center, 2510 N. 47th St., Boulder (303–444–8420)

Brothers Boards, 3330 Arapahoe Ave., Boulder (303–473–0266)

Gear Up, 2426 Arapahoe Ave., Boulder, (303–443–9188)

Powdertools, 2000 30th St., Boulder, (303–444–0954)

Snowshoeing

The growing popularity of snowshoeing is also evident on all the local trails in winter. One needs no real lessons for this simple sport. Just strap on the snowshoes and start walking. Snowshoes provide you with the ability to leave the crowds on the trails and make your own route—and the cross-country skiers would appreciate it if you did. Snowshoes can be rented at most local mountaineering and ski rental shops (listed in the previous "Skiing" section), at a cost of around $12 a day.

Please note: Snowshoers sharing forest trails with cross-country skiers should make their own tracks, wherever possible, and avoid walking in existing ski tracks. This is because cross-country skis work best in ski tracks and don't work well on snowshoe paths. People without skis or snowshoes should not walk in either tracks—it ruins them both, making it frustrating and miserable for skiers and snowshoers alike.

Swimming

Until the really big one hits California, and the Pacific Ocean laps the foot of the Rockies, pools and reservoirs are the main swimming options around Boulder. The three City of Boulder–operated recreation centers (see "Recreational Facilities" in our Boulder Parks and Recreation Centers chapter) all have indoor pools. East Boulder Recreation Center has a water slide and Lazy River with innertubes for kids, plus a mushroom waterfall. Outdoor pools are open during summer months only at Scott Carpenter Park and Spruce Pool (also city-operated and listed in the Parks chapter). Boulder Reservoir's sandy

Insiders' Tip
Keep track! Snowshoers sharing trails with cross-country skiers should make their own tracks, wherever possible, because cross-country skis work best in their own tracks and function poorly in snowshoe tracks. People without skis or snowshoes should not walk in either tracks because it ruins the trail for both skiers and snowshoers, making the going frustrating and miserable for both. Please don't ruin someone else's fun.

swimming beach helps relieve ocean homesickness a bit (no sharks, only carp).

Eldorado Artesian Springs
Eldorado Springs
(303) 499–1316

Just a few miles south of Boulder in Eldorado Springs, look for the resort in this scenic canyon setting. The pool at the springs of this historic resort offers therapeutic mineral water. The thermal pools and snack bar are open from Memorial Day through Labor Day from 10 A.M. to 6 P.M. daily. Rates are $6 for adults, $4 for kids and seniors.

Hyland Hills Water World
1800 W. 89th Ave., Federal Heights
(303) 427–7873

If you are up for a 30-minute drive, there's a world of water waiting at Water World—a kiddie pool with fountains and slides, a wave pool, massive water slides, and a circular lazy river where you can float peacefully around and around. All-day admission is $24.95, $22.95 for kids 4 to 12, free for tots age 3 and under and seniors 60 and older.

Tennis

Free public tennis courts are usually in great demand and short supply in Boulder. Courts can be reserved for $7.50 for 90 minutes through the city-operated North, South, and East Boulder Recreation Centers (303-441-3444, 303-441-3448, and 303-441-4400), and the city offers instruction at various levels. The Boulder Tennis Association (303-442-4282) has tennis ladders and formal and informal tournaments. There's a smattering of free courts around Boulder at various parks and schools including:

Arapahoe Ridge, 1280 43rd Street (two courts)

Base Line Middle School, 700 20th Street (two courts)

Boulder High, 1604 Arapahoe (two courts)

Burbank Middle School, 290 Manhattan Drive (four courts)

Centennial Middle School, 2005 Norwood Avenue (eight courts)

Chautauqua Park, Ninth Street and Baseline Road (one court)

Fairview High, 1515 Greenbriar Boulevard (eight courts)

Martin Park, 36th Street and Dartmouth Avenue (two courts)

Tom Watson Park, 63rd Street and IBM Drive (four courts)

Williams Village, 30th Street and Baseline Road (four courts)

Spectator Sports

College Sports

Basketball
University of Colorado
Athletic Ticket Office, Folsom Field, Colorado Ave., Boulder (303) 492–8337

The women's and men's teams belong to the Big 12 Conference and play home games at the CU Coors Events/Conference Center, on Regent Drive in Boulder on the CU campus; it holds 11,198 fans. The regular season runs from December to March. Individual tickets are $8 to $12 for men's games and $6 to $10 for women's. Students, seniors, and children pay half. Call to order tickets, or for season tickets write to the Athletic Ticket Office, Box 372, Boulder, CO 80309.

Football
University of Colorado
Athletic Ticket Office, Folsom Field, Colorado Ave., Boulder (303) 492–8337

The Golden Buffaloes belong to the Big 12 Conference in NCAA Division I and play home games at Folsom Field, which seats 51,748. The regular season runs from September through November. For season ticket information, call the Athletic Ticket Office at (303) 492-8337.

Fans can watch University of Colorado teams compete in numerous sports throughout the school year.

PHOTO: UNIVERSITY OF COLORADO

Individual game tickets are $40 (the Nebraska game, played here every other year, is $45). Season tickets are available for $290 per seat. Season ticket holders must also contribute $100 to the Golden Buffalo Scholarship Fund. Call the number above for more information.

Volleyball

University of Colorado

Athletic Ticket Office, Folsom Field, Colorado Ave., Boulder (303) 492–8337

The Buffs belong to the Big 12 Conference and play home games at the CU Coors Events/Conference Center on the CU-Boulder campus. The season runs from September into November. Tickets are $6 for reserved seats, $4 for general admission, and $2 for students and children. Call for further ticket information.

Other College Sports

University of Colorado

Other varsity sports teams at CU-Boulder include golf, cross-country skiing, track and field, tennis, and skiing, and there are numerous club sports. For information about varsity sports schedules call (303)

492-7931. For nonvarsity club sports information, call (303) 492-5471.

Professional Sports

Baseball
Colorado Rockies
Coors Field, 2001 Blake St., Denver
(303) 292–0200
The Rockies belong to major league baseball's National League West Division and play their home games at the snazzy Coors Field in Denver (seating capacity 50,249). The season runs from April through September. Individual tickets cost $4 to $37; season tickets run from $405 to $2,977. Tickets are available by calling (800) 388-ROCK; for group tickets (25 people or more) and general customer service, call (303) ROCKIES, or write to the Colorado Rockies Baseball Club, P.O. Box 120, Denver, CO 80201.

Basketball
Denver Nuggets
Pepsi Center, Speer Blvd. and Chopper Pl., Denver
(303) 405–1100,
(303) 893–DUNK (ticket office)
The Nuggets belong to the National Basketball Association's Western Conference and play home games at the impressive Pepsi Center (capacity 19,099). The regular season runs from November into April. Single game tickets range in price from $10 to $180, season tickets from $441 to $7,560. Some discounts are available.

Football
Denver Broncos
Invesco Field at Mile High, 2755 W. 17th Ave., Denver
Denver Broncos Ticket Office, 1900 Eliot St., Denver
(303) 433–7466
With the completion of the bizarrely named 85,000-seat Invesco Field at Mile High in 2001, the Broncos now play on new turf. The Broncos belong to the National Football League's American Conference Western Division. The team won consecutive Super Bowls in the late-'90s, making it one of the most popular teams in the Rockies.

The regular season runs from September through December. For ticket information call the listed number. Season tickets are sold out for the foreseeable future, with a waiting list of more than 5,000 names. Single game tickets, if available, are offered the week prior to each game at the Broncos Ticket Office and cost $30 to $68.

Ice Hockey
Colorado Avalanche
Pepsi Center, Speer Blvd. and Chopper Pl., Denver
(303) 893–6700, (303) 575–1900
Yes, Coloradans are nuts about their 2001 Stanley Cup Champions—and hoping for another championship season. The Colorado Avalanche (formerly the Quebec Nordiques) belong to the National Hockey League and play home games at the Pepsi Center. The regular season runs from October through April, with the playoffs sometimes lasting into June. Individual tickets cost $22 to $125. Call for more information about ticket prices and game schedules. Tickets are also available online through Ticketmaster, (303-830-8497), and at Rite Aid, Foley's, Budget Tapes & CDs, and Tower Records.

Soccer
Colorado Rapids
Invesco Field at Mile High, 2755 W. 17th Ave., Denver
(303) 299–1599, (800) 844–7777
Part of the new and burgeoning major league soccer, the Rapids play home games at the new Invesco Field at Mile High Stadium in Denver, with a seating capacity of 25,000 for soccer. The regular season runs from April through October. Ticket prices range from $13 to $22, season tickets from $176 to $480; tickets are available at King Soopers stores. Call for discount and special group rates.

Neighborhoods and Nearby Communities

As long as you aren't set on oceanfront property, you just might fall in love with a home in one of Boulder's varied neighborhoods. This chapter is for those who enjoy checking out how other people live. It highlights neighborhoods in Boulder and around the county. Boulder's older neighborhoods get the spotlight first. We follow with a description of mountain places, then cities on the plains. If you want more practical information on settling down, check our Real Estate chapter.

Historic Boulder Neighborhoods

If you like historic homes, the first place to call is Historic Boulder (303–444–5192). The organization itself is headquartered in a fanciful turreted gingerbread Victorian at 646 Pearl Street, just a few blocks west of the Pearl Street Mall. If you are up for some walking, you can find booklets there for self-guided tours through seven historic neighborhoods. It's a good excuse to get out and enjoy the usually fine weather while you're gaining an appreciation for the town's past.

Whittier Historic District

The Whittier Historic District is northeast of the Pearl Street Mall. If you're driving, you may have a first encounter here with the raised pedestrian crossings and traffic circles scattered through Boulder neighborhoods to slow speeders and discourage through traffic in residential areas. The trick with traffic circles is to bear right and yield to other cars, bicyclists, and pedestrians already in the circle.

Whittier is a fascinating mix of styles, from the grande old dame to a tiny rental with a couch on the front porch. *Mork & Mindy*'s house, the turreted, gray Victorian at 1619 Pine Street, is a private residence, but you can enjoy it from the sidewalk (the residents lost patience with fame when fans of the show started walking in their front door). At 16th and Spruce Streets, a giant owl guards the home of artist Bob Bellows, who creates sculptures from old farm tools. The "feathers" around the owl's beak are spoons. Some homes are painstakingly authentic; others have been altered with abandon. A city policy of "in-fill" development to increase residential density near downtown produced many backyard alley houses in the Whittier neighborhood.

Step inside the Boulder Victoria Bed and Breakfast Inn, then the Hotel Boulderado, catty-corner from each other at 13th and Pine Streets, if you like historic interiors. Another to check is the whimsical house at 646 Pearl Street that is now Historic Boulder's home (open Tuesday through Friday, 9 A.M. to 4 P.M.). Among a long line of residents of the Arnett-Fullen house were sisters Marion and Ethel

Mann, who took their rope-twirling expertise to New York City's vaudeville circuit, where they learned a few tricks from fellow performer Will Rogers in the basement of Madison Square Garden. When you visit the gift shop, notice the spiral stairs and other 19th-century features.

Mapleton Hill Historic District

Located northwest of Broadway and Pearl Street, Mapleton took its name from the stately maple trees that line the island running down the middle of Mapleton Avenue. Those 100-year-old maples are dear, for this city started as a windblown prairie, and as they age, the city is planting young trees to replace them to maintain the distinctive character of the neighborhood. When lifelong Mapleton resident Judge Horace Holmes died, neighbors planted several new trees in his honor.

The simple stone house at 1019 Spruce Street is Boulder's oldest surviving house. The area is frequently on Historic Boulder's lavish fundraising Christmas tour of homes; if you are hoping for a peek inside, that's your best chance. This neighborhood is a favorite strolling location, and on warm summer evenings the streets and flagstone sidewalks are filled with a quiet crowd enjoying its hometown feel.

Insider's Tip

Boulder homes show up frequently in decorating and design magazines and in compendiums of fine homes. If you like historic homes, check out *Historic Homes of Boulder County* by Jane Valentine Barker. It sells for less than $30.

At the corner of Mapleton and Ninth Street is Mapleton Elementary School, the heart of the neighborhood since it opened in 1888. Step inside and check out the photos of student bodies shod in everything from button shoes to Adidas. At the bottom of Eighth Street is funky little Lolita's market, where neighborhood kids go for a treat and parents stop in for a bare necessity for supper.

University Hill

This historic area continues to attract many university staff, faculty, and students. Its location, tucked between the foothills and the University, is one of the area's greatest pluses, and its greatest source of frustration. Specifically, the neighborhood is reluctant host to thousands of cars that can't find a space on campus, and rental homes can end up overstuffed with students looking for affordable housing.

It's walkable from downtown, but keep in mind you're going to put in some distance, uphill. Head south on Ninth Street from Canyon Boulevard, past the grandly conceived and minimally executed sculpture park, and cross Boulder Creek and the creek path, where you'll see two interesting buildings. The main Boulder Public Library is on your left, and Highland Office Park, a beautiful renovation of an old school, is on your right. The library was designed as a green building, with lots of ambient light and lights in the stacks that turn on and off automatically in response to motion detectors. Live trees in the children's library soar two stories, so adults in the reference department above are in the treetops. During the '60s and '70s, Highland was the funky home of the Free School, which taught tie-dyed adult students to throw pots and create stained glass. Today, it's an upscale office building with an old money ambiance. Farther up Ninth Street at Euclid Avenue is an unusual red brick home with the look of a castle, partially obscured by a wood fence. Legend has it that two Boulder brothers

A morning glory twines around a stone hitching post in front of a Mapleton Hill home, a charming reminder of the long history of this neighborhood, located just north of Pearl Street and west of Broadway.
PHOTO: LINDA CORNETT

who fell in love with the same woman held a house-building contest. The woman chose this octagonal house, which has not a single square room—and the innovative guy who came with it.

Turn left (east) to 1206 Euclid, where you'll find the Boulder Museum of History set in a beautifully landscaped park. The museum was built in 1899 as a summer "cottage" for a New York stockbroker. If this is a cottage, that New Yorker's regular home must have filled three blocks. It now features a Tiffany window, fascinating snippets of Boulder history, and a gift shop. Locals swear the third-floor ballroom is periodically frequented by ghostly revelers and the beloved dogs of a previous owner still prowl the grounds. One block south, at 12th and Aurora, is the serene white building known as Marpa House. With the look of a foreign embassy, complete with flagpoles, Marpa House is a communal residence and meditation center for Boulder's Buddhist community.

Three blocks west, at 970 Aurora, is The Academy retirement community, a blend of new and old. The original building on the site was an isolated Catholic girl's school when it was built—the young students fell asleep to the serenade of coyotes and the howl of the unrestrained wind. The building later housed offices and classrooms for the University of Colorado until CU decided to sell. While sitting empty, it lost its roof and upper floors to fire and became a crumbling home to raccoons, squirrels, and occasional homeless squatters. In 1998, the building was renovated as the centerpiece of a retirement community aimed at former CU faculty. In this area, you will also encounter sorority and fraternity houses, some stately, some in need of a good spruce-up. To the south, at the northwest corner of 12th Street and Baseline Road, is a home designed by local architect Glenn Huntington, whose stately brick buildings set the tone for 1930s University Hill.

Chautauqua Park

Technically, Chautauqua is the name of the historic park and residential area that fills the triangle between Baseline Road, the Flatirons, and a hilly neighborhood of contemporary homes. However, the name Chautauqua has spread to encompass the surrounding neighborhood as well. In the summertime you can still rent a little old wooden summer cabin at Chautauqua Park, a remnant of the days when Texas schoolteachers and their families summered in Boulder to escape the heat. Street names honor mountain flowers, such as the daisy-shaped gaillardia and the nodding blue lupine. South of the big Chautauqua auditorium, site of musical and dance concerts and a summer silent movie festival, it's a short hike up Enchanted Mesa. With the purchase of this meadow of grasses and strong-limbed ponderosa pines in the 1960s, Boulder became the first town in the nation to buy open space through a sales-tax bond. Enchanted Mesa is one reason Boulderites can gaze out their windows and see pine forests, rather than houses, in the foothills. Also check the Chautauqua Rangers' Station on Kinnikinick Road, where you can get information on Boulder Open Space and Mountain Parks. It's staffed part-time every day; take your chances on it being open or call (303) 441-3440 for the latest hours.

Contemporary Boulder Neighborhoods

While you can hoof through Boulder's oldest neighborhoods, you'll probably want to drive to see the newer ones. Many people complain that Boulder is a difficult driving town because it does not always follow a standard grid pattern. If you're lost, remember that if you are facing the mountains, you are facing west. North-south streets are numbered from the mountains, starting with 3rd; Broadway takes the place of 12th Street downtown.

Flagstaff Road

Some of Boulder's most futuristic homes were designed by the late Boulder architect Charles Haertling. The easiest to spot are just up Flagstaff Road. To get there, follow Baseline Road up Flagstaff Mountain. A tenth of a mile past the fire danger sign is a home of round white towers beside one with sand-colored, pyramidal roofs. These are two of Haertling's 52 creations. Haertling, considered one of America's finest architects, often used dramatic and fluid forms. If you are ever invited inside a Haertling home, go gladly, for he designed with reverence for Boulder's vistas. If you haven't driven up Flagstaff Road before, by all means, keep going. The panorama of Boulder Valley is gorgeous, and if you've got a map, you can spot most landmarks from up there. If you don't have a Boulder County license plate on your car, you'll have to pay a $3 parking fee at the overlook parking area. The red roofs you are seeing are the University of Colorado, whose architect imported the red tile roofs of his Italian homeland. The largish bodies of water farther to the east are cooling ponds for the coal-fired Valmont Power Plant, where undisturbed fish are said to grow to phenomenal size in the warm water. If you continue up Flagstaff Road past the park boundary, you'll pass widely scattered homes in diverse styles, from one that resembles a French château to monumental log houses.

Return down the mountain to Baseline and turn left on Sixth Street. Then turn left again at Cascade to Willowbrook Road, then left once more. On your right is a white house that some call a spaceship. It's the Volsky house, a 1960s-era Haertling design that earned him a feature in *Life* magazine.

Martin Acres

If you've had your fill of fancy homes, check out Boulder's first tract-home neighborhood, south of Baseline Road,

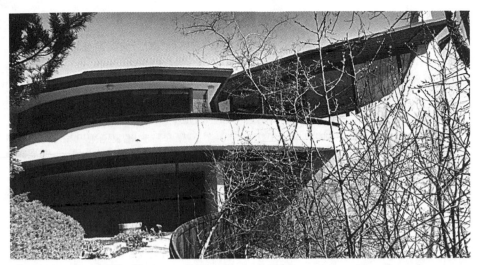

Charles Haertling's Volsky House earned him a feature in Life *magazine.* PHOTO: LINDA CORNETT

north of Table Mesa Drive and east of Broadway. Most of the homes in Martin Acres were built in 1955, when $13,000 bought a three-bedroom ranch house. They now sell for about 15 times that price, and are still among Boulder's most afford- able homes. The trees are now 40 years old. Some renovations are, well, sort of like a kid's party hat on a businessman. But more and more are enthralling transfor- mations. Martin Acres proves that homes from a plain area, filled with interesting people, add character to a neighborhood. Like many Boulder neighborhoods, traffic is the primary concern in the neighbor- hood. Martin Park residents can get reduced-cost bus passes, and the Bear Creek bike path is a lovely way to visit with- out adding pollution or parking problems.

Table Mesa

More 1970s-vintage, and generally pricier than Martin Acres, this is an area of split- levels and raised ranches below the National Center for Atmospheric Research. Table Mesa lies west of Broadway and south of Table Mesa Drive. The Table Mesa Shopping Center is convenient for resi- dents here, as are many mountain trails. The South Boulder Recreation Center on

Gillespie Drive butts up against a lovely park encircling what, in the arid West, passes for a lake—Viele Lake. It's an easy, lovely stroll around the lake, particularly if you are fond of geese. One note: don't wear your finest shoes.

If you long for unobstructed views, fol- low Broadway south to the stoplight at Greenbriar Boulevard. Turn right, and head west past Fairview High School into a neighborhood of earth-toned homes called Shanahan Ridge. Townhomes, con- dominiums, and single-family homes pack the street's north side. The south is open space—a whole valley-ful. Residents awaken to meadowlark songs. One of Boulder's finest achievements is leaving open space near residential areas. People pay a premium to live near open, natural areas. Check out the fresh green growth on the Shanahan Ridge open space, where a prescribed burn in 2000 cleared out dan- gerously dense undergrowth.

Dominating South Boulder is the I. M. Pei–designed National Center for Atmos- pheric Research. This is one of America's finest public buildings, and in typical Boulder fashion, it is also the gateway to easy and popular nature trails, some of them accessible to wheelchairs. NCAR is open to the public for free guided tours at noon Monday through Saturday from June through September; winter tours are at noon Mondays and Wednesdays. You can also take a self-guided tour between 8 A.M. and 5 P.M. Monday through Friday, 9 A.M. and 4 P.M. weekends and holidays. The library and cafeteria are also open weekdays. Call (303) 497–1174. To reach it, drive west on Table Mesa Drive and up to the mesa; keep your eyes open for the deer that roam the mesa (and don't forget to rent Woody Allen's *Sleeper* afterward for an I-was-there experience—also check out the Wonderland Hill neighborhood below for another *Sleeper* reference).

Knollwood Neighborhood

This lovely little neighborhood is tucked away so carefully, many longtime Boulder residents don't know it's there. Driving west on Mapleton, cross Fourth Street and find the sign on your left announcing Knollwood Drive. The long building near the entrance, embracing a boulder, is another Haertling home. Careful of a winter visit, though, as the steep streets can be difficult when icy.

Newlands Neighborhood

Ten years ago this now-trendy place to live didn't even have an official name. But the Newland family once owned the land, and what was once just a collection of houses around North Boulder Park is now one of the hottest real estate markets. This neighborhood is west of Broadway from approximately Alpine on the south to Hawthorn Avenue on the north (from Alpine to the north, east-west street names are pretty much alphabetical). A landscaped island at the intersection of Ninth and Evergreen welcomes visitors to the neighborhood. A sculptor resident donated the statue of a crouching, nude woman in the center of the island; his neighbors have had mixed reactions to the public art. Note the bungalows, some original and others spectacular renovations

and "scrape-offs," where an owner demolishes the old house and builds a bigger one on the site. There is also a subsidized housing unit in the area, but you won't recognize it as such. Approximately 4,899 subsidized units are sprinkled around Boulder, in small, unobtrusive pockets, often close to Boulder's trendiest areas.

A very active neighborhood organization is working hard to build a sense of community here, with activities that include a cooperative childcare and play group, the Junkengrooven swap meet, May Day and Fall Fest picnics, and regular guest presentations for the neighborhood meetings.

Pine Brook Hills

Some of Boulder's grandest modern homes can be found on Linden Avenue in what is called Pine Brook Hills. Back on Broadway, go north past Iris Avenue and turn left (west, toward the mountains) on Linden. These designer homes can't be missed, as many are perched on hillsides with commanding views. Up Linden Avenue is South Cedar Brook Road, and at its very top are the last two homes Haertling designed before he succumbed

Perched in a traffic circle at Ninth and Evergreen in North Boulder, this marble statue of a nude woman serves as a somewhat controversial welcome to the Newlands neighborhood.
PHOTO: LINDA CORNETT

to cancer in his 50s. You can probably find these homes yourself, but here's a clue. One is round and white. The other's roof mimics an aspen leaf, gently curling upward in the wind.

Wonderland Hills

This area was Boulder's first planned multi-unit development and its sense of neighborhood is often appealing to newcomers. To reach the entrance, return to Broadway, going north again, to Poplar Avenue and Wonderland Hills. Several bike paths wind through the neighborhood. In landscaped areas, weeping crab apples, native red-twig dogwoods, and evergreens make homes seem more secluded than in many areas with much larger yards. Within a two-minute walk of the smallest condo are Boulder-style mansions. Did you spot the white "barnacle" house also featured in Woody Allen's futuristic film, *Sleeper*? It's another Haertling home.

Also clinging to this hillside is the huge structure referred to as "the volcano house." Innocuous on the outside, the bizarre home indulges it's owner's childhood fantasies, from a faux volcano with on-command eruptions into bubbling hot tubs, to a fireman's pole connecting the living room with the downstairs foyer. There's even a mini movie theater where every seat is a lounger. The owner has been generous about sharing the ambiance with civic groups holding fund-raisers, so do good and you may get a chance to try out the "snow room"—walls painted with snow scenes and a snow-maker to shower you with the white stuff in the dead of summer.

Go anywhere you want now, and you'll find a new neighborhood. This "point of interest" tour has focused on the older side of Boulder. East of Broadway are many more homes, generally less than 20 years old and more affordable. Dakota Ridge, north of Wonderland Hill, appeals to young families looking for a newly built home. These new areas are ripe for home-owners eager to add their style to a highly creative town.

Mountain Towns

To get an overview of mountain living, take Canyon Boulevard west out of town and head up Boulder Canyon. Turnoffs to Four Mile Canyon, Magnolia Road, and Sugarloaf Road lead to more areas containing mountain homes of various styles. If you continue 17 miles up the canyon, you will reach Nederland and the Peak to Peak Highway (Colo. 72), which leads to other mountain communities. Most of them are along this scenic highway, made up of Colo. Highways 119, 72 and 7. These paved roads are beautiful all year, from the sparkling pine-scented days of summer to the shimmering golden world of an aspen grove in fall to a crisp winter day softened with a comforter of snow. These scenic roads can be steep and curvy, so keep your lower gears in tune and don't let the occasional commuter in a hurry rush you along, as the views along the way are worth the time. Not all mountain towns are listed here, so keep your eyes open to discover one on your own.

Allenspark
8,250 feet;
pop. 800 (winter), 3,000 (summer)
32 miles from Boulder

Founded by Alonzo N. Allen as a mining town, Allenspark was once a stagecoach stop between Ward and Estes Park. Today, Allenspark is a peaceful retirement and vacation community nestled in pine forests on the eastern edge of Rocky Mountain National Park. The style tends to rustic cabins and barns full of trail horses. It has a volunteer fire department and a post office, and offers lodges, cabins, and restaurants. The Fawn Brook Inn (303-747-2556) is a fine dining spot, worth the drive from Boulder. Its hours vary according to the season, so call

Making Things More Neighborly

Not a town to leave things to chance, Boulder has taken a hand in encouraging and helping citizens to organize neighborhood groups.

A full-time neighborhood liaison offers advice on organizational issues, encourages neighbors to get to know each other at down-home events, educates the groups about how to deal with City Hall, and generally makes the town a friendlier place to live.

There are city grants for neighborhood projects—up to $3,000 for large projects. For instance, the small Poplar neighborhood used a city grant to establish a neighborhood composting center. Sprawling Martin Acres installed signs and benches along the Bear Creek bicycle path that runs through the neighborhood.

The city website provides each neighborhood with a profile page that describes its boundaries, its concerns and issues, its successes in addressing those concerns, and a list of neighborhood events and officers.

---

ahead. To reach Allenspark, go to Ward and Nederland and head north on the Peak-to-Peak Highway (Colo. 72). From Lyons, take Colo. 7.

Eldorado Springs
5,760 feet, pop. 650
15 miles from Boulder

This is the closest "mountain" community to Boulder. The gold in these hills comes from the orange and yellow lichens that color the walls of Eldorado Canyon State Park, one of the nation's premier rock-climbing areas. The springs area was the winter home of a Ute Indian tribe. In the early 1900s, these same springs sustained a 40-room resort. Trombone player Glenn Miller used to leave studies at CU to play with the Eldorado Springs resort band. Sweet-faced movie star Mary Pickford was a visitor and soon-to-be-president Dwight Eisenhower and his bride, Mamie, vacationed here. A quarry once yielded Eldorado Canyon's beautiful red rock. It has closed, but that mining scar remains, a reminder of the trade-offs between promoting industry and natural grandeur.

To see Eldorado Springs, drive south on Broadway. Three miles past Table Mesa Drive, turn west on Colo. 170. After 3 more miles, you'll meet a riffraff of cabins, precariously balanced along a steep mountain stream. Welcome to the bumpy dirt roads that some residents say add character and discourage tourists. Most Eldorado Springs residents are romance-smitten commuters. You can see their influence in the flowers that wink in rock gardens, in the misty wash of rainbow colors on a potter's garage, in the blue cow bells cascading near a shake-shingle entry. Drive past the pool and head over the rutted wooden trestles of that one-way bridge. Continue past the caramel-colored chalet called "L'il' Abner," past the '50s-style, minty green place named "Jitterbug," and by that upscale cottage called "Chelsea Morning."

Eldorado Springs pool, fed by underground springs, is a favorite summer swimming hole, the warm water delivered from more than a mile below. The springs also provide clear Eldorado Artesian Springs water, available for home delivery or in local grocery stores.

Jamestown
7,000 feet, pop. 272
18 miles from Boulder

Gold, silver, and fluorspar once brought 10,000 miners to "Jimtown," a town whose name was later "upgraded." Douglas Fairbanks Sr. was born in this shady town. The Jamestown Mercantile Building is a classic false-front store from the mining-town days. The town hall (303-449-1806) is open Monday and Thursday. There's a public elementary school and strong sense of family values in town, including a desire to keep the children safe. So watch for the speed bumps as you enter and leave. Jamestown is northwest of Boulder. Take U.S. Highway 36 to Left Hand Canyon, turning into the mountains and, at the big fork, jogging right.

Lyons
5,375 feet, pop. 1,424
17 miles from Boulder

The red sandstone around Lyons has been the source of much quarry rock, locally called flagstone. Fifteen sandstone buildings, including the Old Stone Congregational Church, are in Lyons's historical district. This dark-brown flagstone church, square with a short steeple, is just north of Main Street, on High Street. The quarries that provided the stone for these buildings still operate around Lyons and are excellent choices if you want flagstone for your patio, classic Colorado stones for your home, or beautiful boulders for your garden. Lyons itself has a small-town atmosphere, with cottonwood trees shading the sparkling St. Vrain River, towering blue spruce trees standing beside turn-of-the-20th-century bungalows, and plenty of pretty contemporary homes. Vacation cabins and high-tech companies are here, plus many good restaurants and antiques shops, some decorated to give a Germanic/Slavic feel to the shopping areas.

Bring your swimsuit and make time to visit Meadow Park on the town's western edge; here the St. Vrain accommodates swimmers with an excellent swimmin' hole with overhanging rocks perfect for cannonballing. There are also baseball diamonds, playgrounds, and lots of places to climb, hike, and picnic.

The prettiest way to reach Lyons is to take 28th Street or Broadway north from Boulder—the two converge into U.S. 36. The route winds beside the foothills, and less than 20 miles from Boulder it dead-ends into Colo. 66. Turn left here, pass roadside shops and eating places, and you're in Lyons. The Town Hall is at 432 Fifth Avenue (303-823-6622).

Nederland
8,236 feet, pop. 1,270
16 miles from Boulder

Nineteen miles up Canyon Boulevard, just past the big blue lake formed by Barker Dam, is Nederland, the largest mountain town near Boulder. Here, the aspen trees shimmer next to pretty plots of colorful mountain flowers during the summer, with mountainsides of pine trees and aspen in every direction. Nederland has a good mix of shopping, tourist-oriented businesses, and basic services. This is a friendly, easygoing community that includes mountain people who wanted to be close to high alpine fields, hippies who came here decades ago to found communes, New Age yuppies, and Boulder intellectuals who retreated from the city below. All this makes for an eclectic, worldly, remote but close-enough-to-it-all mountain town. If you want some fun reading about Nederland history, find a copy of local author Marlys Millhiser's *The Mirror*. This fantasy novel describes a Boulder woman who trades places in time with her Nederland grandmother, then discovers the rigors of being a miner's wife, the challenges of driving a wagon team up a treacherous dirt canyon road, and the red light district that even tiny Nederland supported.

Near Nederland are the Indian Peaks Wilderness and the Eldora Mountain Resort, with its downhill and cross-country skiing. The shops are comfortably close together, picturesque, and easy to amble through. It's worth the trip just to hang out at the Acoustic Coffee House (see our Nightlife chapter), and Annie's is

An 1890s gold strike brought 4,000 people to this greatest gold camp of northern Colorado. Ward merits a footnote to Colorado history, for this is where silver baron (and briefly U.S. Senator) Horace Tabor served as a postmaster toward the end of his life, which he passed in unaccustomed poverty. During the boom, $5 million in gold was taken from veins around Ward, but by 1930 the mines died out, and only three residents stayed behind. Hippies arrived in the 1960s, and many of them have never left; persistent rumors put heiress Patti Hearst in a commune near Ward when she was on the run with the SLA. It's still a place of shaggy hair and beards to match, fringed vests, and love beads. On weekends, intrepid Lycra-clad bicyclists perch outside the general store, with great pride, sucking up cold mineral water and swapping stories about their 23-mile ride from Boulder to reach the hilly streets of Ward. Tourists gaze at the rustic buildings, their colors as faded as sand-washed jeans, within the thick mountain forests. The old Ward School, now the town hall and post office, is typical of wood-framed rural schoolhouses.

Ward has an honor-system public library and a general store. The Millsite Inn (see our Restaurants chapter) sits above town on the Peak to Peak Highway (Colo. 72), about 8 miles north of Nederland. The beautiful alpine hiking area around Brainard Lake is just west of Ward.

a good neighborhood restaurant (see Restaurants). All this means that Nederland has settled, by fits and bounds, into the intriguing community its beginnings hinted at. Originally a gold-, silver-, and tungsten-mining area, Nederland had more than 3,500 residents at the height of the mining boom in 1874. Today, gambling in Blackhawk and Central City, south on Peak to Peak Highway, plus Boulder's spillover prosperity, have fueled Nederland's latest boom. Many residents work in Boulder or elsewhere in the "lowlands" to the east.

Summer events usually include a Kinetic Wind Festival (see our Festivals and Annual Events chapter), a Native American Pow Wow, and a replay of the pioneer days. Check in at the Visitors' Center, on West First Street, where the RTD bus stops. Across from the Visitors' Center is Town Hall (303–258–3266).

Pinecliffe
7,960 feet; pop. 475 (winter), 525 (summer)
20 miles from Boulder

Retired miners and nature lovers live in this enclave southeast of Nederland on Colo. 72. Some are upscale commuters, and some people live "off the grid." That means they're in homes without power, water, or sewage hookups. "Off the grid" can mean rough-hewn cabins or a high-tech home complete with photovoltaic cells to provide solar electricity and heat.

Ward
9,253 feet, pop. 165
23 miles from Boulder

Towns of the Plains

All the towns around Boulder have modern 'burbs, fed by a series of building booms since the 1960s. Here you'll find Boulder County's more affordable housing. Although these towns are more development-friendly and growth-oriented than Boulder, they are beginning to pay more attention to such quality-of-life enhancements as open space. The prosperity of these plains towns is evident in their golf-course competitions and swimming-pool wars. Actually, these aren't wars, but they reflect a trend toward family-oriented community centers.

Stunned by the rate of growth in their towns, east county residents have been increasingly insistent that natural areas be preserved. To keep seeing eagles flying overhead, even as these communities grow, their citizens are beginning to raise more open-space purchase funds. It might not happen in time to save all the favorite local nature walks, but sentiment is growing to preserve more.

These communities have a range of personalities. Rock Creek is nothing but brand-new homes, a huge growth on the side of tiny, historic Superior. Other towns are as old as Boulder, complete with traditional downtowns and beautiful Victorian neighborhoods. Lafayette, Louisville, and Longmont offer the contrast between modern developments and older parts of town known for their quaint atmosphere and lovely trees.

Broomfield
5,200 feet, pop. 41,000
8 miles from Boulder

When the Pony Express needed to get overland mail from Julesburg, Scottsbluff, or Fort Laramie to Denver, carriers changed horses at Broomfield. Travel gave the farming town fame again in 1952, when Broomfield became the site of a toll station on the new Boulder/Denver Turnpike (now known as U.S. 36). The road was especially popular during Saturday CU-Boulder football games. In 1967, it became the nation's first toll road to pay for itself, approximately 13 years ahead of schedule.

That history of a town at the crossroads became a bureaucratic headache as the town found itself in four counties and five different school districts. In 2000, Broomfield became its own county, the first time since 1902, a city and county was created in Colorado. The city is busily creating the government structure, and the buildings, to support that status.

Meanwhile, growth continues at a phenomenal rate. The city's population increased from 24,000 to 41,000 in the past decade. The huge campus-like Inter-

locken high-tech office park continues to expand. The park is home to the Colorado campus of Sun Microsystems, which will incorporate more than a million square feet when completed, and it will house the 800,000-square-foot national headquarters of Level 3. The park is wired with fiberoptic cables to keep the high-tech tenants connected to the world. Interlocken is zoned for at least 25 percent open space, including wetlands and natural grasses, plus a golf course next to a hotel.

Flatirons Crossing Mall opened in 2000, 1.5 million square feet of retail and restaurant space that draws shoppers from all around the region.

As Broomfield grows it is attempting to preserve some open space as well—2,000 acres so far. The Bay, Broomfield's outdoor aquatic park, attracts bathers from around the region. For more information contact the city (and county) of Broomfield, 1 DesCombes Drive, (303) 438–6308.

Erie
5,020 feet, pop. 5,000
8 miles from Boulder

The town was first settled around 1867 by a Methodist pastor who named it after his hometown of Erie, Pennsylvania. Like its namesake, Colorado's Erie is a former coal town. An area of tilled farm fields and new subdivisions, Erie is the site of the 119-acre Tri-County Airport. Some homes near the airport have hangars and taxiways to the airport in their backyards, mirroring the garages and driveways they have in the front. Its current major industries are landfills and junkyards near town. Sound boring? This is Boulder County, remember! Blake's Small Car Salvage has been on national television for being one of the prettiest junkyards around. (See our Shopping chapter for more on this spot.) And a nearby business, Construction Recycling, recycles over 80 percent of the building scraps it receives.

As housing prices push residential development east from Boulder to Lafayette and Louisville to Superior, Erie is beginning to feel the ripple. The traditionally blue-collar town with dirt streets and funky old homes is beginning to spruce up to welcome newcomers and their tax dollars.

You can reach Erie by taking Arapahoe Road east out of Boulder past U.S. Highway 287. You'll be on a dirt road for a while, which dead-ends. Turn left (north). Go about 1.5 miles and you're in Erie. See the woodworking factory? It welcomes visitors. The Town Hall is at Lincoln School, 645 Holbrook Street (303-926-2700).

Gunbarrel
5,145 feet, pop. 9,006
7 miles from Boulder

Great mountain views and fancy homes around a golf course/country club are hallmarks of this large neighborhood of subdivisions. It was first developed in 1963 as a 558-acre subdivision to house the employees of a huge IBM plant across the Diagonal Highway. With Big Blue cutting back on its staff and other high-tech firms moving into the area, Gunbarrel has developed into a more varied community.

The commercial part of Gunbarrel, which includes Celestial Seasonings, IBM and Valleylab, and a small shopping center, is part of the city of Boulder. Much of the residential area is in unincorporated Boulder County. Even though the City of Boulder twice has offered to annex the neighborhood, residents prefer the autonomy of being in the county.

Take the Diagonal Highway (Colo. 119) north toward Longmont. Just out of Boulder, turn right on Jay Road. Keep going. To see the fancy houses, turn left on a street such as Carter Road. To get deeper into Gunbarrel, continue on the Diagonal to 63rd Street and turn right (south). The homes and enterprises of Gunbarrel are both to your right and left. The Boulder Country Club, with a golf course backing up against the yards of dozens of homes, is in the heart of Gunbarrel Greens, south off of Lookout Road. Sorry, members only.

Hygiene
5,100 feet, pop. 265
14 miles from Boulder

In the 1880s, farmers battled grasshopper plagues and other woes to settle this fertile area. The town earned its name when people suffering from tuberculosis moved to a local sanitarium called Hygiene House. Fresh air and sunshine revived many, as the elements still do today. Hygiene is about a mile west of Longmont in an area full of towering old cottonwoods, Siberian elms, ancient lilac hedges, and farm homes with horses mowing the grass. It's at the intersection of North 75th Street and Hygiene Road. A local hangout is Clark's Food Store, the little shop with a rickety, tilting porch awning that hangs like half-closed eyelashes above the front door. Here's a town where the neighbors know each other, and if you decide to hang out for a while, you can be sure they'll talk about you.

Lafayette
5,260 feet, pop. 22,034
11 miles from Boulder

Lafayette Miller ran a farm, a stagecoach, and a hotel. After he died, Mary Miller discovered coal on their late homestead. In 1890, she named a new town after her husband. Coal and farming were the main industries for 50 years. Today, the town is a burgeoning residential community for the high-tech industry, with brand-new home tracts, green patches of lawn, and hopeful baby trees. To reach Lafayette, head 11 miles east on either Baseline Road or South Boulder Road through Louisville.

"Old Town" Lafayette has its tidy little bungalows and big street trees. Efrain's is a good Mexican restaurant (see our Restaurants chapter). The city offices (303-665-5588) are at 1290 South Public Road, the northeast corner of "Four Corners," a new business district at the intersection of U.S. 287 and South Boulder Road. The Lafayette Chamber of Commerce (303-666-9555) is in the old historic district at 309 South Public Road.

Local sentiment favors keeping small-town charm even as affordable and upscale subdivisions boom. There's a move to protect favorite open areas such as Waneka Lake, where people can paddle rented canoes to a blue heron's marshy shallows. So far, the city has 167 acres of developed parks and 467 acres of open space. You can find a map of these places at the recreation center on 111 West Baseline Road (303-665-0469).

The YMCA of Boulder Valley has opened a 55,000-square-foot complex including an ice-skating rink, fitness center, gymnasium, indoor running track, and other facilities on Arapahoe Road and 95th Street to entertain the burgeoning population. The Indian Peaks Golf Course is within city limits.

Lafayette is home to a community of Hmong families, refugees from Laos. It also has one of the nation's few co-housing communities, the Nyland Community Association (303-494-2778). It features 42 passive-solar homes built around a common area and the "community house" with guest rooms, activity rooms, a childcare center, and a dining hall open to residents who don't want to cook evening meals in their homes. Cars are parked outside the community. Only pedestrians are allowed inside.

Longmont
4,979 feet, pop. 71,093
12 miles from Boulder

Longmont, named after Longs Peak, which in turn was named after Major Stephen Long, started as a 30,000-acre farming community and sugar beet center. The city celebrated its 130th anniversary in 2001. It is the county's second-largest town and is sometimes called Boulder's twin. Sure enough, it offers many services similar to Boulder's, including a hospital, school district, daily newspaper, branch of the County Clerk's Office, state Motor Vehicle Division office, and other services. But these twins are not identical. For one thing, Longmont is kind of modest about

how pretty it is, and publicity for local events is often low-key. For another, the two towns come from opposite ends of the political spectrum.

From the old Main Street shopping district to the Boulder County Fairgrounds at 9595 Nelson Road, which hosts dog shows, antiques shows, and the Boulder County Fair in August (see our Festivals and Annual Events chapter), Longmont retains a conservative farming-town hospitality even as it grows and grows. With the exception of Boulder, more homes were sold in Longmont during the first half of 1996 than in any other town in the county, and sometimes it seems that the fields surrounding the town have been planted with house seeds instead of grain. This house crop is sprouting overnight, with townhouses here, single-family homes there and a naked, surprised look to many of these late 20th-century homesteads, as they wait for the saplings in their front yards to catch up and shade their peaked roofs.

To reach Longmont from Boulder, head northeast on Colo. 119 (also called the Diagonal Highway or just the Diagonal for short). Except during rush hour, it's about a 20-minute drive.

To get a feeling for the Victorian houses and tree-canopied streets near Main and Third, check the Callahan House. New houses are in developments all around town. Municipal offices (303-776-6050) are at the Civic Center, at Third Avenue and Kimbark Street. The Longmont Chamber of Commerce (303-776-5295) is at 528 Main Street.

Surrounded by pricey new homes with golf courses attached, the historic heart of Louisville is still a place where people take the time to water the lawn by hand. PHOTO: LINDA CORNETT

Louisville
5,350 feet, pop. 19,500
11 miles from Boulder

Louis Nawatny founded this town in 1878, after discovering coal 200 feet below a settler's farm. Twelve mines eventually thrived in Louisville, providing high wages for sometimes-dangerous work. In the early 1900s, labor organizer Mother Jones spoke to coal miners in the town. During this time, European miners, who occasionally worked as strikebreakers, came to town.

Although the statue of a miner that stands outside city hall is still the town's trademark, Louisville is a coal-mining town that has transformed itself into the epitome of a modern suburb. Two of Boulder County's largest employers, Storage Technology and Neodata, are based here, as is the Centura Avista Adventist Hospital, specializing in maternity and neonatal care. The Coal Creek Golf Course was listed by *Golf Digest* magazine as one of the top 25 new golf courses in 1990. When the golf course first went in, next to U.S. Highway 36, there was concern that errant golf balls would hit cars, but it has not been a problem. The highway interchange is booming, with Louisville's first modern hotels, small shops and huge chain outlets, a 12-plex theater, and practically every chain restaurant you can imagine.

Louisville's population has more than tripled to 19,500 since the 1970s, making it one of Colorado's fastest-growing communities, but the goal is now to stabilize the population around 25,000 and put some effort into preserving open spaces. Most of the population growth has come from young families, with kids galore. Still, Louisville strives to maintain small-town charm with events such as a Fourth of July Community Picnic and a Labor Day food celebration (see our Festivals and Annual Events chapter).

Louisville's city offices are at 749 Main Street (303-666-6565).

Niwot
5,095 feet, pop. 2,666
5 miles from Boulder

The unincorporated town is named after Chief Niwot, whose name means "left hand" in the Arapaho language. The original downtown, which was composed of supply shops and a school for local farmers, is now filled with antique shops and surrounded by brand-new housing developments. The old town center also boasts the Niwot Auction, a big bimonthly mecca for antique hounds, and an annual auction festival in the summer.

To reach Niwot, take the Diagonal Highway (Colo. 119) north toward Longmont. One mile after IBM is Niwot Road. Hang a right, and you're there. It's about a 10- to 15-minute drive from Boulder. Boulderites visit for the antiques and, around Christmas, to mail gifts from the town's small post office.

Superior
5,400 feet, pop. 8,811
9 miles from Boulder

If you had been struck by an unlikely yen to visit the town of Superior a decade ago, you would have found a tiny hamlet of small homes housing 255 souls. Today, you're even more likely to bypass the small old town for the bright lights of a new commercial strip and the broad avenues of a huge new development called Rock Creek, built on land annexed by Superior in 1987 and given water rights in 1990. Rock Creek sprawls across more than 3 square miles of rolling grassland. By 2010, it could eventually include up to 8,000 homes and 15 million square feet of commercial space, extending east along U.S. Highway 36 all the way to the Interlocken Office Park at Broomfield and south to Colo. 128. Some large homes stand beside the meticulously landscaped, new wide boulevards, decorated with statuary and leading to tennis courts and a swimming pool. There are also townhomes and an abundance of smaller single-family homes on more modest lots.

The town is still catching up with much of this growth. Until 1999, Rock Creek's only commercial development was two gas stations. Now there are a slew of new businesses, most of them of the "mega" variety.

The town hall, at 24 E. Coal Creek Drive (303-499-3675), is a good information place, as are Rock Creek's real estate offices and show houses. Superior is just south of the Superior/Louisville interchange on U.S. 36.

Boulder offers a wide variety of houses, one of which you might call home. PHOTO: DAILY CAMERA

Real Estate

In recent years, Colorado generally and Boulder specifi-cally have been among the hottest housing markets in the nation. For a while, the housing market was so hot that Boulder home buyers had a half-hour to run through a home, then sign up before the next buyers beat them to it. In 2000, for example, the number of houses sold climbed 3.5 percent from 1999. Factors including rapid growth of well-paying jobs, the high demand for housing, and a low supply of available homes continues to rank Boulder at the top for average single-family home prices among the metro-area counties. In the past few years buyers scram-bled, and there were many reports of people making two or three offers on houses before they could actually call one their own. Even those moving from high-priced locales such as San Francisco found themselves paying $60,000 more than they had planned. "We expected this to be a cakewalk," said one newcomer from the West Coast. "We made offers on five houses before we got one." Home prices in surrounding communities such as Longmont, Lafayette, and Louisville have climbed sharply even without the benefit of the Boulder postmark. As recently as late 2001, home prices in Boulder and the sur-rounding area showed no sign of dropping. But as you review the statistics and sale prices noted in this chapter, keep in mind that the general downswing in the U.S. econ-omy may affect the region's real estate market in the future.

This chapter provides a general sense of home prices and rental costs in Boulder County. It also includes bargain-hunting tips, ideas on what to look for in a Boulder home and neighborhood, and a list of real estate resources. If you're looking for a Boul-der home, happy hunting!

The Homebuyer's Market

Quality of life, the cachet of a Boulder address, and something called the "Dan-ish Plan" are what have driven local house prices into the stratosphere. Boulder was one of the first cities in the nation to adopt a residential growth-control ordi-nance (called the Danish Plan after City Councilman Paul Danish), which limits the number of permits for new construc-tion that are issued annually. The law of supply and demand is in effect in Boulder, and with limited new construction cou-pled with a strong economy, property val-ues have soared, and the issue of "affordable housing" has become a com-munity hot button.

The strict growth controls, in place since the mid-70s, depress the number of homes that are for sale in Boulder in any given month. That means most are single-family resales with an average price (as of April 2000) of $434,100. The range of prices in Boulder is pretty outrageous, with the lowest-priced house selling for $199,900 in 2000, and the highest priced at $1,995,000. Resales in 2000 increased 26 percent from 1999, while new home sales went up 25 percent. According to one sur-vey, the Denver area, which includes Boul-der, has the sixth-highest price expectation per square foot in the country and the ninth-highest price expectation per home. In other words, don't come looking for a bargain. Just a few years ago it was rare to find a million-dollar home on the market in the Boulder area. In 1999, for instance, there were 33 million-dollar homes on the market in Boulder County. In 2000 there were 74, with 19 of them in Boulder.

Keep in mind that $350,000 will buy you a lot more house just outside the city limits, but if you're looking for the lifestyle or Boulder mystique, $350,000 won't get you much of a house within city boundaries. As the saying goes, location, location, location. Boulder encompasses a wide range of houses and housing styles, from historic cottages, between-the-world-wars Tudor mansions, postwar ranch houses, and new subdivisions with contemporary homes.

In the last 10 years, the appreciation rate for a single-family home in Boulder has been 11.6 percent, while 3 to 4 percent is considered healthy. If you can afford to buy, a house in Boulder is a great investment.

Housing costs considerably less in Boulder County's other communities. The majority of new homes are now built in Erie, Lafayette, Longmont, and Superior. According to Irene Shaffer of RE/MAX of Boulder, during 2000, the average price for a new single-family home was roughly $315,900 in Louisville, $351,800 in Lafayette, $217,200 in Longmont, and $288,000 in Superior. The price for older homes is less, but in new communities such as Superior and Erie, older homes don't exist. Generally, rural lots in both the mountains and plains offer good deals, but price swings are enormous. And if you're thinking about building, you need to take into consideration zoning and the cost of water and utilities. When rural sellers put high price tags on agricultural land, they most likely expect a city to annex the land; when county land does get annexed, the annexing city can change its zoning to allow much greater density. The market price depends, as always, on location, maintenance, and (this being Boulder) the way your horoscope is interacting with current mortgage rates. The Boulder market is softest on the upper end and hottest for con-

dominiums, but no matter what the price, special homes on special lots still sell fast.

Locals, whether tire-kickers or serious buyers, and newcomers alike flock to the open houses (or "open homes," as they are pretentiously called these days) held year-round, rain or shine, on Sunday afternoons. Check the Saturday and Sunday newspapers, or be alert for "Open House" signs if you are out for an afternoon drive to scout neighborhoods. A real estate agent will be on hand to answer questions, pass out leaflets on the property, and perhaps give a very soft sell on the home you're looking at. It's an easy way to comparison shop without the commitment of being taken around by an agent to look at homes by appointment.

Real Estate Resources

So you're sure you want to move to Boulder County, but where do you start? You can get information on buying or renting in Boulder County from the local chambers of commerce and from the area's Board of Realtors. The Boulder Chamber of Commerce, for instance, issues a useful relocation packet, as do many real estate agencies. City halls, listed in our Boulder Neighborhoods chapter, can provide general local information. Recreation centers and most grocery stores display free publications about places to live. *Homes & Land of Boulder County* and *Where to Live in Boulder County* are the two biggest and slickest. You can also call one or more of these groups: Boulder Chamber of Commerce, 2440 Pearl Street, Boulder (303–442–1044); Boulder Area Board of Realtors, 4885 Riverbend Road, Suite A, Boulder (303–442–3585); Office of Human Rights Department of Housing and Human Services, 1101 Arapahoe Avenue, Second Floor, Boulder (303–441–3157).

Real Estate Firms

With the booming real estate market, it seems as if there's an agency on every corner. Most of the bigger agencies serving

The Flatirons serve as a backdrop for many towns and neighborhoods in the Boulder area.

PHOTO: DAILY CAMERA

Boulder County provide newcomer relocation services as well as matching you with a place to live. The Boulder Area Board of Realtors (see contact information listed above) can provide you with a list of real estate agencies, and you'll find others in the phone book, the local newspaper, and such free periodicals as *Where to Live in Boulder County*.

Century 21—The Bernardi Group
3301 30th St., Boulder
(303) 402–6000, (800) 421–2174

This agency burst on the Boulder real estate scene in 1996 with the dazzle and flair of a Roman candle when Karen Bernardi left RE/MAX Realty Consultants of Boulder and started her own agency, affiliated with Century 21. The agency has 14 brokers and specializes in single-family homes, condominiums, and vacant land in Boulder County.

Buyer Brokers of Boulder
4141 Arapahoe Ave., #101, Boulder
(303) 444–6660
(800) 942–8937 (Relocation Hotline)

After 24 years in the business, Alta Drumm left the traditional real estate industry in 1990 to hire her own brokers. They work exclusively for the buyers of real estate, rep-resenting their interests in dealings with the sellers, inspectors, lenders, and title companies.

Coldwell Banker Colorado Landmark Realtors
235034 Broadway, Boulder
(303) 443–3377, (800) 737–6683

Thirty agents work at this downtown Boulder real estate agency, which specializes in upper-end residential and commercial properties, and vacant land. A branch office in Louisville is located at 305 McCasline Boulevard, (303–664–1111).

Coldwell Bank Moore and Company Realtors
3300 28th St., Boulder
(303) 449–5000, (800) 654–4788

This 60-plus-year-old, Denver-based business has 15 branches and 1,000 agents throughout the state. The Boulder County office has 35 real estate agents handling residential and commercial properties.

Colorado Buyer Brokers
4450 Arapahoe Ave., Ste. 100, Boulder
(303) 415–2509

This is a firm that specializes in working with the buyer rather than the seller. It has more than 22 years of experience, although the buyer's broker is still a fairly new concept in real estate. The broker works for the buyer and therefore has no financial stake in selling a particular home.

Fowler Real Estate/Better Homes and Gardens
2970 Wilderness Pl., Boulder
(303) 443–6050, (800) 443–6050

One-hundred thirty agents work here at Boulder's oldest real estate agency. Fowler has grown to be the largest Realtor group in northern Colorado, with branch offices in Longmont at 2432 N. Main Street (303–772–9620), in Nederland at 286 N. Bridge Street (303–258–7020), and a home information center next to JCPenney at Crossroads Mall (303–442–9141).

Prudential Boulder Realtors
4710 Table Mesa Dr., Boulder
(303) 494–7700, (800) 383–6805

A worldwide affiliate, this firm has been established in Boulder for more than 30 years. Twenty-five real estate agents handle both residential and commercial properties.

RE/MAX of Boulder
2425 Canyon Blvd., Ste. 200, Boulder
(303) 449–7000, (800) 825–7000

In 2000, RE/MAX of Boulder ranked No. 1 among RE/MAX Mountain States agencies in terms of volume per agent; that amounts to a lot of sales, since more than 80 agents work out of this office. The agency is particularly strong in relocation services.

RE/MAX Realty Consultants of Boulder
4770 Baseline Rd., Boulder
(303) 499–9880, (800) 373–1282 (Relocation Hotline)

Founded in 1931, this is the county's second-largest realty office, based on volume of sales. The company has more than 70 agents and its own mortgage brokerage service.

Walnut Realty
1911 11th St., Ste. 107, Boulder
(303) 442–3180, (800) 477–3180

Broker Tom Kahn describes Walnut Realty as "Boulder's downtown Realtors,"

and indeed, the office is in a historic building a block from the Pearl Street Mall. The firm specializes in a variety of types of property, from ordinary residential to vacant land, farms, rural and mountain homes, and downtown commercial buildings. It has 28 agents.

Wright-Kingdom Realtors Inc.
1844 Folsom Ave., 4875 Pearl E. Circle, Ste. 100, Boulder
(303) 443–2240, (800) 343–8885

Lew Kingdom and Stuart Wright started this real estate company in 1976, when Boulder was a town of around 60,000 people and the average home cost $85,000. This is one of the longer-established agencies in town. It has 60 associates and includes an international relocation service.

Lone Eagles

Boulder County also has more than 100 single-person realty offices, and some are outstanding. You can check these and other agencies through the Boulder Board of Realtors, although keep in mind that the Board doesn't handle Longmont or Lyons.

About Home Builders

With boom times come large, California-style subdivisions put up by major developers and builders. Boom times also bring the need for more schools, more utilities, more roads, and more services. Communities are leveling "impact fees" at builders, and these fees are built into the price of new construction. Home Builders Association of Metropolitan Denver (303–778–1400) can supply a list of its members, including some large firms building in Boulder County.

Fixer-Uppers

If you've bought a house that needs work, or if you are renovating your current home and are having problems finding suitable contractors, Home Improvement Referral Inc., P.O. Box 26012, Colorado Springs 80936 (303–449–5093 in Boulder area) can help. This 15-year-old firm provides free information and a referral service that lists 300 Colorado contractors and sub-contractors who handle everything from maintenance and repair to custom-built homes.

House-Hunting Tips

Whether you plan to be a yuppie commoner living in a simple condominium or the royal owner of a grand mansionette, the following tips will help you find just the right home in or near Boulder. Spend time looking, and keep location in mind. The closer to a city center, the more you pay, for it puts you closer to the activities and services that make Boulder and other cities so inviting. The lot itself matters—a good mountain view, a babbling creek, adjacent city open space, a golf course, good entertainment, or a public park all add value. So does beautiful, mature landscaping. That's why a tiny Boulder condominium with all these location features might cost more than a spacious single-family home in outlying areas.

On the other hand, Boulder doesn't have many "wrong side of the track" homes, or acres and acres of homogenized housing, although vast housing tracts are blanketing former farmland surrounding outlying communities. One great feature of this city is how mansions can exist right next to apartment buildings, quirky little bungalows, and subsidized public housing. This magical mixture happens because many Boulder neighborhoods add diversity in neighbor-friendly ways. Drive with a real estate agent through sought-after Mapleton Hill, Whittier, University Hill or North Boulder neighborhoods. Look closely, and you'll see how diversity can help a neighborhood thrive. Even in developments where every house seems to have been cloned from the one next door, a mix of high and moderately priced housing often develops as the trees

have grown and people have renovated their properties, whether in modest areas like Martin Acres or more prepossessing ones like Table Mesa. You can find exclusive "mono-communities" in and around Boulder, but if the only thing stopping you from choosing a more eclectic mix is a fear that it would lower your house value, relax. Diverse neighborhoods that are well-loved in Boulder do just fine.

However, an eclectic neighborhood might not be your cup of tea. Perhaps you prefer a brand-new house in a brand-new neighborhood, where you are no more of a newcomer than anyone else. Area developers and Realtors showcase their offerings through annual tours. In 2000 homes ranged in price from $199,900 to $1.995 million, with varying styles for everyone.

What to Look for in a Boulder House

Boulder has a cool semiarid climate, which means most energy goes into heating, not cooling. Insulation matters. Because it's so sunny, passive solar can do wonders. This doesn't mean you must settle for a '70s-style solar home, with a long wall of south-facing glass and sun-blasting black-painted oil drums. Energy-efficient homes can blend into any style and still keep January gas bills low. One regular-looking

An abundance of hiking trails through open space and mountain parks land helps make Boulder an appealing place to live. PHOTO: LINDA CORNETT

Boulder home earned a national energy efficiency award. Its owner, Craig Cristensen, has no heater at all. He relies on passive solar heat, super insulation and a 1,000-gallon hot water storage tank, so that even if a rugby team burst in and asked for showers during a cloudy February week, enough solar-heated water would be on hand to douse them all.

Some homes are energy-efficient but not all. Check winter utility bills before buying. A few summer days get awfully hot, but heat spells tend to be short, and summer nights cool. As long as a home is positioned to keep out the fiercest summer rays, either with deep eaves or shade trees, most residents don't miss air conditioning.

Keeping the garden green is a problem in the dry heat of summer. A sprinkler system is a plus, and a modern, water-saving drip system is a super-plus. While some of Boulder's older, most desirable neighborhoods boast the mixed blessing of large, non-indigenous shade trees that provide atmosphere and character but are not really suitable for the region's climate, xeriscaping is a plus in contemporary homes. Xeriscaping is the art and science of landscaping with indigenous drought-tolerant plants that is increasingly popular in the Southwest and Mountain States. See our Shopping chapter's Close-up on Xeriscaping.

Want to Live in the Mountains?

One of Boulder's most distinctive characteristics is that it is a true city with remote mountain living close by. Is a mountain house your dream? Mountain living is not for the fainthearted. Residents keep their snow chains handy. One winter day, the snow on Magnolia Road hid a steeply tilted skating rink. One woman's sporty truck skidded off near the top and plummeted nearly 100 feet. The truck's bed hit first and collapsed like an accordion. Maybe NASA should study the event to improve their hard-landing techniques, for the lucky lady walked out of that truck alive.

Notice a rocky mountainside covered with charred black sticks marking the 1989 Black Tiger Gulch wildfire. As smoke billowed miles away, one mountain couple packed favorite Navajo rugs in the station wagon. They joked that the scare would end in a few hours, and they'd be unpacking. Suddenly they heard a train-like roar and felt blistering heat. The fire had leapt up their ridge. If they had to do it over again, they would have packed the family photo album instead of those rugs. They raced down their bumpy mountain road and will never forget how it felt to breathe searing, hollow air, the oxygen sucked out by the firestorm. That fire caused $10 million in damage and destroyed 39 homes. Another fire in 1990 burned 2,200 acres and 10 homes. Such fires are a natural part of mountain ecosystems. On dry, windy summer days, even big bomber planes, dropping payloads of slurry, cannot slow the flames.

Icy roads and forest fires are nothing compared to your love of nature? Suppose one dusky evening, a mountain lion eats your dog. The kids are horrified. You're just glad it was the dog. So you build a fence. A mountain lion can jump most fences. And you've blocked land that was open to migrating deer, mountain lions, and everything natural up there. Endangered wildlife is one reason Boulder County has decided to slow mountain developments. A mountain home can be wonderful, but unless you're committed to the mountain lifestyle, you can always visit. The average price for a house in the mountains during 2000 was $348,100.

On the other hand, if you realize the trade-offs you're making and the negative impacts you might create, you can do plenty to minimize the problems. Before you build a home, ask your architect about low-impact choices. One local architect, Dave Barrett of Barrett-Steele (303–449–1141), designs environmentally sensitive homes that have been mentioned in national publications. If you move into an existing home, you can remodel with attention to fire-fighting materials. Consider replacing cedar shingles with tile, slate, metal, or asphalt (if you build new, you won't be permitted to use cedar shakes). Stucco, brick, and stone siding do not burn and will protect the interior better than a wood exterior. Be sure dead brush is kept away from your home. Such changes minimize flammability.

Pop into an eco-shop, such as Planetary Solutions, 2030 17th Street (303–442-6228), which offers materials and consulting services for environmentally sound building. Jade Mountain, 717 Poplar Avenue (303–449-6601), is an appropriate-technology company with solar electric systems and composting toilets. Just being at such a store will give you ideas. Take a course in environmentalism from the University of Colorado (303–492-6301) or the Naropa Institute (303–

> **Insiders' Tip**
> Other things being equal, a new house in the Boulder area costs more than a comparable older one—except in select historic neighborhoods where the rule is, "the older, the better."

Boulder Falls is one of the many natural wonders dotting the region's landscape. PHOTO: DAILY CAMERA

444-0202). Check with the Colorado Division of Wildlife (303-291-7227) to see how to live with animals. The Thorne Ecological Institute, 5398 Manhattan Circle (303-499-3647), is another resource. Train your children about mountain safety, and keep your pets—especially cats—indoors. Mountain lions consider cats tasty tidbits, and cats themselves are miniature mountain lions whose hunting has led to the decline of many rare birds.

A Few, Few Words About Crime

Some Boulder County residents leave their doors unlocked. Others have security systems on everything except their running shoes. Most people take care walking at night, especially when in deserted areas of CU-Boulder, downtown, or the Creek Path. Others head into the dark at 5 A.M. all by themselves and have a grand time listening to the morning birds. Boulder County's biggest law-enforcement concerns involve speeding cars and loud parties. Yes, the county has crimes, including murder and abduction. But there are some, well, endearing criminals, too.

Take the fleet-footed Gunbarrel burglar. Under cover of night, he slipped into homes along golf course greens. He stole silver; he stole jewels. Fifty officers and a helicopter tried an ambush. The SWAT team's fastest sprinter cornered him, but that burglar leapt the fence like a deer. Finally, in 1992, they nabbed him with a backpack full of jewels. Turns out he was a marathon runner. He had girlfriends around the world. They didn't know about each other but had enjoyed his dazzling gifts. Over seven years, the bold, handsome runner had burglarized 244 homes. Golf course communities sleep better now that he runs his laps in prison.

The Renter's Market

Of Boulder's nearly 976,000 residents, 28,000 are CU-Boulder students, and a good majority rent off-campus. They're not the only ones. In the nonstudent population, almost 55 percent of Boulder city residents rent. That's higher than the overall rate in the United States, where less than 35 percent of all households live in rented dwellings. Many people moving here rent while searching for something to buy. Others can't afford to buy and remain renters for years. Many who move from Boulder hang onto their homes while they look elsewhere or contemplate returning. Others move up in the market, then use their former digs as an investment.

So brace yourself. Between 1990 and 2000, the rent for a two-bedroom apartment went up 40 percent, and the rent for a single-family home increased more than 100 percent, compared to 20 percent in the United States overall. Much of this is fueled by an extraordinarily low vacancy rate, which is approximately 1.2 percent. Rents tend to be higher near CU and lower in the county. In recent years, you could get a studio or efficiency in the city for about $550, a one-bedroom apartment for $675, a two-bedroom apartment for about $900, or a five-bedroom house for around $2,400 a month. Reduced rents are available through CU married-student housing and Boulder family assistance programs, but waits for such spaces can run years, so apply early.

Popping into town and finding a place right away is not a sure thing, except in spring or early summer, when relatively few students are in residence and there are more apartment vacancies. Many rental agencies prefer at least 45 days advance notice, and they can match you with a place best if you visit for a few days so they can show you around. To be on the safe side, it's best to rent only a dwelling that is licensed and inspected by the city's inspection office.

The city of Boulder has adopted landlord/tenant laws, which cover such things as security deposits, when a lease is required, when the landlord can raise the rent, and so on. Check these laws before you rent, for your own protection. The Community Mediation Service, 2160

Future owners and volunteers built these cozy houses, one of many efforts to provide affordable housing in Boulder. PHOTO: LINDA CORNETT

Spruce Street (303-441-4364), issues a *Landlord/Tenant Handbook* that covers these subjects and also can help resolve disputes including landlord/tenant relations. Colorado doesn't have many renter-protection laws, so if you rent outside the city your lease is where your rights and responsibilities will be spelled out. Read it while wearing your fine-print glasses. Also, some areas allow only three unrelated people per dwelling, and if you're caught cheating, you can be fined until the situation is corrected, so review the terms in your lease carefully.

Rental Resources

Housing Helpers
2865 Baseline Rd., Boulder
(303) 545-6000

This company offers a number of services, including rental information, roommate or housemate matching for a modest fee, and help with subleasing. There is also a free referral service that helps you select a

Realtor, based on the requirements you outline.

University of Colorado Off-Campus Housing
University Memorial Center, Rm. 336227 (CU-Boulder campus), Boulder
(303) 492-7053

This referral service helps students find rooms, apartments, houses, and roommates. It also provides free copies of Boulder's tenants rights and responsibilities, free model leases and subleases, and general information about renting in Boulder.

City of Boulder Housing Authority
3120 Broadway, Boulder
(303) 441-3150

Subsidized housing in the city is available by application to the Housing Authority. There's a one-year wait for a one-bedroom apartment to a two- to three-year wait for a four-bedroom place. The market, however, is very changeable, so it doesn't hurt to call.

Boulder County Housing Authority
2040 14th St., Boulder
(303) 441–3929

In the county, the waiting list for subsidized housing is two to four years, depending on the house size. The wait is shortest for those who are residents of Boulder County, or who are employed or attend college here.

Questions of Affordability

An ongoing dilemma in Boulder is the issue of housing affordability. The effort to preserve open space limits the addition of new homes, and people's sentimental attachment to the present character of their block often leads to strong opposition to increased density. Managing these issues is like squeezing a balloon: locate new housing away from open space and fearful neighborhoods, and housing prices balloon. That's why more and more people with moderate incomes either choose much smaller places than they originally envisioned or buy homes a long drive from their jobs. Some people say, "Big deal. Things always cost more in a city, but it's worth it." Or they say, "Big deal. Commutes of nearly an hour are common near urban centers." Other people fear that our very success will destroy what's best about Boulder. If the topic of affordability interests you, attend one of the frequent city meetings at which planning experts from around the nation share ideas.

Retirement

Agencies and
Services for
Seniors

Retirement Living

In many ways, Boulder so epitomizes the youth culture that many people don't realize it is a splendid place to retire as well. Excellent community services, an increasing commitment to public transportation, and a benign four-season climate make it congenial for retirees. But "retirement" doesn't automatically equate with "inactivity," and many so-called "retirees" put working folks to shame when it comes to their range of interests.

A "retired" engineer studies ethics at CU-Boulder and works summers at a greenhouse. When his children were young, this high-level manager left escalating salaries and a thirst for fancier things. He and his wife spend more time with their sons now. The dad loves both his scholarly pursuits and his plants. Among the area's other "retirees" is a fifty-something former satellite communications expert who retired early, moved to Boulder, and started hiking, backpacking, and knocking off "fourteeners" (Colorado's 54 peaks that are 14,000 or more feet above sea level). And then there's the eighty-something famous Boulder author who writes less these days because she's so busy managing her very successful stock portfolio. The "Chronologically Gifted" who hike or bike miles might seem intimidating to seniors who plan to age more conventionally. Keep in mind these super seniors impress people a third their age, too. When we grow up, can we do it too? What's their secret?

About 8 percent of Boulder residents are 65 and older, compared with 12 percent nationwide. (Boulder's large student and early post-grad population explains much of the difference.) Although Boulder offers many retirement complexes aimed at the senior market, most older residents opt for more individuality. Two city-sponsored senior centers and even a community Internet link provide a sense of connection with most recreational opportunities and services.

Long-term older residents have shared ideas for improving Boulder. The saltier ones say, "confine the cat" or "send joggers to South America." They are still nostalgic for 19-cents-per-gallon gasoline, passenger trains, and manners. But many say the good old days are now, and 78 percent of the seniors who responded to a *Daily Camera* survey said they're happy. In many cases, especially in Boulder's more traditional neighborhoods, seniors mix comfortably with other age groups.

Agencies and Services for Seniors

Centers

These are the best one-stop shops for senior-related offerings. People who equate senior centers with "old" tend to avoid them, but the centers provide useful services and opportunities for seniors to connect with their peers. When asked why they use the centers, women report that they're interested in learning and improving their lives. Men more often list the challenge of staying active. The county has six urban centers with comprehensive resources and three rural centers open for limited hours and with limited on-site staffing. They can connect you with reduced-cost medical, tax, and legal aid.

Many of the nearby communities aren't large enough to have their own senior centers, so instead they offer the following resource clearinghouses for seniors in Boulder County:

Allenspark Aging Services for Boulder County
Allenspark Nursing Clinic, Colo. Hwy. 7, Allenspark
(303) 747-2592

Lyons Aging Services Resources
Bloomfield Community Room, 722 Fifth Ave., Lyons
(303) 823-9016

Niwot Senior Resources (branch of Boulder County Office of the Aging)
Eagle Place Community Building, 6790 N. 79th St., Niwot
(303) 652-3850

Boulder East Senior Center
5660 Sioux Dr., Boulder
(303) 441-4150
Located at the East Boulder Recreation Center, this facility is operated by the City of Boulder. Because of its location, this is the first choice for seniors who want to combine exercise with socialization and classes. An open floor plan allows the east center to host fairs and art shows, and with the adjacent volleyball courts, seniors create their own tournaments. Classes include ballroom dancing, tai chi chuan, and modern investing. Hours are 7 A.M. to 4:30 P.M.

Boulder West Senior Center
909 Arapahoe Ave., Boulder
(303) 441-3148
Centrally located just west of the downtown public library, this is Boulder's original senior center. Described as a "traditional" facility, many seniors drop in here to socialize. Operated by the City of Boulder, hours are 7 A.M. to 4:30 P.M. on weekdays. Hot lunch is served daily, and dinner is served on Tuesday nights. Information on places to live, medical screenings, and assisted-care options is available here. Classes range from watercolor painting to the art of playing snooker.

Broomfield Senior Center
280 Lamar St., Broomfield
(303) 469-0536
Hot lunch is served weekdays and a sunset dinner is scheduled monthly at this center, which is located in the same building as the Broomfield Recreation Center. Hours are 8 A.M. to 5 P.M. on Monday, Wednesday and Friday; 8 A.M. to 9 P.M. on Tuesday and Thursday. Fitness classes are available on-site, and arts and crafts classes also are offered.

Lafayette Senior Center
103 S. Iowa St., Lafayette
(303) 665-9052
Local entertainers visit this senior social hub regularly, and special events are often scheduled on Saturdays. Enjoy the noon hot meal Tuesday through Friday. Open weekdays from 8 A.M. to 5 P.M., the center also offers travel excursions to the mountains, special events, drop-in activities, daily classes, and educational seminars.

Longmont Senior Center
910 Longs Peak Ave., Longmont
(303) 651-8411
Longmont is a traditional center offering regular exercise programs, card games, craft workshops, educational programs, and day trips. It is open from 8 A.M. to 5 P.M. Longmont's Meals on Wheels prepares its food at this site and also offers daily lunch service here.

Louisville Senior Center
900 W. Via Appia, Louisville
(303) 666-7400
Seniors bring their gym clothes to this center, located inside the Louisville Recreation Center. It's open from 9 A.M. to 4 P.M. Monday through Friday. Specialists from the local hospital offer educational courses on staying healthy, and any holiday is an excuse for a special feast. Lunch is served every weekday (reservations required). Daytrips to wineries, dinner theaters, and casinos are scheduled monthly. Classes range from arts and crafts to tax preparation and computer training.

Education

If you missed out on educational opportunities in your youth, Boulder is the ideal place to be a senior. Many Boulder agencies and private groups offer discounted or age-geared classes to seniors.

Boulder Parks and Recreation
3198 Broadway, Boulder
(303) 441-4400

The city department offers senior yoga, swimming, and tennis classes. The Senior Centers (listed previously) have offerings, too. Other programs include tennis tournaments and a Boulder Creek walking group. Very popular is the 55/Alive Driving Class—a way to brush up on driving skills, learn new driving laws, and often, get a break on insurance.

CU Seniors Auditors Program
1202 University Ave., Boulder
(303) 492-8484

With a professor's permission, a senior may audit virtually any class tuition-free (with a small processing charge).

Nutrition

When you're a senior, grocery shopping and meal preparation may be more challenging than they used to be. Perhaps it's the hassle of getting to the supermarket, or the difficulty of cleaning up after your meal. For those who would rather leave the cooking or shopping to someone else, Boulder has two options:

ElderShare
6363 Horizon Lane, Longmont
(303) 652-3663

Operated by Community Food Share, this service delivers basic groceries twice a month to nearly 500 seniors throughout the county.

Meals on Wheels
2355 Canyon Blvd., Boulder
(303) 441-3907

Insiders' Tip

The City of Boulder Housing and Human Services division produces a quarterly magazine for seniors that lists special events, classes, dining opportunities, information on day trips and overnight travel programs, drop-in activities, sports, clubs and organizations, and community happenings. This free publication, *Boulder Senior Services*, is available at senior centers, public libraries, and grocery stores. For information call (303) 441-3914.

This is Boulder's most frequently requested senior service. It enables people of all ages to eat regular, nutritious meals, even when they're short on money or are unable to handle food preparation and cleanup. A hot meal is delivered at noon, Monday through Friday, with the cost per meal based on an individual's monthly income. This agency serves the elderly, chronically ill, disabled, and those convalescing from illness, accident, or surgery.

Transportation

Senior Centers in Boulder County offer trips to the Denver Center for the Performing Arts, gambling towns, and Denver's Cherry Creek Mall. But it's often the need to get around town that presents the greater challenge. Boulder's commitment

Seniors play shuffleboard near Boulder Creek Path. PHOTO: DAILY CAMERA/JULIE SOTOMURA

to alternative transportation makes it less car-dependent than many Western cities, but there is still plenty of room for improvement. The following services can meet daily transportation needs.

The Hop, The Skip, The Jump, The Leap, and The Bound
1739 Broadway, Park Central Building, Boulder
(303) 441–3266

Five colorful shuttle buses are operated jointly by the Regional Transportation District (RTD) and the Transportation Planning Group, the city's alternate modes division. The Hop takes people between major shopping areas and CU-Boulder for 75 cents. For the same fee, The Skip, a 22-passenger bus, will take you anywhere along Broadway, operating every 10 minutes—every 6 minutes during rush hour. Three new buses debuted in 2001: The Jump offers service between Boulder and Lafayette via Arapahoe; The Leap is a Pearl Street shuttle between 55th Street and the downtown bus station; and The Bound—painted with Superman-inspired graphics—travels along 30th Street between Baseline and Jay Roads. With the introduction of the new services, bus travel in Boulder is much faster and more pleasant. See our Getting Here, Getting Around chapter for more transportation information.

Regional Transportation District (RTD)
14th and Walnut Sts., Boulder
(303) 299–6000

It costs only 25 cents for seniors to ride RTD buses during off-peak hours (not 6 to 9 A.M. or 4 to 6 P.M.). An RTD shopping bus goes from the senior housing sites to grocery stores. Most buses accommodate wheelchairs.

Special Transit
4880 Pearl St., Boulder
(303) 447–9636

Special Transit provides wheelchair-accessible, door-to-door service. This non-profit group charges $1.50 each way within the city, $3 between various cities in the county. It's quite a discount—the real cost of this subsidized service is closer to $16 per person. Those using the service must register first and call a week in advance to schedule a ride.

Special-Interest Organizations and Volunteer Opportunities

Most Boulder seniors consider retirement a chance to do as they please. For others it might mean their first backpack trip to Nepal or that longed-for second career. Many find retirement lonely or just plain boring. In Boulder there are many work and volunteer opportunities for seniors who want to remain active.

Audubon Society
4730 Table Mesa Dr., Suite 1, Boulder
(303) 442-2600, (800) 274-4201
Community education opportunities are offered through the society's Human Population and Habitat Program. The Boulder County chapter schedules daily and extended field trips for those interested in birding and offers a list of what birds to look for in this area. A Christmas bird count is held during a 24-hour period in December; it enlists more than 100 birders and 30 teams who help conduct the local bird census, part of an annual nationwide effort.

Boulder Rotary Club
Angle Pines Country Club, 5706 Arapahoe Ave., Boulder
(303) 554-7074
This service organization works to "build a better community" by hosting fund-raising events and distributing the money to local nonprofit agencies, including Safehouse and Special Transit. The Rotary offers more than $10,000 in scholarships to CU students and funds a study-abroad program for selected CU juniors. Two of the Boulder groups meet weekly for lunch; the third group meets for breakfast.

50+ Employment Opportunities Program
2905 Center Green Ct. S., Ste. C, Boulder
(303) 441-3985

A service of Workforce Boulder County, this program connects people with job-retraining programs and employment possibilities.

Retired and Senior Volunteer Program (R.S.V.P.)
6032 Valmont Rd., Boulder
(303) 443-1933
More than 2,000 registered volunteers in the county participate in this program, both older residents and "junior" volunteers, meaning those younger than 55. One out of every 10 people 60 and older volunteers each year through R.S.V.P., which celebrates its 30th anniversary in 2002. People join because they want to give back to their community while staying active and productive. The Handyman Program, which does fix-it-up jobs for seniors, attracts seniors as volunteers, too.

The Service Exchange
2345 Bent Way, Longmont
(303) 678-3228
Service Exchange is a volunteer-matching service. Volunteers earn service credits (hours) for their work, and then cash them in when they need expertise or assistance from another volunteer.

Volunteer Connection
1136 Alpine Ave., Suite 105, Boulder
(303) 444-4904
Are you stuck in a rut? This service organization has current information on hundreds of volunteer opportunities that could make the difference in your life—while you make a difference in the community. The calendar section of the *Sunday Camera* lists current volunteer opportunities available through Volunteer Connection.

Retirement Living

Often Boulder seniors live in single-family homes, much to the benefit of local neighborhoods. It helps keep the streets safer when retired people are in and out during the day, and it can make for great inter-generational interactions. A child's first job might be watering an older neighbor's lawn or shoveling snow, and seniors may be unofficial substitute grandparents when the real ones live far away. When a favorite local retiree broke her hip, kids came by with flowers. "Guess what!" she told them with a grin. "I have metal parts now. That means I'm a bionic woman!" Her humor delighted them, as does seeing her back on morning walks. Another Boulder senior, when asked by a young neighbor what's the worst thing about growing old, replied, "Where did I put it?"

When they tire of yard work or keep-ing up a big house, many seniors do the Boulder yuppie thing and move to a town-house or condominium. Most housing inquiries at the Senior Centers regard finding affordable independent-living quarters, preferably with no stairs and near bus routes and shopping. But Boul-der offers assisted-living options for sen-iors, too, as well as facilities that offer a range of levels of care.

Assisted Living

The waiting list for assisted-living options can be long—6 to 12, even 18, months. If you want affordable housing with assisted-living services, start checking as soon as you can.

The Beatrice Hover Assisted-living Residence
1380 Charles Dr., Longmont
(303) 772–8102

This facility accommodates 55 residents—eight in double suites and the rest in pri-vate rooms, all with private baths. Opened in the early 1990s, the residence provides three meals per day, housekeeping and laundry services, medication assistance, and a van to take residents to doctors' appointments and outside activities. The rate structure is complex, based on the accommodation's size and location and three levels of service (the third, daily assis-tance with bathing and dressing, is con-sidered the last step before skilled nursing

care is needed); costs range from approxi-mately $2,000 to $3,000 per month. The 121-unit independent-living facility called Hover Manor is nearby. All but 10 percent of these 580-square-foot, one-bedroom apartments are HUD-subsidized and therefore carry strict income guidelines; the 12 nonsubsidized units currently rent for $442 per month.

Crossings Ridge Point Assisted Living Inn
3375 34th St., Boulder
(303) 473–0333

This assisted-living facility, which opened in 1994, has 76 apartments and a 24-hour personal-care staff. The monthly costs are: studio, $2,140; one-bedroom, $2,785; and two-bedroom, $3,110. The rate struc-ture is based on the level of care required. Fees include three meals per day, house-keeping and laundry services, medication assistance, and transportation to outside appointments and recreational activities. RISE (Restoring Independence, Strength and Energy) is a physical fitness program that allows residents to work with a per-sonal trainer; there's a Wellness Spa, too. The facility also offers a daily program for those with memory impairment.

Hawthorn House for Seniors, LLC
3275 23nd St., Boulder
(303) 247–0168

A home with eight private, first-floor bed-rooms with adjacent bathrooms, this facility is nestled in a quiet North Boulder neighborhood next to an open horse pas-ture and private pond. It offers daily social activities; 24-hour personalized care; live-in staff; home-cooked meals; assistance with medication, dressing, bathing and personal care; and house-keeping and laundry services. Fees (depending on need) range from $3,700 to $4,700 per month.

The Legacy at Lafayette
225 Waneka Parkway, Lafayette
(303) 666–0691

Opened in 1997, this 40-room facility offers both a private-pay and Medicaid rate structure. Services include medication management, 24-hour personal care assistance, life enrichment programs, three nutritious meals daily, weekly housekeeping, laundry service, transportation, and a whirlpool and spa. There are four living options: small and large studios, and small and large one-bedroom apartments. Monthly rates range from $2,340 to $2,885. The Legacy is close to shopping in central Lafayette.

The Mary Sandoe House
1244 Gillaspie Dr., Boulder
(303) 494-7317

The Mary Sandoe House has 24 assisted-living rooms that residents furnish with their own belongings. The fee, which for private-pay residents is $2,150 per month, includes three meals per day, housekeeping, medication management, laundry service, and minimal bathing and dressing assistance. The property also has an activity staff. There is a waiting list.

Sterling House
7720 Allison St., Longmont
(303) 682-1066

Sterling House opened in 1998, offering studio units and one-bedroom apartments that look out onto a courtyard. Services include laundry, housekeeping, a 24-hour staff, all meals and special diets, medication assistance, activities, transportation to shopping and medical appointments, and assistance with personal needs. The facility is "committed to quality of life and care while respecting privacy and dignity." Sterling strives to create a sense of family and community by offering a library, living room, TV room, and crafts room. Rates range from $1,500 to $2,000 per month, depending on level of need.

Independent Living

Some retirees move to independent-living facilities to simplify their lives so they can travel and pursue more hobbies while increasing the availability of medical care.

Take the woman who moved to one of Boulder County's independent-housing properties with assisted-care and nursing facilities on the grounds. When she announced that she was renting out the old family home, her children were aghast. She replied, "Well, it's about time. After all, I am going to be 90 this year." She now hosts her women's group in the meeting room of her living center.

Heed this—the independent-living housing market is tight. Although you can get into some places quickly, the waiting list for others is four years long.

The Atrium
3350 30th St., Boulder
(303) 444-0200

The 80 apartments here range from studios to two-bedrooms. Amenities include a craft room, exercise room, beauty parlor and barber shop, underground parking, ice-cream parlor, dining room (serving three meals a day), and free laundry facilities. The Atrium frequently schedules special events such as fashion shows, barbecues, a St. Patrick's Day corned beef and cabbage dinner, and a New Year's Eve dance that's open to both residents and nonresidents (it typically ends at 10 P.M.). Rates at the Atrium range from $1,539 to

> ## Insiders' Tip
> CareLink (303-441-3905) is an "adult daycare" program at the West Boulder Senior Center that provides companionship, structured activities, and medication assistance for Alzheimer's patients and others who are ambulatory but benefit from getting out of the house in a safe, controlled environment.

The library and downtown are within walking distance of Presbyterian Manor, an independent-living residence for seniors. PHOTO: ROZ BROWN

$3,105 a month, including weekly housekeeping, linens, and linen service.

Presbyterian Manor
1050 Arapahoe Ave., Boulder
(303) 444–0642

Presbyterian Manor is a not-for-profit, independent-living facility with modest costs and a four- to five-year waiting list. The 80 units all have small kitchenettes. The monthly rates are: buffet unit, $305; studio, $345; one-bedroom, $405; and two-bedroom, $480. These rents include utilities. The Boulder West Senior Center and the main branch of the Boulder Public Library are practically across the street, and the YMCA will pick up groups of three or more participating in Y programs, so residents don't have problems keeping busy, even though the activity schedule is sparse. The manor puts on an annual Christmas dinner and monthly birthday parties, which are held as picnics from June to September and indoors the rest of the year.

Multilevel Facilities

While various specialized levels of senior housing, including independent and assisted living, respite care, and nursing homes, are available in Boulder, several multilevel facilities provide a range of options and give people the opportunity to move to increasing levels of care if and as needed.

The Academy
970 Aurora Ave., Boulder
(303) 938–1920

Built in 1892, this former private girls school survived the 20th century against all odds. Originally known as Mount St. Gertrude Academy, it was used for classes by the university after the Sisters of Charity closed the school. A fire in 1981 caused severe damage and CU chose not to restore the building. Several proposals for redevelopment were promoted and swiftly rejected by either city planners or the surrounding neighborhood. Finally, in 1996, the plan for a retirement community was approved.

There are three historic buildings on the site including a chapel, conservatory, and the Academy, which now houses 18 apartments. There are a total of 33 apartments, 9 assisted living units and 9 bungalows. The buildings are so beautifully restored that when visitors toured the new facility as a stop on Historic Boulder's 1998 Christmas tour, guests of all ages were ready to move in. The rooms are spacious, with lots of light, and many have beautiful views of the Flatirons. Former Colorado Senator Dorothy Rupert and her husband, Richard, were on the waiting list even before the Academy opened. Monthly fees can range from $3,500 to $4,900, depending on square footage and the view. There is a one-time entry fee of $50,000.

Balfour Retirement Community of Boulder County
1855 Plaza Dr., Louisville
(303) 926–1000

This beautifully landscaped home was designed by award-winning Colorado architects who specialize in retirement housing. In addition to concierge service, the facility offers three meals per day, a private dining room, weekly housekeeping service, scheduled transportation, health promotion and exercise programs, medication management, an in-house beauty salon, a massage therapist, a library, and Internet access. Shopping, restaurants, doctors' offices, hospitals, and cultural events are nearby. Monthly fees for studio apartments begin at $2,260, while one- and two-bedroom apartments range from $4,200 to $4,850 a month. There is an additional charge for a second person, a move-in fee, a pet fee, and a smoker's fee. Balfour's motto is "Never stop growing."

Boulder Good Samaritan
2525 Taft Dr., Boulder
(303) 449–6150

Boulder Good Samaritan offers independent- and assisted-living options as well as a nursing home. Taft Towers is Good Samaritan's lowest level of care, with 66 independent-living units; the largest, two-bedroom, two-bathroom apartments, rent for $1,000 to $1,690 per month. Thirteen assisted-living residents pay $1,725 to $2,220 per month. The nursing home accommodates 60 residents at $150 per day. Good Samaritan has a dining room, transportation services, a full activities program (one winter participants visited the beautiful ice sculptures at Breckenridge), a swimming pool, and housekeeping services. The Older Boulder Wellness Center is at Good Samaritan; it was the first nursing home in the nation to equip its facilities with Nautilus equipment. (How Boulder!) For $72 a month, nonresidents may use the center three times a week.

Originally an isolated Catholic girl's school, then a University of Colorado office and classroom building,
The Academy on University Hill now houses apartments and bungalows for senior citizens.

Frasier Meadows Manor
350 Ponca Pl., Boulder
(303) 499–4888

A continuing-care retirement community since 1960, Frasier offers 200 independent-living units and 15 assisted-living units. There are one- and two-bedroom apartments with a three-month waiting list. Amenities include a flexible meal plan, laundry service, housekeeping, transportation, a rehabilitation program, a computer center, a beauty shop, and recreational opportunities.

Golden West
1055 Adams Circle, Boulder
(303) 444–3967

Golden West was established by the First Christian Church and has been around for more than 30 years. There are currently 255 senior apartments and 56 assisted-living units in three adjacent, interconnected elevator-equipped buildings. There is a 6- to 12-month waiting period for efficiency apartments, which cost $590 to $651 per month, and a 24- to 36-month wait for one-bedroom apartments, which are $500 per month. A meal plan requires residents to purchase either the noon or evening meal for an additional $180 per month. The assisted-living units are 307 square feet and rent for $2,201 per month. The maximum wait, as of this writing, is about three months, and the monthly fee includes 24-hour staffing, three meals a day, snacks, medication monitoring, laundry, housekeeping, and minimal daily-living assistance. On site are a library, computer center, recreation room, wellness center, beauty salon, sitting and guest rooms, a gift shop, and coin laundry facilities. Recreational activities for all residents include exercise classes, educational programs, musical programs (the Kitchen Band is popular), crafts classes, slide presentations, and the Residents' Council.

Childcare and Education

Don't you wish someone could lead you by the hand into the childcare facility or school of your dreams? Boulder offers many good options for childcare and education on all levels. This chapter starts with a rundown of the main childcare information centers and reviews how to screen childcare options. It explains how to find a sitter fast, and then goes on to provide tips on checking out nannies, daycare centers, and preschools. The chapter ends with an overview of Boulder's public and private schools, including its universities. For fun places to go with children and information about summer camps, see the Boulder Kidstuff chapter.

> **Choosing Childcare**
> **Schools**
> **Colleges and Universities**
> **Alternative Schools**

Choosing Childcare

Information Centers

First, head to Boulder's **Children's Services,** 2160 Spruce Street (303-441-3180). Children's Services offers the county's most comprehensive lists of everything: more than 500 family childcare homes, nannies, daycare centers, preschools, babysitting co-ops, public and private school information, financial assistance for housing and food, parenting classes, and more. It also has a library of helpful books and videos. This city-run agency is open 8 A.M. to 5 P.M., Monday through Friday.

If money is a problem, Children's Services now also runs a reduced-rate childcare program and can also tell you which centers/preschools offer a sliding fee or tuition reduction.

There are also other resources for families with young children. **The Colorado Preschool Program** subsidizes the tuition for kids who qualify; placement is made through **Child Find** (303-449-0177). **Head Start** (303-441-3980) operates at two locations in Boulder and two in Lafayette, with preschool enrichment for qualifying 3- to 5-year-olds. The **Parenting Place** in Boulder (303-449-0177) and

Lafayette (303-449-0177) offer low-cost centers with support groups, education, and play groups. You can bring children as old as 5 with you.

Finding a Sitter

You need a sitter, and Children's Services is closed. If the play starts in five minutes, good luck. Boulder might be a spontaneous kind of town, but good sitters get booked fast. Some services advertise that they can provide a sitter with just 24 hours' notice, but don't count on it. It's best to make arrangements for a sitter at least a week in advance.

Before you call a sitter, it's good to prepare a list of questions regarding qualifications. If the sitter you're considering is a teenager or preteen, have they completed the certification course offered by the YMCA? If they are not in the neighborhood, do they drive or will you be responsible for picking them up and getting them home? If your child is a baby, does the sitter have experience with infants? What about rates? Is the sitter prepared to make dinner and play games or help with homework? Does the sitter have references—other families that will vouch for his or her babysitting skills? A list of questions will make it easier to find a suitable match for your family's needs. **Children's**

Alley (303–449–1951) is a YWCA short-term care facility for infants through 12-year-olds. Rates are $1.75 to around $3.75 per hour per child, depending on your income. It's open on weekdays, generally between 7:30 A.M. and 9:45 P.M. (it closes at 5:45 P.M. on Fridays). Call at 4 P.M. the evening before for reservations—you can't call before then, and the place fills up fast. College students interested in babysitting are listed through CU-Boulder's Student Employment Office (303-492-7349), which takes calls 9 A.M. to 5 P.M. Monday through Friday during the school year and until 4:30 P.M. in the summer.

Workforce, Boulder County's 50+ Program (303–441–3985) makes referrals for pre-screened senior sitters, primarily retirees looking for jobs. **Rent-a-Mom** (303–322–1399) has a nanny program. Their pre-screened employees can drive and generally are hired for an evening or up to two weeks. The YMCA (303–442–2778) offers a list of teenagers who have passed a Red Cross babysitting course. If your child is sick but you still need to go to work, call **Heart of Colorado Caregivers** (303–440–0384), **Medix** (303–741–2045), or **Take-A-Break** (303–665–9741). Rates are generally $10 to $12 an hour. Your employer might even cover part of the cost.

If you are visiting Boulder and need a sitter, the hotel's front desk or concierge can probably help. If you've just moved to town and need to find reliable sitters or childcare, ask the mom you see on Pearl Street Mall, call neighborhood churches and schools, and talk with workmates. Ask, ask, ask. It's just like home (or your last home). Sometimes, you find a good sitter fast. Sometimes, you've got to keep trying.

Nannies and Au Pairs

A "nanny" can be anyone from a local college student to a grandmother who regularly cares for your child, either live-in or coming to work in your home every day. An "au pair" is a live-in caretaker, often from Europe. Generally between 18 and 25 years old, the au pair lives with you for a year, providing childcare in exchange for modest pay, room, and board. One service that has worked successfully for the families enrolled is **AuPairCare,** out of San Francisco (800–4AUPAIR). The Yellow Pages and Children's Services both list local referral services.

Daycare Homes and Centers

Every parent wants the best possible environment for their children. Poor-quality childcare can harm a child's self-esteem, ability to learn, and ability to thrive later in life. *Working Mother* magazine regularly lists Colorado in the top 10 states for the quality of childcare, but many experts believe we must set higher standards nationwide. A report by local early childhood expert Mary Culkin recently highlighted infant/toddler care as an area of special concern. She found wide variation in the nurturing and interpersonal interaction at childcare centers, vital indicators of care quality. What's more, the cost of a center did not always correlate with the quality of care provided. That's why visiting prospective daycare centers is an excellent idea.

Full-time childcare in the Boulder area averages more than $175 per week, but cost depends on where you live. Longmont is less; Boulder is more. Smaller

Boulder offers a range of childcare options. PHOTO: DAILY CAMERA/DAVID P. GILKEY

caregiver/child ratios, better caregiver training, more nutritious snacks, and age-appropriate play materials all add up. Check with Children's Services if you need information about sliding scale fees. And keep your screening questions handy to help narrow your search.

The following 17 childcare centers and preschools were accredited as of 2001 by the National Association for the Education of Young Children or the National Association of Family Childcare Providers. These groups provide the only national, voluntary, professionally-sponsored accreditation system for preschools, kindergartens, and childcare centers. They base their decisions on interaction among staff and children, staff and parents, location, staff qualifications, health, safety and physical environment. They are: **Boulder Day Nursery** (303-442-7605), **Children's World in Broomfield** (303-465-2053), **Children's World in Louisville** (303-665-7418), **Children's World South** (303-494-3694), **Children's World on Wedgewood in Longmont** (303-776-6118), **Columbine Preschool** (303-443-0792), **Commerce Children's Center** (303-497-5063), **CU Children's Center**

(303-492-6185), **The Elm Tree** (303-442-7140), **Floc Child Care Center** (303-442-6198), **Harmony Preschool** (303-444-8452), **Kellog Child Development** (303-938-8233), **Messiah Lutheran Preschool** (303-776-2573), **Mountain View Preschool** (303-494-3557), **Peter Pan Cooperative Preschool** (303-499-5231), **Sue Stevens** (303-666-8774), and **Sunflower Preschool** (303-494-2012). The **CU-Boulder Family Housing Children's Center** (303-492-6185) also has national accreditation, but it is only available to University of Colorado student, staff, and faculty families.

The **Colorado Preschool Program** (303-447-5075) conducts developmental screening and subsidizes the placement of nearly 120 students who can benefit from preschool experience at high-quality, community-based preschools, including **Alicia Sanchez Elementary School's** bilingual preschool in Lafayette (303-665-2044); Nederland Elementary School's **Caribou Mountain Preschool** (303-258-7092); the **Child Learning Center** at CU-Boulder's Communications Disorders Clinic (303-492-5375); **Children's House Preschool** (303-444-6432); Kohl Elementary

School's **Cottage Preschool** in Broomfield (303-466-5885); **The Family Learning Center**'s bilingual preschool (303-442-8979); **Friends 'N' Fun Children's Center** in Lafayette (303-666-5111); **Mountain View Preschool** (303-494-3557); **New Horizons Cooperative Preschool** (303-442-7434); and the **Rainbow Tree Preschool** (303-499-3038).

Keep in mind that in addition to the accredited daycare centers listed above, many excellent, nonaccredited daycare homes provide a warm, safe environment with just a few children. Many top-notch daycare centers and preschools have not gone through the fees, paperwork, and visits required for official accreditation. For these reasons, check other places, too, and use our short list to compare.

Extended Care for Older Kids and Other Family Issues

Most local schools offer before- and after-school care and enrichment programs for students whose parents can't be there when their kids come home from school, but who don't want them home alone. If your older child has outgrown such programs, you might connect them with employment or volunteer opportunities.

Church groups, **Boulder Youth Services** (303-441-4357), and your local school are other places that can help. In 1996, **City on the Hill Ministries,** at 7483 Arapahoe Avenue (303-440-3873), built a skateboard park outside the church and welcomes youngsters to use it for free.

Jobs for youngsters, especially those younger than 16, are hard to come by—and vacation periods can stretch interminably for teens with little to do. One of the area's finest summer job programs, is the **Boulder Junior Rangers.** Since it began in 1966, some 4,000 teens ages 14 to 17 have undertaken a variety of construction and maintenance projects in the Boulder Mountain Park System. Digging, hauling, planting, and cleaning have not only provided teens with a modest summer income but also have given them insight into conservation and ecology. At age 18, Junior Rangers may graduate to Assistant Senior Rangers, and at 21 they may become Senior Rangers, supervising teams of 10 to 12 Juniors. The YMCA's **Youth Employment Center,** (303-442-2778 ext. 218), operates as a clearinghouse for jobs from lawn-mowing and babysitting to tutoring younger children. They've helped find work for teens as young as 13.

If your teens are looking for evening entertainment, keep in mind that many local music clubs and pool halls ban anyone under the legal drinking age (21), even if they aren't planning to drink. That explains the popularity of places such as Red Robin (see our Restaurants chapter) or Crossroads Mall (see our Shopping chapter) for younger teens, and coffeehouses for older teens.

Youngsters often take advantage of the programs and facilities available at the YMCA and North, South, and East Boulder recreation centers (see our Parks and Recreation Centers chapter), which have excellent swimming programs, gyms, and

Insiders' Tip

If you have chosen a childcare center but want to make one final check on its reputation, ask the State Department's Office of Child Care Services in Denver (303-866-5958) to share its licensing files. These files contain complaints and reviews about the center. To see a file, make an appointment, or you can order copies of file information at 50 cents per page.

other attractions. The three Boulder Recreation Centers offer free access to gymnasiums for teens every weekday afternoon.

If a family is in real trouble, Children's Services (see "Information Centers" in this chapter) is a source of information about organizations, classes, counseling, and other options to help resolve ongoing family conflicts and even abuse issues. Boulder County's **Family Preservation Program** (303-441-1000), funded by the Boulder County Department of Social Services, Medicaid, and the state's juvenile justice system, draws on the expertise of several agencies to offer intensive short-term intervention to stabilize families in crisis.

Schools

Public Schools

Two school districts serve Boulder County—Boulder Valley and St. Vrain.

The **Boulder Valley District** (303-447-1010) includes Boulder, Broomfield, Gold Hill, Jamestown, Lafayette, Louisville, and Nederland. More than 27,000 students attend 33 elementary schools (including two offering kindergarten through Grade 8), 11 middle schools, one middle/senior high, seven high schools, three charter schools, and one technical education center. Average class size is 25. Most teachers have more than 10 years of teaching experience and hold master's degrees. Some schools offer before- and after-school meals and care, enrichment programs, and summer sessions. The annual budgeted operating expenditure per pupil is $4,800.

The **St. Vrain District** (303-776-6200), serves Dacono, Erie, Firestone, Federick, Hygiene, Longmont, Lyons, Mead, Niwot, Peaceful Valley, and Raymond. It has around 18,300 students in 32 different schools, including 18 elementary schools (including one charter school offering kindergarten through Grade 8), five middle schools, three middle/senior

Insiders' Tip
Boulder's public school system includes magnet schools designed for children with special interests or needs.

high schools, three senior high schools, one alternative high school, one career development center, and one vocational/technical school. It employs 1,050 teachers. Average child/teacher ratio is 24-to-1, and the annual expenditure per pupil is $4,700. Some schools offer before- and after-school meals and care and enrichment programs.

Even though Boulder public schools place quite high in national and statewide rankings, controversies have stirred the system in recent years. Such issues as middle school versus junior high school, individualized learning versus back-to-basics, phonics versus whole language for beginner readers, a disquieting pattern of threatened and rescinded teacher layoffs, and other thorny problems have taken an inordinate amount of community energy. Complicating what appears to be chronic district-wide dissension, the Boulder Valley Schools' "site-based management" approach means that each school sets its own policies within the framework of district goals. Hoping to get back on course, voters in 1997 drummed out a "back to basics" school board majority and overwhelmingly supported four new members seen as being friendly to teachers, whole-language reading curriculum, and middle schools. While voters appeared to be in agreement with many of the previous board's goals, its polarized, divisive interactions were a turnoff.

A huge turnaround began in mid-2000, when the school board hired George Garcia as the new school superintendent. Garcia, with 35 years of teaching and administrative experience, has already had a significant impact on such goals as rais-

Fifth graders celebrate their graduation from Foothill Elementary School, one of Boulder Valley School District's 33 elementary schools. PHOTO: ROZ BROWN

ing academic achievement for all students. There has been across-the-board praise for Garcia from all seven school board members, teachers, parents, and community movers and shakers.

Boulder's Open Enrollment policy means that you have a choice between sending your child to your neighborhood school, a different neighborhood's school, or one of the focus or alternative schools popping up around Boulder. So check around to see which suits you and your youngster.

Boulder students do much better than those in the rest of Colorado—not surprising, considering that Boulder parents are among the most well-educated in the nation. The average SAT score for Boulder's college-bound students is 45 points higher than the national norm. The ACT scores are comparable. St. Vrain's SAT and ACT scores are also higher than the state and national averages. But what do those scores mean? Back-to-basics proponents say the SAT and ACT test firm knowledge and that high scores are necessary to get into a good college. Others believe that

worshipping the Dow Kid Instructional Average can skew education into nothing but a testing drill.

When choosing a school, there are other important matters to consider. What's the school's curriculum? How many children will be in your child's class? What's the ratio of adults to kids? Are parents encouraged to help in the classroom? What's the school's teaching style? Do the desks face forward and do the teachers fill the walls with chemical element charts, or do kids study in a reading nook with old sofas and decorate the walls with their own creations? Testing scores won't tell you which schools are as homogenous as Wonder Bread and which have a richer cultural diversity. Test scores won't tell you what it's like to be at the school. Visits and talks are crucial, for your school is a community, where you and your children can make friends, build memories and learn about life.

Here's one warning: Boulder County has grown fast. That can mean overcrowding. This was a winning theme in a student editorial cartoon contest. In the cartoon, one adult says, "I feel sorry for those goof-offs at our school. They're not getting the education they need." The other adult replies, "I agree. But it's a good thing they ditch class, or we'd have to hold class on the football field." Since 1996, more than 2,000 students have been added to classrooms. Budget constraints mean facilities and staff haven't kept up with increased enrollment, and some new communities are catching up on building schools nearby, forcing children from those communities to face busing to more distant schools or overcrowding. So ask about this "growing" issue.

Public Focus Schools

Some children thrive in any situation, like hardy garden plants. Others need a special environment before they bloom. If you've got a unique bloomer, check out the city's focus and alternative schools, often called "magnet" schools. Some provide more structure than a traditional classroom. Others offer more open-ended explorations. There are programs with specially trained staff for bilingual children or chil-

dren with unusual developmental needs. A few include Family Resource Schools, outreach programs that are as good as having a wonderful aunt or uncle around, ready to help plan after-school activities and improve the school's community.

You'll get the best information about magnet schools if you visit. Each one has distinctive features and programs. See the beautiful rain forest mural kids designed at **University Hill Elementary** (303-442-6735). Also check out Uni Hill's Rainbow Press, where kids edit and publish real books, in English, Spanish, and Asian dialects. **Washington Bilingual School** (303-449-6618) has a goal of 50 percent English-dominant and 50 percent Spanish-dominant children. **Platt Middle School**'s Choice Program (303-499-6800) boasts one of the most interesting science rooms around. Even in politically correct Boulder, **Casey Middle School** (303-442-5235) stands out with its emphasis on multiculturalism and a motto of "Pride in Diversity." Horizons K-8 School (303-447-5580) is one of three charter schools in the Boulder Valley district. The school maintains high academic

Historic Washington Elementary School offers Boulder's premier Spanish-English bilingual program.
PHOTO: ROZ BROWN

and behavioral expectations, offering mixed-age classes and individualized goal setting.

Two additional charter schools will be operating by 2000.

Fairview High School (303–499–7600) has added an International Baccalaureate (IB) program for juniors and seniors. It is designed with more rigorous, internationally regarded academic standards. There were 963 students enrolled in IB in 2000-2001, and more than half took at least three of these challenging courses. **New Vista High School** (303-447-5401) is designed to cultivate students' unique talents and gifts, as well as their ability to be responsible for their own learning. It graduated its first class in 1996, sending 50 percent of its students on to college and boasting one National Merit Scholar. Passages (303-447-5573) is a dropout prevention program for high-school students.

Now in its sixth year of operation, Boulder's **Summit Middle School** (303–499-9511) was founded by parents but operates under the auspices of the school system. This is a tuition-free, public charter school offering grades 6 through 8 a rigorous, academic curriculum designed to meet the needs of students wanting greater challenges.

Another specialized program is the Boulder Valley's **Arapahoe Campus** (303–447-5220), which offers high school students education in trade skill programs. There's also **Halcyon** (303-499- 1121), a day-treatment program for troubled adolescents; it includes around 30 staff people working with 20 students.

Call Boulder Valley School District for more information, and when you do, perhaps you'll learn about even more new focus schools (schools that offer a special, nontypical way of teaching, operated by the school district) or charter schools (schools that offer a special, nontypical way of teaching, funded by the school district but managed by the citizens forming the school) in the works. On one hand, the diversity such schools offer gives people more choices and helps teachers learn from a rich variety of styles. However, there are fears that too much diversity could spread resources thin and create factions that turn attention toward bitter arguments on style rather than letting teaching occur in a nonpolitical, caring environment.

In 1997, St. Vrain opened a charter school, **Twin Peaks Charter Academy** (303-682-9377) for elementary students, grades K through 8. An alternative high school program is offered at **Olde Columbine High School** (303-772-3333). The **Career Development Center** (303-772-3333) is at the same location, 1200 South Sunset. This vocational school is for adults and high school students who take electives in the CDC building. Courses include welding, automotive and building trades, health and dental, agriculture, horticulture, accounting, office systems and other specialties. The **Adult Education Center** at 619 Bowen (303-678-5662) offers adult diploma courses, including classes in citizenship.

Private Schools

You can find private schools run by religious organizations and schools as nondenominational as a pin-striped suit. At some, kids aren't expected to read until they're past 3rd grade. At others, the academic drills start in preschool. Boulder's Children's Services lists private schools in Boulder County. In addition to the local schools below, there are some private schools in Denver that Boulder-area residents attend, despite the commute.

Alexander Dawson School
10455 Dawson Dr., Lafayette
(303) 665–6679

Alexander Dawson offers a tried-and-true basics academic approach for K through 12. About 375 students are enrolled. The sprawling campus east of Boulder includes tennis courts, art rooms, a pottery studio and a theater. The buildings look as clean as new pennies, and the staff takes a rigorous, academic approach, offering courses from Latin through Advanced Placement Biology, plus interscholastic sports and a creative-writing magazine.

Boulder Country Day School
4820 Nautilus Court North, Boulder
(303) 527-4931

Preschool through 5th grade are taught at this very traditional, academically oriented program for 250 students. French and Latin are part of the curriculum. Computers, art, music, and drama are taught here too. Classes have no more than 10 students in the preschool and no more than 15 in the elementary grades. Students wear uniforms, and the principal greets them by name as they arrive each morning, holding an umbrella for them if it's raining. The 4th- and 5th-grade teachers send home biweekly progress reports about how each child is doing.

Bridge School
The Abbey, 6717 S. Boulder Rd., Boulder
(303) 494-7551

One of Boulder's newest private secondary schools for grades 6 through 12 is the Bridge School, designed for motivated, intellectually curious learners. The school also seeks youngsters with good character and a willingness to take risks and challenge themselves. The high school curriculum includes computer competency, an interdisciplinary approach to science, senior seminars in English (including one on literature written before 1914), foreign languages, art, and physical education. Community service is also part of the graduation requirement. Founded with just a handful of students, the school now has an enrollment of about 125.

Friends School
5465 Pennsylvania Ave., Boulder
(303) 499-1999

About 140 kids attend, ranging from 2 years 9 months through 11 years old (preschool through 5th grade). The average class size for preschool is 14 and for elementary about 20, with two teachers per classroom. Lots of hands-on materials, a custom curriculum for each student, and a caring atmosphere characterize Friends School.

Jarrow Montessori
3900 Orange Ct., Boulder
(303) 443-0511

Class sizes are generally small (between 16 and 20) in this school, which has a total enrollment of 210. Located on 3 acres in a pretty, quiet part of North Boulder, Jarrow Montessori offers a toddler program for kids 18 months to 3 years, a primary program for 3- to 6-year-olds, then an elementary program through 6th grade. Different age groups are blended in each classroom. This is a certified American Montessori Society school, with child-guided education. Education here goes from concrete, hands-on experiences to abstract associations.

Sacred Heart of Jesus School
1317 Mapleton Ave., Boulder
(303) 447-2362

This Catholic school has a preschool childcare program then an elementary school from kindergarten through 8th grade. It's well regarded for its traditional academic program and religious course work. Lots of parents volunteer here, helping to add to the community atmosphere. Nearly 400 children attend.

September School
1902 Walnut Ave., Boulder
(303) 443-9933

Hands-on learning and creativity distinguish this high school (grades 9 through 12) of about 100 students. Classes average 8 to 10 students. The teaching staff is dedicated and excellent, including professional scientists and musicians with a knack for communicating with students as peers. The four-building campus includes a small, former church at Canyon and 19th Streets.

When the September School, a private Boulder high school, acquired the old Second Baptist Church for classrooms and events space, art students wasted no time in making the building uniquely their own.

PHOTO: LINDA CORNETT

Shepherd Valley Waldorf School & Garden
6500 W. Dry Creek Parkway, Niwot
(303) 530–2644

Boulder's second Waldorf School opened when the demand at Shining Mountain (below) exceeded space available. This Gunbarrel-area school has preschool through 8th grade. The school relocated in 1999 to a new building on a 38-acre farm site. This allows for a farm and garden atmosphere, making it unique in Boulder for those seeking Waldorf instruction. Class sizes are 15 to 20 students. If you're not familiar with Waldorf schools, see the following entry.

Shining Mountain Waldorf School
999 Violet Ave., Boulder
(303) 444–7697

From preschool through high school, this school offers a rich blend of arts, music, and drama interwoven with academic curriculum. There are 360 students and 50 faculty members. For a chemistry experiment, students might draw what they observe as well as describe it in words. Primary class lessons can include lore about traditional fairy tales, folk stories, and weaving. People who are not familiar with a Waldorf School should give it a visit to observe the warm, comfortable pace at which children learn and the richness of materials available. The philosophy behind Waldorf is more than 75 years old, and in addition to regular accreditation, teachers receive two years of training in Waldorf methods.

The Final Decision

If only Boulder had just one little red schoolhouse, you wouldn't have to agonize over what will be best for your child. Here's a comforting story: One teacher, substituting throughout Boulder County, wore jeans to a school where the children called her by her first name and she read story books to them from a rocking chair. She loved the friendly environment but worried that its open-ended structure let some kids slide. At another school, she wore a business suit, the kids called her "Mrs.," and she lectured from a desk. While academic performance was more easily measured here, she worried that creativity was stifled. Which school was better? She rated them equally good. But at the more casual school, she wove in more structure. At the more traditional school, she slipped in creative moments. If you know a school's program and your child's needs, the fit doesn't have to be exactly, always perfect. You're a parent. You're a wonderful part of your child's life. You can help provide balance, just as this excellent teacher does.

Extra Help

Boulder also has resources for children who need assistance in boosting study skills. Options include **Sylvan Leaning Center,** 1600 38th Street (303-449-1700), and **Huntington Learning Center,** 2317 30th Street (303-545-2100), both offering help with general study skills, reading, writing, and math, as well as motivation and other issues related to improving grades and enhancing self-esteem. **fLearn** (303-499-4386), had a storefront learning center in Boulder for many years but is now available primarily on-line, at flearn.com. It also sponsors summer programs at Learning Power, 1440 28th Street, Boulder (303-938-0136).

School officials also can refer you to private tutors for your child. Some tutors advertise in the local classifieds, and the university is also a reservoir of older students, education majors, and specialists in other disciplines.

Colleges and Universities

Boulder students can choose from a wealth of higher education opportunities. In addition to the colleges and universities

right in the city, thee are numerous other schools within commuting distance of Boulder, including those in Denver: the **University of Denver** (303-871-2000), the **University of Colorado at Denver** (303-556-3287), **Regis University** (303-458-4100), and **Metropolitan State College** (303-556-3058). **Colorado State University** (970-491-1101) is in Fort Collins, roughly an hour north of Boulder. **The Colorado School of Mines** (303-273-3000) and **Red Rocks Community College** (303-988-6160) are in Golden, about a half-hour's drive south of Boulder.

Institutions of Higher Education in Boulder

Front Range Community College
5490 Spine Rd., Gunbarrel
(303) 516–8000
2255 N. Main St., Ste. 118, Longmont
(303) 516–8999
Two-year degree and certificate programs are available at both locations in a variety of subjects. Some programs are specifically designed for students who intend to continue their education at a four-year college or university. Tuition is about half the cost of a four-year college.

The Naropa University
2130 Arapahoe Ave., Boulder
(303) 444–0202, (800) 772–6951
Naropa is an accredited college offering undergraduate and graduate programs in the arts, social sciences, and humanities. The school was founded in 1974 by Chogyam Trungpa Rinpoche, and its educational philosophy is rooted in the Buddhist contemplative tradition. Approximately 800 degree-seeking students attend Naropa. Students can earn bachelor's degrees in music, psychology, dance/movement studies, dance therapy, religious studies, writing and literature, environmental studies, early childhood education, and interdisciplinary studies. Master's degrees are available in psychology, dance therapy, gerontology, art ther-

apy, and writing and poetics. The institute also offers a performing arts series and many workshops, and annually holds the Naropa Summer Institute, drawing faculty and students from around the world. Many courses and workshops are open to the community at large.

University of Colorado at Boulder
Office of Admissions, Regent Administrative Center 125, Campus Box 6, Boulder
(303) 492–6301

With all those red-roofed buildings, CU-Boulder is known as one of the nation's prettiest campuses. It's also close to recreational activities and home to top teams such as the CU Buffs football team and CU women's basketball, both of which make attending CU-Boulder lots of fun. But for academics, it offers excellent opportunities, too.

CU-Boulder is most renowned for its science programs. CU professor Thomas Cech won the 1989 Nobel Prize in chemistry. In 1995 professors Carl Wieman and Eric Cornell were awarded the Fritz London Award for their work in low temperature physics. (Also that year, history professor Patricia Nelson Limerick was awarded a prestigious McArthur Foundation grant, given for intellectual creativ-

ity.) More CU undergraduate and grad-school alumni have become astronauts than graduates of any other school, including the service academies. With such a history, it's no surprise that CU-Boulder got more than $200 million in outside research funds in 2000.

Boulder is the largest campus in a four-campus system. Other campuses are CU-Denver on the three-college Auraria campus; CU-Colorado Springs; and the Health Sciences Center, including the University Hospital, in Denver. Approximately 25,000 students attend CU-Boulder, with 20,000 undergraduates and 5,000 graduates. Psychology, biology and English are among the most popular undergraduate majors. Classics and dance are among the smallest.

As a state school, CU gives tuition breaks to in-state residents, who make up nearly 70 percent of the student population. Nondegree candidates may pay to attend university classes as part of the university's continuing education program. People older than 55 can audit classes for a nominal fee, with the professor's permission; call (303) 492–8484 for details.

Continuing Education

One of the most valuable lessons an educated person can learn is to keep on learning. If you have that attitude, you're going to love Boulder. Young and old, dabblers and those intent on gaining a specific new skill, many local residents take courses from time to time. To get one of the enticing catalogs listing available offerings, call or write the phone numbers below. Or, if you're already in Boulder, head to the library, a recreation center, or a major grocery store, where these catalogs are usually available for free.

Boulder Parks and Recreation
3170 Broadway, Boulder
(303) 441–3412

All three of Boulder's recreation centers offer skill-building courses. Gymnastics for kids and pottery for adults are very popular, as are the dance classes for both

> ### Insiders' Tip
> Thirteen astronauts are alumni of the University of Colorado at Boulder. Other degree holders include retired Supreme Court Justice Byron White, 1958's Miss America Marilyn Van Derbur Atler, film actor/director Robert Redford, and M*A*S*H actor Larry Linville.

age groups. Other courses include yoga, martial arts, guitar, cooking, sign language, investing, and whitewater kayaking. Most of these classes take place at the recreation centers. When the Parks and Recreation offerings first get published each season, the registration phones can be busy for a long time. Sometimes it's quicker to go to any of Boulder's three recreation centers and register in person.

CU-Boulder Continuing Education
1221 University Ave., Boulder
(303) 492–5148,
(800) 331–2801 (out-of-state),
(800) 332–5839 (in-state)

This fabulous catalog offers 300 courses each semester including everything from full-credit, college-level courses taught by CU-Boulder professors to noncredit pursuits such as beginning computer courses and art/poetry workshops. Noncredit classes often are taught by professionals—some just starting out in their fields and willing to share boundless enthusiasm, others nationally famous who will always love teaching. Classes usually take place right on the CU-Boulder campus, in the evenings and on weekends.

Regis University Boulder Campus
6235 Lookout Rd., Suite H, Boulder
(303) 530–9514

Through the School for Professional Studies, adults can complete bachelor of science degrees in business administration, computer information systems, religious studies, and many more subjects by taking accelerated evening classes. Master's degrees are offered in science and management and in computer information science.

Alternative Schools

In addition to schools offering continuing education classes for adults, there are more than 30 schools in Boulder offering training and certification in holistic and spiritual fields. A list of some of the most established schools follows.

Boulder College of Massage Therapy
6255 Longbow Dr., Boulder
(303) 530–2100

The Boulder School of Massage Therapy is a leading massage therapy education center. In 2000 the school celebrated its 25th year as a nonprofit institution. BCMT's diploma program includes in-depth training in a variety of approaches to massage therapy. The program includes human sciences, ethics, movement studies, career development, and professional internships. More than 2,500 students have graduated from BCMT, which has an average annual enrollment of 250.

BMS Center for Clinical Hypnotherapy
75 Manhattan Dr., Ste. 103, Boulder
(303) 494–1001

BMS students can become nationally certified clinical hypnotherapists. Advanced courses also are available to psychologists, social workers, and other licensed professionals. The center is authorized and certified by the National Guild of Hypnotists and the American Association of Professional Hypno-therapists.

Colorado Cranial Institute
1080 Hawthorn Ave., Boulder
(303) 449–0322

The institute offers private, individual training sessions in craniosacral treatments for a wide range of common health problems ranging from back pain to migraine headaches to head, jaw, neck, pelvis, and diaphragm pain.

Colorado Institute for Classical Homeopathy
2299 Pearl St., Boulder
(303) 440–3717

The Colorado Institute offers a two-year program of in-depth homeopathic study. The curriculum is designed to prepare participants for a professional career and the national exam given by the Council for Classical Homeopathy. CICH is a nonprofit organization, and its program is approved and regulated by the Division of Private Occupational Schools, Colorado Department of Higher Education.

The Cooking School of the Rockies
637 S. Broadway, Ste. H, Boulder
(303) 494-7988

Cooking school students can refine their wine-tasting skills, watch famous chefs from around the world demonstrate their favorite techniques, or learn hands-on everything, from professional French cooking to sushi rolling and gingerbread-house baking. A professional chef's course includes a trip to France. The Cooking School has a store with a big kitchen area. It's open 10 A.M. to 6 P.M. weekdays, 10 A.M. to 5 P.M. Saturday, and noon to 5 P.M. Sunday.

Guild for Structural Integration
3107 28th St., Boulder
(303) 447-0122, (800) 447-0150

Dedicated to the traditional teaching of Dr. Ida P. Rolf, GSI offers basic training in the Rolf method of structural integration, continuing education, advanced training, and introductory courses in anatomy and physiology and massage.

Hakomi Institute
1800 30th St., Ste. 201, Boulder
(303) 447-3290, (303) 499-6699

Hakomi Integrative Somatics (HIS) is a body-centered psychotherapy influenced by the techniques of Gestalt, bioenergetics, and Feldenkrais, and by the spiritual principles of Taoism and Buddhism. The institute offers training in healing developmental and traumatic wounds.

International Breath Institute
2525 Arapahoe Ave., Ste. E4-287, Boulder
(303) 444-8615

Founded in 1991, the IBI is a holistic wellness educational organization. It emphasizes personal and professional development through instruction in the Transform-Breathing Energy System (TEMS).

Polarity Center of Colorado
1721 Redwood Ave., Boulder
(303) 443-9847

This center offers professional training and is accredited by the American Polarity Therapy Association. Polarity therapy is a comprehensive health system based on understanding the human energy field; it's founded on the work of Dr. Randolph Stone.

Rocky Mountain Center for Botanical Studies
2639 Spruce St., Boulder
(303) 442-6861

A 10-month Western program includes the study of herbal therapeutics, botany, physiology, earth-centered herbalism, field identification, clinical work, and medicine-making field trips. The center is devoted to in-depth exploration of plants as healing allies.

Rolf Institute
205 Canyon Blvd., Boulder
(303) 449-5903

The Rolf Institute was founded in 1971 and graduates about 75 to 100 students each year from its Boulder school. Developed by Dr. Ida P. Rolf in the 1940s, Rolfing is a series of 10 specific and individualized hands-on sessions designed to realign the body's structure.

The School of Natural Cookery
P.O. Box 19466, Boulder, CO 80308
(303) 444-8068

Established in 1983, this vegetarian cooking school is internationally recognized for its programs for both nonprofessional and professional students. A strong curriculum in the art of preparing whole grains, beans and vegetables includes the techniques of meal composition and improvisation. Classes are held in area homes.

School of Natural Medicine
P.O. Box 7369, Boulder, CO 80306
(888) 593-6173

The School of Natural Medicine was established in 1977 by Director Sharan, also a founder of the British School of Iridology in Cambridge, England. SNM offers natural physician training in iridology, herbal medicine, naturopathy, and transcenDance natural medicine. An extensive summer program in Boulder homes supplements correspondence courses.

Healthcare and Wellness

Many people come to Boulder for the inherently healthful and congenial lifestyle, but even healthy, happy people have babies and sometimes get sick or hurt. This section lists referral services, then describes major medical facilities to assist you with your healthcare needs. We also give you an Insiders' look at how to choose from Boulder's large selection of alternative care providers—in case you're in Boulder County partly because you want to get even healthier.

In Boulder, however, it's not only people who have medical alternatives, but also their furry friends. Boulder's love affair with pets is evidenced by the many options for animal healthcare listed at the end of this chapter.

Emergency

Call 911 if you are any place in Boulder County and need help fast. Not only can you get help, but our 911 is designed to automatically locate you unless you're calling from a party line.

Physician and Dentist Referral Services

After hello, a new neighbor's first question is usually about a doctor, dentist, or orthodontist. Once you know what kind of physician you need, word of mouth is often a good bet for finding someone you're comfortable with. If you don't have a neighbor, friend, or coworker to ask, start by checking the Yellow Pages under "Physicians" or "Dentists" or call one of the area's referral services. The **Boulder County Medical Society** (303-527-3215) lists around 400 doctors, and (800) DOCTORS, operated by **Community Health,** has a local phone number (303-443-2584), which provides referrals to about 300 Boulder-area doctors, dentists, counselors, chiropractors, midwives, and other licensed healthcare professionals. Four of the larger medical clinics also offer referrals. The **Boulder Medical Center's Patient Services** (303-440-3000) lists more than 50 physicians and has two

satellite clinics in Louisville, including one at Centura Avista Hospital. **Centura's Health Advisor** (303-777-6877) is a 24-hour phone line providing referrals, healthcare information, and community information. **Longmont Clinic** (303-776-1234) lists around 40 local physicians. **Kaiser Permanente** (303-440-0884) is a large health maintenance organization; it can also refer its own patients to more than 450 of its associated physicians in the Denver/Boulder area.

Hospitals

**Boulder Community Hospital
1100 Balsam St., Boulder
(303) 440-2273 (general),
(303) 440-2037 (emergency)**

With 265 beds, Community is the largest full-service hospital in Boulder County. It takes pride in its emergency, maternity, cancer (full radiation service), and open-heart surgery centers, among other specialties. It emphasizes high-quality and family-centered care. According to the Colorado Hospital Association's data, Community has one of the state's best records for successful inpatient care, short length of stay, and low-cost service.

The care is first-rate here, and the atmosphere tends toward the friendly and relaxed. Labor and delivery rooms might include old-fashioned rocking chairs and other homey touches, with lots of encouragement for family and new baby to happily bond. A friend who's had surgery in the cancer care center reports that her room's stereo system was top-notch. She's a professional hospital worker from out of state, and she gives the cancer unit an "A+" for the personal attention she received. With advance notice, pet visitation is allowed (be sure the pet's with a trained handler and you have a recent copy of its vaccination record). While there are sort of official visiting hours, the staff tends to be pretty relaxed about visitors if you would like them more often.

A satellite clinic in Lafayette is Community Medical Center, at 2000 South Boulder Road (303-666-4357).

Behavioral-health services at Mapleton include inpatient psychiatric care and day-treatment programs for adults and adolescents. The hotline for emergency evaluation is (303-441-0400).

Centura Health Avista Adventist Hospital
100 Health Park Dr., Louisville
(303) 673-1000 (general), (303) 673-1111 (emergency)

This hospital, commonly referred to simply as Avista Hospital, was built in 1990 in booming Louisville and has beds for 58 patients. This well-regarded, full-service hospital offers 24-hour emergency service, single-room family-centered maternity care, a nursery, a pediatric unit, a cardiac unit, inpatient and outpatient rehabilitation services, and diagnostic services including whole-body MRI and CAT scan . . . the works.

Centennial Peaks Behavioral Health Systems
2255 S. 88th St., Louisville
(303) 673-9990, (800) 842-4673

Centennial has facilities and programs for children, adolescents, adults, and seniors. There are 72 beds for inpatient care, and day-treatment and outpatient programs for anyone with emotional, behavioral, or substance-abuse problems. The Counseling and Assessment Center, a free consultation service, can help determine whether someone needs therapy and suggests where to get assistance from counselors, social workers, support groups, or psychiatrists.

Longmont United Hospital
1950 Mountain View Ave., Longmont
(303) 651-5111 (general),
(303) 651-5000 (emergency)

This 142-bed hospital has a full range of services, from a whole-body CAT scanner to emergency services, home healthcare, a therapy pool, maternity care, psychiatric services, and an adult day-care program. In 1996, the hospital built a medical office building next door and leases space to physicians and other medical providers.

The Mapleton/LUH Rehab is on the hospital grounds. Patients who need minimal rehabilitation as they head home can get transitional care. Longmont United added a cancer care unit in 1995, with full chemo- and radiation-therapy services.

A satellite clinic in Niwot is United Medical Center of Niwot, at 6857 Paiute Avenue (303-652-9135). A second satellite clinic in Lyons is United Medical Center of Lyons, located at 303 Main Street, Unit C (303-823-6535). The unit offers urgent care and family practice.

Mapleton Center
311 Mapleton Ave., Boulder
(303) 443-0230

The Seventh-Day Adventists built their tuberculosis sanitarium here nearly a cen-

The Boulder Creek Path makes it easy for city residents to embrace an active lifestyle. PHOTO: DAILY CAMERA

tury ago. The location is beautiful, near Mount Sanitas Trail and the peace of the foothills. Today the hospital is a division of Boulder Community, offering rehabilitation services for victims of strokes, accidents, brain injuries, developmental disabilities, and more, as well as behavioral health services for people suffering from psychiatric disorders, chemical dependency, alcoholism, depression, drug abuse, eating disorders, and teen behavior problems.

"Easy Street," a special part of the rehabilitation facilities, has stores, curbs, cars, and restaurants so patients can practice real-world situations again. For patients working on balance, there is equestrian therapy and a low-ropes course. In past years therapy for head-injury patients has included a hike up 14,000-foot Pikes Peak to improve physical coordination and self-confidence. A warm-water, nonchlorinated therapy pool is open to anyone; call for hours and fees. A new satellite facility, at 6685 Gunpark Drive, Suite 130 (303-530-4675) in Gunbarrel, offers physical therapy, speed and occupational therapy, and pediatric rehabilitation.

Hospice

Hospice of Boulder County
2825 Marine St., Boulder
2594 Trailridge Dr., Lafayette
(303) 449-7740

This hospice, established in 1978 and one of the first in the nation, offers an interdisciplinary program of home care, counseling, educational services, and bereavement support to meet the needs of terminally ill patients and their family members. Services are provided in patients' homes and in nursing homes; there's no inpatient facility. Care for the terminally ill is provided regardless of a person's ability to pay. The hospice also has a volunteer training program.

County Health Department Clinics

Boulder County residents come to clinics for low-cost immunizations, well-child care, confidential HIV testing, senior clinics, environmental health screening, and more. There's a free directory of services available through the **Boulder County Health Department** (303-441-1100). Clinics are located in Boulder at 3305 N. Broadway (303-413-7500), in Longmont at 529 Coffman St., Suite 200 (303-678-6166), and in Lafayette at 1345 Plaza Court (303-666-0515). The Arc (as it's informally called) is the county's **Addiction Recovery Center,** at 3470 N. Broadway (303-441-1275), offering detox and treating substance abuse and co-dependency. The center also operates an impaired-driver prevention program (303-441-1279).

The **Boulder County AIDS Project,** at 2118 14th Street in Boulder (303-444-6121), offers information about prevention and treatment along with a food bank, counseling, and buddy systems for clients with HIV. The **Mental Health Center of Boulder County,** 1333 Iris Avenue, Boulder, has a crisis line, (303) 447-1665, and a general line, (303) 443-8500. The Mesa **Rape Crisis Team**'s 24-hour crisis line is (303) 443-7300.

The **Boulder Heart Institute,** at 2750 Broadway in Boulder (303-440-3222), offers services ranging from a basic cardiac risk-factor screening to various types of cardiac wellness programs and state-of-the-art exercise testing to assess athletes' fitness levels.

> ## Insiders' Tip
> Boulder County is home to two yoga ashrams or resident communities: the Eldorado Mountain Yoga Ashram in Eldorado Springs and the Shoshoni Yoga Retreat south of Rollinsville. Both communities share the same Hindu- and Buddhist-derived spiritual lineage.

The **People's Clinic** is a healthcare clinic offering comprehensive adult, pediatric, and prenatal care for low-income residents. The Clinic is in Boulder at 3303 N. Broadway (303-449-6050).

Finding Holistic Healthcare

As early as 1896, patients admitted to Boulder's Colorado Sanitarium were given Swedish massage, hydrotherapy treatments, and a vegetarian diet as a cure for illness. Advertised as a resort, the sanitarium encouraged people to come for "refreshment of the mind, body, and spirit," and to that end operators offered their own line of whole-grain cereals and health foods. Many tubercular patients were drawn West to such facilities and soon recovered from what was believed a fatal condition. What was then viewed as radical medical treatment is now tame by comparison to other offerings from Boulder's holistic health community. In Boulder the word "wellness" is used as much or more than "healthcare" or "medicine," and the line between conventional medicine and alternative approaches is blurred.

Holistic doctors believe in treating the whole person, rather than the symptoms of illness. Naturally there is some skepticism about alternative therapies from those who practice traditional medicine, but unless an illness is life-threatening, exploring options can be a first step toward taking control of your health.

Selecting the right therapy and a suitable practitioner can be overwhelming without a few basic guidelines. Holistic medicine defines "complete therapeutic systems" as those based on a philosophy or set of beliefs that include a comprehensive range of treatments. Some examples are Ayurvedic medicine, Chinese medicine, herbal medicine, homeopathy, indigenous medicine, naturopathic medicine, and nutritional therapy. (Chiropractic and osteopathy are sometimes called complete systems but just as often fall under the physical or bodywork category.)

If cycling is popular in health-conscious Boulder, tandem cycling is doubly so. PHOTO: ROZ BROWN

Ayurvedic medicine is central to the culture of India and dates back to 3000 B.C. A variety of healing and prevention techniques are part of Chinese medicine, including the use of herbs, acupuncture, and t'ai chi ch'uan. Once the only source of medicine for ancient cultures, herbal medicine dates back to ancient Egypt but has only recently regained credibility in Western cultures. Homeopathy is based on the 19th century "Law of Similars" and uses the substance causing an illness in minute quantities to cure that same illness. Indigenous medicine, or shamanism, employs a variety of healing techniques found in most tribal communities. Naturopathic medicine is sometimes called "commonsense" medicine because it relies primarily on four components for good health: fresh air and clean water, balanced diet, exercise, and "right living." Finally, nutritional therapy originates from naturopathic medicine, where diet is emphasized as the key to good health.

Not all people seeking a more holistic approach to health want to embrace a complete system of therapy. Perhaps you're suffering from chronic tension or lack of vitality and just want to try a new bodywork therapy. In that case, Boulder is the right place to be. Acupressure, aikido, Alexander technique, Breema, dance therapy, Feldenkrais, Hellerwork, massage, neuro-muscular therapy, polarity therapy, reflexology, Reiki, Rolfing, yoga, and Zen shiatsu are just a few of the offerings available.

There are also techniques that are often, but not always, used in conjunction with the larger, complete "systems" of healing. They include applied kinesiology, aromatherapy, biofeedback, color therapy, crystal and gem therapy, flower essences, hydrotherapy, hypnotherapy, iridology, magnetic therapy, sound therapy, and visualization therapy, to name a few. Practitioners of these techniques also abound in Boulder.

If you feel like an oddball for choosing alternative health options, consider this: Nearly half the population is said to use at least one remedy not prescribed by a doctor; over one-fifth have visited a complementary healthcare practitioner. And the number of adults using some form of alternative therapy continues to rise. According to a 1995 survey in the *British Journal of Clinical Psychology,* many people turn to alternative therapies when they see signs of improvement that conventional medicine failed to provide.

If you decide it's worth your money to seek alternative healthcare, you're not alone, but it will take some research. Finding the right practitioner is complicated by Colorado's vague licensing requirements, which might someday change. For the uninitiated, it's easy to confuse a certified dietitian with one who has one or two years of nonfederally certified training with a registered dietitian who has several years of university training. The same is true with naturopathic physicians. Some have attended federally accredited, four-year programs that have the same basics as medical school, then have had specialized training in the science and counseling skills that can help a person stick with a good diet, exercise, and weight-reduction stress. Others who call themselves naturopathic physicians have taken no more than a six-month correspondence course. Clearly, screening and getting as much information as possible about a practitioner's competence is recommended. Don't be afraid to ask healthcare providers about qualifications. Which program did they attend? What was the program's accreditation—federal or state? How many years of study did they undertake, and what are they qualified to do? Can they provide references?

If you are seeking an expert in wellness counseling, choose carefully. Listen for word-of-mouth recommendations. The *Daily Camera*'s Monday "FIT" magazine includes a regular weekly column featuring three healers (usually an M.D. and two alternative professionals) discussing a health question from different perspectives. It's a great way to compare treatment philosophies and glean names of reputable professionals. Read the local holistic journals such as *Nexus,* which is available at many grocery stores, especially the health-food stores.

Here's the most important aspect of choosing alternative care: Patients of holistic doctors are required to take responsibility for their own wellness, an uncomfortable role for many of us raised on conventional medicine. Don't expect a magical quick fix for improving your health through lifestyle changes, but be aware that confidence in a practitioner is intrinsic to the success of their work.

Interdisciplinary groups and practitioners, as well as specialists, abound. For instance, naturopathic physician Charley Cropley (720–406–9100) is the director of **The Center for Radiant Aliveness** and specializes in nutrition counseling. Chiropractor Jay Wilson (303–449–7414) also is an expert on nutritional issues. Nancy Rao (303–545–021) and JoHanna Reilly (303–541–9600) are among Boulder's half-dozen naturopathic physicians with excellent reputations in the alternative health community.

Medical doctor Bob Rountree of the **Helios Health Center** (303–499–9224) co-authored an excellent reference book, *Smart Medicine for a Healthier Child,* for those wanting to compare conventional and alternative therapies. Co-author Rachel Walton is a Boulder pediatric nurse who teaches classes to new mothers on using natural medicine to care for babies

Insiders' Tip

Practitioners of alternative medicine are regularly listed in or advertise in *Nexus,* Colorado's holistic health, metaphysics, and natural lifestyles directory and magazine. The bimonthly publication is free at health-food stores and is supplied to 300 outlets in Boulder and Denver.

and young children. Helios is an example of physicians and health professionals teaming up because they appreciate the way conventional and alternative healthcare can complement each other. In fact, one of Helios's doctors is a board-certified acupuncturist and homeopath as well as an M.D. Similarly, **Wellspring for Women** (303-443-0321) is a group of women nurse practitioners, acupuncturists, and homeopaths who have designed a practice focusing on the health needs of women. Chiropractor Darryl Hobson (303-449-4498) offers a Reclaiming Your Health seminar, which includes fasting and cleansing. Check out these professionals and clinics, and ask them for referrals to other qualified professionals.

For a sampling of schools offering training and certification in holistic and spiritual fields in Boulder, see our Child Care and Education chapter.

Wellness for Pets

Boulderites love their pets. Owners regularly bring their dogs along to outdoor cafes and especially while running or hiking. In fact, residents feel so strongly about "pet rights" they approved a ballot measure in 1996 to exempt certain park and open-space areas from a city ordinance that required dog owners to keep their pets on a leash.

It's no surprise then that so many options exist for keeping pets healthy. **Allpets Clinic,** at 5290 Manhattan Circle (303-499-5335), stands out because it offers 24-hour veterinary care. This pet clinic has a welcoming fire hydrant out front for the dogs and separate entrances and waiting areas for clients with dogs and cats. In 1992, Allpets received the veterinary economics hospital design award, and in 1993 it was chosen as Boulder's small business of the year. For those in central or north Boulder, the **Boulder Emergency Pet Clinic,** at 1658 30th Street (303-440-7722), may be more convenient. This critical care and trauma center has a doctor on duty all night, every night, and no appointment is necessary.

Other vets specialize. **The Boulder Valley Cat Clinic,** at 2825 Wilderness Place (303-444-6369), deals with feline medical and behavioral problems, offers a low-cost vaccination clinic and boasts of "no barking dogs." **Centennial Valley Animal Hospital,** at 259 Century Circle in Louisville (303-666-9363), handles cats, dogs, and exotics. **Dr. Nancy Loving,** at 2160 James Canyon Drive (303-444-9494), specializes in performance and sport horse care.

In Boulder there are also holistic veterinarians who treat sick pets with such techniques as chiropractic, osteopathy or acupuncture. Holistic veterinarians believe in the animal's ability to heal itself and almost never use antibiotics when confronting illness. While the holistic movement in veterinary medicine is still small, you can locate a holistic veterinarian in the Denver-Boulder metro area by calling (303) 733-2728 or Holistic Care for Animals (303-421-5424).

Media

Newspapers
Magazines
Radio Stations
Television Stations

The story goes that when one of Boulder's early citizens decided the rough mining town needed a newspaper to encourage a sense of community, he simply drove his wagon to a nearby town, loaded up that town's newspaper press, and Boulder had its newspaper. Apparently the notion took, and Boulder has been blessed (or cursed, depending upon your perspective) with a wealth of newspapers ever since. Currently, the town supports one daily, one semi-daily, one alternative weekly, and a number of special-interest newspapers. Boulder was one of the first cities in the nation (outside of the New York metro area) where the *New York Times* became available for home delivery. And the Denver dailies show periodic fascination with the odd little town to the north.

In addition to four local radio stations, the city also has cable television channels for city information, citizen input, and CU programming. Denver's four local television stations also include Boulder in their coverage area.

Newspapers

There's been some disorientation lately in Boulder's newspaper market. The city's only complete, seven-day-a-week newspaper, the *Daily Camera*, was sold to Scripps-Howard after many years of being a member of the Knight-Ridder chain. Scripps-Howard, which then owned the *Denver Rocky Mountain News,* was in a death struggle for supremacy with the *Denver Post* and wanted the *Camera*'s hold on Boulder subscribers to bolster the *Rocky*. Many of the *Camera*'s business functions were dismantled or merged with the *Rocky*'s. Then, the Denver dailies decided to pursue a Joint Operating Agreement. When that agreement was approved by Attorney General Janet Reno, the *Camera* was cut loose from the *Rocky* and found itself having to rebuild.

To complicate matters further, the *Colorado Daily*, a 104-year-old tabloid that publishes not exactly daily, seemed poised to go under in 2000, the victim of mounting expenses and an embezzling employee. The employee-owned newspaper filed for bankruptcy protection, and in 2001 was sold and redesigned.

Also in 2000, the editorially promising weekly *Boulder Planet* died after three and a half years of (money-losing) publication. The all-local newspaper was mourned by a loyal following.

The give-away *Boulder Weekly* continues to dig for local scandal and investigative stories, and specialty papers focusing on topics from business to natural healing to women fill the racks at coffeehouses.

Dailies

Colorado Daily
5505 Central Ave., Boulder
(303) 443–6272

Published since 1897, this free and informative paper continues to serve the university community and Boulder. It's published five days a week; with an extra-large weekend edition on Friday. In summer, it cuts back to two days a week. The paper covers local, regional, and national news with an opinionated style, plus sports and entertainment, and has a very vocal editorial and letters to the editor section. There are also classified advertisements. It's available on campus and at drop sites around town.

The Daily Camera, Boulder's oldest newspaper, fills the corner of 11th and Pearl Streets. The newspaper periodically flirts with the idea of moving part of its operation out of bustling downtown but has so far stayed put. PHOTO: LINDA CORNETT

Daily Camera
1048 Pearl St., Boulder
(303) 442–1202

The *Camera*, Boulder's only complete daily newspaper, provides local coverage of Boulder, neighboring towns, and Boulder County as well as some state news. Regular daily sections and pages present local, national, and international news, business news, and entertainment news. The *Camera*'s award-winning sports section is competitive with Denver dailies and covers local preps, CU, and Denver's professional teams and features special sections on skiing and the Bolder Boulder 10k race.

The *Sunday Camera* includes separate sections for business, lifestyles, and entertainment; a TV guide; color comics; newsfocus stories; local guest opinions; and *The New York Times* crossword puzzle. Among the weekday special-interest sections are "FIT," a weekly health and fitness tabloid aimed at women; "Business Plus"; a food section; "Discovery," a science and technology section; "Get Out," with local recreation information; and "Friday Magazine," covering entertainment in Boulder, Denver, and along the Front Range.

Camera writers, photographers, ads, sections, and the whole paper continue to win awards from various state and national organizations, although readers complain that the paper has lost much of its community savvy due to staff turnover.

Weekly

Boulder Weekly
690 S. Lashley Ln., Boulder
(303) 494–5511

Specializing in investigative news, and arts and entertainment, this edgy tabloid has columns, interviews with local people, plus entertainment news, a classified section and other special sections, and possibly the most adult ads of any paper in the county. The paper is free at numerous local drop sites.

Biweekly

Boulder County Business Report
4865 Sterling Dr., Ste. 200, Boulder
(303) 440–4950

This hefty biweekly newspaper is a leading information source on local and regional trends in real estate, high technology, finance, tourism, and business. A subscription is $29.97 per year in Colorado and Wyoming, and $39.97 in the rest of the country. Or you could just pick it up free at one of the 250 local drop sites.

Magazines

Boulder County Guide
P.O. Box 1075, Boulder, CO 80306
(303) 449–7433

Published annually, this free guide reproduces numerous local restaurant menus and offers information on shopping, services, and recreation, plus a professional directory. Look for it in local shops, bookstores, supermarkets, and other drop sites or visit the packed-with-information online version at guide. boulder.net.

Boulder Magazine
1919 14th St., Ste. 709, Boulder
(303) 443–0600

Published three times a year—summer, fall, and winter/spring—this handy guide has all kinds of local information and interesting articles on local people, places, and things to do. Subscriptions are $15 per year; individual issues are available for $5. The magazine is free at numerous local drop sites. Look for the glorious color photo cover.

Nexus: Colorado's Holistic Journal
1680 Sixth St., Suite 6, Boulder
(303) 442–6662, (888) 644–6662

For more than 20 years, *Nexus* has been devoting its tabloid-size magazine to information about holistic health and natural living "in Colorado and beyond."

Readers will be amazed at the variety of therapies available locally. *Nexus* is published six times a year and includes information on physical health, spirituality, alternative education, complementary medicine, and art. Its lovely color covers are produced by area artists and probably end up on many a reader's walls. Subscriptions are $21 per year (six issues), or pick up *Nexus* for free at 300 locations in health-food stores, bookstores, restaurants, shops, and universities around Boulder and Denver.

Radio Stations

The numerous Front Range radio stations whose broadcasts are received in Boulder are listed here, along with the more popular local stations. The quality of reception is very much dependent on where you are when you're listening (those pesky mountains, again).

Adult Alternative

KTCL 93.3 FM (Modern rock and new music)
KVCU 1190 AM (Independent music from all genres)

Insiders' Tip

Boulder's Community Broadcast Association, Inc., KGNU 88.5 FM, provides the real flavor of Boulder with all types of music, plus talk shows on environment, spirituality, alternative news, and a Grateful Dead Hour. Call (303) 449-4885 for a complete program.

Adult Contemporary

KOSI 101.1 FM
KXPK 96.5 FM

Big Band

KEZW 1430 AM (Nostalgia, Big Band, and easy listening)

Christian

KPOF 910 AM (Christian/talk)
KRKS 990 AM and 94.7 FM (Christian/talk)

Classical

KVOD 92.5 FM (Classical, public radio news)

Community

KGNU 88.5 FM in Boulder/Denver; 93.7 in Ward and the mountain regions (Pacifica, ethnic and world music, much attention to local affairs)

Country

KYGO 98.5 FM
KLMO 1060 AM (Country, Paul Harvey, and ABC News)
KCKK 104.3 FM

Jazz

KHIH 95.7 FM (Jazz, New Age)
KUVO 89.3 FM

News/Talk

KHOW 630 AM (News, local and syndicated talk)
KTLK 760 AM (Business and talk)
KVCU 1190 AM (student-run University of Colorado station)
KWAB 1490 AM (News, talk and opinion)

Oldies

KXKL (KOOL) 105.1 FM
KIMN 100.3 FM

So, you want to be a TV producer . . .

Or a camera-person, or an editor, or an on-air personality? Community Television of Boulder has a spot waiting for you.

The station—CATV, Channel 54, on the local cable line-up—provides training, equipment, and facilities so that citizens can use the digital soapbox to share a vision, a viewpoint, or an interesting slice of Boulder life. CATV studios are in the well-used Dairy Center for the Arts at 2590 Walnut Street (303-440-1000).

Boulder has actually had a community access channel and some equipment for several years. However, the earlier incarnation was in a space so cramped one producer complained that the dangling overhead light burned his hair as he worked. These days, CATV operates more like a real station, with adequate facilities and equipment, trained staff, and reliable funding from a franchise fee paid by AT&T, which provides cable service to the city.

Get started with the free orientation session, held at 5:30 P.M. Wednesdays, then sign up for one of the inexpensive monthly classes. The nine-hour Basic Video class teaches students to use a digital camcorder, microphones, and lighting kits. Next come Basic Editing, and then Basic Studio, where you'll learn how to handle those big, wheeled cameras that show up on your TV screen when Jay Leno wanders off-stage.

Then there you are—you're a producer, a camera-person, an editor, a talent. You're not alone, either. Since the facility opened in June 1996 more than 425 people have been trained. Classes are cheap ($30 each) but if even that is a pinch in the pocketbook, you can work off the cost with a couple of hours of volunteer work around the studio.

CATV provides free access to all the equipment you'll need to produce your oeuvre, but remember, it has to be noncommercial and community-oriented.

A good way to get started is to volunteer to help out with *This Week in Boulder*, a 30-minute collection of short pieces on local events, personalities, and issues. Because the time is shared, no one is burdened with filling a whole show (30 minutes is a very long time when you've run out of things to say), and it gives you a chance to brush up against experienced producers who can teach you a lot about the craft.

Or, if you absolutely, positively have to get something off your chest right now, walk on in and say you want to *Speak Out*. The simple format lets even novices air their views.

Public Radio

KCFR 90.1 FM (Colorado Public Radio, classical, National Public Radio, and local news)
KUNC 91.5 FM (Classical, jazz, oldies, new and alternative music)

Rock

KBCO 97.3 FM Boulder
KKHK 99.5 FM (Classic rock)
KRFX 103.5 FM (Classic rock)
KBPI 106.7 FM (Classic and progressive rock)

Sports

KOA 850 AM (News, talk, sports)
KKFN 950 AM (Sports/talk)

Top 40

KALC 105.9 FM (Alice)

Television Stations

Depending on the location in Boulder, antenna TV reception can be a bit fuzzy to completely nonexistent because of the mountains. Reception without cable is even worse in mountain towns such as Nederland. For this reason most area residents have cable.

Besides the broadcast stations listed below, there are more than 30 cable stations, including Channel 8, the City of Boulder station. The city channel has all types of programs on local issues, such as the environment, seniors, arts, city council meetings, Boulder Valley School Board meetings, sports, and leisure, and information programs on science, travel, and much more.

Channel 54 is Community Access TV of Boulder, with talk shows, performance, community interest and even local cooking programs. CATV offers inexpensive classes to train citizens to produce and edit their own videotapes for presentation on Channel 54. It also provides the audio for Radio Reading Services of the Rockies, which broadcasts audio versions of the *Daily Camera, Denver Rocky Mountain News, Denver Post,* and *Colorado Daily* newspapers, plus BBC News and local weather.

Broadcast Television Stations

KWGN Channel 2 (Independent/WB)
KCNC Channel 4 (CBS)
KRMA Channel 6 (PBS)
KMGH Channel 7 (ABC)
KUSA Channel 9 (NBC)
KBDI Channel 11/12 (Community/PBS)
KTVD Channel 20 (Independent/UPN)
KVDR Channel 31 (Independent/Fox)

Cable Television

There is only one cable supplier for Boulder: AT&T Broadband, (303–930–2000), which also offers the option of digital cable TV and digital cable Internet access. Warning: Be prepared to be shuffled all around the company's phone system before getting your questions answered; there is no central area where you can get information about all of the services. In eastern Boulder County, cable is provided by Comcast Communications, (303–776–6600). For mountain communities, there is Pagosa Vision, (303–258–0304) or Galaxy Cablevision (800–365–6988).

Worship

In the early part of this century, Boulderites often referred to their growing community as "the Athens of the West," and the city's willingness to embrace religious diversity is reflected in that lofty motto.

The Presbyterians were the first to bring worship services to what we now call the Boulder Valley, followed quickly by the Congregationalists, the Baptists, the Episcopalians, the Methodists, of the Roman Catholics. The church sanctuaries seemed large enough when built in the late 1800s, but with the country moving West, nearly all of the faiths quickly outgrew their modest worship halls and built larger churches. Architecturally impressive, many of the truly beautiful downtown Boulder churches were built with local materials.

Boulder is known, however, as much for its eclectic spirituality as its traditional religious offerings. An annual listing compiled by *Nexus*, Colorado's holistic journal, shows more than two dozen "unconventional" spiritual groups meet regularly. This metaphysical emphasis alongside the time-honored religious faiths is one of the best aspects of Boulder.

This chapter begins with some history and an overview of some current events involving Boulder's religious communities. It then describes worship centers located downtown—easy for both tourists and newcomers to reach. It ends by describing other groups that are part of the rich texture of Boulder worship.

From Pioneer Churches to the Gay-Rights Debates

In 1859 a Methodist circuit preacher delivered Boulder's first sermon to 50 people. Churches of other denominations followed, their spires leading pioneers across the prairie. The First Congregational Church, now site of the Carnegie Library on Pine Street, had Boulder's first full-time pastor, building, and church bell. A few churches of historical significance still stand. Longmont's **St. Stephen's Episcopal Church** at 470 Main Street (303–776–1072), was built in 1881. The building now houses the Polar Bear Art Gallery, and worship services are held at a newer and larger sanctuary, at 1303 S. Bross Lane, that is also called St. Stephen's Episcopal Church. Also in 1881, Colorado's original Swedish community built the **Swedish Evangelical Lutheran Church of Ryssby,** on 63rd Street south

of Nelson Road (303–776–2704). They styled it after traditional Swedish churches but built it with local sandstone. Members still hold special midsummer and Christmas ceremonies that include Scandinavian traditions. For the winter service, they decorate the simple chapel with evergreen boughs and candles that make halos on winter-frosted panes. The church is very popular for weddings, and the bride and groom often leave in a horse-drawn buggy. Another historic church is the **Lafayette Congregational Church** (303–665–4206). The plain white structure at 300 E. Simpson Street is currently home to the Mary Miller Theater.

If you enjoy religious history, check with **Historic Boulder,** at 646 Pearl Street (303–444–5192). This nonprofit group occasionally conducts tours of sacred places and sells a guidebook describing a self-guided tour (see our Attractions chapter for details). They also keep lists of historic buildings in which people may hold

367

weddings. The vista from the Flagstaff Mountain Amphitheater, for example makes it a favored wedding site. Boulder's proximity to the foothills, with easy access to nature trails, has created many special places for people to explore their spirituality without manmade structures or traditional ceremonies.

But worship is about more than creating, or finding, special places. **The First Congregational Church** was Boulder's first church. At the dedication ceremony in 1870, the minister encouraged his parishioners to attend every Sunday, but admonished them to "leave the tobacco at home!" Church members helped raise funds to bring CU to town, and for many years, its ministers taught philosophy at the new university. Grandma Dartt was a Seventh-day Adventist who trudged through young Boulder's saloons, distributing temperance tracts and religious information. In 1895, the Seventh-day Adventists began building a tuberculosis sanatorium where Mapleton Avenue heads up Sunshine Canyon. A popular hiking trail, Mount Sanitas Trail, is named after the health center, and the Mapleton Rehabilitation Clinic stands there today. The **Seventh-day Adventist Church** is nearby at 345 Mapleton Avenue (303–442–1522).

If many of Boulder's worship halls were built with sandstone, then their souls are built of wood, tin, lead, and iron. The pipe organs at many of the downtown churches were crafted with loving care and pinched pennies. The three-manual Casavant organ at First Presbyterian is often played for Bach concerts. The Roosevelt organ at First United Methodist sat unused at a Denver church before it was moved to Boulder. By far the largest church organ in the city is enjoyed by parishioners at the First Congregational Church, but even this instrument pales in comparison to the giant at Macky Auditorium on the CU campus. Built in 1923 from contributions by Boulder citizens, the 100-rank organ is housed under the stage and would cost at least $1.5 million to replace. Other notable downtown church organs include the Austin at St. John's Episcopal Church, the hand-built pipe organ at Trinity Lutheran, and the three-manual McManis organ at the First Baptist Church.

The issue of the separation of church and state crops up periodically in this city. During the 1960s the State Board of Education backed religious and civic groups that asked that schools refrain from Christmas pageants. These days, schoolkids may sing songs from many religions at "winter festivals," and the focus is on informing people about various faiths. Still, seemingly small events create a large furor where issues of church and state are concerned. Before Christmas 1995, a big fuss developed after people started hanging little angel ornaments from a tree on public land, and the following spring, law enforcement officials were taken to task for marking sites of fatal vehicular accidents with white crosses as part of a safety awareness campaign.

The **Interfaith Council** (303–442–1787) embodies Boulder's nonsectarian spirit. Its members represent many of the world's major religions. The group includes approximately 40 of Boulder's

Insiders' Tip

The Swedish Evengelical Lutheran Church is all that's left of what was once the town of Ryssby, founded in 1869 by settlers from Ryssby, Sweden. The name refers to a clearing in the forest. The small chapel is now popular for weddings and is decorated for Christmas services.

hundreds of religious communities—Protestant and Catholic churches, synagogues, mosques, and Buddhist and Baha'i worship centers. The Interfaith Council has helped establish the Boulder Shelter for the Homeless, Share-a-Gift the Community Table, and the Boulder Change Program. In 2000 there was an interfaith dialogue on the issue of peace in the Middle East, followed by a piano and violin concert performed by an Israeli Jew and an Israeli Arab. The council also grapples with social issues such as giving women more choices in church leadership and alleviating hunger.

Although no longer based in Boulder, another group with a controversial history is the **Promise Keepers** (303-964-7600, in Denver), founded in 1990 by former CU-Boulder football coach Bill McCartney. With friends, he organized the Promise Keepers as a "Christ-centered ministry, dedicated to uniting men through vital relationships to become Godly influences in their world." Members follow conservative evangelical Christian and Catholic teachings. Gatherings initially held on the CU-Boulder campus are now held nationwide. In 1997 more than 600,000 men gathered on the Mall in Washington, D.C., for a Promise Keepers' rally that was one of the largest religious gatherings in U.S. history. A conference was held in Denver in 2000. Go to www.promisekeepers.org for the most up-to-date information on upcoming conferences.

Worship Centers

Newcomers should check the *Daily Camera's* Saturday religion calendar. The variety of offerings will meet nearly everyone's spiritual needs or desire for spiritual exploration.

Near the Pearl Street Mall

It's no surprise that most of Boulder's oldest—and many of the largest—houses of worship are downtown, within walking distance of the Pearl Street Mall, which has been the civic center of town for a long time. The following is just a sampling of the worship centers downtown.

First Presbyterian, at 1820 15th Street (303-402-6400), has an estimated 2,400 members, with 2,000 attending Sunday services. The original sanctuary celebrated its 100th year in 1995. A major renovation in 1998 added nearly 300 new seats in the main chapel and a 30,000-square-foot children's wing. Members describe it as a reformed, evangelical church with a big, warm congregation. It has large teen, singles, and college groups plus other smaller groups. The church provides space for performances by local music groups, such as the Boulder Bach Festival, the Boulder Chorale, and student groups. It offers a weekly preschool, summer camps, snow camps, and weekly school programs in everything from crafts and cooking to family conflict resolution.

Sacred Heart of Jesus, at 2312 14th Street (303-442-6158), is a Roman Catholic church with more than 1,200 registered households and lots of people who drop in. Sacred Heart School, across the street, is affiliated with the parish (see our Childcare and Education chapter). The large community-outreach program includes a lunch program for transients and distribution of food baskets. The church offers daily masses in English and a weekly Spanish mass.

Karma Dzong Shambhala Center, at 1345 Spruce Street (303-444-0190), is a center for Tibetan Buddhism called "Vajrayana," which translates as "diamond vehicle." The center includes 600 adult members, making it one of the largest communities of practicing Tibetan Buddhists in the West. The top floor, a shrine room, is full of traditional Tibetan red and gold. People are welcome to drop by in the afternoon. Every Sunday morning, there's a 10:30 open house that includes a talk on Buddhism, meditation, and a question-and-answer session. Members say that although Buddhism may sound exotic, it's very ordinary; it's about living your life well, with compassion and wisdom.

St. John's, at 1419 Pine Street (303–442–5246), is a traditional Episcopal Church with very contemporary sensibilities. Among Boulder Episcopalian churches, it's the only "AIDS-aware faith community"—and is one of the few such communities of any denomination. The congregation, which now numbers about 1,000, was founded in 1873 and is one of the oldest in town. The present church, where the big Messiah Sing-along happens each December (see our Festivals and Annual Events chapter), dates back to 1902.

The **First Baptist Church,** at 1237 Pine Street (303–442–6530), was founded in 1872, making it another one of the oldest churches in town. With more than 250 members, it is known for its Chancel Choir and Handbell Choir, which present concerts and cantatas.

First United Methodist Church is at 1421 Spruce Street (303–442–3770). The **Christian Science Reading Room** is on the Pearl Street Mall, at 1434 Pearl Street (303–442–0335). It is an extension of the **Church of Christ Science,** nearby at 2243 13th Street (303–444–1770). The **First Congregational Church,** at 1128 Pine Street (303–442–1787), across from the original Congregational church site, is a medium-size, liberal church with about 850 members. On the opposite corner is **Trinity Lutheran Church-ELCA,** at 2200 Broadway (303–442–2300).

The **Unitarian Universalist Church,** at 5001 Pennsylvania Avenue (303–494–0195), mirrors Boulder's liberalism. The church welcomes people of all races, ages, abilities, sexual orientations, cultures and religious backgrounds to its adult services and children's classes.

VineLife Community Church, at 7845 Lookout Road in Niwot (303–449–3330), is a nondenominational/evangelical/charismatic church started in 1982. More than 1,000 people attend Sunday services, which often include contemporary Christian music, lively sermons, and homey, inspirational stories. Teaching Biblical insights and positive family-raising skills are important parts of the ministry, and the church prides itself on its active and involved children's and youth ministry as well.

The **Boulder Valley Christian Church,** at 7100 South Boulder Road (303–494–7748), is an independent evangelical Christian church with 500 members. Christmas and Easter music programs are popular events.

Unity of Boulder, at 2855 Folsom Avenue (303–442–1411), is a New Age, Christian church. It has grown considerably since 1975, when minister Jack Groverland came to town. He's a dynamic speaker, and sermons are full of both laughter and seriousness. The Unity newsletter goes out to 2,600 people, and 1,000 people attend two different Sunday services. Nearly 3,000 people have taken the church's Course in Miracles, a year-long class that starts each quarter. Unity puts on a professional-quality Christmas play that is both entertaining and enlightening, thanks to the great singing, music, philosophical and religious themes, and humor. The church offers both Sunday school and a summer day camp called Angel Camp. The church houses a metaphysical bookstore and gift shop.

Camp St. Malo, a Catholic conference facility at 10758 Colo. 7, near Allenspark (303-444-5177), is where Pope John Paul II rested on his 1993 trip through Colorado. St. Catherine's, better known as the "Chapel on the Rock," is at the same location. During the summer, it is open to the public, with Sunday masses occasionally held from Memorial Day to Labor Day.

The Sacred Heart of Mary, at 6739 South Boulder Road (303-494-7572), was built in 1873 and is the oldest Catholic church in Boulder County. It started as a Prairie Church and still has an old cemetery in the back. Its priest describes it as a progressive, medium-size congregation with about 700 families, meeting in a beautiful church. The church offers classes in adult education and centering prayer. Drop-ins are welcome at daily mass.

For many years the Benedictine Catholic Abbey of St. Walburga was located next door to Sacred Heart of Mary. Due to growing development and traffic in this once-tranquil area, the Abbey moved in 1996 to a quieter location in Larimer County, at 32109 N. U.S. 287, Virginia Dale (970-472-0612). The Abbey is now home to a private secondary school.

Around 8 percent of the Boulder population is Jewish, according to Allied Jewish Federation surveys. The Jewish community is very active in civic and local affairs. Area synagogues include Bonai Shalom, 1527 Cherryvale Road (303-442-6605), a conservative synagogue of nearly 150 households, nestled near a pretty stream, and Har Hashem, 3950 Baseline Road (303-499-7077), a reform congregation with more than 400 families. Both offer programs for youths, singles, and families, and Hebrew school education. In 1998, Har Hashem built a beautiful new sanctuary and seven new children's classrooms to accommodate its growing membership. The Jewish Renewal Community of Boulder (303-271-3540) is part of an international cross-denominational movement. Approximately 150 members meet for services in members' homes and also hold monthly community Shabbats.

The Second Baptist Church of Boulder, 5300 Baseline Road (303-499-4668), has 300 members and a great musical presence. The Community Choir is open to any church member who likes to sing; the church also has a Men's Chorus; and Angels Without Wings, a chorus for children ages 3 to 13. The Shekinah Glory Choir is a young adult choir of superb voices that has performed all around the Denver area. Boulder Meeting of Friends (303-447-2168), a Quaker group, gathers at 1825 Upland Avenue for Sunday morning meetings. The Boulder Mennonite Church, at 1520 Euclid Avenue (303-443-3889), has a strong emphasis on family, service, and faithful daily living. It founded the Victim-Offender Reconciliation Program, in which volunteers are trained to mediate in the community court system in property-related teen offenses. The Islamic Center of Boulder is at 1530 Culver Court (303-444-6345).

The Jesusonian Foundation, at 4699 Nautilus Court S., #304 (303-581-0456), sells Urantia Books and secondary works. Urantia study groups have approximately 100 members. Mo Seigel, president of Celestial Seasonings, was instrumental in forming the Jesusonian Foundation, which is not a religion, but rather "encourages individuals to live the gospel of Jesus through service."

In Boulder many choices are also available for those who wish to explore their spirituality either through self-examination or meditation. The **Shoshoni Yoga Retreat,** 21614 Colo. 119 (303–642–0116), has log cabins, massage and health therapy rooms, and hiking trails. Many come to practice yoga or meditation or for spiritual renewal. Shoshoni members who founded Rudi's Restaurant, a well-regarded natural-food restaurant, have published a vegetarian cookbook, *The Shoshoni Cookbook.* **Dances of Universal Peace** (303–440–5714) offers attendees a chance to learn key phrases and gestures from many different religions through participatory song and dance. **Followers of Baha'i,** 437 Pine Street (303–443–6422), have been meeting in Boulder for more than 20 years. The **Ridhwan Foundation,** 5869 Marshall Drive (303–447–0025), teaches the "Diamond Approach" and has 250 local members. Members of the **Gurdjieff Foundation** (303–554–8120) meet regularly to study

and practice the teachings of G. I. Gurdjieff. **Followers of Eckankar,** 1800 30th Street, Ste. 208 (303–443–1610), meet monthly for classes and book discussions. **The Church of Gaia,** 8563 Flagstaff Road (303–443–1096), is an Earth-centered church offering training in such Native American traditions as sweat lodges, pipe circles, vision quests, and other ceremonies. Those interested in learning more about Native American worship can also find programs at the 20-year-old **Naropa Institute** at 2130 Arapahoe Avenue (303–444–0202; also see our Childcare and Education chapter). The **Society for the Greater Community Way of Knowledge** (303–938–8401) teaches how to live with certainty, strength, and wisdom in an emerging world.

CU-Boulder also has a Department of Religious Studies (303–492–8041) and offers ethics classes through the Philosophy Department (303–492–6132).

Rocky Mountain National Park

A trip over Trail Ridge Road in Rocky Mountain National Park is a peak experience, literally. The nation's highest mountains, sparkling lakes and streams, abundant wildlife, and stunning wildflowers will leave visitors breathless from both the beauty and the altitude.

Trail Ridge Road transports visitors to a world of different life zones, climates, and vegetation—a trip comparable to driving more than 2,500 miles from Denver to Fairbanks, Alaska. But this world is compressed into just a 50-mile drive over the highest continuous highway in the United States, following the path etched by generations of Native Americans. Trail Ridge Road is one of the few paved roads in the world where a doctor's permission is recommended for those with medical problems. Every 300 feet of elevation equals one degree of latitude or 70 stature miles north. The road provides stunning views of peaks with memorable names—Never Summer Mountains, Mummy Mountain, Lumpy Ridge, Storm Peak, Chief's Head Peak, Isolation Peak, Twin Sisters. Keep your camera handy for the many scenic pullouts. If you ever contemplated investing in a wide-angle lens, this is the trip to make it worthwhile.

From spectacular vistas of endless snowy peaks to tiny, gem-like flowers that grow high above the tree line (one-third of the park's 415 square miles is above this level), Rocky Mountain National Park is without a doubt one of the nation's—and the world's—treasures.

You're almost sure to see grazing deer and elk and, if you're lucky, maybe some Rocky Mountain bighorn sheep, the park's symbol. Above timberline by boulder fields, listen for the whistle of the pikas—cute, furry animals that look like rodents but are related to rabbits. You may spot a yellow-bellied marmot, a large rodent similar to a groundhog, sunning on a rock. Gray jays or spiffy black-trimmed Clark's nutcracker birds will swoop down looking for handouts (but don't feed them, it's illegal and not good for them). It is rare to encounter bears and mountain lions since they are wary of humans; if such a meeting should occur, remember to stand tall, back away slowly, and whatever you do, don't turn and run.

Leave the crowded roadsides, walk a mile or two along one of the park's 346 miles of trails, and you'll begin to feel like one of the first humans ever to set eyes on this beautiful wilderness area.

History

As with the rest of Colorado, the first humans wandered through the area that is now Rocky Mountain National Park some 10,000 to 12,000 years ago. Part of what is now the park's Trail Ridge Road was once part of the Ute Trail, a major route across the mountains for American Indians.

The first Europeans who visited the area were French fur traders collecting animal pelts. The area became U.S. territory in 1803 as part of the Louisiana Purchase. Mineral deposits in the area proved unproductive, so there was never great mining activity.

Because of the astounding beauty, the area was destined to be a tourist attraction from its earliest days. For centuries,

American Indians had visited the area and considered it sacred. Braves visited the area west of present-day Estes Park for vision quests and supposedly climbed Longs Peak to trap bald eagles for their feathers. By the time the settlers arrived, the Ute, having driven out the Arapaho, occupied the area.

After chasing the California Gold Rush in 1849, Joel Estes came looking for Colorado gold in 1859. Estes and his family homesteaded a beautiful parklike valley in 1860. Other settlers arrived slowly to try ranching and farming at elevations below 9,000 feet. Indian agent and soldier Kit Carson built a cabin on the eastern edge of the park in Tahosa Valley.

More visitors began arriving in 1864, determined to meet the challenge of climbing Longs Peak, northern Colorado's highest mountain. William Byers, who was editor of the *Rocky Mountain News* in Denver, was one of the early climbers. He and two friends stayed with the Estes family when they made their attempt at the climb. Although they were unsuccessful, Byers went back to Denver and wrote glowing accounts of the area, calling it Estes Park after his host. In 1868 Byers returned with Major John Wesley Powell (the renowned one-armed explorer of the Colorado River and Grand Canyon), and the two made the first recorded climb to the summit of Longs Peak. Byers wrote another story about Longs Peak and Estes Park, attracting more tourists, hunters, and adventure seekers. Around the area, settlers were finding a good income by housing the increasing number of tourists in their cabins. Later they began building rustic lodges (and even a nine-hole golf course). These lodges eventually evolved into dude ranches, which were popular in the early 20th century.

Had he stayed, Joel Estes might have become one of the richest men in the area, but the long, snowy winter of 1866 did him in. Later that year Estes sold off his claim and cattle for a yoke of oxen and headed south. Griffith Evans bought the Estes homestead, which he operated as a makeshift hostel until he added some cab-

ins and opened a full-scale dude ranch in 1871.

By the 1870s, the area was becoming known around the world for its spectacular scenery. British writer and world traveler Isabella Bird visited the area in 1873 and stayed at the Evans ranch. Her adventures and travels in the area were published in 1879 in the extremely popular book, *A Lady's Life in the Rocky Mountains*. By 1882 the book was in its seventh edition; it's still a best seller at the park gift shops.

Lord Dunraven (the Fourth Earl of Dunraven, Viscount of Mount Earl and Adare) also visited the Evans ranch. It was common for European gentry to visit the United States, and this Irish nobleman and avid hunter liked Estes Park so much that he secretly acquired more than 15,000 acres through third-party purchases and other under-the-table deals, as it was illegal for foreigners to homestead. He then created a private hunting sanctuary for himself and his European hunting cronies. The earl even announced in the *Rocky Mountain News* that "admission to Estes Park, his game preserve, was by invitation only." But eventually the area's beauty defeated even the earl, because it attracted many others who disputed the legality of his claims.

Meanwhile, in 1876, Lord Dunraven invited Western landscape painter Albert Bierstadt to Estes Park to capture its beauty on canvas and to help the earl select a spot for his English Hotel. A lake and moraine in the park are named for the painter, whose exhibited works attracted even more attention—and tourists—to the area.

At his English Hotel near Lake Estes, Dunraven entertained such guests as Buffalo Bill Cody, Kit Carson, Gen. William Tecumseh Sherman, and other notables in the early 1880s. Initially it catered mainly to foreign clientele—the earl's hunting buddies. Its name was later changed to the Estes Park Hotel, which operated until it burned to the ground in 1911.

Settlers continued to homestead and began contesting the earl's land claims.

Dunraven eventually leased the land to ranchers and left. Failing to establish exclusive rights to the preserve and challenged about the legality of his claim, Dunraven stopped visiting Estes Park in 1881. He leased his land and hotel to Theodore Whyte, his property manager, and in 1904 the land was purchased by well-known inventor Freelan O. Stanley (inventor of the Stanley Steamer). Diagnosed with tuberculosis, Stanley, like many of his time, came to be cured in the dry mountain air (and eventually was restored to good health).

In 1905 the town of Estes Park was platted at the confluence of the Fall and Big Thompson Rivers on land sold by John Cleave. Like many locals, Cleave said he "couldn't stand to see the danged place overrun by tenderfeet tourists," so he moved away.

Construction in Estes Park came from logging operations in Hidden Valley, Hollowell Park, and Wild Basin. On the western side of the park, the Kawuneeche Valley, other logging operations provided materials to build dude ranches and develop Grand Lake village, west of the Continental Divide from Estes Park.

Designation of Rocky Mountain National Park

The ever-growing tourism prevalent by the early 1900s and use of the area by individuals and businesses raised concern among residents about preserving the area's pristine beauty.

In 1905 President Theodore Roosevelt had added the area as part of the new national forest system, but many felt that greater protection and preservation were needed, among them H. M. Wheeler, who had opened a national forest office in Estes Park in 1907. Wheeler suggested creating a "wildlife reserve" in the nearby mountains. Enos A. Mills, a 20-year resident of Estes Park and a naturalist, writer, conservationist, and innkeeper, helped promote the park even further. Around 1909 Mills began campaigning to preserve

the area. Other citizens joined Mills, among them the well-known Stanley. The group formed the Estes Park Protective and Improvement Association to protect and preserve the area's scenery and wildlife.

Mills was so eloquent that President Roosevelt commissioned him to tour the country promoting the preservation of wild lands. The national park concept was first formalized in 1872 when designated Yellowstone as the first national park. The stated objectives of national parks were first to preserve natural and historical objects including wildlife, scenery, and ecosystems, and second to promote the enjoyment of these resources by the public.

Finally, in 1915, after years of debate on the size and boundaries of the park, President Woodrow Wilson signed a bill passed by Congress making Rocky Mountain National Park the nation's 10th national park. The new park encompassed 415 square miles of forest, aspen groves, alpine tundra, rich wetlands, and 76 peaks soaring above 12,000 feet. Soon after, the first park superintendent was installed, and rangers were hired to enforce the new restrictions on hunting and cattle grazing.

During the next decades, evidence of human settlement in the park, such as the briefly booming silver mining town called Lulu City in the late 1870s, was removed, and natural vegetation was painstakingly restored.

In 1975 Rocky Mountain National Park was named the 21st biosphere reserve in the world. The biosphere reserve system was established by the United Nations Man and Biosphere Programme to observe and monitor changes in natural ecosystems, especially those resulting from human activities. There are more than 320 biosphere reserves worldwide in 80 countries.

Since 1974, Congress has been pondering a recommendation by then-President Richard Nixon that 239,835 acres of the park be designated as wilderness, prohibiting expansion of roads and buildings in that area; the designation would not affect

From the high and windy Alpine Visitor Center, the view is vast. A telescope helps visitors focus in on the minute. PHOTO: LINDA CORNETT

current activities in the park. Although the designation has not yet been made, National Park Service policy requires that the park be managed as a wilderness until Congress takes action. In 1980, 2,917 acres of the Indian Peaks Wilderness Area were added to Rocky Mountain National Park. Meanwhile, a backcountry/wilderness plan is being prepared to guide park staff in protecting the park from human impact. For more information, write to Wilderness Planning, Rocky Mountain National Park, Estes Park, CO 80517.

Visitor Centers

Perhaps the park's early promoters and protectors realized how popular it would become. Today, more than 3 million visitors come to Rocky Mountain National Park every year. Six visitor centers at the park accommodate this yearly crush of humanity.

The **Beaver Meadows Visitor Center** is 2.5 miles west of Estes Park on U.S. Highway 36 and is open daily year-round. Call the staff at (970) 586–1206 for weather, camping, and other specific information, call (970) 586–1333 for a recorded message; those with hearing impairments can call (970) 586–1319. An orientation film of the park is shown on the half-hour. There are Saturday evening programs at 7 P.M. the rest of the year. Nightly programs are offered from mid-June to mid-August, beginning at 7:30 P.M.

On the west entrance to the park, the **Kawuneeche Visitor Center** (970–627–3471) sits 1.3 miles north of Grand Lake on U.S. Highway 34, and is also open daily year-round. Programs are presented at 7 P.M. each Saturday from mid-June to mid-August. Fall, winter, and spring Saturday evening programs are offered the second Saturday of each month at 7 P.M.

The **Moraine Park Museum** lies 5 miles west of Estes Park on Bear Lake

Road and is open daily from mid-May to Labor Day. You'll find ranger-led programs and a .3-mile nature walk beginning at the center.

Fall River Visitors' Center is on U.S. Rt. 34, 5 miles west of Estes Park, at the Fall River entrance to the park. It is open April through October and, in addition to wildlife exhibits, has a Discovery Room where children can dress up as firefighters or old-time rangers.

Most spectacularly situated of all is the **Alpine Visitor Center** at 11,796 feet atop Trail Ridge Road. It is 25 miles west of Estes Park and is open daily from June through September, weather permitting. Next door, a park concessionaire operates Trail Ridge Store and a snack bar, where diners can enjoy a simple meal along with a panoramic view. Call the main park number (970–586–1206) for information about the Alpine Visitor Center.

Lily Lake Visitor Center, 6 miles south of Estes Park on Colo. 7, is open daily from June to Labor Day, depending upon snow conditions, and open weekends during May and September. There is a wheelchair–accessible trail around the nearby lake.

Besides providing education about the park's different ecosystems, plus maps and directions, the centers remind visitors of the park's regulations:

1. No pets are allowed on trails or away from roadways. Pets must be leashed at all times.

2. Feeding or touching wild animals is prohibited, along with hunting or harassment of wildlife. This includes stalking wild animals for photographs, which frightens them and makes them less viewable for other visitors.

3. Picking wildflowers or plants is prohibited. Removing, disturbing, damaging, or destroying natural features, including rocks and pinecones, is illegal.

4. Fishing requires a valid Colorado state fishing license. Only artificial lures may be used (but children 12 years of age and younger may use bait, in open waters only).

5. Camping is restricted to designated areas.

6. A permit is required for all overnight stays in the backcountry. There are restrictions on the use of pack animals.

7. Gathering firewood is prohibited. Fires may be built only in picnic areas and campsites with grates. Either bring your own wood or ask at the ranger stations or park headquarters about purchasing some.

8. Vehicles must remain on roads or in parking areas. Parking any vehicle or leaving property unattended for more than 24 hours without prior permission is prohibited.

9. Hitchhiking is prohibited.

10. Trail bikes, snowmobiles, and all other vehicles are restricted to roads. Snowmobiles are permitted only on the west side of the park.

11. Firearms are to be kept unloaded.

12. All your own trash must be removed from picnic areas and campsites and disposed of in trash cans and recycling receptacles.

13. Having open containers of alcoholic beverages in a vehicle on Park roads and in parking areas is illegal.

Entrance to the park is $15 per vehicle and $5 for walk-ins and bicyclists; passes are good for a week. An annual pass to Rocky Mountain National Park costs $30, and an annual pass to all national parks is $50.

Recreation

Bicycling

Bicycling in the park is allowed only on roads, and these are heavily used by cars. Since the roads climb from about 9,000 feet to more than 12,000 feet, riding is quite strenuous throughout. No off-road or mountain biking is allowed on any of the trails.

For a challenging ride on a dirt road, follow Old Fall River Road, the first auto route over the Continental Divide, which is described by park officials as a "motor nature trail." You'll be sharing the road with vehicles as it climbs 9.4 miles before joining Trail Ridge Road at the summit of 11,796-foot Old Fall River Pass (see more information under "Driving," below). Old Fall River Road is one-way uphill—for cars and bicycles. Plan to ride down Trail Ridge Road.

Bicycling over 50-mile-long Trail Ridge Road is only for the fittest of the fit, and even they will want to spend the night on the other side at Grand Lake before returning. Trail Ridge Road crosses the Continental Divide, and at its highest point is 12,183 feet, making it one of the world's most spectacular bike rides. But this road, too, is heavily traveled by cars.

Bear Lake Road is a strenuous 10-mile climb of 1,500 feet from the Beaver Meadows Entrance Station to Bear Lake at 9,475 feet.

Remember that you will be riding at a high altitude and be prepared for early afternoon thunderstorms, cold temperatures, icy roads, and thin, thin air.

Camping

To reduce the impact on the park, car camping is allowed only in five roadside campgrounds. Camping reservations can be made five months in advance for individuals and groups at three of the campgrounds, and campgrounds are frequently packed full from mid-June to mid-August, so plan ahead. The maximum stay in the park is seven days during summer and 14 days during winter (only Moraine Park, Timber Creek, and Longs Peak campgrounds are open year-round). At Longs Peak Campground, the limit is three days, and only tents are allowed. Although they can't go on trails with you, pets are allowed in campgrounds (leashed at all times). Reservations can be made online at reservations.nps.gov/index.cfm or by calling (800) 365–CAMP.

Permits are required for all backcountry camping; call the Backcountry Office at (970) 586–1242; there is a $16 a night fee for individual campsites, $30 for group

A relief map at the Estes Park entrance helps visitors grasp the scale of Rocky Mountain National Park.
PHOTO: LINDA CORNETT

camping (at Glacier Basin only). The fee is $10 in off-peak months, when water is turned off.

Remember, you are bedding down in someone else's home; make sure all food is stored in airtight containers in the trunk of your car or suspended high in a tree if you are in the backcountry to avoid a midnight visit from a black bear.

The campgrounds listed below offer a great way to enjoy the park at close range. There are no electrical, water, or sewer connections in any of the campgrounds. Sewer dumping stations are located at Moraine Park, Glacier Basin, and Timber Creek campgrounds. Public telephones are located at Moraine Park, Glacier Basin, Timber Creek, and Aspen Glen. For general information about the park and specific information on recreation, rentals, campgrounds, or even ticks, call the public information office at (970) 586-1206. For emergencies, call (970) 586-1399 or 911.

Aspenglen: Aspenglen is open mid-May through late September on a first come, first served basis. It is located immediately inside the Fall River entrance of the park and has 54 sites for tents, motor homes, or recreational vehicles. The water is turned on in mid-May and turned off in late September.

Glacier Basin: Located 9 miles from Park Headquarters off U.S. Highway 36 on Bear Lake Road, this campground has 152 sites. Reservations are required. The site accommodates tents and recreational vehicles (it has dump stations, but, like all the park's campgrounds, no hookups). The season is from early June through Labor Day.

Group Sites: The park has 15 group sites in Glacier Basin (see above for location) that accommodate groups of 10 to 50 people. They are open early June through Labor Day, with water turned on and off the same times. Dump stations are provided, and there is a public phone. The fees range from $30 to $60, depending on the size of the group. Reservations are required and can be made by calling (800) 365-CAMP, ext. 2267, up to three months in advance. All other times, sites are available on a first come, first served basis at Moraine Park Campground.

Longs Peak: This smaller campground is 11 miles south of Estes Park and a mile west on Colo. 7. It offers 26 tent campsites (no RVs or motor homes) on a first come, first served basis. It's open all year, with water turned on in mid-May and turned off mid-September.

Moraine Park: The park's largest campground, Moraine Park has 250 sites and is located 3 miles west of Park Headquarters off Bear Lake Road. It's open all year and accommodates recreational vehicles and tents. Water is turned on in mid-May and turned off mid-September. Reservations are required Memorial Day through Labor Day.

Sprague Lake Handicamp: This campsite is designed to accommodate visitors with disabilities. From the campsite parking area 7 miles from Park Headquarters, a half-mile wheelchair-accessible nature trail leads to the tent campground for a maximum of 10 people and 5 wheelchairs. There is a three-night limit. For reservations, contact the park at (970) 586-1242.

Timber Creek: Also open all year, Timber Creek is 10 miles north of the Grand Lake entrance to the park and has 100 sites accommodating tents and recreational vehicles. Water is turned on in early June and off in mid-September. The campground operates on a first come, first served basis, with no reservations.

Climbing

The park's climbing challenges are renowned and unlimited. The famous 900-foot Diamond cliff is ranked as one of the top 10 best rock climbs in the world. The diamond-shape granite wall sits atop the east face of Longs Peak—every inch of the sheer face is above 13,000 feet. More than 35 climbing routes challenge the most adventurous climbers.

As with other activities in the park, low-impact techniques are emphasized—motorized drills are prohibited, and climbers are urged to use brown chalk, neutral-colored

amidst the eerie, gnarled krummholz—wind-sculpted trees (Krummholz means "crooked wood" in German)—and up to the alpine tundra above the tree line, comparable to being in the Arctic Circle.

Depending upon weather conditions, the road is generally open from Memorial Day until mid-October. Allow three or four hours for this scenic drive, with stops at the numerous overlooks for stupendous vistas of glacier-carved peaks, snowfields, and cirques, and perhaps a snack at the Alpine Visitor Center on top. Take the short half-hour round-trip Tundra Walk to see the tiny delicate flowers that have adapted to this harsh environment, some of the 900 species of flora found in the park. Be sure to stay on paths because the alpine tundra is fragile and some of the flora is extinct outside the park.

The Bear Lake Road makes another scenic drive, leading to a lovely high mountain basin. Traffic during summer months through the park is quite heavy. A shuttle bus runs in the Moraine Park and Bear Lake areas during the peak summer season—June through Labor Day. Parking lots at Bear Lake and Glacier Gorge Junction will be full between 10 A.M. and 3 P.M. on summer days, so plan accordingly.

Old Fall River Road runs from Horseshoe Park Junction to Fall River Pass. Expect a leisurely pace on the 15-mile-per-hour road as it runs one-way uphill west of Endovalley Picnic Area. A gravel road with many switchbacks, it gives visitors an idea of early travel across the mountains, since it was the first road over the Divide in northern Colorado. A guide booklet is available at the visitor centers describing interesting sights along the way. You can make a loop up Old Fall River Road and return on Trail Ridge Road. Old Fall River Road is west of Estes Park on U.S. Highway 34 at the Fall River Entrance Station. The road is paved for the first 2 miles from the entrance. Take note of the alluvial fan along the way, caused by a flood in 1982. RVs and trailers are not allowed on Fall River Road because of the narrow switchbacks. The road is closed in winter.

webbing, and to follow established routes. Those staying overnight may not build fires and must remove all debris to keep the area pristine for the wild things that live there and other humans who visit. Registration is not required for technical climbers, but be sure to tell a reliable friend or relative of your climbing plans, should you be overdue. If you prefer both feet on the ground, you might catch a glimpse of technical climbers practicing their skills on Lumpy Ridge just north of Estes Park.

Registration is required for overnight bivouacs, and $15 permits are available at Park Headquarters, the West Unit Office, and at most ranger stations for the 269 backcountry sites. Advance reservations are a good idea; call the Backcountry Office at (970) 586-1242 or write to the Backcountry Office, Rocky Mountain National Park, Estes Park, CO 80517.

Driving

The main park drive, Trail Ridge Road, is the highest continuous highway in the United States. It runs 50 miles from Estes Park to Grand Lake over the Continental Divide and was built in 1932. The road climbs through the evergreen forests

Driving Tips

1. There are no service stations in the park. Enter with a full tank of gas.

2. Observe posted speed limits—roads are narrow, winding and heavily used.

3. Travel in early morning or late afternoon. Wildlife is more active at these times, and the light is more beautiful. At midday, traffic can be bumper to bumper.

4. Downshift to lower gears when going up or down steep grades. This will reduce engine stress and keep your brakes from burning out. Manually downshift automatic transmissions. Go down hills in a lower gear than you use to go up.

5. Tap brakes gently and repeatedly on downhills to reduce brake wear and possible overheating (or failure).

6. Be sure to look first and signal at turnouts and parking areas. Watch for oncoming traffic. Sound the horn on blind corners to alert oncoming drivers, if necessary.

7. When you stop, always set the emergency brake, and park in gear if you have manual transmission.

8. Lock your car when unattended; place valuables out of sight or take them with you.

9. Stay in your own lane. Don't drive in the middle to avoid being near the edge. The roads were designed with plenty of room, and you'll only cause an accident by driving down the center.

10. Don't be surprised if your car doesn't perform normally at high altitudes. Cars tuned for lower elevations may overheat or act as though they're not getting enough gas. Drive in a lower-than-usual gear to keep RPMs up and to avoid overheating. Don't pump the accelerator, as it will cause flooding and make matters worse. On warm days some cars may get vapor lock in the fuel line. If this occurs, try to get the car off the road at the nearest pullout. Stop the engine and allow it to cool. If there is snow or cold water nearby, put it on the fuel pump and the line leading to the carburetor. Let the car cool for 15 minutes before trying to start it again.

Fishing

Fly fishers will find four species of trout in the mountain streams and lakes of the park: German brown, rainbow, brook, and cutthroat. The only trout native to the park are the greenback cutthroat and the Colorado River cutthroat; the others were stocked by early settlers and spread throughout the region.

Valid Colorado fishing licenses are required for anglers 16 and older for all fishing in the park; use of live bait is prohibited except for children 12 and younger. See the fishing regulations at Park Headquarters, one of the ranger stations, or the "Fishing" section in our Boulder Sports chapter. No fishing is allowed in Bear Lake, and some lakes and streams on the east side of the park are closed to protect the greenback cutthroat trout, which is being reintroduced to its native habitat.

Only 48 of the Park's 156 lakes have reproducing populations of fish. Cold temperatures and lack of spawning habitat make high-country lakes a bad bet.

Sprague Lake at the east edge of the park is good for catching pan-sized brook trout; however, it's right next to the road and is heavily used. From Estes Park, drive west on U.S. Highway 36 to the Beaver Meadows Entrance Station. Turn left (south) at the first intersection after the entrance, and continue on the Bear Lake Road for about 6 miles.

Insiders' Tip

Pikas are small gerbil-sized creatures found only near the tree line. Though they look like rodents, they are actually related to rabbits. Look for them in rock piles around or above timberline in Rocky Mountain National Park.

At 14,255 feet, Longs Peak towers over Bear Lake in Rocky Mountain National Park. PHOTO: DAILY CAMERA

For a day's outing—a combination hiking and fishing trip—go to Peacock Pool. Begin at the East Longs Peak Trailhead and hike about 4 miles up the trail to a spur that leads to Peacock Pool, 11,360 feet high. This is a hard hike but offers spectacular views. Another 1.5 miles from Peacock Pool is Chasm Lake, with deep water, but according to latest reports, no fish, though it's a scenic spot right under the spectacular Diamond, the east face of Longs Peak. The Longs Peak Trailhead is 9.2 miles south of Estes Park on Colo. 7; turn right at the sign.

Hiking and Backpacking

With 355 miles of trails, Rocky Mountain National Park is prime hiking and backpacking country. There's something for everyone, from wheelchair users to backpackers. Below are some day hikes, rated accordingly. It's best to get a map at one of the visitor centers for detailed descriptions, including distance, elevation, and type of terrain.

Very Easy

The Bear Lake Nature Trail is a half-mile paved path circling Bear Lake. A brochure available at the trailhead describes the subalpine landscape. Elevation is 9,475 feet. Leave from the Bear Lake parking area.

The Sprague Lake Nature Trail, known as the Five Senses Trail, is a half-mile trail around Sprague Lake, at 8,710 feet in altitude. It is also wheelchair-accessible. Take the road to Bear Lake, and turn off at the sign for Sprague Lake.

Easy

Trails from Bear Lake to Nymph, Dream, or Emerald Lakes present a little more challenge, at 3.6 miles round-trip.

The Gem Lake trail, a round-trip hike, makes for a pleasant walk and begins outside the Park on Devil's Gulch Road.

Moderate

Bear Lake or Glacier Gorge to Mills Pond or Black Lake are good 6- to 10-mile round-trip hikes that take a few hours, as does Bear Lake or Glacier Gorge to Sky Pond.

The hike to Chasm Lake is a bit more strenuous at 4.2 miles one-way, but the gorgeous view of the Diamond on Longs Peak and the beautiful lake make it worth the effort. Start at the Longs Peak Trailhead, off Colo. 7, north of Meeker.

Long or Difficult

The trail from Bear Lake to the top of Flattop Mountain is a little more difficult. The hike to Thunder Lake starts at Wild Basin, off Colo. 7 between Allenspark and Meeker, and you should plan on it taking most of the day.

For Ypsilon Lake, start at the Lawn Lake Trailhead at Horseshoe Park on Fall River Road. Don't forget your lunch and rain gear.

A Classic

Longs Peak has always been considered America's Matterhorn. At 14,255 feet high, it is the highest peak in the park and the northernmost "fourteener" in the Rockies (these are peaks of at least 14,000 feet). The dramatic peak has fascinated writers, artists, climbers, and explorers since the first recorded American sighting in 1820 by Stephen Long. The Arapaho are believed to have climbed Longs to obtain eagle feathers on its summit. In 1868 two famed nonnatives made it to the top: one-armed Colorado River explorer John Wesley Powell and Denver newspaperman William Byers.

Climbing Longs is still an exciting accomplishment today. It's an all-day affair—usually taking about 14 hours round-trip. It should be attempted only by strong hikers who are already acclimated to the altitude. The climb should not be attempted by novices. It's crucial to be off the peak and on the way back down by noon to avoid the daily summer thunderstorms and dangerous lightning, which has claimed the lives of many hikers. Remember that fresh snow is possible any day of the year.

The most popular (and only non-technical) route is the East Longs Peak Trail, usually called the Keyhole Route, which starts at the Longs Peak Trailhead and climbs 8 miles and 4,855 vertical feet to the top. The first 6 miles are the easiest and follow an ever-climbing trail through beautiful forests of pine and aspen up to timberline with fantastic views. If you start early enough (say, 3:30 A.M.) you can reach timberline in time to watch the sunrise over Boulder. Those who want to bail out before this point can take the well-marked turnoff to Chasm Lake, at around 4 miles, to a gorgeous lake right beneath the 1,000-foot vertical Diamond on Longs' sheer, spectacular 1,675-foot east face (a popular world-class technical-climbing route). Chasm Lake is 4.2 miles from the trailhead.

But if you continue on the Keyhole Route, at mile 6 you reach the boulder field and hop from boulder to boulder for one mile up to the Keyhole, a prominent rock formation. To the left of the Keyhole is the chilly-looking Agnes Vaille Shelter Cabin. Vaille made the first successful winter ascent of the east face with Walter Kiener in 1925 but collapsed from exhaustion on her way back and froze to death while Kiener went for help.

After passing through the Keyhole, at 13,100 feet, the hard part begins. The route is marked by red and yellow paint circles over the rocky Ledges, which have

Insiders' Tip

Longs Peak in Rocky Mountain National Park is the northernmost of "the Fourteeners"— Colorado's highest peaks, 14,000 feet or more. Longs Peak has an elevation of 14,255 feet and is the 15th-highest peak in the state.

intimidating drop-offs. The Ledges lead to a 600-foot steep couloir of loose gravel and running rivulets called the Trough (or "stairway from hell," as many hikers have renamed it). After climbing the Trough and negotiating the huge boulder at the top, you pass through the notch and cross the Narrows—more rock ledges with even more dizzying exposure. The Narrows lead to the Homestretch, a short, steep couloir to the top, not really difficult, but at this point in the game, a bit much. The Homestretch requires some hand-holds but has solid footing unless slicked by rain. At the top of Homestretch, you have reached the huge summit of Longs, which encompasses four acres. Enjoy the view, do a few push-ups to show how really tough you are, and take a look down the Diamond face, but don't stay too long if noon is approaching. If there is any snow—possible well into July—ice axes are necessary for

safely climbing the Ledges, Trough, Narrows, and Homestretch.

Despite the rigor of the undertaking, don't expect to have the trail to yourself. On some summer days, hikers have complained that the view they saw most was the backside of the hiker ahead of them.

The Longs Peak Trailhead is 9.2 miles south of Estes Park on Colo. 7; turn right at the sign. Those who don't want to do it all in one day can backpack part of the way up Longs and camp in the boulder field, a spectacular but rather inhospitable campground—cold and windy and around 12,000 feet in elevation—among the boulders. But you'll need to reserve your permit well in advance by writing to the Backcountry Office, Rocky Mountain National Park, Estes Park, CO 80517. There are numerous backcountry sites and zones for individuals and groups throughout the park. For more information, maps, or reservations, call the

For those with enough lung capacity and a good pair of hiking shoes, Rocky Mountain National Park offers trails into the sky—like this rocky climb at Alpine Visitor Center. PHOTO: LINDA CORNETT

Backcountry Office at (970) 586–1242, write to the address above, or just show up.

Horseback Riding

Horses, mules, llamas, and other pack and riding animals are not allowed to travel cross-country in the park, but there are more than 260 miles of trails available. Horses and guides can be hired at a number of liveries outside the park, and **Hi Country Stables** has two locations inside the park at Moraine Park and Glacier Basin. Reservations are suggested, call (970) 586–2327 or (970) 586–3244 (only in summer months). Horses and pack animals are not allowed at any campgrounds.

Skiing and Snowshoeing

Though most visitors to the park come in summer, winter offers great cross-country skiing and snowshoeing opportunities. January, February, and March provide the best conditions, sandwiched between the spotty coverage of early winter and the avalanche danger of late winter. Bear Lake and Wild Basin are the park's most popular cross-country skiing areas. The visitor center on U.S. Highway 36, 2.5 miles west of Estes Park, is staffed daily from 8 A.M. to 5 P.M. except Christmas Day. Rangers lead cross-country tours from Kawuneeche Visitor Center on Saturday afternoons, and snowshoe hikes are offered Wednesday, Saturday, and Sunday at Bear Lake. Rangers can answer questions and provide trail maps detailing 40 miles of marked trails around Bear Lake and 88 miles of mainly unmarked trails around Wild Basin. There's a $10 entrance fee per vehicle (don't forget your chains if you don't have snow tires), and $5 for skiers, walkers, or cyclists at all times. For more information call the park at (970) 586–1206.

Equipment can be rented in Estes Park (see "Cross-Country Skiing" in the Estes Park chapter of this book). Precautions to take to heart: don't ski or snowshoe alone; return to the trailhead well before dark; pack in extra food and water to keep your hardworking body fueled, extra clothing, a map and compass, a flashlight, waterproof matches, a space blanket, and a first-aid kit.

Here are a few of our favorite sites:

Glacier Basin Campground: (Easy) Drive 5 miles up Bear Lake Road. Park on the west side of the road at the large parking area (which is the shuttle-bus parking area during summer months) and walk across to the east side to begin skiing on the main trail from the campground, which heads southwest for a mile on level terrain to Sprague Lake. There are many trails in and around the campground as well.

Black Lake: (Intermediate to Difficult) Begin at the Glacier Gorge Junction parking lot, which is about 11 miles up Bear Lake Road. Follow the signs southwest toward Alberta Falls and The Loch. After the intersection of Icy Brook and Glacier Creek, turn south and follow Glacier Creek to Mills Lake. Continue past Mills and Jewel Lakes along the creek. When you leave the trees, continue up the open slope to Black Lake and enjoy the spectacular view of Longs Peak to the east, McHenrys to the west, and Chief's Head Peak to the south.

Wild Basin Trailhead: (Difficult) Drive 13 miles south from Estes Park on

> ### Insiders' Tip
>
> Ptarmigan are birds found only in the Arctic regions or the high mountains such as those in Colorado. They are nearly impossible to spot even when they are right in front of you because they are camouflaged by feathers that perfectly match the rocks. They are the size of pigeons and look something like a quail.

A tourist enjoys the view from Trail Ridge Road. PHOTO: DAILY CAMERA/CRISSY PASCUAL

Colo. Highway 7 (past the Longs Peak Trail at 9.2 miles) to the Sandbeach Lake Trailhead. Turn right and drive another mile to the National Park Service parking lot. The Sandbeach Lake Trail starts at the large sign in the parking area and climbs northeast through the pines 4.2 miles to Sandbeach Lake.

Programs and Tours

Park rangers offer a variety of fun and educational programs and guided tours throughout the year. Among our favorites are the full moon walks in early spring. Reservations are required at (970) 586-1223. For bird lovers there is a spring migration bird walk (bring your binoculars and field guide).

The nonprofit Rocky Mountain Nature Association, created in 1931 to encourage the use of Rocky Mountain National Park as an outdoor classroom and research area, offers almost 100 classes in the park. Classes have such intriguing names as "100 Million Years in a Day," "Rivers of Ice," "Uppity Women of the Rockies," "Close-up Photography

Techniques," "Herbal Medicines," and "Story of Moose." For kids, there are "Fishy Business," "Surviving in the Wild," "Native American Leather and Beads," and others. Fees are quite reasonable, and teachers can earn recertification units. Call (800) 816-7662 or (970) 586-0108 for more information.

If rugged just isn't your style, **Rocky Mountain Park Tours & Limousines** (877-502-5466) offers limo rides through the park lasting three to seven hours for up to eight people.

Auto Tape Tours narrate the drive over Trail Ridge Road. The cassette tapes give highlights of history, facts, legends, and nature, and cost $9.95 at all of the park visitors' centers. Tapes are available starting from either the Estes Park side or the Grand Lake side of Trail Ridge Road.

Safety

A visit to Rocky Mountain National Park can be the experience of a lifetime, but don't ever forget that this is not a climate-controlled theme park—it is the real, wild world with unaccustomed dangers. Don't be afraid to enjoy it, but do use some foresight and common sense.

Altitude sickness: The flu-like symptoms of altitude sickness—nausea, headache, dizziness, rapid heartbeat, breathlessness—may be your body's way of telling you to head to lower ground. Follow its advice. To minimize the effects of the high altitude, avoid alcohol and tobacco, drink lots of fluids, eat frequently and lightly, and rest.

Animals: The park is richly inhabited. As guests here, human visitors must learn the acceptable rules of behavior. Never feed the wildlife; a human diet is not suitable for them and making beggars of them is dangerous for both species. Photographers should take a long lens and shoot from inside a car or from the roadside; aggressive photographers who approach animals may be fined $50. Keep food locked away in airtight containers in your car trunk when in bear country. If you encounter a black bear, stand still or slowly back away; never approach a bear, particularly a female with cubs. If you encounter a mountain lion, stop, pick up small children, stand tall, back away, yell. *Do not* run (running is your signal to the lion that you are game).

Avalanche: Open slopes, particularly after a recent wind or snow storm, can be triggered by as little as a footfall into a massive avalanche. Visitors traveling in such areas should travel in groups, wear electronic transceivers, and carry shovels and poles to use as probes. If you are swept up in an avalanche, discard equipment and swim toward the top of the moving snow.

Giardia: No, it's not just from bad restaurants. Giardia, a microscopic organism that can cause diarrhea, cramps, weight loss (the bad kind), and bloating, lives in the digestive systems of humans and wildlife. It can also flourish in that crystal stream, mountain lake, or enticing snow field. If you must drink the water, boil it for at least five minutes, or use a filtration system capable of removing microorganisms.

Hypothermia: There's a saying in the Rockies—"If you don't like the weather, wait five minutes." A sunny day can suddenly turn overcast, windy, cold, even snowy. Exposure to wet and cold can lead to hypothermia, a lowering of the body's core temperature. Symptoms are confusion, drowsiness, shivering, and slurred speech. A warm, nonalcoholic drink and warm, dry clothing are the treatment; coming prepared for any weather is the prevention.

Snowfields: There's nothing more thrilling than zipping down the slick face of a snowfield or glacier in the middle of summer, either on a tube or sled, or by the seat of your pants. But the thrill can turn to feat when you discover just how difficult it can be to stop. For safety and preservation reasons, snow play and sledding are permitted only at Bear Lake and Hidden Valley, but look for warning signs in those areas as well.

Storms: The high peaks of Rocky Mountain National Park are a favorite target when Thor starts practicing his aim with lightning bolts. Thunderstorms are frequent in early to mid-afternoon. If you're up top when a storm begins, get off ridges or peaks and avoid exposed rocks and trees. If you're on horseback, dismount and put a little distance between you and your horse. Better yet, start out early in the morning so you're down well before practice time.

Sunburn: The high elevation means that you are less protected than normal from ultraviolet radiation, and that dazzling snow also increases the risk of a severe burn. UV-protectant sunglasses, a hat, and covering clothing are a good idea, with heavy-duty sunscreen on exposed skin. Don't forget to slather the kids.

Ticks: Visitors are warned not to take anything from the park, but sometimes it's difficult not to. Ticks, tenacious members of the spider family, love nothing more than hitching a ride on a warm, blood-pumping body passing by. They are plentiful in early spring and summer. To discourage the hangers-on, spray on insect repellent before setting out, keep your ankles covered with thick socks, and if you are wearing pants, tuck them into your boots or socks. Check for ticks periodically throughout your visit to the park, especially in places where your clothing ends, such as your collar, the end of your sleeves, and your pants or shorts legs. If you find one, carefully remove it with tweezers, being sure to get the whole body; remaining embedded parts can cause infection or serious illness like Rocky Mountain Spotted Fever and Colorado Tick Fever (fortunately, no cases of Lyme Disease have been reported in the park).

Water: A beautiful mountain stream can sweep you off your feet—literally. Keep in mind that during spring runoff, even a shallow stream can pick up enough force to knock down adults and carry them away.

Watermelon snow: You know not to eat the yellow snow, but did you know that pink snow is bad news, too? This snow, called watermelon snow because of its color and taste, is actually a colony of algae that can send you running for the nearest port-a-potty.

Estes Park

Estes Park (elevation 7,522 feet) lies 63 miles northwest of Denver and 34 miles northwest of Boulder at the eastern entrance to Rocky Mountain National Park and is the year-round home of more than 5,000 hardy souls (15,000 in summer). It exists primarily as a base camp and service area for visitors to the park, offering hotels, restaurants, shopping, equipment rentals, tours, and other diversions for tourists—with a nearly endless choice during the summer months. Since more than three million visitors come to Rocky Mountain National Park every year—and most of them during summer—things can get a bit hectic along Estes Park's main drag. But those visitors left the town with $5.6 million in sales tax dollars in 2000.

In winter, some of the shops close, and their owners head south, but many others stay open, particularly the art galleries. Some restaurants have abbreviated hours during winter. But winter and other "low-season" months may be the best time to get the flavor of this small town, which is beautifully situated at the base of spectacular Longs Peak and Rocky Mountain National Park.

Estes Park has quite an interesting history all its own. Joel Estes gave his name to the area—which he described as the most beautiful spot he had ever seen—when he topped a ridge and looked down on the valley that is surrounded by 54 peaks 12,000 feet and higher.

Another notable newcomer attracted by the beauty of the mountain valley was Thomas Wyndam-Quin, fourth Earl of Dunraven. Following a series of hunting trips, the Earl in 1874 began acquiring land, through means legal and otherwise, with the intention of creating a grand estate.

In 1877, Dunraven built a hunting lodge in a beautiful setting, calling it the Estes Park Hotel. Locals, who resented the acquisitive foreigner, referred to it as the "English Hotel." Estes Park homesteaders began to join forces against the Earl's purchases and eventually Dunraven moved on to more hospitable areas. The remains of the buildings he left behind have been removed from the park as it is returned to its natural state.

Victorian traveler and writer Isabella Bird wrote extensively and lovingly about the scenic beauty of Estes Park in the fall of 1873. For those interested in the area's history and a fascinating glimpse of life for the first settlers, her book *A Lady's Life in the Rocky Mountains* is required and entertaining reading.

Stephen King wrote more horrifyingly about the malevolent spirits inhabiting the fictional Overlook Hotel (actually the Stanley Hotel, where King lived when he wrote the novel) and their effect on a family hired to "winter over" in the empty hotel. King was so unhappy about the movie version of *The Shining*, starring Jack Nicholson, that he returned to the Stanley to film a television series closer to the novel.

On July 31, 1976, real horror came to Estes Park when the burbling Big Thompson River was transformed by mountain storms into a deadly gusher powerful enough to pick up and carry cars, boulders, homes, bridges, and trees as it crashed down on the tourist-packed town. At least 139 people were killed (7 were listed as missing), and 88 people were injured, making it the largest natural disaster in Colorado history. The flood destroyed 361 homes and 52 businesses. Estes Park has rebuilt, but the flood left as its legacy a heightened awareness of the inextricable connections between humans and the land on which they perch.

Indeed, the history of Estes Park and Rocky Mountain National Park are so deeply intertwined that one would probably not exist without the other. Even the Estes Park Chamber of Commerce brochure begins with "The Park." Major employers are the Park R-3 School District, the Estes Park Medical Center, the town itself, the Holiday Inn, the YMCA of the Rockies, the Harmony Foundation (a drug and alcohol rehab center), the park, Michael Ricker Casting Studio, and Estes Valley Recreation and Park District. The average age of a resident in the 1990 census was 42.6, 10 years younger than the Colorado average. More than half the town's residents are younger than 44, and the median price for a house is $233,000.

Some visitors enjoy connecting with the quieter, community side of an area. Others suddenly need a community service. These days, many visitors stand transfixed by the beautiful surroundings and decide to make Estes Park their permanent home. This chapter provides information for both tourists and newcomers, including details on medical care and worship, real estate and retirement, schools and childcare, as well as information on accommodations, attractions, restaurants, and sports. The following sections are arranged alphabetically.

For information about almost anything in the area, call the Estes Park Visitor Information Center (800) 443–7837 or (800) 44–ESTES. The Chamber of Commerce's Resort Association offers a free vacation planner; call (800) 44–ESTES. The area code for Estes Park is 970 and calls from Boulder are long distance.

Accommodations

Estes Park has so many motels, bed and breakfast inns, lodges, and cabins, visitors will have a large choice and range in quality and atmosphere. But reservations are a good idea during the crowded summer months and a must over holiday weekends. Choose a modern motel, a rustic lodge or cabin, or a place right out of history. All of these accommodations accept major credit cards, with the exception of the cabins at Estes Park Center/YMCA of the Rockies. Pets are not allowed at any of these properties, except for the cabins at Estes Park Center/YMCA of the Rockies. Smoking is prohibited at many inns and bed and breakfasts; if you're a smoker it makes sense to ask in advance.

Price-Code Key

Our code reflects what you'll pay on average for a double room.

$	Less than $50
$$	$50 to $80
$$$	$81 to $100
$$$$	$101 to $150
$$$$$	$151 and more

Alpine Trail Ridge Inn
927 Moraine Ave., Estes Park
(970) 586–4585
$$$$–$$$$$

This tidy blue-trimmed white motel is right on the highway, but its clean and pleasant rooms are a good value. There's a heated swimming pool, and family and kitchen units are available. Enjoy good meals at the Sundeck Restaurant right on the property. Smoking is not allowed at the inn.

Aspen Lodge at Estes Park
6120 Colo. Hwy. 7, Estes Park
(970) 586–8133, (800) 332–6867
$$$$$

Located 7.5 miles south of Estes Park, this beautiful 3,000-acre ranch is a full resort offering hayrides, swimming, fishing, tennis, racquetball, horseback riding, wildlife van tours, mountain biking, hikes, and a great children's program for kids 5 to 12 that includes Indian lore and nature rambles. It's the largest log lodge in the state, according to the owners. There are cozy cabins, a hot tub, saunas, and winter sleigh rides. Three-, four-, and seven-day packages make this all-inclusive resort quite affordable, with all meals and activities included. Smoking is prohibited at this property.

The Baldpate Inn
4900 Colo. Hwy. 7 S., Estes Park
(970) 586–6151
$$$$$

In January 1996, the Baldpate was placed on the National Register of Historic Places. Family-owned and operated as a bed and breakfast, this classic mountain inn and historic local landmark is unsurpassed in charm and history. Built from local wood and stone in 1917, it's the quintessential rustic mountain getaway. The inn is 7 miles south of Estes Park across from the Rocky Mountain National Park Visitor Center at Lily Lake. Guests can stay in the Mae West and Jack Dempsey Rooms, where these and many other stars stayed. The Baldpate Inn has 12 rustic rooms and three cabins with col-orful homemade quilts, calicos, gingham and alluring log-cabin decor. One cabin is a newly redecorated honeymoon suite. There are five massive stone fireplaces and a library. The inn has the world's largest public key collection and an amazing photograph collection.

A three-course breakfast is included in the room rate, and the dining room serves delicious meals with homemade pies, pastries, breads, and soups. Smoking is not allowed. The Baldpate Inn is open Memorial Day until October, weather permitting.

Eagle Manor Bed and Breakfast
441 Chiquita Lane, Estes Park
(970) 586–8482
$$$$$

Bed down in the home of Estes Valley pioneer Frank Bond (as in Bond Park) for a quiet stay. The Tudor-style home, built in 1917, has just four guest rooms (each with cable TV, two with private baths). Lovely oak floors, two fireplaces, and antique furniture remind visitors they are staying in a gracious old home; an indoor swimming pool and sauna and outdoor hot tub satisfy their itch for 21st century amenities. Smoking is not allowed.

Estes Park Center/YMCA of the Rockies
2515 Tunnel Rd., Estes Park
(970) 586–3341
$–$$$$, no credit cards

There's something for almost everyone (except maybe honeymooners) at the Y. This enormous facility, just outside Estes Park, can accommodate 3,469 and runs numerous camps and programs. The Y is the place for families or other groups and offers everything from rustic cabins that sleep four to 10 lodge rooms that sleep four to six. There's a miniature golf course, tennis courts, livery, craft shop, library, museum, post office, and theater. Concerts are given regularly. It's open year-round. Pets are allowed in the cabins but not in the rooms. Smoking is not allowed in any buildings.

Insiders' Tip

For those who want a quiet and more authentic experience with some local people, small inns and bed-and-breakfasts are good alternatives to the motel scene.

Fawn Valley Inn
2760 Fall River Rd., Estes Park
(970) 586–2388, (800) 525–2961
$$$$$

Only a half-mile from Rocky Mountain National Park, these year-round condominiums are set on more than 8 acres along the Fall River. They feature complete kitchens and fireplaces, and there's a heated outdoor pool. Some suites have Jacuzzis. Smoking is not allowed.

H-Bar-G Ranch Hostel
3500 H-Bar-G Rd., Estes Park
(970) 586–3688
$

If you don't mind some togetherness in exchange for very low rates, the H-Bar-G, in operation for more than 25 years, offers cabins, family accommodations, and separate buildings for men and women. There is a tennis court, volleyball court, game room, barbecue pit, and fireplaces to cozy the place up. Guests are expected to bring their own sleeping bags and to contribute a clean-up chore or two. A shared kitchen is available. Visits are limited to three days. The H-Bar-G is a member of Hostelling International, and a membership card gets you a $10 bunk. Memberships are $25 and only members can stay.

Misty Mountain Lodge
232 E. Riverside Dr., Estes Park
(970) 586–4100
$$-$$$$

This attractive and very reasonably priced lodge is a great value right in town. It's set against a hillside, away from the crowd across the river. There are multiroom suites, kitchens and fireplaces, a hot tub, and great off-season rates. Smoking is not allowed.

Romantic River Song Bed & Breakfast Inn
Lower Broadview Rd. (off Mary's Lake Rd.), Estes Park
(970) 586–4666
$$$$$

Reservations are a good idea at this lovely, secluded bed and breakfast set on 27 acres right along the Big Thompson River. Guests like it so much they return year after year, often booking a year in advance. For a stay during the high season, reservations need to be made about 15 weeks in advance. During the rest of the year it's not nearly as busy. Each of the rooms is custom-decorated either with lovely antiques or whimsical handmade furniture. One room has the beautiful 200-year-old bed of the owner's grandmother; another has a delightful bed made of gracefully arching willow twigs complete with (decorative) nesting birds. There's a river stone–faced Jacuzzi in one room and fireplaces in most rooms. The list of amenities goes on and on at this lovely old home. Gourmet breakfast comes with the price of the room. This is a no-smoking inn.

The Stanley Hotel & Conference Center: A Grand Heritage Hotel
333 Wonderview Ave., Estes Park
(970) 586–3371, (800) 976–1377
$$$$$

The stately queen of the area's hotels, and listed on the National Register of Historic Places, the Stanley is truly a classic. The inspiration for Stephen King's book, *The Shining*, the Stanley was also the scene for shooting the 1997 TV miniseries of the same name. King returned in 1996 as screenwriter and executive producer and stayed six months for the shooting. During the filming for the new version, the hotel lobby and MacGregor room were restored to a more authentic turn-of-the-20th-century look by the film directors and Grand Heritage (the company that owns the Stanley), going from white walls back to natural woods and patterned wallpapers.

The hotel was purchased recently by Grand Heritage, which owns and operates castles and historic buildings around the world. Grand Heritage financed a $3.6 million restoration of the Stanley completed in spring of 1997, maintaining the hotel's turn-of-the-20th-century decor. Rooms have canopy beds, Victorian wallpaper, and other period details. Those feel-

The Stanley Hotel, inspiration for Stephen King's The Shining, *has hosted the rich and famous since 1906.* PHOTO: MASES STREET

ing extravagant should ask for the Stephen King Suite. Though there are no skeletons in the closet, it's where the Emperor and Empress of Japan stayed during their visit a few years ago, and other VIPs have lodged there as well.

Historic tours of the hotel are offered year-round, five times a day (see the "Attractions" section of this chapter for more information). The Stanley also hosts free concerts every Sunday, "fairy tale weddings," dinner theater, holiday galas, Big Band dancing, the Colorado Music Festival during summer and the famous "The Shining" Halloween Ball. Smoking is allowed at the Stanley.

Streamside Cabins
1260 Fall River Rd., Estes Park
(970) 586–6464, (800) 321–3303
$$$–$$$$$

Describing itself as a "Village of Cabin Suites," these cabins are for those who want to "rough it" in luxury. They have skylights, fireplaces, wall-to-wall carpeting, private decks, gas grills, steam rooms, and jetted tubs. The cabins are on a wooded hillside on Fall River about a mile

from Estes Park. The 16-acre site offers fishing and solitude. The cabins are listed among the 19 "Best of Estes," by an Estes Park Trail Gazette survey. Special packages are available. Smoking is not allowed.

Sunnyside Knoll Resort
1675 Fall River Rd., Estes Park
(970) 586–5759
$$$$$

This is a resort for couples committed to romance. Each unit has a fireplace, cable television, and a VCR, and many have Jacuzzis for two situated with a fireplace view. There is also a heated outdoor pool and two outdoor hot tubs.

Arts

Estes Park offers the full range of choices for those interested in high-quality art. Shops, galleries, and boutiques dot the main streets with a plethora of Native American art and representations of Rocky Mountain National Park in every medium. Besides the visual arts, the performing arts that may be enjoyed here include theater and classical, jazz, and contemporary music concerts. Larger performing-arts events and festivals generally take place during the summer.

Performing Arts

Chamber Music Society of Estes Park (Cultural Arts Council)
P.O. Box 1331, Estes Park, CO 80517
(970) 586–9203

This society of some 100 chamber-music-loving members sponsors concerts all year in the Estes Park area, inviting different musicians from around the state and nation. The society also sponsors an annual Chamber Music Festival, held over a weekend in fall. Past festivals have featured the American Chamber Players and The Mendelssohn Trio. Information is available on concert locations, dates, and prices from the Cultural Arts Council at the number listed above or from artistic director Louise Dickey in Boulder at (303) 494–8934.

The Estes Park Music Festival
Stanley Concert Hall, Stanley Hotel, Estes Park
(970) 586–9203

Boulder's nationally acclaimed Colorado Music Festival Orchestra comes to Estes Park on Monday evenings from late June through early August. For more information about this better-than-the-best orchestra, see our Boulder Arts chapter. Ticket prices vary.

Music in the Mountains
Rocky Ridge Music Center, Colo. Hwy. 7, 12 miles south of Estes Park
(970) 586–4031, (402) 486–4363 (in winter)

Rocky Ridge offers chamber music and opera. Student and faculty recitals take place here on Fridays and Sundays around 3 P.M. from late June until the end of August. Call for current ticket prices.

The Stanley Hotel
333 Wonderview Ave., Estes Park
(970) 586–3371, (800) 976–1377

For year-round entertainment check the Stanley Hotel, which presents theater and fine arts performances. In fact, the hotel claims to put on more performances than any other private property in the West. The Stanley also hosts free concerts on Sundays. There's a year-round jazz series and a Friday-night dance program. Call for the current schedule of events.

Visual Arts

Charles Eagle Plume Gallery
9853 Hwy. 7, Allenspark
(303) 747–2861

The Charles Eagle Plume Gallery and Museum of Native American Arts has been a local landmark since 1917 and is a favorite stop. Located 10 miles south of Estes Park on Colo. 7, it has a huge collection of art and artifacts, including rugs, jewelry, pottery, baskets, and beautiful beadwork of the Plains Indians. Active in the Native American rights movement, founder Charles Eagle Plume graduated from the University of Colorado in 1932 and was later awarded an honorary Doctorate of Humanities from CU-Boulder. The gallery is open daily April through December, weekends or by appointment January through March.

Galleries of Estes Park Association
P.O. Box 987, Estes Park, CO 80517
No phone

The association publishes the Estes Park Gallery Guide, listing the town's shops and galleries. For information, write to the association or call the Cultural Arts Council, P.O. Box 4135, 160 Moraine Ave., Estes Park, CO 80517, (970) 586-9203. For other information try the Resort Association at (970) 586-4431 or (800) 44- ESTES.

The Glassworks Studio and Gallery
323 W. Elkhorn Ave., Estes Park
(970) 586-8619

This is the only hot-glass studio and gallery in the area. There are free public glass blowing demonstrations daily, year-round, by owner Garth Mudge, who displays the delicate artwork.

The Michael Ricker Pewter Museum, Gallery and Casting Studio
2 miles east of town on U.S. Hwy. 34, Estes Park
(970) 586-2030

Ricker claims to have the world's largest pewter-casting studio, where more than 25,000 pewter sculptures are cast each month, and also the world's largest pewter sculpture (10 feet by 30 feet). Ricker's work has been presented to or commissioned by The White House, the U.S. Olympic Committee, Disney World, and Pope John Paul II, among others. Several of Ricker's pieces are on display in the Smithsonian Institution. Children will enjoy the re-creation of a turn-of-the-20th-century American town. The museum, gallery, and casting studio are open seven days a week year-round. There's also a Ricker Pewter retail shop in town at 167 E. Elkhorn Avenue.

Sundance Center for the Arts
150 E. Riverside Dr., Estes Park

This complex of galleries and frame shops specializing in Western and nature art includes Impressions Ltd. (970-586-6353), and Colorado Essence (970-586-0832), which are the biggest galleries in town with regular programs of shows and openings. Look for animals and other woodcarvings at the Mountain Wood Carvers, also located in the complex (970-586-8678).

Attractions

All of these beautiful mountains could keep you happy for years. But even the most dedicated nature lover sometimes needs a change. There's a lot to see in Estes Park, since much of the early Colorado history was made here by settlers such as Alexander MacGregor and F. O. Stanley— not to mention 19th-century writer Isabella Bird and Enos Mills, the "Father of Rocky Mountain National Park."

Keep in mind, too, that Boulder County is just a stone's throw from the Estes Valley. Some Boulder County attractions are closer to Estes than they are to the city of Boulder. Even events smack on Boulder's Pearl Street Mall are less than an hour away, making them fair game for your fun. Also see the Boulder Festivals and Annual Events and Attractions chapters.

Dick's Rock Museum
490 Moraine Route, Estes Park
(970) 586-4180

Dick's has been in the same location for 30 years, celebrating the varieties and uses of rock from the region. The free museum displays jewelry, fossils, crystals, slabs of rock waiting for shaping, and a 24-inch diamond saw hefty enough to do the job. There are pictures of a bunny, a kissing couple, and other images formed in the natural swirls of rock, a rock farm where everything is carved from rock, and rock "butterflies." Hours vary; call ahead.

Enos Mills Cabin
At the base of Twin Sisters Mountain, Estes Park
(970) 586-4706

The Enos Mills Cabin operates as a nature center and museum today, but it was the home of the well-known "Father of Rocky Mountain National Park." A naturalist, writer, and inn owner in Estes Park, Mills campaigned nationally for the establishment of the national parks in general and specifically for Rocky Mountain National Park. His cabin, built in 1885, is at the base of Twin Sisters Mountain and has several nature trails on the property. His daughter, Enda Mills Kiley (yes, it's Enda, not Edna), and others offer tours of the house, which also has Mills's books, photos, and other memorabilia on display. Copies of his books are for sale. Admission is free. The cabin is open from 11 A.M. to 4 P.M. Tuesday through Sunday, Memorial Day through Labor Day, and other times by appointment.

Estes Park Area Historical Museum
200 Fourth St., Estes Park
(970) 586–6256

This interesting museum shows the history and heritage of the area's first settlers, including an 1859 photograph of just-arrived first settler Joel Estes and 6 of his 13 children. Look for the original National Park Headquarters building out back next to an old homestead cabin. The museum includes a Stanley Steamer, pioneer artifacts, historical photos, and documentation of the founding of Rocky Mountain National Park. In May through October, the museum is open from 10 A.M. to 5 P.M. Monday through Saturday, and from 1 to 5 P.M. Sunday. In March and December it's open from 10 A.M. to 5 P.M. Tuesday through Saturday, and from 1 to 5 P.M. Sunday. It is open by appointment only during the rest of the year. Admission is $2.50 for adults, $2 for seniors (60 and older), and $1 for children ages 5 to 12.

Estes Park Brewery
470 Prospect Village Dr., Estes Park
(970) 586–5421

Open summers from 11 A.M. until midnight, with shorter hours off-season, the brewery offers a free video tour and samples of the nine microbrews it produces. A pub and a restaurant are on-site. See the "Nightlife" section of this chapter for details.

Estes Park Center/YMCA of the Rockies
2515 Tunnel Rd., Estes Park
(970) 586–3341

The YMCA of the Rockies is a huge facility with log cabins, lodges, and a leisurely pace that makes you automatically switch to strolling gear. It offers loads of family-oriented activities. During the winter, when the town is quieter, you can purchase a day pass to use the YMCA's facilities, which include an indoor gym, a roller rink, an indoor swimming pool, plus outdoor volleyball, basketball, and tennis courts. There's also a library and museum.

During the summer, more than 4,000 people stay at the YMCA of the Rockies. (If you'd like to be among them—or to stay during the winter—check the previous "Accommodations" section of this chapter.) Using the facilities in this busy season is limited to those staying as guests or those with proof of membership in a hometown YMCA. Once you've shown that proof, a number of programs are open for your enjoyment. In addition to winter offerings, there's an outdoor mini-golf course here. Complimentary family programs usually give you six options each day, ranging from survival classes and Indian lore to games of water balloon volleyball and campfire songs. For a fee, YMCA registered guests and hometown YMCA members can also enjoy Y-organized horseback riding, mountain bike rentals (including kids' sizes), and whitewater rafting.

The Lulu W. Dorsey Museum (970–586-4331), on the YMCA grounds, explores the history of the facility, which has buildings dating to the early 1900s.

Estes Park Public Library
335 E. Elkhorn Ave., Estes Park
(970) 586–8116

Looking for Internet access? The library has it, plus CD-ROMs that can be checked out. This library is also kid-friendly. It loans toys in addition to books and has a parent-child center with educational activities that change monthly. Librarian Kerry Aiken is a local puppeteer and performer. She does a children's story hour on Thursdays and Saturdays and also works with the parent-child center. The library is open 9 A.M. to 9 P.M. summer weekdays, 9 A.M. to 5 P.M. Fridays and Saturdays, and 1 to 5 P.M. Sundays. During winter the library opens at 10 A.M. Monday through Saturday.

MacGregor Ranch Museum and Education Center
180 MacGregor Ln., off Devil's Gulch Rd.
(970) 586-3749

The MacGregor Ranch Museum and Education Center is a working ranch commemorating the Alexander Q. MacGregor family, one of the valley's largest and most influential ranching families. MacGregor battled the infamous Lord Dunraven over an illegal land claim at Estes Park. Dunraven had bought up all the land for his private hunting reserve. The museum displays domestic items, furniture, silver mining and ranching equipment, plus photos of life in the area in the 1870s through the mid-20th century. Historical photos and documents of MacGregor's battle with Dunraven also are on display. Admission is free, but donations are encouraged. Open Tuesday through Friday from June through August (closed weekends). The facility is open to school groups year-round. It's a half-mile north of Estes Park off Devil's Gulch Road.

The Stanley Hotel
333 Wonderview Ave., Estes Park
(970) 586-3371, (800) 976-1377

The inspiration for Stephen King's *The Shining* (see the "Hotels" section of this chapter), the Stanley continues to be a testament to a grand era. Ghosts aside, the Stanley stands on its own as a showstopper and has hosted the rich and famous since its construction in 1906 by F.O. Stanley, inventor of the Stanley Steamer automobile. Diagnosed with tuberculosis and given little time to live, Stanley came to Colorado for the curative value of the pure mountain air and lived another 30 years. During those years he built his classic hotel and helped promote the establishment of Rocky Mountain National Park.

Among the Stanley's treasures are a 1909 Steinway piano in the music room and a shiny, green Stanley Steamer with brass trim and wooden fenders in the hotel lobby. Stanley proclaimed it was an excellent mountain car because it didn't stall, and to prove his point he once drove the car up the steps of the U.S. Capitol.

Tourists are welcome to visit, and historic tours are offered year-round five times daily; participants are asked for a $5 donation. The tours go through all of the public rooms and down into the tunnel underneath the hotel, which is built on solid rock. Visitors will see fool's gold glittering in the rock that supports the original hotel beams. There's a small museum on the ground level. Many community events take place at the Stanley. You can also stay as a guest.

Education and Childcare

Preschools and Childcare Centers

During the winter, it's easier to find childcare. But as summer brings wildflowers to the mountains, it brings visitors into Estes Park Valley. If you might need summer childcare, even for a week or a few days, daycare centers recommend you start looking at least by midwinter.

To connect with child-related programs in the valley, visit the Estes Park Public Library, 335 E. Elkhorn Avenue (970-586-8116). Parents can check out stuffed animals for their children there, and it also offers a list of babysitters who can come to your home or hotel room. Most are teenagers who have gone through a Red Cross Training Program for first aid and CPR. The library also sponsors summer reading programs for children. Call the Larimer Country Social Services Program in Estes Park (970-577-2150) to request a list of licensed daycare centers and homes, plus applications for reduced-fee services.

Circle of Friends Montessori Preschool
2515 Tunnel Rd., Estes Park
(970) 586-3341 ext. 1137

Located in the Estes Park Center/YMCA of the Rockies, this school has 20 to 30 children, 20 of whom attend full time. There's a parent-toddler program offered in spring for children ages 18 months to 3 years. There is also a kindergarten program.

Kreative Kids
650 Community Dr., Estes Park
(970) 586–6727

This is a private, nonprofit kindergarten/daycare learning center for children ages 5 to 12, located next to the elementary school. It leases space from the school district and has a good relationship with the schools. It's $2.50 per hour for each child. Drop-ins are considered if there is space after the regularly enrolled children arrive.

Mountain Top Preschool
1250 Woodstock, Estes Park
(970) 586–6489

About 60 kids attend the preschool and childcare center at this facility, which is the largest in Estes Park. Drop-ins are not accepted, and there is a short waiting list.

Private Schools

Eagle Rock School and Professional Development Center
2750 Notaiah Rd., Estes Park
(303) 442–7655

This is a year-round, tuition-free, ungraded residential high school. It has been developed and funded by the American Honda Corporation as a public service. A beautiful setting, excellent staff, and facilities for science, arts, and physical education are here. It focuses on young people who are not experiencing success in their current school settings and are willing to commit to growth and change. Individualized learning opportunities are offered to 100 students, who are accepted through a careful application process.

Public Schools

The Park School District R-3 (970–586–2361) includes almost 450 square miles

and the towns of Estes Park, Allenspark, Glen Haven, Pinewood Springs, and the eastern slope of Rocky Mountain National Park. The district employs around 200 people, serving the more than 700 school-age children in the valley.

Though small, Park School District R-3 offers art, music, gifted and talented programs, special education, and reading and sports programs. Volunteers contribute nearly 150 hours each month. The district runs an Aquatic Center, open to the community during nonschool periods. Computer and industrial technologies are part of many classrooms. Around 40 percent of teachers have master's degrees. The pupil/teacher ratio is 16.5 to 1. Nearly 95 percent of Park District children graduate from high school, and 80 percent of these go on to higher education.

For more information write or visit the following schools:
• Park School District R-3 (administrative office), 1501 Brodie Avenue, (970) 586-2361
• Estes Park High School, 1600 Manford Avenue, (970) 586-5321
• Estes Park Middle School, 1500 Manford Avenue, (970) 586-4439
• Estes Park Intermediate School, 1505 Brodie Avenue, (970) 586-7406
• Estes Park Elementary School, 650 Community Drive, (970) 586-9529

Festivals and Annual Events

January

Frost Giant 5K or 10K Race
Municipal Building, 170 MacGregor Ave., Estes Park
(970) 586-8191

You might be a mild-mannered human, but you'll become an Estes Park frost giant if there's a little humidity and freezing weather, for your breath will add lacy frozen filigrees to your eyebrows and hair. If you join the 200 or so runners and walkers who participate, you'll puff up a scenic road to MacGregor Ranch and circle back for a total of either 5 or 10 kilometers (roughly 3 or 6 miles). The 5K race starts around 11 a.m.; the 10K starts at noon. Entrance fees are roughly $18 and include a Frost Giant T-shirt. It costs less if you forgo the T-shirt, more if you register late.

February

Romance of the Rockies
Downtown Estes Park
(970) 586–6641

Simple pleasures bless the 100 or so sweethearts who arrive this weekend to tie the knot. You have two chances to marry or renew wedding vows on Valentine's Saturday or Sunday. The group ceremonies generally are at a nice restaurant or the municipal building. Saying "I do," the sheet wedding cake, and punch cost $5 per couple. Pay extra for champagne and photographs. Then tour the town in antique Stanley Steamer cars, limousines, or hay wagons for a small price. Some years a Valentine's Dance is featured, too. Local hotels and motels offer special sweetheart packages. Call ahead.

Imagine This!
Estes Park High School, 1600 Manford Ave., Estes Park
(970) 586–9203

The rest of this event's title is See It! Hear It! Do It! Be It! This is the single biggest arts event of the year, sponsored by the Cultural Arts Council of Estes Park, which represents all the arts in the area. Artists, musicians, jugglers, and actors give youngsters and adults a chance to create art at more than 26 hands-on activities areas. There's also a silent auction of original artwork, gift certificates, and merchandise. In the evening a benefit performance of dancers, musicians, and other artists from the Estes Valley keeps the entertainment going. Since the event is the main friend- and fund-raiser of the year for the nonprofit Arts Council, a small donation is requested at the door.

Dog Weight Pull
Estes Valley
(800) 44–ESTES

In Jack London's *Call of the Wild*, Buck pulls a 1,000-pound sled over a wager of gold. This isn't quite as dramatic, but it's more the real thing—a four-state, regional dog-pull contest held the last weekend in February. Dogs pull weighted sleds and wagons; winners are those who pull the most weight over the course in a minute. Dogs wear special harnesses to prevent injury, and weights are added incrementally. Small challengers have included a 10-pound poodle mix. A 200-pound Irish Wolfhound was among the largest. The little guy and the bruiser don't face off; they're in different classes and compete against dogs their own size.

Fine Arts Guild of the Rockies Annual Musical
Stanley Concert Hall and various locations, Estes Park
(970) 586–9203

Generally during two weekends in late February or early March, a guest director works with the community to present a favorite musical such as *Mame, Brigadoon,* or *The King and I*. Local guild members star in this community-theater event. The curtain rises at 7 P.M. for the Thursday through Saturday performances, and there's also a 2 P.M. Sunday matinee. Call for exact dates and location.

March

Women's History Month
Various locations, Estes Park
(970) 586–9203

The Cultural Arts Council of Estes Park celebrates female artists and performers with a series of exhibits and programs that run into April. Call for a schedule.

April

Estes Park Oratorio and Chamber Concert
Stanley Concert Hall, Stanley Hotel, 333 Wonderview Ave., Estes Park
(970) 586–9203

This free Sunday concert offers a special way to celebrate Easter with music for the season. Call for the exact date.

May

Duck Fest
Downtown Estes Park
(970) 586–4431, (800) 443–7837
On the first Saturday in May, thousands of floating yellow plastic ducks, each tagged with a sponsor and charity choice, raise more than $20,000 at this annual event. To help you remember the date, the Rotary Club sponsors it on Kentucky Derby Day. But ducks aren't as quick as a thoroughbred. They start at Nicky's Restaurant, 1350 Fall River Road, and depending on the runoff, bobble downtown on the Fall, then, nearly two hours later, reach the Wheel Bar, 132 E. Elkhorn Avenue. The mayor and police chief pull out the winning duck and distribute great prizes, such as trips to Disneyland and Hawaii. Sponsoring a duck costs around $20. Watching is free. Proceeds go to local charities.

Art Walk and Jazz Festival
Downtown Estes Park
(970) 586–9203, (970) 586–6104
More than 20 galleries feature special exhibits and artists' demonstrations as part of the Art Walk, a self-guided studio and gallery tour held Friday through Sunday. Children's art activities are offered, and from 1 to 5 P.M., live jazz concerts put an extra spring in the step of revelers in downtown Estes Park. This festival usually happens the second weekend in May.

Dance Fest
YMCA of the Rockies, Estes Park
(970) 586–3341
This annual celebration of dance is for all ages, with a Saturday night and Sunday afternoon performance early in May. Performers are chosen from local dance studios, and donations are collected at the door. The program includes tap, jazz, ballet, Middle Eastern, and hula.

June

Lake Estes Fishing Derby
Lake Estes Marina, U.S. Hwy. 36, near Lake Estes
(970) 586–2011
Every three weeks during summer, the Division of Wildlife drops 400 fish at many points along the Estes Valley river system, making trout plentiful. They double-stock the rivers and lake for this event, and the town buys some extra-big fish to tempt anglers. What's more, the Cline Trout Farm in Boulder donates some fish for the weekend (the first one in June). All this means contestants in the 8 A.M. to noon fishing derby are likely to pull in fine catches. Entrance fees are around $2.50 in advance, $3.50 on the day of the event. If you want a T-shirt, admission is $12 and $14. Proceeds go to the fire department and local youth programs.

Wool Market
Estes Park Fairground, Community Dr., Estes Park
(970) 586–6104
Tourists are welcome to enjoy this working wool market, the largest natural fiber show in the country. Around 10,000 wander among the market's animal shows. Events start the Thursday prior to the second weekend in June, with workshops and seminars on spinning, weaving, dyeing, raising animals, tax laws, shearing, and grading wool. Throughout the weekend, you can enjoy spinning and weaving contests and a children's tent. See llamas, angora rabbits, alpacas, and sheep, or consider buying one of the beautiful sweaters, yarns, or other wool-related items. Admission is free.

Teddy Bear Picnic
YMCA of the Rockies, 2515 Tunnel Rd., Estes Park
(970) 586–6483
The Talking Teddy Store has sponsored this picnic since 1983. Cute silly events may include a dentist who talks to children about care of their bear's teeth (and chil-

Summertime Horse Shows

This n-e-e-e-i-i-i-g-h-borly valley is full of summer horse shows. Each event brings around 250 sleek beauties to the Estes Park Fairground, on the east side of town near Lake Estes, (970–586–6104). Admission is free for all shows except the Westernaires.

Here's a general calendar:

Around the third week in June, the quarter horses show off their spin-on-a-dime and quarter-mile sprinting skills in barrel racing, roping, pole bending, and riding displays.

The fourth week in June features miniature horses. Some baby miniatures stand only a foot tall, and even adults are less than three feet. These knee-high horses dance to music and can pull a little surrey. Hitch six to a buckboard wagon, and you've got a team. Sometimes, a contestant brings a miniature stagecoach with a team of eight. While miniatures may seem just right for tucking in with a child's toy animals, experts say they act like regular horses. Only cuter.

As June ends and July begins, in thunder the Arabians. The International Arabian Show started here more than 40 years ago then outgrew little Estes Valley. But many of the nation's best Arabians still come here. Two days feature Arabian cattle-cutting championships. It's the second-largest such event in the United States. We promised not to print this but couldn't help ourselves—some local experts say Arabians can be as good or better at cutting cattle as quarter horses. The costume class is the favorite spectator event. Watch for Arabian sheiks and princesses and even horses in flowing capes.

When July ends and August begins, as many as 500 horses leap to the Hunter-Jumper events. They keep three show rings hopping—actually, jumping.

Westernaires normally take on the town during the second weekend in August. The precision riders are dazzling, dedicated, Denver-area teens. In past years, they've done some routines in black lights so their costumes glow, and their lively, Old West skits are always popular. The fee is usually $5 per person for the Friday and Saturday shows, which start around 7:30 P.M.

Don't miss Estes Park's annual Hunter-Jumper horse shows in July and August. PHOTO: TOWN OF ESTES PARK

dren's teeth). Cele-bear-ties, such as Smokey Bear and Celestial Seasoning's Sleepytime Bear, have appeared. There are prizes for the largest bear family, biggest bear, and cutest bear costume. Sandwiches, cake and beverages might be on hand for nibbling. The picnic starts mid-morning and lasts until the teddies get tired. Admission is free to this Father's Day weekend event.

Scandinavian Midsummer Festival
Bond Park, Downtown Estes Park
(970) 586-9203

The local Scandinavian Club's festival includes traditional celebrations for the year's longest day in late June. On Friday, they erect a maypole (*"may"* is a Swedish word for dressing in green), and onlookers decorate it with greens and live flowers. Norwegians, Danes, and Finns used to start a bonfire in a Viking longboat to scare away the evil spirits on this long, long day. The Scandinavian Club hasn't found any people in Estes willing to burn up boats. So enterprising club members hammer one together and launch it near the Lake Estes Marina. The fire reflects on the water, reminding celebrants of Norwegian fiords brooding under tall mountains. Revelers then dance into the evening. All weekend, professional dancers in bright-colored folk costumes invite onlookers to learn new steps. You also can attend workshops, where sages share Scandinavian history. Food booths offer Swedish pancakes with bright red lingonberries. Or nibble potatas korv—a beef, pork and potato sausage. Crafts for sale include wheat-weaving items, painted-wood folk paintings, and rosemaling items, which are painted with traditional flower designs. Proceeds go to pay the dancers, who often come from around the world.

July

Estes Park Fireworks Display
Lake Estes, Estes Park
(970) 586-6104

Locals arrive around 8 P.M. on the Fourth of July, generally gathering in the Stanley Village Shopping Center or near Lake Estes. Outdoor bands entertain the crowds. Around 9:15 P.M., the fireworks shoot up at the edge of the lake, so the reflections bloom in the water below. If you position yourself well, you get to see all this drama with the mountains as a backdrop. The event is free.

Western and Wildlife Art Show
Call for location
(970) 586-9203

Sponsored by the Fine Arts Guild of the Rockies, this annual late-July favorite features more than 30 participating artists from Colorado and the West, with work in a variety of media including painting, sculpture, prints, and more. Western landscapes and characters from the Old West are the main subject matter. There's a "quick draw" and an auction of original works.

Rooftop Rodeo
Estes Park Fairground, Community Dr.,
Estes Park
(970) 586-6104

The rodeo started in 1923 as the Estes Park Stampede, stopped during WWII, but revived right afterward and has been galloping ever since, hanging onto its designation as one of the country's oldest rodeos. A parade through downtown starts it off. Team roping, bulldogging, broncos, and steer wrestling are part of the week's events, which are sanctioned by the Professional Rodeo Cowboys Association. A carnival offers plenty of rides. Cowboy poets read on a stage with a campfire scene. Sometimes, the poet brings his harmonica or strums a guitar. Then there's country-western music, with the likes of Sweethearts of the Rodeo and the Darn Thirsty Cowboys.

Prices vary depending on who's in the main corral. By the way, it's not called "Rooftop Rodeo" because you have to watch from a roof. The name is to remind people of the 7,200-foot elevation and the United States' highest paved highway, Trail Ridge Road.

Fiber Celebration
Call for location
(970) 586–5882
This juried show gives artists who work in fiber their moment in the sun. It's sponsored by the Art Center of Estes Park.

August

Best of the West Estes Brewfest
Estes Park Brewery, Prospect Village Dr.,
Estes Park
(970) 586–5421
Eight kinds of locally brewed beer, brats and hot dogs, and live music under a late summer sun draw an enthusiastic crowd to this annual event.

Throughout the Summer

Cowboy Sing-alongs
Downtown Estes Park
(970) 586–4431, (800) 44–ESTES
This fun chance to yodel your love for the sagebrush is held Thursdays, Fridays, Saturdays, and Sundays from mid-June through mid-August at 7:30 P.M. in Bond Park.

Music in the Mountains
Rocky Ridge Music Center, Colo. Hwy. 7,
12 miles south of Estes Park
(970) 586–4031
The center focuses on both chamber music and opera. Student and faculty recitals take place here on Sundays around 3 P.M. from late June until the end of August. Call for current ticket prices.

The Estes Park Music Festival
Stanley Concert Hall, Stanley Hotel,
333 Wonderview Ave., Estes Park
(970) 586–9203
Boulder's nationally acclaimed Colorado Music Festival Orchestra comes to Estes Park on Monday evenings during the summer from late June through early August. For more about this better-than-the-best orchestra, see the Boulder chapter on Arts. Ticket prices vary.

September

Labor Day Crafts Show
Bond Park, Estes Park
(970) 586–4431
On Labor Day weekend, craftspeople from all over the state set up about 100 booths that sell and display pottery, bronze and wood sculpture, needlework, jewelry, photography, and oil paintings. The local volunteer fire department puts on this event, and it benefits the Muscular Dystrophy Association and the fire department.

Longs Peak Scottish-Irish Festival
Estes Park Fairground, Community Dr.,
Estes Park
(970) 586–6308, (800) 443–7837
This four-day festival in early September, which celebrated its 25th anniversary in 2001, is a 10-ring circus. It's so grand, *USA Today* has listed it as one of the nation's top 10 things to do. At least two and sometimes three top ceremonial bands come to play in the tattoo concerts, which include drums, bugles, and bagpipes. The festival hosts world champion pipe bands, including Simon Fraser University of Canada, Field Marshall Montgomery of Ireland, Victoria Police of Australia, and City of Victoria of Canada. The White House Drum and Bugle Corps has performed here, as have the Governor General's Foot Guard from Canada, and the Royal Highlands Scot Guards. Celtic folk musicians arrive for competitions. Irish step-dancers display their dazzling footwork. Evening concerts thrill Celtic hearts all over town.

Music isn't the only drawing card at this festival. There's jousting, dancing, a dog show, whiskey tasting, and seminars on topics Scottish. Highland games include tossing a stone the size of a shot put, throwing a caber, which is a large log roughly shaped like a telephone pole, and other heavy athletics. Highlanders demonstrate how to shoot antique cannon, and how to fly-fish with lures. Dr. James Durward, founder of this festival, points out

The Longs Peak Scottish–Irish Festival is held each year in early September.

PHOTO: LONGS PEAK SCOTTISH FESTIVAL

that lure fishing had to start in Scotland. After all, a thrifty Scot isn't going to dig up a new worm every time he casts his line!

Altogether, about 3,000 performers participate in this event, and approximately 30,000 people come to see it. Those who like to shop can buy quilts, sweaters, and other crafts related to these island peoples. Hungry revelers can buy scones, which are slightly sweet biscuits; Scotch eggs, hard-boiled then rolled in bacon crumbs; sausages; hot dogs; and pastie, sort of a non-flaking turnover with hamburger inside. Don't forget the shortbread. When you're full, you can quaff it down with Scotch or Irish libations. There's plenty of soda on hand for the lads and lassies.

Ticket prices are around $15 for a one-day field pass and $26 for a two-day pass. Children younger than 15 can get in one day for $7, and the wee bairns who have not yet reached the tender age of 5 get in free. All the money earned by the festival goes back into the festival and other local nonprofits.

Fine Arts and Crafts Show
Bond Park, Estes Park
(970) 586–9203

Sponsored by the Fine Arts Guild of the Rockies, this mid-September event is a juried, national art show. More than 80 booths display everything from pottery and small items to paintings and photography. Estes Park is working to become more of an arts community by bringing in national traveling art shows. This show has been an annual event for more than 20 years and is a pleasant way to pass the afternoon.

Chamber Music Festival
Call for location
(970) 586–9203

Sponsored by the Chamber Music Society of Estes Park, here's a special weekend (in late September or early October) for chamber music aficionados. There's a variety of concerts featuring local and Colorado performers. Call for ticket prices.

October

"The Shining" Costume Ball
Stanley Hotel, 333 Wonderview Ave., Estes Park
(970) 586–3371, (800) 976–1377

Stephen King wrote his horror classic, *The Shining*, after being inspired by a stay at the Stanley Hotel. Once you see what a lovely, elegant place the Stanley is, you'll be even more impressed by how creepily King remade it in his pull-up-the-covers-and-keep-the-lights-on story. You can make a similar transformation by dressing up for the Stanley's annual costume ball, held Halloween night. You don't have to be horrible and ghoulish. Just be sure whatever you wear is good for dancing and easy to sit in for dinner. Admission includes a room, a five-course dinner, the ball, and the costume contest. Only 100 rooms are available and reservations start coming in a year in advance, so plan ahead.

Throughout the Fall

Bull Elk Bugling
Rocky Mountain National Park
(970) 586–1206

Anyone who expects the bull elk's mating call to sound like a royal French horn is in for a surprise. These huge animals belt out a whistling squeal. It might strike you as wimpy, but boy, does it ever carry! The haunting call can travel across valleys and reach high mountain meadows. Forest rangers say the best time to witness (and hear) elk bugling is throughout the fall in the morning, from sunrise to an hour after, and then at dusk, starting about an hour before sunset. Three areas tend to provide good viewing: Moraine Park, Horseshoe Park, and Upper Beaver Meadows. To view wildlife, don't leave the designated trails and roadways. While bull elks rarely charge tourists, there are incidents of rangers charging visitors... and the fine they charge for harassing wildlife can be stiff. The Bighorn Brigade will be around to answer questions and remind you to stay out of the meadows. If you prefer smaller crowds, come on a weekday.

You can also find seminars on helpful subjects like photography. Call for a schedule.

Quaking Aspen
Rocky Mountain National Park
(970) 586–1206

Mother Nature gives us hot dry years when the leaves turn gold early, and she also bestows cool, moist summers when the green leaves never quite believe it's time to change. Because the golden aspen season varies, call the park's information office to learn the best time (generally mid-September through mid-October) and viewing places, which tend to be

Insiders' Tip

In the fall one of the area's top evening attractions is the eerie but beautiful mating call of the elk. (The elk bugle at dawn and dusk.) To discourage individual drivers and traffic jams at Horseshoe Park and other popular listening spots, Rocky Mountain National Park offers bus trips for the public to listen to these impressive animals bugle. Call the Estes Park Chamber of Commerce (800-443-7837), or park headquarters (970-586-1206).

around Bear Lake Road and Moraine Park. Park officials say aspen stands outside the park can be even more spectacular. The highway to Allenspark is designated a scenic byway, with huge aspen stands. Colorado Highways 119 and 72, heading south to Nederland and Central City, are good, too. Wherever you drive, find a chance to step out on a trail and walk. Get the aspens between you and the sunlight to take in their luminescence and brilliant color. Listen to the fluttering leaves. Smell the tannin. While strolling, you may notice elk coming down from the high country to beat the winter snows. Rangers request that you don't pick any aspen leaves, since our thin mountain soil needs their nutrients. To preserve the park's beauty for the future, remember to leave with only your memories and photographs.

November

Christmas Parade
Estes Park Fairground, Community Dr.,
Estes Park
(970) 586–4431, (800) 44–ESTES
When the downtown Christmas lights come on, the parade begins. It starts around 5:30 P.M. the Friday after Thanksgiving, heads through the main shopping district, and ends at the Chamber of Commerce around 7 P.M. Bruiser, a wonderfully dog-like puppeteer, sits atop his doghouse performing tricks. Santa's sleigh is always the last float in line. Onlookers dress in winter woolens, parkas, and blankets. On a mild evening, a jacket will do. If it's cold, some people wear everything they've got. No matter what the thermometer says, the sight is heartwarming—and free. Stores downtown stay open to sell Christmas goods and warm refreshments.

A Christmas Memory
Stanley Hotel Theatre, Stanley Hotel,
333 Wonderview Ave., Estes Park
(970) 586–3371, (800) 976–1377
A Stanley tradition, this dinner-theater production is a funny tearjerker, a family classic about Truman Capote's boyhood with a wise but dotty aunt who makes holiday fruitcakes. The run of the play usually begins the day after Thanksgiving and continues on weekdays and weekends until just before Christmas. Check with the hotel for show times and ticket prices, which are generally $10 for the evening show and around $30 for dinner and the show. Also making a visit to the Stanley a treat is an annual Christmas tree show sponsored by the Estes Park Women's Club with about 50 dazzling, decorated tabletop trees in the main lobby contributed by different local groups (see above).

Miniature Christmas Tree Exhibit
Stanley Hotel, 333 Wonderview Ave.,
Estes Park
(970) 586–4431
Tiny lights twinkle all over the lobby of the Stanley, and lavishly decorated doll-size Christmas trees vie for the attention of visitors to the Miniature Christmas Tree Exhibit. The exhibit is sponsored by the Estes Park Women's Club to benefit local nonprofit organizations. You can buy raffle tickets ($1) and maybe win your favorite tree. The trees are displayed the Monday after Thanksgiving until Dec. 21.

December

Round the Table Sing-Along
Stanley Concert Hall, Stanley Hotel, 333
Wonderview Ave., Estes Park
(970) 586–3371, (800) 976–1377
Generally during the first weekend in December the Estes Park Chorale sings traditional and contemporary songs of the season, and the audience is invited to join in. The sing-along starts around 7 P.M. Contributions are welcomed.

Holiday Home Tour Throughout Estes Park
Valley
(970) 586–4644
Proud owners of six fine Estes Park homes decorate for Christmas, then open their doors on a Saturday in mid-December so

you can wander inside. The Quota Club, a local businesswomen's group, sponsors the event, and profits go to local health and social needs. Usually the tour is from 11 A.M. to 4 P.M.

Oratorio Concert
Community Church of the Rockies,
1700 Brodie Ave., Estes Park
(970) 586–4404

The Oratorio Society and Estes Park Chamber Orchestra perform portions of the *Messiah* in a concert where it's obvious that the performers have practiced and practiced. When you just come for the performance, you can hum along with "The Hallelujah Chorus" if you must, but do it softly—this is a performance, not a sing-along. The concert usually starts around 7 P.M. on a Sunday in mid-December. Donations are appreciated.

Events Central

Here are the phone numbers and locations of the main event centers in town.

Cultural Arts Council
P.O. Box 4135, 160 Moraine Ave., Estes Park,
CO 80517
(970) 586–9203

The CAC represents all the arts in the area with the broad goal of enhancing the quality and accessibility of the arts in the Estes Valley. Call or write to these folks for music, art or theater events and programs.

Estes Park Chamber Resort Association and Visitor Information Center
500 Big Thompson Ave., Estes Park
(970) 586–4431, (800) 44–ESTES

Stop here for local information. To reach the center when coming from Boulder on U.S. Highway 36, go to the second stoplight and make a right. The center is right across from the Taco Bell on U.S. Highway 34. It's open from 8 A.M. to 8 P.M. Monday through Saturday, then from 9 A.M. to 6 P.M. on Sunday.

Estes Park Center/YMCA of the Rockies
2515 Tunnel Rd., Estes Park
(970) 586–3341

To reach the YMCA from Boulder, take U.S. Highway 36 to the second stoplight. Take a left at Elkhorn Avenue. At the second stoplight, turn left on Moraine Avenue. Follow the signs to the YMCA. The tree-lined road winds through a lot of countryside, but you'll soon be there.

Even if you're not staying at the YMCA, it can be a good place to call. They don't publicize their events very much, because they've got a built-in audience. But they often welcome nonguests. For instance, the public is welcome to attend the Christian Artists Music Seminar Concerts held from June through August and featuring all types of music.

Estes Park Fairground
Community Dr., Estes Park
(970) 586–6104

The fairground is off U.S. 36 near Lake Estes. To get there, you take either U.S. Highway 34 or 36 to the east side of town. Right after you pass Lake Estes, turn south onto Community Drive. You'll see arenas, the stables, the covered building for special events, and the ballfields. Numerous events take place here.

The Stanley Hotel
333 Wonderview Ave., Estes Park
(970) 586–3371, (800) 976–1377

Once you're in downtown, you'll see the big white Stanley Hotel on a hill northeast of town. The Stanley Concert Hall is up there too. You can't miss it; but if you do, just pull over anywhere and ask for directions. Everybody knows the Stanley. Call to check on the schedule of events.

Medical Care and Dental Care

Estes Park Dental
343 S. St. Vrain Ave., Estes Park
(970) 586–9330

If you need treatment for a toothache, this clinic has Saturday and evening hours plus same-day emergency care. Other possibilities appear in the Yellow Pages under "Dentists."

Estes Park Medical Center
555 Prospect Ave., Estes Park
(970) 586-2317

This facility has a staff of 10 full-time doctors, plus 20 specialists who visit weekly or monthly. The center includes 24-hour emergency care, radiology, and 16 inpatient rooms. Emergency helicopter service can transport patients to specialized hospitals. Also see the chapter on Healthcare and Wellness.

Timberline Medical
131 Stanley Ave., Suite 202, Estes Park
(970) 586-2343

This family practice also operates an urgent care center for treatment of injuries and illnesses that require immediate care but don't call for hospitalization. It is open 8 A.M. to 8 P.M. weekdays, 9 A.M. to 5 P.M. Saturday, and noon to 6 P.M. Sunday. The clinic closes at 6 P.M. every night in the winter.

Nightlife

Estes Park isn't big on nightlife, but there are a few choices for not-too-weary travelers or residents.

Estes Park Brewery
470 Prospect Village Dr., Estes Park
(970) 586-5421

The brewery has a pub, family restaurant, and outdoor deck, and serves pizza, sandwiches, burgers, and salads. During summer it's open from 11 A.M. to midnight daily. (Check for winter hours, which may vary.) There are free samples of the nine microbrews sold on tap and by the bottle. The Renegade Red has won a gold medal at the Great American Beer Festival.

The Old Gaslight Pub
246 Moraine Ave., Estes Park
(970) 586-0994

DJs provide the varied mix of music on weekends, and there's plenty of room for dancing. Dinner specials include fish and chips, Italian dishes, and other favorites. The bar has some British beers on tap and local microbrews.

Park Theatre
Corner of Moraine Ave. and Rockwell St., Estes Park
(970) 586-8904

Enjoy first-run movies every night from May through September here. The cafe is open until 6 or 7 P.M. during summer.

Park Village Playhouse
900 Moraine Ave., Estes Park
(970) 586-2885

Visit this playhouse to enjoy good, old-fashioned melodrama. The curtain goes up at 8 P.M., doors open at 7 P.M.; reservations are suggested.

The Stanley Hotel
333 Wonderview Ave., Estes Park
(970) 586-3371, (800) 976-1377

The Stanley presents theater and fine arts performances that vary with the season and include free concerts and holiday galas like "The Shining" Halloween Ball and a popular New Year's Eve party. There's a year-round jazz series. Call for the current schedule of events and ask about special honeymoon and "romance" packages.

Wheel Bar
132 E. Elkhorn Ave., Estes Park
(970) 586-9381

This local landmark has been owned and operated by the same family since 1945. The comfortable neighborhood bar offers bottled beers, microbrews on tap, and cocktails at happy-hour prices. Upstairs there's Orlando's steak house for a full meal.

Pet Care

Boarding House for Dogs and Cats
863 Dry Gulch Rd., Estes Park
(970) 586–6606

If you're thinking of leaving your furry friend shut in the car while you wander the lovely local shops don't! Colorado's intense sun can turn a car into an oven within minutes. This can happen even on a cool day—even with a window partially rolled down. Bring your pet here instead. On weekends, the Boarding House books fast, but generally a few days' notice works for short-term boarding. Reservations at least two weeks in advance work best.

Real Estate

Estes Park is becoming a more year-round community. While it has always drawn retirees, lately there's a new demographic in town—computer commuters. As the Front Range booms, industries needing highly skilled workers move closer to Estes Park, increasing its draw as a bedroom community to Boulder. All this means Estes Park is getting younger, drawing families and a wider range of business skills.

In the good old days, you could find a rental when everyone left for the summer, but people aren't leaving so often anymore. For a summer rental, start checking six months in advance. For a long-term rental, get your name in six months early, then check monthly. Homes to purchase are more available than homes for rent, but prices are not cheap. Something for less than $100,000 is unusual; the average price of a home in 1999 was $232,554—up from $141,000 in 1994—and prices continued to rise in subsequent years. The pop of air-gun hammers is more common around town these days and condominiums are springing up all around Estes Park. Through the valley is still a long way from reaching what is said to be its capacity of 22,000 people (valley winter population now is about 10,000), builders are

booked a year in advance. Investors are holding their income properties, and just a few timeshare opportunities are available. All of this information is not meant to discourage you, but rather remind you to start looking.

The Estes Park Chamber Resort Association provides a list of local Realtors.

Restaurants

Estes Park has a large number of restaurants and casual cafes to choose from, ranging from doughnut shops and pizzerias to fine French restaurants and gourmet Italian inns. Italian and Mexican food seem to predominate, but steaks, burgers, and trout are ubiquitous as well. Watch out for "Rocky Mountain Oysters." They're not seafood; in fact they come from a part of the bull that you might not want to consume. Fans say they taste a little like liver.

Even if you can't afford a meal at the historic Stanley Hotel, it's worth a visit for its landmark status, lovely setting, and the shiny green Stanley Steamer automobile parked in the lobby. Those on a budget can still enjoy coffee or afternoon tea at the Stanley on the front veranda or a snack from the Dunraven Grill's bar menu. The Stanley also hosts free classical concerts on Sunday afternoons.

Reservations are not required at most Estes Park restaurants but are accepted and recommended at some of the more popular spots, particularly for groups during the crowded summer season. Almost all restaurants of any size beyond a hole in the wall accept major credit cards.

Price-Code Key

The key below shows the price range for an average dinner for two excluding beverages, appetizers, desserts, or tip.

$	Less than $25
$$	$26 to $50
$$$	$51 to $75
$$$$	$76 and more

The Baldpate Inn
4900 Colo. Hwy. 7 S., south of Estes Park
(970) 586–6151
$-$$

You'll get a lot more than lunch or dinner if you visit the Baldpate Inn. This classic mountain inn and historic local landmark was placed on the National Register of Historic Places in 1996. The inn, which is open Memorial Day until mid- to late October, is 7 miles south of Estes Park at 9,000 feet altitude, across from the Rocky Mountain National Park Visitor Center at Lily Lake. At lunch there's a unique salad bar set in an old claw-foot bathtub, plus delectable homemade soups, breads, and pastries. Dinner is equally charming and delicious; reservations are a must. Mae West, Jack Dempsey and Rin Tin Tin stayed here, and you'll see their photos—along with those of opera singer Tetrazinni and world leaders—in the amazing collection in the dining room assembled by the two original owners. The inn has the world's largest key collection, which is open to the public. It serves lunch and dinner daily.

Black Canyon Inn
800 MacGregor Ave. (Devil's Gulch Rd.),
Estes Park
(970) 586–9344
$$-$$$

This historic mountain lodge offers a romantic fireside atmosphere to complement the fine dining. Seafood and pasta specials include salmon fettuccine and tomato fettuccine with fresh sea scallops. The restaurant also offers some wild game selections, including elk, plus duck and prawns. Black Canyon serves dinner only every day, and reservations are strongly suggested.

La Chaumiere
U.S. Hwy. 36, Pinewood Springs
(303) 823–6521
$$-$$$

Those with sophisticated palates who savor sautéed sweetbreads say La Chaumiere offers the best around. Another popular item is the duck liver paté. Classic French dining in a serene setting, complete with its own deer park, has drawn its faithful patrons to La Chaumiere for years. Though it's a bit out of the way (12 miles southeast of Estes Park), French food lovers don't mind the extra drive for the diverse, changing menu, including specialty game meats, lamb, beef, and seafood. The restaurant has its own smokehouse and organic garden and makes its own ice cream. A six-course, $35 dinner special is served every day. The restaurant is open 5:30 to 10 P.M. Tuesday through Saturday, 2 to 9 P.M. Sunday.

Donut Haus
342 Moraine Ave., Estes Park
(970) 586–2988
$

If it's just a doughnut you're craving, line up at the Donut Haus—there usually is a queue stretching out the door of this tiny doughnut bakery, which also has a large variety of other fresh-baked items. It's right beside the multicolored giant slides. It's closed on Wednesdays.

Dunraven Inn
2470 Colo. Hwy. 66, Estes Park
(970) 586–6409
$-$$

Probably not quite what Lord Dunraven had in mind, the Dunraven Inn calls itself the "Rome of the Rockies" and specializes in Italian food. (Lord Dunraven was the Irish nobleman who bought all of Estes Park in the 19th century to create his own private hunting reserve, but was eventually ousted by locals.) The Dunraven Inn has long been a favorite stop for steak and Italian dishes, including shrimp scampi, lasagna, eggplant Parmesan, and chicken cacciatore, plus a large selection of Italian wines. Be sure to make reservations during the summer months, when the restaurant is packed. Dinner is served daily.

Ed's Cantina and Grill
362 E. Elkhorn Ave., Estes Park
(970) 586–2919
$

In addition to all the Mexican favorites, plus barbecued ribs and sandwiches for lunch and dinner, this comfortable South-of-the-Border spot serves the local microbrew from Estes Park Brewery. Ed's is open 7 A.M. to 10 P.M. seven days a week.

Estes Park Brewery
470 Prospect Village Dr., Estes Park
(970) 586–5421
$–$$

The brewery has a pub, family restaurant, and outdoor deck, serving pizza, sandwiches, burgers, and salads. During summer it's open from 11 A.M. to midnight daily. (Check for winter hours, which may vary.) There are free brewery tours with free samples of the nine microbrews sold on tap and by the bottle. The Renegade Red has won a gold medal at the Great American Beer Festival.

Laura's Fine Candies
129 E. Elkhorn Ave., Estes Park
(970) 586–4004
$

Though it's not exactly a meal, for some it's considered daily bread. Of all the cotton candy and caramel apple stores, Laura's really stands out. The delicious fudge is made with whipping cream—locals have braved the summer weekend crowds packed on Elkhorn Avenue just for a piece of the stuff. Laura's also has homemade cookies, 25 flavors of fudge, and ice cream.

Lazy B Ranch
1915 Dry Gulch Rd., Estes Park
(970) 586–5371
$–$$

For a family night out and a taste of the Old West, sidle up to the chuckwagon where wranglers are dishing out barbecued beef, baked potatoes, beans, and biscuits with coffee or lemonade (no alcohol allowed on the trail, partner). After dinner, there's a live stage show with Western music, stories, and jokes. Souvenir and gift shops are open before dinner and after the show. The Lazy B is open summers only; the schedule varies, so be sure to call ahead.

Mama Rose's
Barlow Plaza, 338 E. Elkhorn Ave., Estes Park
(970) 586–3330
$

This tidy Italian restaurant in a pretty reproduction of an old Victorian home has a large selection of dishes. It offers a very pleasant veranda overlooking the river for dining. Choose from chicken parmesan in wine sauce, seafood fettuccine, fresh basil pesto, baked pasta, and other Italian dishes. Mama Rose's is open 4 to 9 P.M. Monday through Saturday and 11 A.M. to 9 P.M. Sunday.

Molly B Restaurant
200 Moraine Ave., Estes Park
(970) 586–2766
$

For coffee, a light breakfast, or a big meal, try this casual cafe that's open year-round. Along with the usual breakfast foods, you'll also find great choices for lunch or dinner, including seafood, vegetarian dishes, and burgers, and homemade desserts. It's another favorite stop of local mountaineers for an early breakfast or a late snack. Note that the restaurant takes a brief break daily between 3 and 5 P.M.

The Mountaineer
540 S. St. Vrain Rd., Estes Park
(970) 586–9001
$

Fast and friendly service is the hallmark of this unpretentious little cafe, with lots of granny-type knickknacks and corny paintings on the wall. But it's quite cozy and out of the hustle-bustle of downtown Estes Park. It's about a half-mile south on Colo. Highway 7, across the street from the Diamond Shamrock gas station and Estes Park Rehabilitation Center. Open daily for an early breakfast (at 6 A.M.), the restaurant features lots of morning food choices, including homemade biscuits and gravy and cinnamon rolls, and is quite inexpensive. Local climbers and mountaineers (and tourists) like to stop here for a tasty and inexpensive breakfast, lunch, or dinner.

Mountain Home Cafe
Stanley Village, intersection of U.S. Hwys.
34 and 36, Estes Park
(970) 586–6624
$

Formerly known as Johnson's and right in the shopping center, this little cafe isn't glamorous. But the food is quite good, especially the Swedish potato pancakes with sour cream and applesauce and the baked Alaska oatmeal. It's a favorite of area residents for the breakfasts served all day. You can also get lunch here Monday through Saturday, and the cafe is open Sunday for breakfast from 8 A.M. until 1 P.M. (closed afterward).

Nicky's Restaurant and Resort
1350 Fall River Rd., Estes Park
(970) 586–5376
$–$$

Nicky's claim to fame is the delicious prime rib roasted in rock salt. Out a few miles on Fall River Road (a pleasant drive), this large, attractive restaurant has a huge menu with lots of variety, including Italian and Greek specialties, steaks, and a salad bar. It's open year-round, for breakfast, lunch, and dinner daily from June to September, and for lunch and dinner, with breakfasts on weekends only, the rest of the year.

Notchtop Baked Goods & Natural Foods Cafe
and Pub
Upper Stanley Village, intersection of U.S.
Hwys. 34 and 36
(970) 586–0272
$

This local favorite has a pub with its own microbrew—Notchtop, of course. Stop here for delicious pastries or an inexpensive lunch. Very casual, with newspapers and magazines to read (such as *Mother Earth News*), the little cafe is a nice break from the tourist scene and serves nutritious food and natural beverages, plus great locally roasted Silver Canyon coffees. The cafe is open daily from breakfast through dinner. There's live music (no cover) Sunday nights from Memorial Day until Labor Day.

The Other Side
900 Moraine Ave., Estes Park
(970) 586–2171
$

Specializing in an "all-American" menu, this restaurant at the entrance to Rocky Mountain National Park at Mary's Lake Road has a pleasant view of a little duck pond. The menu offers seafood, steaks, prime rib, burgers, and a Sunday champagne brunch. Lunch and dinner are served daily, while breakfast is served Thursday through Sunday. Breakfast is served every day during the summer months.

Poppy's Pizza & Grill
342 E. Elkhorn Ave., Estes Park
(970) 586–8282
$

In the spiffy Barlow Plaza, this pleasant pizzeria has all types of pizza—pesto, Polynesian, Mexican, to name a few—for reasonable prices. Some of the individual pizzas are around $3. There are also homemade soups, salads, desserts, and sandwiches. When the weather cooperates, you can sit outside on the nice patio overlooking the river. Poppy's is open for lunch and dinner year-round, but closes for a time during January.

Safeway
Stanley Village, north of the intersection of
U.S. Hwys. 34 and 36, Estes Park
(970) 586–4447
$

For picnic or camping supplies on the way to Rocky Mountain National Park, look for the big Safeway supermarket up on the hill above the downtown area. There's also a salad bar and deli in the store.

The Stanley Hotel
333 Wonderview Ave., Estes Park
(970) 586–3371, (800) 976–1377
$$–$$$

For a special treat, try the Stanley's Sunday champagne brunch, served year round from 10 A.M. to 2 P.M. in the hotel's MacGregor ballroom. Unlimited champagne or mimosas accompany an unbelievable spread—every pastry you can imagine, and every breakfast dish, plus seafood, prime rib, and much, much, more. An eclectic mix of live music adds to the atmosphere (get dressed up if you want to, but casual is fine, too). For those with time and a hearty appetite, it's a real bargain for the $21.95-per-person price. Dinners at the Stanley are served in the Dunraven Grille, which was just completely renovated and has a brand-new bar. Choices include teriyaki ahi, chorizo-smoked chili rellenos, prime rib, and elk with such side dishes as ahi or duck salad and spicy red bean or beer-cheese soup. The Stanley serves breakfast, lunch, and dinner daily year-round. The Dunraven Grille also offers a bar menu from 11:30 A.M. until 3 P.M. Monday through Saturday. During summer there's usually a long waiting list for tables on the hotel's lovely front veranda, which has a spectacular mountain view, and where breakfast, lunch, and dinner are also served.

Wild Basin Lodge & Smorgasbord
1130 County Rd. 84 West, 13 mi. south of Estes Park
(303) 747-2545
$

Casual, come-as-you-are dining with lots of food and a great view of a rushing river are the highlights of this landmark lodge. In summer, the all-you-can-eat smorgasbord is a daily dinner occurrence Monday through Saturday, and for lunch and dinner on Sunday. After summer the restaurant is open weekends until November 1 and it reopens for weekends again on Palm Sunday. Wild Basin is at the south entrance to Rocky Mountain National Park.

Retirement

Some locals estimate that more than half the full-time residents of the Estes Valley are retired. That doesn't mean nonworking or seniors—many people have jobs because they enjoy keeping busy, and many others have taken early retirement

from big companies. Whatever age they are and whatever "work" residents do, it's true that many people look all over the nation then choose to retire in Estes Valley. If you're among them, visit the Estes Park Senior Center.

A note regarding transportation: one local senior warns that you shouldn't come up here without your own, since there is no public bus system.

Estes Park Senior Center
220 Fourth St., Estes Park
(970) 586-2996

The center is open from 9 A.M. to 3 P.M. Monday through Friday. The Senior Center serves meals five days a week. In the summertime, approximately 40 people enjoy dining here every day. During the winter, the number is in the 30s. About 25 meals a day are transported to seniors' homes. There's a blood-pressure clinic once a month. Exercise classes happen three times a week. The Senior Center is also a good place to connect with town activities, including book groups, lectures, art classes, and pinochle and bridge clubs. It hosts card games twice a week and a weekly oil-painting class. For information on the Retired and Senior Volunteer Program (RSVP), call (970) 586-9486. The local quilt guild and the rock and mineral club hold meetings here, too.

Shopping

Estes Park's shopping area is an attractive but bewildering stretch of gingerbread glitz with a theme and style somewhere between Switzerland and Coney Island. Saltwater taffy in the Rocky Mountains? Unfortunately, some of the clothing, jewelry, knickknacks, "art," and other items found in the shops have nothing to do with Estes Park, Colorado, or the Rocky Mountains. Other offerings are more Southwestern and related to Native American tribes nowhere near the area.

Despite this, a really nice feature of the Estes Park shopping area is the riverside walkway called Confluence Park behind the main street of shops and right on the Big Thompson River. Lots of little wooden bridges provide access across the river to free parking lots all around. Almost all of the shops along the south side of Elkhorn Avenue go through to this very pleasant and relaxing walkway beside the tumbling river, with shade trees, flowers, and lots of benches to rest on.

Canyonlands Indian Arts
146 W. Elkhorn Ave., Estes Park
(970) 577–0479
This shop features top-quality Indian and Southwest jewelry, authentic pottery, kachinas, carvings, and Navajo rugs.

Common Scents
205A Park Lane, Estes Park
(970) 586–5665
The smell is enough to bring you in the front door of this little shop, which sells wax potpourri handmade in Estes Park.

This is a mix-your-own store—make yourself an olfactory apple pie by combining apple, cinnamon, clove, and vanilla. Or, buy one of the ready-mixed blends like Long's Peak Trail—pine, blue spruce, cedar, blue columbine, and lavender. The potpourri can be stored in a ventilated basket to scent a room for weeks, or melted in a potpourri pot to spread aroma through the whole house.

Craftsmen in Leather
135 W. Elkhorn Ave., Estes Park
(970) 586–2400
"Come in and smell the leather," invites this store. You can take a self-guided tour of the shop, try on some of the hats in the huge inventory—which includes everything from fur felt and suede to wool and straw—and learn how to care for leather goods. The store also sells belts and buckles, handbags and luggage, wallets, moccasins, and jewelry.

Downtown Estes Park has an array of gift shops, including Common Scents, which sells wax potpourri in dozens of scents. PHOTO: LINDA CORNETT

Glass Blowers
126 E. Elkhorn Ave., Estes Park
(970) 586-5963

Those who would like a blown-glass hummingbird can find one of the best selections in the area at this shop. Most of the blown glass is made at the shop's other studio in Manitou Springs, Colorado. You'll find hummingbirds in every color of the rainbow here, from red and green ruby throats to copper rufous hummers. All types of other miniature figures are represented in glass as well.

The Hiking Hut
110 E. Elkhorn Ave., Estes Park
(970) 586-0708

This shop offers a nice selection of backpacks, jackets, sunglasses, and other accessories for hiking and camping in the mountains.

MacDonald Book Shop
152 E. Elkhorn Ave., Estes Park
(970) 586-3450

Established in 1928, this large bookstore in an old log cabin was originally the home of turn-of-the-20th-century residents. The owners of the bookstore and adjacent coffee shop (below) have had the bookstore for four generations. *The New York Times* is available, along with a wide selection of hardcovers, paperbacks, children's books, books on cassette, magazines, and calendars. Be sure to read the history plaque out front explaining how the first bookstore on the site was opened in the owners' living room. Colorful Scottish plaid carpet and exposed log beams set the interior mood.

MacDonald Paper & Coffee House
150 E. Elkhorn Ave., Estes Park
(970) 586-3451

Right behind the bookstore of the same name, this cozy coffeehouse has a casual relaxing atmosphere that invites visitors to stay for a while. The shop has a great selection of stationery, greeting cards, gift wrap, and posters and also offers a wide variety of teas, tempting pastries, fresh-squeezed orange juice, Italian fruit drinks, and other beverages. Tables are sprinkled around upstairs and down among the cards. It's light, bright, and pleasant, decorated throughout in blond wood. Sit down with a cappuccino and write a card or letter. The coffeehouse opens daily at 8 A.M.

Moses Street Photography
157 W. Elkhorn, Estes Park
(970) 586-7221, (888) 315-1125,
(800) 634-8401

Okay, it's not exactly shopping, but we thought you might want to know about this service. Moses Street specializes in portraits, but we're not talking about a stool in front of a fake bookcase. In addition to glamour portraits and family reunions captured on film, Moses will actually capture your image at the top of a mountain or canoeing across a crystal lake, if that's where you want to go. "We travel anywhere in the world to do any type of people photography," Moses promises.

Outdoor World
156 E. Elkhorn Ave., Estes Park
(970) 586-2114

Shop here for a great selection of high-quality boots, backpacks, jackets, water bottles, and everything you need for the outdoors.

Park Theatre
Moraine Ave. and Rockwell St., Estes Park
(970) 586-8904

A sprinkling of small shops are nestled around the historic Park Theatre, which was built in 1913. The theatre's impressive white tower—Estes Park's tallest structure—was added to the building by a former owner as a monument to a woman who left him at the altar. The Park Theatre's cafe and snack shops—open from 8 A.M. until 9 P.M. daily—are a good place to stop in summer. Down the lane next to a little shopping mall is Ye Old Tin Shop, at No. 134 (970-586-5129), with a charming collection of reproductions of antique

There's a definite Tyrolean flair to the architecture in downtown Estes Park. PHOTO: LINDA CORNETT

metal tins, including Morton Salt, Lipton Tea, and Hershey's Kisses tins, and many more unusual antique signs and metal plaques—all quite inexpensive.

Rocky Mountain Knife Company
125 Moraine Ave., Estes Park
(970) 586–8419

This tiny shop bills itself as "the Biggest Little Knife Store West of the Mississippi." It's not just knives, though. The walls and shelves are covered with everything from kitchen cutlery to crossbows, swords and battle axes, tomahawks, blow guns and sling shots, water balloons, and martial arts supplies. They sharpen knives, too.

Stanley Village
Intersection of U.S. Hwys. 34 and 36,
Estes Park
(970) 586–6114

This shopping center is located directly below the imposing, white Stanley Hotel, which is perched on a hillside above

town—you can't miss it. Slightly to the east are a Safeway and a shopping area that offers visitors lots of necessary services. To the east of Safeway is a Coast to Coast Hardware store (970–586–3496), for those little gadgets you always end up needing on a trip. There's also the Notchtop Baked Goods & Natural Foods Cafe and Pub, and Mountain Home Cafe (see the previous "Restaurants" section of this chapter for details on each) as well as many other shops and a movie theater.

The Talking Teddy
521 Lone Pine Dr., Estes Park
(970) 586–6483

Visit this fun shop for a mind-boggling assortment of teddy bears in all sizes and styles, teddy bear-related items such as Smokey Bear hats, teddy bear-decorated T-shirts, and individual bears made by various "teddy bear artists." The shop also sells various other plush animals and collectibles.

Western Brands
141 E. Elkhorn Ave., Estes Park
(970) 586–3361

If it's a hat you need, stop here. There's a great selection of cowboy hats plus wonderful felt bowlers, top hats and more. Western Brands also carries lots of Levi's, T-shirts, and jackets, blankets, "cattle drover" coats, and other items to make you feel at home on the range.

Winona Knits
344 E. Elkhorn Ave., Barlow Plaza,
Estes Park
(970) 586–0947

Winona Knits offers an attractive and affordable selection of sportswear with golf, fishing, and tennis themes and other nice casual clothing for the family. Winona's motto: "Life should be comfortable."

Sports

Most people visit Estes Park to see Rocky Mountain National Park and go camping, hiking, or fishing. Yet in addition to these activities, you can participate in everything from sailboarding on Lake Estes to golf and tennis in Estes Park. Horseback riding is a popular activity in the area, with trails leading into the park or the surrounding national forest. Several rafting companies take thrill-seekers to such frothy rivers outside the immediate area as the Poudre and Arkansas. The following are some of the town's many options.

Bicycling

Colorado Bicycling Adventures
184 E. Elkhorn Ave., Estes Park
(970) 586-4241, (800) 607-8765

To rent a bike, or to get information about where to bicycle, stop here—the only bike shop in town. It's a full-service bike shop offering sales and shipping. This shop not only rents brand-new mountain bikes in different models, but also offers several different guided bicycle tours, including a downhill ride from the top of Trail Ridge Road in Rocky Mountain National Park. Cost is $70 per person and includes bike, helmet, and souvenir water bottle plus a continental breakfast. It's about a four-hour trip from Estes Park and back again. No riders under 12 allowed.

There's also a downhill tour in the North Fork Canyon ($46 for adults, $36 for children under 12) suited to riders of all ages—they've taken bicyclists ages 4 to 90. Another tour is in Johnny Park, in Roosevelt National Forest, for more aggressive riders who don't mind a few hills and want to get off-road ($53 per person).

The shop also rents bikes and all types of bike accessories, including trailers to pull children, locks, packs, and car racks. It sells a guidebook of all off-road areas in Roosevelt National Forest and has free maps that show cyclists where to ride right from the store on their own.

Camping

Two campgrounds are run by the Estes Valley Recreation and Park District:

Mary's Lake Campground and Estes Park Campground, but there are also a number of privately owned campgrounds in the area. (See the Rocky Mountain National Park chapter for information on camping in the national park.)

Blue Arrow RV Park and Campground
Colo. Highway 66, adjacent to the south entrance to Rocky Mountain National Park, Estes Park
(970) 586-5342

This is Estes Park's largest RV park and campground. With 170 sites, Blue Arrow offers history along with its views and amenities such as a country store, laundry, playgrounds, and nondenominational church services. The 30-acre site was originally a camping ground for Arapahoe and Ute living in the area. In the 1960s, historical buildings were hauled to the site to create a "frontier town" for moviemakers. Still remaining, and in use, are the original Bear Lake Lodge, built in 1919 and later removed from the park, and a Central City brothel, now used as the camp's recreation hall. All sites are full hookup and rates are $33.25 for RVs and $23.50 for and tent camping.

Elkhorn Lodge Wilderness Camping
600 W. Elkhorn Ave., Estes Park
(970) 586-4416

A 10-minute hike from the Elkhorn Lodge is the opportunity to experience

Indian and Old West camping in your own tent or a rented tepee. Transportation to the campground, water, and a portable toilet are provided. There are no other amenities, but you live surrounded by wildlife and rugged trails leading through wilderness. If you decide to wimp out, there's a restaurant, saloon, swimming pool, and bathing facilities available at the lodge. Rates are $18 per adult and $9 for children 4 to 13 years old.

Estes Park Campground
Hwy. 66 (Tunnel Rd.), a mile past the Estes Park Center/YMCA of the Rockies, Estes Park
(970) 586–4188

Peaceful and secluded, campground has 68 sites, 20 with water and electricity. Head west on U.S. Highway 36 and then turn left on Colo. Highway 66 (which becomes Tunnel Road). Continue for 3 miles; the campground is a mile past the Estes Park Center/YMCA of the Rockies, at the end of a paved road and adjacent to the national park. It is open late May through early September. Costs range from $20 to $26, depending on date and utilities; amenities include showers and restrooms, a playground, a public phone, and firewood and ice for sale. Fishing, with a Colorado license, is available at a neighboring pond. Pets are permitted on a leash.

Jellystone Park
5495 U.S. Hwy. 36
(970) 586–4230, (800) 722–2928

In addition to tent, camper, and RV sites there are housekeeping and camping cabins at this park, which is 5 miles southeast of Estes Park on U.S. 36. The wooded sites are pleasant and quiet. It's open May through September and charges from $23 to $33 per night for two. Children and pets are welcome. Forty-six sites have water and electricity only, and 43 also have sewer.

KOA Campground
Hwy. 34, one mile east of Estes Park
(970) 586–2888

Try out a rented tepee or set up your own tent or RV at this campground with showers, a grocery and gift store, fishing equipment, a game room, mini-golf, and laundry facilities. A tepee that will sleep two to four (mattresses are provided, bring your own linens) is $30 a night; campsites are $23 to $33 a night for two people.

Mary's Lake Campground
Mary's Lake Rd. (directions below)
(970) 586–4411

Though not exactly remote or secluded, Mary's Lake has great views by a pleasant lake plus a heated swimming pool, hot showers, electrical service, a playground and basketball court, a store, and laundry facilities. Drive south of town on U.S. Highway 36 and turn left on Mary's Lake Road. The campground is 3 miles from town and the national park, and is open mid-May through September. Prices range from $22 for tent camping to $28 or $30 per night for RVs, depending upon services chosen.

National Park Resort Campground
2501 Fall River Rd.
(970) 586–4563

Right at the national park's Fall River entrance, this campground has hot showers, hookups, cable TV, a livery, and secluded, terraced sites. The 96-site campground is open May through September. The fee for two people is $25 to $27 per night. There are 68 sites with water and electricity, and another 22 also have sewer hookups.

Paradise RV & Travel Park
1836 Colo. Hwy. 66
(970) 586–5513

Near the YMCA along the Big Thompson River, this adult-oriented park offers 30 sites with RV hookups, cable, bathrooms, fishing, and a laundry. It's open May through September and charges from $22 to $24 for tent camping and $26 to $33 for RVs.

Climbing

Colorado Mountain School
P.O. Box 2062, 351 Moraine Ave.,
Estes Park, CO 80517
(970) 586–5758,
(800) 444–0730 (outside Colorado)

Learn rock climbing or mountaineering at this highly regarded school, ranked one of the top eight in the world by the *Ultimate Adventure Sourcebook*. One-day introductory classes prepare people to begin climbing with guides. The school offers guided hikes, climbs (including technical routes of Longs Peak), and equipment rentals. The school is open year-round, and reservations are requested. Lodging and excursions to other great climbing around the world are also available.

Estes Park Mountain Sports
358 E. Elkhorn Ave., Estes Park
(970) 586–6548, (800) 369–4165

This shop offers instruction and guiding both indoors and out. Learn to climb on the 3,000-square-foot indoor rock-climbing wall and practice these skills on half-day lessons in the field and full-day guided climbs.

Insiders' Tip

Those who would like to rub shoulders with the daring rock jocks who climb the "Diamond" face of Longs Peak (a world-renowned climb) should try an early breakfast at either The Mountaineer or Molly B's. Climbers reputedly have their pre-climb breakfasts at these cafes.

Cross-Country Skiing

See the Rocky Mountain National Park chapter for information on ski trails in the national park. Rental equipment is available in the following outdoor shops in Estes Park. Packages (skis, boots, poles) average $10 for a day, $18 for a weekend.

Estes Park Mountain Sports
358 E. Elkhorn Ave., Estes Park
(970) 586–6548, (800) 369–4165

Stop here for ski and snowshoe rentals, plus a range of other outdoor equipment, clothing, and accessories.

Estes Park Ski Shop
184 E. Elkhorn Ave., Estes Park
(970) 586–4241

This shop also carries downhill skis and snowboards for about $18 a day, and snowshoes for $10 a day.

Fishing

Some local spots include the Big Thompson River, Lake Estes, and Mary's Lake. The best spot on the Big Thompson River is said to be the stretch 8 miles downstream from Lake Estes called Grandpa's Retreat (flies and lures only), where the Colorado Division of Wildlife and the National Forest Service have created several deep holes. The Big Thompson runs along U.S. Highway 34; there are small parking areas along the shoulder. You'll also find several wheelchair-accessible fishing ramps along this stretch.

Lake Estes, on the east side of town between U.S. Highways 34 and 36, is stocked by the Colorado Division of Wildlife with rainbow trout and also has a few German brown trout. Mary's Lake inlet is another good spot to try. Follow U.S. 36 to the east end of town to Mary's Lake Road at the traffic light, turn left and drive 1.5 miles.

You can fish in Colorado without a license only on the first full weekend in June. Otherwise, you must have a license. One-day licenses are available for $5.25; a five-day license is $18.25. Colorado residents can get an annual pass for $20.25; nonresidents must pay almost twice that. Fishing licenses are available at the following locations: Do It Best in Upper Stanley Village (970–586–3496); Estes Angler in Picadilly Square (970–586–2110); Lake Estes Marina on U.S. 34 (970–586–2011); Mary's Lake Campground, 2120 Mary's Lake Road (970–586–4411); Scot's Sporting Goods, Moraine Avenue at U.S. 36 West, (970–586–2877).

Estes Angler
338 W. Riverside Dr., Estes Park
(970) 586–2110, (800) 586–2110

Inquire about the best places and flies to use and pick up everything you need to tie them, plus all types of clothing and equipment. Guided fishing trips and instruction for beginners are also available.

Estes Park Mountain Sports
358 E. Elkhorn Ave., Estes Park
(970) 586–6548, (800) 504–6642

In addition to a complete fly shop and outdoor equipment and clothing, this shop offers rental equipment and instruction and guided trips in and around Rocky Mountain National Park.

Rocky Mountain Adventures
1360 Big Thompson Rd., Estes Park
(970) 586–6191, (970) 493–4005,
(800) 858–6808 in Fort Collins

This company offers year-round guided fly-fishing day trips on Big Thompson River a few miles from Estes Park, and overnights on the Poudre, Upper Colorado, and North Platte Rivers. The company is permitted by the forest service in those locations and licensed by the State of Colorado. The main office in Fort Collins is open year-round. The Estes Park office is open Memorial Day to Labor Day.

Scot's Sporting Goods
2325 Spruce Ave., Estes Park
(970) 586–2877

Stop by and ask owner Scot Richie— the local fishing authority and a third-

generation Rocky Mountain fisherman— where to catch the big ones. He can also recommend and sell the best things to catch them with, including a selection of flies tied by local anglers who know what Estes Park fish like best. The shop also offers fly-fishing lessons and guided trips on the Big Thompson River and rents fishing equipment.

Trout Haven
810 Moraine Ave., Estes Park
(970) 586–5525

For the angler who doesn't want a wilderness experience but rather a guaranteed catch, there's Trout Haven. No license is required and everything is provided— including the cleaning. You pay 50 cents an inch for whatever you catch. It's located a little more than a mile west of downtown on U.S. 36 behind Kentucky Fried Chicken. They'll cook your catch on the spot at the on-site restaurant, or you can have it packed in ice to go. You can even trade it in for smoked trout and take it with you.

Golf

Estes Park Golf Club
1080 S. St. Vrain Rd., Estes Park
(970) 586–8146

This 18-hole course is one of the oldest golf courses in the state, dating from 1912. In early fall, elk wander onto the course—watch out for their divots. The greens fee is $36; $22 after 2 P.M. for nonresidents.

Lake Estes Executive Course
690 Big Thompson Ave., Estes Park
(970) 586–8176

This nine-hole course along the banks of the Big Thompson River provides a good game and a view to go with it. The greens fee is $13 for nonresidents; $9 after 3 P.M. From November through March, you can play all day for just $7; no tee times are required.

Miniature Golf

Miniature golf may be little, but in Estes it's big. Courses are all mini amusement parks, where it's easy to spend money on silly activities. The cost is usually fairly reasonable. During the summer, these places often stay open from early morning until 10 at night.

Estes Park Ride-A-Kart
2250 Big Thompson Ave., Estes Park
(970) 586–6495

This mini amusement park has 36 holes of miniature golf, go-karts, bumper boats, and a miniature train.

Fun City
375 Moraine Ave., Estes Park
(970) 586–2070

Kids will enjoy the 36-hole miniature golf course, bumper cars, video arcade, and two slides at Fun City, which is open every day in the summer, and on weekends only in the spring and fall.

Tiny Town Miniature Golf
840 Moraine Ave., Estes Park
(970) 586–6333

Tiny Town features a 19-hole miniature golf course in a lovely garden setting, with lots of challenging and entertaining features. The course has been in the same family for 46 years, and the friendly owner is a great source of information about other fun things to do in the area.

Hiking and Backpacking

Most hikers head to Rocky Mountain National Park, but the nearby Roosevelt National Forest also offers excellent backcountry trails. Contact the Estes Park Office of Roosevelt National Forest for maps and information about hiking trails: 161 Second Street, (970) 586–3440. See "Hiking" in our Rocky Mountain National Park chapter for other hiking opportunities. You can also stroll along the Big Thompson River corridor from Lake Estes all the way to the YMCA Camp, or get sidetracked by the shop windows downtown and call it a hike. Or follow Highway 7 on a pleasant separate trail.

Crosier Mountain Trail
Devil's Gulch Rd. (directions below)

A moderately difficult 8-mile round-trip that climbs to the top of Crosier Mountain (elevation 9,250 feet), this trail runs through lush meadows and aspen groves past ruins of old homesteads. You'll have superb views from the summit. The trailhead is about 8 miles northeast of Estes Park on Devil's Gulch Road, a mile past Glen Haven. Look for a large gravel cut on the south side of the road to the right.

Fish Creek Trail
U.S. Hwy. 36, Lake Estes

This unpaved 6-mile (one way) hike starts out easy but becomes moderately difficult when you reach the final 2 miles. It follows Fish Creek from its mouth at Lake Estes to its intersection with Colo. Highway 7 south of Mary's Lake.

Lily Mountain Trail
Colo. Hwy. 7 (directions below)

An easy 1.5-mile hike, this trail begins near Estes Park and climbs to 8,800 feet, with fantastic summit views of Estes Park, Longs Peak to the south, and the Continental Divide to the west. The trailhead is 6 miles south of Estes Park on Colo. Highway 7. Just before the 6-mile marker look for a small turnoff on the right, where there's a parking area and trailhead sign.

Lion Gulch
U.S. Hwy. 36 (directions below)

Another pleasant trail of moderate difficulty, Lion Gulch leads to an area of old homesteads and is about 3 miles one way. The trailhead is at mile marker 8 from Estes Park on U.S. 36.

Horseback Riding

Estes Park has numerous stables and outfitters offering everything from kids' pony rides to trail rides and pack trips into the mountains. Most rides head into Rocky Mountain National Park. Virtually all the stables have the same rates—$20 for a one-hour ride and $35 for two hours.

Aspen Lodge
6120 Colo. Hwy. 7, Estes Park
(970) 586–8133, (800) 332–6867

A 3,000-acre ranch resort, Aspen Lodge offers rides into both Rocky Mountain National Park and Roosevelt National Forest. It's south of Estes Park on Colo. Highway 7. There are meadow rides, and steak dinner rides, and a two-hour breakfast ride.

Elkhorn Stables
600 W. Elkhorn Ave., Estes Park
(970) 586–5225

This stable offers breakfast ride; rides ending with a steak dinner, country music, and dancing, hourly rides; and ponies for children. Open year-round, it guides trips into the national park. Take time to tour the 120-year-old lodge and stables.

Sombrero Ranch on the Dam on Lake Estes
U.S. Hwy. 34 E.
(970) 586–4577, (303) 442–0258

Sombrero offers rides into the national forest (not the national park). There's a breakfast ride, a steak-fry evening ride, and an overnight pack trip. Fishing trips are offered, too.

Rafting

There's no rafting to speak of right in the Estes Park area, but there are numerous outfitters that will take you on full- or half-day trips on the Poudre or Arkansas Rivers and rather far afield to the Dolores and Colorado Rivers.

Estes Park Mountain Shop
358 E. Elkhorn Ave., Estes Park
(970) 586–6548, (800) 369–4165

Inquire here about a variety of raft trips on different Colorado rivers; full- and half-day adventures are offered. Estes Park Mountain Sports also offers rock-climbing instruction and has an indoor rock-climbing wall.

Rapid Transit Rafting Ltd.
161 Virginia Dr., Estes Park
(970) 586–8852, (800) 367–8523

Whitewater adventures include full-day trips on the Colorado River and half-day trips on the Poudre River leaving from Estes Park. There's a variety of rafting, from exciting deep canyon rapids to relaxing float water stretches. Trips are suitable for beginners as well as experienced rafters. All the necessary rafting gear, experienced licensed guides, and lunch or snacks are provided. Reservations are recommended.

Rocky Mountain Adventures
1360 Big Thompson Rd., Estes Park
(970) 586–6191, (970) 493–4005,
(800) 858–6808 in Fort Collins

Half- and full-day and overnight trips are offered for whitewater rafting from beginner to advanced levels. Trips are on the Big Thompson, Poudre, and North Platte rivers. All the necessary equipment, plus lunch and snacks are provided, along with licensed guides. The company also provides kayak instruction and lake touring in sea kayaks on Lake Estes. The Fort Collins office is open year-round, and the Estes Park location is open Memorial Day to Labor Day.

Wanderlust
3500 Bingham Hill, Fort Collins
(970) 484–1219

The Cache La Poudre River (apparently named by a French trapper who had left his hunting supplies stored nearby) is the highway for Wanderlust rafting trips, leaving from Estes Park, Fort Collins, and Loveland. Trips range from the Taste Trip (6 miles for rafting newbies) to a full day of whitewater stretching 18 miles and requiring that rafters be in good physical condition. Wanderlust's guides can be seen on reruns of the TV show *Walker—Texas Ranger* involving whitewater rafting. Reservations are required.

Swimming

Estes Park Aquatic Center
660 Community Dr., Estes Park
(970) 586–2340

Just south of Lake Estes, the center has an indoor/outdoor pool. There are separate times for lap swimming, a ladies' night, lessons for first-time swimmers and mothers and babies, and a wading pool for toddlers.

Lake Estes Marina
1770 Big Thompson Ave., Estes Park
(970) 586–2011

The waters of Lake Estes are too chilly for swimming unless you like wearing a wetsuit, which can be rented here, along with sailboarding equipment and other small craft. The marina, which has beaches and picnic areas, is east of town on U.S. Highway 34.

Tennis

Stanley Park
380 Community Dr., Estes Park
(970) 586–8191

Just south of Lake Estes and operated by the Estes Valley Recreation and Park District, Stanley Park has six courts, which are free.

Other Sports Spots

Lake Estes Marina
Lake Estes on U.S. Hwy. 34
(970) 586–2011

This public facility offers fishing access, picnic areas, a hike and bike trail, bike rentals, and rental boats of all kinds—fishing, sport, pontoon, canoes, and paddleboats. There's also a marina store that sells fishing licenses, bait and tackle, snacks and clothing.

Rocky Mountain Athletic Club
1230 Big Thompson Road, Estes Park
(970) 586–8418

With all of the sports and fitness options in the surrounding outdoors, you might not think there's anything to be added by an indoor facility. Well, how about racquetball, handball, and squash court; free weights and resistance equipment with a view of the mountains; aerobics classes; therapeutic massage; and whirlpools and saunas? The Athletic Club offers all that, plus a treadwall that gives a taste of rock climbing and an aerobic workout at the same time. There's also a reaction-time workout station—wield a staff at randomly flashing targets a la Luke Skywalker. The guest fee is $10 per visit. Strangely, the club rules prohibit exposed midriffs, so cover up that hard-won six-pack.

Stanley Park
380 Community Dr., Estes Park
(970) 586–8189

Run by the Estes Valley Recreation and Park District, Stanley Park has a playground; basketball, volleyball, and tennis courts; baseball/softball and soccer fields; shelters; and a picnic area.

Summer Camps

Many lodging places around Estes Park offer special programs for children. Check the previous "Accommodations" section in this chapter for possibilities. Summer camps around Estes Park are also organized by church groups, so check the "Worship" section of this chapter for some phone numbers you can call for more information. For instance, Covenant Heights (970–586–2900) is a conference center with facilities for up to 200 people that is used for a number of children's programs. The programs must be church-related, educational, or nonprofit.

Cheley Camp
(In winter) P.O. Box 6525, Denver, CO 80206
(800) 226–7386
(In summer) 3960 Fish Creek Rd., Estes Park
(970) 586–4244

Cheley's summer camp program has been featured in national magazines such as *Country Living*. It's probably the largest privately owned camp west of the Mississippi and has been around since 1921. Nearly 500 kids enjoy the fun, in camps of 60 each, grouped by age and sex. The camp sessions are four weeks or eight weeks. Mountaineering, with fabulous vistas everywhere, and horseback riding on nearly 150 camp-owned horses are especially popular activities. And with hiking right out the back door, the children get to know the Rocky Mountains. Cheley starts filling up by January, so apply early.

Estes Park Center/YMCA of the Rockies
2515 Tunnel Rd., Estes Park
(970) 586-3341

The YMCA has a summer day-camp program for potty-trained 2-year-olds through high-schoolers. It's from 8:30 A.M. to 3:30 P.M. and programs are grouped according to age. The older kids can participate in leadership programs and adventure hikes. The youngest kids are more likely to stay close by. Pre-registration is required, and parents must either be staying at the Y or be Y members.

Tours

Aerial Tramway
420 E. Riverside Dr., Estes Park
(970) 586-3675

Right in Estes Park, this three- to five-minute ride overlooks the town with great views of Longs Peak and the Continental Divide. The tram takes you to the summit of Prospect Mountain, where you can take your time hiking, picnicking, and photographing the spectacular vista from the observation platform.

American Wilderness Tours
875 Moraine Ave., Estes Park
(970) 586-1626

Six-wheeled vehicles take you off the beaten path and into the backcountry. Some tours include steak dinners and sing-alongs. Tours for private groups are available. Call for prices.

Estes Park Shuttle and Tours
429 W. Elkhorn Ave., Estes Park
(970) 586-5151

This company offers summertime tours over Trail Ridge Road, a Grand Lake Tour, horseback riding trips in the park, Bear Lake hikes and Fall Foliage/Elk Bugling tours, as well as year-round shuttle service from Denver International Airport. Call for current rates.

Worship

Estes Park has more than a dozen churches, with an average church membership of about 300. Many offer Bible School, evening programs and summer camps. Check the Yellow Pages under "Churches" for details. Every Friday, the local newspaper, the *Trail Gazette*, lists services and church news. The Estes Park Center/YMCA of the Rockies (970-586-3341), see listing under "Accommodations" has a full-time pastor on staff, plus facilities for church-related (and secular) events.

Estes Park is less than an hour's trip to Boulder as the angel flies. Some Boulder County churches actually are closer to Estes Park than to the City of Boulder. So you can broaden your choices by also checking the Boulder Worship chapter.

Grand Lake

For those who want to visit Rocky Mountain National Park but also want to avoid the crush and hustle of Estes Park, Grand Lake is an amiable alternative. A little more than a mile from the western entrance to the park and on Colorado's largest natural lake, Grand Lake offers a quieter experience. One of the oldest settlements on the Western Slope, this six-block rustic community of some 320 permanent residents, with picturesque false-front buildings, is surrounded by Shadow Mountain Lake, Grand Lake, Rocky Mountain National Park, and Arapaho National Recreation Area.

Grand Lake's main attraction is the area's beauty, and it prides itself on being a family town. There's no nightlife to speak of, other than a few bars with music in summer and on weekends in spring and fall. There's no movie theater, but in summer there's live professional theater and a good children's recreation program. The town has two tennis courts, a town park, and a beautiful beach on the lake. The Grand Lake Golf Course is one of the top 10 in the state.

The area offers access to some of the state's best hiking, fishing and other outdoor activities. The trio of large lakes—Grand Lake, Lake Granby, and Shadow Mountain Reservoir—offer a variety of watersports, including boating, waterskiing, sailboarding, and fishing. Routt and Arapaho National Forests offer great hiking and backpacking, as does the western side of the Indian Peaks Wilderness Area.

Such is the commitment of natives to outdoor recreation that public schools are open four days a week, and on Mondays any child with a student I.D. can ski for free in area resorts.

Grand Lake lies on the western side of Rocky Mountain National Park. PHOTO: DAILY CAMERA

In summer, Grand Lake's population swells to about 4,000, with many tourists coming through daily on their way to Rocky Mountain National Park or for various outdoor pursuits. In winter, there's excellent cross-country skiing at Grand Lake Ski Touring Center and national forest trails, and downhill skiing nearby at Winter Park and Silver Creek. The town also boasts an ice-skating rink and many sites for ice fishing and sledding.

The Rocky Mountain Repertory Theatre draws young actors from across the country every summer to a professional season of performances.

Because of its more isolated location—literally at the end of the road—Grand Lake never experienced the development of Estes Park, and residents consider this a blessing. Nevertheless, the town and area offer the necessary amenities for visitors, including guest ranches, cabins, motels, and lodges, along with gift shops, galleries, cafes, and fine dining establishments. Abundant camping, fishing, hiking, and natural beauty lure nature lovers to the area.

History

Grand Lake's name comes from the early name for the Colorado River, the "Grand," with headwaters beginning on the Continental Divide just north of the lake. Ute Indians frequented the area for hunting expeditions over the Continental Divide, following trails along Grand Lake's North Inlet and Tonahutu Creek up into the mountains. Arapaho and Cheyenne also visited the area to hunt the plentiful game and fish in the large lake, but relations were not peaceful.

Grand Lake was known as Spirit Lake by the Ute after a particularly tragic incident. During an attack by the Cheyenne and Arapaho, the Ute put their women and children on a makeshift raft and sent them out to the middle of the lake to escape harm. But a storm came up and the raft capsized in the deepest part of the lake, drowning all aboard. Back on land, most of the Ute warriors died in the battle. After this, the Ute never camped near the lake again and believed that the early morning mists and fogs rising from the lake were the spirits of their dead.

The area was settled in 1867 by homesteader Joseph "Judge" Westcott, who supported himself by trapping and fishing and selling the live, boxed fish to hotel restaurants around the region. In the next decade, other families began arriving, and there was a short-lived gold boom.

But it was the area's natural beauty and abundant fishing and hunting that brought other settlers. Wealthy families built summer homes on the beautiful lake in the late 1800s. In 1905, the Grand Lake Yacht Club was registered as the world's highest at 8,369 feet.

The biggest tourist boom started in 1952 when the Colorado–Big Thompson Project was completed, bringing irrigation to the eastern slope through a series of dams, reservoirs, channels, and a 13-mile tunnel under the Continental Divide. The project created Shadow Mountain Lake and Lake Granby, greatly enlarging the area's water recreation opportunities.

The town's history is reflected in the Kauffman House, a former stage stop and hotel built in 1892 and operating today as a history museum.

Getting Around

Grand Lake is 102 miles northwest of Denver, via Interstate 70 west to U.S. Highway 40 (exit 232). Follow U.S. 40 over Berthoud Pass (11,315 feet and well maintained year-round) and through Winter Park, Fraser, and Granby. Grand Lake is 40 miles north of Winter Park. Just past Granby, follow U.S. Highway 34 (and signs to Rocky Mountain National Park) 16 miles north.

Coming from Boulder or Estes Park during the summer, just cross Trail Ridge Road (closed in winter, 44 miles from east to west) through Rocky Mountain National Park to the other side. Grand Lake is 1.3 miles south of the Kawuneeche Visitors Center at the west entrance of Rocky Mountain National Park.

Wooden planks underfoot lead shoppers along Grand Lake's charming main (and virtually only) street.

PHOTO: LINDA CORNETT

Recreation

Bicycling

A map of the area's mountain biking trails can be found at Rocky Mountain Sports, 830 Grand Avenue, Grand Lake (970-627-8124). The shop is open year-round and offers information on local mountain biking. The folks here also rent bikes and other equipment, along with sleds and show-shoes in winter and sailboats in summer.

Camping

There's abundant camping in the area in the national park, forest, and recreation area. The Kawuneeche Visitors Center of Rocky Mountain National Park is 1.3 miles north of Grand Lake and is open daily year-round. For information, call (970) 627-3471.

Sites in Rocky Mountain National Park

Permits are required for all backcountry camping. Permits are limited in number and are available year-round at the West Unit Office at the western entrance of the park on U.S. 34. Permits are available on a first come, first served basis, but may also be obtained in advance by writing to Backcountry Office, Rocky Mountain National Park, Estes Park, CO 80517, or by calling (970) 586-1242; there is a $15 fee Memorial Day through Labor Day.

Timber Creek Campground, 10 miles north of Grand Lake, is the closest developed campsite to Grand Lake. It has 100 sites accommodating tents and recreational vehicles. The fee is $10 per night in winter, $16 in summer. Water is turned on in early June and off in mid-September. The campground operates on a first come, first served basis with no reservations.

Sites in Arapaho National Recreation Area

This area has 350 campsites in four campgrounds, with site fees ranging from $12 to $24 per night. About 3 miles south on U.S. 34, turn left on County Road 66 and go a mile to **Green Ridge Campground** on Shadow Mountain Lake; it has 80 sites and a seven-night limit. Six miles south of Grand Lake on U.S. 34 is **Stillwater Campground** on Lake Granby, with 145 sites and a limit of seven nights.

To reach **Arapahoe Bay Campground** continue a mile south of Stillwater Lake Campground, turn left on County Road 66, and go 10 miles. The campground has 77 sites and a seven-night limit.

For **Willow Creek Campground** go south 8 miles on U.S. 34, turn right on U.S. 40 and go 3 miles to this campground on Willow Creek Reservoir. There are 35 sites and a limit of seven nights.

For more information, call the **Arapaho National Forest,** Sulphur Ranger District Office, at (970) 887-4100; for reservations call toll-free (877) 444-6777.

Sites in Arapaho National Forest

To reach **Sawmill Gulch Campground** go 3 miles northwest of Granby on U.S. 40, turn right on Colo. 125, and go 10 miles. Five sites are available at $9 per night, with a 14-night limit. **Denver Creek Campground,** with 25 sites, is 2 more miles up Colo. 125; it charges $20.

A combination campground, bed and breakfast, and recreation park, privately owned **Winding River Resort Village** (970-627-3215) has more than 160 campsites adjacent to Rocky Mountain National Park with hot showers, RV hookups, a store, and laundry—plus luxurious bed and breakfast rooms. Continental breakfast is included. There's a huge list of activities, including hayrides, horseback riding, a Frisbee golf course, mountain biking, and much more. Drive a mile north of Grand Lake on U.S. 34 and turn left across from the National Park Visitors' Center. Follow the signs for 1.5 miles. Tents cost $20 per night; RV sites cost $23 to $25 per night.

Fishing

Fishing is great in Grand Lake, Lake Granby, Shadow Mountain Reservoir, the Colorado River, Willow Creek, and Monarch Lake. **Budget Tackle** shop owner Bill Leach (970-887-9344) is a good local source of information and has a shop about 3 miles from Grand Lake on U.S. 34 and another in Granby. Check the *Daily Tribune* or the weekly *The Prospectus* for his weekly fishing report. Colorado fishing licenses are required for anyone 15 or older. See the "Fishing" section of our Sports chapter for information on fishing licenses.

Golf and Tennis

Grand Lake Golf Course (970-627-8008) is one of Colorado's most challenging and beautiful, set among the aspen and pines with gorgeous views of the Continental Divide (it doubles in winter as a cross-country ski area). If your ball goes astray on a narrow fairway, it's likely to winter over in the forest—you'll never find it. At an altitude of 8,420 feet, it can be chilly, and afternoon showers are common, so bring a jacket and rain gear. To reach the course go a quarter-mile north

It may not be imaginative, but the name Grand Lake is certainly an accurate description of the lovely lake shimmering below the mountain peaks. PHOTO: LINDA CORNETT

of town on U.S. 34, turn left on County Road 48, and drive another mile. The fee is $45 per person for 18 holes, $25 for 9 holes.

There are public tennis courts at Grand Lake Golf Course and at the park in the center of town (maintained by the Grand Lake Metropolitan Recreation District (970–627–8328); both are free.

Hiking and Backpacking

It's best to pay a visit to the local forest service office or the national park for detailed maps and information about local trails. Maps are available at the **Sulphur Ranger District Office,** 9 Ten-Mile Drive, Granby, CO 80447 (970–887–4100). Grand County also publishes an excellent recreation guide, which is available from the Chamber of Commerce, visitors' centers, or the forest service office. Another good source of information for both hiking and backpacking is **Never Summer Mountain Products,** 919 Grand Avenue, Grand Lake, CO 80447 (970–627–3642).

Sites in Rocky Mountain National Park

Numerous trailheads, including Green Mountain, Onahu Creek, Timber Lake, and the Colorado River Trail are just inside the park. The first two can be short day hikes of a mile or so to the intersection with the Tonahutu Creek Trail, which ventures ever farther into more remote areas of the park. The latter two are more challenging. The **Colorado River Trail**—the easier of the two—goes a scenic 2 miles to Shipler Park and 3.7 miles to Lulu City, an early mining town site, where all vestiges of civilization were removed when the park was created. The more difficult **Timber Lake Trail** winds 4.8 miles up to a lovely, high, tree-lined lake surrounded by wildflowers and with a view of 12,000-foot Mount Ida on the Continental Divide. From Grand Lake there are two nearby trails: the 27-mile, three-day Tonahutu Creek/North Inlet Loop, and the easier, shorter East Inlet Trail, which is better for day hikes. The former is a spectacular trip that crosses Andrews Pass and penetrates the heart of the national park—for experienced backpackers only.

The latter offers several alternatives, including a short trip to beautiful Adams Falls (0.75 miles each way) or a bit farther to a lovely high meadow perfect for lunch. Lone Pine Lake and Lake Verna are another 4.5 and 5.25 miles farther, respectively. To reach the East Inlet Trailhead, follow W.

Portal Road 1.5 miles from Grand Avenue to the end. The Tonahutu Creek/North Inlet Loop begins at the north end of the town at the park boundary.

Sites in Indian Peaks Wilderness Area

Permits are required for overnight camping in the wilderness area and are available at the Sulphur Ranger District Office, 9 Ten-Mile Drive, Granby, CO, 80446. Call (970) 887-4100 for more information. Permits cost $5 for a limit of 14 nights. Group size is limited to 12 (including pack animals). Campfires are allowed in some areas, except when fire danger is extreme. Advance reservations are required for Crater, Jasper, Diamond, and Caribou Lakes. **Arapaho Pass Trail** follows Arapaho Creek 10 miles to the top of the pass at 11,900 feet. The first 8 miles are an easy, gradual climb; the last two are tougher and steeper. The trail begins at Monarch Lake, as does the **Buchanan Creek Trail,** a more difficult hike along Buchanan and Cascade Creeks to Crater Lake, a good spot for camping and fishing. For an alternative and longer trip that climbs the divide, follow the Pawnee Pass Trail east instead of turning south to Crater Lake. It's a difficult 3-mile climb to the top of the 12,541-foot pass. (Also see Pawnee Pass Trail in our Boulder Sports chapter in the "Hiking" and "Backpacking" sections.) To reach Monarch Lake and the trailhead for these routes, take U.S. 34 south to County Road 6, turn left, and go 10 miles to Monarch Lake.

Horseback Riding

Sombrero Stables, 304 W. Portal Road, Grand Lake, CO 80447 (970–627-3514), offers everything from pony rides for kids to breakfast and steak-fry rides for Mom and Dad to pack trips into the park for several days for the more adventurous. Rides are $20 for one hour and $35 for two. Prices vary for rides with meals. Call for reservations. **Winding River Resort Village,** P.O. Box 629, Grand Lake, CO 80447 (970-627-3215), also offers hourly guided rides for around $20 an hour.

Llama Trekking

It's hard to picture John Wayne hitting the trail on a llama, but the sure-footed imports are a natural for Colorado's mountain trails. Groups from **Nature Valley Ranch** (970–627-3425), about 10 miles north of Granby (157 County Road 4480, Grand Lake, CO 80447) sets out on hiking treks with doe-eyed llamas doing the heavy hauling. Treks are daily during the summer, by arrangement at other times of the year. Reservations are required and parties must include six or more participants.

Snowmobiling and Skiing

Grand Lake is the "Official Snowmobiling Capital of Colorado," according to *Snow West* magazine, with more than 300 miles of groomed and ungroomed trails. It's also one of the few places where you can snowmobile right from your front door, out of town and into white solitude. Many local shops rent snowmobiles, among them **Spirit Lake Rentals,** 347 W. Portal Road (970-627-9288), and **Alpine Articat on the Trail,** 1447 County Road 491 (970-627-8866)—both in town. Another rental shop is **On the Trail at Winding River Resort** on Highway 491 (970-627-8866).

Cross-Country Skiing

Green Mountain Trail, a one-way trail in the national park, makes a nice tour if you have two cars: Leave one car at Green Mountain Trailhead and the other at the Tonahutu Creek/North Inlet Trailhead. Starting at Green Mountain Trail, 3 miles north of Grand Lake on U.S. 34, the trail goes uphill for 2 miles then turns right on Tonahutu Creek Trail. It's a pleasant 4-mile downhill run to your waiting second car.

During ski season, the Grand Lake Golf Course becomes the **Grand Lake Touring Center** (970-627-8008), with 25 kilometers of groomed ski trails around the course and a connecting trail to Soda Springs Ranch and other trails. (Directions are given under "Golf.")

At Tabernash, 12 miles north of Winter Park, the **YMCA Snow Mountain Ranch Nordic Center** (970-887-2152) offers many kilometers of groomed trails, lighted night skiing and a whole range of facilities including lodging, pools, and a roller-skating rink.

Farther down the road toward Winter Park in Fraser is **Devil's Thumb Ranch** (970-726-8231), which offers more than 100 kilometers of trails, including some nice meadows and rolling terrain as well as more challenging tracks.

All the touring centers above rent ski equipment, does Grand Lake's **Never Summer Mountain Products,** 919 Grand Avenue (970-627-3642), which also sells ski and other outdoor equipment.

Downhill Skiing

Winter Park Ski Resort is 40 miles south of Grand Lake (central reservations: 970-726-5514 or 800-453-2525) and offers some of the state's best skiing. Adult tickets range from a very reasonable $34 to $56, depending on the time of year. Smaller and quieter, Silver Creek Resort (970-887-3384 or 800-448-9458) is a great family resort for beginning to intermediate skiers. It's 15 miles south of Grand Lake and 17 miles north of Winter Park on U.S. 40. Lift tickets are $34 for adults, $20 for seniors over 61, and $16 for children under 12.

Watersports

This area is known for watersports and there are rental shops galore—especially along the shores of Lake Granby and Shadow Mountain Lake. **Spirit Lake**

Winter in Grand Lake—a perfect time to hitch a ride. PHOTO: ROZ BROWN

Cool year-round, the lake provides a brisk relief from the high-altitude summer sun for waders, paddleboaters, sailors, rowers, water-skiers, and just about anyone else who isn't afraid to get wet.

PHOTO: LINDA CORNETT

Marina, 1030 Lake Avenue (970–627–8158), offers boat rentals and lake tours from mid-May through mid-October. Bumper boats (like bumper cars) are also available to rent. **Grand Lake Marina,** 11246 Lake Avenue (970–627–3401), rents a variety of watercraft, including motorboats, fishing boats, canoes, and paddleboats.

Annual Events

July 4th Fireworks Extravaganza
(970) 627–3402

Watch the fireworks reflect over beautiful Grand Lake in this free show sponsored by the Grand Lake Chamber of Commerce.

Western Week Buffalo BBQ
(mid-July) Grand Lake
(970) 627–3402

This event takes place in mid-July and is an old-time celebration. Included in the week of events is the Spirit Lake Mountain Men Rendezvous, a parade down Grand Avenue, a 5K run, and, of course, a grand barbecue with all the fixin's.

Lipton Cup Regatta
(early August)

Named for English tea baron Sir Thomas Lipton, who was wined and dined by early members of Grand Lake's Yacht Club, this race is not open to the public. Spectators, however, can watch the yacht club sailors compete for the prestigious sterling silver Lipton Cup.

Other local events include a Memorial Day weekend auction and parade, and the Grand Festival of the Arts in August. For the more sedate, there's Bingo Friday and Saturday nights at the Town Park.

Grand Lake is alive and well in the winter months as well with ice-fishing derbies, snowmobile drag races, an ice-golf tournament, ice/snow-sculpture competition, concerts, sled-dog races, and other events.

Call the Chamber of Commerce (970-627-3402 or 970-627-3372) for a complete schedule and details.

Restaurants

Grand Lake's six-block main street, Grand Avenue, is lined with numerous small eateries with a variety of offerings, from beer and burgers to cappuccino and pastries. There are also a few fine dining establishments tucked away at both ends of town and a little ways out of town. For a tasty treat, stop in at the Rocky Mountain Chocolate Factory about midway down Grand Avenue.

Most restaurants have sections for smokers and nonsmokers, and the ones we've noted here accept major credit cards.

Price-Code Key

The price code is based on dinner for two people, excluding cocktails, beer or wine, appetizer, dessert, tax, and tip.

$ .... Less than $25
$$ .... $26 to $50
$$$ .... $51 to $75
$$$$ .... $76 and more

Caroline's Cuisine
9921 U.S. Hwy. 34 (Soda Springs Ranch), Grand Lake
(970) 627-9404
$$

For quite a reasonable price, enjoy French-American cuisine and an extensive wine list at this attractive restaurant. There's a children's menu and a full bar. Caroline's is open for dinner daily except Mondays.

Chuck Hole Cafe
1131 Grand Ave., Grand Lake
(970) 627-3509
$

Stop in for a hearty morning meal, with selections from a full breakfast menu. Lunch choices include burgers, chili, sandwiches, salads, homemade pies, and cappuccino. The Chuck Hole serves breakfast and lunch daily.

Daven Haven Lodge
604 Marina Drive, Grand Lake
(970) 627-8144
$$

Dinner is served daily at 5 P.M. at this restaurant on the lake. Steaks, seafood, and pasta are the specialties. There's a menu for kids, and seniors can split entrees.

E.G.'s Garden Grill
1000 Grand Ave., Grand Lake
(970) 627-8404
$$

Sit outside and watch the Grand Lake scene pass while chowing down on your choices from the varied menu—everything from light fare like salads and sandwiches to gourmet burgers and ribs.

Grand Lake Lodge Restaurant
0.25 mile north of Grand Lake off U.S. Hwy. 34, Grand Lake
(970) 627-3967
$$

Enjoy an evening cocktail or full meal on the lodge's open porch, or enjoy the same vista inside the comfortably rustic dining room. Either way, you'll have a glorious view of the lake and surrounding area. The restaurant specializes in Continental cuisine and has an open grill. Full breakfasts and a spectacular Sunday champagne brunch are served, too. There's weekly entertainment in the bar. The dining room is open for breakfast, lunch, and dinner daily from Memorial Day through the week after Labor Day.

Grand Pizza
717 Grand Ave., Grand Lake
(970) 627-8390
$

Pizza, pasta, calzones, and salads fill the menu of this fun restaurant. Interesting toppings include artichoke hearts, feta cheese and spinach, and refried beans, salsa, jalapenos, and hamburger.

The Mountain Inn
612 Grand Ave., Grand Lake
(970) 627-3385
$

A crowded parking lot is usually a good sign and so are the full tables inside this cozy restaurant, specializing in "Grandma's cooking." The catch of the day complements the menu, which features homemade chicken pot pie, old-fashioned stews, real mashed potatoes (which seem to be a big item in Grand Lake), and Mexican food. The restaurant is open year-round.

Pancho & Lefty's
1101 Grand Ave., Grand Lake
(970) 627–8773
$

No Colorado town is complete without a Mexican cafe, and here it is. The Pancho & Lefty combo means both Mexican and American dishes. Have a tasty taco, burrito, burger, or steak, and there's a full bar, too. The cafe is open daily for lunch and dinner.

The Rapids Lodge and Restaurant
Downtown Grand Lake, left at end of Grand Lake Ave.
(970) 627–3707
$$$

Elegant dining with Italian specialties and an extensive wine list set the Rapids apart from the usual more casual local restaurants. Specialties include linguine with prawns, chili oil, limes and Asian seasonings, and grilled New Zealand rack of lamb with a papaya-mint jalapeno glaze. In addition to a fine selection of beef

dishes, the Rapids also serves elk medallions in a sour cherry port wine sauce.

Rocky Mountain Coffee Company
915 Grand Ave., Grand Lake
(970) 627–5005
$

True to its name, the Coffee Company offers rich coffee and espresso, along with tea, homemade soup, sandwiches, and some sinful pastries. It's open at 7 A.M. for folks eager to hit the slopes or the trails or the lakes or the shops.

Terrace Inn
813 Grand Lake Ave., Grand Lake
(970) 627–3000
$$$

It's about ambiance in this charming circa 1920s inn on Grand Lake's main street. Breakfast, lunch, and dinner are served in the upscale dining room.

Accommodations

Grand Lake has a large selection of lodges, motels and cabins. Many are right on the lake; others are along scenic creeks tumbling down from the mountains. Below are some recommended places to stay. It's always a good idea to ask to see a room before you put your money down, should you decide to strike out on your own.

All the accommodations listed accept major credit cards.

Price-Code Key

Our price code is based on the average cost of a double occupancy room.

$	Less than $50
$$	$51 to $75
$$$	$76 to $90
$$$$	$91 to $120
$$$$$	$121 and more

Columbine Creek Ranch Bed and Breakfast
14814 U.S. Highway 34, Grand Lake
(970) 887–2429
$$$

There's a catch-and-release pond right outside the five cabins and one apartment that make up the ranch; if you can't give up your catch, you can keep it for a fee. Cabins all have gas grills and there's a hot tub for guests. Minimum stay is two nights, three nights over holidays.

Grand Lake Lodge
0.25 mile north of Grand Lake; look for the sign, and turn on U.S. Hwy. 34, Grand Lake
(970) 627–3967 (in-season),
(970) 759–5848 (off-season)
$$–$$$$$

Perched on a hilltop overlooking the lake, the historic, log-beamed main lodge is very inviting. This classic mountain lodge lies on the boundary of Rocky Mountain National Park with an inviting heated swimming pool right in front. The lodge's window-lined dining room sprawls out onto a front porch affording a grand view for an alfresco meal. In the evenings, guests gather in the friendly, relaxed main lodge to watch a movie, play cards, or warm their toes around the big circular freestanding fireplace. A 14-person hot tub has been added. The cabins, tucked away in a lodgepole pine forest up the hillside, don't share the lodge's grand view. The comfortable, austere (no phones or TV) cabins range from two-person modern duplexes to the Ford Cabin (where Henry Ford stayed in 1927), which sleeps 10 people. The lodge opens the first weekend in June and stays open through the second weekend in September (minimum stays of two and three days are required on weekends and holidays, respectively). Smoking is allowed, pets are not.

Lemmon Lodge
East end of town behind yacht club; turn right at the end of Grand Ave., Grand Lake
(970) 627–3314 (summer), (970) 725–3511 (winter)
$$$–$$$$$

Situated right on Grand Lake's lapping edge, Lemmon Lodge offers a variety of small and large (up to 12 persons) cabins in a pleasant, wooded area of five private acres. There are kitchens in all but one of the cabins, barbecue grills and picnic tables on the grounds, and a children's playground right on the beach. The lodge's location on the North Inlet of the lake offers great fishing and a private boat slip, so bring your rod and boat. Cabins are often reserved a year in advance, and there's a four-day minimum stay required from late June to early September (three-day minimum over Memorial and Labor Day weekends). Smoking is allowed in some of the cabins; pets are not.

Mountain Lakes Lodge
10480 Hwy. 34
(970) 887–8448
$$–$$$$$

Dogs are welcome at this hewn-log lodge, built in 1955 on the waterway between Lake Granby and Shadow Mountain Reservoir. Ten cabins and a log house have private decks and barbecues, color TV, and kitchenettes. There's a two-night minimum on summer weekends and a three-night minimum on holidays.

The Rapids Lodge
East end of town; turn left at end of Grand Ave., Grand Lake
(970) 627–3707
$$$–$$$$$

The oldest lodge in Grand Lake, built in the early 1900s, the Rapids Lodge looks quite rustic from the outside. But once inside, guests will be charmed by the lovely restored Victorian decor and antiques. The dining room looks out on the rushing Tonahutu River—a feast for the eyes with its frothy water spraying over large boulders. It was the river that powered a generator, making the Rapids the first electrified building in Grand Lake. Carpeted and comfortable, the rooms in the lodge are a nostalgic treat, with lace curtains and hearts-and-flowers wallpaper. Each room has a big brass bed or a four-poster wooden one, mounded with fluffy quilts. You can easily imagine yourself back at the turn of the century in this delightful retreat. Those who relish the sight and sound of the rushing water should ask for a room on the creek side. Nonsmoking rooms are available in the adjacent Rapids Chalet; there are also individual cabins and bright, modern condominiums along the creek that sleep up to 12 people. The lodge is open year-round.

Trail Mountain Bed & Breakfast
4850 County Rd. 41 (6 miles south of Grand Lake or 8.4 miles north of Granby on U.S. 34)
(970) 887-3944
$$$

Ideal for adult couples or small groups looking for privacy in a pristine setting with a taste of luxury, this bed and breakfast inn is close to lots of area activities such as golf and skiing. Each of the three large guest rooms has a private bath, shower, gas fireplace, and two-person Jacuzzi. Each room has a deck, and two rooms have private entrances. There's a big fireplace in the great room, near the dining area, plus a wet bar. Smoking and pets are not allowed.

Index

About the Authors

Roz Brown

A South Dakota native, Roz studied close to home before finding the closest thing to nirvana, Boulder, and transferring to the University of Colorado. A transfer student from the University of South Dakota to CU-Boulder, she was awed by mascot Ralphie the Buffalo, in spite of the Buffs' lack of bragging rights in that decade.

In college she began working in radio and upon graduation in 1979 was hired by Boulder's KBOL. While she was serving as News Director there, the station received the 1983 Colorado Associated Press "News Station of the Year" award.

After the birth of her first child, Roz began freelancing for Denver's KOA as the Boulder Bureau reporter. She has been an adjunct professor for CU's Journalism School, teaching production classes to aspiring broadcasters, and has twice served as president of the Boulder Press Club. She has also written and published newsletters for the City of Boulder since 1982 and has been a contributor to *Nexus, Colorado's Journal of Holistic Health,* since 1992. In 1997 she worked for CBS radio as a correspondent covering the Timothy McVeigh, Oklahoma City bombing trial in Denver, and has covered the Boulder murder case of JonBenet Ramsey. Since 2000 she has written and done voice-over work for Ball Aerospace.

Roz and her daughters, 15-year old Collier and 11-year old Grey, live in north Boulder, where a herd of mule deer are daily visitors. Much to her teenager's mortification, Roz is actively involved at the neighborhood middle school as PTO Co-President. She also enjoys hiking, biking, reading, antique shopping, entertaining, and accompanying friends and family at the piano.

Linda Cornett

Born in Oak Ridge, Tennessee, Linda Cornett moved with her parents to Idaho Falls, Idaho, when she was three. The family fell in love with the majestic scenery and the outdoor activities of their new home. When a nuclear explosion forced closure of the experimental aircraft site where her father (and many of Idaho Falls' breadwinners) worked, the family moved South again, to Huntsville, Alabama, and the NASA facility there.

Alabama never "took," and after graduating from Auburn University with a degree in journalism and working for a year at the local newspaper, Linda packed up books, clothes, a couple of pots, a rocking chair, and a waterbed, and headed back West.

Avoiding Denver traffic jams, she saw a road sign to a place with the odd name of Boulder. She stumbled into a town that had shed its rough mining origins to embrace the sophisticated liberalism of a college town. Stopping for supper, she was served black bean soup by a waitress in bare feet and a tie-dyed skirt who casually enlisted the help of the long-haired clientele to suggest a cheap place to stay. For a spot so geographically, socially, and politically removed from family and Alabama, it felt a lot like home.

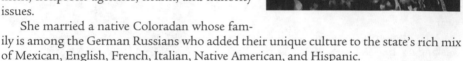

Within a week, she was settled in a house with a group of University of Colorado students and within two weeks she had a job at the Boulder *Daily Camera*, the local newspaper, where she would work on and off for 18 years.

The *Camera*—and a one-year stint at the *Denver Post*—opened the door to the community and the region, as Linda covered everything from public schools and the University of Colorado, to city and county government, to entertainment, nonprofit agencies, health, and minority issues.

She married a native Coloradan whose family is among the German Russians who added their unique culture to the state's rich mix of Mexican, English, French, Italian, Native American, and Hispanic.

In 1997, after a total of 20 years in the daily education that is journalism, Linda headed in a new direction, returning to college to work on a master's degree in computer information systems with an emphasis on multimedia. It was a logical choice, since Colorado's Front Range has become a mini–Silicon Valley, and the centrally located state is a headquarters for communications giants like TCI. She did public relations and web design for the Boulder Valley School District and the city of Boulder before landing at Red Rocks Community College in Lakewood, south of Boulder.

Linda shares her downtown Boulder home with her dog Gloria and Gloria's dog, Jackson, who provided insight for the dog parks portion of this book. Shy, the cat, kept his opinions to himself.

Her two children have the strong sense of place that comes from growing up in a smallish town where a walk down any street turns up a friend or acquaintance. Artis, 22, is a junior at the University of Colorado planning to get a degree in education. She spends her free time with a close group of lifelong friends. Bayard, 19, is a graduate of a private Boulder high school, September School; a student at Red Rocks; a dedicated *otaku* (fan of japanimation); and an aficionado of role-playing games. They're both ready to spread their wings into the wider world, but they will always know where home is.